"十三五"江苏省高等学校重点教材（编号：2018-2-100）
"江苏高校品牌专业建设工程"资助项目
国家"双一流"建设学科"南京大学中国语言文学艺术"资助项目
南京大学"十三五"规划教材

汉语言文学本科专业核心课程
研究导引教材

主编　徐兴无
　　　徐雁平

语言学

罗琼鹏　彭馨葭　编

南京大学出版社

汉语言文学本科专业核心课程研究导引教材

顾　问

[学校按汉语拼音顺序排列]

北京大学	陈晓明
北京师范大学	过常宝
复旦大学	陈引驰
华东师范大学	朱国华
吉林大学	张福贵
南开大学	沈立岩
武汉大学	涂险峰
中山大学	彭玉平

序

徐兴无

任何一所大学的本科课堂教学,都要随着知识内涵和教学手段的更新而不断地改进。课堂教学改进的途径是多种多样的,在当下中国高等教育"以本为本,植根课堂",打造"金课"的基调中,中国的高校主要在三个方面下功夫:一是培育教学名师和优秀教学团队;二是变革教学方式,有所谓"线下课堂"、"线上课堂"、"线上线下混合课堂";三是打造精品教材,"精品"是一个流行词汇,应该指有内涵、高等级的产品,包括文化产品。这三方面的核心是提高学生的知识积累和学习能力。

但是,不同的学科、不同的培养目标,其课堂教学的三个方面各有其规律与特点。汉语言文学是基础性人文学科,按照英国学者托尼·比彻和保罗·特罗勒尔所著《学术部落及其领地》中形象的学科分类,属于所谓的"纯软科学",其知识带有整体性和有机性的特点,关注事物的特殊性和复杂性,包含着人的主观色彩以及价值观与信仰,本质上是人类对世界的理解或阐释,因而涉及的领域广,问题分散,甚至很难有共识。上述特点,决定了人文学科的主要传授方式就是讲学与讨论,古人叫做"讲习"、"讲论"或者"讲辩"。"讲"的本义,就是不同观点与思想的商议,《说文解字》曰:"讲,和解也。"段玉裁注曰:"不合者调和之,纷纠者解释之,是曰讲。"从孔子、苏格拉底这些人类文明"轴心时代"的思想家开始直到现代大学的人文学科教育,无不如此,既古老,又现代,即便线上课堂也应设计讨论的场域,但终究不如面对面,"见而知之"。这和具有普遍性、规律性、客观性的知识传授不同,后者主要通过验证事实、计算推理、技能训练等方式教学。

因此,尽管不需要很多物质条件的支撑,人文学科的教学永远是成本最高的教学,因为它对人力资源的要求最为苛刻,所以荀子在《劝学篇》中说:"学莫便乎近其人。学之经莫速乎好其人。"这里的人,指的是知识渊博、富有智慧而且能以人格和道德魅力影响学生的师长。人文学科的教学方式,绝不是一两本教材、一张嘴、一支笔、一块黑板或一个PPT、一教室的学生、一两张考试卷子。人文学科教学的第一步,就是要真正地将"一言堂"改进为"多言堂",由集中讲授与平行小班研讨共同构成课堂教学的实践过程。只有学会聆听不同的声音,才能提出问题;只有学会与他者对话,才能克服偏见;只有学会自我陈述,才能主动学习。需要特别指出的是:这样的理想绝不是什么先进的教学改革理念,而是大学人文学科教学方式的"题中之义"和"应然"的状态,只是当下的"实然"状态,与此相差甚远。作为研究型大学的人文学科,如果具备师资基础和教学投入能力,与其不断地创新教学方式,还不如让课堂教学回到其"应然"状态。

随着知识信息的网络化和云端化,人文学科的主要教学目标必须由获得与掌握系统化知识或纯粹的信息,转变为培养问题意识、提升理解与阐释能力。这就要求教师的教学水平要从讲授技巧的提升转变为讲授内容的提升:集中讲授讲得少,讲得精,讲成有新意有深度的学术讲座。还要求教师从一个讲授者转变为训练者与组织者:在平行小班研讨课上和助教一道,向学生抛出有启发性的问题,提供研习材料与书目,训练、督促学生开展阅读、讨论、报告,辅导课程论文、习题训练,管理学生的学习环节和评价环节;既要避免漫谈式的研讨,又要避免小班化的"一言堂"。

传统的中文本科专业,以通史、通论和作品选作为专业核心课程的教材形式,旨在传授系统的知识和经典作品的内容。现在看来,这些常识性的知识只能是工具性的,起到接引和背景坐标的作用,而不是教学内容的主体。如果以问题作为教学的核心内容,就要围绕问题设计一系列的研讨活动与研究课题,这就需要有面向"应然"的课堂教学,并为其提供示范的教材。早在2006年,南京大学就已经规划编纂文史哲等人文学科本科专业的"大学研究型课程专业系列教材",由周宪教授担任总主编,并出版了其中"中国语言文学类导引系列"8种,部分教材如《中国古代文学研究导引》、《文学理论研究导引》等已经在南京大学汉语言文学本科教学中使用,受到师生们的广泛好评,作为"中文本科专业研究型课程体系建设"的成果之一,荣获2009年国家优秀教学成果二等奖。随着一流学科建设的开展,创新型人才培养的教学改革逐步深化,南京大学文学院自2018年起,对汉语言文学本科和戏剧影视文学本科专业的核心课程实行全面提升计划,实施集中讲授与平行小班研讨教学,编纂了《核心课程助教手册》,各核心课程的任课教师也编纂了《小班研讨教学资料汇编》、《学生研讨会论文集》等,边实践边总结,积累了一些经验。在此基础上,我们决定对2006版"中国语言文学类导引系列"8种的内容进行改编,有的重新编纂,有的修订三分之一以上的内容并修改体例,经过各专业一年的努力,推出这套新编的"汉语言文学本科专业核心课程研究导引"教材。

这套教材的编纂思路体现在三个方面:

一、以问题建构教材的内容体系。在每门课程的知识领域内,结合本课程的教学实践与科研成果,提炼最主要的问题集群。这些问题既是本课程的核心知识集群,又是本学科基础性或前沿性乃至带有方法论启示性的科研课题。通过对问题的发现、分析和研究,培养学生的问题意识和科研能力。

二、围绕问题,选择具有权威性、文献性、可读性与引导性的经典学术文献。通过对这些典范性文献和研究方法的解析,训练学生把握或体会研究方法和理论。

三、设计研讨、研究和课外延展学习的方案。这些方案,既可以为平行小班研讨课程提供参考,又可以为本科生的学年论文与毕业论文写作提供前期训练,甚至对研究生的学习也具有参考价值。

梁启超先生说过:"教科书死物,教员所讲则活物也。"在人文学科中,任何教材都是知识或学术的"导游图",在使用时,既不能指定教材,也不能"照本宣科",绝不能将"导游图"当成在场的体验。因此,我们将这套教材定义为一个开放的体系,它的目的只是"导引"而已,老师和学生可以参考教材的体例与功能,在具体的教学过程中,创造性地自行拓展问题,选择研讨文献,设计研究方案,深化、更新教学内容。我们衷心地希望这套教材能够帮助、启发师生进入学术对话的场域,变被动接受知识为主动探求知识,从而创新中文本科专业教材的形式。更希望广大师生在教学实践中对这套教材提出批评与建议。

前　言

　　我从2011年秋季学期开始,一直承担南京大学文学院汉语言文学专业本科核心课程"语言学概论"的教学工作。在多年的教学实践中,深感有必要针对中文系的学生编写一本深入浅出的入门级教材。理想的教材应兼具全面性、基础性和前沿性这三个方面:(一)基础性:要能涵盖当代语言学中最基础的概念、理论和研究方法;(二)全面性:要能较为全面地反映语言学各个分支、各个领域的重要进展;(三)前沿性:语言学科发展神速,新的理论和思潮层出不穷,跨学科研究越来越受到重视,语言与心理、语言与社会、语言与大脑、语言与人工智能等的研究如火如荼,语言学教材要着眼于未来,能让学生感受到这一学科的前景与未来发展趋势。但由于种种原因,这一教材编写计划一直没能实现。

　　2018年8月,南京大学文学院为落实教育部"以本为本",加快建设高水平本科教育、全面提高人才培养能力的要求,启动了汉语言文学专业七门核心课程的教学改革工作,全面实施"大班讲授+小班研讨"的授课模式,即在主讲教师传授完基本的知识点后,再通过小班研讨的形式,补充课堂知识点,探讨前沿课题,拓展学生视野。新的教学模式需要全新的教材。以此为契机,南京大学文学院组织力量编写一本全新的语言学方向的入门教材。正是得益于这一契机,本教材才有了最终面世的机会。我们期待这本教材既可以作为小班研讨课的教材,亦可以作为"语言学概论"课的补充教材。

　　在编写过程中,我们努力让本教材在以下几个方面有自己鲜明的特色:(一)发展史观指引下的当代性。以往类似教材侧重于介绍语言学史上的各种流派的基本情况(如历史比较语法、结构主义语言学、描写主义语言学等),很少针对当代语言学的基本理论和研究方法进行介绍。本教材将采纳半个世纪以来主流的生成语法作为基本理论框架,以弥补这一不足。(二)经典与前沿兼顾。以往的类似教材主要选取经典文献,但这些文献往往历史久远,并不能完全反映语言学的勃勃生机,因而,我们对文献的选取进行了精心编排,争取做到既有经典文献,又有学术前沿中被学界广为接受的新观点、新文献。除了以上提到的追流溯源外,本教材也会介绍及收录当今最前沿的研究成果。(三)中西合璧,兼容并蓄。语言学的研究往往受限于所研究的语言样本。一味地只看基于西方语言发展出的语言学理论,会发现它们往往无法完全解释中国的语言现象。而如果只看中国本土的研究,难免显得与世界脱节,故步自封,缺乏全球视角。本教材收录的论文既有用英语写作的语言学理论经典,也有以中国语言为研究对象的中文论文,两者均以原文呈现。(四)全面性。本教材涵盖当代语言学的各个主要分支,如句法学、语义学、语用学、音系学、形态学、语言习得、语言类型学等,有助于学生掌握当代语言学的全貌。

　　在体例和内容安排方面,本教材也有自己的特色。每一章内容分为"导引"、"选读"、"思考和练习"、"延伸阅读"等四个方面。"导引"部分主要是阐述最基本的概念,"选读"提供原文(或经典译文),帮助读者加深对基本概念的认识,"思考和练习"鼓励读者进一步思考,"延伸阅读"提供必要的参考文献,以便读者进一步跟踪学习。为了让读者体会到更为原汁原味的语言学,"选读"中的选文(译文),我们尽可能保持原文的格式(包括体例符号、术语译名、参考文献等),不作无必要之调整。我们还在最后增加了"语言学基本术语中英文对照表"这一附录部分,以期培养读者对中英文专业术语的熟悉度和敏感度。

　　本教材各章节的编写分工如下:罗琼鹏编写第一章、第三章、第四章、

第五章、第六章、第七章，彭馨葭编写第二章、第八章、第九章、第十章、第十一章、第十二章，最后由罗琼鹏统稿编辑。没有同为编者的彭馨葭老师的工作和付出，本书的完成是不可能的。在本书编写过程中，我们还得到了多位同学的协助，尤其是南京大学文学院语言学专业 2014 级博士生刘凡协助整理了部分选文，语言学专业 2017 级硕士生张晨阳、2018 级硕士生王蕴寰和夏小雨协助对书稿进行了仔细校对。谨致谢忱！

这本教材中由本人编写的部分，主要基于以往几年的讲义，潜移默化中还受到两本我个人最推崇的语言学教材的影响：*An Introduction to Language*（第 8—10 版）（由 V. Fromkin、R. Rodman、N. Hyams 等编写）以及 *Contemporary Linguistics：An Introduction*（第 4—7 版）（由 W. O'Grady、J. Archibald、M. Aronoff 等编写）。和这些经典语言学教材相比，这本仓促编写的教材要学习借鉴的地方还很多。只言片语，无法表达我对那些对当代语言学的发展做出过巨大贡献，并深深影响我的语言学之路的前贤们的敬意。感谢这些年来上过我的"语言学概论"课的所有同学，寓教于乐，学生们对这门课的兴趣，是我在语言学这一领域痛并快乐着坚持至今的原因之一。我还要感谢南京大学文学院的领导和本专业的同事，谢谢他们一直以来的支持和鼓励。

编写一本好的教材殊为不易。因为编者水平有限，加之时间仓促，缺陷和不足在所难免。我们恳请读者提出反馈意见，以便改进。

罗琼鹏

2019 年 1 月于南京仙林

目 录

图表索引 ··· (001)

第一章 语言与语言学 ··· (001)
  1.1 导引 ·· (001)
    1.1.1 语言概说 ··· (001)
    1.1.2 语言的定义与研究取向 ·· (002)
    1.1.3 语言的甄别性特征 ·· (004)
    1.1.4 语言的语法 ··· (006)
    1.1.5 语言与思维 ··· (008)
  1.2 选读 ·· (010)
    索绪尔(1916)《普通语言学教程》选读 ························· (010)
    布龙菲尔德(1933)《语言论》选读 ································ (019)
    乔姆斯基(2006)《语言与心智》选读 ··························· (029)
  1.3 思考和练习 ··· (043)
  1.4 延伸阅读 ·· (044)

第二章 语音学 ··· (046)
  2.1 导引 ·· (046)
    2.1.1 语音概说 ··· (046)
    2.1.2 发音语音学 ··· (047)
    2.1.3 音素 ·· (047)

2.1.4　音节 …………………………………………………… (052)
　　　2.1.5　超音段特征 ………………………………………… (053)
　　　2.1.6　声学语音学 ………………………………………… (055)
　　　2.1.7　听觉语音学 ………………………………………… (058)
　2.2　选读 ………………………………………………………… (058)
　　　罗常培,王均(2002)《普通语音学纲要》选读 …………… (059)
　　　赖福吉(1975)《语音学教程》选读 ……………………… (066)
　　　杨顺安(1992)《语音合成与语音学研究》选读 ………… (075)
　2.3　思考和练习 ………………………………………………… (084)
　2.4　延伸阅读 …………………………………………………… (085)

第三章　音系学 ……………………………………………………… (086)
　3.1　导引 ………………………………………………………… (086)
　　　3.1.1　音系概说 …………………………………………… (086)
　　　3.1.2　音位和音位变体 …………………………………… (087)
　　　3.1.3　最小对立对 ………………………………………… (089)
　　　3.1.4　互补分布 …………………………………………… (089)
　　　3.1.5　音系特征 …………………………………………… (090)
　　　3.1.6　音节结构 …………………………………………… (091)
　　　3.1.7　音系规则 …………………………………………… (093)
　　　3.1.8　结语 ………………………………………………… (094)
　3.2　选读 ………………………………………………………… (095)
　　　乔姆斯基(2006)《语言与心智》音系部分选读 ………… (095)
　　　David Odden (2013) *Introducing Phonology* 选读 ………… (103)
　　　Alan Prince & Paul Smolensk (2004) *Optimality Theory*:
　　　　Constraint Interaction in Generative Grammar 选读 …… (131)
　3.3　思考和练习 ………………………………………………… (142)
　3.4　延伸阅读 …………………………………………………… (143)

第四章　形态学 ……………………………………………………… (145)
　4.1　导引 ………………………………………………………… (145)

         4.1.1 形态概说 ……………………………………………… (145)
         4.1.2 语素与词的内部结构 ………………………………… (146)
         4.1.3 派生形态 ……………………………………………… (149)
         4.1.4 屈折形态 ……………………………………………… (153)
         4.1.5 词的层级结构 ………………………………………… (156)
         4.1.6 基于形态的语言类型 ………………………………… (158)
         4.1.7 小结 …………………………………………………… (161)
   4.2 选读 …………………………………………………………… (161)
         布龙菲尔德(1933)《语言论》选读 …………………………… (161)
         吕叔湘(1979)《汉语语法分析问题》选读 …………………… (167)
         朱德熙(1984)《关于向心结构的定义》选读 ………………… (174)
         Di Sciullo & Williams (1988) On the Definition of Word 选读
           ……………………………………………………………… (178)
   4.3 思考和练习 …………………………………………………… (198)
   4.4 延伸阅读 ……………………………………………………… (198)

第五章 句法学 ………………………………………………………… (200)
   5.1 导引 …………………………………………………………… (200)
         5.1.1 句法概说 ……………………………………………… (200)
         5.1.2 句法范畴 ……………………………………………… (201)
         5.1.3 句子的结构依存性 …………………………………… (205)
         5.1.4 短语结构 ……………………………………………… (209)
         5.1.5 普遍语法中的原则与参数 …………………………… (215)
         5.1.6 小结 …………………………………………………… (217)
   5.2 选读 …………………………………………………………… (217)
         乔姆斯基(2006)《语言与心智》选读 ………………………… (217)
         黄正德(1982)《汉语生成语法——汉语中的逻辑关系及语法理论》
           选读 ……………………………………………………… (234)
         Rizzi (2001) "Relativized Minimality Effects" 选读 ………… (244)
   5.3 思考和练习 …………………………………………………… (263)
   5.4 延伸阅读 ……………………………………………………… (264)

第六章 语义学 ································ (266)
6.1 导引 ···································· (266)
6.1.1 语义概说 ·························· (266)
6.1.2 词之间的意义关系 ················ (266)
6.1.3 句子之间的意义关系 ·············· (268)
6.1.4 真值条件语义学 ···················· (271)
6.1.5 组合性原则 ························· (272)
6.1.6 题元角色 ···························· (273)
6.1.7 小结 ································· (274)
6.2 选读 ···································· (275)
Russell (1905) "On denoting" 选读 ············ (275)
Heim & Kratzer (1998) *Semantics in Generative Grammar* 选读 ································ (285)
Partee (2004) *Compositionality in Formal Semantics* 选读 ································ (297)
6.3 思考和练习 ····························· (306)
6.4 延伸阅读 ································ (306)

第七章 语用学 ································ (308)
7.1 导引 ···································· (308)
7.1.1 语用概说 ·························· (308)
7.1.2 语用的规律性 ······················ (311)
7.1.3 预设与衍推 ························· (314)
7.1.4 会话涵义 ···························· (317)
7.1.5 言语行为 ···························· (326)
7.1.6 小结 ································· (332)
7.2 选读 ···································· (333)
莱文森(1986)《语用学》选读 ··················· (333)
7.3 思考和练习 ····························· (374)
7.4 延伸阅读 ································ (377)

第八章 语言习得 ……………………………………………… (379)

8.1 导引 ……………………………………………………… (379)
8.1.1 引言 …………………………………………………… (379)
8.1.2 语言发展的几个理论 ………………………………… (380)
8.1.3 基于使用的语言观 …………………………………… (383)
8.1.4 第一语言发展 ………………………………………… (385)
8.1.5 第二语言习得 ………………………………………… (386)
8.1.6 语言习得的研究方法 ………………………………… (390)
8.1.7 小结 …………………………………………………… (390)

8.2 选读 ……………………………………………………… (391)
乔姆斯基(1959)《评斯金纳著〈言语行为〉》选读 …………… (391)
Ibbotson & Tomasello (2018) "Evidence Rebuts Chomsky's Theory of Language Learning"选读 ………………………… (400)
Schmidt (1983) "Interaction, Acculturation, and the Acquisition of Communicative Competence: A Case Study of An Adult" 选读 ……………………………………………………… (413)

8.3 思考和练习 ……………………………………………… (426)
8.4 延伸阅读 ………………………………………………… (428)

第九章 语言与社会 ……………………………………………… (429)

9.1 导引 ……………………………………………………… (429)
9.1.1 引言 …………………………………………………… (429)
9.1.2 变异社会语言学 ……………………………………… (430)
9.1.3 话语分析 ……………………………………………… (434)
9.1.4 广义社会语言学 ……………………………………… (436)

9.2 选读 ……………………………………………………… (438)
Labov (1972) "The Social Stratification of (r) in New York City Department Stores"选读 ……………………………… (439)
鲍明炜(1980)《六十年来南京方音向普通话靠拢情况的考察》选读 ……………………………………………………… (452)

Zhang (2008) "Rhotacization and the 'Beijing Smooth Operator': The social meaning of a linguistic variable" 选读 ……… (459)
9.3 思考和练习 ……………………………………… (469)
9.4 延伸阅读 ………………………………………… (470)

第十章 语言类型学 ……………………………… (472)
10.1 导引 …………………………………………… (472)
 10.1.1 类型学的研究目的 ……………………… (472)
 10.1.2 类型学的起源 …………………………… (472)
 10.1.3 类型学的分类 …………………………… (474)
 10.1.4 汉语类型学研究 ………………………… (478)
 10.1.5 类型学的解释 …………………………… (479)
 10.1.6 类型学的发展 …………………………… (480)
10.2 选读 …………………………………………… (480)
 格林伯格(1963)《某些主要跟语序有关的语法普遍现象》选读 …………………………………… (481)
 Charles Li & Sandra Thompson (1976)《主语与主题：一种新的语言类型学》选读 ……………… (491)
 Hilary Chappell (2001) "Language Contact and Areal Diffusion in Sinitic Languages" 选读 ……… (503)
10.3 思考和练习 …………………………………… (512)
10.4 延伸阅读 ……………………………………… (513)

第十一章 历史语言学 …………………………… (514)
11.1 导引 …………………………………………… (514)
 11.1.1 引言 ……………………………………… (514)
 11.1.2 历史比较语言学 ………………………… (514)
 11.1.3 语言谱系 ………………………………… (518)
 11.1.4 语言演变的类型 ………………………… (521)
 11.1.5 语言演变的过程 ………………………… (524)
 11.1.6 语言演变的动因 ………………………… (525)

11.2　选读 ··· (525)
　　　　梅耶(1925)《历史语言学中的比较方法》选读 ··············· (526)
　　　　Jerry Norman (1988) "The Methodology of Middle Chinese
　　　　　　Reconstruction"选读 ··· (535)
　　　　梅祖麟(1991)《从汉代的"动、杀"、"动、死"来看动补结构的发展》
　　　　　　选读 ·· (546)
　　　　Cavalli-Sforza et al. (1988) "Reconstruction of Human Evolution"
　　　　　　选读 ·· (556)
　　11.3　思考和练习 ··· (568)
　　11.4　延伸阅读 ·· (568)

第十二章　语言与大脑 ·· (570)

　　12.1　导引 ··· (570)
　　　　12.1.1　引言 ·· (570)
　　　　12.1.2　大脑皮层的语言区 ······································· (570)
　　　　12.1.3　大脑语言区的几个理论 ································ (572)
　　　　12.1.4　大脑语言区对语言理论的启示 ······················ (574)
　　　　12.1.5　脑功能成像技术 ·· (575)
　　　　12.1.6　语言与电脑 ··· (577)
　　12.2　选读 ··· (577)
　　　　祖里夫(1990)《语言与大脑》选读 ······························· (578)
　　　　Ding et al.(2016) "Cortical Tracking of Hierarchical
　　　　　　Linguistic Structures in Connected Speech"选读 ······ (587)
　　　　迈因策尔(2018)《人工智能与机器学习》选读 ················ (601)
　　12.3　思考和练习 ··· (611)
　　12.4　延伸阅读 ·· (611)

附录:基本术语中英文对照表 ·· (613)

图表索引

图 2.1　国际语音学会制定的国际音标(2015年版)　　　　　　　(049)
图 2.2　普通话一级元音格局图(以北京话为样本)　　　　　　　(052)
图 2.3　一个英文语音片段的频谱图(上)和波形图(下)　　　　　(056)
图 2.4　0.016秒的元音/a/(左)和塞音/s/(右)的波形图　　　　(056)
图 2.5　普通话的/a,i,u/频谱图　　　　　　　　　　　　　　　(058)
图 8.1　一个简化的联结主义模型的图示　　　　　　　　　　　(383)
图 9.1　"r"卷舌音在纽约市不同人群的发音情况　　　　　　　(432)
图 10.1　声调语言在全球的分布　　　　　　　　　　　　　　　(475)
图 11.1　四种语言中的与格(dative case)变位　　　　　　　　　(516)
图 11.2　世界语系分布图　　　　　　　　　　　　　　　　　　(519)
图 11.3　施莱赫尔构建的印欧语谱系树　　　　　　　　　　　　(520)
图 11.4　汉藏语系的"落叶模型"　　　　　　　　　　　　　　(520)
图 12.1　"威尼克-格施温德模型"　　　　　　　　　　　　　　(573)
图 12.2　布洛卡区的分布　　　　　　　　　　　　　　　　　　(574)
图 12.3　听单词时不同大脑区域激活情况(fMRI图像)　　　　　(576)

表 2.1　普通话的辅音分布　　　　　　　　　　　　　　　　　(050)
表 2.2　普通话四声的不同表示方法　　　　　　　　　　　　　(054)
表 4.1　现代英语中的屈折语素　　　　　　　　　　　　　　　(153)
表 4.2　屈折形态和派生形态变化对比　　　　　　　　　　　　(155)
表 5.1　英语中常见的句法范畴　　　　　　　　　　　　　　　(202)

表 5.2	英语中的词汇范畴及其屈折形态后缀	(204)
表 5.3	名词、动词、形容词的分布特征	(204)
表 7.1	话语形式和言语行为之间的对应性	(331)
表 8.1	二语习得是否存在"关键时期"的正反面的证据	(387)
表 9.1	10个国家和地区社会语言学研究关键词	(437)
表 10.1	格林伯格(1963)疑问词位置和语序的六分表	(473)

第一章 语言与语言学

1.1 导引

- 语言概说
- 语言的定义与研究取向
- 语言的甄别性特征
- 语言的语法
- 语言与思维

1.1.1 语言概说

我们无时无刻不在使用语言:使用语言进行交际、表达思想、传递情感、抒发情怀……人类语言的复杂性和能产性超过了任何已知动物的交际系统。人类语言具有巨大的变异性。根据"民族语言志"(www.ethnologue.com)最新(2018年)的统计结果,目前世界上已知的语言有 7097 种,这还不包括大大小小的方言。仅中国境内,就有 299 种语言,其中 275 种为本土语言(indigenous language),24 种为非本土语言。[①] 绝大多数中国人每天使用的汉语普通话仅仅是这 299 种语言之一。语言从何而来? 语言是如何演化的? 语言的本质是什么? 语言和心智有什么关系? 人类如何使用语言? 这些问题自古以来就困扰着人类,构成了语言研究中的核心问题。

---

① 参见"民族语言志"(www.ethnologue.com) 2018 年的统计资料:https://www.ethnologue.com/country/CN。

英语中的"语言"(language)一词,源自原始印欧语中的"$*dn\dot{g}^hwéh_2s$(意为 tongue、speech)"、拉丁语中的"lingua(speech, tongue)"以及古法语中的"langage"。这一古老的词源表明了人类对语言思考历史的悠久。关于语言的思辨,比较有名的是古希腊哲学家高尔吉亚(Gorgias)和柏拉图(Plato)的争辩。高尔吉亚认为语言既不能反映客观经验,也不能传递主观经验,因而,交际和真理的表达是不可能的;柏拉图则认为交际是可能的,因为语言所表达的思想和概念,独立于或者先于语言产生。

语言可以表达概念、传递思想、进行交际,这是从语言的功能角度而言的。实际上,作为严肃的学术研究对象的"语言",有两层主要的意思:语言作为一个抽象的概念,以及语言作为一个特定的系统(如汉语、法语、英语、拉萨藏语等)。有"现代语言学之父"之称的瑞士语言学家索绪尔(Ferdinand de Saussure)把语言视为一种抽象概念(他用法语词"langage"表示),并明确区分了两个概念:"语言"(langue)和"言语"(parole),前者是某一特定的语言系统,后者是特定语言中语言的具体使用。

1.1.2 语言的定义与研究取向

语言学是对语言的科学研究(the scientific study of language)。如果把语言视为广义的抽象概念,会产生不同的定义,不同的定义侧重语言现象的不同方面。不同的定义蕴含理解和研究语言的不同取向,这些不同的取向导致了不同的,甚至彼此对立的语言学理论。虽然本书作者采取了形式语言学[或称生成语法(Generative Grammar)]的理论取向,但是了解语言的不同定义(以及由此形成的不同语言学思潮)也相当必要。

1.1.2.1 语言作为一种符号体系

有一种定义认为语言是一个关于符号的形式系统。这个系统由语法规则组成。这一定义强调人类语言可以表述为由"符号—意义"对应规则组成的封闭的结构系统。这种结构主义语言学的观点由索绪尔提出,影响深远。索绪尔把语言学分为历时语言学(Diachronic Linguistics)和共时语言学(Synchronic Linguistics),把语言活动分为语言和言语,并主张语言学的真正任务是研究共时系统中的语言。在这个系统中,某一特定语言符号的价值并不取决于自身,而是取决于这个系统中的其它符号,因而,"语言是形式而不是实质"。索绪尔语言学的核心是对比与对立;通过对比与对立提取语言单位(包括语音单位和语法单位），确立语言规则，最终建立一套共时语言结构体系。索绪尔的观点为20世纪初期的结构主义语言学的兴起和发展提供了重要的理论基础，如哥本哈根学派、布拉格学派等的理论源泉可以直接追溯到索绪尔语言学。

1933年，美国语言学家布龙菲尔德（Leonard Bloomfield）出版了著名的《语言论》（*Language*），标志着美国结构主义语言学理论走向成熟。布龙菲尔德的语法体系以层级性（hierarchy）为基础，它包含两个方面：一个是不同层级的语法形式，如语素（morpheme）、词（word）、短语（phrase）、句子（sentence）；另一个是语法规则，包含语法形式的推导规则及语类的推导规则。语法形式的推导规则论述语素、词、短语与句子之间的相互关系，如语素与语素结合成词、词与词结合成短语、短语与短语结合成句子等等。语类的推导规则是在向心结构和离心结构的分立下展开的，语类推导离不开单位的形式类，词类是根据句法功能确定的形式类别，句法从词类出发可以得到充分描写。结构主义语言学的思想和分析手段对当代语言学产生了深远的影响。

1.1.2.2 语言作为一种心智能力

1957年，乔姆斯基（Noam Chomsky）的《句法结构》（*Syntactic Structure*）的问世标志着生成语法的诞生，实现了语言学研究从结构主义语言学向生成语法转变，人类对语言的探索由"外"而"内"，由对现象的探索转向对制约现象的内在机制的探索。相信生成语法的学者认为，语言是人类独有的一种心智能力。语言学探索不仅仅要追求描写充分（descriptive adequacy），即对语言规则的详细构拟，更要追求解释充分（explanatory adequacy），即对规则所依赖的语言能力做出充分的刻画和说明。对语言的这一定义强调语言能力的普遍性以及语言的生物基础。有许多证据表明，语言能力是天生的，譬如认知正常的儿童，不分语言、地域、财富、社会地位等，只要给予一定的语言刺激，均可以在三岁左右发展出成熟的语言能力。乔姆斯基区分了语言能力（linguistic competence）和语言表现（linguistic performance），前者是语言行为背后的心智能力，后者是语言具体的使用。乔姆斯基认为，语言研究的终极目标是要探索理想状态下语言使用者的语言能力，而不是语言表现。因为语言能力是人类独有的能力，对语言能力的探索，也是对人类语言的普遍语法（Universal Grammar, UG）的探索。经过半个多世纪的发展，对普遍语法的探索，已经成为当今语言学的主流理论思潮。

1.1.2.3 语言作为一种交际工具

学界也有观点将语言视为人类用于交换符号性内容的交际系统。该观点的出发点是语言的社会功能，即人类用语言来表达自身、改造环境。功能语法理论以交际功能来解释语法结构，将语法接受视为服务使用者交际需要的适应性过程的结果。这一取向的研究也往往和语用、认知和交互性框架、社会语言学（Sociolinguistics）、语言人类学（Linguistic Anthropology）紧密关联。功能学派还将语言视为动态现象，在被说话人使用的同时也在不断地变化。该观点也使得语言类型学（Linguistic Typology）的重要性得以凸显。这种根据结构特征的分类，还可呈现出部分取决于结构的语法化（grammaticalization）轨迹。在语言哲学里，这一思潮和维特根斯坦（Wittgenstein）晚期哲学有密切关联，此外奥斯汀（J. L. Austin）、格莱斯（Paul Grice）、赛尔（John Searle）和奎因（W. O. Quine）等语言哲学家也均属于这一阵营。

1.1.3 语言的甄别性特征

虽然基于不同的研究取向对语言的界定各异，但仍然有一些广为认可的特征可用于区分语言与其它符号系统。

1.1.3.1 创造性（Creativity）

人类语言具有创造性，即允准对新的想法、经验和情境做出新颖和创造性的回应。语言创造性的背后是一个复杂的心智系统，该系统界定了创造性发生的边界。典型的操作如基于名词创造动词，如"bottle"（瓶子）一般被视为名词，可以说"put the wine in bottles"（把酒装到瓶子里），动词用法的"bottle"（"bottle the wine"）也能表达相似的意思，类似用法的还有"beach、ground、string、spear、mop"等，这就为语言表达创造了很多的新形式。但创造性也有边界，如果表达相同内涵意义的词已经存在，动词一般不易被创造，像我们已经可以用"jail the robber"来表达"put the robber in jail"（将抢劫犯关入监狱），就无法对"prison"（监狱）也进行相同的创造性用法，即只能说"put the robber in prison"，而不会说"prison the jail"。系统性的限制对于创造性而言是非常必要的。试想一下，如果已经建立好的词项总是不停地被新创造出的词项所替换，那么语言的词汇将变得极其不稳定，甚至会危及交际。

人们对句子的产出和识解也是创造性的集中体现。除了常见的固定用语和招呼用语外，人们每天大部分所说、所听、所读的句子可以说都是新的。

在对话、课堂、新闻和课本里，人们总是会遇到词项的新组合、对新想法的表征和全新的信息，比如你此刻正在阅读的段落。然而这些句子对人们而言都是可以识解的，并全然不同于以往所见过的任何表征。当然，这种可以产出、理解新话语的能力并不意味着人们就能理解或使用任意词项的随意组合，即语言的创造性受到系统性的限制。

1.1.3.2 普遍性（Universality）

普遍性认为语法在根本上是相似的。不同的语言在表面形式上无疑有很多区别，如语音系统、词汇、词序等，但这并不是说人们可以毫无限制地接受和使用任意类型的语法。当前研究表明，有一些重要的语法原则（grammatical principles）和趋向为所有的人类语言所共享。以否定的表达为例，如果没有任何限制，那么如(1)的四种语序都是可能的，并且可以预测四种语序应有相近的出现频率：

(1) a. Not Pat is here.
    b. Pat not is here.
    c. Pat is not here.
    d. Pat is here not.

但事实上，第一种(1a)和第四种(1d)相当少见。在所有的语言里，形如"not"这样的谓词性否定成分不是直接出现在谓词前，就是居于谓词后。其它成分的语序也受到一些限制，如对于"Australians like cricket"这样的陈述在逻辑上应有六种语序可能：

(2) a. Australians like cricket.
    b. Australians cricket like.
    c. Like Australians cricket.
    d. Like cricket Australians.
    e. Cricket Australians like.
    f. Cricket like Australians.

有趣的是，世界上的绝大多数语言都采用前三种语序(2a–c)，仅有极少的语言采用后三种(2d-f)为基础语序,这也再度印证了各异的语言间存在共同的限制和偏好。值得注意的是,这些现象都并非孤例,在本书的后面章节我们将展示:语法范畴(grammatical categories)和原则具有普遍性,即使存在各异的表征(如词序),但仍然被限制在有限的可能性里。

1.1.3.3 可变性(Changeability)

所有语言的语法都处在不停的变化中。有些变化微小并迅速出现,如语言中浮现的新词;有些变化巨大并耗时甚久,如古汉语到现代汉语的语序变化,又如英语的否定结构,在公元1200年之前,必须同时将"ne"放在动词前且"not"置于动词后;在公元1400年左右,"ne"渐渐不常用了;之后不到200年,英语否定式逐渐发展为当前的面貌,即"not"只能出现在有限的几个词(如"do、have、will")之后。这充分显示了语法随着时间而变化。语言的变化与语言的规范互有交织,有些语法学家为了维护语言的纯洁性编写了规定语法,我们将在下一节予以介绍。也有语言学家并不赞同必须保护某一时期的语言,他们也不认为连续的变化会污染、腐化语言。基于所有语言都是平等的这一出发点,他们认为没有一种语法必然优越于另一种语法,变化本身并不会毁掉任何语言。

1.1.4 语言的语法

乔姆斯基等曾一针见血地指出:我们使用的"语法"一词呈现出了系统的歧义。一方面,它指称语言学家所构建的明晰理论,并描述了说话人的语言能力;另一方面,它又指向这个能力本身(Noam Chomsky and Morris Halle, *The Sound Pattern of English*, 1968)。当我们在谈论"语法"时,并不是基于其最日常的意义。在语言学家看来,语法是说话人具有的关于语言单位和规则的知识。声音与词组合的规则被称为音系学(Phonology),词的内部组合的规则被称为形态学(Morphology),词组成短语、短语组成句子的规则被称为句法学(Syntax),指派意义的规则构成语义学(Semantics)。语法和包含词项的心理词典[即词库(lexicon)]一起构成语言能力。要理解语言的本质必须先理解语法的本质。在各类与语法有关的表述中,常见的有以下四种。

1.1.4.1 描写语法(Descriptive Grammar)

每个会说某种语言的人都了解这种语言的语法。当语言学家想要描述一种语言时,他们需要清晰地描述在说话人心智里既已存在的语言规则,这在不同的说话人之间可能存有差异,但也必然存在共识。正是说话人所共享的这部分语法知识,使得通过语言进行交流成为可能。当语言学家的描述构建了说话人语言知识的真实模型时,即被视为对该语法和语言本身进行了恰当的描写,该模型即被称为描写语法。

需要注意的是,描写语法并不规定如何说话,而是对基本语言知识进行描述。它只是阐明了言说和识解的可能性,判断其合法性,并表述了说话人所知该语言的声音、词项、短语和句子。当我们说某个句子是合乎语法的(grammatical),即指和语言学家描述的心智语法一致;当我们认为一个表征不合乎语法(ungrammatical),即认为它在某种程度上偏离了规则。有时语言学家所描写的规则可能与你的直觉不同,这意味着该描写语法与你的语言能力所表征的心智语法有差异,可以认为你的语法和语言学家所表述的并非同一种语法。就语言学意义而言,没有哪种语言或语言变体[即方言(dialect)]必然比其它的优越,每种语言都是同样复杂、具有逻辑的,而且具有表征任何思想的无限集合的能力。

1.1.4.2 规定语法（Prescriptive Grammar）

然而,并非所有的语法学家都秉持上述"语法平等观"。一些语言的"纯洁主义者"坚信一种语言的某些版本比另一些更优越,它是所有受教育者应该读写的"正确"形式,而语言变化是一种污染。他们倾向于规定,而非描写语法,由此产生了规定语法。这种思潮从公元 1 世纪的希腊亚历山大学派就已经存在,至今仍然争议不断。本书从语言学的立场坚信所有的人类语言和方言都是充分具有表达性、完整性和逻辑性的,其两百年甚至两千年前的面貌也是如此。我们认为所有的语言和方言都受规则管辖,无论说话人贫富贵贱、识字与否。不可否认的是,标准方言(standard dialect)可能在某些工作或社会地位上具有事实上的优势,但这种社会优势并不意味着在语言学意义上它们具有更好的语法。

1.1.4.3 教学语法（Teaching Grammar）

描写语法描写的是说话人内化语言的规则,而教学语法则不同,后者用于学习另一种语言或方言。教学语法对于不说标准和优势方言的学习者往往很有帮助,也可用于第二语言的教学课堂。这种语法一般给出词项和读音,并清晰地陈述语言规则。对于第二语言的学习者来说,正式的教学是非常必要的。教学语法会假设学生已经通晓一种语言(即学习者的母语),并将其和目标语(target language)进行对比。如词项的意义往往以逐词对译的注释(gloss)形式来展现。目标语里如有学习者母语里没有的语音形式,也往往需要以学习者所熟知的语音形式来呈现。对于语法的学习也需要比较学习者的母语和目标语,如 Sibusiso Nyembezi 所著的祖鲁语的教材就会提到"祖鲁语没有无定和有定冠词'a'和'the'",这类表述都以学生熟知的母语的语法规则为出发点。虽然教学语法也尝试向学习者规定在目标语里区分合乎语法和不合乎语法的结构,但是其目的明显有别于规定语法。

1.1.4.4　普遍语法(Universal Grammar)

不同的语言无疑有其特殊的语法,如英语、阿拉伯语和祖鲁语显然由不同的规则支配;但也存在适切于所有语言的规则。这种普遍规则正是我们了解人类"语言官能(faculty of language)"的窗口。纵观学术史,学者们很早就开始了对语言普遍性的探索。早期学者致力于发展"通用语法(General Grammar)"的理念,并与"特殊语法(Special Grammar)"相区别,通用语法试图揭示所有语言共有的特征。随着人们对语言探索的深入,越来越多的证据支持乔姆斯基的观点,即普遍语法是具有生物基础的人类语言官能。可以将普遍语法视为所有语言都遵守的规则,同时它构成儿童语言习得内在能力的一部分。它明晰了语法里不同单位的构成及相互关系,以及这些单位组合、交互的规则。可以认为,当前语言学理论的重要目标就是探索普遍语法。语言学家的目标是揭露人类语言的法则,这和物理学家的任务是揭露物理宇宙的法则同出一辙。基于语言的复杂性,想完全实现这一目标无疑会很难,但不失为一个值得努力的方向。

1.1.5　语言与思维

语言和思维的关系一直是热门话题,也涌现出相当多的理论,其中最负盛名的当属语言学家萨丕尔和他的学生沃尔夫提出的"萨丕尔—沃尔夫假说(Sapir-Whorf Hypothesis)"。萨丕尔指出:"人类并不是单独生存于客观世界或是社会活动的世界里,得益于语言作为表征和社会的媒介……我们得以极大程度地看到、听到、体验到社区里其他语言习惯的诠释取向"(Sapir 1929:207)。沃尔夫则有更强势的表述:"各个语言的背景语言系统(即语法)并不仅仅是思想的发声工具,其本身也塑造着思想、个体的认知活动"(Whorf and Garroll 1956)。

萨丕尔—沃尔夫假说的强势版本被称为"语言决定论（linguistic determinism）,因为其直接认为是人们言说的语言决定人们如何感知和思考所处的世界。在此观点下,语言更像是一个真相的过滤器。支持该说法的一个论据来自于霍皮印第安人（Hopi Indian）与欧洲人不同的感知时间方式,因为霍皮语没有语法时态,而英语则有"did、will、shall、-s、-ed、-ing"等多种表征。

该假说的弱化版本则为"语言相对论"（linguistic relativism）,认为不同的语言编码了不同的范畴,所以该语言的言说者也以不同的方式观照世界。比如不同的语言对颜色光谱有不同的界定,比如对纳瓦霍人（Navaho）而言绿色和蓝色是一个词,而俄语则区分深蓝（siniy）和浅蓝（goluboy）,英语则需要额外词如"dark"（深）和"light"（浅）。美洲印第安祖尼语（Zuni）则不区分黄色和橘色。

不同的语言在词库和语法上无疑会呈现差异,但问题的关键在于这些差异在多大程度上决定或影响了言说者感知和处理世界的方式。萨丕尔—沃尔夫假说一直饱受争议,但其强势版本"语言决定论"明显是错误的。人们的感知和思维并不是由其所言说的语言决定的,人并不是语言的囚徒。如果人们无法去思考其言说语言中不存在的词,那么除非真正学了第二语言,否则理解翻译在理论上也是不可能的。比如英语没有一个单独的词去表达内角和外角,但是英语说话人可以很轻易地用多个词项来表征,如"inside of a corner"和"outside of a corner"。如果人们不能在母语里用不存在的词项来思考,那么婴儿们又如何去学习第一个词项呢？"语言决定论"的一些论据也站不住脚,霍皮语虽然没有语法时态,但有其它的词项来表征时间,如表示一天内的早晚、昨天、明天、星期几、月份、季节等,可见他们仍然有完善的时间概念。

人们能够理解所处的世界,显然不是像萨丕尔所认为的那样"得益于所说的语言"。但是语言与思维的关系问题仍然值得我们思考：语言是否能在某种程度上"影响"认知。在颜色范畴的领域,如果一种语言缺乏"红色"表述,那么其言说者去辨别红色物体会变得困难。这样看来,有一个标签至少能更便于记忆和回溯其指涉。此外,也有实验表明,俄语说话人比起英语说话人更擅长辨别深蓝和浅蓝色,因为俄语直接对这两种颜色进行区分。

总之,当前的研究表明,语言并不决定我们如何认知和感受世界。语言对认知,特别是记忆、范畴化等因素的影响,有待进一步研究。

1.2 选读

- 索绪尔(1916)《普通语言学教程》选读
- 布龙菲尔德(1933)《语言论》选读
- 乔姆斯基(2006)《语言与心智》选读

索绪尔(1916)《普通语言学教程》选读①

◆ 作者简介

费尔迪南·德·索绪尔②(Ferdinand de Saussure, 1857—1913),现代语言学奠基人。索绪尔出生于日内瓦,他的祖先是法国人但早已加入瑞士籍,祖父和父亲都是自然科学家。索绪尔从小受到家中一位世交,语文学者阿道夫·皮科特(Adolphe Pictet)的指引,掌握了法语、德语、英语、拉丁语等多种语言,并对语言学产生了浓厚的兴趣,但 1875 年中学毕业后他还是按照父母的意愿进入日内瓦大学学习物理和化学专业。一年后他转学到德国莱比锡大学专攻语言学,在那里结识了青年语法学派的几位重要人物。1879 年他转学到柏林大学,同年发表了成名作《论印欧系语元音的原始系统》("Mémoire sur le système primitif des voyelles dans les langues indo-européennes"),从理论上解决了印欧语元音原始系统中的一个疑难问题。1880 年他回到莱比锡大学完成了博士论文《论梵语绝对属格用法》(De l'imploi du genitive absolu en sanscrit),获博士学位。在法国巴黎高等研究学院任教十年后,1891 年他回到瑞士担任日内瓦大学教

---

① 索绪尔,《普通语言学教程》,高名凯译,商务印书馆 1999 年版。
② 图片来源:https://en.wikipedia.org/wiki/Ferdinand_de_Saussure,拍摄者为 F. Jullien Genève。

授；在1906年开设普通语言学这门课之前，索绪尔已经把印欧系主要语言（梵语、波斯语、希腊语、拉丁语、古日耳曼语、古高地德语、古英语）都讲了一遍或几遍。他深知历时比较语言学的缺陷，决心走一条崭新的道路，在普通语言学这门课中他提出了现代语言学的基本观点。1906—1911年，他应学生的要求先后三次讲授普通语言学课程，但是出于严谨的治学态度，始终没有把教程写成一本书。索绪尔去世后，他的学生巴利（Ch. Bally）和薛施霭（Albert Sechehaye）等根据同学们的笔记和索绪尔本人的札记进行整理，编成《普通语言学教程》(Cours de linguistique générale)。该书于1916年在瑞士洛桑初版，随后多次再版并被翻译成多国语言，世界上各种重要的语言差不多都有这本教程的译本。

◆ 正文节选

第三章　语言学的对象

§ 1. 语言；它的定义

语言学的又完整又具体的对象是什么呢？这个问题特别难以回答，原因将在下面说明，这里只限于使大家了解这种困难。

别的科学都是对预先确定了的对象进行工作，接着就可以从不同的观点去加以考虑。在我们的领域里，情况却不是这样。有人发出法语 nu "赤裸裸的"这个词，一个肤浅的观察者在这里也许会看到一个具体的语言学对象；但是仔细考察一下，人们将会按照不同的看法连续找到三四个完全不同的事物，如把它看作一个声音，一种观念的表达，一个跟拉丁语 nūdum 相对应的词①等等。那远不是对象在观点之前，人们将会说，这是观点创造了对象，而且我们也没法预先知道，在这种种看法中，哪一种比其他的优越。

此外，不管我们采用哪一种看法，语言现象总有两个方面，这两个方面是互相对应的，而且其中的一个要有另外一个才能有它的价值。例如：

（1）人们发出的音节是耳朵听得到的音响印象，但是声音没有发音器官就不能存在；例如一个 n 音只因有这两个方面的对应才能存在。所以我们不能把语言归结为声音，也不能使声音脱离口头上的发音；反过来说，撇开了音

---

① 法语的 nu 这个词和民间拉丁语的 nudo 相对应，到十一世纪末才由民间拉丁语的 nudo 变成了现代法语的 nu。它跟古典拉丁语的 nūdum 没有直接最佳剧作联系。德·索绪尔在这里认为法语的 nu 和拉丁语的 nūdum 相对应，这是一种比较简单的说法。

响印象也就无从确定发音器官的动作。

　　(2)就算声音是简单的东西,它是否就构成言语活动了呢?不,它只是思想的工具;它本身不能单独存在。在这里又出现了一种新的可怕的对应:声音是音响·发音的复合单位,它跟观念结合起来又构成了生理·心理的复合单位。事情还不只是这样:

　　(3)言语活动有个人的一面,又有社会的一面;没有这一面就无从设想另一面。此外:

　　(4)在任何时候,言语活动既包含一个已定的系统,又包含一种演变;在任何时候,它都是现行的制度和过去的产物。乍一看来,把这个系统和它的历史,把它的现状和过去的状态区别开来似乎很简单;实际上两者的关系非常密切,很难把它们截然分开。假如我们从起源方面去考虑语言现象,例如从研究儿童的言语活动开始,问题会不会变得简单些呢?不,因为就言语活动来说,认为起源的问题和恒常条件的问题有什么不同,那是非常错误的;所以我们还是跳不出圈子。

　　因此,我们无论从哪一方面去着手解决问题,任何地方都找不着语言学的完整的对象;处处都会碰到这样一种进退两难的窘境:要么只执着于每个问题的一个方面,冒着看不见上述二重性的危险;要么同时从几个方面去研究言语言语活动,这样,语言学的对象就象是乱七八糟的一堆离奇古怪、彼此毫无联系的东西。两种做法都将为好几种科学——心理学、人类学、规范语法、语文学等等——同时敞开大门;这几种科学,我们要把它们跟语言学划分清楚,但是由于用上了错误的方法,它们都将会要求言语活动作为它们的一个对象。

　　在我们看来,要解决这一切困难只有一个办法:一开始就站在语言的阵地上,把它当做言语活动的其他一切表现的准则。事实上,在这许多二重性当中,看来只有语言可能有一个独立的定义,为人们的精神提供一个差强人意的支点。

　　但语言是什么呢?在我们看来,语言和言语活动不能混为一谈;它只是言语活动的一个确定的部分,而且当然是一个主要的部分。它既是言语机能的社会产物,又是社会集团为了使个人有可能行使这机能所采用的一整套必不可少的规约。整个看来,言语活动是多方面的、性质复杂的,同时跨着物理、生理和心理几个领域,它还属于个人的领域和社会的领域。我们没法把它归入任何一个人文事实的范畴,因为不知道怎么去理出它的统一体。

相反,语言本身就是一个整体、一个分类的原则。我们一旦在言语活动的事实中给以首要的地位,就在一个不容许作其他任何分类的整体中引入一种自然的秩序。

也许有人会反对这样一个分类的原则,认为言语活动的运用要以我们的天赋机能为基础,而语言却是某种后天获得的、约定俗成的东西,它应该从属于自然的本能,而不应该居于它之上。

我们可以这样回答:

首先,人们还没有证明,说话时所表现的言语活动的功能完全出于天赋,就是说,人体之有发音器官是为了说话,正如双腿是为了行走一样。语言学家关于这一点的意见很不一致。例如辉特尼就把语言看作一种社会制度,跟其他一切社会制度一样。在他看来,我们之所以使用发音器官作为语言的工具,只是出于偶然,只是为了方便起见;人类本来也可以选择手势,使用视觉形象,而不使用音响形象。他的这番议论无疑太绝对了;语言并不是在任何一点上都跟其他社会制度相同的社会制度。此外,辉特尼说我们之所以选择发音器官只是出于偶然,也未免走得太远;这选择在某种程度上其实是自然强加于我们的。但是在主要论点上,我们觉得这位美国语言学家是对的:语言是一种约定俗成的东西,人们同意使用什么符号,这符号的性质是无关轻重的。所以,对于发音器官的问题,在言语活动的问题上是次要的。

这种想法可以用人们对于所谓 langage articulé(分节语)所下的定义来加以证实。拉丁语 articulus 的意思是"肢体、部分,一连串事物的小区分"。就言语活动来说,articulation(分节)可以指把语链分成音节,也可以指把意链分成意义单位;德语的 gegliederte Sprache 正是就这个意义来说的。根据这个定义,我们可以说,对人类天赋的不是口头的言语活动,而是构成语言——即一套和不同的观念相当的不同的符号——的机能。

卜洛卡(Broca)[1]发现说话的机能位于左大脑第三额回,人们也就根据这

---

[1] 原书注解:"卜洛卡(1824—1880),法国解剖学家兼外科医生。他研究人脑结构,曾发现人们的语言发动中枢位于左大脑第三额回,它跟语言音响中枢和书写中枢有紧密联系。这些神经中枢受到损害,就会引起失语症和失书症。"卜洛卡,现多译为布洛卡。——编者注

一点认为言语活动有天赋的性质。但是大家知道,这个定位已被证明是跟言语活动的一切,其中包括文字,有关的。这些证明,加上人们对于因为这一部位的神经中枢受损害而引起的各种形式的失语症所作的观察,似乎可以表明:(1)口头言语活动的各种错乱跟书写言语活动有千丝万缕的联系;(2)在任何失语症或失书症的病例中,受影响的,与其说是发出某些声音或写出某些符号的机能,不如说是使用某种工具——不管是什么工具——来唤起正常的言语活动中的符号的机能。这一切使我们相信,在各种器官的运用上面有一种更一般的机能,指挥各种符号的机能,那可正好是语言机能。我们上述的结论就是从这里得出的。

　　为了使语言在言语活动的研究中占首要地位,我们最后还可以提出这样的论据:人们说话的机能——不管是天赋的或非天赋的——只有借助于集体所创造和提供的工具才能运用;所以,说语言使言语活动成为统一体,那决不是什么空想。

§2. 语言在言语活动事实中的地位

　　要在整个言语活动中找到与语言相当的部分,必须仔细考察可以把言语循环重建出来的个人行为。这种行为至少要有两个人参加:这是使循环完整的最低限度的人数。所以,假设有甲乙两个人在交谈:

甲　　　　　　　　　　　　乙

　　循环的出发点是在对话者之一例如甲的脑子里,在这里,被称为概念的意识事实是跟用来表达它们的语言符号的表象或音响形象联结在一起的。假设某一个概念在脑子里引起一个相应的音响形象,这完全是一个心理现象。接着是一个生理过程:脑子把一个与那音响形象有相互关系的冲动传递给发音器官,然后把声波从甲的口里播送到乙的耳朵:这是纯粹的物理过程。随后,循环在乙方以相反的程序继续着:从耳朵到脑子,这是音响形象在生理上的传递;在脑子里,是这形象和相应的概念在心理上的联结。如果轮到乙方说话,这新的行为就继续下去——从他的脑子到甲方的脑子——进程跟前

一个完全相同,连续经过同一些阶段,可以图示如下:

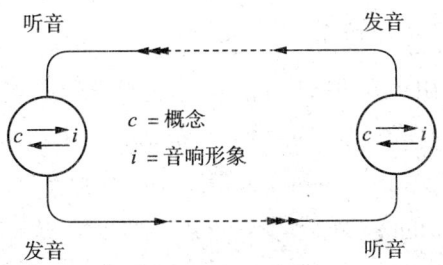

这分析当然不是很完备的;我们还可以区分出:纯粹的音响感觉,音响感觉和潜在的音响形象的合一,发音的肌动形象,等等。我们考虑的只是大家认为是主要的要素;但是上图已能使我们把物理部分(声波)同生理部分(发音和听音)和心理部分(词语形象和概念)一举区别开来。重要的是不要把词语形象和声音本身混为一谈,它和跟它联结在一起的概念都是心理现象。

上述循环还可以分为:

(a) 外面部分(声音从口到耳的振动)和包括其余一切的里面部分;

(b) 心理部分和非心理部分,后者既包括由发音器官发出的生理事实,也包括个人以外的物理事实;

(c) 主动部分和被动部分:凡从说话者的联想中枢到听者的耳朵的一切都属主动部分,凡从听者的耳朵到他的联想中枢的一切都属被动部分;

最后,在脑子里的心理部分中,凡属主动的一切($c \rightarrow i$)都可以称为执行的部分,凡属被动的一切($i \rightarrow c$)都可以称为接受的部分。

此外,我们还要加上一个联合和配置的机能。只要不是孤立的符号,到处都可以看到这个机能;它在作为系统的语言的组织中起着最大的作用。

但是要彻底了解这种作用,我们必须要离开个人行为,走向社会事实,因为个人行为只是言语活动的胚胎。

在由言语活动联系起来的每个个人当中,会建立起一种平均数:每个人都在复制(当然不是很确切地,而只是近似地)与相同的概念结合在一起的相同的符号。

这种社会的晶化是怎么来的呢?上述循环中的哪一部分可能是跟它有关的呢?因为很可能不是任何部分都同样在里面起作用的。

我们首先可以把物理部分撇开。当我们听到人家说一种我们不懂的语言的时候，我们的确听到一些声音，但是由于我们不了解，我们仍然是在社会事实之外。

心理部分也不是全部起作用的：执行的一方是没有关系的，因为执行永远不是由集体，而是由个人进行的。个人永远是它的主人；我们管它叫言语。

由于接受机能和配置机能的运用，在说话者当中形成了一些大家都觉得是相同的印迹。我们究竟应该怎样去设想这种社会产物，才能使语言看来是完全跟其他一切分立的呢？如果我们能够全部掌握储存在每个人脑子里的词语形象，也许会接触到构成语言的社会纽带。这是通过言语实践存放在某一社会集团全体成员中的宝库，一个潜存在每一个人的脑子里，或者说得更确切些，潜存在一群人的脑子里的语法体系；因为在任何人的脑子里，语言都是不完备的，它只有在集体中才能完全存在。

把语言和言语分开，我们一下子就把(1) 什么是社会的，什么是个人的；(2) 什么是主要的，什么是从属的和多少是偶然的分开来了。

语言不是说话者的一种功能，它是个人被动地记录下来的产物；它从来不需要什么深思熟虑，思考也只是为了分类的活动才插进手来，这将是我们在后文所要讨论的问题。

相反，言语却是个人的意志和智能的行为，其中应该区别开：(1) 说话者赖以运用语言规则表达他的个人思想的组合；(2) 使他有可能把这些组合表露出现的心理·物理机构。

应该注意，我们是给事物下定义，而不是给词下定义，因此，我们所确立的区别不必因为各种语言有某些意义不尽相符的含糊的术语而觉得有什么可怕。例如，德语的 Sprache 是"语言"和"言语活动"的意思；Rede 大致相当于"言语"，但要加上"谈话"的特殊意味。拉丁语的 sermo 无宁说是指"言语活动"和"言语"，而 lingua 却是"语言"的意思，如此等等。没有一个词跟上面所确定的任何一个概念完全相当。因此，对词下任何定义都是徒劳的；从词出发给事物下定义是一个要不得的办法。

语言的特征可以概括如下：

(1) 它是言语活动事实的混杂的总体中一个十分确定的对象。我们可以把它定位在循环中听觉形象和概念相联结的那确定的部分。它是言语活动的社会部分，个人以外的东西；个人独自不能创造语言，也不能改变语言；它只凭社会的成员间通过的一种契约而存在。另一方面，个人必须经过一个见习期才能懂得它的运用；儿童只能一点一滴地掌握它。它是一种很明确的东西，一个人即使丧失了使用言语的能力，只要能理解所听到的声音符号，还算是保持着语言。

（2）语言和言语不同，它是人们能够分出来加以研究的对象。我们虽已不再说死去的语言，但是完全能够掌握它们的语言机构。语言科学不仅可以没有言语活动的其他要素，而且正要没有这些要素掺杂在里面，才能够建立起来。

（3）言语活动是异质的，而这样规定下来的语言确是同质的：它是一种符号系统；在这系统里，只有意义和音响形象的结合是主要的；在这系统里，符号的两个部分都是心理的。

（4）语言这个对象在具体性上比之言语毫无逊色，这对于研究特别有利。语言符号虽然主要是心理的，但并不是抽象的概念；由于集体的同意而得到认可，其全体即构成语言的那种种联结，都是实在的东西，它们的所在地就在我们脑子里。此外，语言的符号可以说都是可以捉摸的；文字把它们固定在约定俗成的形象里。但是要把言语行为的一切细节都摄成照片却是不可能的；一个词的发音，哪怕是一个很短的词的发音，都是无数肌肉运动的结果，是极难认识和描绘的。相反，语言中只有音响形象，我们可以把它们译成固定的视觉形象。因为把言语中实现音响形象的许许多多动作撇开不谈，那么，我们将可以看到，每个音响形象也不过是若干为数有限的要素或音位的总和，我们还可以在文字中用相应数量的符号把它们唤起。正是这种把有关语言的事实固定下来的可能性使得一本词典和语法能够成为语言的忠实代表；语言既然是音响形象的堆栈，文字就是这些形象的可以捉摸的形式。

§3. 语言在人文事实中的地位：符号学

语言的这些特征可以使我们发现另外一个更重要的特征。在言语活动的全部事实中这样划定了界限的语言，可以归入人文事实一类，而言语活动却不可能。

我们刚才已经看到，语言是一种社会制度；但是有几个特点使它和政治、法律等其他制度不同。要了解它的特殊性质，我们必须援引另一类新的事实。

语言是一种表达观念的符号系统，因此，可以比之于文字、聋哑人的字母、象征仪式、礼节形式、军用信号等等，等等。它只是这些系统中最重要的。

因此，我们可以设想有一门研究社会生活中符号生命的科学；它将构成社会心理学的一部分,因而也是普通心理学的一部分;我们管它叫符号学(sémiologie①,来自希腊语 sēmeîon"符号")。它将告诉我们符号是由什么构成的,受什么规律支配。因为这门科学还不存在,我们说出它将会是什么样子,但是它有存在的权利,它的地位是预先确定了的。语言学不过是这门一般科学的一部分,将来符号学发现的规律也可以应用于语言学,所以后者将属于全部人文事实中一个非常确定的领域。

确定符号学的恰当地位,这是心理学家的事,语言学家的任务是确定究竟是什么使得语言在全部符号事实中成为一个特殊的系统。这个问题我们回头再谈,在这里只提出一点:如果我们能够在各门科学中第一次为语言学指定一个地位,那是因为我们已把它归属于符号学。

为什么大家还不承认符号学是一门独立的科学,像其他任何科学一样有它自己的研究对象呢?因为大家老是在一个圈子里打转:一方面,语言比任何东西都更适宜于使人了解符号学问题的性质,但是要把问题提得恰当,又必须研究语言本身;可是直到现在,人们差不多老是把它当作别的东西,从别的观点去进行研究。

首先是大众有一种很肤浅的理解,只把语言看作一种分类命名集,这样就取消了对它的真正性质作任何探讨。

其次是心理学家的观点,它要研究个人脑海中符号的机构;这方法是最容易的,但是跨不出个人执行的范围,和符号沾不上边,因为符号在本质上是社会的。

或者,就算看到了符号应该从社会方面去进行研究,大家也只注意到语言中那些使它归属于其他制度,即多少依靠人们的意志的制度的特征。这样就没有对准目标,把那些一般地只属于符号系统和特殊地属于语言的特征忽略了。因为符号在某种程度上总要逃避个人的或社会的意志,这就是它的主要的特征;但这正是乍看起来最不明显的。

正因为这个特征只在语言中显露得最清楚,而它却正是在人们研究得最少的地方表现出来,结果,人们就看不出一门符号科学有什么必要或特殊效用。相反,依我们看来,语言的问题主要是符号学的问题,我们的全部论证都

---

① 仔细不要把符号学和语义学混为一谈。语义学是研究语义的变化的,德·索绪尔没有作过有系统的阐述;但是在(原文)第112页我们可以找到他所表述的基本原理。

从这一重要的事实获得意义。要发现语言的真正本质,首先必须知道它跟其他一切同类的符号系统有什么共同点。有些语言的因素乍一看来似乎很重要(例如发音器官的作用),但如果只能用来使语言区别于其他系统,那就只好放到次要的地位去考虑。这样做,不仅可以阐明语言的问题,而且我们认为,把礼仪、习惯等等看作符号,这些事实也将显得完全是另一种样子。到那时,人们将会感到有必要把它们划归符号学,并用这门科学的规律去进行解释。

布龙菲尔德(1933)《语言论》选读①

◆ 作者简介

布龙菲尔德②(Leonard Bloomfield,1887—1949),美国语言学家,北美结构主义语言学的先导人物之一。他出生于美国芝加哥,1903—1906 年在哈佛学院学习,获得学士学位。1907 年他在芝加哥大学继续深造,在伍德(Francis A. Wood)教授的指导下完成了论文《日耳曼语次元音交替的语义差异》,1909 年获博士学位。1913—1914 年他赴德国莱比锡大学和哥根廷大学进修,并结识了新语法学派的代表人物布鲁格曼(Karl Brugmann)和雷斯琴(August Leskien)等,受到该学派理论的深刻影响。布龙菲尔德从研究日耳曼语系和印欧语系入手,继而研究了普通语言学、阿尔表琴语等其它语言。他曾在很多大学执教,最后执教于耶鲁大学,并任该校高级语言学教授。《语言论》是他最有影响力的著作,该书提出了美国结构语言学派研究语言的基本原则和描写语言结构的总框架,他本人也成为美国结构主义学派的奠基者和最重要的代表人物,该学派在二十世纪三四十年代的美国语言学界占有主

---

① 布龙菲尔德,《语言论》,袁家骅、赵世开、甘世福译,商务印书馆 1997 年版。
② 图片来源:https://ling.yale.edu/history/leonard-bloomfield。

导地位，1933—1950年在美国语言学史上甚至被称为"布龙菲尔德世纪"，足见他对语言学界的深刻影响。

◆ 正文节选

第二章　语言的用途

2.1　在语言研究中，最困难的一步就是第一步。过去的学者虽然一次又一次地接近了语言研究，然而并没有真正地进入这个领域。语言科学是从人们关心的一些比较实际的问题产生的，例如文字的使用，文学、特别是年代较古的文献的研究，以及优美的言辞的规则；可是人们尽管在这些事情上花了许多时间，仍然没有真正进入语言研究的领域。因为个别学者难免重复推迟历史的前进，我们不妨好好地把这些问题谈一谈，以便把我们研究的主题区别开来。

文字并不是语言，而只是利用看得见的符号来记录语言的一种方法。在某些国家，例如中国、埃及和美索不达米亚，几千年以前就使用文字了，但是今天人们说的语言，大多数是在不久以前才有文字，或者现在还没有文字。再说，在印刷术通行以前，识字只限于很少数的人。是在整个历史时期，一切语言几乎都是不会读书写字的人使用的；不会读书写字的民族的语言，和会读书识字的民族的语言同样地稳定、有规则和丰富。一种语言不论使用哪一种文字体系来记录，总还是那种语言，正如一个人不论怎样给他照相，总还是那样的一个人。日本人已有三套文字体系，如今正在发展第四套。土耳其人1928年采用了拉丁字母代替阿拉伯字母，可是他们仍旧像过去那样讲话。为了研究文字，我们必须懂得一些有关语言的指示，但是并非必须有关于文字的知识才能研究语言。固然，我们主要从文字记载知道过去语言的情况——为了这个原因，在另外有关问题上我们将研究文字的历史——但是我们发现要这样做也有一重障碍。我们必须十分小心地把文字符号译成实际的言语；可是我们往往做不到这一点，因而我们总是觉得有听得见的话语更好。

文学，不论是口语形式或是我们现在习用的书写形式，总是由优美的或者其他出色的话语构成。研究文学的人，细心研究某些人的话语（譬如说，像莎士比亚），只关心其内容和异乎寻常的形式特点。语文学家的兴趣更广些，因为他所涉及的是他所阅读的材料的文化意义和背景。语言学家可不同，他一视同仁地研究所有人的语言。一个伟大作家的个人语言特点，区别于他同时同地的普通语言，这对语言学家来说，并不比任何个人的言语特点更饶兴趣；如果拿这和所有说话的人的共同特点相比，那兴趣就更少得多了。

优美的或"正确的"言语的区分，是一定社会条件的副产品，语言学家必须观察，和观察其它语言现象一样。把某些说话的人的言语形式标明为"好的"、"正确的"，有的标明为"坏的"、"不正确的"，这个事实往往是语言学家有关这个言语形式的一部分资料。不用说，语言学家不容忽视一部分资料或是把记录歪曲，语言学家应当毫无偏见地观察一切言语形式。语言学家的任务，有一部分就是查明在什么样的条件下说话的人们赞许或非难某个形式，而且对于每一个具体形式都要查明为什么会有人赞许或非难。比方说，为什么很多人说 ain't(不是)是"坏的"，而 am not(不是)是"好的"。可是，这只是语言学的问题之一，而且并不是根本问题，所以只有在很多别的东西搞清楚之后才能研究。奇怪的是，没有语言学训练的人偏偏白费气力讨论这个题目，其实只是进一步研究语言本身才能拿找出解决问题的关键。

研究文字、文学、语文学或修辞正言的学者，假如他是坚持不懈、治学谨严的话，在浪费了一些气力之后，准会认识到他最好还是首先研究语言，然后再回到这些问题上来。我们只要转过头来观察一般言语，就能够不走这段弯路了。现在就让我们来看看在简单的情况下发生的言语行为。

2.2 假设杰克和琪儿正沿着一条小路走去。琪儿饿了。她看到树上有个苹果。于是她用她的喉咙、舌头和嘴唇发出一个声音。杰克接着就跳过篱笆，爬上树，摘下苹果，把它带到琪儿那里，放在她的手里。琪儿就这样吃到了这个苹果。

这一连串的事项可以从很多方面来加以研究，但是我们这些研究语言的人，很自然地会把言语行为和其他事情区别开来，那些其它事情，我们叫做实际事项。假如按照这种方法来观察的话，那么根据时间的先后，这件事情包括三个部分：

A. 言语行为以前的实际事项；

B. 言语；

C. 言语行为以后的实际事项。

我们首先来考察一下实际事项 A 和 C。A 项主要是关于说话人琪儿的一些事。她饿了，也就是说，她的某些肌肉在收缩，有些液体，特别是胃液，分泌了出来。或许她还渴：她的舌头和喉咙是干的。光波从红色的苹果那儿反射到她的眼睛里。她看到杰克在她的身边。她和杰克过去的关系现在应当加以说明；我们假设这是某种一般的关系，如兄妹的关系或是夫妻的关系。所有这些在琪儿说话以前已经存在并且和她有关的事项，我们叫做说话人的刺激。

现在我们再来看看发生在琪儿说话以后的实际事项C。这些事项主要是关于听话人杰克，包括他去摘苹果，把苹果交给琪儿。这些在说话以后发生而且和听话人有关的实际事项，我们叫做听话人的反应。这些说话以后发生的事项也关系到琪儿，而且关系很大：她把苹果拿到手里而且吃了。

这里还可以看出，整个故事还决定于一些与AC有关但是隔了一层的条件。并不是每一个杰克和琪儿都会像我们所说的那样做。假如琪儿害羞，或者上过杰克的当，她可能虽然肚子饿了并且看到了苹果，可是什么也不说；假如杰克对她没有好感，就算琪儿求他，他也不一定会给她摘苹果。言语行为的发生（以及怎样措辞，这一点我们将要谈到），和行为发生以前和以后的全部实际事项的过程，都决定于说话人和听话人的全部生活史。在目前情况下，我们假定所有这些决定性的因素正好引起我们所讲的这个故事。假如是这样的话，那么我们就想知道言语（B）在这个故事里起着什么样的作用。

假如琪儿是单独一个人，她可能同样的饿了，渴了，而且看到了同一个苹果。假如她有足够的气力和本领去翻过篱笆爬上树，那么她就可以拿到苹果吃下去了；要不是这样，她就只好挨饿。这位没人陪伴的琪儿和不会说话的动物几乎处于同样的地位。假如动物饿了并且看到或是闻到事物，它就会向食物的方向移动；至于能否得到食物，要决定于它的力气和本领。饥饿的状态和看或闻到食物是一种刺激（我们用S来代表），朝向事物方面移动就是反应（我们用R来代表）。没有人陪伴的琪儿和不会说话的动物的行为只有一种方式，这就是：

$$S \longrightarrow R$$

假如这样行之有效的话，他们就得到食物；假如不行——譬如说没有足够的力气和本领去采取行动R来拿事物——他们就只好挨饿。

当然，从琪儿的利益来说，拿到苹果是很重要的。在多数情况下，这还不是什么生死问题，虽然有的时候确实是生死问题；然而，从长远来看，琪儿（或是动物）如得到食物，便更有可能在地球上生存和繁殖。所以，任何增加琪儿获得苹果的机会的办法，对她都是有极大的价值的。在我们的故事里说话的琪儿正是利用了这样的办法。首先，她和没人陪伴的琪儿或者不会说话的动物同样有获得苹果的机会。然而，除此以外，说话的琪儿比其余二者还多了一个其他两个所没有的机会。她不用费劲去翻篱笆和爬树，只要在喉咙和嘴巴里做一些小动作，发出一点儿声音。她这么一来，杰克就为她做出反应，做了超出琪儿力气的动作，因而琪儿终于得到了苹果。语言可以在一个人受到刺激(S)时让另一个人去做出反应(R)。

理想的情况应该是，在彼此对话的一群人里，每一个人都可以随自己的意愿利用别人的力气和本领。这些人越是各有特殊本领，那么每个人所能利用的力量范围也就越大。爬树的能手只要一个，因为他可以给所有其他的人采果子；能干的渔夫也只要一个，因为他可以把鱼供给其他的人。劳动分工以及人类社会按分工原则进行活动，都依靠语言。

2.3 我们还必须考察我们这故事中的语言事项B。作为语言研究者，我们主要关心的当然就在于此。在我们所有的工作中我们都在研究B，A和C之所以同我们有关，只是因为和B有联系。多亏有了生理学和物理学，我们才能充分了解到这个言语事项原来一共包括三个部分：

(B1) 说话人琪儿使声带(在喉结内的两片小肌肉)，下颚，舌头等等活动，让空气形成声波。说话人的这些活动是对于刺激S的一种反应。她不去作实际的(或者干活的)反应R——也就是说，实际动手摘下苹果——而去做这些发音动作，即言语(speech)的反应(我们把它叫做替代性反应)，这个反应我们用小写字母r来代表。所以总起来说，作为说话人的琪儿不光有一种而是有两种对刺激起反应的方式：

$$S \longrightarrow R (实际的反应)$$

$$S \longrightarrow r (语言的替代性反应)$$

在目前情况下，她所作的是后一种反应。

(B2) 琪儿口腔里空气中的声波使周围的空气形成类似的波形振动。

(B3) 空气里的声波冲击杰克的耳膜，使它颤动，这样就对杰克的神经发生了作用：杰克听到了言语。这听到的话对于杰克就是一种刺激；我们看到他跑去摘苹果，把它放在琪儿的手里，就好像是琪儿所感到的饥饿与苹果的刺激作用于杰克本身一样。假如有谁从另外一个星球来这儿进行观察，并且不知道人类语言为何物，他一定会认为杰克身体的某部分有一种感觉器官告诉他说："琪儿饿了并且看到那上面有一个苹果了"。总之，杰克作为一个能说话的人，对两种刺激作出反应：大写字母S一类的实际刺激的反应(如饥饿和看见食物)和小写字母 s 所代表的言语(或叫替代性)刺激的反应,也就是耳膜的某种颤动。当我们看到杰克做某件事情(譬如说摘苹果)的时候,他的行为可能不只是像一个动物的动作那样,由于实际刺激(如胃部饥渴或者看到苹果),而且往往是由于言语的刺激。他的行为 R 可能不是一种刺激,而是两种刺激所引起的:

(实际刺激)S⟶R

(语言的替代性刺激)s⟶R

显然,在琪儿的语音活动(B1)和杰克的听话行为(B3)之间的联系,是不会有什么不确实,不稳定的毛病,因为这联系只是在空气中传送的声波(B2)。加入我们用虚线来表示这样一种联系,那么我们就可以用下面两种图式来表示人类回答刺激的两种方式:

无言语的反应:S⟶R

用言语作中介的反应:S⟶r⋯s⟶R

这两种类型之间的差别是明显的。无言语的反应总是发生在受到刺激的同一个人身上;受到刺激的人是唯一能够作出反应的人。所以反应也仅仅限于接受刺激的人能做出任何行为。与此相反,用言语作中介以激起的反应可能在没有受过实际刺激的人身上;受到刺激的人可以激起另外一个人的反应,而这另外一个人也许能够做出说话人本身所不能做的事情。在我们图式里的箭头代表在一个人身上的一系列事项——我们认为这些事项的发生是由于神经系统的某种属性。所以无言语的反应只能发生在受到过刺激的人的身上。另一方面,在用言语作中介的反应里,就有虚线所代表的联系,这就是空气中的声波:用言语作中介的反应可以发生在任何听到言语的人的身上;由于不同的听话人可能具有做出各式各样的行为的能力,所以反应的可能性也就大大地增加了。说话人和听话人身体之间原有一段距离——两个互不相连的神经系统——由声波作了桥梁。

从生物学看来,无论在无言语或是有言语的情况下,S(肚子饿和看到食物)和 R(取得食物的行为或者拿不到食物的行为)都是同等重要的。这是事情的两个实际方面。语言行为 s⋯r 只是一种手段,使 S 和 R 在不同的人的身上发生。一般正常的人只对 S 和 R 有兴趣;虽然他运用言语而且获益不浅,但是他并不加以注意。说"苹果"这个词或者听到别人说这个词,都不能给任何人充饥。这个词和其他言语里的词,是获得伙伴帮助唯一手段。然而作为研究语言的人,我们所关心的恰恰正是言语的事项(s…r)。它本身虽然没有价值,但却是达到某种巨大目的的手段。我们把语言即我们所研究的主题,与真实的或者是实际的事项,即刺激和反应区别开来。当任何表面看来并不重要的事物,却和比较重要的事物密切地联系起来,我们便说,这里总是有"意义";也就是说,它"意味着"重要的事物。所以我们说,本身微笑而不重要的话语也是重要的,因为它具有意义:这意义就在于言语(B)和重要的事情即实际事项(A 和 C)相联系。

2.4 有些动物在一定程度上也能因彼此刺激而起反应。很显然,一群蚂蚁或者蜜蜂能够很好地合作,必定是由于有某种相互感应的方式。以声音来互相感应,是相当普遍的,例如蟋蟀用摩擦式,即用腿摩擦身体发出唧唧声,来呼唤其他的蟋蟀。有些动物,像人一样,用发音器官发出声音。鸟用肺部顶端一对芦笛似的器官即鸣管发出声波。较高级的哺乳动物有一个喉头,是在气管顶端由软骨构成的匣子似的东西(在男子就叫做喉头隆起)。在喉头里面,沿着左右两边喉壁各有两层肌肉;这两层肌肉即是声带,要是拉紧了,那呼出的气息就使它们有规则第颤动,由此产生声响。我们把这种声响叫做发音器官的声音。

人类的语言和动物做出的类似信号的活动不同,甚至和那些使用发音器官的动物也不同,因为人类语言的声音是很复杂的。譬如狗只能发出两种或者三种声音——吠声、咆哮声和嗥声:一只狗可以用这几种不同的信号使另一只狗做某种行动。鹦鹉可以发出很多种不同的声音,但显然对不同的声音不能做不同的反应。人能发出很多种语音而且利用这些不同的语音。在一定类型的刺激下,他发出一定的语音,他的同伴听到了这些声音就做出相应的反应。简单地说,在人类的语言里,不同的声音具有不同的意义。研究一定的声音和一定意义如何配合,这就是研究语言。

这种配合使得人们能够十分准确地相互感应。譬如有一所房子,某人从来没有看到过,我们把地址告诉他,这时,我们就是做着没有一个动物能做的事。不仅每个人可以使许多其他人发挥所长来为自己效劳,而且这种合作是十分准确的。协作规模的大小和准确程度的高低,是衡量我们社会组织成效大小的标准。社会或者社会机构这些术语,并不是一种隐喻。人类集体比起单个动物来,的确是高一级的单位,正好像多细胞动物比起单细胞动物来是高一级的单位一样。在多细胞动物身体里边,单细胞是靠着神经系统这样的组织来协作的；在人类社会里，各个人是靠声波来协作的。

　　我们从语言得到各种好处，这事儿是如此明显，这儿只要提几点就够了。我们可以传递消息。当有些农民或者做生意的人说："我们要求在这条小河上造一座桥"的时候，这消息就会传到市民大会、州议会、公路局、工程处以及承建商人办事处那里，这其间通过了许多说话人而且多次经过语言的传递；直到最后，由于对农民最初所作的刺激起了真正的（实际的）反应，一群工人架起桥来了。在性质上和语言传递密切相关的是语言的抽象性。在实际的刺激发出以后，实际的反应发生以前，那一连串的语言传递并没有直接的实际效果。所以这一连串语言传递可以采取各种不同的形式，只要在作最后实际反应之前能正确地变成原有的刺激就行了。设计桥梁的工程师，并不一定真要去搬动大小钢梁，他仅仅和语言形式（如计算时所用的数字）打交道；假如他算错了，他并不要拆毁任何材料，只要在开始正式筑桥之前用一个正确的语言形式来代替那个错误的语言形式（一个错误的数字）就行了。自言自语或是思维的价值就在于此。我们小时候常对自己大声说话，但是因为长辈禁止，不久便学会抑制发声动作而代之以很轻微的听不到的声音：我们"用词来思维"。思维的用处可以用计算过程来加以说明。我们如不使用语言，计算数目的能力是十分有限的，这只要用眼睛扫视一下书架上的一排书，就可以知道。所谓两组东西"数目相同"，意思是这样：假如我们从第一组东西里拿出一件，放在第二组一个东西的旁边，而且依次放下去，每件东西只放一遍，那么，最后就不会有不配对的东西剩下来。然而，我们不可能永远这样做。这些东西也许太重了，搬不动，也许是在世界不同的地方，也许存在于不同的时间（譬如说在暴风雨之前和暴风雨之后的一群羊）。这时候语言就有用了。一、二、三、四这些数目字，只不过是我们学会顺序说出的一连串单词，用来代替上述的做法。我们可以用这些数目字来"计算"任何一组东西，让那些东西和数目字一对一（如数学家所说的），譬如说，有一个东西就说一，到了另一个就说二，到下一个就说三，依此类推，要注意每件东西只用一次，直到东西全部点完。假如当我们数到十九的时候，再没有东西剩下了。以后，在任何时间或者任何地方，碰到一组新的东西，我们只要把它照此再计算一遍，就可以确定这一组新的东西是否和第一组东西数目相同。数学是语言最理想的运用，可是它只不过是把这样一种过程复杂化而已。数字的运用是自言自语发生作用最简单也最清楚的例证，此外，还有许许多多其他的情况。我们总是先思而后行。

2.5 在不同的人群里,对某些特殊的刺激所发出的特殊的语音是不同的;人类讲多种的语言。使用同一个语法符号系统的一群人,称一个语言社团。显然,语言之用处,就在于人们以同样的方式来使用它。每一个社会集团成员必须在适当的场合发出适当的语音,而且当他听到另外一个人发出这样一些语音时,也必须作出适当的反应。他必须说得人家懂,而且也必须懂得别人说的是什么。甚至最不开化的社群,也是如此;无论在哪儿,只要看见有人,他们总是会说话的。

在各个集团里生出来的每一个小孩儿,从几岁起就学会了那个集团的言语习惯和反应。这无疑是我们每一个人都要学会的智力上最大的本领。小孩儿究竟怎么样学会讲话,还不很清楚;也许是这样一种过程吧:

(1) 在各种刺激下,小孩儿发出一些声音,以后又重复发出。这似乎是一种遗传下来的特性。假如他发出一个声音,我们姑且用 da 代表它,当然,他的实际动作和发出的相应的声音和任何正规使用的英语可能不同。当这孩子不断重复发音动作时,声波就冲击着他的鼓膜。这样就形成了一种习惯:每当一个类似的声音冲击着他的鼓膜时,他往往做同样的口腔动作,再发出 da 这个音。这种无意义的发音动作教会他照样去发出冲击他的耳朵的声音。

(2) 有个人,譬如说母亲,在孩子面前发出了一种声音,和小孩儿咿呀学语的音节类似;例如,她说 doll(洋娃娃)。当这些声音冲击小孩儿的耳朵时,他的习惯(1)就起作用了,他发出了最接近 doll 的音节 da。在这个时候,我们说他开始"模仿"了。成年的人们似乎到处都看得到这种情况,因为每种语言都似乎有类似婴儿学语的一些词,如 mama(妈妈),dada(爸爸)等等。毫无疑问,这些词儿广泛地流行,是因为小孩儿很容易学会。

(3) 当适当的刺激出现时,母亲自然得用她自己的词来说话。当她真的给婴儿看洋娃娃或者把洋娃娃给他时,她就说 doll。看到,拿到洋娃娃,和听到,说出 doll(也就是 da)这个词,多次一块儿出现,一直到这个小孩儿形成了一种新的习惯:每当他看到并接触到洋娃娃时,他就会说出 da 来。这时候他就懂得一个词的用法了。成年人也许觉得,这个词听起来不像他们所用的任何一个词,但这仅仅是由于发音不正确。看起来孩子们不会创造一个新词。

(4) 看到洋娃娃就说 da,这个习惯引起了另一个习惯。譬如说,每天在小孩儿洗完澡以后,接着就给他洋娃娃(而且小孩同时说 da,da,da);那么它就有了一种在洗澡后说 da, da 的习惯;这就是说,假如有那么一天母亲忘了给他洋娃娃,他在洗完澡以后还是会喊 da, da 的。母亲说:"他在要洋娃娃呢"。这话说得对,因为无疑地,成年人在"要求"或者"要"东西时,情况也是相同,只不过是形式更为复杂而已。小孩儿到这时候,已经会运用抽象的或者转移的(abstract or displaced)言语了:甚至当某个东西不在面前的时候,他也会说出那个东西的名称。

(5) 小孩子的言语,由获得效果而逐渐完善。假如他的 da, da 说得相当好,那么长辈就中的他的意思,给他洋娃娃。在这种情况下,看到和摸到洋娃娃就成了一种附加的刺激,这小孩儿也就屡次地使用他这有效的变了音的词。另一方面,假如他的 da, da 说得不完全——也就是说,和成年人们惯用的形式 doll 有很大的差异——那么他的长辈就没受到刺激,也不给他洋娃娃了。当他没有得到看见与拿到洋娃娃这些附加的刺激,却受到了另外一种使他精神错乱的刺激,或者洗澡以后不像平时那样得到洋娃娃,他发脾气了,这就打乱了他最近的印象。总之,他在言语上比较成功的尝试,往往由于重复而加强。而他的失败往往就在精神混乱中被抹去了。这个过程一直不停止。再过好些时候,假如他说:Daddy bringed it(爸爸把它拿来了),他只能得到失望的回答,No! You must say "Daddy brought it"(不! 你得说"爸爸把它拿来了");可是假如他说"Daddy brought it",他往往会再一次听到这个形式:Yes, Daddy brought it,这样他就得到了一个有利的实际的反应。

与此同时而且经过同样的过程,小孩儿也在学听话。当他拿着洋娃娃的时候,他听到自己说 da, da,而母亲说 doll。过了一个时期,听到了 doll 这个声音,就能使他去拿洋娃娃。当小孩儿自动向父亲招手,或者母亲举起他的手摇一摇的时候,母亲就会说:Wave your hand to Daddy(向爸爸招手)。小孩儿在听到别人说话时就养成了按约定俗成的方式行动起来的习惯。

言语习惯这种二重性变得越来越一致了,因为二者总是一块儿发生的。每当小孩儿学会了把 S⟶r 联系起来时(例如,当他看到他的洋娃娃时就说 doll),他也就学会把 S⟶R 联系起来(例如,当他听到 doll 这个词的时候,他的手就伸向洋娃娃或者把它拿起来)。在他学会了许多这样的双重联系以后,他就逐渐养成一种习惯,把某一类联系和另一类联系结合在一起:每当他学会说一个新词的时候,他就能在听到别人说这个词的时候做出反应;反过来也是如此,每当他学会如何对一个新词作出反应时,他通常也能在适当的场合把这词说出来。在二者当中,后一种转换似乎是比较困难些;在以后的生活中,我们会发现,一个说话人懂得很多的言语形式,那是他自己在言语里很少用它或者根本没有用过的。

乔姆斯基(2006)《语言与心智》选读[①]

◆ **作者简介**

诺姆·乔姆斯基[②](Noam Chomsky, 1928—)出生于美国宾夕法尼亚州的费城,本科就读于宾夕法尼亚大学,并在那里遇见了哈里斯(Zegllig Harris),这对乔姆斯基的一生产生了深远的影响。1949年乔姆斯基本科毕业,论文主题为研究现代希伯来语,后来被进一步扩展为他的硕士论文。1955年他在宾夕法尼亚大学取得语言学博士学位,然而他的大部分博士研究是用四年时间以哈佛年轻学者的身份在哈佛大学完成的。
在博士论文中,他开始提出自己的一些语言学思想,后来他将这些进一步阐发,于是有了著名的《句法结构》。

乔姆斯基之所以重要,主要是因为他证明了世界上实际只有一种人类语言,人们所听到的身边数以万计、复杂纷呈的不同语言乃是同一语言的不同变体。他引发了语言学革命,也因此在哲学界引发热议。他重新发展了天赋论思想,证明人类相当一部分知识由基因遗传决定。他使沉静了几个世纪的理性主义思想得以复苏,证明了无意识的知识是我们说话与理解能力的寄出。他颠覆了行为主义学派在心理学领域的统治地位。简而言之,他改变了人类对自己的认知地位,在思想史上的地位几乎等同于达尔文或笛卡尔。此外,他还花费大量时间致力于异议政治和激进主义运动,揭示政府的谎言,被

[①] 乔姆斯基,《语言与心智(第三版)》,熊仲儒、张孝荣译,中国人民大学出版社2015年版。
[②] 图片来源:https://en.wikipedia.org/wiki/Noam_Chomsky。

称为"西方的良心"。

《语言与心智》是乔姆斯基关于语言与心智的杰出论文集,前六章初版于二十世纪六十年代,对语言学理论做出了突破性的贡献。第三版对其进行了补充,增加了新的一章和新的序言,将乔姆斯基有影响力的研究方法带入了二十一世纪。

◆ 正文节选

第四章 自然语言的形式和意义

我们在研究人类语言(human language)的时候,也在接近可称之为"人类本质"(human essence)的东西,它是心智的特有品质,就我们所知,它是人类所特有的,不管从个人还是从社会来说,它都跟人类存在的任何关键时期不可分离。因此,这项研究的魅力跟它面临的困难不相上下。困难来自如下事实,即尽管研究有很大的进展,但我们仍然像早先一样抓不住人类语言的核心问题。在我看来,掌握一门语言,一方面,听话者可以理解无数的语言表达式,这些语言表达式相对于其经验而言是全新的,跟构成其语言经验的别的语言表达式之间没有简单的物理相似,也绝不简单地类同;另一方面,说者可以在合适场合通过或多或少的技能产生语言表达式,尽管这些语言表达式是全新的并且独立于可察觉的刺激结构(detectable stimulus configuration),但它可以被共享这一至今仍神秘的能力的其他人所理解。从这个意义上看,语言的正常使用是一项创造性的活动。语言正常使用的创造性是将人类语言区别于任何已知的动物交际系统的基本因素。

语言表达式的创造性是语言使用的正常模式,这种表达式虽然新奇但是很合适,记住这一点是很重要的。如果某人很大程度地将自己局限在有限的语言模式上,或局限在对刺激结构的一些习惯性的反应上,或局限在现代语言学意义上的"类推(analogy)"上,那我们就会认为他有心智缺陷,不像人类,而更像动物。他会被直接地从普通人类中区分出来,因为他不能理解正常的话语,或者不能以正常的方式参与话语。这种正常的方式具有创新性,不受外部刺激的控制,并且对新的、不断变化的情景是合适的。

用这些属性区分人类言语(human speech)并不是什么新鲜的观点,但这个观点必须一次次地被我们重新认识。随着我们对语言、思想和行为的机制的理解的每一次进步,逐渐出现了一种趋势,这种趋势让我们相信已经找到了理解人类心智那明显独特的属性的钥匙。这些进步是真实的,但是诚实的评价是：我认为这些进步还远远没有提供这样的钥匙。我们也都知道，其实我们并不理解，也可能永远也不会理解是什么使正常的人类智力将语言作为自由表达思想和感觉的工具成为可能的；或许就此而言，我们也不理解智力的创造性活动涉及到心智的什么属性。智力的创造性活动，在真实的人类存在(human existence)中，是特有的而非唯一的和例外的。

我认为这是一种需要强调的重要事实，这不仅是为了那些以此为研究中心的语言学家和心理学家，更是为了那些希望在工作中学到有用的东西并希望从其研究想到语言和思维的人们。对大学教师来说，认识到理解的局限性非常重要；对一般学校中的教师而言，更是如此。有一股很强的压力逼迫着这些教师根据最新的科学进步去利用新的教育技术并设计课程和教授方法。这样做虽然没有什么好反对的，但对这个真实存在的危险保持警惕却是非常重要的：新的知识和技术虽然可以明确教什么与怎么教的本质，但是却不能对建立在其他基础之上且使用其他术语加以表述的教育目标的实现做贡献。让我说得更具体点。在语言教学、算术教学以及其他领域中，虽然能够获得快速有效地传授熟练行为所需的技巧甚至科技，但相应地，也存在一种真实诱惑，即用新科技定义的术语去重建课程。利用"行为控制"的概念或者通过提升技术等方式创造一个基本原理并非难事，设计一些肯定能证明这种方法在达到某种目标方面的有效性的客观测试(objective test)也不难，这些目标已经被融进了这些测试。但这类成功并不能证明重要的教育目标已经达到，也不能证明集中发展学生的熟练行为很重要。我们对人类智力不多的了解至少可以证明一些不同的事情，即不管是减少向勇于求索的心智所呈现材料的范围和复杂性，还是在固定模式里设置行为，这些方法都可能会伤害、扭曲创造性能力的正常发展。我不想细究这个问题。我可以肯定的是，不论是谁，他都有能力从自己的经验中发现这样的例子。在知识或某一特定的研究领域里去尝试探索真实的进步，这是非常正确的。向哪个方向研究，应该考虑可行性与根本意义，可以说，这种考虑是不可避免的，也是非常合适的。对可行性与重要性的考虑很有可能导致完全不同的道路，如果不是不可避免的话。对于那些希望把一个学科的成果应用到解决另一个学科中的问题的人来说，弄清楚这些成果的确切本质非常重要，弄清楚这些成果的局限性同样也很重要。

我刚提到过：语言正常使用的创造性方面不是新的发现。它为笛卡尔的心智理论及其机械解释的限制研究提供了重要的支撑。后者又反过来为建构启蒙运动中的反独裁主义的社会和政治哲学提供了一个重要的要素。而且,事实上,也有努力地根据语言正常使用的创造性方面建构艺术创造性理论的。比如说,施莱格尔(Schlegel)认为诗歌在艺术作品中有独特的地位,他的例证是两个不同的术语:"诗性"(poetical)与"音乐性"(musical),前者用来指称任何艺术成就中的创造性想象力的元素,后者隐喻性地用来指称感觉元素。为解释这种不对称性,他观察到艺术表达的每种模式都利用某种媒介,诗歌(语言)的媒介在那种语言中是唯一的,像人类心智的表达而非自然的产物,它在范围上是无限的,并被建构在递归性原则的基础上,递归性原则准许每种作品都可以作为新的创作活动的基础。因此,它在艺术形式以语言为媒介的艺术中处于中心地位。

天生就有创造性的语言为人类唯一拥有,这种信念当然也并非没有争议。笛卡儿哲学的一个解释者安托万(Antoine Le Grand),他提到过"东印度群岛的一些人的(观点),这些人认为他们周围数目极大的猿和狒狒都拥有理解力,也认为它们会说话但不说,因为它们害怕被雇用,并被安排工作。"我不知道是否有更严肃的证据支持其他灵长类动物也和人类一样有语言能力的论断。事实上,对我而言,我们拥有的任何证据似乎都支持这样的观点:习得和使用语言的能力是人类这一物种所特有的能力,有很深层的和限制性的原则决定着人类语言的本质,并且这些原则被深根于人类心智的特性之中。很显然,与该假设相关的论据不会是决定性的或结论性的,但在我看来,即使就我们现有的知识来看,证据仍然值得考虑。

有很多问题都可能会引导人们从事语言的研究。就我个人而言,激发我兴趣的是通过语言研究可以学到揭示人类心智固有属性的东西。对于语言正常使用的创造性,我根本说不出什么特别翔实的信息。我认为我们正在慢慢地理解使语言的这种创造性用法、语言被用作自由思维与表达的工具成为可能的机制。再从个人观点的角度来说,对我而言,当代语法研究中最有趣的方面,一是试图制定语言的组织原则,而这些原则被认为是对心智属性的普遍反映;二是试图表明特殊语言的某些方面可以根据这些假设得到解释。根据以上观点,语言学只是人类心理学的一部分:该领域旨在确定人类心智能力的本质和研究这些能力是如何运作的。很多心理学家都会拒绝用这些术语来描述他们的学科,但这种反应对我而言似乎只是他们对心理学构想的严重不足,而不是公式化方法本身的缺陷。无论如何,在我看来,总会有一些合适的术语可用来为当代语言学设置目标和讨论其得失。

我认为现在可以就人类语言的组织给出一些相当明确的建议,并对它们进行经验上的测验。转换生成语法学理论正沿着几种不同并且时而相互冲突的道路发展,在其发展过程中也提出了这种建议;在过去的几年里,出现了一些成果非常丰富而又有启发性的研究,这些工作试图完善和重构人类语言底层的操作与底层的结构的形式化方法。

语法学理论关心的问题是:人的语言知识的本质是什么?知道某种语言的人都掌握了一套规则系统,这套规则系统以确定的方式为无数种可能的句子指派声音和意义。因此,每种语言,(某种程度上)都是由无数成对的声音和意义组成。当然,知道语言的人并没有意识到已经掌握了这些规则或正在使用这些规则,也没有任何理由假定语言规则的这种知识能够被带入意识中。通过内省,人们会慢慢积累起语音—意义关系的很多证据,这种关系是由他所掌握的这种语言的规则决定的;没有任何理由可以假定,他可以远远地超出这些语料的表面层次,以至可以通过内省发现决定语音与意义的这种对应关系的底层规则和原则。准确地说,发现这些规则和原则是一个典型的科学问题。我们收集了各种语言中语音—意义(即语言表达式的形式和解释)之间的对应关系的语料。我们力图为各种语言确立解释这些语料的规则系统。我们还想更深入地为各种人类语言建立起支配形成这些规则系统的原则。

详细说明所给定语言中的音义关系的规则系统,可以称之为这种语言的"语法",或许还可以用一个更专业的名称"生成语法"(generative grammar)。说语法"生成"一个确定的结构集合,只是简单地说它以非常明确的方式详细说明了这个集合。在这个意义上,无论用哪一种形式属性或构型作为音义关系的中介,我们都可以说,每种语言的语法都可以生成"结构描写"(structural description)的无限集,每个结构描写都是决定特定声音、特定意义的某类抽象客体。举例来说,英语语法生成了我正在说的这些句子的结构描写,或许还可以用一个更简单的例子来说明。比如说,英语语法将会为以下这些句子生成结构描写。

(1) John is certain that Bill will leave.
　　约翰坚信比尔会离开。

(2) John is certain to leave.
　　约翰肯定会离开。

我们每个人都已经掌握，并内部表征了向这些句子指派结构描写的语法系统；我们在说出这些句子或理解别人说出的这些句子的时候，是完全没有意识，甚至是在没有产生这种意识的可能性的情况下使用这方面的语言知识的。结构描写包括句子的音系表达式和具体的语义内容。在例(1)和例(2)里，结构描写必须大致传达以下的信息：在例(1)中必须指示，一个特定的心理状态（即"坚信比尔会离开"）系"约翰"所有；而在例(2)的情况下，一个特定的逻辑属性（即某一"肯定"的属性）系命题"约翰会离开"所有。尽管这两个句子的形式表面上非常相似，但是通过语法生成的结构描写必须表明这两个句子的意义有很大的不同：一个将心理状态归结给"约翰"，另一个将逻辑属性归结给抽象命题。第二句可以用非常不同的形式解释：

(3) That John will leave is certain.
　　约翰会离开是肯定的。

例(1)没有这样的解释。也许有人会说，在解释(3)中，(2)的"逻辑形式"(logical form)被表达得更为直接。(2)和(3)的语法关系十分相似，尽管表面形式有区别；(1)和(2)中的语法关系具有较大不同，尽管表面形式很相似。诸如此类的语言事实，为英语语法结构的考察，更一般地说，也为人类语言普遍属性的考察提供了出发点。

为了更进一步地讨论语言的属性，请允许我引入"表层结构"这一术语用来表示构成语言表达式的短语表达式和这些短语所属的类别。在例(1)中，表层结构的短语包括：完整命题"that Bill will leave"、名词短语"Bill"和"John"、动词短语"will leave"和"is certain that Bill will leave"及其他。在例(2)中，表层结构包括动词短语"to leave"和"is certain to leave"，但例(2)的表层结构不包括"John will leave"这种命题形式，尽管这种命题表达了"John is certain to leave"的部分意义，并在其解释"that John will leave is certain"的表层结构中作为短语出现。从这个角度说，表层结构不必准确地显示决定句子意义的各种结构和关系。在例(2)"John is certain to leave"中,表层结构无法显示以下事实:"John will leave"这一命题表达了句子的部分意义,尽管在我所给的另外两个句子中,表层结构能非常直接地显示语义上非常重要的关系。

接着让我引入另外一个更专业的术语"深层结构",这一术语用来表示在句子的语义解释上发挥更重要作用的短语表达式。在例(1)和例(3)中,深层结构和表层结构可能差别不大,但在例(2)中,深层结构和表层结构却相差很大,因为它包括像"John will leave"这样的命题和应用于这一命题的谓词"is certain",尽管在表层结构里没有这样的表达。一般而言,除了那些最简单的例子外,句子的表层结构和深层结构的差别还是非常大的。

英语的语法会为每个句子生成一个深层结构并包含显示深层结构和表层结构如何关联的规则。表达深层结构与表层结构之间关系的规则被称为"语法转换"(grammatical transformation)。所以这种语法又叫"转换生成语法"(transformational-generative grammar)。除了定义深层结构、表层结构以及这两者之间的关系的规则外,英语语法还包含着其他规则,这些规则一方面关联着这些"句法体"(syntactic object)(即成对的深层结构与表层结构)与语音表达式,另一方面关联着这些句法体与意义表达式。一个获得英语知识的人,已经将这些规则内化了,并用这些规则理解或说出上面所给的例句或无数其他句子。

支持这种方法的证据是:英语句子的一些很有趣的属性可直接用指派给它们的深层结构进行解释。我们重新分析句子(1)中的"John is certain that Bill will leave."和句子(2)中的"John is certain to leave."。句子(1)的深层结构和表层结构完全相同,句子(2)的表层结构和深层结构却非常不同。句子(1)有一个对应的名词性短语,即"John's certainty that Bill will leave (surprised me)";但句子(2)却没有这种对应的名词性短语。我们不说"John's certainty to leave surprised me."。我假定这后一种名词性短语是可以理解的,但它在英语中是不合格的。英语说话者非常清楚这样的事实,尽管他很可能说不出原因。这种事实是英语非常普遍的属性的一个特殊案例,即句子的表层结构与深层结构差别很小时,有对应于句子的名词短语;句子的表层结构与深层结构差别很大时,没有对应于句子的名词短语。"John is certain that Bill will leave"这句话,因为其表层结构和深层结构接近,所以对应于名词短语"John's certainty that Bill will leave"。但是没有对应于句子"John is certain to leave"的名词短语"John's certainty to leave",因为这个句子的表层结构跟其深层结构差别很大。

"差别很小"(closeness)、"差别很大"(remoteness)这两个概念可以弄得更准确些。当我们把它们弄准确后,就可以解释为什么名词化在一些例子中适用,而在其他情况下却不适用,尽管它们可以出现在不适用的语境,而且通常也相当容易理解。这个解释取决于深层结构这个概念,实际上,它表明名词化必须反映深层结构的属性。有许多实例可以说明这个现象。重要的是,它支持了如下观点:深层结构是存在的,并且通常都很抽象,它在我们用来产生和解释句子的语法操作中起着重要作用。这些事实,又支持着下一个假设,那就是这类在转换生成语法中被假定存在的深层结构是实实在在的心智结构。深层结构规则,跟关联深层结构与表层结构的转换规则,关联深层结构、表层结构与语音表达式、语义表达式的规则,这三种规则,会一门语言的人都已经掌握了。这些规则构成了人的语言知识。当人在说话或理解时,这些规则就派上用场了。

以上我所给出的例子阐释了深层结构在决定意义方面的作用,同时也表明即使在非常简单的情况中,深层结构也有可能与表层结构相距甚远。大量事实表明,句子的语音形式是由其表层结构决定的,所用的原则既特别有趣又错综复杂,在这里我就不讨论了。从这些事实可以得出:表层结构决定语音形式,而深层结构所表征的语法关系则决定意义。另外,如前文所述,有一些诸如名词化的语法操作只能用抽象的深层结构表达。

其实,情况比这更复杂,因为表层结构在决定语义解释方面也起一定的作用①。这个问题的研究是当前工作中最有争议的一个方面,同时,在我看来,它也有可能是最有成果的工作之一。如果要解释的话,英语中的现在完

---

① 我在《深层结构与语义解释》这篇文章里较为详细地讨论了这个问题,该文载于雅克布逊与川本茂雄主编的《一般语言学与东方语言学研究》,本期是专门纪念服部四郎先生(Shiro Hattori)的(N. Chomsky, "Deep Structure and Semantic Interpretation", in R. Jakobson and S. Kawamoto, eds., Studies in General and Oriental Linguistics, commemorative volume for Shiro Hattori TEC Corporation for Language and Educational Research, Tokyo, 1970)。

成时的一些特征就是一个很好的例子,如"John has lived in Princeton."(约翰住在了普林斯顿)这类句子。这一时体有一个非常有趣却很少被提及的特征,那就是它暗含着"主语还活着"这个预设。正因为如此,说"I have lived in Princeton"(我住在了普林斯顿)是合适的,但是,由于大家都知道爱因斯坦已逝世,我就不能说"Einstein has lived in Princeton."(爱因斯坦住在了普林斯顿)。相反,我会说"Einstein lived in Princeton."(爱因斯坦在普林斯顿住过)(当然,还有很多复杂的情况存在,但粗略地说这是准确的。)现在,请思考一下现在完成时的主动和被动形式,假如我们知道约翰已经死了而比尔还活着,那么我们就可以说"Bill has often been visited by John(比尔经常有约翰来拜访)"、"John often visited Bill(约翰过去经常拜访比尔)",却不能说"John has often visited Bill(约翰经常拜访比尔)"。同样,我可以说"I have been taught physics by Einstein(爱因斯坦教我物理学)"、"Einstein taught me physics(爱因斯坦教过我物理学)",不能说"Einstein has taught me physics(爱因斯坦现在教我物理学)"。一般而言,主动语态和被动语态具有相同的意义与本质相同的深层结构。但在这些情况下,主动和被动形式的差别在于他们所表达的预设。简单地说,预设是表层主语所指称的人是活着的。在这个方面,表层结构对这个句子的意义有贡献,它跟确定句子使用中的预设有关。

把这个问题再往深处拓展,我们可以观察到当出现一个联合主语时,情况又有所不同。比如我们知道希拉里还健在,马可·波罗却已过世,那么我们可以说"Hilary has climbed Mt. Everest"(希拉里爬了珠穆朗玛峰)、"Marco Polo climbed Mt. Everest"(马可·波罗爬过珠穆朗玛峰),而不能说"Marco Polo has climbed Mt.Everest"(马可·波罗爬了珠穆朗玛峰)(同样,我忽略了一些微妙和复杂的情况)。现在,请思考这个句子"Marco Polo and Hilary (among others) have climbed Mt. Everest"[马可·波罗和希拉里(和其他人一起)爬了珠穆朗玛峰],在这个例子中,没有"马可·波罗在世"这样的预设。像被动句"Mt. Everest has been climbed by Marco Polo (among others)"[珠穆朗玛峰有马可波罗(和其他人一起)爬]一样,它也没有这种预设。

我们进一步注意到,当我们从正常语调转到一个包含对比重音或表达重音的语调时,情况又发生了很大的变化。就预设而言,这些语调的效果十分复杂。下面我将用一个简单的例子来说明。请看"The Yankees played the Red Sox in Boston"(洋基队跟红袜队在波士顿比赛)这个句子。从正常语调来看,如果主重音与音高的位置落在 Boston(波士顿)这个单词上,则可以用来回答这些问题:"Where did the Yankees play the Red Sox?"(in Boston);"What did the Yankees do?"(They played the Red Sox in Boston);"What happened?"(The Yankees played the Red Sox in Boston)。但是假如对比重音落在"Red Sox"(红袜队)上,"The Yankees played the RED SOX in Boston",现在,这个句子只能用来回答"Who did the Yankees play in Boston?"注意,这个句子预设了"Yankees played someone in Boston"。如果根本就没有比赛,那么说"The Yankees played the RED SOX in Boston"就是不合适的,而不仅仅是为真值上的"假"(false)。相比之下,如果根本就没有比赛,但用正常的语调说"The Yankees played the Red Sox in Boston",那就只是为"假",但并非不合适。因此,对比重音携带了正常语调所没有携带的预设,尽管正常语调在另外的意义上也携带预设。因而它用"The Yankees played the Red Sox in Boston"(正常语调)来回答"Who played the Red Sox in Boston"这个问题是不合适的。在所谓的分裂句中也可以看到对比重音的相同特征。句子"It was the YANKEES who played the Red Sox in Boston"的主重音落在 YANKEES 上,预设是有人在波士顿跟红袜队比赛。假如根本没有比赛的话,这个句子就不合适,而不仅仅为假。当对比重音的语义作用被提出来后,这些现象一般就被忽略了。

为进一步解释表层结构在决定语义上的作用,让我们考虑"John is tall for a pygmy"(就俾格米人而言,约翰算高的了)这类句子。这个句子预设了约翰是一个俾格米人,而俾格米人一般是很矮的。如果我们了解"Watusi"(瓦图西人),那么说"John is tall for a Watusi"(就瓦图西人而言,约翰算高的)就不正常了。另一方面,也可以想想如果我们把"even"这个词插入这个句子会发生什么。如果把它放在"John"之前,我们就可以得到"Even John is tall for a pygmy"(就俾格米人而言,连约翰都算高的),同样,其预设是约翰是个俾格米人,俾格米人很矮。但是再看看"John is tall even for a pygmy"(甚至对俾格米人而言,约翰都算高的)。这个预设是俾格米人是高的,所以它是一个反常的句子,而根据我们的常识,如果我们说"John is tall even for a Watusi"(甚至就瓦图西人而言,约翰都算高的),这就很正确。原因在于,"even"

在"John is tall for a pygmy"这个句子中的位置决定了一个跟俾格米人平均身高有关的预设。

不过,"even"这个词的位置只是表层结构的问题。根据以下事实我们可以看出这一点:"even"这个词可以跟在深层结构上没有任何表达式的短语发生关联。再看下面这个句子,"John isn't certain to leave at 10; in fact, he isn't even certain to leave at all"(不能确定约翰是否在10点离开;实际上,甚至完全不能确定他是否离开),在这里,跟"even"这个词发生关联的是"certain to leave",正如前文提到的,这个短语不出现在深层结构里。因此,在这种情况下,表层结构的属性在确立一个句子的预设时同样起作用。

代词化①现象再一次证明了表层结构在决定意义时的作用。因此如果我说"Each of the men hates his brothers.",单词"his"可以指这些人中的任何一个。但是假如我说"The men each hate his brothers.",单词"his"则一定指其他人,不会指句子中任何一个人。不过,我们有足够的证据去说明"each of the men"和"the men each"来自同样的深层结构。同样,就像先前提到的,重音的位置在决定代词的指称上起着很重要的作用。让我们来看下面这个语段"John washed the car; I was afraid someone ELSE would do it",这个句子隐含着我希望John去洗车,并且我很高兴他这么做。但是现在请看下面的句子"John washed the car; I was AFRAID someone else would do it.",重音落在"afraid"上,这个句子隐含着我希望John不去洗这辆车。"someone else"的指称在两个例子中是不同的。有很多例子说明表层结构在决定代词的指称方面起重要作用。

使问题变得更为复杂的是,深层结构在决定代词化方面也起着重要的作用。接下来请看"John appeared to Bill to like him"(约翰好像喜欢比尔)这个句子,在这里,代词"him"应该是指 Bill 而不是 John。比较一下"John appealed to Bill to like him"(约翰请求比尔喜欢他),这里的代词"him"是指

---

① 原书注:"接下来的例子来源于多尔蒂(Ray Dougherty)、阿卡马基恩(Adrian Akmajian)和杰肯道夫(Ray Jackendoff)。我的文章可以参见雅克布逊与川本茂雄主编的《一般语言学与东方语言学研究》。"该文章为"N. Chomsky, Deep Structure and Semantic Interpretation, in R. Jakobson and S. Kawamoto, eds., *Studies in General and Oriental Linguistics*, TEC Corporation for Language and Educational Research, Tokyo, 1970"。

John 而不是 Bill。因此，我们能说"John appealed to Mary to like him"（约翰请求玛丽喜欢他），但不能说"John appealed to Mary to like her"（约翰请求玛丽喜欢她），在这里，"him"是指 John。另一方面，我们可以说"John appeared to Mary to like her"，但不能说"John appealed to Mary to like her"，其中"her"指 Mary。同样，反身代词在"John appealed to Bill to like himself"中指 Bill，但在"John appeared to Bill to like himself"中则指 John。这些句子表层结构上是大致相同的。是深层结构的差别决定了代词的指称。

因此，代词的指称依赖于深层结构和表层结构。知道英语的人都掌握了一种利用深层结构和表层结构的属性确定代词指称的规则系统。再重复一遍，他们不能通过内省发现这些规则。实际上，这些规则至今尚不为人所知，尽管它们的一些属性是清楚的。

概括一下：语言的生成语法规定了结构描写的无限集，每一个结构描写都包含深层结构、表层结构、语音表现、语义表现以及其他形式的结构。关联深层结构和表层结构的规则，即所谓的"语法转换"，在某些细节上已经被研究，而且能够被很好地理解。关联表层结构和语音的规则也能被很好地理解（我不想暗示这个问题是不可争议的，其实远非如此）。深层结构和表层结构似乎都能决定意义。深层结构能够提供述谓、修饰等语法关系，这些语法关系都能决定语义。另一方面，焦点与预设、话题与述题、逻辑成分的辖域和代词的指称等问题，似乎至少部分是由表层结构决定的。关联句法结构与意义的表达式的规则根本不好理解。事实上，"意义表达式"（representation of meaning）或"语义表达式"（semantic representation）这个概念本身是极具争议性的。语法对意义确定的贡献，与所谓的"语用考虑"（如事实和信仰的问题与说话语境等）对意义确定的贡献，这两种贡献能否严格区分一点也不清楚。关于"语音表达式"所引起的类似问题大概也值得一提。尽管后者是语言学理论中建构得最好的也是较少争议的概念之一，然而，我们仍可以提出以下问题：它是不是合法的抽象，对语言使用的深入理解是不是可能不会显示出超出语法结构的因素以一种逃脱不掉的方式决定感知表达式与物理形式，而且这种因素不能从将表层结构解释为语音形式的形式规则中毫无扭曲地分离出来。

到目前为止，语言研究已经在某些抽象的基础方面有所进展。也就是说，我们从语言的使用条件中进行抽象，并考虑关联它们的形式结构与形式操作。这些形式结构是句法结构,即深层结构与表层结构,也是语音表达式与语义表达式,它们是通过合格操作与句法结构关联的某些形式客体。这个抽象的过程绝不是非法的,但是,我们必须理解它表达了一种观点,即一个有关心智本质的假说,那并不很清晰。它表达了一种工作假设,即我们可以从语言如何使用的问题中用抽象的方式继续研究"语言知识","语言知识"也常被称做语言能力。采用这个工作假设时所获得的成功,证明这个工作假设是合理的。在这个假设的基础上,大量的语言机制,我更想说的是心智本质,已经获知。但是我们必须意识到,当我们尝试研究语言使用的时候,研究语言的这种方法至少在部分上,是由我们的观念使我们失望这一事实强加给我们的。我们陷入陈词滥调,或如下观察之中:这些观察虽然很有趣,但并不适用于通过我们可以获得的知识工具对其进行系统研究。另一方面,我们能够把丰富的经验和理解带入形式结构及其关系的研究之中。在这点上,我们可能面临着重要性与可行性之间的冲突问题,这类冲突我们在之前曾提到过。虽然我不相信一定如此,但相信这是有可能的。对语言形式机制的研究进行抽象是合适的,我对此相当的自信。我的自信基于这样的事实,即许多非常优美的结果是在抽象的基础上获得的。谨慎仍然是需要的。语言研究下一步大的发展可能需要锻造新的知识工具,这个工具允许我们考虑大量已被扔进"语用学"这一垃圾桶的问题,以便我们可以继续研究如何用一种可理解的形式描述的问题。

  如前所述,我认为对语言能力的抽象是合理的。更深入地说,我坚信现代心理学无力应对人类智力问题,至少部分是由它不愿研究心智的抽象结构与机制造成的。注意,我们所描述的研究语言结构的方法有非常浓烈的传统味道。我认为可以真实地说,这个方法使这样的观点更加准确,这种观点为17、18世纪普遍语法的重要文献所固有,并且在语言和心智的理性主义与浪漫主义哲学中以各种方式得到发展。这个方法在很多方面偏离了更为现代的观念,依我看,现代的观念是相当错误的。现代的观念认为语言知识可以用习惯的系统,或用刺激—反映关系的术语,或用"类推"与"概括"的原则或用其他观念进行解释,这些其他的观念是20世纪语言学与心理学所探讨的并发展自传统经验主义的构想。我相信,所有这些方法的致命的不适应性来源于他们不愿意从事语言能力的抽象研究。如果自然科学受类似的方法限制,我们可能仍然处于巴比伦天文学时代。

　　再次出现于近期研究中的一个传统观念是"普遍语法"的观念,我想用一句话总结这个话题。有两种类型的证据表明,所有语言的语法都能满足深层次的形式条件。第一种证据由大量不同语言的研究提供。在试图为多种语言构建生成语法时,研究者反复被引向关于这种生成系统的形式与组织的类似假设。一个更有说服力的关于普遍语法的证据是由个体语言的研究提供的。它第一眼看上去可能很矛盾,对单个语言的深入研究为普遍语法提供相关证据,但是稍微想想这件事情就会知道这是一个很自然的结果。

　　为了看出这一点,请考虑一下使语言习得成为可能的心智能力的决定问题。如果语法(语言能力)的研究涉及对语言使用的抽象,则使语法习得成为可能的心智能力的研究涉及进一步的二阶抽象。从这里我看不到错误。我们可以描述决定未知属性的装置的内部特征的问题。这种装置接受儿童学习第一语言所获得的语料,并以之为"输入";产生那个语言的生成语法,并以之为"输出"。在这种情况下,"输出"是内部表征的语法,所掌握的语法构成了语言知识。我们如果不墨守成规或心怀偏见地研究语言习得装置的内部结构,就能得到一些结论,这些结论尽管是初步的,但对我而言,却是重要的并且是有根据的。我们必须把足够的结构赋予这种装置,以便语法能够在经验上受限的时间与语料的基础上构建。我们必须满足经验上的条件,即相同语言的不同说话者,他们尽管经验与所受的教育都不相同,却都能获得非常相似的语法,同时,我们可以从他们沟通的难易程度和对新句子解释时新句子间的对应关系来决定这些经验上的条件。显而易见的是,儿童可以得到的语料是很有限的——与他以合适的方式所能直接理解和所能产生的句子的数量来比,他一生寿命的长度是很短的。了解所习得语法的特征与可获得的语料的有限性之后,我们能够构想出十分合理且非常强大的经验性假设,该假设跟语言习得装置的内部结构有关,语言习得装置根据给定的语料建构所假设的语法。当我们仔细研究这个问题,我相信,我们会把对可能语法形式进行限制的一种非常丰富的系统归功于这种装置;否则,将无法解释儿童在时间和语料获得的已定条件下,是如何构建这类经验上似乎很充分的语法的。此外,如果我们假设儿童不是天生地倾向于学习一种语言而非另一种语言,那么我们得到的关于语言习得装置的结论是关于普遍语法的结论。这些结论可以被证明是错误,比如说,它们不能解释其他语言的语法构造;这些结论也可以被证明是正确的,如果它们能解释其他语言的事实。总的来说,这一论点对我来说是非常合理的,如果仔细地研究下去,即使研究的是个别的语言,它也会引导我们发现关于普遍语法的强大的经验性假设。

我讨论了语言研究的一种方法,这种方法将语言研究看作理论心理学的一门分支。它的目标是展示和阐明使人类学习和使用语言成为可能的心智能力。众所周知,这些能力是人类特有的,并且任何其他生物体都没有与之具有显著相似性的能力。如果这个研究的结论接近正确,那么人类必须被赋予一组充足且明确的心智属性,使之能够在数量有限且颇有缺陷的语料的基础上决定语言的特殊形式。此外,他们创造性地利用心智中表征的语言,这种语言尽管受规则限制,但可以自由地用来表达新的想法,这些新的想法只以差别较大的与抽象的方式关联过去的经验或当前的情感。如果这是正确的,那么通过刺激条件、强化训练的安排、习惯结构的建立、行为模式之类进行的人类行为的"控制"研究就没有什么前景了。当然,研究者可以设计一个受限制的环境,让这类的控制和模式能在该环境中被展示,但没有任何理由去猜测,用这种方法了解人类潜能的范围将会比在监狱或军队里或是在教室里观察人有更多的收获。这些探索常常会忽视人类心智的本质属性。如果我最后的这些"非专业"评述能获得谅解,我会非常满意这个结果。

1.3 思考和练习

1. 人类语言最重要的特征是可以利用有限的规则生产出无穷无尽的表达式,如:

张三喜欢语言学。
李四知道张三喜欢语言学。
王五知道李四知道张三喜欢语言学。
我知道王五知道李四知道张三喜欢语言学。
……

请问上述现象体现了语言的哪个本质特征?你可以再举出一些类似的

例子吗?

2. 根据本章关于"语法"的阐述,我们通常所说的"现代汉语语法"属于哪一个范畴?什么样的汉语语法研究才是具有语言学理论价值的研究?

3. 根据"民族语言志"的统计,世界上有7097种语言,其中有使用人数最多的语言(汉语普通话),也有应用范围最广泛的语言(英语),还有只有几个人使用的语言(某些美洲印第安语和澳洲土著语言),以及其它濒危语言。请问这些语言的地位是平等的吗?语言会不会因为使用人数多寡、应用范围广泛与否,亦或使用人群的区别而存在不同?

4. 如果语言学的终极目标是探索人类的普遍语法(Universal Grammar, UG),那么该如何推进汉语语言学,尤其是汉语语法研究,从而促进对人类语言本质的探索?汉语研究如何才能增进全人类对语言本质的认识?

5. 语言既有共性(语言普遍性),也有个性(语言特殊性)。如何在具体的研究实践中把握二者的关系?

6. 乔姆斯基曾说过一句话:"要说猿猴具有语言能力,就好比在某个孤岛上,人类教不会飞行的鸟学会飞行一样(不可能)。"你怎么看待乔姆斯基这个观点?为什么猿猴不具有像人类一样的语言能力?

1.4 延伸阅读

Anderson, S. R. 2008. The logical structure of linguistic theory. *Language*: 785-814.

Chomsky, N. 1986. *Knowledge of Language: Its Nature, Origin, and use*. New York and London: Praeger.

Crystal, D. 2010. *Cambridge Encyclopedia of Language*. Cambridge, UK: Cambridge University Press.

Fromkin, V., Rodman, R. & N. Hyams. 2014. *An Introduction to Language (the 10th edition)*. Boston: Wadsworth.

Jackendoff, R. 1997. *The Architecture of the Language Faculty*. Cambridge, MA: The MIT Press.

Napoli, D. J. 2003. *Language Matters: A Guide to Everyday Thinking about Language*. New York: Oxford University Press.

O'Grady, W., Archibald, J., Aronoff, M. & J. Rees-Miller. 2017. *Contemporary Linguistics: An Introduction (the 7th edition)*. Boston: Bedford/St. Martin's.

Pinker, S. 2003. *The Language Instinct: How the Mind Creates Language*. London: Penguin.

第二章 语音学

2.1 导引

- 语音概说
- 发音语音学
- 音素
- 音节
- 超音段特征
- 声学语音学
- 听觉语音学

2.1.1 语音概说

语音学是对人类语言声音的研究，其主要的研究范畴包括发音语音学 (Articulatory Phonetics)、声学语音学 (Acoustic Phonetics) 以及听觉语音学 (Auditory Phonetics)。口语是人类语言最基本，也是最普遍的实现形式，而人类具有的发音、听音、辨音的能力，是实现口语交流的基础，因此也是语言学的主要研究对象。

有一些语言发源的理论认为，人类最原始的语言形式并不是声音，而是手势。但是，手语的弊端在于说话者必须面对面，有距离的限制；而声音传播的距离很远，打破了这个限制，因此口语取代了手语，成为语言主要的形式。但这并不意味着手语在语言的准确性和复杂度方面劣于口语。对于一些听力或发音器官受损的个体(有时是一个家族或村落)，手语帮助他们实现无异于口语的语言沟通。广义的语音学研究对象既包括口语的语音,也包括手语的手势。由于篇幅限制,本章仅对口语的语音做介绍。

2.1.2 发音语音学

发音语言学研究的是人类使用语言时发音的人体生理机制。如果把人说话看成是一个生理活动,其实就是"一股股的热气流"。从物理学上来讲,声音的本质是声波,是由物体的颤动产生的,而人类的发音颤动体是人的声带。人类之所以能发出来各种各样的声音,是因为人类具有复杂的发音器官,让从肺里呼出来的气流发生了变化。

通常,我们用以辨识语音的要素有四个:音高、音强、音长和音色。当气流从肺往外送时,气流会经过喉管、咽腔、口腔和(或)鼻腔,人类通过控制这些器官,比如通过绷紧或放松某些肌肉,扩大或缩小气流通过的空间和位置,就可以改变声波,从而产生了我们听到的不同声音。

声波的振动频率决定了音高,通过控制声带的肌肉使其变长缩短或紧绷放松,可以改变音高。声波的振幅大小决定了音强,试想当我们要大喊时往往要先大吸一口气,其实就是通过制造更大的气流,产生振幅更大的声波,也就是音强更大的声音。时间的长短决定了音长,这个非常好理解。以上这三个方面的声音变化,我们在大部分的飞鸟走兽身上也都能看到。

但是让人类语言的声音如此丰富、复杂的关键,是人类语言的共鸣器:口腔、咽腔、鼻腔;共鸣器的作用是改变声音的音色。普通话的"波"和"泼"的声母的区别,"波"和"八"的韵母的区别,都是通过对共鸣腔的控制实现的。关于人类的发音器官,罗常培在《普通语音学纲要》一书中做了详细的介绍,本章也节选了相关的内容。了解发音器官对于语言学研究极为有必要。以下我们将看到,人类语音基本的分析单位主要是按照发音器官(部位)的不同来分类的。

2.1.3 音素

人类语音非常丰富复杂,但如果要对其进行记录和分析,最基本的分析单位应该是音素(phone)。根据音质的不同,语言学家对人类语言发音进行了区别划分,形成了不同的音素。音素是具体存在的物理现象;一个音素对应的是一个发音动作。

根据目前发现的人类语言,国际语音学会制定了国际音标(International

Phonetic Alphabet,IPA,或称为"国际语音学字母",见图2.1)。这些国际音标与全人类语言的音素一一对应,用以准确记录人类的任何语言。国际音标的官网有所有音素的音频,感兴趣的读者可以前往听取。①

在使用国际音标标注语音时,可以遵循两种方法。如果严格按照国际音标来标注语音,一般会加方括号表示(如[p]),这种方法称为严式标音法。还有一种用斜杠(如/p/)来标注语音的方法,称为宽式标音法,一般不代表国际音标的发音,而是一个语言中的某个音位,我们会在下一章谈到。

图2.1中我们可以看到,音素大致可分为元音(vowel)和辅音(consonant)两大类。以普通话为例,汉语拼音中的韵母a、o、e、i、u、ü是单元音,而声母b、p、m、f等代表的是辅音。

2.1.3.1 辅音

一般来讲,辅音的发音过程是气流从肺腔发出到达共鸣腔,经历"成阻——持阻——除阻"的过程。从图2.1顶端第一个大表"肺部气流音"(pulmonic consonant),我们可以看到辅音一般按照发音部位(place of articulation)和发音方法(manner of articulation)两个维度进行划分。

该表中的横轴表示的是不同的发音部位。辅音的发音部位指的是气流受到阻碍的部位。根据人体的共鸣器不同的发音部位,我们把这些辅音归类为:双唇音(bilabial)、唇齿音(labiodental)、齿音(dental)、齿龈音(alveolar)、龈后音(postalveolar)、卷舌音(retroflex)、硬腭音(palatal)、软腭音(velar)、小舌音(uvular)、咽音(pharyngeal)、声门音(glottal)。这些不同的发音位置可参见本章选文的发音器官图。

该表中的竖轴表示的是不同的发音方法。辅音的发音方法指的是气流破除发音阻碍的方法。如果把这些不同的辅音按发音方法来归类,可以分为:塞音(plosive)、鼻音(nasal)、颤音(trill)、闪音(flap or tap)、擦音(fricative)、边擦音(lateral fricative)、通音(approximate)、边通音(lateral approximate)。塞音的发音方式是口腔和鼻腔一开始完全阻碍,由气流冲破口腔阻碍后爆破发出;鼻音则是阻碍后打开鼻腔通路,气流颤动声带,从鼻腔通过。发颤音时,发音器官有弹性的部分,如双唇、舌尖、小舌,迅速颤动,使气流忽通忽塞,急速交替,形成颤音;闪音的发音方式类似于颤音,只是不连续

---

① http://www.internationalphoneticalphabet.org/ipa-sounds/ipa-chart-with-sounds/.

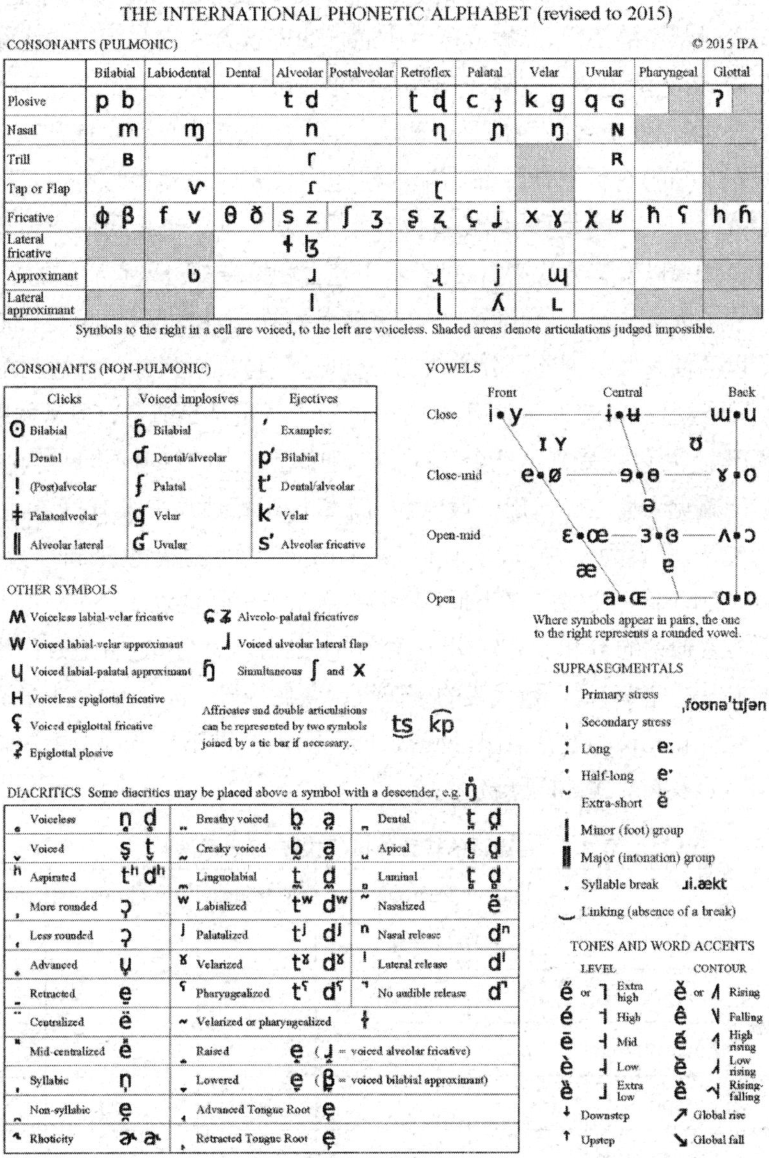

图 2.1　国际语音学会制定的国际音标（2015 年版）①

---

① 图片来源：https://www.internationalphoneticassociation.org/sites/default/files/IPA_Kiel_2015.pdf。

颤动,只是闪动一下。擦音发音的阻碍是相近的发音部位形成的窄缝,气流经过口腔时从窄缝挤出,摩擦成声。边通音的发音方式则是舌尖与齿龈相接构成阻碍,舌头两边留有空隙,气流从舌头两边经过形成。

另外,根据发辅音时声带是否颤动,可以分为清辅音和浊辅音。且看该表中最左上角的双唇塞音[p][b]那一格,[p]代表的是发音时声带不颤动的清辅音,而[b]代表的是和[p]发音位置相同、发音方法也相同但声带颤动的浊辅音。如果以发音方式来看,可以看出塞音和擦音都可以有清浊的区分。

世界上大部分语言(包括英文)的辅音都存在清浊的区别,可是普通话的辅音不以清浊来做主要的区分方法,而是以送气与否来区分。普通话里的 b-p、d-t、g-k 这几组塞音发音时声带不颤动,可以确定都是清音。但是如果把手放在嘴巴前,可以感受到这几个塞音发音时嘴巴送出的气流不同:发 p、t 和 k 的时候能感觉到嘴巴会送出一股气流,而发 b、d、g 时几乎没有气流,因而称前者为送气,后者为不送气。j-q、z-c、zh-ch 这三组塞擦音也是同理,皆为清音,以送气不送气来区分。在国际音标中,送气这一特征以一个上标的 h 来表示,例如,普通话的 b 和 p 分别用[p]和[pʰ]来标注(注:[pʰ]右上方作为上标出现的 h 是一个变音符号,代表的是送气。变音符号(diacritic)是为了更精确地表现辅音和元音的发音情况,见图 2.1 左下角)。以下是普通话中的辅音分布(表 2.1),及其对应的国际音标。

表 2.1 普通话的辅音分布(国际音标表示法)①

		Labial	Denti-alveolar	Retroflex	Alveolo-palatal	Velar
Nasal		m	n			ŋ
Stop	aspirated	pʰ	tʰ			kʰ
	unaspirated	p	t			k
Affricate	aspirated		t͡sʰ	t͡ʂʰ	(t͡ɕʰ)	
	unaspirated		t͡s	t͡ʂ	(t͡ɕ)	
Fricative		f	s	ʂ	(ɕ)	x
Liquid			l	ɻ		

---

① 图片来源:https://en.wikipedia.org/wiki/Standard_Chinese_phonology。

辅音除了肺部气流音以外，还有非肺部气流音，指的是不需要从肺部送气的辅音（见图 2.1 第二排左侧"non-pulmonic consonants"）。非肺部气流音同样可以用发音方式和发音部位来区分。如果以发音方式来区分，有搭嘴音（click）、内爆音（voiced implosive）和挤喉音（ejective）。使用非肺部气流音的语言多见于非洲，非洲南部的科依桑语系（Khoisan languages）就使用许多不同的非肺部气流辅音。虽然普通话中不存在这些辅音，但我们在日常生活中其实也经常听到。比如我们逗小孩的时候弹舌头、表示惋惜的时候咂舌都属于搭嘴音，而我们在模仿亲嘴的动作发出的"啵啵"的声音则是内爆音。

2.1.3.2 元音

元音的发音方式与辅音不同，不需要经过"成阻——持阻——除阻"的过程。发元音时，气流经过口腔不受到阻碍，并且发声时各发音器官部位保持均衡的紧张。上面提到，辅音有清浊之分，也就是声带颤动与否的区别，但是发元音时声带肯定是颤动的，所以元音的声音都很响亮。元音也有送气不送气的区别，但是和辅音相比，发元音时的气流非常弱，我们几乎感受不到。

最基本的元音每一个只有一个发音位置，称为单元音（monophthong）。拼音中的 a、o、e、i、ü 就属于单元音。两个或三个单元音组合一起，则构成复合元音（双元音 diphthong 或三元音 triphthong），比如拼音中的 ao、ou、iu。复合元音的发音过程是由一个元音向另一个元音滑动，因此复合元音也叫滑动元音（gliding vowel）。

舌头和嘴唇是元音发音的共鸣腔，决定了元音的音质。舌头升降（或口腔开闭）、舌位的前后、圆唇不圆唇是区分单元音的三个维度。国际音标的元音表是一个四角图（见图一第二排右测），代表的就是舌头处在不同位置（舌位高低前后的四个极限边缘）所发出的元音音素。而在同一个位置前后的两个元音，比如舌高前位（四角图左上角）的［i］和［y］则代表的是不圆唇与圆唇时的音素。

我们可以通过发汉语拼音中的几个单元音来感受一下舌头和嘴唇的变化。试着发拼音的 a，我们可以感觉到嘴巴是张着的，舌头贴着下面的；而发 e，甚至 i 的时候舌头会抬高的，嘴巴也会变小；当我们发 i 的时候把嘴唇噘成圆形，就变成了 ü；而从 ü 到 u，我们感觉到舌头往后缩；从 u 到 o，我们能感觉嘴巴的张口变大。

普通话的单元音是一个倒三角形，而非国际音标表中的四角形，因为我们的低元音 a 只有一个位置,没有舌位前后之分。早期的学者认为,普通话的单元音有十个,但有学者认为,普通话的元音如果仅按基础音来计算,排除掉边际音和派生音,应该只有七个(见图 2.2)。这些基础音在不同的条件下出现局部音变产生的音素,实际来讲应视为同一音位(phoneme)的音位变体(allophone)。

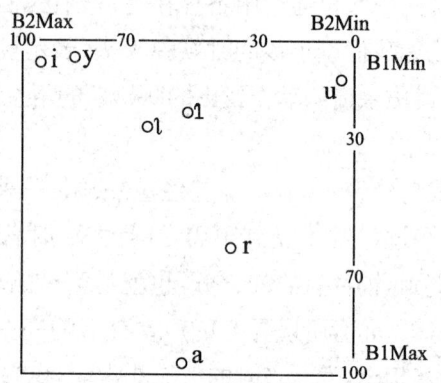

图 2.2　普通话一级元音格局图(以北京话为样本)①

2.1.4　音节

音素是语音的最小单位,而音节(syllable)是听觉能感受到的最自然的语音单位。即使没有受过语音训练的人,也能很容易地感知到音节这一概念。汉语中通常一个字对应的是一个音节,例如,"音节"这个词有两个音节,"音"是一个,"节"是另一个;而英文的"syllable"这个单词则由[si]-[lə]-[bl]三个音节构成,依此类推。

一个音节内部一般由一个或几个音素按一定规律组合在一起。以汉语为例,如果用辅音(C)和元音(V)的组合来表示汉语音节结构的话,汉语方言普遍只有 CV、V、CVC、VC 四种音节结构(其中 V 可以是一个或多个元音的组合)。

音节中不同的位置所允许出现的辅音在不同的方言内部存在不同的规则。例如,普通话虽然一共有 22 个辅音,但是出现在音节末尾的辅音韵尾(coda)的只有[n]和[ŋ]这两个鼻音,并且[ŋ]只出现在韵尾,不能出现在音节

---

①　图片来源:石锋,2002,《普通话元音的再分析》,《世界汉语教学 4》,5—9.

开始的声母(onset)位置上。而汉语的其他方言中，例如粤语、闽南语和客家语，能出现在韵尾的辅音除了[m]、[n]和[ŋ]三个鼻音以外，还有[p]、[t]、[k]三个塞音。印欧语系的音节结构则要比汉语复杂得多。例如，英语单词 strengths [strɛŋθ] 就包含了多达8个音素。

对于汉语音节结构的划分，中国传统的音韵研究更倾向于把汉语的音节结构分为声母和韵母(rhyme)两部分，即音节中元音之前的辅音为声母，元音以及元音后面的辅音合并称为韵母。《广韵》、《切韵》等中国历史上的韵书都是基于对声母、韵母等的划分进行编排分类的。

2.1.5 超音段特征

以上我们所讨论的辅音和元音的各种区别属于音色上的区别。而我们之前提到，辨识语音的要素除了音色以外还有音高、音强和音长几个特征。在语音学研究中，后面这几个属性都属于超音段特征(suprasegmental feature)。之所以称之为"超音段"，是因为这几项语音特征的作用单位可能大于某个语素(比如汉语的声调作用单位是音节)。图2.1右下角的 suprasegmantals(超音段标记)以及 tones and accents(声调和重音)这两部分列举了常见的超音段特征及其标注方法。之所以要研究超音段特征，是因为有些语言采用了某个方面的超音段特征作为区分词义的手段。

2.1.5.1 声调

首先谈谈音高。在语音学研究中，我们称语音的音高为声调(tone)。声调在汉语中具有区分语义的作用。比如，在大部分的语言中[ma]这个音节只有一个意思，代表的是"母亲"这个概念，或者作为对母亲的称谓。但如果我们赋予[ma]普通话的四个不同声调，在普通话的语境中，它可能分别代表"妈"、"麻"、"马"、"骂"这四个字，具有不同的，但是固定的语义。而如果把这带四声的[ma]放在英语的语境中，它的区别可能只在于呼唤母亲时所带有的不同感情色彩，比如亲切、引起注意、娇嗲、不耐烦、愤怒、震惊、怀疑等等。注意这种语气所传达的感情色彩并非是固定的，而是会随着语境发生变化的。

类似于汉语利用声调来区分语义的语言称为声调语言(tonal language)。除汉语外，藏语、泰语、老挝语、越南语都是较为典型的声调语言。声调通常负载于整个音节或音节中的韵母之上，对于声调语言来说，声调属于音节的一部分。在这些语言中，声调需要通过两方面来描述，一是通过声调升降

(contour)来描述,比如:音高是保持不变的(平调),从低音往高音走(升调),从高音往低音走(降调),或是先降后升、先升后降等(曲折调)——以上是几种基本的调类。二是从调值来描述。虽然声调的音高可以通过测量频率进行科学的记录,但是在语言沟通中,我们并不是通过绝对音高来判断声调,而是通过音高的相对高低和跨度来判断。赵元任先生受到音乐五线谱的启发,提出用五度标记法来表示声调的音高,即音值从低到高可分为低、次低、中、次高、高;如果用符号表示,就是把一条竖线分成五段,用连接竖线的纵线位置来表示音值;或者也可以用数字1—5来表示从低到高的五个音值。国际音标表中表示声调音高的符号(声调符号)就是赵元任先生发明的。如果声调是平调,则可以用单个声调符号表示音值;如果声调有升降,则可以通过排列声调符号来表示声调的升降变化。表 2.2 分别用国际音标的声调符号、曲线法和数字法表示了普通话的四声。

除了汉语这一类声调语言以外,大多数声调语言在音节内并没有声调的升降,只有一个平调,仅区分调值高低。班图语系(Bantu)的许多语言,如津巴布韦的绍纳语(Shona)和南非的祖鲁语,它们的声调就只有高低之分;西非的约鲁巴语的声调有高中低三种。这些语言的声调和汉语一样,有辨义的作用。日语的方言中也会用高低音调结合重音区别词汇,例如,[haçi]的两个音节在高低音调不同时可以有三个意思:当把重音放在第一个音节时,第一个音节的声调比第二个音节高,意思为"筷子";如果重音放在第二个音节,第二个音节的声调比第一个音节高,意思为"桥";如果两个音节都没有重音,音高在同一个水平,此时意思为"边缘"。

表 2.2 普通话四声的不同表示方法

	声调符号	曲线法示例	数字法示例
一声(高平调)	ˉ	mā	ma^{55}
二声(高升调)	ˊ	má	ma^{35}
三声(降升调)	ˇ	mǎ	ma^{214}
四声(全降调)	ˋ	mà	ma^{51}

2.1.5.2 重音

在语音学中,语言的音强称为重音(stress)。重音是以音节为单位的。有辨义作用的重音多见于日耳曼语系的语言,如英语、德语。英语中的很多词汇利用重音的位置来区分词性,比如 insult、record、permit 这几个词,作为动词时重音在第二个音节,而名词的重音则在第一个音节。德语中的"unterstellen"一词,当重音出现在词首,意为"储存";当重音出现在第三个音节,意为"暗示"。汉语中也能见到一些零星的例子。例如北京话中的"大姑娘"一词,如果把重音放在第一个字"大"上,意为"第一个女儿";而如果重音出现在第二个字"姑"上面,则意为"已成年的女孩子"。

在有些语言中,重音虽然不具有辨义作用,但仍是一个单词的有机组成部分。有些语言有固定的重音位置,例如,西班牙语的重音默认落在倒数第二个音节上。

严格来讲,重音不是一个可以完全孤立分析的超音段现象。从发音机制上看,重音是通过加强肺部气流来实现的,因此它会改变重音音节中不同音素产生的听觉效果,比如送气辅音的气流会更长,而高元音会听起来更高,或低元音听起来更低。同时,由于气流增加,重音也会改变重音音节的声调,使其音高上升。比如,在上一部分日语的高低音声调的例子中,其实不同前后两个音节也有音强上的区别。

2.1.5.3 音长

音色、音高、音强和音长这四个辨识语音的因素中,在汉语唯一没有体现辨义作用的是音长。但在有些语言中,元音的长短构成不同的音素,并且在构词时能造成词义的区别。国际音标系统中长元音通常用元音后加冒号":"表示,不加冒号的则是相对短的元音。英语中的 [fiː] "feel" 和 [fɪ] "fill",[siːt] "seat" 和 [sɪt] "sit",[fuːl] "fool" 和 [ful] "full" 这几组语义截然不同的最小对立对(minimal pair)的主要差别就在其元音音长。

2.1.6 声学语音学

声学语音学研究的是语音的声学特征,也就是从声波的频率、振幅、时长等物理属性对语音进行描述和分析。

声学语音学的发展离不开各种现代科学仪器和精密测量技术的推动。1877 年,爱迪生发明了留声机,意味着转瞬即逝的声音终于可以被记录下来,并且可以不断地回放重听。到了 20 世纪,声音的图像化手段开始陆续出现。示波器以波形图(sound waveform)的形式记录声音,而声谱仪(1945 年美国贝尔公司发明)则能直接把声波信息转为频谱图(spectrogram),提供更多有用的信息。

图 2.3 是一个英文语音片段的频谱图(上)和波形图(下),图 2.4 是元音/a/(左)和塞音/s/(右)的波形图。波形图和频谱图的横轴都是时间轴,通过查看中间的音素标注行,可以发现每个音素对应的波形和频谱都有较为明显的特征。

波形图直观地表现了语音的声波能量(频率、振幅)。波形图的纵轴(幅值)对应的是声音的响亮度(因此有音素的另一种分类方法:响音和阻音,也就是把发音时声带颤动的辅音归为响音)。在图 2.3 的波形图中我们可以看出:元音声波的振幅最大,边通音/l/和鼻音/n/次之,塞音/d,g/和擦音/z/最弱。如果把波形图放大来看,会发现元音的声波具有稳定的频率和周期,而声带不颤动的辅音则显得杂乱无章。波形图的横轴(时间)显示的是声波能量在时间轴上爆发的形态。因此,波形图可以帮助我们大致地判断音素的类别,但却无法做到精确的描述。

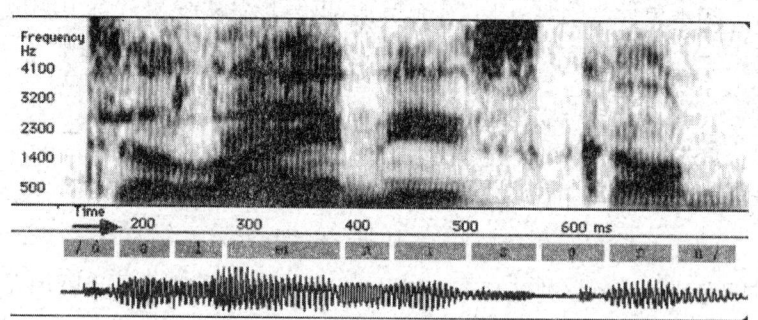

图 2.3　一个英文语音片段的频谱图(上)和波形图(下)①

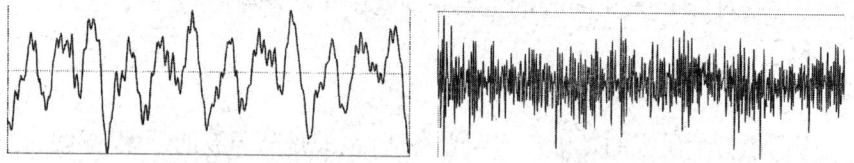

图 2.4　0.016 秒的元音/a/(左)和塞音/s/(右)的波形图 ②

---

① 来源于 University of New English 的一个交互式网上语音入门课程。该网站还有许多与语音相关的交互式内容与练习。图片来源网页:http://australianlinguistics.com/acoustic-analysis-2/spectrograms/。

② 声音来源为作者录音,图像由 Praat 生成。

而频谱图则包含非常丰富的信息。频谱图是由声波信息经傅里叶变换处理而生成的。简单地讲,波形图所体现的声波其实是不同频率的波的叠加,而傅里叶变换则可以把这些不同频率的波分离出来。频谱图的横轴同样是时间,但纵轴代表的是不同频率上的波的幅值——纵轴越往上,代表波的频率越高;坐标中的点颜色越深,则代表该频率的波能量越大。这些能量较强的波在时间轴上的延伸形成了横向黑带,每一条黑带称为一个共振峰(formant)。

共振峰之所以产生,是因为声音在经过共振腔时受到了腔体的滤波作用,频域中不同频率的能量被重新分配,一部分因为共振腔的共振作用得到强化,另一部分则受到衰减。由于能量分布不均匀,强的部分犹如山峰一般,故而称之为共振峰。不同的音素由于其发音部位的不同,会形成各异的共振峰,因此共振峰可以用来判断和分析音素。语音频谱图中(如图 2.5 上图)往往存在多个共振峰。我们可以利用软件对共振峰数值进行划线测量,但大部分语音处理软件都可以自动分析并给出不同共振峰的数值。图 2.5 下图就是语音处理软件 Praat 以红点的方式标注出来的几个共振峰。最靠近下方的红点组成的线,也就是频率最低的共振峰,被称为第一共振峰 f_1;以此类推,第二低的是第二共振峰 f_2,第三低的是第三共振峰 f_3。

一般来讲,元音仅靠 f_1 和 f_2 便可进行区别判断。图 2.5 中,f_1 从低到高是 /i/ < /u/ < /a/,其中 /i, u/ 的数值非常接近,它们的数值都远小于/a/。f_2 从高到低是 /i/ > /a/ > /u/,其中/i/的数值要远高于/a, u/。事实上,f_1 的数值代表的是舌位的高低,数值越小,舌位越高;f_2 代表的是舌位的前后,数值越大,舌位越靠前。

相比元音的声学分析,辅音声学要复杂得多。本文节选了经典的语音学课本——赖福吉的《语言学教程》中关于辅音声学的内容供读者入门。对声学语音学感兴趣的读者,可进一步参阅 Stevens(1998)的《声学语音学》[1],这本著作整合并发展了五十年的声学语言学的研究,对各种元音和辅音都做出了前无古人后无来者的详细分析。关于汉语的声学语音学研究,则可参阅《实验语音学概要》[2]。

---

[1] Stevens, K.N. 1998. *Acoustic Phonetics*. Cambridge, Mass.: The MIT Press.
[2] 鲍怀翘、林茂灿主编,《实验语音学概要(增订版)》,北京大学出版社 2014 年版。

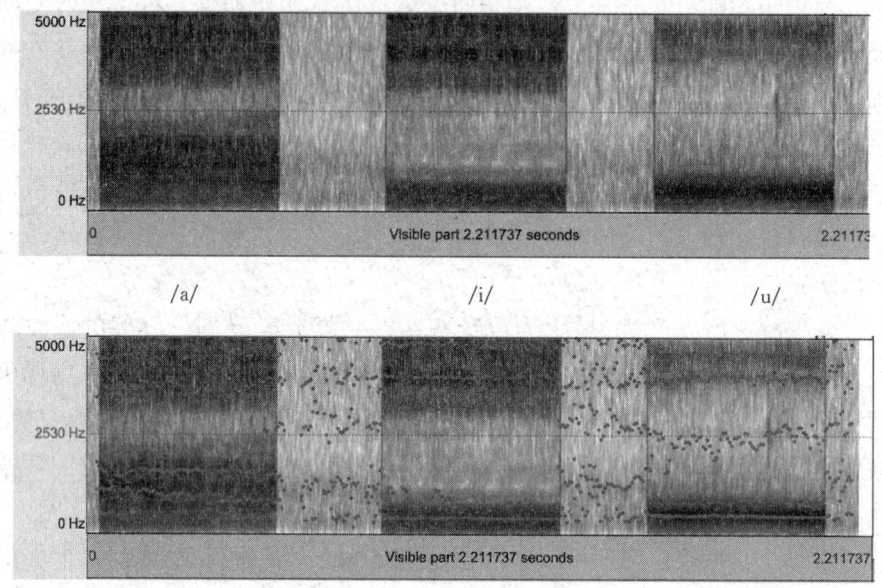

图 2.5　普通话的/a, i, u/频谱图①

2.1.7　听觉语音学

听觉语音学（或称感知语音学）与发音语音学恰好相对，研究的是人们如何接收并处理语音信息，包括人的听觉器官的结构、听觉功能实现的机制、听觉器官与大脑神经元之间信号的传递和转换等等，与人体生理学和神经科学更为相关。本章在此便不多做介绍，感兴趣的读者可参阅《实验语音学概要》中的相关章节。

2.2　选读

- 罗常培，王均(2002)《普通语音学纲要》选读
- 赖福吉(1975)《语音学教程》选读
- 杨顺安(1992)《语音合成与语音学研究》选读

---

① 声音来源为作者录音，图像由 Praat 生成。

罗常培,王均(2002)《普通语音学纲要》选读[1]

◆ 作者简介

罗常培[2](1899—1958),当代著名语言学家、语言教育家,是中国语言学界公认的"继往开来的一代宗师"。罗常培1919年毕业于北京大学中文系。从1923年起,他曾先后在国立西北大学、厦门大学、广东中山大学、西南联合大学、北京大学任教授,并在美国讲学,讲授的课程包括中国语言学、中国音韵学、中国语音学等课程。1928年他参与了中央研究院历史语言研究所的筹建工作,之后也在研究所内从事专职研究多年。罗常培不仅  参与创办了《国文月刊》(1939年),也是《中国语文》创刊后(1959年)的总编辑;他还参与了建国后多项文字规范工作和少数民族语言调查。

罗常培一生勤苦力学。他的语言学著作丰富,专著十余部,文章一百多篇,在汉语音韵学方面和语言学其它方面,特别是语音学方面,有很高的造诣。主要著作包括《汉语音韵学导论》(1949年初版,1956年新版)、《汉魏晋南北朝韵部演变研究第一分册》(与周祖谟合作,1958年)等。这些重要论著,用现代语音学的方法,结合我国音韵学的传统,对音韵学上的一些关键性的术语,做了科学的阐明,使音韵学成为一门比较容易理解的学科。

本选文节选自与王均合著的《普通语音学纲要》,该纲要最初以文章的形式连载于《中国语文》1951年1月到1955年5月,共14期,1957年合并为集子出版。

◆ 正文节选

第二章 语音的基础

第二节 语音的生理基础——发音器官

1. 发音器官的三个部分

前面说过,人的发音器官是一个巧妙的乐器。现在还拿乐器来比。一切

---

[1] 罗常培、王均主编,《普通语音学纲要(修订本)》,商务印书馆2002年版。
[2] 图片来源:http://p0.qhmsg.com/dr/270_500_/t014c5ae885cea198dc.png。

声音的构成由于物体的颤动，物体的颤动总有一个原动力。胡琴不拉不响，笙笛不吹不鸣，拉胡琴、吹笙笛都是使胡琴的弦和笙簧笛膜颤动的原动力，人类发音的原动力是呼吸的气流；因此，人类发音器官的第一部分就是呼吸器官。

一般地说，气流虽是发音的原动力，但还不是发音体的本身。跟胡琴的弦和笙簧笛膜相当的人类发音的颤动体是喉头里的声带。声带是使气流乐音化的器官，是人类发音器官的第二部分。

人的发音器官跟乐器一样，除了颤动体还有共鸣器。人在说话的时候，主要的共鸣器是口腔。常常用得着鼻腔，有时也用得着咽腔。上一章说过，人体发音的共鸣器，构造复杂，形状不规则，而且变化多端，因此形成人类说话跟任何乐器不同的特殊音色。口腔以及鼻腔、咽腔和喉头是人类发音的共鸣器，同时是节制声音、形成各种音素的重要器官，这是发音器官的第三部分。

2. 呼吸器官

呼吸的气流是声音的原动力，所以呼吸器官是声音的发动机。语言的发音和呼吸是分不开的，关于呼吸器官不能不谈一谈。呼吸器官是一连串的管道，从鼻腔口腔开始，经过咽头，通到喉头，再向下由气管、支气管到达肺脏。肺脏是呼吸气流的总仓库，它在发音方面的作用相当于风琴中的风袋。肺的外面是一架鸟儿笼子似的胸廓（由肋骨前连胸骨、后接椎骨构成），下面是一层横隔膜。肋骨和膜隔膜因筋肉的作用，可以上下伸缩推动，协助肺部的呼吸。

呼吸器官中的肺和气管对于呼吸的作用比较明显，用不着细说。肋骨和横隔膜的作用也是不宜忽视的。咱们吸气的时候胸部一定得扩大，呼气的时候胸部自然得缩小。胸部怎会扩大或缩小呢？这就在乎肋骨和横隔膜的作用了。在肋骨之间有所谓"肋间内肌"和"肋间外肌"。肋间外肌收缩可以把肋骨提起而使胸腔增大，帮助吸气；肋间内肌收缩可以让肋骨下降而使胸腔缩小，帮助呼气。横隔膜的膈肌也是行呼吸作用的主要肌肉，当它收缩时，横隔膜就给拉下去，因而胸腔扩大，可以协助吸气；它一松弛，横隔膜又缩上去了，因而胸腔缩小，可以协助呼气。好像拉风箱一样：你把风箱的拉手一抽，里面的空间大了，外面的气自然就会流进去；你把风箱一推，里面的空间小了，风箱里的气就会被驱逐出去。肋肌和膈肌对呼吸的作用就是这样。以上肌肉的运动由肋间神经和膈神经管理。胸部的扩大或缩小，有时肋骨跟横隔膜同时起作用，有时是其中之一起作用。横隔膜起作用比较容易，所以我国唱旧戏的人讲究所谓"丹田之气"，学声乐的人也主张多练腹式呼吸，就是这个道理。（试把手放在腹部之上，或胸腔外边，连发 a 音；轻重相间，你会感觉那筋肉或肋骨的动作。）

3. 喉头和声带

人类发音器官的颤动体——声带——藏在喉头里边。这一部分对于语音的重要性是不用讲的了。咱们且来看看喉头的构造：

从外表看，颈部正中突起的一块，就是喉头。这一部分上通咽喉，下接气管，是由许多软骨衬着一些黏膜互相连接起来造成功的。这些软骨的名字是：甲状软骨，环状软骨，杓状软骨（又称披裂软骨或破裂软骨）。

甲状软骨是喉头最大的软骨。这块软骨卫护着喉头，像个盾甲，所以叫做甲状软骨。左右两片，略成方形，在脖颈的前部正中的地方合而为一，可以用手摸到。男人因为角度较尖，特别突出，称为喉结（北京话叫"颏勒嗦"）。左右两边各有上下两个角。甲状软骨的上面有一块像马蹄铁样的骨头，叫做舌骨。

环状软骨前低后高，像个带着印章的指环，前面在甲状软骨底下，纤维把它跟甲状软骨连在一块儿；下面纤维又把它跟气管的第一节软骨环连接起来。

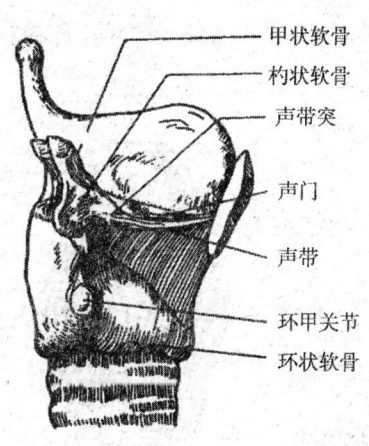

图 8　喉的侧面（甲状软骨的右半已除去）

杓状软骨在环状软骨后面那个印章似的板状部分的上边，左右各一，有点儿像两个椎形的杓儿。它的前角叫做声带突，声带就附着在这里。

在甲状软骨的后边还有一块树叶儿形的软骨，叫做会厌软骨。会厌软骨好比一扇活门，可以开关自如。会厌软骨的柄附着在喉结内壁，当咱们呼吸或说话的时候，它就升起，使气流容易出来；当食物下咽的时候，会厌软骨就被推弯，盖住喉门，不让食物走错了道儿，跑到气管里去。咱们说话跟咽东西的时候就可以看出喉头一上一下地活动。这一套软骨（包括甲状软骨、环状软骨、杓状软骨和会厌软骨）筑成一个很精巧的筋肉的小室，这个小室当中就是咱们发音的颤动体——声带。

喉部两旁的黏膜并不是平坦得像个筒儿似的。有两处皱起,做成皱襞,形成两对门户,上一对门户关不拢,在发音上也不很重要,叫做假声带;下一对形似两唇,是发音上最重要的器官,这就是咱们上面说的,人类发音的颤动体——真声带。这一对声带,左右能分开,也能并合。中间的通路叫做声门,依声带的张缩而开闭:在真假两声带之间,左右还各有一个小窦,叫做喉室,也可以叫做声窦,从声门出来的声音在这两窦间能够发生反响。

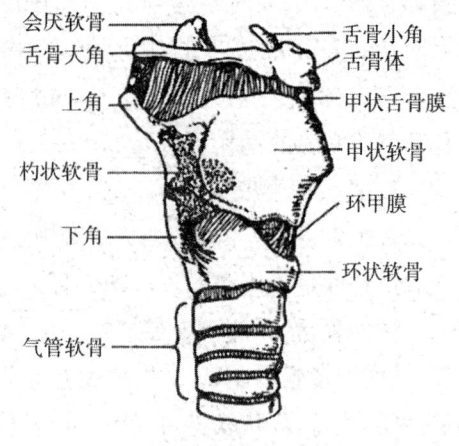

图9　喉软骨侧面

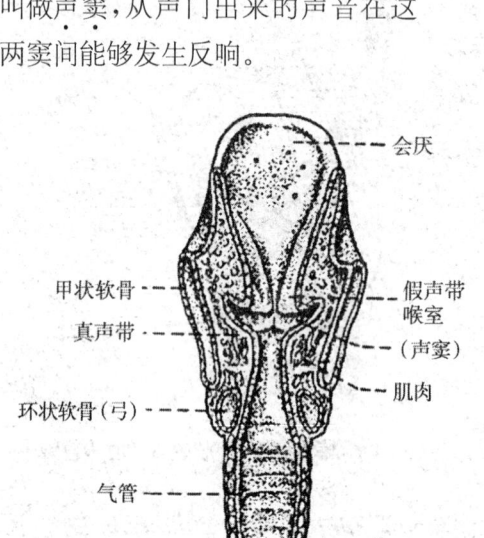

图10　喉的直剖

以上所讲的声门还可分为两部分:(1) 音声门——靠前而窄,前端接于甲状软骨,长度约相当于真声带三分之二。(2) 气声门——靠后而宽,刚好在两块杓状软骨的声带突之间,长度约相当于真声带三分之一。男人跟女人的声带长度不同,大约男人的比女人长十分之三弱,所以女人的声音比男人高。

在喉头各软骨之间有各种肌肉,这些肌肉的作用,能牵引杓状软骨转动,使声带或紧或松,声门也随着呈现出不同程度的开闭状态。

1. 声门闭紧,暂时气息完全不通,忽然急激地冲出气来,就发出破裂的声音,最剧烈的就是咳嗽。

2. 平时呼吸时因环杓背侧肌的作用,使杓状软骨往外推,声门就张开。一般地声门略呈三角形,深呼吸或喘气时差不多就扩大成菱形。

3. 耳语(打喳喳)的时候,因甲杓肌的作用,使声门的前半关闭而后半相接近。这时,气流由声带的后部,气声门的间隙中出来,接触到声带的边缘发出细致的音响,就是耳语。

4. 发声音时因杓肌的作用,使音声门和气声门一齐关闭,气流通过声门时得从声带当中挤出来,因而使声带颤动,这时发生的声音是清晰响亮的,和前面所说

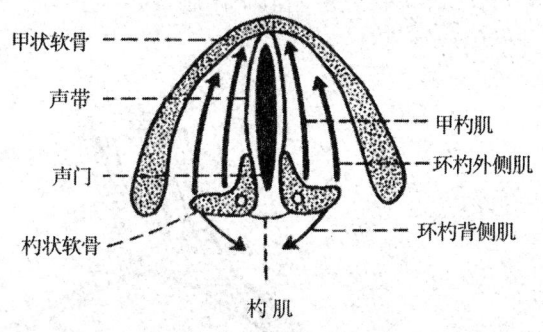

图 11　声门及喉肌的作用(横断面)

唏嘘的气息、细微的耳语完全不同。声带紧而短的时候发高音,松而长的时候发低音。作为人类交际工具的语言主要得靠这种乐音化的声音。

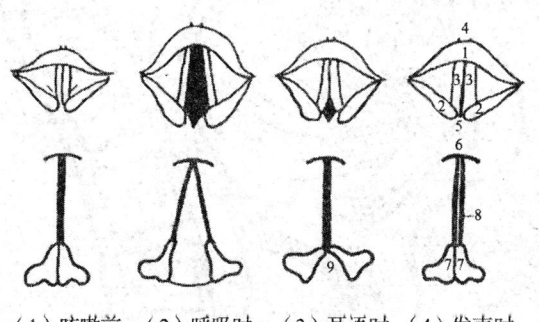

(1) 咳嗽前　(2) 呼吸时　(3) 耳语时　(4) 发声时

图 12　声带的状况

(上图表示喉头镜中所见喉的入口的一部分,下图表示甲状软骨与杓状软骨之间声带开合的情况)
1. 会厌　2. 会厌破裂　3. 声带　4. 前联合　5. 后联合
6. 甲状软骨　7. 杓状软骨　8. 音声门　9. 气声门

4. 口腔和鼻腔

人类的语言跟鸟兽的啼叫不同,是因为语言作为人们交流思想的工具,不仅能表现情感,而且能表达思想。人类的语音所以能用来作为交流思想的工具,全由于不同的音素结合起来,在约定俗成的情况下表示出一定的意思。鸟兽也能发音,但是它们发出的声音很少变化,不像人类能发出多种音素的复杂声音。人类语言里多种音素的不同,无论是乐音化的声音还是没有乐音化的气流,都是由于在它们通过口腔或鼻腔的路程上受到节制,发生种种变化。口腔和鼻腔不仅是人类发音的共鸣器,而且是不同音素的制造厂。(当

然,有些音素喉头也起节制作用,以后咱们还要讲到;但绝大多数的音素的节制作用是在口鼻。)

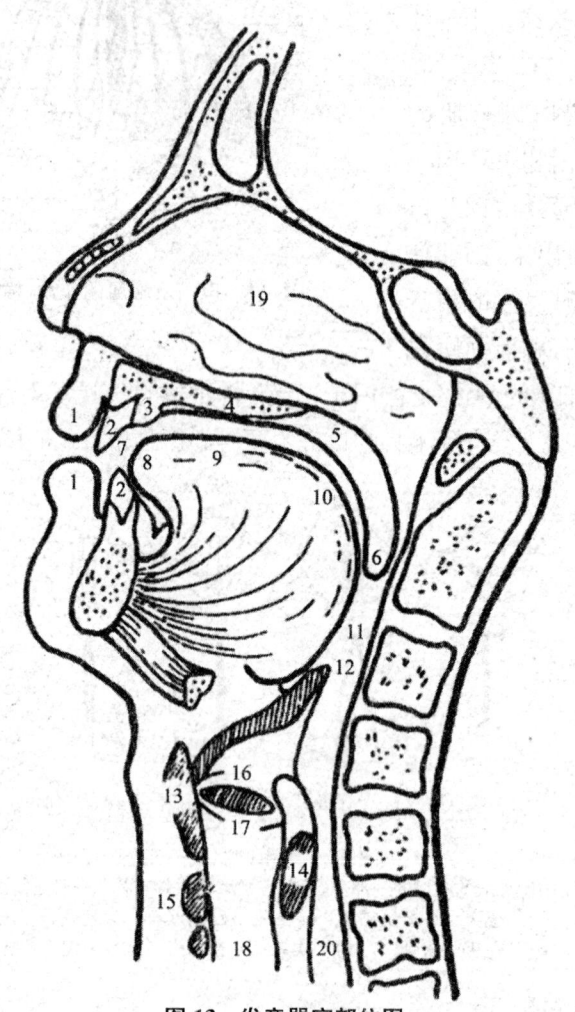

图 13 发音器官部位图
1.上下唇 2.上下齿 3.齿龈 4.硬腭 5.软腭 6.小舌 7.舌尖
8.舌叶 9.舌面前部 10.舌面后部 11.咽腔 12.会厌
13.甲状软骨 14.环状软骨(后板) 15.环状软骨(前弓)
16.假声带 17.声带 18.气管 19.鼻腔 20.食道

咱们可以把口腔分作三部分来讲:一部分是口壁,包括唇、齿、齿龈、上颚、小舌;一部分是舌;一部分是咽头。

口腔的大门是上唇和下唇。小孩儿开始学话,最先能学会的词就是"妈妈""爸爸",因为 a 是容易发的元音,而别人发双唇音[p]和[m]的动作是看得见的，这也是最容易发的两个辅音。

上齿和下齿是口腔的二门，也是一张开嘴就看得见的。再从牙齿往里看，紧靠着上齿的稍微凸出的部分叫齿龈。上齿龈往里是口腔的天花板，咱们管它叫上颚，又叫口盖。上腭前部坚硬，叫硬腭；后部柔软，叫软腭；软腭后边连着一个小肉坠儿，叫做小舌，又叫悬壅垂。

口腔下部最活动的一部分是舌头，舌头是很灵活的，人们所以能发出各种不同的声音，主要就因为舌头的活动造成口腔形式各种各样的变化。

舌头又可分为舌尖、舌叶、舌面、舌根四部分。

舌尖是舌的尖端。

舌叶是舌头放平时，在舌尖的靠上靠后的部分。

舌叶还可细分为前舌叶和后舌叶两部分。

舌面在舌时之后。舌面还可分为舌面前、舌面中、舌面后三部分。当舌头自然平放时，舌面前部和舌面中部正在硬腭的下面，舌面后部正在软腭的下面。过去我国的习惯，称舌面后部为舌根，实际舌根是在舌面后部的下后方。

口腔的后面有一个管状的三叉路口，上通鼻腔，中通口腔，下通喉头，这就是咽腔。咽腔在发音上也是共鸣室的一部分。咽腔的后面叫做咽壁。

口腔上面是鼻腔，鼻腔也是人类发音的一个共鸣室。假如把上腭比作楼板，那么鼻腔是楼上的共鸣室，口腔是楼下的，软腭跟小舌有些像一个活动的楼门。咱们呼吸的时候，小舌悬在当中，既不靠舌根，也不碰到咽壁，这时咽头的三叉路口大开，气流可以分别从口腔和鼻腔直通喉头。咱们咽食物的时候，软腭伸直，挡住咽头上部（所谓鼻咽部）的通路，舌根向下压，把喉头的会厌闭起来，就把食物送进食管，使它不致误入气管。说话的时候如果软腭小舌伸直，抵到咽壁那儿，挡住鼻腔的通路，气流只能从口腔出去，这时发出的声音就是单纯的口音；如果软腭下垂，口腔有一个部位闭塞起来，气流只能从鼻腔出去，这时就会发出一种鼻音来；如果三条路都通，从下面来的气流可以同时从口腔跟鼻腔两路出去，这就造成一种口鼻音（或称半鼻音、鼻化音）了。

唇、舌、软腭、小舌、声带，是发音器官中活动的部分，也是发音器官中最主要的部分，有人管它们叫发音器官中的主动器官。此外，下腭的动作和口腔的开合也颇有关系。人类语言各个音素的造成是跟它们的活动分不开的。

在学习语言的各个音素以前，咱们一定得把发音器官的部位弄清楚，进一步理解并且学会控制咱们的发音器官,才能正确地发出所要发的音来。最好随身带一面小镜子,发音时注意观察它们的活动部位。镜子里看不到声带,有一种语音学仪器,叫做喉头镜,可以用来观察声门开闭的情况。此外,为检查舌头和口盖接触的地带,还可以利用假腭。理解每个音素发音器官的部位是掌握正确发音的必要条件。

赖福吉(1975)《语音学教程》选读①

◆ 作者简介

彼得·赖福吉②(Peter Ladefoged,1925—2006),加州大学洛杉矶分校终身荣誉语音学教授,1959年博士毕业于苏格兰爱丁堡大学,1962年创立了加州大学洛杉矶分校的语音实验室,并一直担任实验室主任(1962—1991)。赖福吉曾任美国语言学学会主席(1978)以及国际语音学会主席(1986—1991)。任国际语音学会主席期间,他推动了1989年版国际音标的改革,以更准确地记录世界上新发现的各种语言。

赖福吉热衷于田野语言学记录和实验语音学分析,对世界的语言,特别是非洲的语言尤有深入的研究,与Ian Maddieson合著了《世界语音》③一书。但赖福吉最广为人知的还是《语音学教程》一书,也是以下文章的来源。该书作为语言学专业使用最多的语言学教材,从1975年第一版出版至今已更新修订至第七版(2014),并被翻译成多种语言。

① 彼得·赖福吉,《语音学教程(第五版)》,张维佳译,北京大学出版社2008年版。
② 图片来源:https://senate.universityofcalifornia.edu/_files/inmemoriam/html/images/clip_image001_002.jpg。
③ Ladefoged, P. & I. Maddieson, 1996. *The Sounds of the World's Languages*. Oxford, UK; Cambridge, Mass.: Blackwell Publishers.

◆ 正文节选

第八章 声学语音学

共振峰

本书第一章讨论了语音在音高、音强和音质上的不同。在讨论音质差异时我们注意到元音音质取决于它的陪音结构，换种说法，一个元音同时包含许多不同的频率。其中一个即所谓基频，其他都是陪音频率，是它们赋予这个元音独特的音质。我们通过这些陪音差异将此元音跟其他元音区别开来。回顾一下前面说过的内容，我们发现每个元音都有三个共振峰，三个凸显的陪音频率。频率最低的共振峰，是第一共振峰，记为 F1。当带嘎裂声来发元音时它最易被听见。你可以听到（你自己的发音或 CD 第一章的录音），当带有嘎裂声（本身并没有真正的音高）来发 heed, hid, head, had 中的元音时，它们的频率在一定程度上会升高。当低声发这些元音时，能更容易听出第二个共振峰（F2）频率的下降。第三个共振峰（F3），可以增加音质的区别度，但我们没有明显感知它的简单方法。

这些共振峰是如何产生的？答案是，声道中的空气就像音管里或者瓶子里的空气那样运动。当你拍击它时，它就会振动。如果你张开嘴，发一个喉塞音，并朝脖子接近颌下的地方轻弹手指，就会听见一个音，就像拍瓶子听到的声音一样。当你轻弹时，如果把头稍稍向后倾将脖子的皮肤拉紧，你可能会更清楚地听到这个音。要小心保持元音的调音部位，不要将舌根抬起碰上软腭。如果你用这个方法检测发一组完整元音 [i, ɪ, e, ɛ, æ, ɑ, ɔ, ʊ, u] 的部位，你就会听见前四个元音第一共振峰频率依次抬高，后四个元音依次降低。

可以根据共振峰给元音分类，不同的共振峰是不同声道形状的结果。任何空气，比如声道或瓶子中的空气，会根据由声道大小和形状决定的方式来振动。如果对着一个空瓶子的瓶口儿吹气，你就会发出低频音。如果给瓶子灌点儿水，使瓶子的容积变小，你就能发出带有高频的音。被变小的瓶子容积，跟钢琴的细音管或风琴细琴弦相似，可以形成更高的频率。发元音时声道形状复杂，使不同空气产生许多陪音。

声道里的空气随着声带运动而振动。每一次声带的开合都伴有从肺部出来的气流脉冲。这些脉冲就像声道中的气流受到猛烈拍击一样，使共鸣腔振动，从而产生大量不同的领率。就像你同时敲打不同的瓶子一样。不考虑声带振动频率,只要保持调音器管位置不变,声道中的气流就和这些频率产生共鸣。由于声道形状复杂,空气会同时产生不同的振动。声道后部的气流可能会以一种方式振动,形成如图 8.1 最上面的波形。同时舌前较小空间里的气流,可以用另一种方式振动,产生图中第二个波形。声道中第三种气流的振动方式可能产生图中第三个波形。实际上我们听到的是这些波形的叠加形式。

请看图 8.1 上面的波形。它像是在声道上轻拍了一下发出的,是一个振幅递减的波(随着时间变小)。你可以从图底部的时间轴上看到 10 毫秒内(即一秒的百分之一)有 5 个气压峰。相当于一秒里有 500 个峰值。换句话说,这是一个 500 Hz 的波,大约是元音[ə]的第一共振峰值。图中另外两个波有更高的频率——10 毫秒中有更多的气压峰值。它们相当于 1500 和 2500 Hz 的波,即元音[ə]的第二和第三共振峰频率。如果声道中的空气振动源单一,会产生像图 8.1 中比较规则的音波。如果有很多振动源,如气流通过振动的声带,这些波形会重复产生,给这些陪音频率加上一个基音频率。

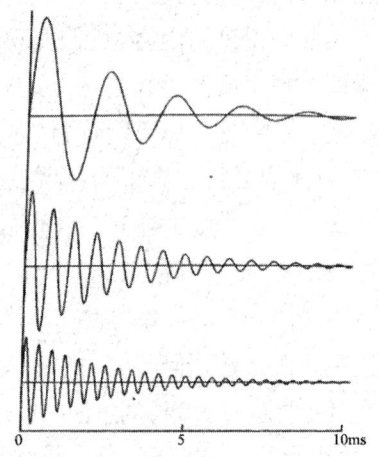

图 8.1 声道中气流轻拍所形成的三个波形

我们在书中不会详细涉及声道形状和共振峰频率之间的关系。我的另一本书《声学语音学纲要》(1996)对这个问题有很好的研究。这种关系实际上比气流以一种方式在声道后部振动和以其他方式在其他部位振动都更复杂。这里我们将只关注一个事实,即在发大多数浊音时,每次声带振动会产生三个共振峰。注意声道中气流振动速率和声带振动速率无关。声带可能振动得更快或更慢,形成一个较高或较低的音高,但是只要声道形状没有变化共振峰频率也就不会改变。

辅音声学

辅音的声学结构通常比元音复杂。在很多情况下,可以说辅音是元音开头或结尾的一种特殊发音方式,辅音本身发音不具有区别性特征。因此[b, d, g]三个音的持阻实际几乎是一样的,[p, t, k]持阻过程也完全一样。因为在持阻阶段几乎是无声的。

每个塞音都通过影响邻近的元音来展现它的音质。我们已经看到,像[æ]这样的元音在发音过程中,共振峰与声道特定形状保持一致,如发音节[bæ]时,它的这些共振峰将呈现为嘴唇开启。嘴唇开启那一瞬间的特定形状决定了这些共振峰的频率。随着嘴唇的张大和声道形状开始变化,共振峰也会发生相应的变化。双唇闭塞导致所有共振峰频率下降。因此,音节[bæ]开始时共振峰频率相对较低,到发[æ]时突然迅速上升,通过这个特征使它不同于其他音节。同样,在[æb]音节中,[æ]的共振峰频率会随着双唇闭塞的形成而降低。因此,无论是闭塞形成时或是闭塞解除时都将出现由特定共振峰频率表示的特定声道形状。

比如,当你说 bib 或 bab 时,在词的开头嘴唇甚至还闭合时,舌头就会预先处于准备发元音的位置。除阻瞬间的共振峰频率是由整个发音过程的声道形状决定的,因此元音也会影响辅音共振峰的变化。我们将每个调音部位共振峰的明显起始点称为那个调音部位的**音轨**(**locus**)①。共振峰起始点决定于邻近元音。这是因为跟辅音闭塞无关的舌头部位大多是邻近元音的调音部位。

图 8.7 是 a bab,a dad,a gag 等词的语图,是由图 8.3 中元音的美式英语发音人念的。他在每个词前发一个 a「ə」来给辅音可视段加上浊音(基于同样理由,我也将这张语图做得比通常的要黑)。你可以看到[b, d, g]音标上方接近底线处的模糊带声条纹。这些音节起始处的条纹没有结尾处的明显。在辅音持阻阶段,语图底线附近出现的浊音证据被称为**浊音杠**(**voice bar**)。

在这三个词中,第一共振峰都从低处上升,这只是一个塞音持阻的标志,而不会在区分调音部位方面起主要作用。这三个塞音的主要区别表现为第二和第三共振峰的首尾。共振峰起首用箭头标在图 8.7 中。bab 开头音的第二和第三共振峰频率比 dad 开头音的要低。第二共振峰音轨从相对低的[b]开始明显上升。这个词末尾降得不很明显,这是由这个元音复音化造成的。但第三共振峰频率有明显的下降。dad 中的第二和第三共振峰开始时都相

---

① 译按:音轨(locus),是指在语图中一组共振峰的明显音源点,即所有具体元音的共振峰都将弯头指向所邻接辅音的同样频率点。

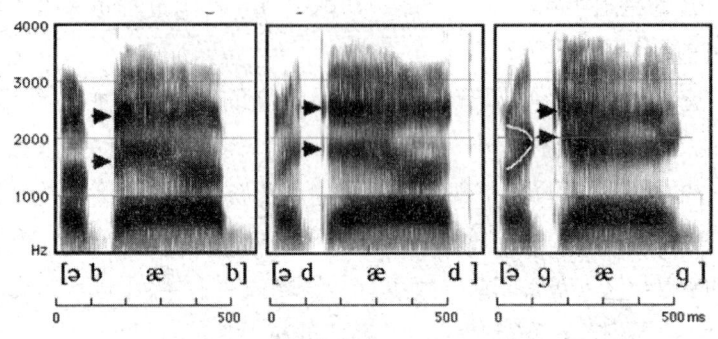

图 8.7 *a bab*，*a dad*，*a gag* 语图

当稳定。词末第三共振峰频率也相对稳定，不像它在[b]前下降得那么厉害，而且由于元音复音化，第二共振峰在降低后有一个明显抬高。*gag* 最显著的特征是第二和第三共振峰的间隔变窄。第二共振峰上升持续影响到整个元音，使得这个元音不再是一个复化元音。第二和第三共振峰用 *gag* 前[ə]音节里的白线标注。它们好像共同指向一个点。第二和第三共振峰非常接近，有时被称为软腭音源点，它很好地体现了软腭辅音的特征。

相应的清塞音[p, t, k]出现在 *a Pam*，*a tan*，*a kang*，如图 8.8 所示。当然不存在 *kang* 这个词，它只是 *kangaroo* 一词的前部分。这里再一次将 a [ə]放在每个音节之前。送气塞音的除阻标志是噪音爆发起始处的一条尖锐的竖线。噪音模式具有相对的随机性，主要分布在高频区。*Pam* 中[p]的爆发频率最低。语图中[t]和[k]的噪音延伸至 4000 Hz 以上，这些我们会在后面图中看到。最高频率实际出现在[t]而不是[k]的爆发中。如果悄声以[t, k, p]的顺序发辅音序列[t, t, t, k, k, k, p, p, p]，你可以听出最高音是[t]，其次是[k]，最低是[p]。你也可以听到[t]最响，[k]次之，[p]最低。[p]的音强有时非常低，因此在语图上很难找到冲直条印记。由于送气清塞音后的共振峰音渡发生在送气期间，在图 8.8 中它们就不像图 8.7 中浊塞音之后的那么明显。但是你可以看到，在 *Pam* 的送气阶段（在[ʰ]之上），第二、第三共振峰上升。此外，也容易察觉到它们之前元音向塞音的音渡。在[p]前的[ə]末尾处，第二和第三共振峰频率下降；在[t]之前第二共振峰频率升高，第三共振峰频率则保持不变。三个词中变化最显著的是，因为软腭音源点的缘故，第二、第三共振峰在[k]之前彼此接近。

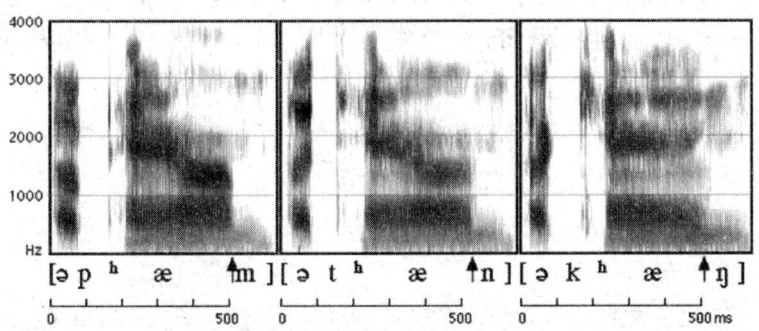

图 8.8 *a Pam*, *a tan*, *a kang* 的语图。箭头表示口腔鼻塞形成鼻辅音。

图 8.8 还显示了鼻音[m, n, ŋ]。鼻音（或者我们将要看到的边音）的明显标志是调音器官闭塞形成的那一刻，语图会有一个很突然的变化，图 8.8 用箭头标注在鼻音音标前。鼻音共振峰结构和元音相似，不同地方是浊音杠更弱，并位于由鼻腔共鸣特征决定的特别频率位置上。在鼻辅音中，第一共振峰非常低，通常约为 250 Hz。第二共振峰位置较高，在第一共振峰和第二共振峰之间的很大区域里通常没有能量。图中发音人第二共振峰很弱，频率值恰好低于 2000 Hz。鼻辅音之间的差异主要取决于它们前面元音末出现的不同共振峰音渡。[m]前元音的第二共振峰下降，*kang* 末尾软腭鼻音之前的软腭音源点使第二和第三共振峰彼此接近，但是它们起始点有时候不是很清楚。

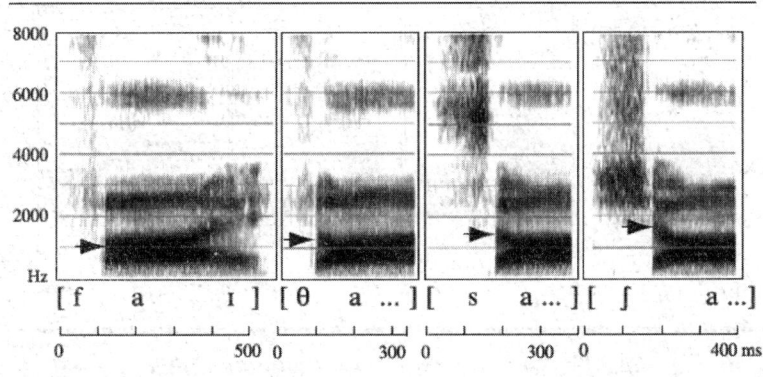

图 8.9 *fie*, *thigh*, *sigh*, *shy* 的语图。频率刻度提高到 8000 Hz，箭头指向第二共振峰起始处。语图只将第一个词完全呈现，其他词中复合元音第二部分的语图被删去。

图 8.9 是用以解释清擦音的 *fie*，*thigh*，*sigh*，*shy* 等词的语图。这些语图将频率刻度增加到 8000 Hz，作为擦音发声的最高频率。[s]中随机噪音延伸甚至远远超过这张语图的最高频率限度。第一个词 *fie* 的语图显示了词中的复合元音。其中第一和第二共振峰在央低元音的位置开始接近，然后分开，在复合元音结尾处，两个共振峰的间距如同图 8.3 中的[ɪ]。鉴于复合元音的共振峰模式在 *fie*，*thigh*，*sigh*，*shy* 里都一样，所以后面三个词只呈现其中第一部分元音的语图。

所有这些音都拥有频率分布范围很宽的随机能量。[f]和[θ]的模式几乎一样。区分这两个词的是移向后接元音的第二共振峰变化，图中用箭头表示。[f]中第二共振峰变化非常小，而[θ]在大约 1200 Hz 处开始下降。由于这两个音之间的差别非常小，所以在噪音背景下它们常常混淆在一起，而且在一些英语地方口音中它们被归为一个音。比如伦敦东区考克尼腔中，就不区分 *fin* 和 *thin*。

[s]的噪音集中于高频区，图 8.9 中在 5000 到 6000 Hz 之间。[ʃ]要更低一些，下延至 2500 Hz。由于[s]、[ʃ]声学强度都相当大，所以它们所形成的语图也比[f]和[θ]更黑，而且也有明显的共振峰音渡标记。在四个词中第二共振峰明显的音渡源点（音轨）依次抬高，*shy* 中已到了跟元音[i]相当的位置，然后再显著降下来。

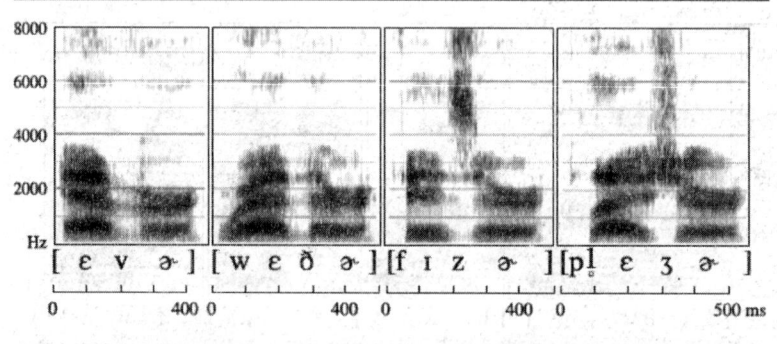

图 8.10 *ever*，*weather*，*fizzer*，*pleasure* 的语图

图 8.10 是元音之间[v, ð, z, ʒ]的语图。图中浊擦音跟清擦音[f, θ, s, ʃ]的对立不在词首的位置上。清声和浊擦音的语图模式相似，只是浊擦音具有带声直纹。*ever* 的摩擦成分[v]甚至比 *face* 的[f]还要弱，它只出现于后接

元音的开头。带声直纹在整个发音过程中都很明显。whether 中的[ð]也是如此。与含有清擦音[f，θ]的词一样，这些词是由相邻元音的共振峰来区别的。这张图中擦音都出现在[ɛ]和[ə]之间。[ð]前后的第二共振峰比[v]的要高。

在[z]、[ʒ]的高频区，擦音能量非常显著。[z]中有一个很弱的浊音杠，而[ʒ]中却很难看到。在擦音噪音开始时，6000—8000 Hz 范围内只有很少的带音直纹。从[z]到元音[ə]，共振峰音渡很平稳，但从[ʒ]开始下降显著。最后一个词是 pleasure，它还可以让我们看到，送气塞音(如[p])后接近音(如[ɹ])时会发生怎样的变化。绝大多数[l]是清音，只有在[p]爆发和送气噪音的作用下才能听到它。

最后要考察的英语辅音是边、央近音[l, r, w, j]。图 8.11 是 led, red, wed, yell 等词的语图，边、央近音就在其中。所有这些浊近音的共振峰跟元音共振峰几乎一样。在第一个词的词首边音中，三个共振峰中心频率约为 250、1100、2400 Hz(强度很低)，但到元音开始处音强突变。正像我们上面注意到的，共振峰模式的显著变化是浊鼻音和边音的特点。但在词末，这种显著变化可能要少一些，如图 8.11 的 yell。发词末边音时由于舌尖跟龈接触面可能很小或者根本没有接触，所以所发的音并非一个真正的边音，而是一个后、不圆唇元音。共振峰频率为 1100 Hz 或 1200 Hz 左右，这是大多数人发词首边音的典型模式。

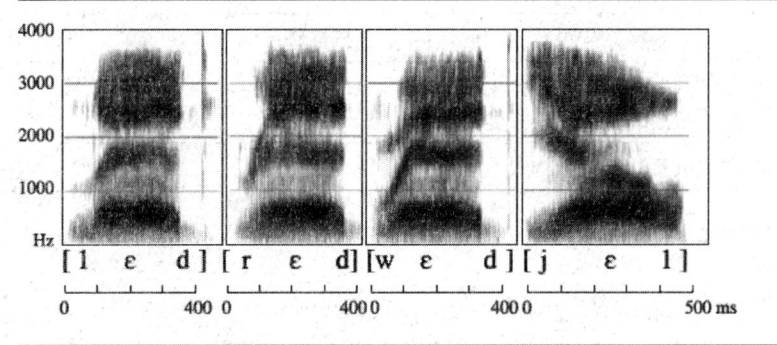

图 8.11 led, red, wed, yell 的语图

图 8.11 第二个词 red 解释了近音[r](要记住，本书英语宽式音标[r]是近音[ɹ])。[r]最明显的特征是第二和第三共振峰频率较低，尤其是第三共振峰

频率非常低,例中它(显示在[r]音标之上)约开始于 1600 Hz。*red* 和 *wed* 之间有很多相似点,这就是儿童在学着发这两个音时有时难于区分它们的原因。近音[w]始发时,三个共振峰的位置都很低,但第二共振峰随后陡升。[w]的共振峰滑动就像是从非常短的[u]滑开一样。最后,[j]的共振峰变化,也像距非常短的[i]很远的那个元音的共振峰。如 *yell* 或 *yes*。因此,将[w]、[j]称为半元音比较合适。

这里,我希望前面章节很多模糊的解释,能让你认识到语图所呈现的通常也不是非常清晰的。表 8.1 简要总结了一些调音器官特征的声学关联。但本书不可能给出完整而详细的发声学解释。我们应该将上面的声学描述视作只是一个粗略的指向,而不是对语图所示的一成不变的声学结构解释,任何音段当处于不同语音环境时,可能会有非常不同的声学结构。

表 8.1 辅音特征的声学关联。注意:这些描述应该视作只是一个粗略的指向。实际的声学关联在很大程度上取决于一个音中的特定组合以及邻近的元音。

浊音	有跟声带振动对应的直纹。
双唇音	第二和第三共振峰的音轨相对较低。
龈音	第二共振峰的音轨大约 1700—1800 Hz。
软腭音	第二共振峰的音轨通常较高,第二和第三共振峰音渡有共同源点。
卷舌音	第三和第四共振峰通常低。
塞音	缺乏噪音模式,其后有清塞音爆发或带声塞音共振峰的尖锐结构。
擦音	随机噪音模式,特别在高频区,但是也取决于调音部位。
鼻音	共振峰结构跟元音相似,但三个共振峰频率约为 250、2500 和 3250 Hz。
边音	共振峰结构跟元音相似,但邻近区域三个共振峰为 250、1200 和 2400 Hz。较高的共振峰在强度上显著下降。
近音	近音共振峰结构跟元音相似,但经常变化。

杨顺安(1992)《语音合成与语音学研究》选读[①]

◆ **作者简介**

杨顺安[②](1941—1992),中国社会科学院语言研究所语音研究室研究员。1978年他考入中国社会科学院研究生院语言学系,师从著名语音学家和语言学家吴宗济先生和林茂灿先生,1981年毕业后留任社科院从事汉语语音合成技术的研究工作。

杨顺安结合汉语语言学和语音学的研究成果,开展普通话语音参数合成,特别是在共振峰规则合成技术方面进行了开创性研究,包括普通话的声源动态特性、普通话元音声学特性和动态模型、声调和调连模型、轻声特性及其合成规则。他提出了SIFS合成框架模型,并实现了单音节、多音节词语和语句的合成;在《中国语文》、《声学学报》、*Speech Communication*等国内外重要期刊上发表了一系列重量级的文章。他毕生围绕汉语普通话合成技术进行研究,集中体现在他的专著《面向声学语音学的普通话语音合成技术》中。

引文着重介绍了由汉语语音特征所决定的汉语语音合成技术的一些重点和难点。

◆ **正文节选**

言语是人类特有的、最迅速、最方便和最自然的一种通信系统。在当今的世界上,能力非凡的电脑已迈出试验室,来到了工厂、办公室乃至家庭。如果我们能教会电脑说话和听话,赋予它言语功能,实现人——机——人的言语通信,那么,将会给我们的工作和生活带来多么大的便利和乐趣啊!

语音合成(speech synthesis)技术,是一种教会电脑说话的技术,也泛指利用电脑技术或数字信号处理技术重新产生人类言语声音的技术。语音合成技术与电脑"听话"的语音识别(speech recognition)技术相结合,就有可能

[①] 杨顺安,1992,《语音合成与语音学研究》,《语文建设》,35—42。
[②] 图片来源:https://senate.universityofcalifornia.edu/_files/inmemoriam/html/images/clip_image001_002.jpg。

实现人——机——人语音通信，那时，人们就无需叩击令人眼花缭乱的键盘，而可以直接用话音向电脑发号施令了；也无需目不转睛地盯着屏幕，因为电脑会用清晰的话音及时向你报告各种信息。

[……]

此外，在语言学中，语音合成又是研究语音特性的一种重要手段。人们可以利用合成技术人为地产生出各种语音，通过对这些语音的听辨，从而进一步探讨语音产生和语音感知的机制。"如今，没有经过合成的验证，没有谁敢于发表语音产生方面的重要理论"（Coker, 1972, p.319）。

下面，我们将着重讨论普通话语音合成技术中的语音学和语言学问题。

语音合成技术的基本原理

就汉语而言，语音合成技术大体上可分为两类：编码式合成和参数式规则合成。在编码式合成中，以语句、短语、词或音节为合成单元，录音后直接进行数字化编码，经适当的数据压缩，这些单元的语音数据就驻留在存储器中，组成一个合成语音库；重放时，根据待输出的信息，由语音库中取出一个一个的单元的数据，串接（concatenation）或编辑在一起，经解码还原出语音。这种合成方式的原理与录音机相似，也叫录音编辑合成。例如，在一种自动报站系统中，设计者事先将下列词语"录入"电脑存储器中："东单王府井""天安门""复兴门"等站名和"车站到了""下车的乘客请往车门口走"等常用语句。车快到天安门，售票员一按标有"天安门"的按钮，就从存储器中顺序调出下列单元："天安门""车站到了""下车的乘客请往车门口走"等，经解码还原成话音输出出去。采用这种方式的系统，结构简单，价格低廉，开发较容易，在合成的语汇量很少时，其合成音质较好。如今，已陆续用于自动报时、报号、报站或报警等装置中。

在规则合成（synthesis-by-rule）系统中，合成语音库中所存的是较小的语音单位（如音素、双音素、半音节或音节）的声学上的合成参数。合成时，输入一串代码来指定每一语音单元的音色、音高、音强和音长，合成系统中有一套合成规则，对某些合成参数进行必要的修改和调节，而后，由语音合成器合成出连续的语句来。合成器在特定的合成参数控制下，能模拟人们产生语音的三个过程：声源（浊或清）激励、声道（即咽腔、口腔和鼻腔的总合）共鸣和口鼻辐射。

比较而言，编码式合成技术对语音学的依赖性不大。而参数式规则合成系统的开发却一步也离不开语音学的研究。下面，我们就开发普通话规则合成系统中的合成单元的选取、合成音质的流畅性和自然度等方面,来讨论一下语音学研究的作用问题。

普通话语音的特点与合成单元的选取

这里所说的合成单元是指在一种合成系统中,为了合成无限词语的语句而选取的语言学上的某种基本单元或基本单位。这种单元选定后,就可以在该合成系统中为这些基本单元建立一个合成参数的数据库,要合成一篇文本(text)或一句话时,从数据库中取出有关合成参数,这些参数经过有关规则作适当的修改后,送入语音合成器,就可以合成出语句来。

合成单元的选取是开发语音合成系统中的关键问题之一。合成单元的大小要兼顾到:(1) 合成音质的好坏;(2) 数据库的大小;(3) 合成程序的复杂性或硬件实现的难易。

我们可选音位做基本单元,对任何一种语言来说,语音学上的音位数目总是很少的。普通话中,只有 21 个辅音和十来个元音,这样的语音数据库是很小的。然而,在自然的语流中,五花八门的音变无所不在,在人们头脑中,可能存在着像音位这类的分离的语言学单元,但输出的语音波却是一种连续的声学信号。各语音单元间会相互作用,使某个单元出现或多或少的变异。一个音位会有许多个音位变体。目前,从声学语音学来看,我们对普通话中音位这一级上的音变规律,知之甚少,所以无法选取音位来做合成单元。

与其他语言(如英语等)相比,普通话中的音节有如下几个特点:首先,它是普通话中最自然和最基本的语音单位,除极少数例外,普通话的一个音节,写下来就是一个汉字,而且还具有一定的意义,也就是说,一个音节是形音义的结合体;其次,在音节相连的语流中,虽然同样存在着音节之间的协同调音效应,但效应的作用范围较小,在听感上,基本上可以分出一个个音节,每一音节的声学表现有其相对的稳定性;第三,普通话的音节数较少,不计声调只有四百多个,而英语多达 4030 个,俄语也有 2960 个(高汉平等,1983,p.70)。

据资料统计,在大多数普通话语音合成系统中,都是以音节作为合成单元的。在合成语句时,就将一个个单音节串接起来。这些系统的合成音质,清晰度尚好,但是其自然度和流畅性恐怕就差一些了。为了使合成的词语更连贯些,可以选用单词做合成单元,但普通话中的基本词条的数量是相当大的,所以,这恐怕是一条实现不了的途径。

为了开发出合成音质较好的普通话语音合成系统,我们应当选取比音节更小的语音单元,多在声学语音学方面下功夫,寻找出各种语音层次上的音变规律,适时地调整合成参数,这样就有可能获得较高音质的合成语句。普通话语音体系中的声母和韵母就可以充当这种意义上的合成单元。

声学分析表明,普通话中的声母和韵母,虽然没有什么一成不变的声学表现与之一一对应,但还是可以进一步划分出若干"特征音段"。在大量分析了普通话中有代表性的音节的语谱图以及反复的合成试验后,我们提出了一种用于合成普通话音节的"音节—声母/韵母—音段框架模型(Syllable-Inatial/Final-Segments Model),简称 SIFS 模型(图1)。

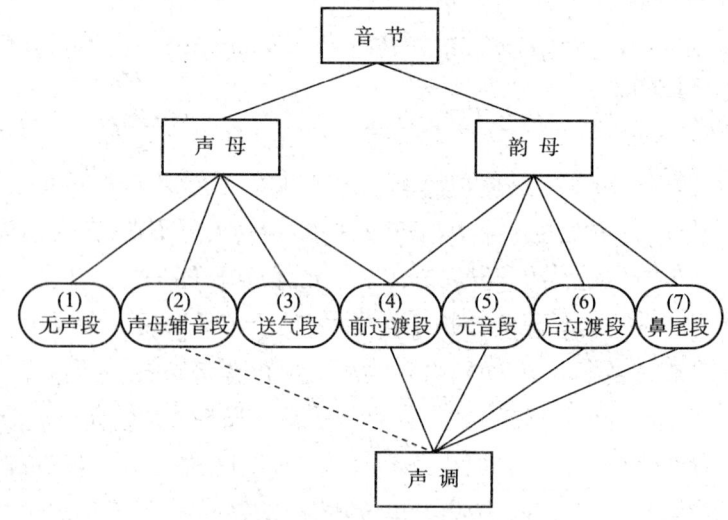

图1 普通话音节的 SIFS 模型

根据这种 SIFS 模型,从普通话的一个音节里可划分出 7 种特征音段,如果按照表示出现先后的序号排列,它们是:(1) 无声段,(2) 声母辅音段,(3) 送气段,(4) 前过渡段,(5) 元音段,(6) 后过渡段,(7) 鼻尾段。对某一个具体的音节来说,可能具有 1—7 种音段,也可能只具有其中某几段。表1列举了几个音节的声母、韵母及其在 SIFS 模型中的配列。

由表中的例子看到,任何音节都少不了元音段,而且只要声母不是零声母,一般都会有前过渡段。在最后一个例子中,因为声母辅音/tɕ/和韵母元音/i/的调音部位相同,通常无过渡,所以也就无前过渡段。在模型中,不论单元音韵母,还是复合元音韵母,都只有一段元音段,至于复合元音中的共振峰频率的动态变化,另有别的模型来处理(杨顺安,1986a)。整个音节的声调由字调模型来处理(1986b)。

应该说明的是,这种模型中的音段,并不对应着语音学中的某一种公认的语音单位,它们只是从合成的需要出发,以普通话音节的声学特性为依据,人为地划分出来的。它既可比音位大,如一个元音段(5)中,可以包括三个音位组成的复合元音,也可以比音位小,如一个送气塞音须由模型中的无声段(1)、声母辅音段(2)、送气段(3)和前过渡段(4)组成。

根据对大量语谱图的分析和反复的合成调试,我们建立了一个以60个声母变体和40个韵母为存储单元的合成参数库,用此参数库不但能合成出普通话的全部单音节(Yang & Xu,1988),还能按规则合成出普通话中颇具特色的儿化音节和轻声音节(杨顺安,1991a;1991b)。

表1 一些音节的声母、韵母及其在 SIFS 模型中的配列

音节	声调	声母	韵母	SIFS 模型时序号						
				1	2	3	4	5	6	7
爱	4	0	ai					*		
恩	1	0	en					*	(*)	*
大	4	d	a	*	*			*		
小	3	x	iao		*			*		
天	1	t	ian	*	*	*	*	*	(*)	*
然	2	r	an		*			*	(*)	*
机	1	j	i	*				*		

音节的协同调音效应与合成语音的流畅性

如前所述,用一串单音节拼连出来的合成语句是不流畅的,是不自然的。因为在自然的语流中,一个个语音的调音和发声是会相互影响的,存在着大量的复杂的发生在音系学层面上的和语音学层面上的音变效应,即协同调音(co-articulation)效应和协同发声(co-phonation)效应。这里,协同调音是对语音的音段特征(即音色)而言的,协同发声是对超音段特征(即音高、音长、音强)而言的。

先讨论协同调音效应。对普通话来说,传统语音学家(如徐世荣,1980,p.159)早已注意到属于协同调音效应的所谓连读音变现象,如"面/mian/"和"包/pao/"连读时,/n/会被同化为/m/等。调音动作的不同必然会在语音声

学特性上产生不可忽略的差异。近年来,还通过声学分析,从不同的角度考察了普通话的协同调音效应现象(许毅,1986;Chen,1989;Wu & Sun,1990;1991、杨顺安,1990)。

要改善合成语句的自然度和流畅性,就必须寻求到协同调音效应的规律,在合成参数的过程中设法模拟它。对那些以音节为合成单元的合成系统来说,要模拟协同调音效应是比较困难的,在我们开发的以特征音段为合成单元的合成系统中,这种模拟就比较容易。我们通过对几百个双音节词的语谱图的观测,初步归纳出音节间的协同调音效应的一些明显规律,在所开发的普通话语音合成系统中,增添了五条协同调音规则(Yang,1990a),合成出音质比较清晰和流畅的多音节词语。下面举一例来说明。

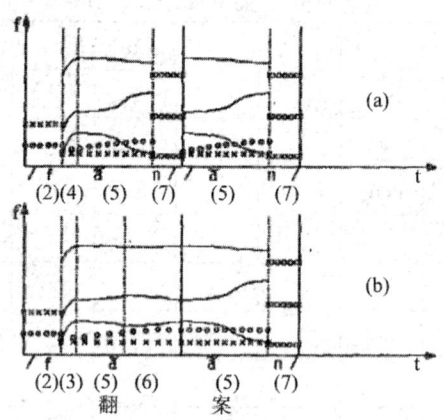

图 2　音节间的协同调音效应的模拟

图 2 示出了合成单音节"翻"/fan/和"案"/an/(图 a)以及双音节词"翻案"/fan an/(图 b)时各音段的控制参数。图中,竖实线表示音节界线;竖虚线表示音段界线;实曲线自下而上分别表示共振峰频率 F1、F2 和 F3 的轨迹;XXX 线表示鼻音或鼻化元音的极点频率轨迹;OOO 线表示零点频率轨迹。为便于比较,音节时长方面没有处理。根据协同调音规则,合成双音节的前音节时:(1)增添后过渡段,取后音节元音/a/的共振峰频率作目标值;(2)前音节鼻尾脱落,后音节元音被鼻化;(3)后音节元音/a/的共振峰频率降低与前音节的共振峰平滑衔接。这样一来,就比较圆满地模拟了语流中音节间的协同调音效应,改善了合成词语的流畅性。

普通话的韵律特性与合成语句的自然度

在普通话的自然语流中,每一音节的音高、音长和强度都会随语境而变,人们说出来的话,抑扬顿挫、轻重相随、缓急相间、节奏分明,有如唱歌一般。这样的韵律特性对于合成语句的自然度关系极大。到目前为止,关于普通话的韵律的研究多限于一般语音学的范围,声学语音学方面的研究刚刚开始,尚无适合于合成应用的韵律模型。因此,几乎所有的普通话语音合成系统的合成音质,其自然度和流畅性都不尽如人意,一听就有一股子"机器味儿"或"洋腔洋调"。

为了改善合成语句的自然度,人们进行过许多探索。例如,李子殷(1985)采用了15种双音节调型的基频曲线来合成双音节词。张家禄(1990)在其开发的系统中,借用了瑞典语的Lund语调生成模型,以手工方式为该模型中的参数附加语调标志后,再由模型生成出所需要的语调曲线。在四川大学的系统中,有6条调节能量的规则,有6条调节音节时长的规则,有3种停顿,6种声调模式(于鸿洋等,1990)。在台湾大学开发的"国语"语音合成系统中,有14种音节调型和8条变调规则、重音规则、语调规则、音节时长规则和能量调整规则(Lee et al,1989)。

韵律特征涉及语音中的音高、音长和音强等方面的属性,千头万绪,从何入手?传统语音学的研究指出,"汉语的重音首先扩大音域和持续时间,其次才是增加强度"(赵元任,1968,p.23);"重音音节的音量大。音量的增强,影响主要元音变得长些,声调调值特别分明,或者显得高些"(徐世荣,1980,p.133)。这就告诉我们,普通话中的重音是一个影响着声调、时长和强度的重要参量。一些声学分析也证实了这种看法(如林茂灿等,1984;陆致极,1984;颜景助等,1988)。因此,在研究多音节词语的合成中,我们就把语流中各音节的重音等级,当作控制韵律特性的主要参量,根据每一音节的轻重等级,调节这个音节的调域、声韵母时长和浊声源幅度。

一个词语的轻重格式,是在长期使用过程中"约定俗成"的,经过语音学家的归纳,从音系学的角度加以标定。例如,在"头昏眼花,不辨南北和东西"和"他去买东西"这两句话中,前一句话中的"东西",要读成"中重"格;后一句的要读成"重轻"格,否则,会引起语义上的误会,或者听起来不自然。一个词语的轻重格式虽然被定下来了,但在语流中还会有语音学层面上的变化。仍以上面两例句来说,同一字形的"东西",在音系学上被变成两种轻重格式的读法;如果把第一句改为:"……不辨东西和南北",则这个"东西"的轻重格式,要发生语音学层次上的音变,不再是"中重"格,"西"反比"东"读得轻。

我们把按音系学规定下来的某一音节在一个词中的重音的轻重程度,称之为重度(stress degree),表为 Sd。在语境中,该音节的轻重格式发生了变化。目前,关于普通话中"一个"的轻重格式尚无定论,拿双音节词来说,一般认为,有中重格和重轻格两种。但也有人认为,还有重中格和重次轻格,音节的轻重等级要分成四级:重、中重(或次重)、次轻和轻声(如:殷作炎,1982;徐世荣,1982;陆致极,1984;俞敏,1988)。根据我们的实验,音节轻重分为四级是必要的,即:4(重)、3(中)、2(次轻)、1(轻声)。

在普通话语流中,一个语句(尤其是较长的语句)是被分成为一个个短语说出来的,一个短语一般由几个词组成。在由词组成短语的过程中,短语中的各音节的重度会发生语音学层次上变化,此时各音节的重度分配受所谓"位置效应"和"音节数效应"的支配,某一音节的重度 Sd′由下式算出:

$$Sd' = Sd - Dp - Dn \tag{1}$$

式中 Sd 为该音节原来的重度,Dp 和 Dn 分别叫作"位置效应减量"和"音节数效应减量",它们皆可用经验公式求得(Yang,1990b)。在几个短语组成句子时,各音节的重度还会受停顿、意群重音、强调重音、感情重音、句长效应等的影响,而改变其值。

在我们的合成系统中,合成词语的韵律特性参数是通过声调协调规则、时长协调规则和幅度协调规则来调整的。下面,举个实例来说明声调协调规则的作用。

现在,要合成的语句是"姐姐和我去看绘画展览",图 3 示出了用此声调协调规则最终生成整句话的基频曲线的全过程:

(a) 单音节处理:首先给定每一单音节的调整型码和重度,这是由音系学上定下来的。图中每一小框表示一个音节的基频曲线,框长代表该音节的时长,框中的纵虚线代表清声母和韵母的分界线,框高代表该音节的调域,这里的单音节的重度都被标定为4,框中横虚线代表音节的调基值。在此阶段,因为都作单音节处理,所以,各音节不相连,各小框互相分开。

(b) 词处理阶段:按音系学上的约定,在由单音节组成词的过程中,为每一音节分配一个调型码和重度。此例中有如下词:"姐姐""和""我""去""看""绘画""展览"。在此阶段有几条音系学层面上的变调规则。例如,"展"和

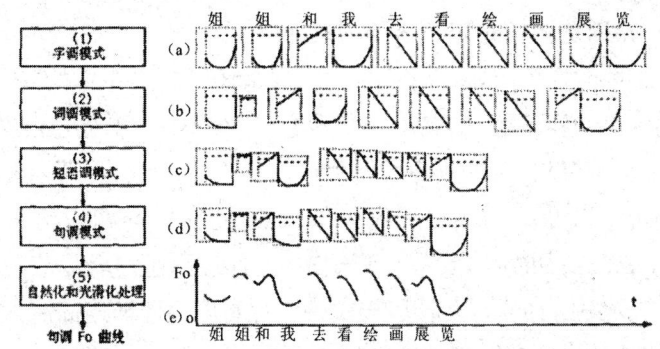

图 3　同声调协调规则最终生成整句话的基频曲线的过程示意图

"览"组成"展览"时,"展"变成阳平,"姐姐"的后音节是轻声音节,后音节就变阴平,前音节变半上声。

图(b)中的小框有大有小,这是因为各音节的重度不同,因而时长和调域随之不同。另外,同一词中的几个音节的调基值也要依次略降。

值得一提的是,用这种声调规则可以较合理地解释许多语音学中讨论的连读变调现象,例如:语音学指出,两个去声音节组成一个"中重"格的词时,前音节的声调要变为半去,其调值为53。按我们的模型,这种变调属于语音学层次上的变调,由于前音节的重度小于后音节,其调域相应地小些,所以,其调值自然是53,并非发音人刻意产生的(参见图 b 中"绘画"一词的调形)。再如,语音学指出,一般三音节词按"中轻重"格读音时,第二音节会变成阴平,用本模型来解释,这也是由于该音节的调域减小的缘故。

(c) 短语处理:按公式(1),重新分配各音节的重度,进而计算调域。

(d) 句子处理:该句为陈述句,主语"姐姐和我"比谓语略轻,重度稍减,句尾音节"览"的调基值略降。

(e) 声调曲线自然化和光滑化:所谓"自然化",是给每一音节的声调曲线,加上适当的"弯头"和"降尾",使得合成音质更加自然;而"光滑化"是对那些浊声母或零声母音节而言的,如此例中"我"和"览",它们的基频曲线应与前一音节的光滑相连。合成程序会自动地判定应进行光滑处理的音节。

应用包括了声调协调规则、时长协调规则和幅度协调规则在内的韵律规则,在我们的普通话语音合成系统上,合成了大量的多音节词、短语和短句,合成音质在自然度和流畅性上,都比用单音节拼接的有较明显提高,有些合成词语几乎听不出什么"机器味儿"。但由于规则还不够完善,所以合成出来的有些词语,特别是较长的句子,还不那么自然。

从上述规则的描述中,可以看出,这些规则还是相当粗糙的,规则的制定缺乏充足的定量的实验数据,带有很大程度的经验性。例如,在这种声调协调规则中,虽然也有句子处理阶段,但到目前为止,关于普通话中各种语气的语句的语调规律以及语调和字调的纠葛问题,还在研究和争论之中(沈迥,1985;吴宗济,1982;胡明扬,1987),尚无定论。最近,还发现音节间有协同发声效应(Lin & Yan,1991)。所以,合成语句时的声调处理还需深入探索。再者,普通话语流的音节的时长特性是较为复杂的,就单个音节而言,音节的时长与该音节的构成有关,还与该音节的声调有关。进入语句平面,某个音节的时长就会与该音节读音的轻重、所处的位置、上下文的语法结构关系等因素密切相关。而且,时长特性还与若干非语言学的因素有关,如语速、个人习惯等。通过声学测量研究普通话音节的时长特性的工作已逐步展开(冯隆,1985;Cao,1991;王晶、王理嘉,1991),这些研究对进一步完善时长协调规则是有益的。

2.3 思考和练习

1. 普通话的辅音和英语的辅音有哪些音素是对方语言里所没有的?请列出。

2. 普通话有以下韵母,请试着用国际音标一一标注出来。(建议完成练习前先熟悉国际音标的元音表。)

　　(1) a o e i u ü er (y)e (zh)i

　　(2) ai ei ui ao ou iu ie iao uo ua uai üe er

　　(3) an en in un ün ian uan ang eng ing ong iang iong uang

3. 思考上题中的 a o e i u ü 代表的音素。在不同的韵母中,比如 a 在 ta 和 tian,或者 o 在 fo 和 tuo 中,它们代表的是同一个音素吗?

4. 北京人喜欢把"中央电视台"说成"装垫台","西红柿炒鸡蛋"说成"胸是炒鸡蛋"。请用国际音标标注出这四个词的发音并进行比较,在音素的层面解释北京话发音的特征。

5. 据你的观察，男性和女性的发音除了音高不同，还有哪些区别？请用发音语音学的术语解释这些区别。

6. 参考第二篇选文的内容，试指出以下谱图中可能有哪些辅音，并说出你判断的根据。

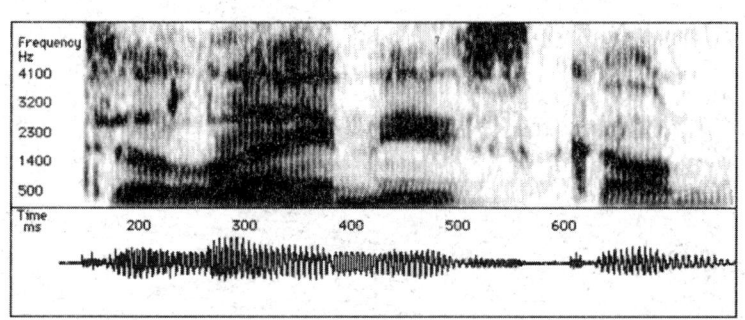

2.4 延伸阅读

鲍怀翘,林茂灿,(2014)《实验语音学概要(增订版)》,北京：北京大学出版社。

罗常培,王均,(2002)《普通语音学纲要(修订本)》,北京：商务印书馆。

Ladefoged, P. & K. Johnson. 2015. *A Course in Phonetics* (*Seventh Edition*). Stamford, CT: Cengage Learning.

Laver, J. 1994. *Principles of Phonetics*. Cambridge: Cambridge University Press.

Li, Y.-H. 2007. *The Sounds of Chinese*. Cambridge: Cambridge University Press.

Stevens, K. N. 1998. *Acoustic Phonetics*. Cambridge, Mass.: The MIT Press.

第三章 音系学

3.1 导引

- 音系概说
- 音位和音位变体
- 最小对立对
- 互补分布
- 音系特征
- 音节结构
- 音系规则
- 结语

3.1.1 音系概说

上一章讨论了语音学。语音学研究语音的物理特性、产生机制和感知规律。和语音学不同，音系学研究语音的模式（the sound pattern），即语音的组织规律。语音学中的基本单位是单音（phone），而音系学中的基本单位是音位（phoneme）。语音学和物理学中的声学、人工智能研究中的语音识别有很多交叉，而音系学则是相对纯粹的语言学分支。在这一章，我们将介绍音系学中的常用概念，如音位、音位变体、互补分布、最小对立对、音节结构等。我们也将简要介绍如何进行音系分析。

3.1.2 音位和音位变体

在第二章里我们提到，人类可以产生和感知相当数量的语音（sounds）。在自然语言中，没有哪一种语言穷尽性地使用到所有可能的语音。每一种语言都是有选择的从语音库藏里面，选择某些"独特"的语音进行组织和搭配，形成一个具有对立性和规律性的语音系统。这个语音系统，就是音系系统，比如我们通常所说的汉语音系、英语音系、拉萨藏语音系等。研究音系系统规律的，就是音系学。

某一语言的音系系统分为三个层次。最明显的层次就是音段（segment）层次，主要是指不同的语音（如元音和辅音）之间的相互关系；比音段高一层的是音节，研究不同的音段组成比音段更大的单位；比音段低一层的是音系特征，每一个音段都可以分解为若干音系特征。我们之所以觉得两个音不同，就是因为组成它们的特征不同。音系系统的三层分立结构如（1）所示：

(1) 音系特征→音段→音节（结构）

我们先从音段开始。我们经常会觉得某个人说话带有独特的口音，一个说普通话的北方人不需要在南京生活多久就会发现，老派的南京人经常把"大南京"读成"大蓝鲸"；我们也可以一耳就能听出"爸"和"怕"是两个不同的词——凡此种种，都和音系有关。换言之，音系的对立可以归结到音系中的基本单位——音位——的对立上。"爸"（发音[pa]）和"怕"（发音为[pʰa]）之所以是两个不同的词，是因为它们涉及到两个不同的音位：不送气的[p]和送气的[p]（为以示区别，一般把送气的[p]记为[pʰ]）。

语言学家把具有对立意义、能够区分不同词的语音叫做音位。音位具有辨义作用。在汉语中，送气的[p]和不送气的[p]就代表了不同的音位（因为它们可以区别意义）。属于同一个音位，但是不具有区别意义的语音叫做音位变体（allophone）。如果某些人经常把"大南京"读成"大蓝鲸"，一个可能的原因就是在这些人的音系系统中，[l]和[n]属于同一个音位的变体（也有可能是在它们的音系系统中，不存在和[n]相对应的音位）。语音系统的差异，主要是音位上的差异。语言不同，音位也不同。在汉语普通话中，送气的[p]和不送气的[p]表示不同的音位，但是在英语中不是。"pit"（发音[pɪt]）和"spit"

(发音[spɪt])中[p]的发音不同,前者是送气音,后者是不送气音,存在音质上的差异,但是英语母语者并不觉得音位具有辨义功能。也就是说,如果一个人把"spit"发成[spʰɪt],听话人会觉得奇怪,但是不会认为这和"spit"是不同的词。然而,[sbit]和[spit]却有本质的区别,前者是浊爆破音,后者是清爆破音。清浊对立在英语中具有辨义功能。所以我们说[b]和[p]在英语中表示不同的音位,而英语中送气的[pʰ]和不送气的[p]就是音位变体。

为了区分音位和语音(以及音位变体),语言学家一般用"/ /"表示音位,用方括号"[ ]"表示人耳所感知到的具体的语音。如下(2)是英语中音位和音位变体之间的示意图:

(2)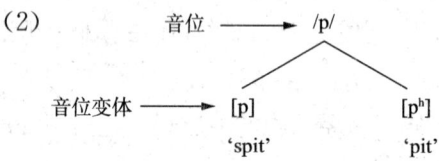

在英语中,送气的[pʰ]和不送气的[p]属于音位/p/的不同变体。但是在汉语普通话中,送气的[pʰ]和不送气的[p]则属于不同的音位。母语为汉语普通话的使用者无法将两者视为同一个音位的变体,因为它们可以区别不同的词,具有辨义功能。如(3):

(3) a. 怕[pʰa4]、趴[pʰa1]、爬[pʰa2]、啪[pʰa]
    b. 爸[pa4]、把[pa3]、吧[pa]、八[pa1]

(3a)中的是送气的[pʰ],(3b)中的是不送气的[p](1、2、3、4 分别表示第一声、第二声、第三声、第四声,没有标记表示轻声)。(3a)和(3b)表示不同的词。在汉语普通话中,送气的[pʰ]和不送气的[p]分别代表不同的音位,如(4):

(4)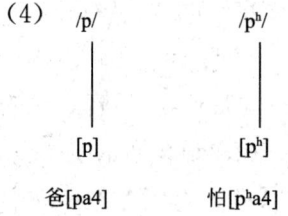

音位和音位变体的概念存在的前提是语言的音系有两个层次:音位变体是语音音段的物理实现,是具体的;而音位存在于说话人的音系系统中(储藏于人脑的语言知识中),是抽象的。音位变体是抽象的音位的实现。音位变体和音位之间是实现和被实现的关系。

3.1.3 最小对立对

音位是具有辨义功能、能够产生对立的语音。要确定两个音是不同的音位亦或同一音位的不同变体,一般通过最小对立对来判断。所谓最小对立对,指的是两个词(或其它语言单位)在所有位置上的音都一模一样,仅在同一个地方存在区别,且这个区别导致了两个词的意义不同,则认为这两个词组成一对最小对立对。上文提到的"怕"[pʰa]和"爸"[pa]就是一对最小对立对:它们在所有位置上的音都相同,只在词首的辅音存在区别,并且这一区别导致了两个不同的词。同理,"妈"[ma]和"爸"[pa]也是一对最小对立对。通过最小对立对,我们可以得出,[m]、[p]、[pʰ]属于不同的音位。但是,"怕"[pʰa]和"提"[tʰi]不是一对最小对立对,因为这两个词的音并不是只在同一个地方存在区别,相反,这两个词的音在每一个位置都存在区别。

下面的(5)和(6)各举了一些英语和汉语中最小对立对的例子。通过建立最小对立对,可以很直接地判定两个音属于不同的音位。

(5) 布[pu4]　铺[pʰu4] 音位:/p/ vs. /pʰ/
　　 读[tu2]　图[tʰu2] 音位:/t/ vs. /tʰ/
　　 稿[kao3]　考[kʰao3] 音位:/k/ vs. /kʰ/
　　 脚[tɕiao3]　巧[tɕʰiao3] 音位:/tɕ/ vs. /tɕʰ/
　　 声[ʂəŋ1]　身[ʂən1] 音位:/ŋ/ vs. /n/
(6) lacy [lejsi]　lazy [lejzi] 音位:/s/ vs. /z/
　　 sum [sʌm]　sun [sʌn] 音位:/m/ vs. /n/
　　 sing [siŋ]　sin [sin] 音位:/ŋ/ vs. /n/

3.1.4 互补分布

用最小对立对可以区分两个不同的音位。那么,如何区分同一音位的不同变体呢？语言学家通常采用互补分布(complementary distribution)的方法来区分音位变体。所谓互补分布，就是没有区别意义的两个音在不同的位置出现，并且这两个音出现的环境互相排斥。用通俗的话来说，假设 x 和 y 是两个不同的音，x 音出现的地方，不会出现 y 音，反之亦然，那么这样的现象就叫做互补分布。

英语中的长元音[iː]和短元音[i]的出现就呈现互补分布。[iː]一般出现在浊塞音(voiced obstruent)之前，而[i]则出现在别的地方，譬如清塞音之前、鼻辅音之前等等。我们可以得出下面的规则：

(7) [iː]和[i]的互补分布
  a. [iː]出现在浊塞音之前，如 heed、seize、leave 等。
  b. [i]出现在别的地方，如 heat、cease、leaf、seen 等。

总而言之，两个不同的音可能会(也可能不会)产生词的对立，可能具有(也可能不具有)辨义功能。如果两个音导致了词的对立，具有辨义功能，则这两个音属于不同的音位；如果两个(不同的)音不会导致不同的词，不具有辨义功能，则这两个音属于同一音位的音位变体。我们用最小对立对来确定音位。同一音位的音位变体之间则存在互补分布。

3.1.5 音系特征

前文提到过，音系系统存在三个层次：(一) 特征层次；(二) 音段层次；(三) 音节层次。上文讨论到的音位属于音段层次。在下一小节我们会介绍音节层次的结构。在这一小节，我们简单介绍一下音系特征。

音段可以分解为若干音系特征。各种音都是由特征组成的。音系特征来源于语音特征(见第二章)，音系上音位的对立就是因为特征的对立造成的。不同的特征会导致音的不同。有的时候，某一个特征的不同也会导致音位的不同。能导致音位变化的特征叫做甄别性特征(distinctive features)。音系是因语言而异的，所以，一个语言中的甄别性特征，可能在另一个语言中不具有甄别音位的作用。在汉语中，送气/不送气的对立是甄别性特征，但是这一特征在英语中不具有甄别音位的作用，而是属于音位变体的语音特征。在英语中，清浊对立(voiced/voiceless)(又称"带声/不带声")是甄别性特征，如[b]和[p]是不同的音位。它们之间的差异,就在于前者是带声的,后者是不带声的。

我们可以用音系特征分析法来描写音位。以汉语普通话中不送气的[p]和送气的[pʰ]为例,它们的音位特征可以用特征矩阵(feature matrix)描述如下:

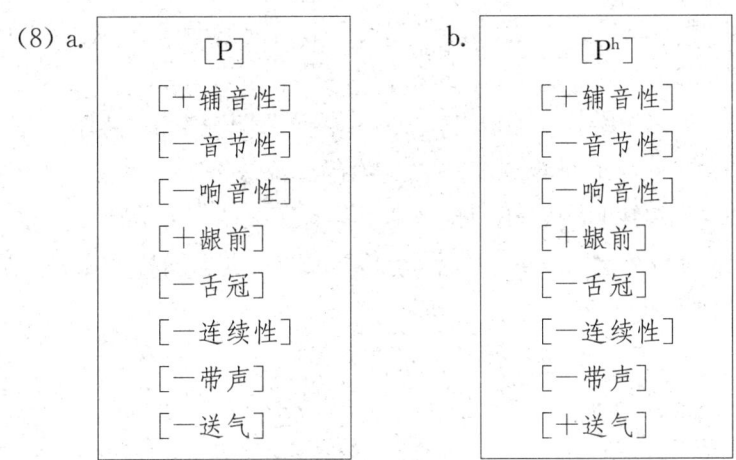

上述特征矩阵很直观地描述了汉语普通话中不送气的[p]和送气的[pʰ]的重合与差异:它们除了在[±送气]这一特征上存在差异外,其他所有特征都相同。而[±送气]正是甄别这两个音的关键。

3.1.6 音节结构

音系系统分为三个层次:特征层次、音段层次和音节层次。前文分别讨论了音段层次和特征层次。这一小节讨论音节层次。两个或两个以上的音段组成音节。音节是比音段更大的单位。最简单的音节由元音组成(如英语中的"I"),常见的音节由辅音加上元音组成,形成 CV 结构(C:consonants;V:vowels)。不同语言的音节结构是不一样的。汉语普通话中的音节一般是 CV(如果是 CVC 的话,音节末的 C 只能是鼻音,如"南"[nan])。汉语普通话不允许在音节首出现辅音串(consonants clusters),CCV 结构不存在于汉语中,至少不存在于现代汉语普通话中。但是,很多语言允许在音节首出现辅音串。英语就是其中之一,如(9):

(9) a. CCCVC,例:stream [strɪm]
    b. CVCCCC,例:sixths [siksθs]

英语允许音节首最多出现 3 个辅音:第一个一般是丝擦音[s],后面跟随一个不带声爆破音(如[t]),第三个音一般是流音或边音,如[r]或者[l]。在音节尾,英语最多允许出现四个辅音,如(9b)的音节末就是四个辅音串(CCCC)。

俄语的音节结构比英语更为复杂。俄语大量允许辅音串出现在音节首,如"vprog"(发音:[fprɔk]),就有三个辅音出现在音节首。

和语言中其他的结构一样,音节也具有层级性。用希腊字母σ表示音节,Onset 表示音节首,Rhyme 表示韵部,Nucleus 表示韵核,Coda 表示音节尾(韵尾),典型的音节结构如(10)所示:

(10) 音节结构

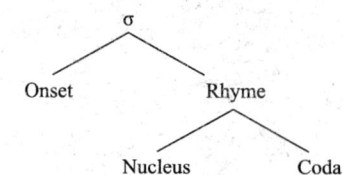

(11) [bin]

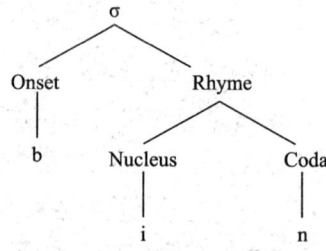

如果一个词由多个音节组成,我们也可以像绘制树形图一样的,把多个音节连接起来,如(W 表示词):

(12) phonetics [fənɛtiks]

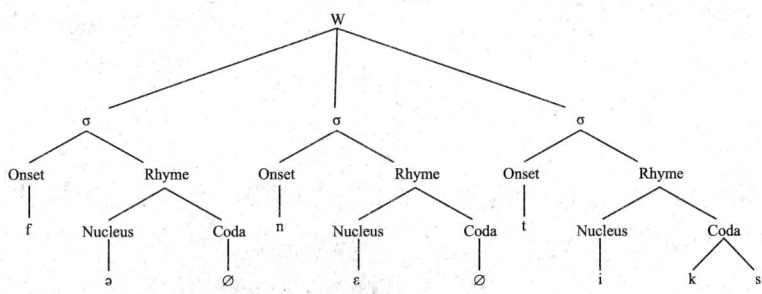

[fənɛtiks]由三个音节组成，第一个音节的 coda 为空（用空集符号∅表示），第二个音节的 coda 也为空，第三个音节的 coda 有两个辅音。

当一种语言的词被"借入"另一种语言中的时候，如果这两种语言的音节结构不同，通常借入的词要进行音节化（syllabification）。如英语中的 Amsterdam 由三个音节组成，但是译成汉语，却成了五个音节（阿-姆-斯-特-丹）。音节化是借词音系中一个很常见的现象。

3.1.7 音系规则

前文我们区分了音位和音位变体（语音）。音位和音位变体分别代表了音段的两层表征。音位对应的是抽象的、语言使用者大脑中关于音系知识的表征，我们把这一层叫做音系表征（phonological representation）或底层表征（underlying representation, UR）。音位变体对应的是音位的实现，我们把这一层叫做语音表征（phonetic representation）或表层表征（surface representation, SR）。和音系表征不同，语音表征包含了一些和具体发音相关的信息。

我们感知到的语音是通过应用音系规则生成出来的。音系规则作用于音系/底层表征，生成语音/表层表征。这一构拟音系系统的方式，叫做推导（derivation）。推导总是通过规则来实现的。推导模型如(13)所示：

(13)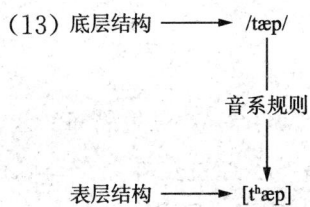

音系规则可以通过形式化的方式来表述。在当代音系学中,音系规则一般采用(14)的范式来表述:

(14) A→B / X_____Y

在表达式(14)中,A 表示规则的作用对象(输入),B 表示应用规则后所得到的结果(输出),"/ X_____Y"是规则所适用的环境,其中"/"表示"在……环境中","_____"表示受影响的音所出现的位置。这一规则非正式的表达是:"A 变成 B 当 A 出现于 X 和 Y 之中的时候"。

我们可以通过一个简单的例子来说明这一规则是如何运作的。英语可数名词的规则变化是在词尾加"s",如:dog-s, student-s, teacher-s, desk-s 等。但是,当名词以[s, z, ʃ, ʒ, ʧ, ʤ]中的任意一个结尾时,在复数标记"s"和相应的名词中间要插入一个中性元音(schwa)"ə"。这一点也反映在拼写上:当相应的名词以 s、z 结尾时,复数标记要改为"es"。如:

(15) bus-es [bʌsəz], bush-es [buʃəz], badg-es [bædʒəz], garag-es [gæraʒəz], etc

这一现象可以通过一条插入规则(epenthesis)来刻画:

(16) 中性元音插入规则
∅→ə/[丝擦音]_____[丝擦音]

规则(16)可以读成:在两个丝擦音中间插入中性元音 ə。这一规则可以很直观地描述(15)所示的现象。

更多音系分析的实例,见 Fromkin et al. (2013)第 6 章。

3.1.8 结语

人类语言中的音段可以区分三个层次:(一) 音位特征;(二) 音位;(三) 音节。我们通过最小对立对来确定音位,通过互补分布来确定音位变体。音节分为音节首和韵部两个部分,其中韵部又可以分为韵核和韵尾两个部分。音位所对应的是音位表征(底层表征),我们感知到的具体的语音所对应的是语音表征(表层表征)。音系规则作用于底层表征的音位,生成表层表征层面上具体的语音。

3.2 选读

- 乔姆斯基(2006)《语言与心智》音系部分选读
- David Odden (2013) *Introducing Phonology* 选读
- Alan Prince & Paul Smolensk (2004) *Optimality Theory: Constraint Interaction in Generative Grammar* 选读

乔姆斯基(2006)《语言与心智》音系部分选读[①]

第五章 语言的形式属性

音系部分的结构

生成语法的句法部分定义(即生成)成对(D, S)的无限集合,其中 D 是深层结构,S 是表层结构。语法的解释部分为 D 指派语义表达式,为 S 指派语音表达式。

我们首先考虑向表层结构指派语音表达式的问题。像上文关于普遍语音学的讨论一样,我们将语音表达式看作普遍语音字母的符号串,每个符号都分析作有特定值的区别特征。相同的观念如果用稍微不同的方式陈述的话,那么我们可以把语音表达式看作一个矩阵,其中"行"对应于普遍系统的特征,"列"对应于连续的音段(语音字母表中的符号),每个条目都是个整数,这个整数规定了所探讨的特定音段的特征值。我们需要确定以下问题:一是

[①] 乔姆斯基,《语言与心智(第三版)》,熊仲儒、张孝荣译,中国人民大学出版社 2015 年版。作者简介请见第一章"选读"部分。

哪些信息必须被包含在表层结构中,二是语法的音系部分的规则怎样用这些信息来规定所描述的这类语音矩阵。

再考虑例(4),为表述方便我们重新写作(5):

(5) What ♯ disturb-ed ♯ John ♯ was ♯ be-ing ♯ dis-regard-ed ♯ by ♯ every-one.

粗略看来①,我们可以将(5)看作构成要素"what、disturb、ed、John、was、be、ing、dis、regard、ed、by、every、one"的序列,其联结处用符号"♯"和"—"表达,如(5)所示。这些联结符号(juncture)指明了构成要素的组合方式,为音系部分的解释规则提供了信息。事实上,联结符号必须分析为特征集合,即单列矩阵(single-column matrix),其中"行"对应于联结系统中的某些特征,每个条目都是两个特征值中的一个,特征值我们表征为"+"或"—"。同样,每个构成要素将分析为矩阵,其中"列"代表连续的音段,"行"对应于某种范畴特征(categorial feature),每个条目或为"+"或为"—"。所以,(5)整个句子可看作条目为"+""—"的单个矩阵。②

范畴特征包括语音系统的普遍特征与附加特征(diacritic feature),附加特征实质上指明的是规则的例外情况。在一些方言中"what"所对应的语音表达式为[wat],所以,对应于"what"的矩阵包含三个音段,第一个规定为唇滑音(labial glide),第二个规定为低元音、后元音与非圆唇元音,第三个是清辅音、齿辅音与塞辅音(这些规定完全用普遍语音系统提供的特征值"+"和"—"表示)。在这种情况,音系部分的规则会将这些用"+"和"—"值表示的规定转化为用整数表示的更加详细的规定,即每个音段的语音特征(如舌位的高度、送气的程度等),它所显示的值达到预设的普遍语音理论所要求的精确程度,并在语言所准许的变异范围之内。在这个例子中,被指派的值将把(5)中"what"的底层矩阵中的分歧简单地修正为"+"和"—"值。

上面所引例子非常简单。一般来说,音系部分的规则不但会对底层的"+"和"—"值有较好的规定,而且也会极大地改变特征值,并且可能还会插

---

① 这里所给的分析主要是为了讲解方便,为了经验上的充分性这个分析将会改进。
② 注意,每两个连续的构成要素都要由联结符号隔开,为保持构成要素的结构,将(5)的表达式当作单个的矩阵是有必要的。根据当前的目的,我们可以认为,构成要素的每个音段相对于所有的联结符号的特征而言是无标记的,每个联结符号相对构成要素的每个特征而言是无标记的。

入、删除或重组音段。比如说，构成要素"by"被表征为包含两列的底层矩阵，其中的第二列被规定为高元音、前元音（用特征值进行规定）。然而，相应的语音矩阵将包含三列，第二列被规定为低元音、后元音，第三列为上颚滑音（这里的规定要求在语音矩阵中用整数值的条目表示）①。

　　(5)的表层结构被表征为矩阵，两个特征值中的一个出现在矩阵的每个条目中。只有两个特征值可以出现的事实表明底层的矩阵确实起着纯粹分类的作用。每个句子按有别于其它句子的方式进行分类，也按照决定音系部分的规则如何向特定位置指派语音值的方式进行分类。我们看到普遍语音系统的区别特征在构成表层结构一部分的底层矩阵中有分类功能（classificatory function），在构成所探讨句子的语音表达式的矩阵中有语音功能（phonetic function）。只在前一种功能中区别特征才一律两分，只在后一种功能中它们接受直接的物理解释。

　　刚刚所描述的底层分类矩阵并没有穷尽解释性的音系规则所需要的信息。除此，也有必要了解所探讨的句子是如何被划分作各种长度的短语以及这些短语的类别的。就(5)而言，音系解释需要如下信息：disturb 与 disregard 为动词，what disturbed John 是名词短语，John was being 不是短语等。相关信息可以用带标记的括号在句子上标示出来②。包含在成对括号[$_A$ 和]$_A$ 中的单位为 A 类短语。比如说(5)中的序列"what ＃ disturbed ＃ John"将用括号"[$_{NP}$]$_{NP}$"封闭，表示它是个名词短语；构成要素"disturb"将用括号"[$_V$]$_V$"封闭，表示它是个动词；(5)中的整个表达式将用括号"[$_S$]$_S$"封闭，表示它是个句子；序列"John was being"不能用成对的括号封闭，因为它根本不是短语。再举个极为简单的例子，如句子"John saw Bill"可按以下方式表征为表层结构，其中每个由正字法表征的项目都可当作一个分类性矩阵：

　　(6) [$_S$[$_{NP}$[$_N$John]$_N$]$_{NP}$[$_{VP}$[$_V$saw]$_V$[$_{NP}$[$_N$Bill]$_N$]$_{NP}$]$_{VP}$]$_S$

　　这个表达式表明"John"与"Bill"是名词(N)，"saw"是动词(V)，"John"与

----

① 这种分析的理由已超过这里的讨论范围，详细分析可参见我和哈勒的《英语语音模式》(N. Chomsky and M. Halle, *Sound Pattern of English*, New York: Harper & Row, 1968)。

② 这是显然的。比如说，"[$_A$...[$_B$...]$_B$...[$_C$...]$_C$...]$_A$"就是用括号对符号串的合适标记，就带标记的括号"[$_A$]$_A$、[$_B$]$_B$、[$_C$]$_C$"而言，下面没有哪一个是合适的括号标记：[$_A$...[$_B$...]$_A$；[$_A$...[$_B$...]$_A$...]$_B$。

"Bill"是名词短语(NP),"saw Bill"是动词短语(VP),"John saw Bill"是句子(S)。语法的音系部分在解释句子的时候,似乎总是需要可以按上文所描述的方式进行表征的信息,所以我们假定句子的表层结构是用括号对构成要素和联结符号的分类矩阵的合适标记。

语法的音系部分将表层结构转化为语音表达式。我们已经粗略地规定了"表层结构"与"语音表达式"这两个概念,但仍然需要描述音系部分的规则与它们被组织起来的方式。

目前可获得的证据表明音系部分的规则是按照序列 R_1、……R_n 的方式线性排列的,并且规则的序列按以下方式循环应用于表层结构。在应用的第一个循环中,规则 R_1、……R_n 按这种顺序应用于无内部括号的表层结构中最大的连续部分。这些规则中的最后一个应用后,最内部的括号被删除,而应用的第二个循环被引进。在这个循环中,规则又一次按这种顺序应用于无内部括号的表层结构中最大的连续部分。然后最内部的括号被删除,第三个循环被引进。这种操作一直持续,直到到达音系操作的最大范围(简单的例子就是整个句子)。某些规则应用于词内时会受限,只有当应用范围是完整的词时它们才能应用于循环。有些规则在应用的任何阶段都可以自由反复。注意:循环应用的原则是高度本能的。这实际上是说有个固定的规则系统,该系统根据组成部分的(理想的)形式决定着由其组成的较大单位的形式。

我们可以用英语中的重音指派规则说明循环应用规则。似乎有这样一个事实:英语的语音表达式必须允许重音的区别特征能取五六个不同的值,然而,所有音段在表层结构中却没有标记重音。也就是说,对英语而言,重音没有区别特征那样的范畴功能(除了最边缘的)。语音表达式的复杂重音曲线由规则(7)(8)决定[①]:

(7) 在名词中,向最左边的两个主重元音指派主重音(primary stress)。

(8) 向最右边的重音峰(stress-peak)指派主重音,在某一范围内如果没

[①] 为了讲解的目的,这些被简化了。更精准的解释请参见我与哈勒的《英语语音模式》(N. Chomsky and M. Halle, *Sound Pattern of English*, New York: Harper & Row, 1968)。注意,我在这里的讲解有歧义地使用了"apply"(运用)这一术语,其一是说"a-vailable for application"(适用),另一是说"actually modifies the sequence under consideration"(确实改变所考虑的序列)。

有哪个元音比某一元音 V 更重,则该元音 V 在该范围内为重音峰。

规则(7)适用于有两个主重音的名词,规则(8)适用于任何种类的语言单位。这些规则按由(7)到(8)的顺序循环应用。根据规约,当主重音被指派到某一位置,所有其他的重音都弱化一个等级。注意,如果某一范围内没有重读元音,则规则(8)会向最右边的元音指派主重音。

我们用(6)的表层结构说明这些规则。根据循环应用的基本原则,规则(7)与(8)首先应用于最内层的单位[$_N$ John]$_N$、[$_V$ saw]$_V$ 与[$_N$ Bill]$_N$。规则(7)应用不起来,只能应用规则(8),首先向这些例子中的单个元音指派主重音,然后,最内层的括号被删除。下一个循环需要处理的单位是"[$_{NP}$ John]$_{NP}$"和"[$_{NP}$ Bill]$_{NP}$",根据规则(8),简单地向单个元音重新指派主重音。然后删除最内层的括号,我们得到作为规则应用范围的单位[$_{VP}$ saw Bill]$_{VP}$。规则(7)又不能应用,因为"saw Bill"不是名词;规则(8)向"Bill"的元音指派主重音,并把"saw"的重音弱化到第二级。删除最内层的括号,我们得到作为应用范围的单位[$_S$ John saw Bill]$_S$。规则(7)又不能应用,规则(8)向"Bill"指派主重音,并弱化其他重音,其结果是John saw Bill,作为重音曲线的理想表达式,这是可接受的。

考虑一个稍微复杂的例子"John's black-board eraser"。在第一个应用循环中,规则(7)与(8)应用于最内层被括起来的单位"John""black""board"与"erase",规则(7)不能应用,规则(8)给每个例子中最右侧的元音指派主重音(前面三个例子都只有一个元音)。下一个循环涉及的单位有"John's"与"eraser",但没有意义①。下一个循环的应用范围是[$_N$ black board]$_N$。作为名词,这个单位受规则(7)支配,规则(7)向"black"指派主重音,并在第二级弱化"board"的重音。删除最内层的括号,下一个循环的应用范围是[$_N$ black board eraser]$_N$。接着应用规则(7),向"black"指派主重音,并弱化其他重音一个等级。在最后的一个循环里,规则的应用范围是[$_{NP}$ John's black board

---

① 在这个阶段,单词"eraser"为双音节。

eraser]$_{NP}$。因为这是个完整的名词短语,不能应用规则(7)。规则(8)向最右边的主重元音指派主重音并弱化所有的其他重音,其结果是John's black board eraser。按这种方式,复杂语音表达式由独立激发而且非常简单的规则决定,规则根据循环的一般原则进行应用。

这个例子有典型性,说明了几个很重要的方面。英语语法必须包含规则(7)和规则(8),前者用来解释名词"blackboard"(黑板)中的重音曲线这一事实,后者用来解释短语"black board"(黑色的板子)中的上升曲线。严格地说,循环原则不是英语语法的一部分,而是普遍语法的一部分,它决定着英语或其他语言中特殊规则的应用,不管这些规则是什么样的。在上述例子中,循环应用的一般原则正如所示的那样指派复杂的重音曲线。有了循环原则和规则(7)与规则(8),人们就会知道①各种语言表达式的合适的重音曲线,这些语言表达式可以是"John's blackboard eraser",也可以是他可能从未听过的。这是一个语言基本属性的简单例子。某些普遍原则必须跟特殊规则相互作用以决定全新的语言表达式的形式(和意义)。

这个例子也为某些较微妙又深远的假设提供了证据。毫无疑问的是,像英语里重音曲线这种现象是一种感知现实(perceptual reality)。比如说,经过训练的观察者能在记录他们母语中的新话语时达到很高的一致性。但没有理由认为这些重音曲线能够反映物理现实(physical reality)。这可能是因为重音曲线不能像感知到的细节那样表征在物理信号之中。这里没有矛盾。如果在物理信息中仅有两个重音层次被区分,则对于一个正在学习英语的人来说,他会有足够证据去建构规则(7)和规则(8)(如果 blackboard 和 black board 有对立的话)。假定这个人知道循环原则,那么即使重音曲线不是信号的物理属性,他也将能够感知到"John's blackboard eraser"的重音曲线。目前已获得的证据有力地表明这是英语中重音如何被感知的准确描述。

有一点很重要,就是必须明确这种描述中不存在任何神秘之处。原则上,设计这样一种自动机是没有问题的,这种自动机使用规则(7)和规则(8)、

---

① 像早先一样,我们把"知道"看作"隐性的"(tacit)或"潜在的知识"(latent knowledge),这种知识通过适当的注意可能能够进入意识,但一定是出现在"不能控制的直觉"中。

英语句法的规则和转换循环原则,并且甚至能够向根本没有表征重音的话语(比如,由传统正字法拼成的句子)指派多层次的重音曲线。把这种自动机粗略地看作言语感知模型(请参见 103 页的(1)①),我们可以认为听话者运用物理信息中已选定的性质去确定形成了什么样的句子,并为之指派出深层结构和表层结构。无论重音是否和所呈现的信号的任何物理性质的信息相一致,任何人只要他全神贯注,都能"听"出由其语法中音系部分所指派的重音曲线。

宽泛地说,对言语感知的这种解释的假定是,话语的句法解释部分是详细"听"出语音表达式的先决条件。这样也排除了两种假定:一种假定是言语感知需要语音形式的全面分析,并且这种分析是有序的,即语义解释之后是句法结构的全面分析,句法结构的全面分析之后是语音形式的全面分析;另一种假定是所感知的语音形式是信号的点对点的精确表达式。需要记住的是:这里并没有证据表明这些已被否定的假设是正确的,也没有证据表明这些刚刚提到的能否定这些假设的观点有什么神秘之处。事实上,刚刚提到的观点貌似具有很高的可信度,因为一方面,它可以排除一些主张,即在识别话语的一些目前还不能觉察的物理属性时,其精确度甚至超出理想条件下实验可论证的东西;另一方面,它可以根据非常简单的假定对新话语②的重音曲线的感知进行解释,这些假定是规则(7)、规则(8)与循环应用的一般原则可以被感知系统利用。

关于各种感知模型的相对优势,有许多可说的。这个话题暂且不说,让我们进一步考虑这样一个假设:规则(7)、规则(8)与循环应用的一般原则可以被感知系统利用并按所提出的方式执行。很显然,规则(7)、规则(8)可能是从升降曲线等简单例子中学会的(如"black board"与"blackboard"的对立)。但问题是:人是如何学会循环应用原则的?在直面这个问题之前,有必要解决另一逻辑上先于它的问题:为什么假定原则完全是学会的?原则被执行的证据有很多,但这并不能推出原则是被学会的。事实上,很难想像这些原则是如何被所有说话者完全一致地学会的;是否有充足的证据在物理信号

---

① 此处指原书页码。——编者注
② 还有其他方面。事实上,该观点是非常普遍的。必须记住,即使信号被严重扭曲,言语感知也很少被削弱,甚至根本没有被削弱。这一事实很难跟以下观点协调,即详细的语音分析是句法结构和语义结构分析的前提。

中被用来证明这个原则的正当性也根本不清楚。因此,最合理的结论似乎是:原则根本不是学会的,它只是学习者完成语言习得任务的概念才能(conceptual equipment)的一部分。普遍语法的其他原则也可做类似论证。

需要再次提醒的是,上述结论并不奇怪。原则上,设计这样一种自动机根本没有什么困难,它融合了普遍语法的原则,并用这些原则确定它所探讨的语言中的哪一种语言是可能的语言。从先验上说,假定这些原则是学会的,这一假定并不比另一假定有更多的理由,即人们用直线、角、曲线、距离等来解释视觉刺激是学会的,或者说,其实连人们有两个手臂也是学会的。这完全是个经验事实的问题,目前没有任何关于一般的外部语言类的信息可用来支持如下假设:一些普遍语法的原则是学会的,或是天赋的,或是(从某些方面来说)两者兼备。如果语言事实似乎表明一些原则是不能学会的,则没有理由认为这个结论是矛盾的或是奇怪的。

回到对普遍语法的原则的详细描述上来,语法中的音系部分似乎是由一系列的规则构成的,如上文所述,这些规则按循环的方式应用,并向表层结构指派语音表达式。语音表达式是语音特征规定的矩阵,表层结构是构成要素所带的具有合适标记的括号,其中构成要素本身又是用范畴区别特征的标记进行表征的。目前所获得的证据都支持这些假设,这些假设又为解释语音事实中的许多奇怪特征提供了基础。

值得重视的是,语法中音系部分的这些属性没有先验的必然性。普遍语法的这些假设将可能的人类语言的种类限制在可设想的"语言"集合的一个非常特殊的子集中。我们手头所获的证据表明这些假设属于106页[①]的语言习得装置 AM,如(3),它们构成先天程式的一部分,儿童用它来解决语言学习问题。很显然,这种程式必须非常精确并且高度受限。如果不是这样,在时间、机会和变异等经验上已知的限制下,语言习得就会是难以理解的神秘现象。先前讨论所涉及的各种想法跟确定先天机制的性质这一问题直接相关,因此,这些想法非常值得认真研究和关注。

[①]　此处指原书页码。——编者注

David Odden（2013）*Introducing Phonology* 选读[①]

◆ 作者简介

大卫·奥登（David Odden，1954—　），美国知名音系学家，1975 年在华盛顿大学取得学士学位，1981 年在伊利诺伊大学取得博士学位，曾先后在华盛顿州立大学、密歇根州立大学、耶鲁大学执教，现为俄亥俄州立大学语言系教授。他在音系学、描写语言等方面颇有建树，特别是在非洲语言声调、班图语言描写、强制调形原则（obligatory contour principle）方面做出了突出贡献。

◆ 正文选读

Chapter 3　Feature theory

➢ This chapter explores the theory for representing language sounds as symbolic units. You will:

◆ see that sounds are defined in terms of a fixed set of universal features

◆ learn the phonetic definitions of features, and how to assign feature values to segments based on phonetic properties

◆ understand how phonological rules are formalized in terms of these features

◆ see how these features make predictions about possible sounds and rules in human language

➢ **Key terms**: observation, predictions, features, natural classes

3.1　Scientific questions about speech sounds

One of the scientific questions that need to be asked about language is: *what is a possible speech sound ?* Humans can physically produce many more kinds of sounds than are used in language. No language employs hand-clapping, finger-snapping, or vibrations of air between the hand and cheek caused by release of air from the mouth when obstructed by the palm of the

---

① David Odden. 2013. *Introducing Phonology*. New York: Cambridge University Press.

hand (though such a sound can easily communicate an attitude). A goal of a scientific theory of language is to systematize such facts and explain them; thus we have discovered one limitation on language sound and its modality—language sounds are produced exclusively within the mouth and nasal passages, in the area between the lips and larynx.

Even staying within the vocal tract, languages also do not, for example, use whistles or inhalation to form speech sounds, nor is a labiolingual trill (a.k.a. "the raspberry") a speech sound in any language. It is important to understand that even though these various odd sounds are not language sounds, they may still be used in communication. The "raspberry" in American culture communicates a contemptuous attitude; in parts of coastal East Africa and Scandinavia, inhaling with the tongue in the position for schwa expresses agreement. Such noises lie outside of language, and we never find plurality indicated with these sounds, nor are they surrounded by other sounds to form the word *dog*. General communication has no systematic limitations short of anatomical ones, but in language, only a restricted range of sounds are used.

The issue of possible speech sounds is complicated by manual languages such as American Sign Language. ASL is technically not a counterexample to a claim about modality framed in terms of "speech sounds." But it is arbitrary to declare manual language to be outside the theory of language, and facts from such languages are relevant in principle. Unfortunately, knowledge of the signed languages of the world is very restricted, especially in phonology. Signed languages clearly have syntax: what isn't clear is what they have by way of phonologies. Researchers have only just begun to scratch the surface of sign language phonologies, so unfortunately we can say nothing more about them here.

The central question is: what is the basis for defining possible speech sounds? Do we use our "speech anatomy" in every imaginable way, or only in certain well-defined ways?

3.1.1 Possible differences in sounds

One way to approach the question is to collect samples of the sounds of all of the languages in the world. This search (which has never been conducted) would reveal massive repetition, and would probably reveal that the segment [m] in English is exactly the same as the segment [m] in French, German, Tübatülabal, Arabic, Swahili, Chinese, and innumerable other languages. It would also reveal differences, some of them perhaps a bit surprising. Given the richness of our transcriptional resources for notating phonetic differences between segments, you might expect that if a collection of languages had the same vowels transcribed as [i] and [ɪ], then these vowels should sound the same. This is not so.

Varieties of phonetic [i] vs. [ɪ]. Many languages have this pair of vowels; for example, Matuumbi has [i] and [ɪ]. But the actual pronunciation of [i] vs. [ɪ] differs between English and Matuumbi. Matuumbi [i] is higher than in English, and Matuumbi [ɪ] is a bit lower than English [ɪ]—to some people it almost sounds like [e] (but is clearly different from [e], even the "pure" [e] found in Spanish). This might force us to introduce new symbols, so that we can accurately represent these distinctions. (This is done in publications on Matuumbi, where the difference is notated as "extreme" i, u versus "regular" i, u.) Before we embark on a program of adding new symbols, we should be sure that we know how many symbols to add. It turns out that the pronunciation of [i] and [ɪ] differs in many languages: these vowels exist in English, Kamba, Lomwe, Matuumbi, Bari, Kipsigis, Didinga, and Sotho, and their actual pronunciation differs in each language.

You do not have to go very far into exotic languages to find this phonetic difference, for the difference between English [i] and German [i] is also very noticeable, and is something that a language learner must master to develop a good German or English accent. Although the differences may be difficult for the untrained ear to perceive at first, they are consistent, physically measurable, and reproducible by speakers. If written symbols are to represent phonetic differences between languages, a totally accurate transcription should represent these differences. To represent just this range of vowel differences involving [i] and [ɪ], over a dozen new symbols would need to be introduced. Yet we do not introduce large numbers of new symbols to express these differences in pronunciations, because phonological symbols do *not* represent the precise phonetic properties of the sounds in a language, they only represent the essential contrast between sounds.

Other variants of sounds. Similar variation exists with other phonetic categories. The retroflex consonants of Telugu, Hindi, and Koti are all pronounced differently. Hindi has what might be called "mild" retroflexion, where the tip of the tongue is placed just behind the alveolar ridge, while in Telugu, the tip of the tongue is further back and contact is made between the palate and the underside of the tongue (sublaminal); in Koti, the tongue is placed further forward, but is also sublaminal. Finnish, Norwegian, and English contrast the vowels [a] and [æ], but in each of these languages the vowels are pronounced in a slightly different way. The voiced velar fricative [ɣ] found in Arabic, Spanish, and the Kurdish language Hawrami are all phonetically different in subtle but audible ways.

The important details of speech. Although languages can differ substantially in the details of how their sounds are pronounced, there are limits on the types of sound differences which can be exploited contrastively, i. e. can form the basis for making differences in meaning. Language can contrast tense [i] and lax [ɪ], but cannot further contrast a hyper-tense high vowel (like that found in Matuumbi), which we might write as [i⁺], with plain tense [i] as in English, or hyper-lax [ɪ⁻] as in Matuumbi with plain lax [ɪ] as found in English. Within a language, you find at most [i] vs. [ɪ]. Languages can have one series of retroflex consonants, and cannot contrast Hindi-style [ʈ] with a Telugu-style phoneme which we might notate as [ʈ⁺]. The phonology simply has "retroflex", and it is up to the phonetic component of a language to say exactly how a retroflex consonant is pronounced.

It is important to emphasize that such phonetic details are not too subtle to hear. The difference between various types of retroflex consonants is quite audible—otherwise, people could not learn the typical pronunciation of retroflex consonants in their language—and the difference between English and German [i] is appreciable. Children learning German can hear and reproduce German [i] accurately. Speakers can also tell when someone mispronounces a German [i] as an English [i], and bilingual German-English speakers can easily switch between the two phonetic vowels.

One thing that phonological theory wants to know is: *what is a possible phoneme?* How might we answer this? We could look at all languages and publish a list. A monumental difficulty with that is that there are nearly 7,000 languages, but useful information on around only 10 percent of these languages. Worse, this could only say what phonemic contrasts happen to exist at the present. A scientific account of language does not just ask what has been actually observed, it asks about the fundamental nature of language, including *potential* sounds which may have existed in a language spoken 1,000 years ago, or some future language which will be spoken 1,000 years hence. We are not just interested in *observation*, we are interested in *prediction*.

In this connection, consider whether a "bilabial click" is a possible phoneme. We symbolize it as [⊙]—it is like a kiss, but with the lips flat as for [m], not protruded as for [w]. Virtually all languages have bilabial consonants, and we know of dozens of languages with click consonants (Dahalo, Sotho, Zulu, Xhosa, Khoekhoe), so the question is whether the combination of concepts "bilabial" and "click" can define a phoneme. As it happens, we know that such a sound does exist, but only in two closely related languages, !Xoo and Eastern ≠ Hoan, members of the Khoisan language family. These languages have under 5,000 speakers combined, and given socioeconomic factors where these languages are spoken (Namibia and Botswana), it is likely that the languages will no longer be spoken in 200 years. We are fortunate in this case that we have information on these languages which allows us to say that this is a phoneme, but things could have turned out differently. The languages could easily have died out without having been recorded, and then we would wrongly conclude that a bilabial click is not a possible phoneme because it has not been observed. We need a principled, theoretical basis for saying what we think might be observed.

Predictions versus observations. A list of facts is scientifically uninteresting. A basic goal of science is to have knowledge that goes beyond what has been observed, because we believe that the universe obeys general laws. A list might be helpful in building a theory, but we would not want to stop with a list, because it would give us no explanation why that particular list, as opposed to some other arbitrary list, should constitute the possible phonemes of language. The question "what is a possible phoneme?" should thus be answered by reference to a general theory of what speech sounds are made of, just as a theory of "possible atoms" is based on a general theory of what makes up atoms and rules for putting those bits together. Science is not simply the accumulation and sorting of facts, but rather the attempt to discover laws that regulate the universe. Such laws make predictions about things that we have yet to observe: certain things should be found, other things should never be found.

The Law of Gravity predicts that a rock will fall to earth, which says what it will do and by implication what it will not do: it also won't go up or sideways. Physicists have observed that subatomic particles decay into other particles. Particles have an electrical charge—positive, negative or neutral—and there is a physical law that the charge of a particle is preserved when it decays (adding up the charges of the decay products). The particle known as a "kaon" (K) can be positive (K^+), negative (K^-) or neutral (K^0); a kaon can decay into other particles known as "pions" (π) which also can be positive (π^+), negative (π^-) or neutral (π^0). Thus a neutral kaon may become a positive pion and a negative pion ($K^0 \rightarrow \pi^+ + \pi^-$) or it may become one positive, one negative, and one neutral pion ($K^0 \rightarrow \pi^+ + \pi^- + \pi^0$), because in both cases the positives and negatives cancel out and the sum of charges is neutral (0). The Law of Conservation of Charge allows these patterns of decay, and prohibits a neutral kaon from becoming two positive pions ($K^0 \rightarrow \pi^+ + \pi^+$). In the myriad cases of particle decay which have been observed experimentally, none violates this law which predicts what can happen and what cannot.

Analogously, phonological theory seeks to discover the laws for building phonemes, which predict what phonemes can be found in languages. We will see that theory, after considering a related question which defines phonology.

3.1.2 Possible rules

Previous chapters have focused on rules, but we haven't paid much attention to how they should be formulated. English has rules defining allowed clusters of two consonants at the beginning of the word. The first set of consonant sequences in (1) is allowed, whereas the second set of sequences is disallowed.

(1) pr pl br bl tr dr kr kl gr gl
 *rp *lp *rb *lb *rt *rd *rk *lk *rg *lg

This restriction is very natural and exists in many languages—but it is not inevitable, and does not reflect any insurmountable problems of physiology or perception. Russian allows many of these clusters, for example [rtut^j] 'mercury' exemplifies the sequence [rt] which is impossible in English.

We could list the allowed and disallowed sequences of phonemes and leave it at that, but this does not explain why these particular sequences are allowed. Why don't we find a language which is like English, except that the specific sequence [lb] is allowed and the sequence [bl] is disallowed? An interesting generalization regarding sequencing has emerged after comparing such rules across languages. Some languages (e.g. Hawaiian) do not allow any clusters of consonants and some (Bella Coola, a Salishan language of British Columbia) allow any combination of two consonants, but no language allows initial [lb] without also allowing [bl]. This is a more interesting and suggestive observation, since it indicates that there is something about such sequences that is not accidental in English; but it is still just a random fact from a list of accumulated facts if we have no basis for characterizing classes of sounds, and view the restrictions as restrictions on letters, as sounds with no structure.

There is a rule in English which requires that all vowels be nasalized when they appear before a nasal consonant, and thus we have a rule something like (2).

$$(2)\ \begin{matrix} \varepsilon\ e\ \text{\i}\ i \\ a\ \mathfrak{o}\ o\ \upsilon \\ u\ \mathfrak{a}\ \text{æ} \end{matrix} \rightarrow \begin{matrix} \bar{\varepsilon}\ \bar{e}\ \bar{\text{\i}}\ \bar{i} \\ \bar{a}\ \bar{\mathfrak{o}}\ \bar{o}\ \bar{\upsilon} \\ \bar{u}\ \bar{\mathfrak{a}}\ \bar{\text{æ}} \end{matrix} /\_\text{m, n, ŋ}$$

If rules just replace one arbitrary list of sounds by another list when they stand in front of a third arbitrary list, we have to ask why these particular sets of symbols operate together. Could we replace the symbol [n] with the symbol [t^j], or the symbol [ō] with the symbol [ø], and still have a rule in some language? It is not likely to be an accident that these particular symbols are found in the rule: a rule similar to this can be found in quite a number of languages, and we would not expect this particular collection of letters to assemble themselves into a rule in many languages, if these were just random collections of letters.

Were phonological rules stated in terms of randomly assembled symbols, there would be no reason to expect (3a) to have a different status from (3b).

(3) a. $\{p, t, t^j, k\} \rightarrow \{m, n, \textipa{\textltailn}, \text{ŋ}\} / \_\{m, n, \textipa{\textltailn}, \text{ŋ}\}$
    b. $\{b, p, d, q\} \rightarrow \{d, q, b, p\} / \_\{s, x, o, \i\}$

Rule (3a)—nasalization of stops before nasals—is quite common, but

(3b) is never found in human language. This is not an accident, but rather reflects the fact that the latter process cannot be characterized in terms of a unified phonetic operation applying to a phonetically defined context. The insight which we have implicitly assumed, and make explicit here, is that rules operate not in terms of specific symbols, but in terms of definable classes. The basis for defining those classes is a set of phonetic properties.

As a final illustration of this point, rule (4a) is common in the world's languages but (4b) is completely unattested.

(4) a. k, g → t^j, d^3/_i, e
    b. p, r → i, b/_o, n

The first rule refers to phonetically definable classes of segments (velar stops, alveopalatal affricates, front vowels), and the nature of the change is definable in terms of a phonetic difference (velars change place of articulation and become alveopalatals). The second rule cannot be characterized by phonetic properties: the sets {p, r}, {i, b}, and {o, n} are not defined by some phonetic property, and the change of [p] to [i] and [r] to [b] has no coherent phonetic characterization.

The lack of rules like (4b) is not just an isolated limitation of knowledge—it's not simply that we haven't found the specific rules (4b) but we have found (4a)—but rather these kinds of rules represent large, systematic classes. (3b) and (4b) represent a general kind of rule, where classes of segments are defined arbitrarily. Consider the constraint on clusters of two consonants in English. In terms of phonetic classes, this reduces to the simple rule that the first consonant must be a stop and the second consonant must be a liquid. The second rule changes vowels into nasalized vowels before nasal consonants. The basis for defining these classes will be considered now.

3.2 Distinctive feature theory

Just saying that rules are defined in terms of phonetic properties is too broad a claim, since it says nothing about the phonetic properties that are relevant. Consider a hypothetical rule, stated in terms of phonetic properties:

> all vowels change place of articulation so that the original difference in formant frequency between F_1 and F_3 is reduced to half what it originally was, when the vowel appears before a consonant whose duration ranges from 100 to 135 ms.

What renders this rule implausible (no language has one vaguely resembling it) is that it refers to specific numerical durations, and to the difference in frequency between the first and third formant.

An acoustic description considers just physical sound, but a perceptual description factors in the question of how the ear and brain process sound. The difference between 100 Hz and 125 Hz is acoustically the same as that between 5,100 Hz and 5,125 Hz. The two sets are perceptually very different, the former being perceived as "more separate" and the latter as virtually indistinguishable.

The phonetic properties which are the basis of phonological systems are general and somewhat abstract, such as voicing or rounding, and are largely the categories which we have informally been using already: they are not the same, as we will see. The hypothesis of distinctive feature theory is that there is a small set, around two dozen, of phonetically based properties which phonological analysis uses. These properties, the **distinctive features**, not only define the possible phonemes of human languages, but also define phonological rules.

The classical statement of features derives from Chomsky and Halle (1968). We will use an adapted set of these features, which takes into consideration refinements. Each feature can have one of two values, plus and minus, so for each speech sound, the segment either *has* the property (is $[+F_i]$) or *lacks* the property (is $[-F_i]$). In this section, we follow Chomsky and Halle (1968) and present the generally accepted articulatory correlates of the features, that is, what aspects of production the feature relates to. There are also acoustic and perceptual correlates of features, pertaining to what the segment sounds like, which are discussed by Jakobson, Fant, and Halle (1952) using a somewhat different system of features.

3.2.1 Phonetic preliminaries

By way of phonetic background to understanding certain features, two phonetic points need to be clarified. First, some features are characterized in terms of the "neutral position", which is a configuration that the vocal tract is assumed to have immediately prior to speaking. The neutral position, approximately that of the vowel [ɛ], defines relative movement of the tongue.

Second, you need to know a bit about how the vocal folds vibrate, since some feature definitions relate to the effect on vocal fold vibration (important because it provides most of the sound energy of speech). The vocal folds vibrate when there is enough air pressure below the glottis (the opening between the vocal folds) to force the vocal folds apart. This opening reduces subglottal pressure, which allows the folds to close, and this allows air pressure to rebuild to the critical level where the vocal folds are blown apart again. The critical factor that causes the folds to open is that the pressure below the vocal folds is higher than the pressure above.

Air flows from the lungs at a roughly constant rate. Whether there is enough drop in pressure for air to force the vocal folds open is thus determined by the positioning and tension of the vocal folds (how hard it is to force them apart), and the pressure above the glottis. The pressure above the glottis depends on how effectively pressure buildup can be relieved, and this is determined by the degree of constriction in the vocal tract. In short, the configuration of the vocal folds, and the degree and location of constriction above the glottis almost exclusively determine whether there will be voicing.

If the pressure above and below the glottis is nearly equal, air stops flowing and voicing is blocked. So if the vocal tract is completely obstructed (as for the production of a voiceless stop like [k]), air flowing through the glottis rapidly equalizes the pressure below and above the glottis, which stops voicing. On the other hand, if the obstruction in the vocal tract is negligible (as it is in the vowel [a]), the pressure differential needed for voicing is easily maintained, since air passing through the glottis is quickly vented from the vocal tract.

A voiced stop such as [g] is possible, even though it involves a total obstruction of the vocal tract analogous to that found in [k], because it takes time for pressure to build up in the oral cavity to the point that voicing ceases. Production of [g] involves ancillary actions to maintain voicing. The pharynx may be widened, which gives the air more room to escape, delaying the buildup of pressure. The larynx may be lowered, which also increases the volume of the oral cavity; the closure for the stop may be weakened slightly, allowing tiny amounts of air to flow through; the velum may be raised somewhat to increase the size of the air cavity, or it may be lowered somewhat to allow small (usually imperceptible) amounts of air to pass through the nose. The duration of the consonant can be reduced—generally, voiced stops are phonetically shorter than corresponding voiceless stops.

Certain sounds such as vowels lack a radical constriction in the vocal tract, so it is quite easy to maintain voicing during such sounds, whereas with other sounds, specifically obstruents, voicing is difficult to maintain. Some accounts of this distinction, especially that of Chomsky and Halle (1968), refer to "spontaneous voicing", which is grounded on the assumption that voicing occurs automatically simply by positioning the vocal folds in what we might call the "default" position. For sounds that involve a significant obstruction of the vocal tract, special actions are required for voicing. The features [sonorant] and [consonantal] directly relate to the obstruction in the vocal tract, which determines whether the vocal folds vibrate spontaneously.

3.2.2 Major class features

One of the most intuitive distinctions which feature theory needs to capture is that between consonants and vowels. There are three features, the so-called major class features, which provide a rough first grouping of sounds into functional types that includes the consonant/vowel distinction.

syllabic (**syl**): forms a syllable peak (and thus can be stressed).

sonorant (**son**): sounds produced with a vocal tract configuration in which spontaneous voicing is possible.

consonantal (**cons**): sounds produced with a major obstruction in the oral cavity.

The feature [syllabic] is, unfortunately, simultaneously one of the most important features and one of the hardest to define physically. It corresponds intuitively to the notion "consonant" (where [h], [j], [m], [s], [t] are "consonants") versus "vowel" (such as [a], [i]): indeed the only difference between the vowels [i, u] and the corresponding glides [j, w] is that [i, u] are [+syllabic] and [j, w] are [−syllabic]. The feature [syllabic] goes beyond the intuitive vowel/consonant split. English has syllabic sonorants, such as [r], [l], [n]. The main distinction between the English words (American English pronunciation) *ear* [ɪr] and *your* [jr] resides in which segments are [+syllabic] versus [−syllabic]. In *ear*, the vowel [ɪ] is [+syllabic] and [r] is [−syllabic], whereas in *your*, [j] is [−syllabic] and [r] is [+syllabic]. The words *eel* [il] and the reduced form of *you'll* [jl] for many speakers of American English similarly differ in that [i] is the peak of the syllable (is [+syllabic]) in *eel*, but [l] is the syllable peak in *you'll*.

Other languages have syllabic sonorants which phonemically contrast with nonsyllabic sonorants, such as Serbo-Croatian which contrasts syllabic [r] with nonsyllabic [r] (cf. *groze* 'fear (gen)' versus *groce* 'little throat'). Swahili distinguishes [mbuni] 'ostrich' and [mbuni] 'coffee plant' in the fact that [mbuni] is a three-syllable word and [m] is the peak (the only segment) of that first syllable, but [mbuni] is a two-syllable word, whose first syllable peak is [u]. Although such segments may be thought of as "consonants" in one intuitive sense of the concept, they have the feature value[+syllabic]. This is a reminder that there is a difference between popular concepts about language and technical terms. "Consonant" is not strictly speaking a technical concept of phonological theory, even though it is a term quite frequently used by phonologists—almost always with the meaning "nonpeak" in the syllable, i.e. a [−syllabic] segment.

The definition of [sonorant] could be changed so that glottal configuration is also included, then the laryngeals would be [−sonorant]. There is little compelling evidence to show whether this would be correct; later, we discuss how to go about finding such evidence for revising feature definitions.

The feature [sonorant] captures the distinction between segments such as vowels and liquids where the constriction in the vocal tract is small enough that no special effort is required to maintain voicing, as opposed to sounds such as stops and fricatives which have enough constriction that effort is needed to maintain voicing. In an oral stop, air cannot flow through the vocal tract at all, so oral stops are [−sonorant]. In a fricative, even though there is some airflow, there is so much constriction that pressure builds up, with the result that spontaneous voicing is not possible, thus fricatives are [−sonorant]. In a vowel or glide, the vocal tract is only minimally constricted so air can flow without impedance: vowels and glides are therefore [+sonorant]. A nasal consonant like [n] has a complete obstruction of airflow through the oral cavity, but nevertheless the nasal passages are open which allows free flow of air. Air pressure does not build up during the production of nasals, so nasals are [+sonorant]. In the liquid [l], there is a complete obstruction formed by the tip of the tongue with the alveolar ridge, but nevertheless air flows freely over the sides of the tongue so [l] is [+sonorant].

The question whether *r* is [+sonorant] or [−sonorant] has no simple answer, since many phonetically different segments are transcribed as *r*; some are [−sonorant] and some are [+sonorant], depending on their phonetic properties. The so-called fricative *r* of Czech (spelle6d *ř*) has a considerable constriction, so it is [−sonorant], but the English type [ɹ] is a sonorant since there is very little constriction. In other languages there may be more constriction, but it is so brief that it does not allow significant buildup of air pressure (this would be the case with "tapped" r's). Even though spontaneous voicing is impossible for the laryngeal consonants [h, ʔ] because they are formed by positioning the vocal folds so that voicing is precluded, they are [+sonorant] since they have no constriction above the glottis, which is the essential property defining [+sonorant].

The feature [consonantal] is very similar to the feature [sonorant], but specifically addresses the question of whether there is any major constriction in the oral cavity. This feature groups together obstruents, liquids and nasals which are [+consonantal], versus vowels, glides, and laryngeals ([h, ʔ]) which are [−consonantal]. Vowels and glides have a minor obstruction in the vocal tract, compared to that formed by a fricative or a stop. Glottal stop is formed with an obstruction at the glottis, but none in the vocal tract, hence it is [−consonantal]. In nasals and liquids, there is an obstruction in the oral cavity, even though the overall constriction of the whole vocal tract is not high enough toprevent spontaneous voicing. Recent research indicates that this feature may not be necessary, since its function is usually covered as well or better by other features.

The most important phonological use of features is that they identify classes of segments in rules. All speech sounds can be analyzed in terms of their values for the set of distinctive features, and the set of segments that have a particular value for some feature (or set of feature values) is a **natural class**. Thus the segments [a i r m] are members of the [+syllabic] class, and [j h ʔ r m s p] are members of the [−syllabic] class; [a r j ʔ r m] are in the [+sonorant] class and [s z p b] are in the [−sonorant] class; [a i w h ʔ] are in the [−consonantal] class and [r m r m s p] are in the [+consonantal] class. Natural classes can be defined in terms of conjunctions of features, such as [+consonantal, −syllabic], which refers to the set of segments which are simultaneously [+consonantal] and [−syllabic].

When referring to segments defined by a combination of features, the features are written in a single set of brackets—[+cons, −syl] refers to a single segment which is both +consonantal and -syllabic, while [+cons] [−syl] refers to a sequence of segments, the first being +consonantal and the second being −syllabic.

Accordingly, the three major class features combine to define five maximally differentiated classes, exemplified by the following segment groups.

(5)

	a,i,u	r,l,m	j,w,h,ʔ	r,l,m	s,z,p,b
syllabic	+	+	−	−	−
sonorant	+	+	+	+	−
consonantal	−	+	−	+	+

Further classes are definable by omitting specifications of one or more of these features: for example, the class [−syllabic, +sonorant] includes {j, w, h, ʔ, r, l, m}.

One thing to note is that all [+syllabic] segments, i.e. all syllable peaks, are also [+sonorant]. It is unclear whether there are syllabic obstruents, i.e. [s], [k]. It has been claimed that such things exist in certain dialects of Berber, but their interpretation remains controversial, since the prin-ciples for detection of syllables are controversial. Another gap is the combination [−sonorant, −consonantal], which would be a physical impossibility. A [−sonorant] segment would require a major obstruction in the vocal tract, but the specification [−consonantal] entails that the obstruction could not be in the oral cavity. The only other possibility would be constriction of the nasal passages, and nostrils are not sufficiently constrictable.

3.2.3 Place of articulation

Features to define place of articulation are our next functional set. We begin with the features typically used by vowels, specifically the [+syllabic, −consonantal, +sonorant] segments, and then proceed to con-sonant features, ending with a discussion of the intersection of these features.

Vowel place features. The features which define place of articulation for vowels are the following.

>**high**: the body of the tongue is raised from the neutral position.
>**low**: the body of the tongue is lowered from the neutral position.
>**back**: the body of the tongue is retracted from the neutral position.
>**round**: the lips are protruded.
>**tense**: sounds requiring deliberate, accurate, maximally distinct gestures that involve considerable muscular effort.
>**advanced tongue root**: produced by drawing the root of the tongue forward.

The main features are [high], [low], [back], and [round]. Phonologists primarily distinguish just front and back vowels, governed by [back]:

front vowels are [−back] since they do not involve retraction of the tongue body, and back vowels are [+back]. Phonetic central vowels are usually treated as phonological back vowels, since typically central vowels are unrounded and back vowels are rounded. Distinctions such as those between [ɨ] and [ɯ], [ɜ] and [ʌ], [y] and [ʉ], [ɵ] and [œ], or [a] and [ɑ] are usually considered to be phonologically unimportant over-differentiations of language-specific phonetic values of phonologically back unrounded vowels. The phonologically relevant question about a vowel pronounced as [ʉ] is not whether the tongue position is intermediate between that of [i] and [u], but whether it patterns with {i, e, y, ø} or with {u, ɯ, o, ʌ}—or does it pattern apart from either set? In lieu of clear examples of a contrast between central and back rounded vowels, or central and back unrounded vowels, we will not at the moment postulate any other feature for the front-back dimension; though section 3.6 considers possible evidence for the phonological relevance of the concept "central vowel". Given the phonologically questionable status of distinctive central vowels, no significance should be attributed to the use of the symbol [ɨ] versus [ɯ], and typographic convenience may determine that a [+back, −round] high vowel is typically transcribed as [ɨ].

Two main features are employed to represent vowel height. High vowels are [+high] and [−low], low vowels are [+low] and [−high]. No vowel can be simultaneously [+high] and [+low] since the tongue cannot be raised and lowered simultaneously; mid vowels are [−high, −low]. In addition, any vowel can be produced with lip rounding, using the feature [round]. These features allow us to characterize the following vowel contrasts.

(6)

	i	y	ɨ	u	e	ø	ə	o	æ	œ	ɑ	ɒ
high	+	+	+	+	−	−	−	−	−	−	−	−
low	−	−	−	−	−	−	−	−	+	+	+	+
back	−	−	+	+	−	−	+	+	−	−	+	+
round	−	+	−	+	−	+	−	+	−	+	−	+

Note that [ɑ] is a back low unrounded vowel, in contrast to the symbol [ɒ] for a back low rounded vowel.

Vowels with a laxer, "less deliberate," and lower articulation, such as [ɪ] in English *sit* or [ɛ] in English *set*, would be specified as [−tense].

(7)	I	Y	ɨ	ʊ	ɛ	œ	ʌ	ɔ
high	+	+	+	+	−	−	−	−
low	−	−	−	−	−	−	−	−
back	−	−	+	+	−	−	+	+
round	−	+	−	+	−	+	−	+
tense	−	−	−	−	−	−	−	−

Korean has a set of so-called "tense" consonants but these are phonetically "glottal" consonants.

One question which has not been resolved is the status of low vowels in terms of this feature. Unlike high and mid vowels, there do not seem to be analogous contrasts in low vowels between tense and lax [æ]. Another important point about this feature is that while [back], [round], [high], and [low] will also play a role in defining consonants, [tense] plays no role in consonantal contrasts.

The difference between *i* and *ɪ*, or *e* and *ɛ* has also been considered to be one of vowel height (proposed in alternative models where vowel height is governed by a single scalar vowel height feature, rather than by the binary features [high] and [low]). This vowel contrast has also been described in terms of the feature "Advanced Tongue Root" (ATR), especially in the vowel systems of languages of Africa and Siberia. There has been debate over the phonetic difference between [ATR] and [tense]. Typically, [+tense] front vowels are fronter than their lax counterparts, and [+tense] back vowels are backer than their lax counterparts. In comparison, [+ATR] vowels are supposed to be generally fronter than corresponding [−ATR] vowels, so that [+ATR] back vowels are phonetically fronter than their [—ATR] counterparts. However, some articulatory studies have shown that the physical basis for the tense/lax distinction in English is no different from that which ATR is based on. Unfortunately, the clearest examples of the feature [ATR] are found in languages of Africa, where very little phonetic research has been done. Since no language contrasts both [ATR] and [tense] vowels, it is usually supposed that there is a single feature, whose precise phonetic realization varies somewhat from language to language.

Consonant place features. The main features used for defining consonantal place of articulation are the following.

coronal: produced with the blade or tip of the tongue raised from the neutral position.
anterior: produced with a major constriction located at or in front of the alveolar ridge.
strident: produced with greater noisiness.
distributed: produced with a constriction that extends for a considerable distance along the direction of airflow.

Place of articulation in consonants is primarily described with the features [coronal] and [anterior]. Labials, labiodentals, dentals, and alveolars are [+anterior] since their primary constriction is at or in front of the alveolar ridge (either at the lips, the teeth, or just back of the teeth) whereas other consonants (including laryngeals) are [—anterior], since they lack this front constriction. The best way to understand this feature is to remember that it is the defining difference between [s] and [ʃ], where [s] is [+anterior] and [ʃ] is [—anterior]. Anything produced where [s] is produced, or in front of that position, is [+anterior]; anything produced where [ʃ] is, or behind [ʃ], is [—anterior].

(8) [+anterior]   [−anterior]

  f ɸ p θ s t̪ t   ʃ tʲ ʂ ʈ ç x k q ʕ h ʔ

Remember that the two IPA letters <tʲ> represent a single [−anterior] segment, not a combination of [+anterior] [t] and [−anterior] [ʃ].

Consonants which involve the blade or tip of the tongue are [+coronal], and this covers the dentals, alveolars, alveopalatals, and retroflex consonants. Consonants at other places of articulation-labial, velar, uvular, and laryngeal—are [−coronal]. Note that this feature does not encompass the body (back) of the tongue, so while velars and uvulars use the tongue, they use the body of the tongue rather than the blade or tip, and therefore are [−coronal]. The division of consonants into classes as defined by [coronal] is illustrated below.

(9) [+coronal]   [−coronal]

  t̪ θ t s ʃ n l r ɲ ʈ   p ɸ f k q ʕ

Two other features are important in characterizing the traditional places of articulation. The feature [distributed] is used in coronal sounds to distinguish dental [t̪] from English alveolar [t], or alveopalatal [ʃ] from retroflex [ʂ]: the segments [t̪, ʃ] are [+distributed] and [t, ʈ, ʂ] are [−distributed]. The feature [distributed], as applied to coronal consonants, approximately corresponds to the traditional phonetic notion "apical" ([−distributed]) versus "laminal" ([+distributed]). This feature is not rele-vantfor velar and labial sounds and we will not specify any value of [distributed] for noncoronal segments.

The feature [strident] distinguishes strident [f, s] from nonstrident [ɸ, θ]: otherwise, the consonants [f, ɸ] would have the same feature specifications. Note that the feature [strident] is defined in terms of the aerodynamic property of greater turbulence (which has the acoustic correlate of greater noise), not in terms of the movement of a particular articulator—

this defining characteristic is accomplished by different articulatory configurations. In terms of contrastive usage, the feature [strident] only serves to distinguish bilabial and labiodentals, or interdentals and alveolars. A sound is [+strident] only if it has greater noisiness, and "greater" implies a comparison. In the case of [φ] vs. [f], [β] vs. [v], [θ] vs. [s], or [ð] vs. [z] the second sound in the pair is noisier. No specific degree of noisiness has been proposed which would allow you to determine in isolation whether a given sound meets the definition of strident or not. Thus it is impossible to determine whether [ʃ] is [+strident], since there is no contrast between strident and nonstrident alveopalatal sounds. The phoneme [ʃ] is certainly relatively noisy—noisier than [θ]—but then [θ] is noisier than [φ] is.

[Strident] is not strictly necessary for making a distinction between [s] and [θ], since [distributed] also distinguishes these phonemes. Since [strident] is therefore only crucial for distinguishing bilabial and labial fricatives, it seems questionable to postulate a feature with such broad implications solely to account for the contrast between labiodental and bilabial fricatives. Nonetheless, we need a way of representing this contrast. The main problem is that there are very few languages (such as Ewe, Venda, and Shona) which have both [f] and [φ], or [v] and [β], and the phonological rules of these languages do not give us evidence as to how this distinction should be made in terms of features. We will therefore only invoke the feature [strident] in connection with the [φ, β] vs. [f, v] contrast.

Using these three features, consonantal places of articulation can be partially distinguished as follows.

(10)

	p	t̪	t	tʲ	ṭ	c, k, q, ʕ, ʔ
anterior	+	+	+	−	−	−
coronal	−	+	+	+	+	−
distributed		+	−	+	−	−

Vowel features on consonants. The features [high], [low], [back], and [round] are not reserved exclusively for vowels, and these typical vowel features can play a role in defining consonants as well. As we see in (10), velar, uvular, pharyngeal, and glottal places of articulation are not yet distinguished; this is where the features [high], [low], and [back] become important. Velar, uvular, and pharyngeal consonants are [+back] since they are produced with a retracted tongue body. The difference between velar and uvular consonants is that with velar consonants the tongue body is raised, whereas with uvular consonants it is not, and thus velars are [+high] where uvulars are [−high]. Pharyngeal consonants are distinguished from uvulars in that pharyngeals are [+low] and uvulars are [−low], indicating that the constriction for pharyngeals is even lower than that for uvulars.

One traditional phonetic place of articulation for consonants is that of "palatal" consonants. The term "palatal" is used in many ways, for example the postalveolar or alveopalatal (palatoalveolar) consonants [ʃ] and [tʲ] might be referred to as palatals. This is strictly speaking a misnomer, and the term "palatal" is best used only for the "true palatals," transcribed as [c ç ɟ]. Such consonants are found in Hungarian, and also in German in words like [iç] 'I' or in Norwegian [çø:per] 'buys'. These consonants are produced with the body of the tongue raised and fronted, and therefore they have the feature values [+high, −back]. The classical feature system presented here provides no way to distinguish such palatals from palatalized velars ([kʲ]) either phonetically or phonologically. Palatalized (fronted) velars exist as allophonic vari-ants of velars before front vowels in English, e.g. [kʲip] 'keep'; they are articulatorily and acoustically extremely similar to the palatals of Hungarian. Very little phonological evidence is available regarding the treatment of "palatals" versus "palatalized velars": it is quite possible that [c] and [kʲ], or [ç] and [xʲ], are simply different symbols, chosen on the basis of phonological patterning rather than systematic phonetic differences.

With the addition of these features, the traditional places of articulation for consonants can now be fully distinguished.

(11)

	p	t̪	t	tʲ	ṭ	c, kʲ	k	q	ʕ	ʔ
anterior	+	+	+	−	−	−	−	−	−	−
coronal	−	+	+	+	+	−	−	−	−	−
distributed		+	−	+	−					
high	−	−	−	−	−	+	+	−	−	−
back	−	−	−	−	−	−	+	+	+	−
low	−	−	−	−	−	−	−	−	+	−

The typical vowel features have an additional function as applied to consonants, namely that they define secondary articulations such as palatalization and rounding. Palatalization involves superimposing the raised and fronted tongue position of the glide [j] onto the canonical articulation of a consonant, thus the features [+high, −back] are added to the primary features that characterize a consonant (those being the features that typify [i, j]). So, for example, the essential feature characteristics of a bilabial are [+anterior, −coronal] and they are only incidentally [−high, −back]. A palatalized bilabial would be [+anterior, −coronal, +high, −back]. Velarized consonants have the features [+high, +back] analogous to the features of velar consonants; pharyngealized consonants have the features [+back, +low]. Consonants may also bear the feature [round]. Applying various possible secondary articulations to labial consonants results in the following specifications.

(12)

	p	pʲ	pˠ	pʷ	pq	pˤ	pq	pº	pᵒ
high	−	+	+	+	+	−	−	−	−

back	−	−	+	+	−	+	+	+	−
low	−	−	−	−	−	+	−	−	−
round	−	−	−	+	+	−	−	+	+

Labialized (p^w), palatalized (p^j), velarized (p^γ) and pharyngealized (p^ς) variants are the most common categories of secondary articulation. Uvularized consonants, i.e. p^q, are rare; uvularized clicks are attested in Ju/'hoansi. It is unknown if there is a contrast between rounded consonants differing in secondary height, symbolized above as p^w vs. p^o or p^q vs. p^o. Feature theory allows such a contrast, so eventually we ought to find examples. If, as seems likely after some decades of research, such contrasts do not exist where predicted, there should be a revision of the theory, so that the predictions of the theory better match observations.

This treatment of secondary articulations makes other predictions. One is that there cannot be palatalized uvulars or pharyngeals. This follows from the fact that the features for palatalization ([+high, −back]) conflict with the features for uvulars ([−high, +back]) and pharyngeals ([−high, +back, +low]). Since such segments do not appear to exist, this supports the theory; otherwise we expect—in lieu of a principle that prohibits them—that they will be found in some language. Second, in this theory a "pure" palatal consonant (such as Hungarian [ɟ]) is equivalent to a palatalized (i.e. fronted) velar. Again, since no language makes a contrast between a palatal and a palatalized velar, this is a good prediction of the theory (unless such a contrast is uncovered, in which case it becomes a bad prediction of the theory).

3.2.4 Manner of articulation

Other features relate to the manner in which a segment is produced, apart from the location of the segment's constriction. The manner features are:

continuant (**cont**): the primary constriction is not narrowed so much that airflow through the oral cavity is blocked.

delayed release (**del.rel**): release of a total constriction is slowed so that a fricative is formed after the stop portion.

nasal (**nas**): the velum is lowered which allows air to escape through the nose.

lateral (**lat**): the mid section of the tongue is lowered at the side.

The feature [continuant] groups together vowels, glides, fricatives, and [h] as [+continuant]. Note that [continuant] is a broader group than the traditional notion "fricative" which refers to segments such as [s], [ʃ], or [θ].

The term "fricative" generally refers to nonsonorant continuants, i. e. the class defined by the conjunction of features [+continuant, −sonorant]. Since continuants are defined as sounds where air can flow continuously through the oral cavity, nasals like [m n ŋ] are [−continuant], even though they allow continuous airflow (through the nose).

Affricates such as [tʲ, pf] are characterized with the feature [+delayed release]. Necessarily, all affricates are [−continuant], since they involve complete constriction followed by a period of partial fricative-like constriction, and therefore they behave essentially as a kind of stop. This feature is in question, since [pf tʲ kˣ] do not act as a unified phonological class; nevertheless, some feature is needed to characterize stops versus affricates. Various alternatives have been proposed, for example that [kˣ] might just be the pronunciation of aspirated [kʰ] since velar [kˣ] and [kʰ] never seem to contrast; perhaps the feature [strident] defines [tˢ] vs. [t]. The proper representation of affricates is a currently unresolved issue in phonology.

The feature [+nasal] is assigned to sounds where air flows through the nasal passages, for example [n] as well as nasalized vowels like [ã]. Liquids and fricatives can be nasalized as well, but the latter especially are quite rare. L-like sounds are characterized with the feature [lateral]. Almost all

[+lateral] sounds are coronal, though there are a few reports of velar laterals. Detailed information on the phonetics and phonology of these segments is not available.

Examples of the major manners of articulation are illustrated below, for coronal place of articulation.

(13)

	t	n	t^s	s	l	ĩ	t^l
delayed release	—	—	+	—	—	—	+
continuant	—	—	—	+	+	+	+
lateral	—	—	—	—	+	+	+
nasal	—	+	—	—	—	+	—

3.2.5 Laryngeal features

Three features characterize the state of the glottis:

spread glottis (s.g.): the vocal folds are spread far apart.
constricted glottis (c.g.): the vocal folds are tightly constricted.
voice (voi): the vocal folds vibrate.

Voiced sounds are [+voice]. The feature [spread glottis] describes aspirated obstruents ([p^h], [b^h]) and breathy sonorants ([m̤], [a̤]); [constricted glottis] describes implosives ([ɓ]), ejective obstruents ([p']), and laryngealized sonorants ([m̰], [a̰]).

How to distinguish implosives from ejectives is not entirely obvious, but the standard answer is that ejectives are [−voice] and implosives are [+voice]. There are two problems with this. One is that implosives do not generally pattern with other [+voiced] consonants in phonological systems, especially in how consonants affect tone (voiced consonants, but typically not implosives, may lower following tones). The second is that Ngiti and

Lendu have both voiced and voiceless implosives. The languages lack ejectives, which raises the possibility that voiceless implosives are phonologically [−voice, +c.g.], which is exactly the specification given to ejective consonants. You may wonder how [−voice, +c.g.] can be realized as an ejective in languages like Navajo, Tigre or Lushootseed, and as a voiceless implosive in Ngiti or Lendu. This is possible because feature values give approximate phonetic descriptions, not exact ones. The Korean "fortis" consonants, found in [k'ata] 'peel (noun),' [ak'i] 'musical instrument,' or [alt'a] 'be ill,' are often described as glottalized, and phonetic studies have shown that they are produced with glottal constrictions: thus they would be described as [− voice, + c. g.]. Nevertheless, they are not ejectives. Similarly, Khoekhoe (Nama) has a contrast between plain clicks ([!àm] 'deep') and glottalized ones ([!'ám] 'kill'), but the glottalized clicks realize the feature [+c.g.] as a simple constriction of the glottis, not involving an ejective release.

The usual explanation for the difference between ejectives in Navajo and glottalized nonejective consonants in Korean or Khoekhoe is that they have the same phonological specifications, [−voice, +c.g.], but realize the features differently due to language-specific differences in principles of phonetic implementation. This is an area of feature theory where more research is required.

The representations of laryngeal contrasts in consonants are given below.

(14)

	p	b	ɓ	p'	pʰ	bʱ
voice	−	+	+	−	−	+
c.g.	−	−	+	+	−	−
s.g.	−	−	−	−	+	+

3.2.6 Prosodic features

Finally, in order to account for the existence of length distinctions, and to represent stressed versus unstressed vowels, two other features were proposed:

long: has greater duration.
stress: has greater emphasis, higher amplitude and pitch, longer duration.

These are obvious: long segments are [+long] and stressed vowels are [+stress].

A major lacuna in the Chomsky and Halle (1968) account of features is a lack of features for tone. This is remedied in chapter 9 when we introduce nonlinear representations. For the moment, we can at least assume that tones are governed by a binary feature [±high tone]—this allows only two levels of tone, but we will not be concerned with languages having more than two tone levels until chapter 9.

Alan Prince & Paul Smolensk(2004) *Optimality Theory*: *Constraint Interaction in Generative Grammar* 选读[①]

◆ 作者简介

艾伦·普林斯(Alan Prince,1946—),本科就读于加拿大麦吉尔大学,1975年在麻省理工大学取得博士学位,曾先后执教于布兰德斯大学、马萨诸塞大学安姆斯特分校、罗格斯大学新布朗斯维克分校。他是优选论的两位主要创始人之一。

---

① Alan P. and Paul S. 2004. *Optimality Theory: Constraint Interaction in Generative Grammar*. Oxford: Blackwell Publishing.

保罗·斯摩棱斯克(Paul Smolensk, 1955—　)曾先后在哈佛大学、印第安纳大学大学取得物理学学士、硕士学位,并最终取得数学物理博士学位。他曾先后执教于科罗拉多大学波尔得分校、约翰霍普金斯大学。他是优选论的两位主要创始人之一。

◆ 正文节选

Chapter 1　　Preliminaries

1.1　Background and Overview

As originally conceived, the *RULE* of grammar was to be built from a Structural Description delimiting a class of inputs and a Structural Change specifying the operations that altered the input (e.g. Chomsky 1961). The central thrust of linguistic investigation would therefore be to explicate the system of predicates used to analyze inputs—the possible Structural Descriptions of rules—and to define the operations available for transforming inputs-the possible Structural Changes of rules. This conception has been jolted repeatedly by the discovery that the significant regularities were to be found not in input configurations, nor in the formal details of structure-deforming operations, but rather in the character of the *output* structures, which ought by rights to be nothing more than epiphenomenal. We can trace a path by which "conditions" on well-formedness start out as peripheral annotations guiding the interpretation of re-write rules, and, metamorphosing by stages into constraints on output structure, end up as the central object of linguistic study.

As the theory of representations in syntax ramified, the theory of operations dwindled in content, even to triviality and, for some, nonexistence. The parallel development inphonology and morphology has been underway for a number of years, but the outcome is perhaps less clear—both in the sense that one view has failed to predominate, and in the sense that much work is itself imperfectly articulate on crucial points. What is clear is that any serious theory of phonology must rely heavily on well-formedness constraints; where by 'serious' we mean 'committed to Universal Grammar'. What remains in dispute, or in subformal obscurity, is the character of the interaction among the posited well-formedness constraints, and, equally, the relation between such constraints and whatever derivational rules they are meant to influence. Given the pervasiveness of this unclarity, and the extent to which it impedes understanding even the most basic functioning of the grammar, it is not excessively dramatic to speak of the issues surrounding the role of well-formedness constraints as involving a kind of conceptual crisis at the center of phonological thought.

Our goal is to develop and explore a theory of the way that representational well-formedness determines the assignment of grammatical structure. We aim therefore to ratify and to extend the results of modern research on the role of constraints in phonological grammar. This body of work is so large and various as to defy concise citation, but we would like to point to such important pieces as Kisseberth 1972, Haiman 1972, Pyle 1972, Hale 1973, Sommerstein 1974, where the basic issues are recognized and addressed; to Wheeler 1981, 1988, Bach and Wheeler 1981, Broselow 1982, Dressler 1985, Singh 1987, Paradis 1988ab, Paradis & Prunet 1991, Noske 1982, Hulst 1984, Kaye & Lowenstamm 1984, Kaye, Lowenstamm, & Vergnaud 1985, Calabrese 1988, Myers 1991, Goldsmith 1991, 1993, Bird 1990, Coleman 1991, Scobbie 1991, which all represent important strands in recent work; as well as to Vennemann 1972, Hooper [Bybee] 1972, 1985, Liberman 1975, Goldsmith 1976, Liberman & Prince 1977, McCarthy 1979, McCarthy & Prince 1986, Selkirk 1980ab, 1981, Kiparsky 1981, 1982, Kaye & Lowenstamm 1981, McCarthy 1981, 1986, Lapointe & Feinstein 1982, Cairns & Feinstein 1982, Steriade 1982, Prince 1983, 1990, Kager & Visch 1984ab, Hayes 1984, Hyman 1985, Wurzel 1985, Borowsky 1986ab, Itô 1986, 1989, Mester 1986, 1992, Halle & Vergnaud 1987, Lakoff 1988, 1993, Yip 1988, Cairns 1988, Kager 1989, Visch 1989, Clements 1990, Legendre, Miyata, & Smolensky 1990bc, Mohanan 1991, 1993, Archangeli & Pulleyblank 1992, Burzio 1992ab, Itô, Kitagawa, & Mester 1992, Itô & Mester 1992—a sample of work which offers an array of perspectives on the kinds of problems we will be concerned with—some close to, others more distant from our own, and some contributory of fundamental representational notions that will put in appearances throughout this work (for which, see the local references in the text below). Illuminating discussion of fundamental issues and an interesting interpretation of the historical development is found in Goldsmith 1990; Scobbie 1992 reviews further relevant background.

The work of Stampe 1973/79, though framed in a very different way, shares central abstract commitments with our own, particularly in its then-radical conception of substantive universality, which we will assume in a form that makes sense within our proposals. Perhaps more distantly related are chapter 9 of Chomsky & Halle 1968 and Kean 1974. The work of Wertheimer 1923, Lerdahl & Jackendoff 1983 (chs 3 and 12), Jackendoff 1983 (chs 7 and 8), 1987, 1991, though not concerned with phonology at all, provide significant conceptual antecedents in their focus on the role of preference; similarly, the proposals of Chomsky 1986, and especially 1989, 1992, though very different in implementation, have fundamental similarities with our own. Perlmutter 1971, Rizzi 1990, Bittner 1993, Legendre, Raymond, & Smolensky 1993, and Grimshaw 1993, are among works in syntax and semantics that resonate with our particular concerns.

The basic idea we will explore is that Universal Grammar (UG) consists largely of a set of constraints on representational well-formedness, out of which individual grammars are constructed. The representational system we employ, using ideas introduced into generative phonology in the 1970s and 1980s, will be rich enough to support two fundamental classes of constraints: those that assess output configurations *per se* and those responsible for maintaining the faithful preservation of underlying structures in the output. Departing from the usual view, we do not assume that the constraints in a grammar are mutually consistent, each true of the observable surface or of some level of representation or of the relation between levels of representation. On the contrary: we assert that the constraints operating in a particular language are highly conflicting and make sharply contrary claims about the well-formedness of most representations. The grammar consists of the constraints together with a general means of resolving their conflicts. We argue further that this conception is an essential prerequisite for a substantive theory of UG.

It follows that many of the conditions which define a particular grammar are, of necessity, frequently violated in the actual forms of the language. The licit analyses are those which satisfy the conflicting constraint set *as well as possible*; they constitute the optimal analyses of underlying forms. This, then, is a theory of optimality with respect to a grammatical system rather than of well-formedness with respect to isolated individual constraints.

The heart of the proposal is a means for precisely determining which analysis of an input *best satisfies*—or least violates—a set of conflicting conditions. For most inputs, it will be the case that every possible analysis violates many constraints. The grammar rates all these analyses according to how well they satisfy the whole constraint set and declares any analysis at the top of this list to be *optimal*. Such an analysis is assigned by the grammar as output to that input. The grammatically well-formed structures are exactly those that are optimal in this sense.

How does a grammar determine which analysis of a given input best satisfies a set of inconsistent well-formedness conditions? Optimality Theory relies on a conceptually simple but surprisingly rich notion of constraint interaction whereby the satisfaction of one constraint can be designated to take absolute priority over the satisfaction of another. The means that a grammar uses to resolve conflicts is to rank constraints in a *strict domination hierarchy*. Each constraint has absolute priority over all the constraints lower in the hierarchy.

Such prioritizing is in fact found with surprising frequency in the literature, typically as a subsidiary remark in the presentation of complex constraints.[①] We will show that once the notion of constraint-precedence is

---

① One work that uses ranking as a systematic part of the analysis is Cole 1992; thanks to Robert Kirchner for bringing this to our attention.

brought in from the periphery and foregrounded, it reveals itself to be of remarkably wide generality, the formal engine driving many grammatical interactions. It will follow that much that has been attributed to narrowly specific constructional rules or to highly particularized conditions is actually the responsibility of very general well-formedness constraints. In addition, a diversity of effects, previously understood in terms of the triggering or blocking of rules by constraints (or merely by special conditions), will be seen to emerge from constraint interaction.

Although we do not draw on the formal tools of connectionism in constructing Optimality Theory, we will establish a high-level conceptual rapport between the mode of functioning of grammars and that of certain kinds of connectionist networks: what Smolensky (1983, 1986) has called 'Harmony maximization', the passage to an output state with the maximal attainable consistency between constraints bearing on a given input, where the level of consistency is determined exactly by a measure derived from statistical physics. The degree to which a possible analysis of an input satisfies a set of conflicting well-formedness constraints will be referred to as the *Harmony* of that analysis. We thereby respect the absoluteness of the term 'well-formed', avoiding terminological confusion and at the same time emphasizing the abstract relation between Optimality Theory and Harmony-theoretic network analysis. In these terms, a grammar is precisely a means of determining which of a pair of structural descriptions is more *harmonic*. Via pair-wise comparison of alternative analyses, the grammar imposes a harmonic order on the entire set of possible analyses of a given underlying form. The actual output is the most harmonic analysis of all, the optimal one. A structural description is well-formed if and only if the grammar determines it to be an optimal analysis of the corresponding underlying form.

With an improved understanding of constraint interaction, a far more ambitious goal becomes accessible: to build individual grammars directly from universal principles of well-formedness, much as Stampe 1973/79 and

Bach 1965 envisioned, in the context of rule theories, building grammars from a universal vocabulary of rules. (This is clearly impossible if we imagine that constraints or rules must be surface- or level-true and hence non-interactive.) The goal is to attain a significant increase in the predictiveness and explanatory force of grammatical theory. The conception we pursue can be stated, in its purest form, as follows: Universal Grammar provides a set of highly general constraints. These often conflicting constraints are *all* operative in individual languages. Languages differ primarily in the way they resolve the conflicts: in how they rank these universal constraints in strict domination hierarchies that determine the circumstances under which constraints are violated. A language-particular grammar *is* a means of resolving the conflicts among universal constraints.

On this view, Universal Grammar provides not only the formal mechanisms for constructing particular grammars, but also the very substance that grammars are built from. Although we shall be entirely concerned in this work with phonology and morphology, we note the implications for syntax and semantics.

1.2 Optimality

The standard phonological rule aims to encode grammatical generalizations in this format:

(1) A → B / C—D

The rule scans potential inputs for structures CAD and performs the change on them that is explicitly spelled out in the rule: the unit denoted by A takes on property B. For this format to be worth pursuing, there must be an interesting theory which defines the class of possible predicates CAD (Structural Descriptions) and another theory which defines the class of possible operations A → B (Structural Changes). If these theories are loose and uninformative, as indeed they have proved to be in reality, we must entertain one of two conclusions:

(i) phonology itself simply doesn't have much content, is mostly 'periphery' rather than 'core', is just a technique for data-compression, with aspirations to depth subverted by the inevitable idiosyncrasies of history and lexicon; or

(ii) the locus of explanatory action is elsewhere.

We suspect the latter.

The explanatory burden can of course be distributed quite differently than in the re-write rule theory. Suppose that the input-output relation is governed by conditions on the well-formedness of the *output*, 'markedness constraints', and by conditions asking for the *exact preservation of the input* in the output along various dimensions, 'faithfulness constraints'. In this case, the inputs falling under the influence of a constraint need share no input-specifiable structure (CAD), nor need there be a single determinate transformation (A→B) that affects them. Rather, we generate (or admit) a set of candidate outputs, perhaps by very general conditions indeed, and then we assess the candidates, seeking the one that best satisfies the relevant constraints. Many possibilities are open to contemplation, but some well-defined measure of value excludes all but the best.[①] The process can be schematically represented like this:

(2) **Structure of Optimality-Theoretic Grammar**
    (a) Gen (In_k)   → {Out_1, Out_2, ... }
    (b) H-eval (Out_i, $1 \leqslant i \leqslant \infty$)   → Out_{real}

The grammar must define a pairing of underlying and surface forms,

---

① This kind of reasoning is familiar at the level of grammar selection in the form of the Evaluation Metric (Chomsky 1951, 1965). On this view, the resources of UG define many grammars that generate the same language; the members of that set are evaluated, and the optimal grammar is the real one.

(input$_i$, output$_j$). Each input is associated with a candidate set of possible analyses by the function Gen (short for 'generator'), a fixed part of Universal Grammar. In the rich representational system employed below, an output form retains its input as a subrepresentation, so that departures from faithfulness may be detected by scrutiny of output forms alone. A 'candidate' is an input-output pair, here formally encoded in what is called 'Out$_i$' in (2). Gen contains information about the representational primitives and their universally irrevocable relations: for example, that the node σ may dominate a node *Onset* or a node μ (implementing some theory of syllable structure), but never vice versa. Gen will also determine such matters as whether every segment must be syllabified—we assume not, below, following McCarthy 1979 *et seq.*—and whether every node of syllable structure must dominate segmental material—again, we will assume not, following Itô 1986, 1989. The function H-eval evaluates the relative Harmony of the candidates, imposing an order on the entire set. An optimal output is at the top of the harmonic order on the candidate set; by definition, it best satisfies the constraint system. Though Gen has a role to play, the burden of explanation falls principally on the function H-eval, a construction built from well-formedness constraints, and the account of interlinguistic differences is entirely tied to the different ways the constraint-system H-eval can be put together, given UG.

H-eval must be constructible in a general way if the theory is to be worth pursuing. There are really two notions of generality involved here: general with respect to UG, and therefore cross-linguistically; and general with respect to the language at hand, and therefore across constructions, categories, descriptive generalizations, etc. These are logically independent, and success along either dimension of generality would count as an argument in favor of the optimality approach. But the strongest argument, the one that is most consonant with the work in the area, and the one that will be pursued here, breaches the distinction, seeking a formulation of H-eval that is built from maximally universal constraints which apply with maximal breadth over an entire language. It is in this set of constraints, Con, that the substantive universals revealed by the theory lie.

Optimality Theory, in common with much previous work, shifts the burden from the theory of operations (Gen) to the theory of well-formedness (H-eval). To the degree that the theory of well-formedness can be put generally, the theory will fulfill the basic goals of generative grammar. To the extent that operation-based theories cannot be so put, they must be rejected.

Among possible developments of the optimality idea, it is useful to distinguish some basic architectural variants. Perhaps nearest to the familiar derivational conceptions of grammar is what we might call 'harmonic serialism', by which Gen provides a set of candidate analyses for an input, which are harmonically evaluated; the optimal form is then fed back into Gen, which produces another set of analyses, which are then evaluated; and so on until no further improvement in representational Harmony is possible. Here Gen might mean: 'do any *one* thing: advance all candidates which differ in one respect from the input.' The Gen $\leftrightarrows$ H-eval loop would iterate until there was nothing left to be done or, better, until nothing that could be done would result in increased Harmony. A significant proposal of roughly this character is the *Theory of Constraints and Repair Strategies* of Paradis 1988ab, with a couple of caveats: the *constraints* involved are a set of parochial level-true phonotactic statements, rather than being universal and violable, as we insist; and the *repair strategies* are quite narrowly specifiable in terms of structural description and structural change rather than being of the general 'do-something-to-α' variety. Paradis confronts the central complexity implicit in the notion 'repair': what to do when applying a repair strategy to satisfy one constraint results in violation of another constraint (i.e. at an intermediate level of derivation). Paradis refers to such situations as 'constraint conflicts' and although these are not conflicts in our sense of the term—they cannot be, as Robert Kirchner has pointed out to us, since all of her constraints are surface- or level-true and therefore never disagree among themselves in the assessment of output well-formedness—her work is of unique importance in addressing and shedding light on fundamental complexities in the idea of well-formedness-driven rule-application. The 'persistent rule' theory of Myers 1991 can similarly be related to the notion of Harmony-governed serialism. The program for *Harmonic Phonology* in Goldsmith 1991, 1993, is even more strongly of this character; within its lexical levels, all rules are constrained to apply harmonically. Here again, however, the rules are conceived of as being pretty much of the familiar sort, *triggered* if they increase Harmony, and Harmony itself is to be defined in specifically phonotactic terms. A subtheory which is very much in the mold of harmonic serialism, using a general procedure to produce candidates, is the 'Move-x' theory of rhythmic adjustment (Prince 1983, Hayes 1991/95).[①]

A contrasting view would hold that the *Input* → *Output* map has no internal structure: all possible variants are produced by Gen in one step and evaluated in parallel. In the course of this work, we will see instances of both kinds of analysis, though we will focus predominantly on developing the parallel idea, finding strong support for it, as do McCarthy & Prince 1993a. Definitive adjudication between parallel and serial conceptions, not to mention hybrids of various kinds, is a challenge of considerable subtlety, as indeed the debate over the necessity of serial Move-α illustrates plentifully (e.g. Aoun 1986, Browning 1991, Chomsky 1981), and the matter can be sensibly addressed only after much well-founded analytical work and theoretical exploration.

Optimality Theory abandons two key presuppositions of earlier

---

① An interesting variant is what we might call 'anharmonic serialism', in which Gen produces the candidate set by a nondeterministic sequence of constrained procedures ('do one thing; do another one') which are themselves not subject to harmonic evaluation. The candidate set is derived by running through every possible sequence of such actions; harmonic evaluation looks at this candidate set. To a large extent, classical Move-α theories (Chomsky 1981) work like this.

work. First, that grammatical theory allows individual grammars to narrowly and parochially specify the Structural Description and Structural Change of rules. In place of this is Gen, which defines for any given input a large space of candidate analyses by freely exercising the basic structural resources of the representational theory. The idea is that the desired output lies somewhere in this space, and the constraint system is strong enough to single it out. Second, Optimality Theory abandons the widely held view that constraints are language-particular statements of phonotactic truth. In its place is the assertion that the constraints of Con are universal and of very general formulation, with great potential for disagreement over the well-formedness of analyses; an individual grammar consists of a ranking of these constraints, which resolves any conflict in favor of the higher-ranked constraint. The constraints provided by Universal Grammar must be simple and general; interlinguistic differences arise from the permutations of constraint-ranking; typology is the study of the range of systems that re-ranking permits.

Because they are ranked, constraints are regularly violated in the grammatical forms of a language. Violability has significant consequences not only for the mechanics of description, but also for the process of theory construction: a new class of predicates becomes usable in the formal theory, with a concomitant shift in what we can think the actual generalizations are. We cannot expect the world to stay the same when we change our way of describing it.

3.3 思考和练习

1. 很多说汉语方言的人不能区分[n]和[l]以及[f]和[v],在这些方言中,[n]和[l]以及[f]和[v]属于不同的音位还是同一音位的音位变体?请结合自己的方言(或者熟悉的方言)加以论述。

2. 请使用特征分析法,列出汉语普通话中的辅音和元音的音位特征。

例：[k]：[－带声]，[＋软腭]，[＋塞音]。

3. 考虑下列韩语(韩国的官方语言)的语料：

pʰul	'glue'	pap	'food'
pam	'night'	pʰal	'arm'
sɨlpʰə	'sad'	apʰə	'hurt'
pi	'rain'	pul	'fire'
pʰjo	'ticket'	pan	'half'

回答问题：韩语中的[p]和[pʰ]属于不同的音位还是同一音位的变体？说出你的判断根据。

4. 请使用本章中提到的音系规则，构拟至少三条汉语中的音系规则(也可以使用你熟悉的语言或者方言为语料)。

5. 除了汉语普通话，你还了解中国境内其它语言(如藏语、维吾尔语、蒙语等)或者方言(吴方言、赣方言、湘方言、闽方言、粤方言、江淮方言等)吗？这些语言的音系系统是怎么样的？如果你去做田野调查，会如何确定这些语言(方言)中的音位？

3.4 延伸阅读

Chomsky, N. 1967. Some general properties of phonological rules. *Language* 43：102–128.

Chomsky, N. & M. Halle. 1969. *The Sound Pattern of English*. New York：Harper and Row.

Fromkin, V. Rodman, R. & N. Hyams. 2014. *An Introduction to Language* (*the 10th edition*). Boston：Wadsworth.(第 6 章)

Halle, M. & G. N. Clements. 1983. *Problem Book of Phonology：a Workbook for courses in Introductory Linguistics and Modern Phonology*. Cambridge, Mass.：The MIT Press.

Kenstowicz, M. 1994. *Phonology in Generative Grammar*. Oxford：

Blackwell.

Kenstowicz, M. & C. Kisseberth. 1979. *Generative Phonology: Description and Theory*. New York: Academic Press.

Maddieson, I. 1984. *Patterns of Sounds*. Cambridge: Cambridge University Press.

O'Grady, W., Archibald, J., Aronoff, M. & J. Rees-Miller. 2017. *Contemporary Linguistics: An Introduction (the 7th edition)*. Boston: Bedford/St. Martin's.

Odden, D. 2013. *Introducing Phonology*. New York: Cambridge University Press.

Prince, A. & P. Smolensk. 2004. *Optimality Theory: Constraint Interaction in Generative Grammar*. Oxford: Blackwell Publishing.

第四章 形态学

4.1 导引

- 形态概说
- 语素与词的内部结构
- 派生形态
- 屈折形态
- 词的层级结构
- 基于形态的语言类型
- 小结

4.1.1 形态概说

形态学是英语 morphology 的直译。"morphology"源自古希腊语。"morph"在希腊语中意为形式(form)。形态学是研究词法的语言学分支,主要关注词的内部结构、构词规律,以及和词有关的形态变化等。本章主要关注的问题有:(1)如何分析词的内部结构?(2)如何通过增加前缀、中缀和后缀等产生新词?(3)如何把已有的两个或多个词结合起来产生新词?(4)词的屈折形态变化,即词如何标记数、格、呼应、时态、体态等语法概念?问题(2)和(3)关注词的派生形态(derivational morphology),问题(4)关注词的屈折形态(inflectional morphology)。派生形态和屈折形态都是形态学研究的主要对象。

4.1.2 语素与词的内部结构

对语言而言,可能没有什么东西比词更重要。和音位、音节等不同,词是意义的载体;和可以随意创造和使用的句子不同,词可以永久地储藏在语言使用者的心理词库中。哪怕一个人对另一种语言的句法规则一无所知,只要他能认识其中的某些词,也可以在一定条件下完成交际功能。词是实现交际最重要的材料。那么,什么是词呢?

语言学家把词定义为最小的自由形式。所谓自由形式,指的是不需要在固定位置出现的语言单位。很多时候,词可以单独出现。考虑下面的例子:

(1) a. Students like linguistics.
　　b. *Student-s like linguistics.

例(1a)中的"students"由两个部分组成:student 和复数标记-s。很明显,前者是词,而后者不是。前者是自由形式,可以单独使用,位置不固定;后者不是自由形式,不能单独使用,只能附在可数名词后面。

"students"的例子说明词具有内部结构。词由比它更小的单位组成。我们把词的下一级单位叫做语素。语素是一种语言中最小的、具有意义的单位。语素在这一点上和音位不同。音位是语言中最小的单位,但是音位不是意义(或语法功能)的载体。"students"由两个语素构成:student 和-s。这两个语素分别代表了语言中两类不同的语素:自由语素(free morpheme)和黏着语素(bound morpheme)。自由语素不需要依附于其它语素,可以独立成词(如 student、read、like、pretty 等);黏着语素不能独立成词,必须依附于其它语素,如上文提到的复数标记-s。黏着语素一般由词缀(affix)、依附成分(clitic)等构成。"-s"就是英语中的复数词缀。

同一概念在不同语言中的实现方式不同。有的概念在一种语言中用自由语素表示,在另一种语言中则可能用黏着语素来表示,反之亦然。如英语中的进行体标记-ing,在英语中是黏着语素,必须附着于动词才能使用,但在汉语中是一个可以独立成词的自由语素"在",比较(2a)和(2b):

(2) a. John is reading a book.

b. 小张在看书。

一个形式上较为复杂的词一般由一个词根语素(root)和一个(或多个)词缀组成。词缀所依附的语素又叫词干(stem)(也有学者叫做词基(base))。词根是承载词的意义的核心单位。词根可以是自由语素,也可以是黏着语素。如"reader、writer、painter、professor"等词中的"read、write、paint、profess"等是词的词根,但它们是自由语素。而在"perceive、conceive、receive、deceive"等词中的"ceive"(意为感知)是这些词的词根,但"ceive"本身不是自由语素。

词干是一个相对的概念,每一个词缀所依附的单位都是一个词干。在"reader、writer、painter、professor"等词中的"read、write、paint、profess"等是词的词根,同时也是词干。但是在"readers、writers、painters、professors"等词中,复数标记-s所依附的词干是"reader、writer、painter、professor",词根依然不变。而相对词缀-er而言,词干则分别是"read、write、paint、profess"。下图说明了词根和词干的区别(N:noun;Af:Affix):

(3)
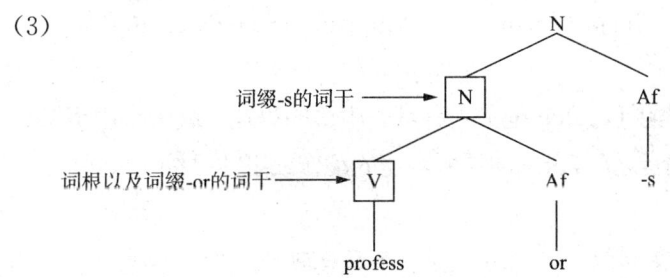

自然语言中依附于词干的词缀一般分为四种类型:(一)前缀(prefix);(二)后缀(suffix);(三)中缀(infix);(四)环缀(circumfix)。

(一)**前缀**　在线性序列上位于词干之前的词缀叫做前缀。汉语中"老师、老虎"中的"老","阿大、阿二、阿华"中的"阿",英语中的"prefix、prejudge、premeditate"中的"pre","bipolar、bisexual、biannual"中的"bi"都是前缀。

(二)**后缀**　线性序列上位于词干之后的词缀叫做后缀。汉语中的"老子、儿子、桌子"中的"子",粤方言中的"靓仔、烂仔"中的"仔"都是典型的后缀。英语中的"singer、writer、painter、cleaner"中的"er","worked、delayed、passed、liked"中的"ed"都是后缀。同一个概念,在一个语言中用前缀表示,可能在另一个语言中需要用后缀表示,反之亦然。如英语中的复数-s 是后缀,依附于词干之后。但是在墨西哥的 Isthmus Zapotec 语中,复数标记 ka-是前缀,需要位于词干之前:

(4) zigi '下巴'　kazigi '复数-下巴'
　　 zike '肩膀'　kazike '复数-肩膀'
　　 diaga '耳朵'　kadiaga '复数-耳朵'

(三) 中缀　还有些语言有中缀。中缀位于两个语素之间。菲律宾的 Bontoc 就具有中缀。Bontoc 有一个形/名转动词的中缀"um"。"um"位于形容词或名词的第一个辅音之后,把相应的形容词或名词转换为动词,如(5)所示:

(5) 名词/形容词　　　动词
　　 fikas 'strong'　　fumikas 'to be strong'
　　 kilad 'red'　　　kumilad 'to be red'
　　 fusul 'enemy'　　fumusul 'to be an enemy'

菲律宾的 Tagalog 是另一种具有中缀的语言。有一个中缀"in"位于动词的第一个辅音之后,表示动词所表述的动作或事件已经完成:

(6) 词根　　　　　加了中缀后的形式
　　 bili 'buy'　　　b-in-ili 'bought'
　　 basa 'read'　　 b-in-asa 'read(PAST)'
　　 sulat 'write'　　s-in-ulat 'wrote'

还有一种中缀现象属于非组合型形态范畴,比较典型的有阿拉伯语和其它闪米特语(Simitic)。阿拉伯语中典型的词根一般由三个辅音组成,在辅音中插入不同的元音可以表示不同的语法对立,如(7)所示:

(7) **ktb** 'write'
　　 katab 'he wrote'

kataba 'wrote'
kutib 'has been written'
a**k**tub 'am writing'
kaatib 'writer'
kitaab 'book'
kutub 'books'

（四）环缀 有些语言还有环缀，即同时位于词干前后的语素。这些语素属于非连续性语素。比较熟悉的环缀现象是德语中规则动词的过去分词变位。德语规则动词的过去分词变位要同时在动词词根的前面加上 ge-，同时在后面加上-t，形成 ge-X-t 的结构（X 表示动词词根），如(8)所示：

(8) **ge**-lieb-**t** 'loved'
   ge-spiel-**t** 'played'
   ge-hör-**t** 'heard'
   ge-sag-**t** 'said'
   ge-arbeit-**et** 'worked'

在美国俄克拉荷马州的 Chickasaw 中，否定形式也是通过环缀构成的。这种语言的否定形式一般是在表示肯定的词干前面加上 ik-，在后面加上-o，如(9)所示：

(9) 肯定   否定
   chokma 'he is good'   ik＋chokma＋o 'he isn't good'
   lakna 'it is yellowed'   ik＋lakn＋o 'it isn't yellowed'
   palli 'it is hot'   ik＋pall＋o 'it isn't hot'
   tiwwi 'he opens it'   ik＋tiww＋o 'he doesn't open it'

4.1.3 派生形态

形态学研究词的内部结构，也研究词的形成规律。词的形成分为两种类型:一种类型是以某一个词根为基础,通过加上各种词缀形成一个新词,新词的词类和词根可能相同,也可能不同,这种方式叫做派生(derivation);另一种类型也是以某一个词根为基础,通过加上各种词缀形成,但是这些词缀只具有语法上的意义,如时、体、数、格等,新词和词根的词类相同,这种方式叫做屈折(inflection)。通常我们说的形态,实质是派生形态和屈折形态的交集。单独讨论某一类形态都是偏颇的。这一小节主要讨论派生形态,下一小节讨论屈折形态。

派生的结果是产生一个新词。通过把派生语素附着于某一词干之上得到的新词叫做派生词(derived word)。英语中有丰富的派生语素,它们有的是前缀,有的是后缀。派生一般改变词类,如原来是动词的,通过附加派生语素后,变成了名词;原来是形容词的,通过附加派生语素之后,变成了副词。派生语素一般有明确的语义内容,如"-able"表示具有某种能力之意,"-er"表示做某事之人之意,"-ize"表示某种过程之意,等等。从这一角度来说,派生语素就是词,只是不具有词的独立地位。

英语中常见的改变词类的派生语素和派生过程如下面的例子所示:

(10) a. 名词→形容词

　　boy ＋ -ish→boyish

　　virtu ＋ -ous→virtuous

　　picture ＋ -esque→picturesque

　　affection＋ -ate→affectionate

　　alcohol ＋ -ic→alcoholic

b. 动词→名词

　　clear＋-ance→clearance

　　accus＋ -ation→accusation

　　predic＋ -ion→ prediction

　　sing ＋ -er→singer

　　comform＋-ist→conformist

c. 形容词→副词

　　happy＋-ly→happily

d. 名词→动词

moral＋-ize → moralize
vaccin＋-ate → vaccinate
hast＋-en → hasten
im＋prison → imprison
be＋friend → befriend
en＋joy → enjoy
in＋habit → inhabit

e. 形容词 → 名词
tall＋-ness → tallness
specific＋-ity → specificity
feudal＋-ism → feudalism
free＋dom → freedom

f. 动词 → 形容词
creat＋-ive → creative
migrat＋-ory → migratory
run＋-y → runny
read＋-able → readable

g. 形容词 → 动词
en＋enlarge → enlarge
en＋dear → endear
en＋rich → enrich

还有一些派生语素，虽然不会改变原来词干的词类，但是会改变意义。如下是一些英语中的例子：

(11) a. 名词 → 名词
friend＋-ship → friendship
human＋-ity → humanity
America＋-n → American
auto＋biography → autobiography
dis＋advantage → disadvantage

ex＋wife→ex-wife
un＋employment→unemployment

b. 动词→动词
un-＋do→undo
re-＋cover→recover
dis-＋believe→disbelieve
auto＋destruct→autodestruct

c. 形容词→形容词
pink＋-ish→pinkish
red＋-like→redlike
a-＋moral→amoral
il-＋legal→illegal
in-＋accurate→inaccurate
semi-＋annual→semiannual
sub-＋minimal→subminimal

有些词可能不止涉及到一次派生过程。派生过程可以多次发生，产生新词。这样的词具有多层的内部结构。我们可以通过树形图（tree-diagram）来形象地表述词的内部结构，如下：

（12）*activation*

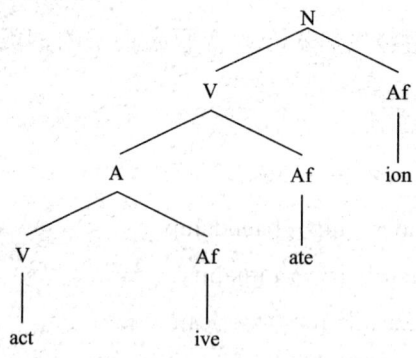

派生是普遍的构词手段。很多语言都用派生的方式生成新词。虽然汉语的屈折形态不发达，但是汉语中仍然存在相当数量的派生形态。如"椅子、桌子、杯子"中的"子"就是典型的派生后缀，"老师、老虎"中的"老"是派生前缀，"阿大、阿二"中的"阿"也是派生前缀。所以汉语绝对没有形态变化这一说法是不严谨的。

4.1.4 屈折形态

自然语言中还有很多语素只表示纯粹的语法功能，如人称、性、格、数等范畴。这类语素叫做屈折语素（inflectional morpheme）。通过将屈折语素附着于词干之上表示各种各样的语法信息的方式叫做折变化。曲折变化属于屈折形态。考虑下面的例子：

(13) a. I sail the ocean blue.
　　　b. He sail-s the ocean blue.
　　　c. John sail-ed the ocean blue.
　　　d. John has sail-ed the ocean blue.
　　　e. John is sail-ing the ocean blue.

上面的几个句子都涉及同一个动词（sail），但是形式各不相同。例(13b)中的"-s"是表示呼应的语素，表示动词的主语是第三人称单数的现在时，(13c)中的"-ed"表示动词所描述事件的发生时间在参照时间之前，(13d)中的"have -ed"表示事件的发生时间在参照时间之前，并且参照时间和说话事件重合，(13e)中的"-ing"表示动词所表述的动作正在进行。以上种种，呼应、时、体等，都是语法功能，相应的，"-s、-ed、-ing"都是屈折语素。

相比而言，现代英语不是屈折形态十分丰富的语言。现代英语中只有 8 个屈折语素，2 个和名词有关，2 个和形容词有关，还有 4 个和动词有关，如下表：

表 4.1　现代英语中的屈折语素

名词	
复数标记 -s	the students
领属标记 's	Mary's novels

	续 表
动词	
第三人称单数非过去式 -s	He likes linguistics.
进行体 -ing	He is studying linguistics.
过去时 -ed	He studied linguistics.
过去分词 -ed/-en	He has studied linguistics.
形容词	
比较级标记 -er	the bigger one
最高级标记 -est	the biggest one

很多语言的屈折形态远比英语发达。在罗曼语言（由拉丁语分化出来的语言）中，动词依据人称的不同，有六种变位形式。如下面西班牙语的例子：

(14) hablo 'I speak'
　　 hablas 'you speak'
　　 habla 'she/he speaks'
　　 hablamos 'we speak'
　　 hablais 'you.PL speak'
　　 hablan 'they speak'

屈折形态变化和派生形态变化存在根本性的不同。具体而言，可以通过以下四条标准区分两种不同的形态变化。

（一）**词类改变**　屈折形态变化不改变词类，"walks、walked"中的"-s"和"-ed"虽然表示不同的语法意义，但是不改变词干"walk"的词类。相反，派生形态变化一般会改变词类，如"-ly"附加于形容词之后生成形容词（happy＋ly→happily），"-ness"附加于形容词之后生成名词（happy＋ness→happiness），"-er"附加于动词之后生成名词（write＋-er→writer）。

（二）**语序**　当一个词中同时有屈折语素和派生语素的时候，屈折语素要位于派生语素之后，形成"［词根＋派生语素］＋屈折语素"的格局，如：

(15) neighbor-hood-s
  * neighbor-s-hood

（三）**能产性**　屈折形态变化远比派生形态变化能产。除去极少数的不规则动词,表示过去时的"-ed"可以附加于几乎所有动词之后。相比之下,派生形态变化则受到严格的限制。如"-ment"可以附在动词后面生成名词,但是只有一部分动词有这样的形态变化方式:

(16) confine confined confinement
  align aligned alignment
  treat treated treatment
  arrest arrested * arrestment
  straighten straightened * straightenment
  cure cured * curement

（四）**语义透明性**　通过屈折形态变化得到的新词和词干在语义上基本一致,语义是透明的,但是通过派生形态变化得到的新词,和原来的词干在语义上并不完全一致。"-ment"可以附在动词后面生成名词,如"government"可以表示机构,也可以表示(管理)行为,但是"abandonment"则只有表示(抛弃)行为的意思,没有表示地点的意思。

屈折形态变化和派生形态变化的区别如下表:

表 4.2　屈折形态和派生形态变化对比

	屈折形态	派生形态
承载功能	语法功能	词汇功能
是否改变词类	否	是
是否改变意义	否	是
是否由语法规则决定	是	否
是否位于词尾	是	不一定
是否能产	是	否

语素示意图如下(以英语为例):

(17) 英语中的语素

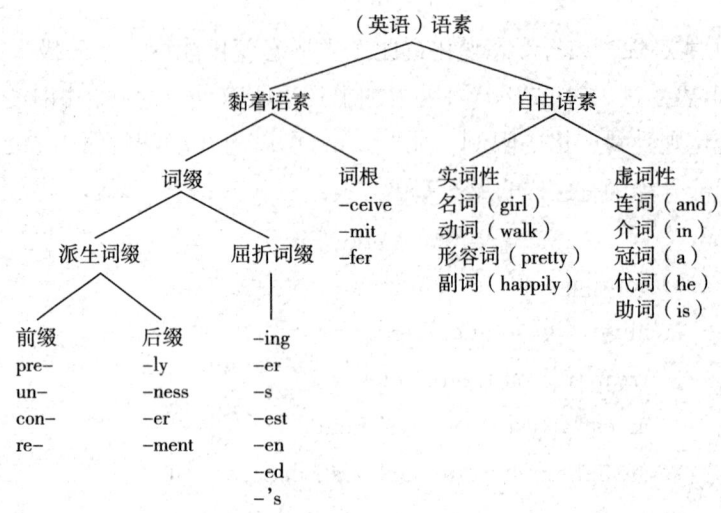

4.1.5 词的层级结构

层级性是人类语言最重要的属性之一。词的内部也是有层级结构的。前文提到过,不同类型的语素以固定的顺序排列(屈折语素位于派生语素之后)。这一语素之间的顺序实质上体现了词内部不同组成部分之间的层级结构。换言之,在一个由两个或两个以上语素组成的词中,这些语素不是单纯的线性序列排列,而是存在内部结构。

词的内部结构可以用倒置的树形图表示。词根犹如树的根,其它黏着语素犹如树的枝杈。下面用例子来说明。

(18) unsystematically

"unsystematically"这个词由词根 system 和 un-、-atic、-al、-ly 等五个语素构成。这五个语素之间的排列遵循严格的规则,体现了词的层级结构。用树形图来表示,如(19)所示:

(19) 词的层级结构

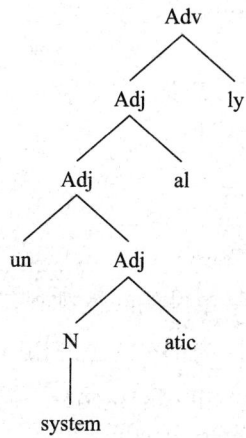

　　有些具有结构歧义的词可以非常清晰地反映词的层级结构。所谓结构歧义,是指一个词可以同时有两个不同的意思。比如英语中的"unlockable"。"unlockable"的一个意思是门不能被锁住(not able to be locked)。想象一个情景:一个人在屋里,想要静处,结果却非常沮丧地发现,门没法上锁。"unlockable"的另一个意思是门锁可以被打开(able to be unlocked)。想象另一个情景:一个人在屋里要出去,结果却惊喜地发现,门锁可以被打开。这两个意思对应两种不同的层级结构,分别如(20a)和(20b)所示:

(20) a. unlockable = not able to be locked

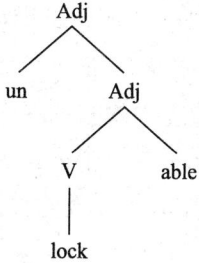

b. unlockable = able to be unlocked

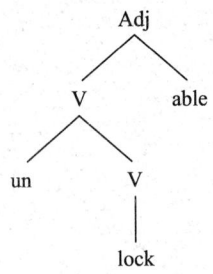

如果词的各个组成语素是单纯的线性排列,我们将无法解释像"unlockable"这样的歧义现象。正是因为词有内部结构,相同的语素可以导致不同的结构,我们才能正确得出(20a)和(20b)这两种不同的意义。这一现象也说明,语言的意义是由结构决定的,不同的结构导致不同的意义。

4.1.6 基于形态的语言类型

所有的语言都有语素和词。因而,形态学可以帮助我们更好地认识世界上语言的类型。所谓语言类型学,就是依据特定语言是否可以通过语素合并以及如何合并的规律,对语言的特性做出的归纳和总结。一般而言,基于形态特征的语言类型可以分为两大类四小类:分析型(analytic)和综合型(synthetic),后者又可以分为三个次类:黏着型(agglutinating)、溶合型(fusional)以及复综型(polysynthetic)。

(一) 分析型

分析型语言避免或几乎不适合用以词缀来构词。每一个词就是一个(自由)语素。在这种类型的语言中,词和语素的比率几乎达到 1∶1。分析型语言的典型代表就是孤立语(isolating language)。汉语就是一种具有很强的孤立语倾向的语言。在汉语中,绝大多数的词都由一个(自由)语素组成。一个词就是一个语素,一个语素就能组成一个词。汉语不适合用屈折语素来表示各种语法上的对立。譬如汉语中表示完成的体标记"了",在句中没有固定的位置,就是明证:

(21) a. 张三吃饭了。
　　 b. 张三吃了饭。

分析型语言大多集中在东南亚、大洋洲以及非洲中部地区,在美洲和欧洲分布较少。典型的分析型语言(孤立语)有汉语、越南语、泰语、高棉语(柬埔寨)、老挝语等。

(二) 黏着型

黏着型语言中,一个词可以由两个或两个以上的语素构成。黏着型语言广泛使用(黏着)语素,并且每一个语素都有独立的、可以辨析的意义。土耳其语就是典型的黏着型语言。如:

(22) a. [kœk] 'village'
  b. [kœk-leɾ]
   village-PL
   'villages'
  c. [kœk-leɾ-in]
   village-PL-GEN
   'of the villages'

如上面的例子所示,在土耳其语中,后缀"leɾ"是复数标记,"in"是属格标记。一个词由多个语素组成,并且一个语素对应一个独立的意义,这是黏着型语言的典型特征。

(三) 溶合型

溶合型语言的词也是由"词根+词缀"组成,即一个词可以由两个或超过两个以上的语素组成。但是,和黏着型语言不同,在溶合型语言中,一个语素可以同时表示多个(语法)意义。俄语是典型的溶合型语言。如俄语的后缀"-u",可以同时表示阴性、单数、宾格等语法范畴,如(23)所示:

(23) My vidim ruk-u
  we see hand-FEM.SG.ACC
  'We see a/the hand.'

(四) 复综型

在复综型语言中,一个词由若干语素组成,并且一个词表达的意义在其它语言中可能需要用一个句子来表示。Inuktitut（因纽特语）就是典型的复综型语言。如例(24)：

(24) Qasu-iir- sar -vig -ssar -si -ngit -luinar -nar -puq
tired-not-cause-to be palce-for suitable find not completely someone 3.SG

'Someone did not find a completely suitable resting place.'

绝大多数美洲印第安语，如 Inuktitut、Cree（克里语）、Sarcee（萨西语）等，都是复综型语言。

以上是基于形态的语言类型分布。但是实际上，很多语言属于混合型（mixed type），即在某些方面呈现一种类型的特征，但是在另一些方面又呈现另一种类型的特征。英语就是典型的混合型。现代英语只有8个屈折形态变化，从这一点看，英语有孤立语的倾向。但是英语中存在大量的派生语素，又呈现黏着型语言的特征。另外，如果仅仅从代词系统来看，英语当归属于溶合型语言。英语中的"he"可以同时表示第三人称、单数、阳性等语法概念。所以，有学者提出，分析与综合的概念，应该因语言结构而异，而非因语言而异。我们把这一观点留给读者自行思考。

通过对世界上语言的形态的仔细考察，我们可以得出一些行之有效的归纳和总结，这就是蕴涵共性（implicational universals）。以下两种蕴涵共性被发现广泛存在于自然语言中：

(25) 关于形态分布的蕴涵共性

a. 如果一个语言存在屈折词缀，那么它必然会有派生词缀。如现代英语既有屈折词缀，又有派生词缀。现代汉语则只有派生词缀，没有屈折词缀。

b. 如果一个词中同时存在屈折词缀和派生词缀，则派生词缀在结构上和词根联系更紧密。在英语中，屈折词缀要跟随派生词缀，而非派生词缀跟随屈折词缀：writ-er-s 对比 * writ-s-er。

4.1.7 小结

形态学主要研究自然语言中词的结构和构成。语素是构成词最基本的建筑材料。语素的另一个定义是"语言中最小的、具有意义的单位"。语素可以分为自由语素和黏着语素。黏着语素可以进一步分为前缀、后缀、中缀和环缀。自然语言中存在两种不同类型的语素:派生语素和屈折语素。和前者有关的叫派生形态,和后者有关的叫屈折形态。说汉语完全没有形态是不对的。汉语中存在一定数量的派生形态(但是汉语没有屈折形态)。汉语在语言类型上具有很强的孤立语倾向。

4.2 选读

- 布龙菲尔德(1933)《语言论》选读
- 吕叔湘(1979)《汉语语法分析问题》选读
- 朱德熙(1984)《关于向心结构的定义》选读
- Di Sciullo & Williams (1988) *On the Definition of Word* 选读

布龙菲尔德(1933)《语言论》选读[①]

第十三章 词法

13.1 我们所谓一种语言的词法(morphology),意思就是粘附形式出现于组成成分中的结构。从定义上讲,这种合成形式也诈是粘附形式也许是词,但决不是短语。因此,我们可以说,词法包含词和词的一部份的结构,而句法包含短语的结构。短语词[jack-in-the-pulpit(天南星草)]和有些复合词(blackbird)可以当作边缘地带,因为它们的直接成分里没有粘附形式,然而在某些方面所显示的,与其说是句法的不如说是词法的结构类型。

---

① 布龙菲尔德,《语言论》,袁家骅、赵世开、甘世福译,商务印书馆 1997 年版。作者简介参考第一章"选读"部分。

一般讲来，词法结构比句法结构更为繁琐。变音和变调的特征更是层出不穷，而且往往是不规则的——即只限于特殊的成分或结合体。组成成分的次序大致都是十分固定的，不容许有如 John ran away：Away ran John 这样一些涵义上有所不同的变体。选择特征对可以组成复合形式的成分常加以细微的和变幻莫测的限制。

因此，各种悟言的区别，在词法上比在句法上更大。由于语言的种类繁多，所以，就词法而论，还找不到一个简单的语言分类法。一种分类法是把很少使用粘附形式的分析（analytic）语跟大量使用粘附形式的综合（synthetic）语区别开来。一个极端，是完全的分析语，如现代汉语。在这样的语言中，每个词是一个单音节词素或是一个复合词或短语词；另一个极端，就是高度的综合语，如爱斯基摩语，这样的语言把长串的粘附形式联成单词，例如[a:wlisa-ut-iss?ar-si-niarpu-ŋa]（我正在找点合适的东西来做一个钓鱼绳）。然而，除了前述的那一极端的一些例子以外，这种区别是相对的；任何一种语言在某些方面也许比其它的语言更具有分析性，而在另一些方面也许更具有综合性。另一种分类法是把语言分成四种词法类型：孤立的（isolating）、粘附的（agglutinative）、多形综合的（polysynthetic）和屈折的（inflecting）。孤立语是那些像汉语一样的语言，不使用粘附形式；在粘附语中，被认为是把粘附形式一个随着一个地加上去，土耳其语就是一个现成的例子；多形综合语利用粘附形式来表示语义上的重要成分如动词性的宾语（verbal goal），爱斯基摩语就是这种情况；屈折语把语义上的不同特征或是体现在一个单一的粘附形式中或是合并在多个紧密结合的粘附形式中，例如拉丁语的一个形式如 amō "我爱"中的后缀 -ō，可以表达几种意义：如"说话人作为施事者"，"只有一个施事者"，"现在的动作"，"真实的（不只是可能发生的或假定的）动作"。这些区别不是相互并列的，而且后三类的定义的界限从来就是不明确的。

13.2 既然说话人不能用单独讲出粘附形式的方式来把它分离开来，所以他通常不能把词的结构加以描写。对形态作一番叙述需要系统的研究。古代的希腊人在这方面有些成就，但是，我们的技术大体上是由过去的印度的一些语法学家发展起来的。我们的方法无论多么精密，难于捉摸的意义的本质总会造成一些困难，尤其是含糊的意义关系又伴有形式上的不规则变化。在 goose（雌鹅）、gosling（小鹅）、gooseberry（醋栗、鹅莓）、gander（雄鹅）这个系列中，我们或许会同意头两个形式在意义上是有形态的关系的：即

gosling 中的[gɔz-]是 goose 的变音，但 gooseberry 中的[guz-]就跟这个意义不相称了。在另一方面，goose 和 gander 在形式上的相似点[g-]仅仅是这么一点儿，以致人们会怀疑是不是这么一点儿相似点就真能使实际的意义关系体现为语言形式。最后提到的这种难以对付的问题也出现在 duck（母鸭）：drake（公鸭）这一对词中，因为都有[d...k]。我们很快就会知道：我们不能指望说话人给我们解答，因为他们没有受过词法分析的训练；如果我们拿这样一些问题来麻烦他们，他们就会给一些自相矛盾或可笑的回答。如果我们了解了一种语言的历史，我们往往发觉这种含糊情况并不存在于该语言的较古阶段——例如几世纪以前"goose-berry"原是 * grose-berry 而跟 goose 毫无关系——但是这一类的事实并不能明确地告诉我们这种语言现阶段的活动情况是怎么回事。

为了要描写出现于句法中的变调和变音，我们自然而然地会把一个词或短语的绝对形式当作我们的出发点，但是对待一个出现于几种形状中的粘附形式，我们就会根据怎样选择一个基础交替形式（basic alternant）而采取几种截然不同的描写方式。譬如，英语名词的复数后缀通常以三种形状出现：[-iz]glasses（玻璃杯）、[-z] cards（卡片）、[-s] books（书）；如果把这三种形状当中的每一种依次序拿来作为我们的出发点，我们就会得到三种截然不同的事实的描述。

往往还有另外一些困难情况。有时一种语法特征如语音变换——用来表达通常利用一种语言形式来表达的意义，如 man：men，这儿元音的变换代替了复数后缀。在另一些情况下，连什么语法特征也没有：一个单一的语音形式，以同音形式来表示通常利用语言形式来区别意义，如在 sheep (grazes)：sheep (graze)中的单数和复数名词。关于这点，印度人曾想到一个表面上是虚构的而实际上显然很有用的所谓零成分（zero element）的方法：在 sheep：sheep 中，复数后缀被零式——即被不存在的任何东西——所代替。

13.3　由于这些和另一些困难情况，任何不合理的工作程序都可能在词法的描述上造成混乱。最重要的是，我们必须遵守直接成分（§10.2）的原则。这个原则引导我们在一开头就可根据直接成分（immediate constituents）来区分词的分类：

A. 次要词（secondary words），包含自由形式：

1. 复合词(compound words)，包含一个以上的自由形式：doorknob(门上捏手)，wild-animal-tamer(野兽驯养者)。这些内含的自由形式是复合词的成员(members)：在我们的例子中，成员是 door、knob、tamer 这些词和 wild animal 这个短语。

2. 派生次要词(derived secondary words)，包含一个自由形式：boyish(孩子气的)，old-maidish(老处女似的)。内含的自由形式叫做基础形式(underlying form)：在我们的例子中，基础形式是 boy 这个词和 old maid(老处女)这个短语。

B. 基本词(primary words)，不包含自由形式：

1. 派生基本词(derived primary words)，包含一个以上的粘附形式：re-ceive(收到)，de-ceive(欺骗)，con-ceive(想像)，re-tain(保留)，de-tain(扣留)，con-tain(包含)。

2. 语素词(morpheme-words)，只含有一个单一的(自由)词素：man，boy，cut，run，red，big。

直接成分的原则会引导我们把一个形式加以类归，比方说，把 gentlemanly(绅士风度的)这样一个形式不作为一个复合词而作为一个派生次要词来归类，因为直接成分是粘附形式-ly 和基础词 gentleman(绅士)；于是 gentlemanly 这个词便是一个次要派生词(所谓再复合词 de-compound)，它的基础形式碰巧是个复合词。同样，door-knobs(门上捏手——复数)不是一个复合词，而是由粘附形式[-z]和基础词 door-knob 组成的再复合词。

直接成分的原则引导我们观察组成成分的结构次序。组成成分的结构次序跟它们的实际序列(actual sequence)是不同的；比方，ungentlemanly(非绅士风度的)由 un-和 gentlemanly 组成，把粘附形式加在开头，但 gentlemanly 是由 gentleman 和-ly 组成的，把粘附形式加在末尾。

13.4 作为比较简单的词法配列的例子，我们可以把出现在英语复数名词[glass-es(玻璃杯)]和过去时动词(land-ed 登陆了)中的次要派生结构拿来加以阐述。

就选择而论，粘附形式在两种情况下都是独特的，但基础形式属于两个大的形类：复数名词是由单数名词派生而来的(如 glasses 来自 glass)，而过去时动词是由不定式动词派生而来的(如 landed 来自 land)。其它一些附属的选择法位留在以后再讨论。

就次序而论，粘附形式在上两种情况下都是在基础形式以后讲出来的。

按照几乎所有的英语形态结构所共有的重音变易特征来讲，基础形式保留它的重音，而粘附形式没有重音。

变音法位更为繁复些，我们将看到由此而产生的一些特点出现在许多语言的形态里。

首先，一个粘附形式出现了几个交替形式（alternants）这样的例子是几个不同的词形意味着变音特征：

glass（单数）：glasses [-iz]（复数）

pen（单数）：pens [-z]（复数）

book（单数）：books [-s]（复数）

如果我们把这些例子集中起来看，我们立刻就会发觉：粘附形式的形状是由伴随形式的最后一个音位规定的：[-iz]出现在嘶擦音（sibilants）和塞擦音后面[glasses，roses（玫瑰花），dishes（盘子），garages（汽车库），churches（教堂），bridges（桥）]；[-z]出现在所有其它的浊音音位后面（saws（锯子），boys，ribs（肋骨），sleeves（袖子），pens，hills（小山），cars（车））；[-s]出现在所有其它的清音位后面[books，cliffs（悬崖）]。既然这三个交替形式[-iz, -z, -s]之间的区别能根据语音变换来描写，我们就可说它们是语音交替形式（phonetic alternants）。既然这三个交替形式的分布是依照伴随形式在语言上可以认出的特征而规定的，我们就可说这种交替是规则的。最后，既然伴随形式的决定特征是音位性的（即最后一个音位的识别），我们就可说这种交替是自动的。

规则的交替在大多数语言的形态中占有很重要的地位。不是所有的规则交替都是语音的或自动的。比方，在德语里，单数名词根据某些句法特征分成三种通常称为性属的形类（§12.7）；那么，德语的复数名词就是利用附加一些粘附形式的方法从单数形式派生而来的，这些粘附形式是依基础单数形式的性而各有不同：

阳性名词加[-e]，带有某些元音变化：der Hut [hu:t]"帽子（单数）"：Hüte ['hy:te]"帽子（复数）"；der Sohn [zo:n]"儿子（单数）"：Söhne ['zɸ:ne]"儿子（复数）"；der Baum [bawm]"树（单数）"：Bäume [bojme]"树（复数）"。

中性名词加[-e]，不带有元音变化：das Jahr [ja:r]"年（单数）"：Jahre

['jaːre]"年（复数）"；das Boot [boːt]"船（单数）"：Boote ['boːte]"船（复数）"；das Tier [tiːr]"动物（单数）"：Tiere [tiːre]"动物（复数）"。

阴性名词加[-en]：die Uhr [uːr]"钟、表（单数）"：Uhren ['uːr-en]"钟、表（复数）"；die Last [last]"负担（单数）"：Lasten ['lasten]"负担（复数）"；die Frau [fraw]"女人（单数）"：Frauen ['frawen]"女人（复数）"。

这种交替（除了那些我们不需要考虑的特殊的特征以外）是规则的，但它不是语音性的，因为在带有元音变化的[-e]、[-e]和[-en]这三个交替形式中，最后的一个跟头两个在该语言的系统中没有语音上的联系；因此这种交替不是自动的，而是语法的(grammatical)，因为它不是因基础形式的语音特征而是因基础形式的语法（在这个例子上，即句法）特征而定的。

第十四章 形态类型

14.1 根据组成成分的性质可以区分三种形态结构类型——即复合结构、次要派生结构和主要派生结构（§13.3）——其中以复合词的结构最像句法结构。

复合词在其直接成分中有两个（或两个以上）自由形式(door-knob'门上捏手')。依据直接成分的原则，各种语言通常能把复合词跟短语派生词[如old-maidish(老处女似的)，含有基础短语 old maid(老处女)的次要派生词]和再复合词[如 gentlemanly(绅士风的)含有基础复合词 gentleman(绅士)的次要派生词]区别开来。在复合词的范围内，上述原则通常包含一定的结构次序；比方说，复合词 wild-animal-house(野兽房)不是由 wild，animal 和 house 三个成员，也不是由 wild 和 animal-house 两个成员组成的，而是由 wild animal(一个短语)和 house 这两个成员组成的；同样，复合词 doorknob-wiper（门上捏手揩布）明显地是由 doorknob 和 wiper 这两个成员组成的，而不是——比方说——由 door 和 knob-wiper 组成的。

那些导致我们认识复合词的语法特征，在不同的语言是有所不同的，有些语言毫无疑义地是没有这一类的形式的。在词和短语之间可以分成很多层次；却往往不能定出严格的区别。那些被我们归入复合词的形式，具有某些在该语言中表明是单词而异于短语的特征。

在意义上，复合词通常比短语更有所特指；例如，blackbird 指的是一种特殊的鸟，它比指同一颜色的鸟所用的短语 black bird(黑色的鸟)较为特殊。试图利用这种差别作为区分的标准是一个非常普通的错误。我们不能十分精确地给意义作出归纳；再者，许多短语在意义上跟任何复合词一样特殊化；在短语 a queer bird"一个怪癖的人"和 meat and drink"酒食"中，bird 和 meat 这些词完全跟它们在复合词 jailbird（囚徒）和 sweetmeats（糖果）中一样特殊化了。

吕叔湘(1979)《汉语语法分析问题》选读①

◆ 作者简介

吕叔湘②(1904—1998)，江苏省丹阳市人。1926 年他毕业于国立东南大学（现南京大学）外国语文系；1936 年赴英国留学，先后在牛津大学人类学系、伦敦大学图书馆学科学习；1938 年回国后任云南大学文史系副教授，后又任华西协和大学中国文化研究所研究员、金陵大学中国文化研究所研究员兼中央大学中文系教授以及开明书店编辑等职；解放后，1952 年起任中国科学院语言研究所（1977 年起改属中国社会科学院）研究员、中国科学院哲学社会科学学部委员、语言研究所副所长、所长、名誉所长。吕叔湘先生是近代汉语学的拓荒者和奠基人。

◆ 正文节选

二 单位

8 对语言进行语法分析，就是分析各种语言片段的结构。要分析一个语言片段的结构，必须先把它分解成多少个较小的片段，这些小片段又可以分解成更小的片段。结构就是由较小的片段组合成较大的片段的方式。所以，要做语法结构的分析，首先得确定一些大、中、小的单位，例如"句子"、"短语"、"词"。

---

① 吕叔湘，《汉语语法分析问题》，商务印书馆 1979 年版。
② 图片来源：https://en.wikipedia.org/wiki/Lü__Shuxiang。

中国的传统的用语是"字"和"句"。再上去就"章"和"篇",按照现代的学科分工,已经不在语法论述的范围之内了。传统的"字",既指书面上的一个个方块字,也指说话里边的一个个音节,不管它在多大程度上独立地起表达作用。传统的"句"指说话和读书的时候两个停顿之间的一个片段,不管意义上是否告一段落。用传统的"字"和"句"来分析古汉语的语法结构,也许还可以试试,用来分析现代汉语,显然行不通了。现在用"词"和"句子"来代替"字"和"句","词"比"字"大,"句子"比"句"大。多少跟"字"相当的单位,现在管它叫"语素";多少跟"句"相当的单位,有的管它叫"小句"(分句),有的管它叫"短语"(词组)。讲西方语言的语法,词和句子是主要的单位,语素、短语、小句是次要的。(这是就传统语法说,结构主义语法里边语素的地位比词重要。)讲汉语的语法,由于历史的原因,语素和短语的重要性不亚于词,小句的重要性不亚于句子。

9 语素。最小的语法单位是语素,语素可以定义为"最小的语音语义结合体"。也可以拿"词素"作最小的单位,只包括不能单独成为词的语素。比较起来,用语素好些,因为语素的划分可以先于词的划分,词素的划分必得后于词的划分,而汉语的词的划分是问题比较多的。(这里说的"先"和"后"指逻辑上的先后,不是历史上的先后。)语素有三方面的问题:大小问题,异同问题,以及与汉字对应的问题。

10 汉语的语素,单音节的多,也有双音节的,如疙瘩、逍遥,还有三个音节以上的,如巧克力、奥林匹克,都是译音。有很多双音节,里边是两个语素还是一个语素可以讨论,例如含胡(比较含混、胡涂),什么(比较这么,那么,怎)。这是语素大小问题。

11 一个语素可以有几个意思,只要这几个意思联得上,仍然是一个语素,例如工有工作、技术、精巧等意思,都联得上,只是一个语素。如果几个意思联不上,就得算两个语素。例如公有共同、公平等意思,又有公[侯]、公[婆]、公的[母的]等意思,这两组意思联不上,得算两个语素。有时候,几个意思联得上联不上难于决定,例如快速、锐利的快和愉快、痛快的快。这是语素异同问题。

这两个问题都可以说是"一个还是两个?"的问题,不过前一个是一根绳子切不切成两段的问题,后一个是一根绳子掰不掰成两股的问题。

12 辨认语素跟读没读过古书有关系。读过点古书的人在大小问题上倾向于小,在异同问题上倾向于同。大小问题如<u>经济</u>,一般人觉得它跟<u>逻辑</u>一样,不能分析,读过古书的人就说这是"经世济民"的意思,经和济可以分开讲,是两个语素。异同问题如书信的<u>信</u>和信用、信任的<u>信</u>,一般人觉得联不上,念过古书的人知道可以通过信使的<u>信</u>(古时候可以单用)把前面说的两种意思联起来,认为<u>信</u>只是一个语素。

13　语素和汉字。汉语的语素和汉字,多数是一对一的关系,但是也有别种情况。语音、语义、字形这三样的异同互相搭配,共有八种可能:两同一异的有三种,一同两异的有三种,全同的和全异的各一种。

(音)	(义)	(形)	(例)	(语素)	(字)
同	同	同	圆	1	1
同	同	异	園、园	1	1(异体字)
同	异	同	会_合 会_能	2	1(多义字)
异	同	同	妨 fāng～fáng	1	1(多音字)
异	异	同	行 xíng～háng	2	1(多音多义)
异	同	异	行、走	2	2(同义字)
同	异	异	圆、園	2	2(同音字)
异	异	异	圆、方	2	2

以上所说三个问题的情况,都是在一定程度上简单化了的。实际情况比这复杂,疑难问题是不少的。

14　关于语素,还有一个问题。有时候一个语素可以用于两个词类,意思密切相关,例如<u>一把锁</u>和<u>锁上门</u>的<u>锁</u>,<u>一个姓</u>和<u>他姓姚</u>的<u>姓</u>。是一个语素、一个词呢,还是两个语素、两个词? 一般认为词类不同就得算两个词,可是基本意义不变只是一个语素,这样就该作为一个语素、两个词。如果可以这样处理,那么像把门的<u>把</u>,<u>把门锁上</u>的<u>把</u>,<u>一把锁</u>的<u>把</u>,就是一个语素三个词了。

15　词。比语素高一级的单位是词。词的定义很难下,一般说它是"最小的自由活动的语言片段",这仍然不十分明确,因为什么算是"自由活动"还有待于说明。最好是用具体事例来给词划界。词在两头都有划界问题:一头是如何区别单独成词的语素和单独不成词的语素;另一头是如何决定什么样的语素组合只是一个词,什么样的语素组合构成一个短语。

先说第一个问题,即一个语素成词不成词的问题。第一条,可单独作为一句话来说的,比如可以回答问话的,是不成问题的词。第二条,一句话里边把所有可以单说的部分都提开,剩下来不能单说,可也不是一个词的一部分的,也是词。例如<u>我下午再来</u>这句话里边,把<u>我</u>,<u>下午</u>,<u>来</u>提开,剩下<u>再</u>是一个词,虽然它不能单说。可是如果在<u>比赛现在开始</u>这句话里边,把<u>比赛</u>,<u>现在</u>提开之后,又把<u>开</u>提开,说<u>始</u>是剩余下来的词,那就不对,因为<u>始</u>是<u>开始</u>这个词的一部分。上面定义里边说的"自由活动",不但包括<u>来</u>这一类语素,也包括<u>再</u>这一类语素,但是不包括<u>始</u>这一类语素。

大概说来,能单说的多数是实词,少数是虚词;大多数虚词是靠第二条划出来的,少数实词也靠这一条。

16 以上有意把问题说得简单些,借以突出要点。实际情况比这复杂,下面是几种值得研究的情况。

(1) 一般不单用,但在一定的格式里可以单用('单用'包括<u>来</u>等和<u>再</u>等两类)。

楼:楼房,大楼,前楼,后楼(一般);但三号楼。

院:医院,剧院,研究院(一般);但院领导,院一级。

(2) 一般不单用,但在专科文献里可以单用。

氧气(一般);氧(化学)。

叶子,树叶(一般);叶(植物学)。

(3) 一般不单用,成语、熟语里可以单用。

老虎(一般);前怕狼,后怕虎(成语)。

言语(一般);你一言,我一语(熟语)。

(4) 说话不单用,文章里可以单用。

云彩(说话);云(文章)。

时候(说话);时(文章)。

像这些情况该怎么处理?按说,能单用的语素不一定只能单用,有时候也跟别的语素组合成词,比如<u>来</u>也出现在<u>来源</u>,<u>来宾</u>,<u>将来</u>,<u>往来</u>这些词里,<u>再</u>也出现在<u>一再</u>,<u>再三</u>,<u>再会</u>,<u>再版</u>这些词里。能不能援这个例,无条件地承认<u>楼</u>,

叶,虎等等也是能单用的语素,是一般的词呢?要是这样,就抹杀了一个重要的事实:这些语素在一般场合是不能单用的。

17　一个语素可以有互相联系的好几个意义,其中有的能单用,有的不能单用。例如工,在工人,工艺,工业这些意义上是不能单用的,在工作(如上工),工程(如开工),计工单位(如三工)这些意义上是可以单用的。遇到这种情形,如果受汉字的拘束,就要在工字是词不是词上头决断不下。可不可以说:工这个语素有两个变体(似乎不必作为两个语素),一个能单用,是词,一个不能单用,是构词的语素?

18　总起来说,语素可以分成四种。(1) 能单用的,单用的时候是词,不单用的时候是构词成分。(2) 一般不单用,在特殊条件下单用的,单用的时候是词。(3) 不单用,但是活动能力较强,结合面较宽,有单向性,即只位于别的语素之前,或别的语素之后,或两个语素之间。这是所谓"前缀","后缀","中缀",可以总的称为"词缀"或"语缀"。"语缀"这个名称也许较好,因为其中有几个不限于构词,也可以加在短语的前边(如第)或后边(如的)。语缀和词的界限也难划,例如单音方位词和某些量词就很像后缀。(4) 不单用,结合面较窄,但不限于在前或在后,专作构词成分,可以称为"词根"。

19　词和短语。现在来讨论第二个问题,一个语素组合是词还是短语的问题。前面谈一个语素是词不是词的问题,要考虑的只有一个因素:能不能单用。语素组合的问题就复杂了,大致涉及五个因素:第一,这个组合能不能单用,这个组合的成分能不能单用;第二,这个组合能不能拆开,也就是这个组合的成分能不能变换位置或者让别的语素隔开;第三,这个组合的成分能不能扩展;第四,这个组合的意义是不是等于它的成分的意义的总和;第五,这个组合包含多少个语素,也就是它有多长。这个因素不是互不相关,可是不相一致,常常有矛盾,问题讨论起来够复杂的。这里不能详细讨论,只能提出几个问题来谈谈。

20　先说一个组合的成分能不能单用的问题。除了所有的成分都不能单用就不可能是短语外,似乎成分的能不能单用跟整体的能不能单用、是词还是短语,没有一定的关系。看下面的例子:

单用＋单用	→短语	工人农民	
	→词	田地	
	→不单用	高射	
单用＋不单用	→短语	老师同学们	
	→词	高速	
不单用＋不单用	→词	典型	
	→不单用	微型	

单纯用有没有不单用的成分来决定一个组合是词还是短语，显然行不通。有一个过去常引用的例子，说是如果因为驼和鸭不能单用，所以驼毛和鸭蛋是词，因为羊和鸡可以单用，所以羊毛和鸡蛋是短语，那是非常可笑的。应该认为羊毛和鸡蛋也是词。

再说，如果一个组合里有一个不单用的成分就认为这个组合是词，那么，一个带语助词的句子就也得算是一个词，因为语助词是绝对不能单用的。能有那么长的词吗？

21　其次，整个组合如果能单用就是词(或短语)，如果不能单用就不是词而只是构词的成分，这样规定看上去是合理的。可是遇到一个问题：比如说高射不是词，高射炮才是一个词，孤立起来看这个例子，说得通，但是高射机关枪呢？就有点为难了。高射不能单说，这是事实，能不能算是可以单用呢？值得考虑。有很多语素组合是属于高射一类的，这一类组合又常常跟别的组合(不能单用的和能单用的)连成很长一串，例如袖珍英汉词典，大型彩色纪录片，同步稳相回旋加速器，多弹头分导重入大气层运载工具，等等。说这些都只是一个词，行吗？从语法理论这方面讲，没什么不可以，但是一般人不会同意。一般人心目中的词是不太长不太复杂的语音语义单位，大致跟词典里的词目差不多。这可以叫做"词汇的词"，以区别于"语法的词"。咱们不能忘了，词这个东西，不光是语法单位，也是词汇单位。二者有时候一致，有时候不一致，因为所用标准不同。袖珍、英汉、大型、彩色、同步、稳相、多弹头，这些都可以算是词汇词。语法上是不是也可以承认它们是词呢？要找根据也不难，语助词不都是不能单说的吗？还有介词、多数连词和多数副词，也都是不能单说的。

上面举的是名词的前加成分的例子，同样的情况也见于动词的前加成分,如<u>超额</u>完成,<u>加倍</u>努力,<u>按劳</u>分配,<u>准时</u>到达,<u>定期</u>汇报,<u>高价</u>收购。这里边的<u>超额</u>,<u>加倍</u>,<u>按劳</u>,<u>准时</u>,<u>定期</u>,<u>高价</u>,也都是不能单说的,但是如果不承认它们可以单用,因而可以算是词,就不好办。

22 从词汇的角度看,双语素的组合多半可以算一个词,即使两个成分都可以单说,如<u>电灯</u>,<u>黄豆</u>。四个语素的组合多半可以算两个词,即使其中有一个不能单说,如<u>无轨电车</u>,<u>社办工厂</u>。三个语素的组合也是多数以作为一个词较好。例如<u>人造丝</u>可以向<u>人造纤维</u>看齐,作为两个词,但是<u>人造革</u>只能作为一个词,与其把<u>人造丝</u>和<u>人造革</u>作不同处理(类似鸡蛋和鸭蛋问题),不如让<u>人造丝</u>和<u>人造纤维</u>有所不同。同类的例子有<u>耐火—材料</u>:<u>耐火砖</u>|<u>生物—制品</u>:<u>豆制品</u>|<u>高压—电线</u>:<u>高压线</u>|<u>自由—体操</u>:<u>自由泳</u>。不妨说,拿到一个双语素的组合,比较省事的办法是暂时不寻找有无作为一个词的特点,而是先假定它是词,然后看是否有别的理由该认为是短语。同样,拿到一个四语素的组合,可以先假定它是两个词,然后看是否有别的理由该认为是一个词。在这里,语素组合的长短这个因素起了很大的作用。

23 现在来谈谈有没有专门意义的问题。向来有一种意见,认为如果一个组合的意义等于它的成分的意义的总和,那么这个组合是一个短语;如果不是这样,这个组合就是一个词。同一个<u>吃饭</u>,如果吃的是米饭,吃饭是短语;如果吃的是馒头或者面条,<u>吃饭</u>是"进餐"的意思,那就是一个词。又如<u>大车</u>是个词,因为不是所有大的车都能叫做<u>大车</u>,只有牲口拉的两个车轮的载重车才叫大车;相反,<u>大树</u>是个短语,因为意思就是大的树。这个意见也是从词汇的角度考虑的结果。有专门意义的组合是一个新的词汇单位,没有专门意义的组合没有增加新的东西。从语法的角度看,有没有专门意义只有参考价值,没有决定作用。拿吃饭来说,只是<u>饭</u>的意义不同,吃和<u>饭</u>的关系没有什么不同,一切语法格式变化,如吃着饭,<u>饭</u>不吃了等等,对两种意义的吃饭都适用,没什么两样。同样,大树和大车在语法上也难于分别。

24 <u>大树</u>和<u>大车</u>都是形容词加名词。我们知道,形名组合不是很自由的,特别是单音形容词。例如我们说<u>高山</u>,不说<u>高树</u>,说<u>错字</u>,不说<u>错数目</u>,说<u>脏衣服</u>,不说<u>脏鞋</u>,说<u>闲工夫</u>,不说<u>闲日子</u>,不说<u>巧手</u>,不说<u>笨手</u>,说<u>热炕头</u>,不说<u>冷炕头</u>,等等。组合不自由,就是有熟语性,这是复合词的特点。短语的组成,原则上应该是自由的,应该是除意义之外没有任何限制的。

朱德熙(1984)《关于向心结构的定义》选读[1]

◆ 作者简介

朱德熙[2](1920—1992),苏州人,著名语言学家、教育家。1939年考取昆明西南联大物理系,第二年转入中文系学习,并受到罗常培、唐兰、陈梦家等先生的教导和赏识。1945年毕业后曾在昆明中法大学、清华大学、北京大学任教。朱先生以其精湛的汉语语法和古文字方面的研究成果而蜚声于国内外的汉语语言学界,先后赴保加利亚、美国、法国、泰国、香港、新加坡、澳大利亚等地区讲学,并培养了一大批汉语语言学的人才,为我国的语言研究和教育事业做出了卓越的贡献。

◆ 正文节选

§1 布龙姆菲尔德[3](L. Bloomfield)把句法结构分为两类,至少有一个直接成分跟整体的语法功能相同的结构叫向心结构(endocentric construction)向心结构里跟整体功能相同的直接成分叫做这个向心结构的核心(head)。所有的直接成分都跟整体的语法功能不同的结构叫离心结构(exocentric construction)。例如汉语的偏正结构(包括定语加中心语的名词性偏正结构和状语加中心语的谓词性偏正结构)的语法功能跟它的后一个直接成分(中心语)相同,述宾结构的语法功能和它的前一个直接成分(述语)相同,因此都是向心结构。所有由虚词组成的句法结构如介词结构、"的"字结构的语法功能和它的两个直接成分都不一样,所以是离心结构。联合结构的语法功能跟它的每一项直接成分都相同,是一种多核心的向心结构,布龙姆菲尔德管它叫并列式向心结构(coordinative endocentric construction)。

§2 布龙姆菲尔德关于向心结构的定义是有毛病的。譬如汉语里 NN(木头房子)一类格式本身是名词性结构,两个直接成分也都是名词。按照布

---

① 朱德熙,1984,《关于向心结构的定义》,《中国语文》第6期。
② 图片来源:https://en.wikipedia.org/wiki/Zhu_Dexi。
③ 布龙姆菲尔德(L.Bloomfield),美国著名语言学家,现多译为"布龙菲尔德",后文不再一一说明。——编者注

龙姆菲尔德的定义,应该说有两个核心。这显然不合理。因为我们凭直觉就知道"木头房子"跟"新房子"一样,只有一个核心——"房子"。"木头"虽然跟"木头房子"语法功能相同,它并不是这个向心结构真正的核心。所以会产生这样的矛盾,是因为布龙姆菲尔德完全根据语法功能给"核心"下定义,实际上"核心"这个概念跟语义密切相关。完全撇开语义,就无法把"核心""向心结构""离心结构"等等概念说清楚。曾经有人修正布龙姆菲尔德的说法,提出向心结构和它的核心的关系是"在语法上等价"(grammatically equivalent),至少接近于等价;可是并没有说明所谓语法上等价的准确的含义是什么。在我们看来,所谓等价不能仅仅指语法功能相同。它要比语法功能相同多出一点东西,这多出来的东西就是语义。因此光从字面上说,"语法上等价"的"语法上"三个字就不够妥当。可是我们也不能把"语法上"改成"语义上",因为"白马非马","木头房子"和"房子"语义上也并不等价。

§3 我们认为,向心结构和它的核心的关系包括语法和语义两方面。从语法上说,功能相同;从语义上说,受到相同的语义选择限制(semantic selection restriction)。所谓语义选择限制就是语义上的搭配关系。举例来说,"木头房子"里的"房子"是核心,"木头"不是。这是因为"房子"和"木头房子"受到的语义选择限制相同,而"木头"和"木头房子"受到的语义选择限制不同。比较:

住木头房子	住房子	住木头
木头房子盖好了	房子盖好了	木头盖好了
一所木头房子	一所房子	一所木头
*锯木头房子	*锯房子	锯木头
*木头房子的纹理	*房子的纹理	木头的纹理
*一块木头房子	*一块房子	一块木头

§4 "木头的房子"(N的N)跟"木头房子"(NN)不同。"木头房子"只有一个核心"房子";"木头的房子"有两个核心,一个是"房子",另一个是"木头的"。我们说"木头的房子"里的"木头的"也是一个核心,因为"木头的"不但跟"木头的房子"语法功能相同,而且受到的语义选择限制也一样。例如:

住木头的房子　　　　　　住木头的
木头的房子盖好了　　　　木头的盖好了
一所木头的房子　　　　　一所木头的

根据上文所说，我们可以把向心结构的定义修正如下：

向心结构指的是至少有一个直接成分与整体在语法上功能相同、在语义上受到相同的语义选择限制的句法结构。向心结构中与整体功能相同并且受到相同的语义选择限制的直接成分是它的核心。

§5　上文指出"N的N"是包含两个核心的向心结构。其实不仅是"N的N"，所有由"的"字结构和量词组合充任定语的向心结构都包含两个核心。例如：

A的N：
住新的房子　　　　　　　住新的
新的房子盖好了　　　　　新的盖好了
一所新的房子　　　　　　一所新的
V的N：
住刚盖好的房子　　　　　住刚盖好的
刚盖好的房子就塌了　　　刚盖好的就塌了
一所刚盖好的房子　　　　一所刚盖好的
QN：
住那所房子　　　　　　　住那所
那所房子盖好了　　　　　那所盖好了

我们把以上讨论到的几类格式统称为同位性向心结构。

"美国首都华盛顿"也是包含两个核心的同位性向心结构。这类格式的特点是由整个向心结构造成的判断和由它的两个核心造成的判断的真值（truth value）相同。例如"白宫在美国首都华盛顿"是真的，那末"白宫在美国首都"和"白宫在华盛顿"两个命题也是真的。为了跟一般的同位性向心结构区别,这类格式可以称为同一性向心结构。

"黄河长江"也是包含两个核心的向心结构,布龙姆菲尔德称之为并列式向心结构。它跟上文说的同位性向心结构有两点区别。第一,这类格式可以扩展成包含任意个核心的向心结构。例如:

黄河长江($n=2$)→ 黄河长江珠江($n=3$)→ 黄河长江珠江鸭绿江($n=4$)……

第二,这类格式可以插入连词而不改变其基本结构。例如:

黄河长江→黄河和长江　　黄河长江珠江→黄河、长江和珠江

§6　现在我们来讨论由动词(指广义的动词,包括形容词在内)充任中心语的名词性偏正结构。例如:

技术的进步(N 的 V)非常快。
他的死(N 的 V)很悲惨。
这种谦虚(QV)是假的。

这类格式本身是名词性的,中心语是动词,语法功能不同。按照布龙姆菲尔德的定义,这里的动词中心语不是核心,真正的核心应该是前边充任修饰语的"的"字结构(N 的)和量词组合(Q)。采取这种看法,那么"N 的 V"和"QV"都是核心在前的单核心向心结构,跟双核心向心结构"N 的 N"和"QN"构造很不相同。可是我们如果采用修正以后的关于核心的定义,那末"N 的 V"和"QV"也可以看成跟"N 的 N"和"QN"一样,都是双核心向心结构。因为这类格式的中心语虽然跟整体的语法功能不同,可是它们受到的语义选择限制却是相同的。比较:

技术的进步非常快　　　　进步快
他的死很悲惨　　　　　　死得很悲惨
这种谦虚是假的　　　　　假谦虚

严格说起来,"N 的 V"和"QV"并不符合上文给向心结构下的定义。因为这两类格式里的中心语与整体语法功能不同。此外,就"N 的 V"来说,修饰语"N 的"不能离开中心语独立。换言之,"N 的"不能指代"N 的 V"("木头的房子"可以光说"木头的","技术的进步"可不能光说"技术的"),因此也就谈不上修饰语和整体受到相同的语义选择限制。尽管如此,这两类格式跟"N 的 N"和"QN"仍有许多重要的共同点,可以看成是一种广义的同构。

Di Sciullo & Williams（1988）*On the Definition of Word* 选读[①]

◆ 作者简介

安娜·玛利亚·迪西洛（Anna Maria Di Sciullo）,1977 年在罗马大学取得学士学位,1975 年在蒙特利尔魁北克大学取得语言学硕士学位,1981 年在蒙特利尔大学获语言学博士学位,现为蒙特利尔魁北克大学语言学系教授。她的主要研究领域是理论语言学、计算语言学和生物语言学。

艾德温·威廉姆斯（Edwin S. Williams）,1970 年在普林斯顿大学获英语学士学位,1974 年在麻省理工学院师从乔姆斯基获博士学位,曾先后执教于马萨诸塞大学阿默斯特分校、普林斯顿大学。他的主要研究领域是句法学和形态学。

◆ 正文节选

The Notion "Word"

There are three different ideas of what a word is. Our purpose here is to sort them out, and in this introductory section we will do this in a preliminary way. The notion central to this text concerns the *form* of a certain set of objects; the definition of this set is the theory of morphological form. The theory defines the set by means of a set of atoms (morphemes) and rules of combination (affixing, compounding). We will call the members of this set

---

[①] Di Sciullo, A.-M. & E. Williams. 1988. *On the Definition of Word*. MA: The MIT Press.

morphological objects and assert that the central task of morphology is to determine the laws of form that determine membership in this set. Just as morphology has atoms, so does syntax, and words are commonly taken to be the atoms of syntax. We will call words in this sense *syntactic atoms*. This notion of word is conceptually and factually distinct from that of word as "morphological object". We will discuss an important class of items that are syntactic atoms (insertable in X^0 slots in syntactic structures) but that do not have morphological form (in fact they have syntactic form). Finally, the third notion of word we want to discuss is the one from which most confusion about words derives—the notion of words as the "listed" units of language. For this notion of word, which we believe to be of no interest to the grammarian (though perhaps it is to the psychologist), we coin the term *listeme*. We will show that the listemes of a language correspond to neither the morphological objects nor the syntactic atoms of a language.

Morphology and syntax are similar in that each has a set of atoms and some rules of combination. It is our thesis that the difference between these two subtheories is exactly a difference in the atoms and in the properties of the rules of formation. There are of course other imaginable ideas of what constitutes the difference between syntax and morphology. For example, one might conceive of morphology as a theory of the lexicon, an innocuous-sounding conception but one from which we feel flows a great deal of confusion. Another perhaps related idea of the difference is that syntax is a characterization of the "productive" aspects of language and morphology a characterization of the semi-or unproductive aspects. These views tend to equate *listeme* and *morphological object*. Under such a view, the following diagram characterizes the "ideal" language:

	Word	Phrase
Listed	yes	no
Unlisted	no	yes

Of course there are exceptions in every cell of this diagram. The question is, Are these exceptions deviations from an ideal, or is the ideal misconceived in the first place? A difficult question.

For example, there are vast veins of productive (and so we assume unlisted) morphology, such as the words ending in *-ness* in English. In addition, there are unproductive and therefore listed veins of idiomatic syntactic constructions, such as the verb-particle construction in English. In fact we can show that all cells in this diagram are substantially filled and should be marked "yes".

But our objection to the diagram is more fundamental than these factual observations would suggest. The diagram itself, however the cells are filled, is an artifact of the confusion we seek to address.

The distinction between word and phrase is a distinction in the theory of grammar. The listed/unlisted distinction has nothing to do with grammar. Syntax and morphology are both recursive definitions of sets of objects—but of different sets, with different atoms and different rules of combination. These are the only differences the grammarian need acknowledge.

The most immediate consequence of this view is that productivity and listedness are not grammatical concepts. We will explore this in chapter 1, where we will examine the property of "listedness". A second consequence is that the lexicalist hypothesis (which we call here the *thesis of the atomicity of words*) is not a principle of grammar but rather a consequence of the conception that grammar contains two subparts, with different atoms and different rules of formation. We will take this up in chapters 3 and 4, which concern the notion "syntactic atom". In chapter 2 we will present a substantive account of the laws and rules of word formation, which we take to constitute the notion "morphological object".

In sum, then, we postulate three empirically and conceptually distinct notions of word: listeme, syntactic atom, and morphological object. In fact, though, there is a fourth, which we will essentially ignore here: the notion of phonological word. We take it up briefly at the end of chapter 4 mainly to draw the contrast with the other senses of word.

Chapter 1 Listeme: The Property of Listedness

Knowledge of language involves in some way a knowledge of particular linguistic objects—for example, the word *transmission* and the knowledge that it (1) has a certain morphological form and (2) refers to a part of a car; that *take to task* has a certain syntactic form and means "rebuke". To the extent that an object does not have the form or interpretation specified by the recursive definitions of the objects of the language, that object and its properties must be "memorized". We have dubbed such memorized objects *listemes*, and this property of being memorized, *listedness*. Our overall point is that listedness is no more intrinsically characteristic of words than it is of phrases. Some words and some phrases are listed, but infinitely many of each are not.

If conceived of as the set of listemes, the lexicon, is incredibly boring by its very nature. It contains objects of no single specifiable type (words, VPs, morphemes, perhaps intonation patterns, and so on), and those objects that it does contain are there because they fail to conform to interesting laws. The lexicon is like a prison—it contains only the lawless, and the only thing that its inmates have in common is lawlessness.

This view of the lexicon is quite unfriendly to most current proposals, which by and large can be traced to the influential view of Jackendoff (1975). According to Jackendoff, all words of a language are listed in the lexicon, whether or not they conform completely to the laws of form and meaning for words. The rules of morphology are conceived of as redundancy rules, by means of which the "cost" of a lexical item is computed. Those that are totally predictable will have no cost.

We do not take issue with the view that the "cost" of a word is a function of its deviation from the rules of morphology. As noted, a structured item is easier to memorize than an unstructured one. But we do take issue with the idea that the rules of morphology are essentially redundancy rules over a finite set of objects in a way that syntactic rules are not. To us this makes no more sense than to say that VP → V NP is a redundancy rule over the set of VPs, most but of course not all of which have zero redundancy.

Jackendoff acknowledges that there are phrases in the lexicon (idioms) and that "possible words" that are not in the lexicon can be created and used, but these aberrations do not deter him from conceiving of the lexicon as a list of all the words of a language, and of the rules of morphology as a "theory" of that list.

A related view that we reject is the idea that "productivity" is characteristic of syntax and "unproductivity" is characteristic of morphology. Fabb (1984, 38), for example, explicitly considers this a criterial difference, and many others implicitly consider it as such. Selkirk (1981), for example, proposes that productive compounds are derived in syntax and unproductive or idiosyncratic ones are listed in the lexicon. In our view, to the extent that productivity is phenomenally perceived to distinguish syntax and morphology, this is something to explain, not something that follows from the intrinsic nature of these two systems, and the explanation is not all that interesting (see section 1.2.3).

Another related view that we reject is the idea that the lexicon has structure. As mentioned, it is simply a collection of the lawless, and there neither can nor should be a theory directly about it, for it can only be understood in terms of the laws it fails to obey. This is not to say that the space of words in a language is not structured—in fact the space of words has a rich structure, imposed first by the rules of word formation and second by the paradigmatic matrices that words enter into (see Williams 1981). But the lexicon contains only some of the words that enter into this structure (the ones that do it least well), and it contains much else besides. In sum we reject the idea that listedness is a grammatical property—the lexicon is a collection of semigrammatical objects, some of them words and others phrases. The set of listed items has no structure, and the property of being a member of this set is no more essential to the nature of words than it is to the nature of phrases.

Of course this is not to say that knowledge of the listed items of a language is not part of knowledge of that language. Rather, if we think of the rules of formation for words and phrases as defining the grammatical items of the language, then we might regard the lexicon as containing a finite list of some semigrammatical objects that are a part of the language.

In the next two sections we will explore somewhat the reasons for distinguishing the lexicon from the space of words of a language. We will concentrate on the two important types of case for which these two concepts fail to coincide: (1) the listed syntactic objects and (2) the unlisted (and unlistable) morphological objects.

1.1 Listed Syntactic Objects

The listed syntactic objects are the idioms. Although these are like some words in that their meanings cannot be compositionally computed, this very feature makes them unlike most words.

As far as we can see, there is nothing more to say about them than that (1) they are syntactic objects and (2) they are listed because of their failure to have a predictable property (usually their meaning).

It is not trivial to say that an item is a syntactic object: it means that the item is a syntactic unit of some kind—an NP, VP, and so on. It is certainly conceivable that some concatenation of words that was not a unit could be an idiom, or that some particular string of words, such as *park saw* in *The man in the park saw the woman*, could contribute an unpredictable element of meaning to a sentence, but idioms do not work like this—they are always units.

They do not always look like units. For example, the VP *take NP to task* looks like a discontinuous unit, wrapped around the object NP—in fact it has been proposed (by Emonds (1969) for one) that *take to task* is a complex V and not a VP at all (with *to task* extraposed by a rule).

This description, which would enormously complicate the morphological notion "verb", is not forced on us, because we can assign the idiom the following structure:

(1)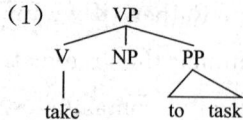

This idiom contains an unfilled position, the NP object; nevertheless, it is formally a VP and functions as one when inserted for the node VP in a sentence.

There are many such VPs in English (*take in hand*, *push too far*), all of whose properties follow if they are viewed simply as listed VPs. There are probably as many such VPs as there are noncompositional words ending in-*ion*, so this should not be viewed as a minor appendix to the dictionary.

Another set of such VPs in English consists of verb-particle constructions (*look up*, *throw up*, and so on), which are listed VPs consisting of a V, a particle, and an (optional) open NP position. We will discuss this system shortly.

The discontinuity these VPs exhibit follows from allowing one free open position. This need not be in the object position—it can be inside the direct object position (for example, *bite NP's head off*). In general it can probably be anywhere.

French exhibits a more interesting discontinuity—idioms that include clitics such as *en* (see Di Sciullo 1983):

(2) [en mettre plein la vue]_{VP}
'to impress greatly'
[en voir de toutes les couleurs]_{VP}
'to have a hard time'

These clitics can wind up in S-Structure separated from the rest of the idiom, as in the following examples:

(3) Jean en voit de toutes les couleurs
Jean en a vu de toutes les couleurs
Jean en fait voir de toutes les couleurs

The separation is exactly what one would expect if the VPs in (2) were inserted for VP nodes in S and cliticization were then to apply. Incidentally, these apparently provide strong evidence for a cliticization rule—the clitic attaches to the first finite verb, whether or not it is part of the idiom. Again, the discontinuity is no obstacle to calling these syntactic units, specifically, VPs.

Calling idioms listed syntactic units means not only that they will be units in the first place but also that they will have the internal structure of other syntactic units in the language and will behave as other units do in syntax; and, as is clear from these examples, this is the case.

We are further led by this view to expect to find listed syntactic units of all kinds—NP, AP, PP, VP, S—and we do:

(4) AP   all wet
PP   in the dark about NP
S   the cat has got NP's tongue
N'   that son of a bitch
NP   The Big Apple

The great wealth of such expressions in languages substantiates half of the view that there is nothing special about listed words. In fact there are listemes among all the syntactic categories, perhaps as many as there are words. Further, these listemes have quite regular internal syntax, syntax of the kind given by phrasal syntax, not by morphology.

1.2 Unlisted Morphological Objects

The second part of our argument that there is no correspondence between listedness and morphological objecthood is the demonstration that there are unlisted morphological objects. Actually this is quite widely recognized; all theories of morphology acknowledge, for example, the ability of speakers to make up new words. Thus Halle (1973) cites the series of words *anti-missile missile*, *anti-anti-missile missile missile*, and so on—an infinite series of words, each with a determinate meaning different from that of all the others.

Most views, though, attach grammatical significance to the use of a new word—when a speaker makes up a new word, he changes his grammar by adding the word to his lexicon, even if the word's form and meaning are completely determined by regular rule (see, for example, Jackendoff 1975). But in our view the listedness of a regular form is of no grammatical significance, and whether or not it is listed will vary from speaker to speaker, determined by such factors as its frequency of use in the speaker's daily life.

Most views of morphology distinguish it from syntax in some way that has to do with productivity: use of a new (but regular) syntactic phrase does not result in that phrase being listed in the dictionary, but the use of a new word will. This, so the story goes, is because syntax is inherently productive, whereas morphology is inherently nonproductive or only marginally or spottily productive. This difference is related to a second difference: "blocking" of one form by another (in the sense of Aronoff 1976) only obtains among morphological objects, not among syntactic objects.

In the next two sections we will argue that neither of these distinctions between syntax and morphology is real—that both systems are productive in the same way and that blocking, to the extent that it holds at all, holds in both systems and in fact holds across both systems.

1.2.1 Productivity

It is often noted (and great consequence is attached to it) that *-ness* is more productive than *-ion*. Thus practically any adjective can have *-ness* attached, but only a few select verbs have nominalizations in *-ion* (*breakion*, *cution*, *bition*, *killion*). These two affixes are said to differ in productivity. We might imagine assigning a productivity index to each affix, where we arrive at the index by dividing the number of forms that the affix actually attaches to by the total number of items belonging to the part of speech (C) that the item attaches to:

$$(5) \quad P_{af} = \frac{size(X\text{-}af)}{size(C)}$$

But as Aronoff (1976) understood, the productivity of an affix is not uniform across an entire part of speech; *-ion*, for example, is highly productive (in fact P = 1) for verbs of the form X-*ate* (*emancipate*, *calibrate*). This provokes us to ask, Why compute productivity over a part of speech? Why not a smaller domain (verbs ending in *-ate*) or a larger *domain* (the entire lexicon)? Is there any answer to this that is not arbitrary?

Suppose that we compute productivity within the contextual restrictions of the affix itself. Thus *-ness* is restricted to As, so the productivity is computed with respect to size (A). But *-ion* is restricted to the Latinate subvocabulary in English. In that subvocabulary *-ion* is extremely productive; perhaps P = 1.

It may be objected that this computation of P_{-ion} is artificial because the only way to identify the Latinate subvocabulary is to see what *-ion* attaches to in the first place. But in this case the charge is not true; there are other ways to identify the subvocabulary. For example, consider the class of words that *-ive* attaches to. The affix *-ion* is 100 percent productive across that independently identified class. Actually the Latinate vocabulary is a closed class to start with, but *-ion* is extremely productive within that class, just as *-ness* is productive across its class (the class of all As). The only difference between *-ion* and *-ness* is that *-ness* is initially defined for a larger class.

In fact *-ion* is productive in the most basic sense of the word—it can be used to make up new words. Of course the base word must be of the right type, which happens to be a relatively closed class to begin with, so most of the possible -*ion* attachments already "exist." But if one encounters a new verb ending in -*ate* (say, *lucubrate*), one does not have to guess, one knows, that a word can be derived from it by adding -*ion* (*lucubration*).

It may seem that we want to regard -*ion* as productive. But productive compared to what? Compared to the class of words it is defined to attach to. But this class is defined in terms of a nonuniversal rule feature, the feature + Latinate. If productivity can be defined with respect to such features, can any affix be less than 100 percent productive? The answer is not obvious.

We have so far drawn into question any firm conclusions based on differences in productivity among rules of morphology. What about differences in productivity between morphology and syntax? To illuminate this discussion, we will examine two subsystems of English verbs.

One subsystem is the Latinate subsystem, consisting of Latinate prefixes (*de-*, *in-*, *re-*, *sub-*, and so on) and stems (-*duct*, -*ject*, -*fer*, -*sist*); our discussion is based on Aronoff 1976:

	-ject	-sist	-fer	-duct
de-	*	*	*	*
in-	*	*	*	*
re-	*	*	*	—
sub-	*	*	—	*

As the chart reveals, this space of words is quite dense, at least for this (carefully chosen) sample. Does this mean that this morphology is productive? It is difficult to say, for two reasons. First, there are a finite number of Latinate prefixes and stems, so there are only so many possible forms of this kind, and most of them exist. Second, because there is no productive semantics for the class of forms, they must all be listed in any case. A good example is *subduct*—this word was probably invented in the service of the new theory of plate tectonics, and its meaning is technical and was invented simultaneously (similar to *subjacency* in linguistics).

We are not as interested in determining whether this system is productive as we are in comparing it with another system in English, the verb-particle system (*look up*) mentioned in section 1.1. This system is undoubtedly phrasal—a VP, with the head verb on the left: the left element takes inflection (*looks up*); the right element can be modified by adverbs (*look right up*); syntactic elements can intervene (*look it up*); and so on. Consider the following array:

	give	throw	stand	look	call
up	*	*	*	*	*
down	—	•	•	•	*
in	*	•	*	*	*
out	*	*	*	*	*

Consider the similarities between this chart and the one of Latinate verbs. Again the space is dense—every form for these verbs and particles exists but one. Again there is no rule for giving the meaning of most of the forms (" * " designates noncompositional forms and "." compositional forms). And again the particles seem to be restricted to a subvocabulary—a particle with a Latinate verb is uncommon (* *donate up*).

There seems to be no essential difference between the Latinate prefix-stem system and the verb-particle system with respect to either productivity or compositionality. But one of these systems is lexical and the other syntactic; that is, one is a part of the definition of English word, and the other is a part of the definition of English phrase. This suggests that it would be wrong to consider productivity as a criterial difference between syntax and morphology. There are both productive and unproductive phrase types and word types.

Of course some theoreticians have considered the verb-particle system to be lexical, and then we can draw no such conclusions. However, the only reason to consider this system to be lexical is in fact the lack of productivity and compositionality just considered. The system interests us precisely because it is formally phrasal and at the same time unproductive, which can be denied only at great cost—a jerrymandered definition of "word."

Chapter 2 Morphological Objects: The Rules of of Word Formation
2.1 The Rules of Formation
2.1.1 Phrase Structure of Words and Heads of Words

The work mentioned above (especially Selkirk 1982) is based on the idea that word formation rules are phrase structure rules, that is, rules specifying the concatenation of formatives that compose various morphological classes of object. For example, we might have the following rules for English:

(1) a. stem→af stem
　　b. stem→stem af
　　c. word→af word
　　d. word→word af
　　e. word→stem
　　f. word→ word word

Although these rules can "eliminated" in favor of principles or slogans such as "Affix α," there is nevertheless sufficient variation in what veins of word formation various languages exploit to wonder whether there might not be some notion of "rule". For example, English has few compounds of the form V-N (*bartend* is one exception), whereas some languages, such as Algonquian and Iroquois, have completely general compounding of this type. Is this due to the presence in these languages (and the absence in English) of the rule V→N V? See Selkirk 1982 for a discussion of various gaps in the English word formation system.

The theories of Williams (1978a, 1981a) and Selkirk (1982) are based on the notion that words have heads, just as phrases in syntax do. The identifying feature of heads in both syntax and morphology is that the properties of the head are those of the whole; in general, there is complete agreement of features between the head and the whole.

In syntax the head of a phrase is identified as the item with one less bar level than the phrase (or simply as the lexical daughter of the phrase):

(2) $X^n \rightarrow ... YP ... X^{n-1} ... ZP ...$

The head in syntax can be identified by virtue of an intrinsic property— the number of bar levels. The head of a phrase is the only daughter of the phrase that is not a maximal projection.

In morphology, however, such an identification of the head is impossible; the daughters of a compound are not intrinsically distinct from one another:

(3)
```
        N
       / \
      N   N
      |   |
    light house
```

There is no way to know which is the head of this compound, because the two elements are both of the same level, namely, N.

Morphology avails itself of a different means of identifying the head of a word, a contextual means:

(4) The head of a word is the rightmost member of a word.

In compounds the role of the head is clear; it determines the category, plurality, and other general features of the word:

(5) $[\text{bar}_N \text{ tend}_V]_V$
$[\text{apple}_N \text{ pie}_N]_N$
$[\text{jet}_N \text{ black}_A]_A$
$[\text{parts}_{PL} \text{ supplier}_{SG}]$ (singular)
$[\text{part}_{SG} \text{ suppliers}_{PL}]$ (plural)

In each of these cases the rightmost element determines the category of the word, and in the last two cases this element also determines the plurality of the word.

The role of the head in compounding is the same as it is in syntax; in syntax the head determines the category and plurality of the phrase, among other things.

The notion of head and its identification as the rightmost element can be extended to words formed by affixation, as proposed by Williams (1978a). The affixation rules give us two structures, one for prefixes and one for suffixes:

(6)   word   word
      /   \   /   \
     af   word   word   af

The identification of head in morphology tells us that suffixes (but not prefixes) will be the heads of their words. This predicts that suffixes (but not prefixes) will determinethe category, plurality, and so on, of their words, a prediction documented by Williams (1978a, 1981a). For example, the suffix *-ion* always derives nouns, but the prefix *counter-* (Williams 1978a) derives verbs (*counterscrew*), nouns (*counterspy*), and adjectives (*counterrevolutionary*), depending on the category of the word it attaches to.

How does a suffix determine the category of its word? Williams (1978a, 1981a) proposes that suffixes themselves belong to the categories N, V, and A, just as words do. There is no harm in regarding *-ion* as a "noun," so long as it is a bound form and thus cannot surface independent of a stem to which it is attached.

The notion "head of a word" allows for inflectional morphology to be reduced to derivational morphology. The principal mark of an inflectional affix is that it must appear outside derivational affixes; for example, the plural inflectional affix *-s* appears outside the derivational affix *-hood*:

(7) a. nounhoods
    b. *nounshood

It is not necessary to posit an extra level of morphology, either in morphology proper or in syntax, to account for this fact about inflectional morphology. Rather, it follows from the identification of heads in words. Inflectional morphemes are the ones that participate in syntax. This participation is greatly limited by the lexicalist hypothesis (see chapter 3), but one mode of participation remains: an affix may determine the properties of its word, and syntax may determine the distribution of words according to these properties. For an affix to determine the properties of its word, it must appear in the "ultimate" head position (the head of the head of the h e a d...), which explains why it must appear outside derivational affixes—if it appeared inside one of them, it would not be in head position.

In fact the real generalization about inflectional affixes is that they must appear in head position, not that they must appear "outside" all other word formation—the latter is partly a consequence of the former, although there are cases in which the former holds but the latter does not; for example, in (8) the plural appears "inside" the second element of the compound and yet determines the plurality of the entire compound because it appears in "ultimate" head position:

(8)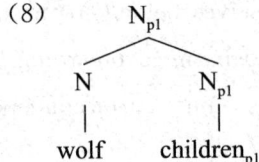

2.1.2 Problems with the Notion "Head of a Word"

Several problems have accrued against the notion "head of a word", causing some researchers to restrict its applicability in various ways and others to reject it entirely. In this section we will review these problems and propose that instead of being rejected or restricted, the notion "head" should be relativized. The relativization capitalizes on the fact that heads in morphology (as opposed to syntax) are identified contextually.

First, Jaeggli (1980) observes that the diminutive suffix in Spanish can attach to almost any part of speech and that the resulting word belongs to the same category as the word to which the diminutive attaches:

(9) Adjective: poco   poquita
               'little'
    Noun: chica   Chiquita
               'girl'
    Adverb: ahora   ahorita
               'now'

This means that the diminutive does not determine the category of the derived word and so is not a likely head even though it occupies the rightmost position.

We feel that we can account for these facts and preserve the notion "head of a word" by relativizing the notion "head". Because the diminutive does not determine the category of the word to which it attaches, there is no reason (for the child or the linguist; see Williams 1980) to assign the diminutive to a lexical category; so the diminutive, like prefixes, is unspecified for category. Now, how can we get the category of the left member of these forms to determine the category of the whole? Suppose we define "head" as follows:

(10) Definition of "head_F" (read: head with respect to the feature F):
The head_F of a word is the rightmost element of the word marked for the feature F.

Because the left-hand elements of the forms in (9) are (by default) the rightmost elements of the forms marked for category specification, they are "$\text{head}_{\text{category}}$" (head with respect to category), and so the whole must agree with them in category.

The notion "relativized head" is peculiar to morphology (it has no analogue in syntax), and for good reason. In syntax the head is identifiable by an intrinsic feature (it is a nonmaximal projection), not contextually; so there can be no relativization of the head in syntax because there is only one potential head in the first place. The relativization of the head in morphology thus exploits the contextual definition of head in morphology.

The notion "relativized head" permits the possibility that words could have two heads, a head_{F_1} and a head_{F_2}, where F_1 and F_2 are different features:

(11)
$$\begin{array}{c} X \\ \diagup \diagdown \\ Z \quad\quad Y \\ \begin{bmatrix} \text{unmarked} \\ \text{for } F_1 \\ -F_2 \end{bmatrix} \begin{bmatrix} +F_1 \\ +F_2 \end{bmatrix} \end{array}$$

Here Y is the head_{F_1} of X, and Z is the head_{F_2}. There is nothing incoherent or disturbing about this situation, and in fact there are certainly cases of this kind.

Selkirk (1982) points out that Williams's (1981) explanation for the fact that inflectional affixes appear outside derivational affixes, which requires that inflectional affixes appear in head position, incorrectly entails that there can be only one inflectional affix per word. *Amabitur*, for example, is a Latin word with two inflectional affixes:

(12) ama   bi   tur
               +fut +passive

She concludes (p. 77) that inflectional affixes cannot be heads, and she provides a means of passing up features that is independent of the notion "head".

We may instead suppose that amabitur has two heads, where *bi* is the head$_{future}$ and *tur* is the head$_{passive}$.

This account permits us to maintain that inflectional affixes are not separated from derivational morphology in any way; Selkirk's treatment accords them a special rule (p. 66) and percolation mechanisms not based on the notion "head" (p. 76).

Actually the peripherality of inflectional elements does not follow from the theory of relativized heads by itself. Suppose that alongside singular *boy* and plural *boys* there also existed unmarked *boy*, neither singular nor plural. Then in the following compound the plural on the left element, *choir*, could mark the entire compound as plural:

(13)
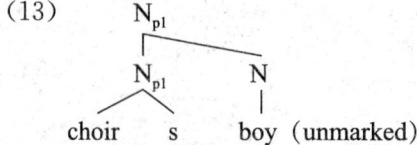

The problem is specific to the theory of relativized heads and did not arise under the theory of fixed heads in Williams (1978a, 1980).

To avoid this prediction, we must assume that all nouns are marked for number. In fact we must assume that all nominal elements are marked for number, in order to preserve the prediction in (7). And we must assume in general that if a feature is defined for a category, then all members of that category are marked for that feature.

Another instance of relativized head concerns argument structure and inflection. In general the argument structure of a form is determined by the argument structure of the head (which is not to say that it *is* necessarily the argument structure of the head; see sections 2.2 and 2.3 for proposals). However, for reasons already discussed, inflectional endings on verbs must appear in head position. So it would seem that a verb and the inflectional affix compete for head position, the former to determine the argument structure of the whole and the latter to pass up its inflectional features. Again, though, we may appeal to the notion "relativized head"— inflectional affixes are not marked with argument structures, so the head$_{\text{argument structure}}$ will be the verb stem and not the inflectional affix, while the inflectional affix will still be the head$_{\text{inflectional features}}$:

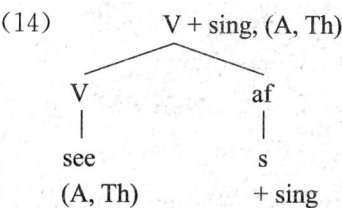

In sum the notion "head$_F$" solves several different problems that have accrued against the idea that suffixes are heads of words and permits unified treatment of inflectional and derivational morphology (a distinction that we think is mythical in any case; see section 3.8). It exploits a possibility inherent in the fact that the head in morphology, as opposed to syntax, is identified contextually.

4.3 思考和练习

1. 什么叫"词"？如何确定汉语普通话中的词？
2. 汉语普通话中，"字""词""语素"这几个概念如何区分？
3. 很多人认为汉语没有形态，你同意吗？请结合本章的内容，对这一观点提出批判性的建议。
4. 简要论述汉语合成词的构词规则。
5. 举例说明什么是向心结构？什么是离心结构？
6. 如果汉语只有派生形态变化，没有屈折形态变化，那么，汉语如何表示那些在别的语言中需要通过屈折形态变化表示的语法范畴（如人称、性、数、格、时、体、情态等）？试举例说明之。

4.4 延伸阅读

Anderson, S. 1982. Where's morphology? *Linguistic Inquiry* 13: 571-612.

Anderson, S. 1992. *A-Morphous Morphology*. Cambridge: Cambridge University Press.

Aronoff, M. 1994. *Morphology by itself: Stems and inflection classes*. Cambridge, Mass.: The MIT Press.

Baker, M. 2003. *Lexical Categories: Verbs, Nouns, and Adjectives*. Cambridge: Cambridge University Press.

Bybee, L. 1985. *Morphology: A Study of the Relation between Meaning and Form*. Amsterdam: Benjamins.

Bonet, E. 1991. *Morphology after Syntax*. Cambridge, Mass.: The MIT Press.

Di Sciullo, A.-M. and E. Williams, 1988. *On the Definition of Word*. Cambridge, Mass.: The MIT Press.

Halle, M. & A. Marantz. 1993. Distributed Morphology and the pieces of inflection. In K. Hale & S. J. Keyser (eds.), *The View from Building 20: Essays in Linguistics in Honor of Sylvain Bromberger*, 111 - 176. Cambridge, Mass.: The MIT Press.

Huang, C.-T. J. 1984. Phrase structure, lexical integrity, and Chinese compounds. *Journal of the Chinese Language Teachers Association* 19(2): 53 - 78.

O'Grady, W., Archibald, J., Aronoff, M. & J. Rees-Miller. 2017. *Contemporary Linguistics: An Introduction (the 7th edition)*. Boston: Bedford/St. Martin's.

Stump, G. T. 2001. *Inflectional Morphology: A Theory of Paradigm Structure*. Cambridge: Cambridge University Press.

第五章 句法学

5.1 导引

- 句法概说
- 句法范畴
- 句子的结构依存性
- 短语结构
- 普遍语法中的原则与参数
- 小结

5.1.1 句法概说

短语和句子的各个组成部分之间并非简单的线性排列(linear sequencing)，而是存在内在的结构。考虑下面来自汉语和英语的例子：

(1) 张三在火车上写字。
    a. 张三写字，人在火车上。
    b. 张三写字，字写在火车上。
(2) wealthy men and women
    a. [有钱的男人]和女人(只有男人有钱)
    b. 有钱的[男人和女人](男人和女人都有钱)
(3) Nicole saw the man *with binocular*.
    a. Nicole [$_{VP}$ saw [$_{NP}$ the man with binoculars]]. (Nicole 看见了拿着双筒望远镜的男人。)

b. Nicole [$_{VP}$ saw [$_{NP}$ the man] with binoculars]. (Nicole 用双筒望远镜看见那个男人。)

上述句子都有歧义。歧义的产生说明了短语和句子存在内部结构。就短语和句子存在内部结构这一点而言,英语和汉语没有区别。实际上,所有的自然语言都有内部结构性;所有自然语言的句子都不是简单的线性排列。研究短语和句子内部结构规律的语言学分支叫做句法学。自从乔姆斯基在1950年代提出普遍语法这一概念以来,句法学的一个根本目标就是探寻制约自然语言句法现象的普遍规律。句法学和语义学,一个研究语言的结构,一个研究语言的意义,是当今语言学的两大基础性学科之一,是最重要的两个分支。这一章主要介绍句法学中的基本概念。

5.1.2 句法范畴

所谓句子的结构,其实由两个部分组成:一个是抽象的,即句子的构造规则;另一个是具体的,即组成句子的各种语法单位。用盖楼来打比方,句子的构造规则相当于楼房的构造规律,这些构造规律要遵循基本的力学原理,而组成句子的各种语法单位则相当于盖楼需要的砖瓦门窗等建筑材料。句法研究就是通过对语言单位的组合规律的观察和分析,进而得出关于语言结构的具有一般意义的原理性的结论。

句法研究中最重要的语言单位是词。和自然语言中的词相关的一项根本属性是:词可以根据一定的标准归为某一个自然类(natural class)。这样的自然类叫做句法范畴(syntactic category)[传统语法中叫做词类(parts of speech)]。句法范畴的划分和一系列的因素有关,主要有:(a)词所表达的意义特征;(b)词本身的形态特征(主要体现在不同的词和不同类型的语素的结合能力);(c)词在句子中的分布特征,即在句子结构中的位置(如充当主语、宾语、谓语等)。

词汇范畴(lexical category)与**功能范畴**(functional category)　　句法范畴可以分为词汇范畴与功能范畴两大类。词汇范畴是具有实际词汇意义的范畴。最常见的词汇范畴有:名词(noun,用 N 表示)、动词(verb,用 V 表示)、形容词(adjective,用 A 表示)、副词(adverb,用 Adv 表示)。也有一些语法书把介词(preposition,用 P 表示)归为词汇范畴。这些范畴在句法构造中扮演重要的角色。除了词汇范畴之外,自然语言还包含非词汇范畴或功能范畴,常见的有:限定词(determiner,用 Det 表示)、助动词(auxiliary verb,用 Aux 表示)、连词(conjunction,用 Conj 表示)、程度副词(degree words,用 Deg 表示)。这类词汇范畴的意义空灵,很难像词汇范畴那样可以定义。比如说,限定词 the 的语义就很难定义,类似的还有汉语中结构助词"的"的意义(汉语"的"的语义本质是什么,一直是汉语语法中的难题)。相比之下,词汇范畴的意义一般较为具体,如"手机"可以定义为手持的电话机,"汽车"是燃烧汽油的小型交通工具等。

下表罗列了英语中常见的句法范畴(参考 O'Grady et al. 2017:169):

表 5.1 英语中常见的句法范畴

词汇范畴		功能范畴	
词类	示例	词类	示例
Noun (N)	Harry Porter, boy, wheat, beer, Nanjing University	Determiner (Det)	the, a, this, that
Verb (V)	arrive, discuss, communicate, talk, like	Degree word (Deg)	too, so, very, quite, more
Adjective (A)	good, tall, sharp, intelligent, pretty	Auxiliary Modal/Non-modal (Aux)	will, would, can, may, might, must, should
Adverb (Adv)	slowly, quietly, always, now, perhaps		be, have, do
Preposition (P)	to, in, on, near, at, by	Conjunction (Conj)	and, or, but

划分句法范畴的一个难点在于:很多时候,同一个词可以归为不同的范畴(即所谓的词类兼用现象)。英语和汉语中都存在大量的词类兼用现象。(4—5)是英语的例子,(6—7)是汉语的例子。例(4)中的"stone"既可以充当名词,也可以充当动词;例(5)中的"near"可以充当介词、动词和形容词;例(6)中的"骄傲"可以充当形容词,也可以充当名词;例(7)中的"在"可以做介词用,也可以做动词用。

(4) a. "stone"充当名词

John has two stones.

b. "stone"充当动词

John stoned two birds.

(5) a. "near"充当介词

　　　The child stood near the fence.

　b. "near"充当动词

　　　The runners neared the finish line.

　c. "near"充当形容词

　　　The end is nearer than you might think.

(6) a. "骄傲"充当形容词

　　　小张很骄傲。

　b. "骄傲"充当名词

　　　小张的骄傲害了自己。

(7) a. "在"充当介词

　　　小张在厨房洗碗。

　b. "在"充当动词

　　　小张在厨房里。

　　我们可以从三个标准来划分句法范畴：(一)词所表达的意义特征；(二)词本身的形态特征；(三)词在句子中的分布特征。

　　(一) 意义标准　　不同的词类表示不同的意义。名词通常指称个体，表示人(Harry Porter)或者物(book、desk)。动词表示动作(run、jump)、感觉(feel、hurt)或者状态(be、remain)。形容词表示名词所指称的个体具有的属性或性质。当我们谈及某个人的时候，可以用"聪明、漂亮、伶俐"等来修饰这个人：聪明的学生、漂亮的小女孩、伶俐的小姑娘。与形容词类似，副词表示动词所述动作、感觉或状态所具有的属性。下面的例(8a)表示 Janet 离开的方式，(8b)表示 Janet 离开的时间：

(8) a. Janet left quickly.

　b. Janet left early.

　　单纯从意义的角度来划分范畴会面临一些问题。实际上，意义和范畴类别之间不存在严格的一一对应关系。有些名词，如"骄傲、高尚、谦虚"等并不指称严格意义上的个体。虽然动作倾向于用动词表示，但有些名词也可以表示动作,如英语中的"give some a push, have a run"等。

（二）**形态标准** 不同的词具有不同的形态特征。我们可以通过不同的词的屈折形态变化(inflection)来划分词类/范畴。以英语为例,名词可以加上复数后缀、领属格后缀；动词可以加上表示时态(tense)变化的语素、表示体态(aspect)变化的语素等；形容词有比较级和最高级变位,如表 5.2（参考 O'Grady et al. 2017：171）：

表 5.2　英语中的词汇范畴及其屈折形态后缀

范畴	曲折后缀	例子
Noun	复数标记 -s	books, professors, doctors, students
	属格标记 's	John's, Mary's, that man's
Verb	过去时态 -ed	arrived, melted, hoped, killed, liked
	进行体 -ing	arriving, melting, hoping, killing
	第三人称单数 -s	arrives, melts, boils
Adjective	比较级 -er	taller, faster, smarter
	最高级 -est	taller, fastest, smartest

单纯从曲折形态变化很难完全判定词的范畴。譬如并非所有英语中的形容词都有比较级或最高级后缀(*intelligenter、*beautifulest),许多名词也不能带复数比较(*moistures、*braveries、*knowledges)。

（三）**分布标准** 另一种相对而言比较可靠的标准是从词的分布特征来确定词的范畴。不同的词与其他语言单位的组配能力不尽相同。名词前面通常可以出现限定词,动词前面可以出现助动词,形容词前面可以出现程度副词。英语中名词、动词和形容词的分布特征如表 5.3（参考 O'Grady et al. 2017：171）：

表 5.3　名词、动词、形容词的分布特征

范畴	分布特征	例子
Noun	和限定词共现	a teacher, the wheat
Verb	和助动词共现	has gone, will go
Adjective	和程度副词共现	very rich, too smart

违反了搭配限制,通常会导致不合语法,如：

(9) *will destruction, *the destroy, *very appreciate

在分析具体语言时，通常要将意义标准、形态标准和分布标准这三类标准相结合，以确定某一语言单位的句法范畴。

词汇范畴与功能范畴的区分，大致对应到传统语法中的实词(content words)和虚词(function words)之分，但它们的外延不尽相同：前者的外延比后者的外延大。当代句法学研究更多的是关注范畴之分，而非简单的虚实之分。

5.1.3 句子的结构依存性

任何事物都是有组织、有层级性的，而不是杂乱无章的堆积和排列。结构性和层级性是宇宙万物的普遍属性。物理学中分析物质的构成，也是一层一层地剥离其基本单位：分子由原子组成，原子由粒子组成，粒子由更小的夸克单位组成，夸克可能由更小的上帝粒子组成等等。生物组织也是如此：生物体由各种系统组成，系统由各种器官组成，器官由组织组成，组织有细胞组成，细胞由更小的分子单位组成。语言也不外如是。每一个大的语言单位，都可以离析出更小的单位。语素组成词，词组成短语，短语组成句子，句子构成语篇等等。

句子的各个组成部分不是简单的线性序列，而是有组织有规律的组成。句子中各个组成部分排列的规律性，受制于句法原则。对汉语母语者而言，(9a)是可以接受的句子，而(9b)是不可接受的句子(不合语法)：

(9) a. 我们喜欢语言学。
　　b. *喜欢我们语言学。

句子(9a)由三个成分组成：主语"我们"、谓语"喜欢"、宾语"语言学"。从逻辑上看，这三个成分可以组成三种不同的层级结构，分别如(10a-c)所示：

(10) a.

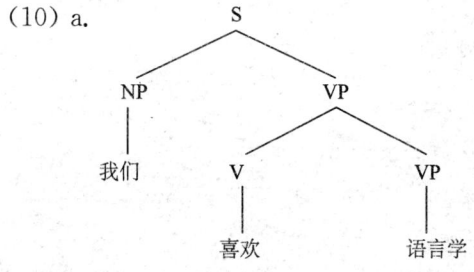

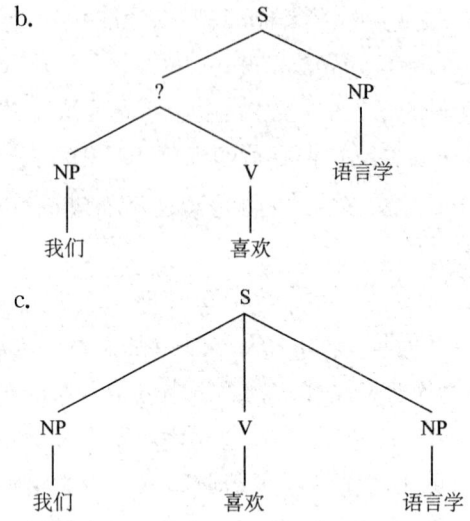

用 S 表示句子，V 表示动词，NP 表示名词短语。上述三种结构中，只有(10a)是合法的，即 V"喜欢"先和宾语位置的 NP"语言学"组成一个成分(constituent)(用 VP 表示)，然后这个成分 VP 再和主语位置的名词短语 NP"我们"组成句子。用成分测试(constituent test)可以检验这样的分析的正确性。

成分测试一般有三种方法：(一) 独立法(stand-alone test)；(二) 替代法(replacement test)；(三) 位移法(displacement test)。

先来看独立法。句子的成分可以独立使用，比如可以用来单独回答问题。如果可以，则可以认为这个单位是一个成分。还是以"我们喜欢语言学"为例。"语言学"、"喜欢语言学"、"我们"都可以独立使用，用来回答问题。相比之下，"我们喜欢"、"喜欢"则比较困难：

(11) A：谁喜欢语言学？
　　 B：我们。
(12) A：我们喜欢什么？
　　 B：语言学。
(13) A：我们有什么爱好？
　　 B：喜欢语言学。
(14) A：*/? 语言学？

B:* 我们喜欢。
(15) A: 我们怎么语言学?
B:?? 喜欢。

再来看替代法。句子的成分可以被其它同范畴的成分替代而不影响合法性。如果一个句子可以被别的成分替代,则可以认为它是一个成分。很明显,(10a)的结构满足替代法的测试:

(16) a. 我们喜欢<u>语言学</u>。
b. 我们喜欢<u>它</u>。
(17) a. <u>我们</u>喜欢语言学。
b. <u>小张</u>喜欢语言学。
(18) a. 我们<u>喜欢语言学</u>。
b. 我们<u>有这个兴趣</u>。

最后来看位移法。如果一个单位可以作为一个整体进行位移,则可以认为它是一个成分。在"我们喜欢语言学"这个句子中,"我们"、"喜欢语言学"、"语言学"都可以进行位移:

(19) a. 语言学,我们喜欢。
b. 爱好,我们有喜欢语言学。
c. 我们啊,喜欢语言学。

句子的层级性不但体现在句子各个组成部分排列的规律性和原则性,还体现在这种排列是以结构为单位的,即不完全依据线性序列。这一属性叫做句法的结构依存性(structural dependency)。考虑下面的句子:

(20) a. 张三$_1$知道李四$_2$喜欢自己$_{1/2}$。
b. 张三$_1$的姐姐$_2$知道李四$_3$喜欢自己$_{*1/2/3}$。

汉语"自己"的一个特性是它需要在一定范围内(一般是"自己"所在句子)存在先行语(antecedent),并且先行语和"自己"同指(指称同一个体)。例(20a)中的"自己"的先行语可以是张三,也可以是李四,分别表示:张三知道李四喜欢(自己=张三);张三知道李四喜欢(自己=李四)。

从表面看,"张三"和"李四"都在线性序列上位于"自己"的前面。是不是只要在线性序列上位于"自己"的前面的名词性短语都可以成为"自己"的先行语,和它同指呢？(20b)的现象表明,答案是否定的。在(20b)中,"张三"位于"自己"的前面,但是"张三"和"自己"不能同指[该句不能表达:张三的姐姐知道李四喜欢(自己=张三)]。究其原因,在于"张三"位于一个更大的名词性结构(张三的姐姐)中。整个名词性成分"姐姐"可以和"自己"同指,但是"张三"不能。这一现象充分说明句法规则的结构依存性。

结构依存性在自然语言中普遍存在。考虑下面的英语例子:

(21) a. The boy will win.
b. Will the boy win?

英语构成一般疑问句的规则是:如果句子中有助动词,则把助动词移位到句首。(21b)就是通过把助动词"will"前置到句首生成的。由此可以得出一条规则,如(22):

(22) 英语一般疑问句生成规则
将句子中的助动词前置到句首位置。

这一规则是否具有普遍适用性呢？考虑(23)的句子:

(23) a. The boy who can sleep well will win.
b. *Can the boy who sleep well will win?
c. Will the boy who can sleep well win?

如果将线性序列的第一个助动词(can)移动到句首,我们会得到(23b)的句子,而这显然是错误的。正确的疑问句应该是(23c),尽管(23c)中的"will"并不是线性序列的第一个助动词。如果句法规则具有结构依存性,那么这一现象很容易解释。因为"can"虽然是线性序列的第一个助动词,但是它位于另一个结构之中。也就是说,从结构上来看,整个句子的主助动词是"will"而不是"can"。

结构依存性还体现在其它方面。在某些语言中,存在主谓呼应(agreement)现象,即如果主语是单数,相应的谓语也是单数;如果主语是复数,则相应的谓语也是复数。在下面英语的英语句子(24a)中,尽管离动词最近的"children"是复数,但是动词仍然和"the mother"呼应,是单数形式。类似的现象也会出现在意大利语、德语和斯瓦西里语(Swahili)中(黑体部分表示呼应):

(24) a. The **mother** with many children work**s** a lot.
　　 b. La **madre** con tanti figli lavor**a** molto.
　　 c. Die **Mutter** mit den vielen Kindern arbeite**t** viel.
　　 d. **Mama** anao watoto wengi **a**najitahidi.

只要承认句法具有结构依存性,上述现象可以很容易得到解释。

5.1.4 短语结构

不同的词会组成短语(传统语法中一般把词与词结合的单位叫做词组)。短语是比词更高一级的语法单位。一个短语至少包含两个词。词与词构成短语不是任意的,要受到严格的规则的制约。这些规则,一般称为短语结构规则(phrase structure rule, PSR)。先来考虑几组短语:

(25) a. NP: the mother *of John*
　　 b. VP: visit *Nanjing University*
　　 c. AP: afraid *of snakes*
　　 d. PP: over *the hill*

上述例子分别是名词短语（NP）、动词短语（VP）、形容词短语（AP）和介词短语（PP）。值得注意的是，每一个短语都包含一个和相应的短语类型相同的范畴，如 NP 中存在名词 N（"mother"），VP 中存在动词 V（"visit"），AP 中存在形容词 A（"afraid"），PP 中存在介词 P（"over"）。可以认为，NP、VP、AP、PP 就是由 N、V、A、P 扩展而来的。用数学的术语来说，NP 就是 N 的投射（projection），VP 是 V 的投射，AP 是 A 的投射，PP 是 P 的投射，依此类推。投射和相应范畴的关系如（26）所示：

(26) a. NP→... N ...
　　 b. VP→... V ...
　　 c. AP→... A ...
　　 d. PP→... P ...

（26）表达式中的符号"→"读作"转写符号（rewrite）"，意为 NP 由 N 扩展而来（NP 必须包含 N），VP 由 V 扩展而来（VP 必须包含 V）等等。这里的 N、V、A、P 分别是 NP、VP、AP、PP 的中心语（核心）（head）。换言之，任意一个短语（XP）必定有一个中心语 X，并且 X 和 XP 的类型相同。

例（25）表明，短语除了中心语之外，还可能包含别的成分，如 NP 中的"of John"，VP 中的"Nanjing University"，AP 中的"of snakes"，PP 中的"the hill"。这些成分可以出现，也可以缺省。在语义上，它们是对中心语的补充说明（如 NP 中的"of John"是对 mother 的进一步说明）。我们把这些成分叫做补足语（complement）。

除了补足成分之外，一个短语还可能有包含表示指示语（specifier），如"the mother of John"中的"the"。前面提过，定冠词"the"属于限定词，用 Det 表示。指示语是一个纯粹的结构上的概念。

短语中的指示语、中心语、补足语可以通过句法树来表示。句法树又称树形图，是一个比喻，用来描绘句子之间各个成分之间的层级结构，犹如一棵树一样（根——树干——树枝——树叶），层次清楚。句法树一般是双分叉结构（binary branching）。以名词短语 NP 为例，其结构如（27）所示（"Spec"表示指示语，"Comp"表示补足语）：

(27) the mother of John

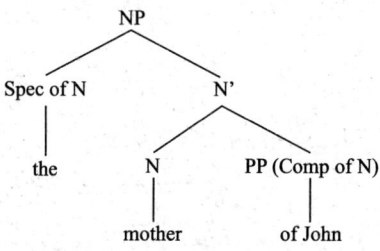

我们也可以通过转写规则,把上述结构转写如下:

(27) a. NP→Spec N'
b. N'→N PP

中间的 N' 读作 N-标阶,用来表示 N 和 NP 之间的中间成分。用通俗的话来说,N' 是一个介于词与短语之间的中间成分。如果用变量 X 来表示各种范畴,用 XP 表示以 X 为中心语的各类短语,上述思路可以进一步概化为一种假设:"X-标杆理论"(X-bar Theory),即任意的短语,都必然有(且只有)一个中心语,可能包含指示语和补足语。X-标杆理论的图示如(28):

(28) X-标杆理论

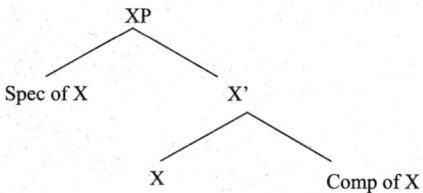

需要注意的是,XP 中的中心语是必须出现的,但是 Spec 和 Comp 是可以缺省的。所以,单纯的专有名词,如 John Smith,就是一个名词短语 NP。和上述 NP 不同的是,这个名词短语没有 Spec 和 Comp。

X-标杆理论可以推广到自然语言中的所有短语结构,即所有短语结构,都有类似(28)的结构。应用 X-标杆理论,前面提到的例子"visit *Nanjing University*""afraid *of snakes*""over *the hill*"的结构分别如下面的树形图所示:

(29) a. VP: visit *Nanjing University*

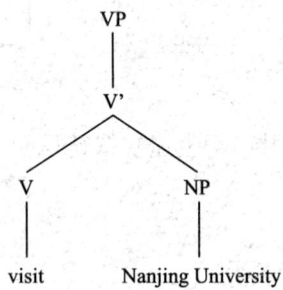

b. AP: afraid *of snakes*

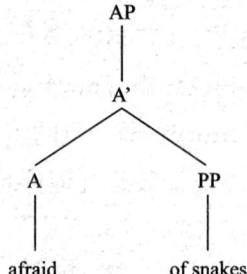

c. PP: over *the hill*

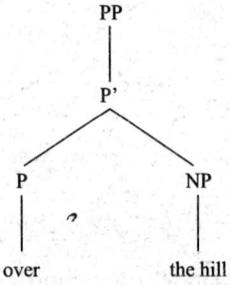

将每个组成部分的结构都完整表述出来,下面的例(30)(the boy over the hill visited Nanjing University)的结构如图(31)所示:

(31) a. The boy over the hill visited Nanjing University.

b.
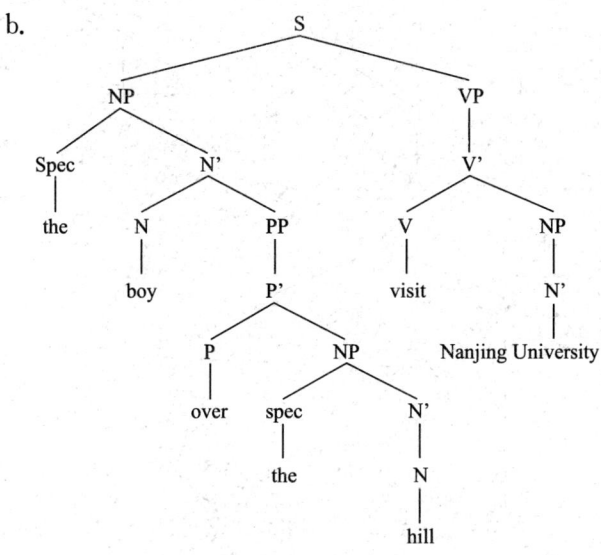

在(31b)的图中,NP 之下还可以包含 NP,同样,PP 之下可以包含 PP 等等。这一特性体现了自然语言的递归属性(recursion)。

短语结构规则可以充分说明句子因结构而产生的歧义。考虑(32):

(32) 张三在火车上写字。
    a. 张三在写字,张三人在火车上。
    b. 张三在写字,字写在火车上。

例(32)有歧义,分别可以表示(32a)和(32b)。在第一种解读中,张三人在火车上;在第二种解读中,字写在火车上。这两种语义解读分别对应到不同的句法结构,如(33a)和(33b)所示:

(33) a.

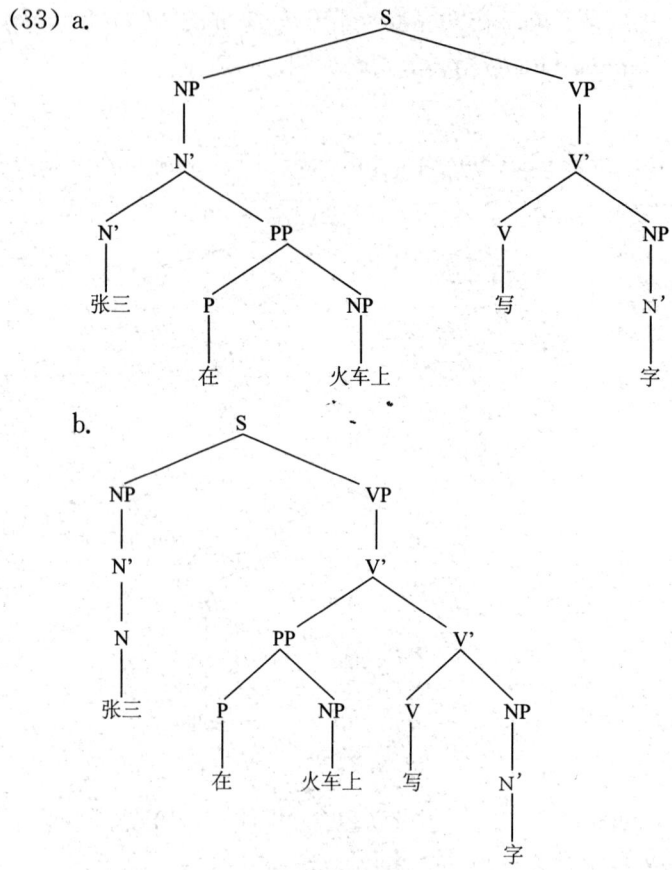

b.

这一歧义的来源是介词短语 PP"在火车上"所附接的成分不同。在(33a)中,PP 附加于主语 NP;在(33b)中,PP 附加于谓语。为了以示区分,我们把中心语的姊妹节点叫做补足语,X' 的姊妹节点叫做附加语。

附加语在句法上的位置比较灵活。当附加语附加于不同的句法位置时,一般会导致歧义。在英语中也是如此,如:

(34) The boy touched the magician with a wand.
 a. The boy touched the magician, the boy has a wand.
 b. The boy touched the magician who has a wand.

如(34a)和(34b)所示,(34)具有结构歧义,有两种不同的语义解读。这两

种语义解读源于不同的句法结构。这两种结构可以分别用括号表示法表示如下。(有兴趣的读者可以把括号转写为句法树)

(35) a. [s[NP The boy] [VP[V'[V touch [NP the magician]]] [PP with a wand]]]]
b. [s[NP The boy] [VP[V'[V touch [NP[Spec the] [N'[N' [N magician]][PP with a wand]]]]]]

X-标杆理论可以应用于自然语言中所有短语的内部结构,被认为是普遍语法的重要组成部分之一。

5.1.5 普遍语法中的原则与参数

"X-标杆"结构作为普遍语法的组成部分,规定自然语言的短语都可以投射为一个由指示语、中心语和补足语组成的 XP 结构。在英语的 VP 结构中(以及物动词为例),补足语一般跟随在中心语的后面,如(36):

(36) a. VP→Spec V'
b. V'→ V NP

但是并非所有自然语言中的 VP 都具有和英语 VP 一模一样的结构。在有的语言中,补足语可以位于中心语之前。如日语:

(37) a. Taro found a dog.
b. Taro-ga   inu-o   mitsuketa.
    Taro-subject marker dog-object marker found

和英语 SVO 语序不同,日语属于 SOV 语言,如(37b)所示。这一跨语言的差异可以归根于一个基本参数的不同:即中心语在前(head-initial)还是中心语在后(head-final)。当一个语言选择中心语在前,则补足语跟随中心语,否则中心语跟随补足语。日语显然选择了中心语在后的设置。不但在 VP 层次如此,在 PP 层次也是如此。英语中 PP 的补足语要跟随介词,形成[P+

Comp]("in the garden")的结构,但是日语中 PP 的补足语在介词之前,形成[Comp+P]的结构,如(38):

(38) Inu-ga   niwa-de   asonde iru.
     dog-subject marker   garden-in   playing is
     'The dog is playing in the garden.'

比较英语和日语,可以得出两类不同的 XP-标杆结构:

(39) a. 英语

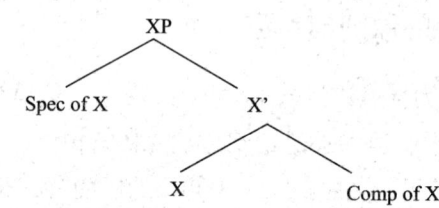

b. 日语

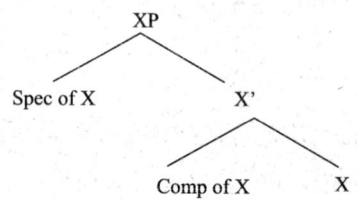

仔细比较(39a)和(39b)的两种结构,可以发现它们同中有异,异中有同。共同之处在于它们都由指示语、中心语、补足语组成,不同之处在于中心语和补足语在线性上的排列存在差异。这一刻画同中有异,异中有同的句法学思路,就是原则与参数理论(Principles and Parameters, P&P)。普遍语法既规定了语言中不变的那一部分(原则),也规定了可变异的范围(参数)。原则与参数相结合,可以对自然语言既存在共性,又具有个性特征这一现象做出更具原则性的解释。原则与参数理论是当前句法学中的重要思潮。

5.1.6 小结

句法学研究短语和句子的内部构造。句子的构造不是各个语言单位杂乱无章的排列,也非纯粹的线性序列,而是有其内在的规律性和结构性。研究句子内部的规律性和结构原则的语言学分支叫做句法学。句法学把句子的组成部分分为不同的范畴:词汇范畴和功能范畴,短语结构图可以反映不同范畴之间的排列组合关系和层级结构。X-标杆理论可以用于分析自然语言的短语结构,被认为是普遍语法原则的一部分。普遍语法既包含不变的原则,也包含可异的参数。原则与参数相结合,解释了自然语言既具有共性,又具有个性这一特性。

5.2 选读

- 乔姆斯基(2006)《语言与心智》选读
- 黄正德(1982)《汉语生成语法——汉语中的逻辑关系及语法理论》选读
- Rizzi(2001) "Relativized Minimality Effects"选读

乔姆斯基(2006)《语言与心智》选读[1]

第五章 语言的形式属性

句法部分的结构

语法的句法部分必须生成配对(D, S),其中 D 是深层结构,S 是与之关联的表层结构(关于"生成"请参见 112 页注释[2])。表层结构 S 是一串带标记的构成要素和联结符号的括号,深层结构也是带标记的括号,它决定着一套成分及其组合的语法功能和语法关系。很显然,句法部分必须包含有限数目的

---

[1] 乔姆斯基,《语言与心智(第三版)》,熊仲儒、张孝荣译,中国人民大学出版社 2015 年版。作者简介参考第一章"选读"部分。
[2] 此处指原书注释。——编者注

规则(或规则程式),这些规则必须被组织起来以生成无限数目的深层结构与表层结构的配对(D, S),对应于语言中的每个被解释的句子(即语音结构与语义解释)①。原则上,该系统有各种组织方式。比如说,它可能是由生成深层结构与表层结构的独立规则与关联两者的相容性条件(condition of compatibility)组成,也有可能是由生成表层结构的规则与将表层结构映射到相关深层结构的规则组成,也有可能是由生成深层结构的规则与将深层结构映射到相关表层结构的规则构成②。选择哪种组织方式是事实问题,而不是决策问题。我们必须问:对各种语言现象而言,哪种组织方式使最深层的概括与最深远的解释成为可能?和普遍语法的其他方面一样,我们这里正在处理的是经验问题,关键证据可能很难获得,但我们不能据此得出结论,即原则上,问题没有对错。

对这些可选的组织方式而言,目前所获的语言事实似乎一贯都指向这样的一种结论,即句法部分是由生成深层结构的规则与将深层结构映射到相关表层结构的规则构成。我们把规则的这两种系统分别称为句法的基础部分与转换部分。基础系统(base system)可进一步分为两个部分,即范畴系统(categorial system)与词库(lexicon)。句法的这三个子部分,每部分对运用都有特殊的功能,并且存在严格的决定其形式与相互关系的普遍原则。语法的一般结构可用图(13)进行描述:

(13)

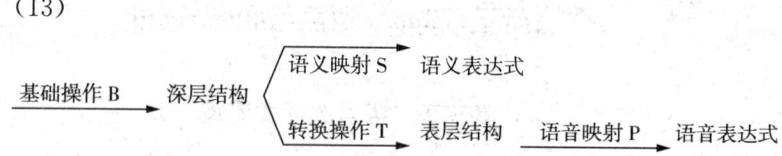

语义映射 S 由语义部分执行,转换操作 T 由转换部分执行,语音映射 P 由音系部分执行。由基础系统(通过基础操作 B)生成深层结构,这是由范畴

---

① 事实上,我们可以将语言理解为将语义解释指派给所有可能的句子(在普遍语音学和语义学的理论中,这是清晰的概念),包括那些偏离语言规则的句子。但这是一个我们在这里不能深入的问题。

② 关于句法部分是如何组织的问题不应跟发展运用(造句或感知)模型的问题搞混,不过时常会有搞混。事实上,刚刚所描述的各种组织可以用作各种运用理论的基础。

系统与词库决定的。

词库是词条的集合；每个词条相应地可理解为各种类型特征的集合,如我们已经简略提过的音系特征和语义特征。音系特征可以理解为位置索引(即第一、第二等);除此之外,在不规则的情况下,每个特征都简单地指示着某个普遍的区别特征(distinctive feature,在这里可视为范畴功能)的标记或关于附加特征(diacritic feature,见114页①)的标记。因此,像早先描述的那样,位置索引的音系特征构成了带有"＋"或"－"值条目的区别特征矩阵。语义特征构成了"字典中的定义"。如前所述,其中的一些语义特征至少是很抽象的。此外,各类语义特征之间可能有各种各样的内在联系,这种关联有时被称为"语义场结构"(field structure)。词条还包含句法特征和规则,句法特征决定了所讨论的词条可能占据的位置,规则应用于包含该词条的结构并将其转化为表层结构。通常来说,词条包含所探讨词项的所有信息,这些信息不能用一般规则来解释的。

除了词条之外,词库中也会包含一些冗余规则,这些冗余规则将会根据一般的规则修正词条的特征内容。举一个例子来说,元音是有响度的(voiced)与人类是有生命的,这些都是事实,不需要在特定的词条中特别提及。毫无疑问,词条的大多冗余信息都是由一般的规约提供(即普遍语法的规则),而不是由特定语言的冗余规则提供。

词典考虑个体词条的所有属性,包括特殊的属性或者冗余的属性。基础的范畴部分决定深层结构的其他方面。看来,范畴部分是所谓的简单的或者是上下文自由的短语结构语法(context-free phrase-structure grammar)。这样的一个系统是什么样的,看一个简单的例子就很容易明白。假设我们有规则(14):

14 S→NP VP
    VP →V NP
    NP → N
    N → △
    V → △

---

① 此处指原书114页。——编者注

根据(14)中的这些规则,我们按以下方式构造出了(15)的推导过程。首先写下符号 S,把它作为推导式的第一行,我们将(14)中的第一条规则解释为 S 可以被 NP VP 替换,得到(15)中的第二行推导式。用同样的方式来解释(14)中的第二条规则,我们得到(15)中的第三行推导式,其中 VP 由 V NP 替换。以同样的方式解释规则 NP→N,我们将该规则应用于(15)中的第三行推导式中的两个 NP,得到(15)中的第四行推导式。最后,我们通过应用规则 N→△ 和 V→△ 得到(15)中的最后两行推导式。

(15)   S
       NP VP
       NP V NP
       N V N
       △ V △
       △ △ △

我们也可以用树形图(16)清晰地表征推导式(15)中的必要成分,如:

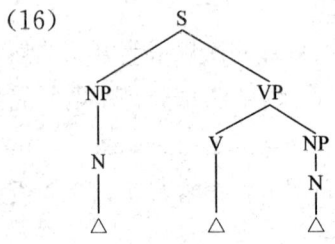

在树形图(16)中,每个符号都支配着在构成(15)的过程中被替换的符号。事实上,我们可能把(14)中的规则当作简单描述(16)这样的树形图的构造方式。很显然,(16)是(17)中括号标记法的另一种表达。

(17)   [$_S$[$_{NP}$[$_N$△]$_N$]$_{NP}$[$_{VP}$[$_V$△]$_V$[$_{NP}$[$_N$△]$_N$]$_{NP}$]$_{VP}$]$_S$

(16) 中被符号 A 支配的成分(如 V NP 被 VP 支配)在(17)中用括号标

记法封装在"[ₐ]ₐ"里。如果我们有这样一个词库,它告诉我们当符号△受 N 支配时(即可封装在"[ₙ]ₙ"里),"John"与"Bill"可以替换符号△,当△受 V 支配时"saw"可以替换△,则我们可以扩展(15)中的推导式以推导出"John saw Bill",相关结构如(6)所示。事实上,(6)是由(17)通过替换推导出来的,如"John"替换第一个△,"saw"替换第二个△,"Bill"替换第三个△。

注意,规则(14)有效地定义了语法关系,相关定义可参见 121—122 页①。因此,(14)中的第一条规则定义的是主—谓关系,第二条定义的是动—宾关系。同样,语义上非常重要的其他语法功能和关系可用这种形式的规则定义,也可用所指出的方式进行解释。

以一个更加正式和一般的方式来重述这些见解,基础的范畴部分是一个形式为"A →Z"的规则系统,其中的 A 是一个范畴符号,如 S(句子)、NP(名词短语)、N(名词)等。Z 是一个符号或多个符号构成的序列,它可能还是范畴符号,也可能是终端符号(终端符号不出现于任何基础规则的箭头的左边)。根据这种系统,我们可以形成推导式。推导式是一连串满足如下条件的"行":第一行只是个符号 S(代表句子);最后一行只包含终端符号;如果 X、Y 是两个连续的行,则 X 的形式必须是"…A…",Y 的形式必须是"…Z…",其中"A →Z"是一条规则。推导式以显而易见的方式为终端符号串带上括号标记。所以,如果连续的行是"X = …A…"与"Y = …Z…",其中 Y 通过规则"A → Z"由 X 推导,则我们可以说由Z(或者 Z 自身,如果 Z 是终端符号)推导的符号串用"[ₐ]ₐ"封装。同样的,我们也可以用树形图表征括号标记,在树形图中,(这个例子中)以 A 标记的节点支配连续的节点,这些连续的节点由 Z 中的连续符号标记。

我们假定范畴部分的终端符号之一为空符号△。非终端符号中有很多代表词汇范畴的,特别是 N(名词)、V(动词)、ADJ(形容词)。只有当 Z 为△时,词汇范畴 A 才能出现于规则"A→Z"的箭头左边。词条通过不同种类的规则将被插入推导式以取代△,这扩展了由范畴部分提供的推导式。△指示词库中的词项可以出现的位置,除了△,范畴部分的终端符号也可以是 be、of 等之类的语法成分。由范畴部分的规则引进的一些终端符号有固有的语义内容。

---

① 此处指原书 121—122 页。——编者注

由基础规则生成的带标记的括号被称为基础短语标记(base phrase-marker),基础规则,也就是范畴部分的短语结构规则与上一段所提到的词汇插入规则。更一般地说,我们这里用术语"短语标记"指由带标记的括号正确括起来的任何成分串①。转换部分的规则以某种固定方式更改短语标记。这些规则按"$T_1,\cdots,T_m$"的序列安排。这列规则以循环的方式应用于基础部分的短语标记。首先,它应用于受 S 支配的构型,即"$[_S\cdots]_S$"构型,该构型不包含 S 的其他出现。当转换规则应用于所有这些构型之后,下一步就会应用于受 S 支配的构型,包含规则已经应用的且只受 S 支配的构型。这种过程一直持续到规则应用于完整的短语标记,该短语标记在基础短语标记中受 S 的第一次出现的支配。这时,就有了表层结构。转换操作的顺序条件可能比较松散——对转换操作集$\{T_1,\cdots,T_m\}$可能有某种顺序条件,也可能是在循环的某个阶段,如果转换不违反这些条件,一系列转换就可以应用——但我在这儿不能深入探讨这个问题。

句法部分的属性可以通过例子更清晰说明(这个例子自然必须过分简化)。考虑英语的子部分,它的词库(18)与范畴部分(19)可如下表示:

(18)　词库:it, fact, John, Bill, boy, future　(名词 N)
　　　　　dream, see, persuade, annoy　(动词 V)
　　　　　sad　(形容词 ADJ)
　　　　　will　(情态动词 M)
　　　　　the　(限定词 DET)

(19)　S → (Q) NP AUX VP
　　　　VP → be ADJ
　　　　VP → V (NP) (of NP)
　　　　NP → (DET) N (that S)
　　　　AUX → past
　　　　AUX → M
　　　　N, V, ADJ, DET, M → △

---

① 可能需要更概括的概念"短语标记",但我们在这里将撇开这个问题。

在(19)中,圆括号用来表示该成分在规则中可能出现也可能不出现。所以(19)中的第一行是两个规则的简写形式,一种规则中的 S 可重写为"Q NP AUX VP",另一种规则中的 S 可重写为"NP AUX VP"。同样,(19)中的第三行实际上是四个规则的简写形式。(19)中的最后一行代表五种规则,其中的每一个规则都将左边的一个范畴符号重写为空的终端符号。

这个范畴部分提供了如下的推导式:

(20)　a. S

　　　　　NP AUX VP

　　　　　NP AUX be ADJ

　　　　　N AUX be ADJ

　　　　　N past be ADJ

　　　　　△past be △

　　b. S

　　　　　NP AUX VP

　　　　　NP AUX V NP of NP

　　　　　DET N AUX V N of DET N that S

　　　　　DET N M V N of DET N that S

　　　　　△　△△△△ of △ △ that S

　　　　　△　△△△△ of △ △ that NP VP

　　　　　△　△△△△ of △ △ that NP AUX V

　　　　　△　△△△△ of △ △ that N AUX V

　　　　　△　△△△△ of △ △ that N past V

　　　　　△　△△△△ of △ △ that △ past △

这些推导式按上述方式建构,可用带标记的括号法表示。为清晰起见,我们将用等价的树形图表示:

(21) a.

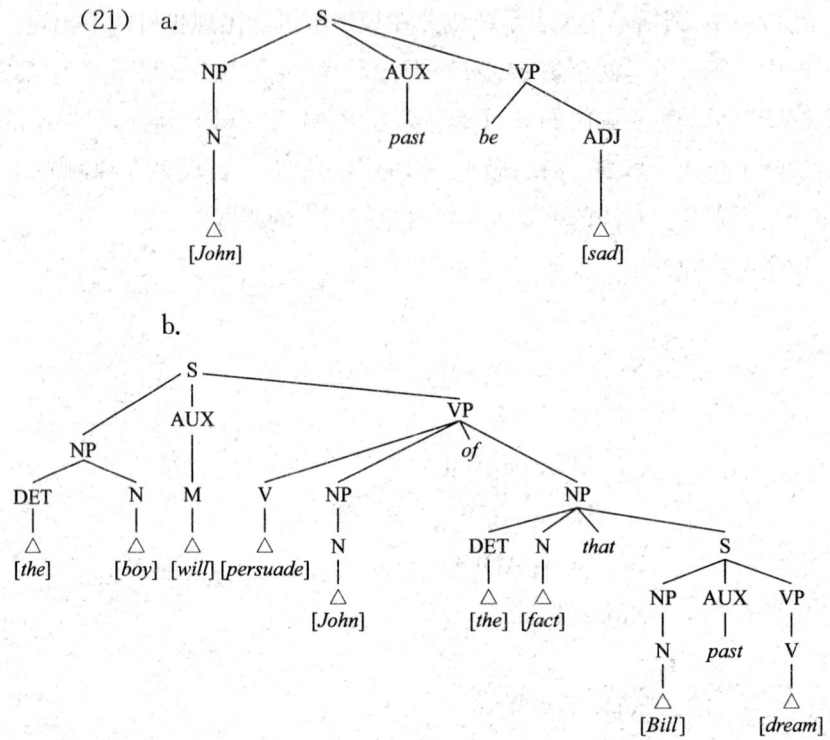

b.

我们现在用词库完成基础推导式(20a)与(20b)。词库中的每个词条包含着句法信息，这些句法信息识别推导式中词条可以替换的△的出现。比如说，(18)中五行项目可以替换△的出现，在(21)的树形图中△分别受 N、V、ADJ、M、DET 等范畴符号的支配。

但限制比这还要窄得多。(18)中的动词(第二行)，只有"persuade"可以替换受 V 支配的△的出现，但 V 的这个出现在 VP 中由"NP of NP"紧随其后，我们可以得到"…persuade John of the fact."，但得不到"…dream（see, annoy）John of the fact."。同样，(18)中的名词(第一行)，只有"fact"可以出现于"DET__ that S"语境中(如"the fact that John left")；只有"it"可以出现于"__ that S"形式的 NP 中①；只有"fact、boy 与 future"可以出现于"DET __"形式的 NP 中("the fact"、"the boy"、"the future")。忽略细节，这种限制的一般属性相当清楚。因此，如果假定词条包含了合适的词汇特征，通过在(21)

---

① 这可能不清晰，我们直接回到例子。

中插入被封闭在括号中的项目,则可以将(20)中的基础推导式扩展为(22)这种终端符号串。

(22)　a. John past be sad
　　　　b. the boy will persuade John of the fact that Bill past dream

对推导式做其他选择的话,我们也可以构成像(23)这样的终端符号串。

(23)　Q the boy will dream of the future
　　　　it that John past see Bill past annoy the boy
　　　　John will be sad
　　　　John past see the future

我们按如下方式构成完整的基础推导式:先使用范畴部分的规则,然后根据词条的句法特征,用词条替换空符号△的特定出现。相应地,我们得到如(21)所表征的那样的带标记的括号,其中词条按允许的方式替换了△的出现。这些都是基础短语标记。

请注意,向基础短语标记引进词条的规则,它在特征上完全不同于范畴部分的规则。我们用来构成(20)的规则(19)是非常基本的。每一个这样的规则都允许符号串"...A..."中的某个符号 A 被重写为某个符号串 Z,这种重写在推导式中不依赖于 A 的语境与 A 的来源。但在引进词条以替换△时,我们必须考虑△所出现的短语标记的被选择的方面。例如,如果△在短语标记中受 N 支配而不是受 V 支配的话,它的一个出现可以被"John"替换。因此,词汇插入规则,像范畴部分的规则一样,确实不适用于范畴和终端符号串,但适用于(21)这样的短语标记。应用于短语标记,并以某种方式改变短语标记的规则,用当前的术语可称之为(语法)转换。因此,词汇插入规则是转换规则,而范畴部分的规则是简单的重写规则。

现在让我们回到例子(22a)和(22b)。首先考虑(22a),其基础短语标记为(21a)①。我们立刻看到(21)只包含句子"John was sad."的深层结构所需要

---

① 所以,如其所示,我们假定(21a)与(21b)插入合适的词项扩展成完整的短语标记。

的信息。显然，符号串"past be"只是构成要素"was"的表达式，就像"past see"表征为"saw"与"past persuade"表征为"persuaded"一样。通过应用将"past be"转化为构成要素"was"的规则，我们得到句子"John was sad."的表层结构。此外，如果我们用前面所描述的方式定义语法功能和语法关系，则(21)表示"John"和"past be sad"之间存在主谓关系，它也包含了意义负载项"John、past、sad"的语义信息；事实上，我们可以假设，"past"本身就是一个普遍的有固定语义内容的终端字母；也可以假设，像词条的语音特征一样，从上面讨论的表达式的普遍系统中，选择词条"John"和"sad"的语义特征。总之，(21a)包含语义解释所需的所有信息，因此，我们可以把它当作句子"John was sad."底层的深层结构。

这个例子的正确性在于其非常普遍的正确性，即由范畴部分和词库生成的基础短语标记是决定语义解释的深层结构。在这种简单的情况下，只需要一个规则就可以将深层结构转化为表层结构，如将"past be"转化为构成要素"was"的规则。这个规则很显然同样适用于形式为"past V"的任意符号的规则的特殊情况，因此它确实是非常简单的转换规则（用刚刚给出的术语来说），胜于我们在范畴部分所发现的那类基本规则。这种观点可以概括化，即把深层结构转化为表层结构的规则是转换规则。

假定我们构成的是一个非常类似于(20)的推导式，而不是(20a)这个推导式。该推导式的短语标记如下：

(24)   S
        Q NP AUX VP
        Q NP AUX be ADJ
        Q N AUX be ADJ
        Q N M be ADJ
        Q △ △ be △
        Q John will be sad

我们想让符号Q表示有固定语义解释的普遍终端字母的符号，即相关句子为疑问句。假定句法的转换部分包含着这样一种规则，它能将"Q NP AUX…"形式的短语标记转化为相对应的"AUX NP …"形式的短语标记（即转换操作只用 Q 替换 AUX,其他短语标记不变)。该规则作用于(24)这样的短语标记,可得到句子"Will John be sad?"的带标记的括号,即形成该句的表层结构。

假定我们用重写 AUX 为 past 的规则取代(24)。上段的疑问句转换所给出的结果将是终端符号串为"past John be sad"的短语标记,跟(24)中给出的结果"Will John be sad?"相同。很显然,我们必须修正疑问句转换规则,使得它不仅仅倒置"past",而且在某些情况也能倒置符号串"past be",以至于能最后推导出"Was John sad?"。当这些规则被正确应用的时候,这种修正实际上很直接。

在(24)中,无论我们选择 M 还是"past",生成的基础短语标记都有资格充当深层结构。根据先前提出的定义,"John"跟"will(past)be sad"的语法关系,在(24)中跟在(20a)中完全相同,这也是经验上的充分性的要求。当然,表层形式并不直接地表达这些语法关系;正如我们早先的观察那样,重要的语法关系很少在表层结构中直接表达。

现在让我们转向更复杂的例子(20b)—(21b)—(22b)。(22b)的基础短语标记是(21b),它表达了句子"The boy will persuade John of the fact that Bill dreamt"的语义解释所需的信息,这个句子就是由(22b)推导出来的,其中就用了将"past dream"转化为"dreamt"的转换规则。因此,(21b)可以看作这个句子背后的深层结构,正如(21a)为"John was sad"的深层结构一样,也如对应于(24)的短语标记为"Will John be sad?"的深层结构一样。

假设在重写(20b)中第三行的 NP 时,我们所选不是"DET N that S"而是"N that S"[请看(19)的第四行],则(18)中出现于 N 的出现位置的唯一词项为"it"。因此,我们推导出的是(25)而不是(22b):

(25)　　the boy will persuade John of it that Bill past dream.

这两个句子中相关成分的语法关系与语义内容都没有改变。现在,假定句法的转换部分有如下效应的规则:

(26)　　a. it 在 that S 之前被删除
　　　　b. of 在 that S 之前被删除

按(26a)和(26b)的顺序依次对(25)进行操作,并用把"past dream"转化为"dreamt"的规则,我们推导出"The boy will persuade John that Bill dreamt."的表

层结构。对应于(25)的基础短语标记为这句话背后的深层结构。

注意,规则(26a)更为普遍。假设我们选择名词短语 NP "it that Bill past dream"做"past annoy John"的主语,这也受规则(18)(19)准许。由此得到:

(27)　it that Bill past dream past annoy John

应用规则(26a)(与形成动词过去式的规则),我们得出"That Bill dreamt annoyed John."。我们也可以应用有(28)效应的转换规则:

(28)　形式"it that S X"的短语标记被重组为对应的形式"it X that S"的短语标记

对(27)应用规则(28),我们得到"It annoyed John that Bill dreamt"。在这种情况下,(26a)是不适用的。因此(27)有两个表层结构,一个取决于(28),另一个取决于(26a);由于具有相同的深层结构,这两个表层结构同义。在(25)这种情况下,(28)是不适用的,因此,我们只有一个对应的表层结构。

考虑其他的转换规则,我们可以进一步探讨例(25)。假定内嵌句中选择的不是"Bill",而是第二次选择"John"。英语和其他语言都有一个一般性的转换规则,即对重复项进行删除。应用该规则和其他显而易见的辅助性规则,我们将由深层结构推导出(29):

(29)　The boy will persuade John to dream

该深层结构包含而且必须包含一个子短语标记,该子短语标记表达了"John"为"dream"的主语这一事实。事实上,在这种情况下,深层短语标记会稍微有些不同,不过这种不同在这概略性的描述中可以忽略。

现在假定我们添加了一个转换规则,它以非常显然的方式将形式为"NP AUX V NP"的短语标记转化为相应的被动形式[①]。将这个规则应用于跟(21b)非常像的短语标记,如(25)与(29),我们将会得到句子"John will be

---

[①] 注意,这个转换将修改它所应用的短语标记,其方式比上文讨论的还要彻底,但原则仍然相同。

persuaded that Bill dreamt (by the boy)"与"John will be persuaded to dream (by the boy)"的表层结构。在每种情况下,语义解释都是对底层短语标记的解释;在某些情况下,重要的语法关系在表层结构中会被完全遮蔽。因此,在句子"John will be persuaded to dream"中,"John"为"dream"的实际主语这一事实,在表层结构中没有显示出来,但在底层的深层结构中却被直接表达出来了,像我们之前所观察的那样。

从这些例子中,我们可以看到一系列的转换是怎样形成非常复杂的句子的,句中成分之间非常重要的关系并没有以任何直接的方式呈现。事实上,只有在人为的简单例句中,深层结构和表层结构才会对应得紧密些。在日常的普通句子中,语法关系非常复杂,因为在将底层结构转化为表层结构的过程中应用了一长串的转换。

我们所用的例子都是生硬的和不自然的。只用较少的基本语法,就可以提供更加自然的例子。例如,我们可以用更能让人接受的句子取代由(26)通过规则(27)或(28)形成的句子,如"That you should believe this is not surprising."和"It is not surprising that you should believe this."等。事实上,我们所用例子的不自然,正好阐明了一个简单但又常常被忽视的观点,那就是一个句子的固有意义及其语法功能是由规则决定的,而不是由使用条件、语境和内部成分的频率等决定的①。因此,上面的几段例子在一些说话者的经验中(或者说,在语言的历史中)可能从不会产生,但是它们作为英语句子的身份,理想语音和语义解释是不会受这一事实的影响。

因为一系列的转换会造成短语标记中的重大修改,所以我们对以下事实的发现不必感到惊讶:单一的结构②可能源于两个完全不同的深层结构,即某个句子具有歧义性[参见 110 页例句(4)③]。歧义句能够特别清晰地表明表

---

① 尽管这些因素可能会影响运用。因此,它们可能影响物理信号,并在决定人们如何解释句子方面起作用。在产生和理解句子时,听—说双方都利用理想的语音解释与语义解释,但其他因素也会起作用。说话者可能只对让自己所说的被听懂感兴趣,说话者可能只对确定说话者的意图感兴趣(这可能跟他所生成的句子或句子片段的字面语义解释不同)。我们必须再一次坚持区分运用与能力的必要性,如果其中的某一个需要认真研究的话。

② 更准确地说,两个表层结构足够接近,以致能决定相同的语音表达式。

③ 原书前文的例句为:What disturbed John was being disregarded by everyone.(困扰约翰的是众人的漠视。)——编者注

层结构作为深层关系的表达式是不充分的。①

更普遍的是,我们可以很容易地找到这样的成对的句子,它们在本质上有着相同的表层结构,却有着完全不同的语法关系。这里只举一个例子,请比较(30)中的句子:

(30) a. I persuaded the doctor to examine John.
  我劝医生检查约翰。
 b. I expected the doctor to examine John.
  我希望医生检查约翰。

它们的表层结构在本质上是相同的。例句(30a)跟例句(29)的形式相同。(30a)由一个和形式(31)大致相同的深层结构推导而来:

(31) *I past persuad the doctor of it that the doctor AUX examine John*

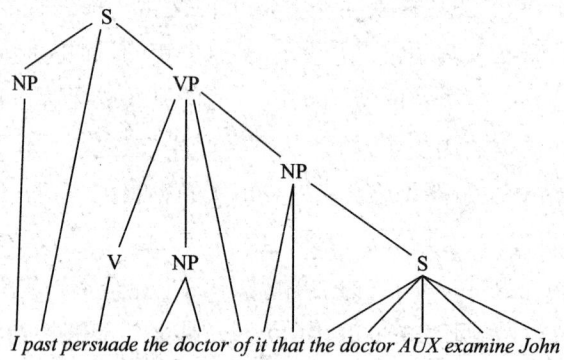

I past persuade the doctor of it that the doctor AUX examine John

这个深层结构在本质上和(21b)是一样的,通过与例句(29)有联系的转换过程,我们由它推导出例句(30a)。但是在例句(30b)中,没有像"I expected

---

① 作为研究工具,现代语言学也偶尔使用语言的这种属性。最先概括讨论如何使用歧义阐释句法结构某些概念的不充分性的是霍凯特的《语法描写的两种模型》(C. F. Hockett, Two Models for Grammatical Description, *Word*, Vol. 10, 1954, pp. 210-31, reprinted in M. Joos, ed., *Readings in Linguistics One*, 4th ed., Chicago: University of Chicago Press, 1966)。

the doctor of the fact that he examined John"、"…of the necessity(for him) to examine John"等有关的结构,而在例句(30a)中有。相应地,没有理由将(30b)分析为由(31)这样的结构推导而来的,(30b)底层的深层结构应该像(32)这样(再次省略细节):

（32） *I past expect it that the doctor AUX examine John*

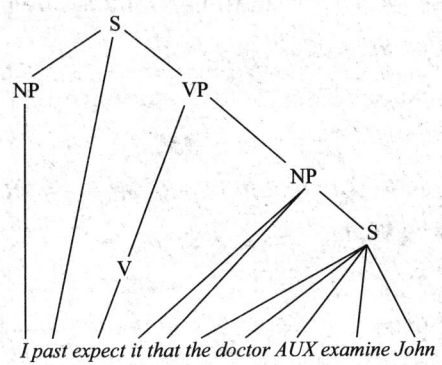

有很多其他事实支持(30a)与(30b)的这种分析。比如说,我们可以根据(32)这样的结构形成"What I expected was that the doctor (will, should, etc.) examine John",所用规则跟由"NP－V－NP"结构"I saw the book."的底层结构推导出"What I saw was the book"的规则相同。但我们不能形成对应于(30a)的"What I persuaded was that the doctor should examine John",因为(31)这一底层结构不是转换所需要的"NP－V－NP"形式。对(32)应用规则(26a),我们推导出"I expected that the doctor (will, should, etc.) examine John."。通过使用得出(29)的相同规则,我们推导出(30b),其中内嵌句包含的是"to"而不是"that",在这种情况,内嵌句不包含范畴AUX的其他表达式。

忽略无关细节,我们看到(30a)由(31)推导而来,(30b)由(32)推导而来,所以,尽管(30a)与(30b)的表层结构几乎等同,但它们的深层结构却非常不同。深层结构中必须有这种分别的说法也根本不是显而易见的①。但如果我

---

① 事实上,英语的现代语法学者与传统的语法学者好像都没有关注这种现象。

们考虑以下效应,就会很清楚,如用被动形式"John to be examined by the doctor"替换(30a)与(30b)中的"the doctor to examine John",分别得到待考察的(33)与(34):

(33) a. I persuaded the doctor to examine John [=30a]
我劝那个医生检查约翰。

b. I persuaded John to be examined by the doctor.
我劝约翰由那个医生检查。

(34) a. I expected the doctor to examine John [=30b]
我希望那个医生检查约翰。

b. I expected John to be examined by the doctor.
我希望约翰由那个医生检查。

(34)中一组句子的的语义关系完全不同于(33)中一组句子的语义关系。我们可以通过考虑真值中的关系看出这点。(34a)和(34b)在真值上必然相同:如果"我希望那个医生检查约翰",那就是"我希望约翰由那个医生检查",反过来也是如此。但是(33a)和(33b)在真值上没有必然的关系:"我劝那个医生检查约翰",并不意味着"我劝约翰由那个医生检查",反过来也如此。

实际上,从某种非常清晰的意义上说,内嵌句中主动与被动的互换在(30b)中而不是在(30a)中保持意义不变。这种解释直接来自对这些句子底层的深层结构的考虑。用被动形式替换(32)中的主动形式,我们接着推导(34b),其方式跟由(32)推导(30b)相同。但要推导(33b),我们不仅要对(31)中的内嵌句进行被动化,而且必须选择"John"而不是选择"the doctor"作动词"persuade"的宾语;否则,删除重复的名词短语的条件将不能得到满足,像(29)的推导一样需删除重复的名词短语。所以,(33b)与(33a)的深层结构完全不同。不仅是内嵌句需要被动化,而且(31)中的宾语"the doctor"也必须换成"John"。因而,这种语法关系是完全不同的,相应地,语义解释也不同。这一直是事实,在这两种情况中,被动化不会改变意义(这里是就相关的"意义"而言)。在(30a)中,当"the doctor to examine John"被换成"John to be examined by the doctor"时,意义会发生变化,意义的变化是由语法关系的变化引起的,现在深层结构中动词短语的直接宾语是"John",而不是"the doctor"。

就(34a)来说,它没有对应的变化,因此当它的深层结构变为被动语态时,意义保持不变。

例子(30a)和(30b)再次说明:表层结构在表征语义上的重要的语法关系时表现不充分(而且,总体来说是不相干的)。有的带标记的括号传达的是语音解释所需的信息,有的带标记的括号传达的是语义解释所需的信息,一般来说两种括号标记很不相同。例子(30a)和(30b)的也说明了把一个人的"语言直觉"变成意识可能非常困难。我们已经看到,英语语法作为能力的体现(参考102页的注释①),为了描写的充分性,必须向(30a)和(30b)中的句子指派不同的深层结构。每个说话者内化的语法的确都能够区分这些深层结构,我们可以从如下事实中看出:任何英语说话者都有能力理解用被动形式替换(30)中两句的内嵌句有什么后果。但即使仔细地观察说母语者,都可能会忽略他内化语言能力的事实。

这些例子或许能够展现语言句法结构的特点。总结我们关于句法部分的观察,得到的结论是,它包括一个基础与一个转换部分。基础生成深层结构,转换规则把深层结构转化为表层结构。基础的范畴部分定义了语言中重要的语法关系,把合理的顺序指派给底层短语,而且以各种方式决定应用哪种转换②。词库详述了各个词项的独特属性。基础的这个部分似乎能够一起为语义解释提供相关的信息,从我们使用这个术语的角度看,也受制于前面所提到的条件。转换规则将短语标记转化为新的短语标记,影响了各种重新排序与重新组织。会受影响的变化种类是极其有限的;但是,我们在这里将不会深入讨论这个问题。然而,顺次应用转换,可能会非常彻底地影响基础短语标记的组织。因此,转换提供了种类繁多的表层结构,它们与它们起源的并且表达语义内容的基础结构没有直接或者简单的关联。

非常重要的事实是:由深层结构到表层结构的映射不是一步达成的,而是可分析为一系列连续的转换步骤。对由深层结构到表层结构的映射有贡献的转换,可以用许多不同的方式联合在一起,这取决于它们应用的深层结构的形式。既然这些转换顺次应用,每个转换就都要为下个转换的应用产生一类结构。在我们的形式描述中这个条件被满足,因为转换应用于短语标记

---

① 此处指原书102页的注释。——编者注
② 这种决定是否是唯一的,目前尚无定论。

并将它们转化为新的短语标记。这里有一个很好的经验证据,即决定语音形式的表层结构实际上是短语标记(即构成要素的括号标记)。因而可以断定,在我们的形式描述中,最初应用转换的深层结构自身也应该是短语标记。

原则上,一套语法关系可以用很多种方式表现出来。我们选择的是短语标记的方法,短语标记是由基础规则生成的。选择短语标记的方法的一个主要原因正好是如下事实:转换必须顺次应用,所以也必须应用于它们自身所产生的客体,最终应用于跟表层结构有着相同形式属性的短语标记①。

黄正德(1982)《汉语生成语法——汉语中的逻辑关系及语法理论》选读②

◆ 作者简介

黄正德③(C. T. James Huang),1948 年出生于台湾,在台湾师范大学取得学士、硕士学位,1982 年在麻省理工学院取得博士学位,曾先后于夏威夷大学、台湾清华大学、康奈尔大学、加州大学尔湾分校等学校任教,现为哈佛大学语言学系教授。2014 年他获台湾语言学会终身成就奖,2015 年当选为美国语言学会会士(fellow),2016 年当选为台湾"中央研究院"院士。他致力于生成语法框架下英语和汉语的研究,出版了若干高水平的学术论文和专著,在汉语语法结构方面做出了杰出贡献,被认为"引领了汉语句法学的开拓和发展"。

---

① 这里还有其他的支持理由。一方面,总的来说,语法关系不是词间的关系,也不是语素间的关系,而是短语间的关系。另一方面,经验主义的探讨一致地显示出在底层结构中有一个最理想的短语顺序,这与底层结构由上面讨论过的基础系统生成的假设相一致。
② 黄正德,《汉语生成语法——汉语中的逻辑关系及语法理论》,宁春岩、侯方、张达三译,黑龙江大学科技处,1983 年 6 月。
③ 图片来源:https://static.hwpi.harvard.edu/files/styles/profile_full/public/linguistics/files/huang2x.jpg。

◆ 正文节选

第二章　短语结构及 $\bar{X}$ 理论

2.0　引言

在一种特定的语言中,确定逻辑关系的一个最重要的因素是这种语言的句法结构。所以,我们的讨论应该从汉语的短语结构开始谈起,主要看一看汉语中有哪些事实符合最优的短语结构理论。讨论时将首先勾划一下基本的短语结构式,然后再简要地讨论一下汉语的语言类型学方面的问题。我们将会看到,要想对汉语的句法结构做出充分的描述,最好是从恰当的 X 理论及从这一理论推导出来的类型学方面来考虑。汉语和英语在词序上均属 SVO 语言,但这两种语言在结构上的共同点大多数限于这一方面。从短语结构理论上看,英语适用于全部中心词在前的结构,而汉语中大多数为中心词在后的结构,只有很少的一部分结构是中心词在前的。在汉语的表层结构中,中心词只能一次左接分枝,即中心词出现在分枝节结的右侧,或者说在多次分枝的最低层次上。英语允许各种各样的左分枝结构产生,而汉语却是一种严格的右分枝语言。汉语的这个特点可以用来说明有关表层可接受性的语言事实,并对大量的语言结构做出可能的解释。第三、四章还将提到汉语的这个特点,这在确定汉语的量词域和其他成分的逻辑域时将成为一个重要的类型学上的特点。

本章讨论中心为 NP,VP,AP 和 PP 等短语范畴,此外还讨论量词短语的结构以及包含补语化成分和话题化短语的结构问题。

2.1　基本结构短语

汉语的基本词序是主语——谓语——宾语,而副词修饰语一般出现于主语和谓语动词之间。

(1) 张三昨天在学校看见了李四。

以形容词为主句谓语的句子也呈现为同样的格式:

(2) 他在学校很高兴这件事。

及物句的词序变化一般是:动词的宾语出现在以介词"把"为首的动词前

PP中。这就是所说的"把"字结构。下面两句话的主题结构是一样的,(3)中动词后面的 NP 和(4)中动词前面的 PP 都具有同样的主题关系,都是动词的"受事"。

(3) 他骗了李四。
(4) 他把李四骗了。

从(3)变到(4)的变化以往称之为"把字变换",按照这个规则,动词后面的宾语要提到动词前面。像(2)这样的及物性形容词句中,动词后的宾语也可在以"对"字开头的 PP 形式中出现。

(5) 他很高兴这件事。
(6) 他对这件事很高兴。

从这些句子中可以看出:谓语的语义上或主题上的宾语在表层结构中可出现在谓语动词之前,也可出现在谓语动词之后。但是,在句法上,一个宾语只有当嵌套在 PP 之中时,才可出现在动词之前;如果没有介词时,宾语得出现在动词之后。但是,在句法上,一个宾语只有当嵌套在 PP 之中时,才可以出现在动词之前;如果没有介词时,宾语得出现在动词之后[像话题化(topicalization)这种"远程移动"(long distance movement)除外]。这种规则适用于 VP,AP 也适用于 PP。按照句法范畴 NP 的宾语一定在中心词之后的规定,PP 的内部结构应该是一个 P 后面跟着它的宾语 NP。与 VP 及 AP 不同的是,PP 中的 P 之前永远不会出现修饰语。

名词短语的内部结构基本上与 VP 和 AP 的内部结构相同,即所有的修饰成分在中心名词之前。这种修饰成分包括所有性质的短语、"限定词——数词——量词"短语(以下简称 QP)、形容词及其他的修饰语:

(7) [NP[NP他的] [QP那双 [VP会说话的] [AP漂亮的] 眼睛]]

NP 同其他范畴之间的一个重要差别是:名词的宾语补语只能在名词之前,而不能在名词之后;但对于 AP 和 VP 来说,如果宾语作为一个不受 PP 管辖的NP出现时,那么这个宾语只能位于动词之后,而不能位于动词之前。从语义上看,没有理由说名词不可带有宾语,尤其当名词是动词的名物化形式时更是如此。应该注意到,不及物动词可在不改变词序的情况下直接变成名物化的形式,(8)就是这种例子。但及物动词则做不到这点,(9)(10)便是这种例子。

(8) a. 耶稣复活了。
　　b. 耶稣的复活
(9) a. 他热爱祖国。
　　b. *他的热爱祖国
(10) a. 他了解这件事情。
　　 b. *他的了解这件事情

(9)(10)可接受的名物化形式应该是(11)(12)的样子,其中的宾语补语出现在"对"引出的PP之中。

(11) 他对祖国的热爱
(12) 他对这件事情的了解

如果从作为人类的一种固有的认知能力的普遍语法(UG)出发,这些事实会向我们提出这样一个重要问题:普遍语法(UG)的词序和短语结构原则是什么? 这些原则的参数又是什么,当它们确定下来之后,语法就会在学习汉语的儿童的大脑中"生长"? 我们提到的这些汉语语言事实更有意义的方面在于它们本身构成了Greenberg(1966)著名普遍词序格式的反例。比如,按照Greenberg的框架,如果一种语言中的定语从句在中心名词之前,那么这种语言则是后置性(postpositional)语言。可是,这和我们看到的汉语中定语从句在中心词之前而汉语却是前置性(prepositional)的事实相矛盾。另外,按照Greenberg的理论框架,汉语应是SOV语言,因为在这种语言中名词、动词和形容词的修饰成分都在中心词之前。如果,把宾语限制在NP范畴之内,那么汉语则是绝对的SVO语言。这类显然相互矛盾的事实最近使人们陷入是否应概括地把语言分成要么单纯是SOV语言,要么单纯是SVO

语言的争论。比如，戴浩一(1973a)建议把汉语的潜在结构看成为 SOV，而再用转换机制推导出表层的非 SOV 特征来。对于这种观点有人赞同，有人反对，在反对的人中有梅广(1980)和屈承熹(1980)等学者。事实上，汉语的确具有 SVO 语言的一整套系统性的特点，但同时又具有 SOV 的系统性特点。因此，无论把汉语看成是 SVO 语言，还是把汉语看成是 SOV 语言，都必须解释说明非 SVO 的特点或非 SOV 的特点。但，以我来看，这两种努力迄今还没有产生出什么令人信服的成果，汉语究竟属哪种语言仍悬而未决。

汉语中明显的不规律的词序使李讷和 Thompson(1976b, 1978)对 Greenberg 的词序类型理论提出质疑，他们甚至认为不可能用 Greenberg 的类型学来描写汉语。他们提出了一种基于"话题——突出"/"主语——突出"("topic-prominence" VS. "subject-prominence")这类概念基础上的语用类型学(pragmatic typology)。这样，汉语中词序的可能性便主要取决于语用和语义因素，而与语法结构无关。这种理论主张实际上避免了人们所争论的问题。虽然，从语用或功用的角度看待语言类型问题不无道理，但是没有充分的理由得出汉语中的词序可能性与语法结构无关。按他们的意见，像汉语这种语言是"话题——突出"的语言，而像英语这类语言是"主语——突出"的语言。从这点出发，他们已对这两种语言间的差别做了一些描述，其中有些差别从其他方面是无法解释的。可是，很难解释为什么"话题——突出"的语言使用名词前定语从句，"主语——突出"的语言使用名词后定语从句，而两者又均是前置性语言。如果，语用和语义因素是决定汉语词序的全部因素，那么，我们似乎能在这种语言中找到全部可以想象得出来的词序，这当然是不符合汉语事实的。

第 2.2 节中指出：如果把 Greenberg 的类型理论放到更普遍的 UG 框架中，汉语中的似乎是无规律的词序问题也可应刃而解了。现在，有些学者(Hale 1979, 1980, Stowell 1981, Farmer 1980)显然采用了这种方法。如果，把 Greenberg 的类型学中所使用的主要特征看成是 UG 一般原则的参数化结果，即 X 阶标理论(X-bar theory)原则的参数化结果，而不是采用独立的类型学理论，那么，汉语中的词序问题不会比英语中的词序问题更难解决。

2.2 独立的类型学和 X̄ 类型学

Greenberg 研究中提到的一个重要事实是：典型的 VSO 语言中的词序特征群正好构成了典型的 SOV 语中词序特征群的镜象。除了一些例外，在大多数情况下，的确像他所指出的那样，一种语言不是具有(13)中的四个属性，就是具有(14)中的四个属性：

(13) a. SOV
b. 后置性
c. 名词修饰语位于中心词之前
d. 副词位于主要动词或形容词中心词之前
(14) a. VSO
b. 前置性
c. 名词修饰语位于中心词之后
d. 副词位于主要动词或形容词中心词之后

Greenberg 把这些特征群列成为许多"内涵性共项"（implicational universals）。但是，这种方法使许多重要问题没有得到解决。比如，没有解释为什么要有这些内涵性共项，即为什么一种属性的存在要蕴含着另一种属性的存在。另外，在汉语中出现例外的情况下（象上面讨论过的那样），这种方法缺乏解释这些例外现象的原则基础，也无法解释为什么其他一些可以想象出来的例外却不太容易出现。比如，在 Greenberg 列出的 142 种语言中，具有 VSO 特征和后置属性的语言及具有 SOV 特征和前置属性的语言均为这种少见的例外。

我认为，Greenberg 理论的主要缺点是他把类型学建立在一种独立的理论考虑之上。他把 SVO：SOV：VSO 作为语言类型分类的基本的独立的参数，此外又加上了前置：后置参数和 Adj-N：N-Adj 参数作为区分标准。这样就不可能在确定 SOV：SOV：VSO 参数后，使待确定的前置：后置参数值自动地确定下来。

为要弄清为什么可从(13)和(14)的特征群中会得出内涵共项来，有必要搞清这些特征间的共性。(13a-d)中最明显的共性是，在一个短语范畴结构中，中心词出现在位于所有外围成分，即修饰成分和补足成分之后的最后位置上。(14a-d)的共性是：在一个短语中，中心词出现在外围成分之前的位置上。(在有的文献中，有人认为：许多语言中的 V 或 VP 是句子的中心词。(13-a)与(13b-d)呈相同形式，(14-a)同(14b-d)呈相同形式，这支持了上述看法。)从这种观察出发，为什么(13)(14)中的特征群中会产生内涵共项的问题则不复存在了。如果，一种语言是中心词在后的语言，那么当然它也便是典型的动词在后、名词在后、形容词在后的语言及后置性或副词在后的语言。中心词在前的语言恰好与此相反。这么讲没有什么奇怪的，如果大多数语言具有(13a,c)的特点而又具有(14b,d)的特点那倒奇怪了。

对(13)和(14)的正确概括是：语言应该分为两类，一类是全部为中心词在后的内向(endocentric)结构语言；另一类是均为中心词在前[范畴交错的(cross-categorilly)]的内向结构语言。Greenberg 的类型学中没有做出这种概括，可很容易在 Chomsky(1970)的 $\bar{X}$ 短语结构理论中做出。Chomsky 的这一理论原用来作为名物化理论的基础。X 阶标理论的最基本的内容是：n 层次上的范畴 X 直接管辖由 n-1 层次上同 X 相同之范畴构成的串，这个串的前面或后面有时可有一个或多个外围短语。X 阶标理论的主要规则可分别写成(15)和(16)的样子：

(15) $X^a \rightarrow VP^* \ X^{a-1}$

(16) $X^a \rightarrow X^{a-1} \ YP^*$

这两个规则当然也可以并为一个镜象规则。在(15)(16)的形式中箭头的两侧都出现了相同的范畴符号，这便可以得到短语结构的内向性。另一方面，范畴交错现象可通过把 X 当作 N,V,A,P 的变量来表达。这样，变量则当作特征群[$\alpha N, \beta V$]（其中，α 和 β 代表＋或－）的缩写。概括性弱一点的办法是对 X 的特征群中的 α, β 值作部分规定。

X 阶标类型学与 Greenberg 的独立性类型学不同，把(15)和(16)看成为一种参数的两个值。这种类型理论认为，语言间的类型上的主要分界点在于对(15)这一中心词在后规则和(16)这一中心词在前规则进行选择上，无论(15)还是(16)，X 可为任何一种范畴。从语言获得的角度讲，由于 UG 的作用，一个儿童在形成符合(13)或(14)中所表达的语言知识之前，只须确定(15)或(16)即可。一种优化类型理论不应是独立的，而应像 Ken Hale 所说的那样,是 UG 理论的副产品。

至于说到那些不易按(15)和(16)作类型分辨的语言,我们认为可以把它们看作同时适用于中心词在前和中心词在后的规则,但运用的方式是不相同的。中心词在后/中心词在前的参数值不必为所有的范畴及其层次确定下来。比如说,很可能是,在短语结构的某个层次上(如双阶标层次上)某种语言运用的是中心词在后的规则,而在低一级的层次上运用的是中心词在前的规则。在每一个层次上,对(15)(16)的选用不必一次为所有范畴做出,而只应为某一种自然的次范畴种类或一个范畴种类做出。这种 $\bar{X}$ 理论特征系统的简洁度反映了(13)(14)不能描写的语言中的相对的标记性。比如说,在某一层次上,短语范畴不用同一种规则的语言,可以被看作是相对具有使用同一种规则的语言的标记,这是因为这种语言包括有更为复杂的语法,其中要求有更多的规则,更多的特征,但应用的范围较小。据我观察,对语言标记性的这种预测基本上是正确的,至少在范畴交错的基础上是这样的,诚然问题要比这复杂的多,因为一种 VSO 语言否真地比大量的 SVO 语言的标记性弱,这是不得而知的事。如果 V 是句子的中心词,那么 VSO 语言只须(16)这一种中心词在前的规则,而 SVO 则须用(15)和(16)两种规则。假设内向 $\bar{X}$ 结构必须是中心词在后或中心词在前的,那么"中心词在中间"(head-medial)的结构就必须运用(15)和(16)这两种规则了。英语就是具有这种结构的语言,很难说英语的 NP,AP 和 PP 的内部结构是否是先用中心词在后的规则,再用中心词在前的规则,如:

(17) a. $[_{\bar{N}}$ Their $[_{\bar{N}}[_{\bar{N}}$ destruction$]$ of thecity$]]$
b. $[_{\bar{A}}$ How $[_{\bar{A}}[_{A}$ happy$]$ about the news$]]$
c. $[_{\bar{P}}$ So much $[_{\bar{P}}[_{P}$ off$]$ the track$]]$

另外,有些学者(如 Jackendoff 1977,Marantz 1980)认为英语中的动词是从句的中心词。根据这一看法,句子形式的结构同(17)这种短语结构相同:

(18) $[_{\bar{V}}$ They $[_{\bar{V}}[_{V}$ destroyed$]$ the city$]]$

也有人(Chomsky 1981,Hale 1978 等)认为英语句子的中心词不是动词而是 INFL(屈折变化成分)或 AUX(助动词)。按照这种做法,一个句子的内部结构同(17)相同,其中 INFL 与 VP 构成一个成分(Chomsky 1965):

(19) [$_{\overline{\text{INFL}}}$ They [$_{\overline{\text{INFL}}}$ [$_{\text{INFL}}$ did] destroy the city]]

在(17)—(19)的各个结构中,我们在扩展单一短语范畴时既使用了中心词在后的规则又使用了中心词在前的规则,这样就有必须至少分出两个短语结构层次:$\overline{\overline{X}}$和$\overline{X}$英语的组列便可据此做出。在典型的中心词在后或中心词在前的语言中,(15)和(16)中只须选用一个,而不是两个。在比$\overline{X}$更高的结构层次上不必如此。因此,日语可能具有一种"平直"(flat)结构,所有的外围成分都按线性顺序出现在中心词的左侧(见 Hale 1980, Farmer 1980)。有些人(Chomsky 1981a)建议用确立[±组列性]这一参数的方法把语言分为组列性语言(Configurational language)和非组列性语法(non-configurational language)。很明显,这种区别可能取决于一种语言是否有高于一个阶标的结构层次。一种语言如果具有高于一个阶标的结构层次的$\overline{X}$结构其一原因之一就是为它具有"中心词在中间"的性质,需要使用(15)(16)这两种规则。

使某种语言中$\overline{X}$结构高于一个阶标的另一个因素可能是在一个特定的短语中某些成分成为该短语内的一种子成分。比如说,虽然马拉格西语(Malagasy)中句子的词序只要求中心词在后的规则,但有些学者(如 Keenan 1976)认为动词和宾语构成一个 VP。同样,我们满有理由说,英语中动词和它的补语之间的关系要比定语从句和它的中心名词之间的关系更紧密。因此,Jackendoff (1977)认为:既然名词短语的补语受 N 后之 $\overline{N}$ 管辖,最好把限制性定语从句或其他修饰语看成是受 $\overline{\overline{N}}$ 管辖,非限制性定语从句受 $\overline{N}$ 管辖。同样应该把英语的状语短语看成是受高于动词宾语层次之短语节结管辖。

下面回到汉语上来。先让我们研究一下它在 X 阶标类型理论中属于哪种。像英语一样,汉语在描写短语结构时,同时需要(15)和(16)这两种规则。这是因为动词和形容词出现在宾语和非宾语之间。这说明汉语是一种至少需要双阶标结构的组列性语言(如果句子的中心词是 V 或 A 时,$\overline{\overline{V}}$和$\overline{\overline{A}}$分别表示句子)。但是,汉语同英语有两点不同。汉语中,中心词在先的规则只用于 VP,AP,PP 三个范畴,不用于 NP 范畴。这可以直接看作是汉语在范畴交错方面的一个有标记的特性,虽然可能在某个层次上可做出更好的概括来。这也就是说,虽然人们趋于对所有语言的所有的范畴,一次性把[±中心词在后]和[±中心词在前]的参数确定下来,但是可以对每一种语言的一个个范畴分别确定这些参数。这样,英语则选用[＋中心词在后]和[＋中心词在前]的参数,并用于全部范畴。与英语不同的是,汉语对 NP 只选用[＋中心词在后]而不是[＋中心词在前]的参数。同英语相比,汉语的另一个不同的特点是在使用中心词在后及中心词在前这两种规则的范畴中,中心词之后只能是补语成分,不可能是状语从句或短语这些修饰成分。而在英语中,不仅名词和动词的补语可出现在中心词之后的位置上,而且它们的修饰成分(定语从句、状语从句等)亦可出现在中心词后面的位置上。另外,汉语允许在中心词前面的位置上出现各种各样的外围性短语,而英语中中心词前面成分的种类十分有限,一般说来,只限于起限定词(specifiers)、主语、强调语(intensifiers)和单个起的修饰语(形容词、副词)作用的范畴;而其他非名词性状语短语或从句必须位于中心词之后。为说明汉英两种语言间的差异,可以提出这种论断:对每一种语言,[±中心词在后]和[±中心词在前]的参数可在短语扩展的每一个层次上确定。汉语只在短语扩展的最低层次上,即$\overline{X}$层次上,选用中心词在前的规则,而在 VP, AP, PP 这些短语中允许补足语出现在中心词的右侧。但在其他高一级的扩展层次($\overline{\overline{X}}$,$\overline{\overline{\overline{X}}}$等)上,要求使用中心词在后的规则,主语、限定语及所有的修饰语位于中心词左侧。而英语中,只有一两个扩展的最高层次(X^{max}, X^{max-1})允许使用中心词在后的规则,但其他所中心词在前的规则。汉语主要用中心词在后的规则,在细微末节上使用有层次都需用中心词在前的规则;英语与之相反,主要使用中心词在前的规则,在细微末节上使用中心词在后的规则。然而,两者均属 SVO 语。

有(15)和(16)这两个规则,再加上有关语言可以从范畴类型和层次方面确定参数的假说,那么就没理由说什么存在着"典型的 SVO 语言"了,或者说有什么"典型的"中心词在中间的而语言了。从某种意义上来说,所有的中心词在中间的语言都是"偏离"于中心词在后和中心词在前这两种"典型"语言的,因而在不同程度便成为"不典型"的了。说英语是"典型的 SVO 语言"(参见 Lehman 1978)似乎也没有什么意义。汉语中有关词序的事实既然并不是"典型的 SVO"类的事实,也就没有必要据此来讨论汉语的词序了,也不会产生在某一抽象的层次上提出 SOV 顺序的动机。

Rizzi（2001）"Relativized Minimality Effects"选读[1]

◆ **作者简介**

Luigi Rizzi[2]（1952—　），意大利语言学家，先后在意大利比萨大学、法国巴黎第八大学学习，曾任教于麻省理工学院、加州大学洛杉矶分校、巴黎高等师范学院、日内瓦大学等，现为锡耶纳大学全职教授。他多年来专注于句法理论和语言习得的研究，在制图理论、局域性理论和比较句法等方面做出了突出贡献。

◆ **原文节选**

0 Introduction

Natural language expressions are potentially unbounded in length and depth of embedding, as a consequence of the recursive nature of natural language syntax. Nevertheless, the core of syntactic processes is inherently local, in that such processes are bound to apply within limited structural domains. The search for the relevant locality principles is one of the central topics of generative grammar. In this chapter I would like to report on a subclass of locality effect which has been the focus of intensive research since the late 1980s or so. Such effects are all amenable to the following abstract form: in the configuration:

(1) ... X... Z... Y...

Y cannot be related to X if Z intervenes and Z has certain characteristics

---

[1] Luigi Rizzi, 2001, "Relativized Minimality Effects," In Mark Baltin and Chris Collins (eds), *The Handbook of Contemporary Syntactic Theory*, Oxford: Blackwell.
[2] 图片来源：https://upload.wikimedia.org/wikipedia/commons/3/32/Luigi_Rizzi.jpg。

in common with X. So, in order to be related to X, Y must be in a minimal configuration with X, where Minimality is relativized to the nature of the structural relation to be established. The major cases illustrating such Relativized Minimality (RM) effects involve the theory of chains: in the general case, a chain cannot be built between X and Y in configuration (1). In the first part of this chapter, I will present Relativized Minimality effects on the different types of chain through a representational formulation of the relevant locality principle, as in Rizzi (1990). I will then focus on A'-chains and refine the approach to deal with complex patterns of Minimality effects induced by different kinds of adverbial modifier. This part will also contain a brief comparison with the derivational approach proposed by Chomsky (1995b). I will conclude with a discussion of Minimality effects in head-phrase interactions.

1 Relativized Minimality

It is a central property of natural languages that elements can be pronounced in positions different from those in which they are interpreted as thematic arguments, as theta-assigners, as modifiers of various sorts, etc. By "chain" I mean the connection between a displaced element and its traces, down to the relevant interpretive position. I will not take a position here on the question of whether such a connection is established by movement (an operation distinct from the fundamental structure-building operation, which perhaps simply consists in stringing together two elements into a third element, "Merge" in Chomsky's 1995b sense) or is read off configurations (Rizzi 1986) created by the fundamental structure-building operation uniquely. When I mention movement from now on, I simply use the term metaphorically, to refer to an abstract relation between two structural positions.

On the other hand, following Chomsky's (1995b) approach, I will assume that traces are silent copies of antecedents, and I will express them as fully specified positions within angled brackets (as in Starke 1997; in other environments I will use more standard symbols for traces such as "t" or "___

_".). So, (2a) will have a representation like (2b):

(2) a. How did you solve the problem?
b. How did you solve the problem <how>?

Now, it is well known that certain structural environments block chain formation; for instance, a *wh*-chain starting from an adverb position fails across an indirect question:

(3) a. I wonder who could solve the problem in this way.
b. *How do you wonder who could solve this problem <how>?

It is natural to think of (3b) as illustrating pattern (1): a chain cannot connect *how* and its trace in (3b) because another *wh*-element intervenes in the lower Spec of C.

In order to express the effect precisely, I will adopt the following principle (a simplification and updating of RM in Rizzi 1990):

(4) Y is in a Minimal Configuration (MC) with X iff
there is no Z such that
(i) Z is of the same structural type as X, and
(ii) Z intervenes between X and Y

So, if we think of Y as the position from which the relevant relation is computed, and X as the target of the computation (i.e., in the case of chain formation, the trace Y seeks for an antecedent X), the two elements are in a minimal configuration when there is nointervening element having certain structural characteristics in common with the target. A proper typology of positions is critical for the system to work; i.e., we must achieve the result that none of the intervening positions blocks the chain in the well-formed

(2b), while at least one position does in (3b). The typology must involve at least two irreducible distinctions:

> (5) (i) between heads and phrases and, in the latter class,
> (ii) between positions of arguments (A'-positions) and of non-arguments (A'-positions).

Intervention could be defined hierarchically, in terms of c-command (Z c-commands one but not the other), but it could also be relativized to the kind of relation looked at (particularly if we want to extend the system to deal with locality in ellipsis, on which see below).

We can now define a chain through the notion of minimal configuration (4), as follows:

> (6) $(A_1, ..., A_n)$ is a chain iff, for $1 \leqslant i < n$
> (i) $A_i = A_{i+1}$
> (ii) A_i c-commands A_{i+1}
> (iii) A_{i+1} is in a MC with A_i

So, each chain link involves identity (under the copy-theory of traces), c-command and Minimality.

Going back to (3b), chain formation between how and <how> fails because the two are not in a minimal configuration due to the intervention of *who*, an element of the same structural kind as *how*, an A'-specifier.

Notice that locality as expressed by (4) does not involve c-command. It seems to be the case that prominence (expressed by c-command) and locality (expressed by (4)) are two fundamental and independent configurational notions that natural languages use. Chains require both prominence and locality to hold, but other complex relations dissociate them. For instance, the possibility of interpreting a pronoun as a variable bound by a quantified expression requires c-command, hence (8) is out, but it is totally insensitive to locality, as in (7):

(7) a. *No candidate* can predict how many people will vote for *him*.
b. *Every politician* is worried when the press starts attacking *him*.
c. *Which politician* appointed the journalist who supported *him*?

(8) *The fact that *no candidate* was elected shows that *he* was inadequate.

The converse case may also exist: certain kinds of ellipsis seem to involve locality but not c-command. E.g., the gapped verb in (9) can be interpreted as identical to the local verb *buy*, not to the non-local verb *sell* (see Koster 1978 for relevant discussion):

(9) John sells books, Mary buys records and Bill V newspapers.

We have seen that chains involve both locality and c-command to hold. The fourth case may also exist: simple coreference requires neither:

(10) The question of whether *John* met Mary worries the people who support *him*.

Going back to chains, they divide into three fundamental kinds, depending on the nature of the displaced element and on the nature of the position it occupies. The first crucial distinction is between X chains and XP chains; then within the latter class, we want to distinguish at least between Argument chains (involved in passive, raising, and in fact any movement to subject position under the VP internal subject hypothesis, as well as object movement to various IP internal positions) and operator chains (involved in questions, relatives, exclamatives, focus movement, etc.). By and large, argument chains involve IP internal positions, while operator chains involve the CP system of the clause, the left periphery, even though the distinction is not absolute (see below). Different descriptive locality conditions hold of the three kinds of chain, head chains being by far the most local, and operator chains the most liberal. The system sketched out here is an attempt to subsume such descriptive conditions under a unified principle. We will now consider the different kinds of chain separately.

2 Head Chains

In general, heads cannot move across other heads: heads can be displaced over significant distances in the tree provided that they move through all the intervening head positions; as soon as one position is skipped, ill-formedness results. This is the Head Movement Constraint of Travis (1984). It is illustrated, for instance, by the fact that only the highest functional verb can move to C in English:

(11) a. They have left.
  b. Have they <have> left?

(12) a. They could have left.
  b. * Have they could <have> left?
  c. Could they <could> have left?

or by the fact that lexical verbs, unable to reach I in Modern English (as in 13c), cannot be moved to C in interrogatives (as in 13d):

(13) a. He has often seen Mary.
  b. He *I* often sees Mary.
  c.* He sees often <sees> Mary.

d. *Sees he *I* often <sees> Mary?

In earlier phases of English, when movement of the lexical V to I was possible, the continuation of the movement to C was also allowed (Roberts 1993b). Modern French allows (in fact, requires) movement of the lexical V to I (Pollock 1989), and the continuation of this movement to C in interrogatives:

(14) a. Il a souvent vu Marie.
"He has often seen Marie."
b. Il voit souvent <voit> Marie.
"He sees often Marie."
c. Voit-il <voit> souvent <voit> Marie?
"Sees he often Marie?"

Consider also the fact that in Italian gerundival (Rizzi 1982) and participal (Belletti 1981) clauses the non-finite verb moves to C; but the participle cannot move across the gerundival auxiliary:

(15) a. Essendo Mario <essendo> tornato a Milano, ...
"Having Mario come back to Milan, ..."
b. Tornato Mario <tornato> a Milano, ...
"Come back Mario to Milan, ..."
c. *Tornato Mario essendo <tornato> a Milano ...
"Come back Mario having to Milan, ..."

The same constraint is also illustrated by the fact that non-finite functional verbs in English can optionally move to the left of *not* (Pollock 1989), but can never cross the infinitive marker *to*:

(16) a. Not to be

b. To not be
c. To be not
d. * Be to not
e. * Be not to

Assuming that *to* can occupy at least two functional head positions, higher and lower than *not*, and the latter is the specifier of NegP, *be* can optionally move head to head across *not* (16c), but cannot cross *to*.

The impermeability of *to* to movement is only a special instance of the general fact that particle like elements in the inflectional system have the effect of blocking V-movement. For instance, in Creole languages, in which the inflectional field is typically realized by a rich system of particles designating tense, mood, and aspect, we never find V-movement to C in interrogatives and related constructions. For example, Haitian Creole does not involve movement of the verb to C in interrogatives, contrary to French, etc. Evidently, the particles do not enter into head movement to C, but their presence suffices to block head movement to C of some lower verbal element, as expected under RM. Of particular interest here is the case of mixed systems, pointed out by Guglielmo Cinque. Cinque (1999) observes that languages having both affixes and particles to express properties of the inflectional field may give rise to configurations like:

(17) ... Aff... Prt ...V...

where a structurally higher property is expressed by a verbal affix and a lower property by a particle in the inflectional field. In such cases, the language never resolves the situation by having the V move to the affix by jumping across the particle; rather the language reverts to the insertion of an auxiliary in a position higher than the particle, a semantically empty verb capable of supporting the relevant affix. Evidently, a strong structural constraint is operative to block movement here, forcing the language to complicate the representation in order to achieve morphological well-formedness. A case in point discussed by Cinque is Welsh: tense and agreement suffixes are normally attached to a main verb, but if aspectual particles *wedi* (perfective) or *yn* (progressive) are present, the language reverts to an auxiliary verb (be) to carry tense and agreement suffixes:

(18) a. Cana   i   yfory.
       sing-Fut-1Sg I tomorrow
       "I will sing tomorrow."
    b. Bydda   i wedi canu erbyn saith o'r gloch.
       be-Fut-1Sg   I Perf sing by seven o'clock
       "I will have sung by seven o'clock."
    c. Bydda   i'n canu yfory.
       be-Fut-1Sg   I Prog sing tomorrow
       "I will be singing tomorrow."

All these cases straightforwardly follow from the assumption that chain links must satisfy RM, as formally expressed by our principles (4) and (6).

3 A-Chains

A subject raised to a higher subject position cannot skip an intervening subject position; the banned configuration has been called "Super Raising":

(19) a. It seems that it is likely that John will win.
    b. It seems that John is likely t to win.
    c. John seems t to be likely t to win.
    d. *John seems that it is likely t to win.

One could think that the impossibility of (19d) is related to the impossibility of extracting the subject from the tensed clause:

(20) *John seems (that) t will win.

If A-movement is triggered by Case, one could think that the DP simply moves to the closest case position, so it cannot move further from the embedded subject position in (20) and cannot skip the embedded subject position in (19d).

But in fact, the problem is more general: a pure Case approach is not plausible for cases of languages allowing raising out of tensed clauses, such as the dialect of Turkish discussed in Moore (1998). These languages clearly dissociate (19d) and (20):

(21) Biz san-a viski-yi iç-ti-k gibi gorun-du-k.
We-Nom you-Dat whiskey-Acc drink-Past-1Pl like appear-Past-1Pl
"We appeared to you (we) have drunk the whiskey."

(22) Cok viski iç-ti san-dl-n gibi gorun-du-0
Much whiskey drink-Past-1Sg believe-Past-2Sg like appear-Past-3Sg
"It appears you believed I have drunk a lot of whiskey."

(23) *Cok viski iç-ti san-dl-n gibi gorun-du-m
Much whiskey drink-Past-1Sg believe-Past-2Sg like appear-Past-1Sg
"I appear you believe (I) have drunk a lot of whiskey."

As raising is possible in this variety from the subject position of a finite clause, where the raised DP could receive Case (as in 21a), the locality effect shown by (21c) seems to be independent from attraction to the closest Case position. What this pattern suggests is that intervening subject positions of the kind involved in the satisfaction of the Extended Projection Principle (EPP) block any kind of A-chains, regardless of case considerations, as Moore points out.

This is also shown by the fact that intervening subjects also block A-chains not aiming at another (cased) subject position, but to a different kind of A-position. Consider for instance past participle agreement, triggered by a dis-placed object in French (e.g. in a *wh*-construction):

(24) Les voitures qu'il a t' conduites t
"The cars that he has driven(FP)"

I will assume (following in essence Kayne 1989) that agreement is triggered by the passage of the displaced object through a specifier position of the relevant agreement head (t' in (24)). It has been observed (Kayne 1989a, Déprez 1989) that this agreement is local. For instance, in case of *wh*-extraction of the object, it cannot be triggered on the verb of the higher clause:

(25) Les voitures qu'il a dit(*es) qu'il a conduit(es)
"The cars that he has said(FP) that he has driven(FP)"

The structure involving the higher agreement could have a representation like the following:

(26) Les voitures qu'il a t''' dites (t'') qu'il a t' conduites t

(t, t') is a well-formed link of an A-chain, but (t', t''') is not: if t'' is present in the spec of some C-projection, the chain moves from an A-position to an A'-position back to an A-position, a case of improper movement. If t'' is not there, the link (t', t''') crosses a subject position, again a Super Raising violation. All these cases are excluded by RM for X, Z = A specifiers.

4 A'-Chains: The Asymmetries

Huang (1982) observed that the effect shown in (3) is not fully homogeneous. While adverbial elements strongly resist *wh*-extraction from *wh*-islands, *wh*-arguments are at least marginally extractable, as is shown by near-minimal pairs like the following (only the relevant extraction trace is indicated):

(27) a. ? Which problem do you wonder how to solve <which problem>?
b. *How do you wonder which problem to solve <how>?

So, while adverbs fully manifest the expected RM effects for A'-chains, arguments somehow manage to escape, at least in part. Since the mid-1980s, much work has been devoted to the exact structural characterization of the asymmetries, and to theidentification of the class of "interveners" determining RM effects in A'-chains. Let us consider these two issues in turn.

If much work in the 1980s treated the contrast in (27) as an asymmetry between arguments and adverbs (or adjuncts), later it became clear that a more accurate characterization should set aside arguments from everything else. An instance of this wider generalization is offered by cases in which part of an argument can be moved out of the DP, apparently in free alternation with movement of the whole DP, as with *combien* extraction in French:

(28) a. Combien de problèmes sais-tu résoudre _____?
"How many of problems can you solve?"
b. Combien sais-tu résoudre [_____ de problèmes]?
"How many can you solve of problems?"

Now, extraction of the whole direct object out of a *wh*-island is marginally acceptable, but extraction of *combien* alone is barred:

(29) a. ? Combien de problèmes sais-tu comment résoudre _____?

"How many of problems do you know how to solve?"

b. *Combien sais-tu comment résoudre [_____ de problèmes]?

"How many do you know how to solve of problems?"

So, here we have an asymmetry between an argument and a proper part of an argument, the latter resisting extraction. Moreover, if pied-piped arguments are marginally extractable from *wh*-islands, pied-piped predicates are not (Baltin 1992):

(30) a. How many people do you consider _____ intelligent?

b. How intelligent do you consider John _____?

(31) a. ?? How many people do you wonder whether I consider _____ intelligent?

b. *How intelligent do you wonder whether I consider John _____?

In conclusion, the asymmetry appears to be between arguments and everything else: predicates, adverbs and proper subparts of arguments resist extraction from *wh*-islands.

An additional restriction, more subtle but clearly detectable in many cases, was then brought to light. It was observed that *wh*-arguments are optimally extractable only with a special interpretation, i.e., when the range of the variable is pre-established in discourse, or presupposed (Comorovski 1989, Cinque 1990b). This disourse-linked (D-linked: Pesetsky 1987) or presupposed interpretation is favored or forced by certain lexical choices for the *wh*-operator (e.g. by *which* in English), while certain types of *wh*-phrase like *what the hell*, *what on earth* are incompatible with it

(Pesetsky's "aggressively non-D-linked" *wh*-expressions), whence such contrasts as:

(32) a. ? Which problem do you wonder how to solve ____ ____?
b. * What the hell do you wonder how to say _____?

The necessity of a pre-established range emerges with clarity also in the interpretation of other *wh*-operators. Consider the following contrast in Italian (and see Frampton 1991 for the discussion of similar pairs in English):

(33) a.? Quanti problemi non sai come risolvere _____?
"How many problems don't you know how to solve?"
b. * Quanti soldi non sai come guadagnare _____?
"How much money don't you know how to make?"

While it is natural to assume that there may be a known set of problems of which (33a) can be asked, in general (33b) will not be asked about a known set of objects (say, sums of money pre-established in discourse). On the other hand, even sentences like (33b) can improve if the partitive form of the interrogative DP is used, explicitly stating that the question bears on a specific sum of money:

(34) ? Quanti dei soldi che ti servono non sai come guadagnare _____?
"How much of the money that you need don't you know how to make?"

In conclusion, *wh*-extraction from a *wh*-clause is generally barred, as expected under RM. A systematic exception involves D-linked argumental *wh*-phrases, which are marginally extractable. In order to accommodate the exception, it was proposed in Rizzi (1990) that such *wh*-phrases can be related to their traces through a mechanism different from ordinary chain formation as expressed by (6), and as such are not submitted to locality. As the theory must admit a way to relate positions non-locally in order to accommodate long distance binding of a pronoun by a quantified expression (see (7) and the related discussion), the proposal was made that D-linked argumental *wh*-phrases can exploit such a mechanism to be related long distance to their traces. This idea was implemented in Cinque (1990b) and Rizzi (1990) by assuming that only D-linked and argumental (theta-marked) *wh*-phrases could bear (and share with their traces) a referential index capable of ensuring the antecedent-trace connection non-locally. Much of the discussion on this approach was centered on the legitimacy and appropriateness of using referential indices as a technical device to permit long distance dependencies (see Frampton 1991 for a critical discussion, Chomsky 1995b on the possibility of dispensing with indices, and Manzini 1992 for a different view on the asymmetries).

Here I would like to suggest a different implementation, which does not resort to indices and fully exploits the analogy with (7). Let me first introduce a mechanism to deal with the latter case and, in general, with long distance binding of pronouns from quantified expressions. Following fairly standard assumptions, I will assume that binding holds when the following conditions are met:

(35) A binds B iff:
    (i) A and B are non-distinct DPs, and
    (ii) A c-commands B.

It is natural to restrict binding to DPs (possibly to DPs and CPs), the only categories that can enter into referential dependencies. Featural non-distinctness is needed to ensure feature matching between the binder and the bindee (here we cannot require the stronger condition of full structural identity as in (6i); a bound pronoun is not identical to its binder); and c-command must hold (cf. (8)).

Now, suppose that (35) is the grammatical device that can be used as an alternative to "being in a minimal configuration" in chain formation (condition (6iii)). Given the fact that (35) is restricted to DPs, the non-local mechanism is not available with *wh*-dependencies involving adjuncts (27b), predicates (31b), or parts of DPs (29b). What about non-D-linked *wh*-DPs? Following Frampton (1991) I will assume that in such cases "reconstruction" must apply, leaving the bare *wh*-operator in the left periphery, and reconstructing the rest of the DP in situ. If we adopt the core idea of the theory of reconstruction in Chomsky (1995b), exploiting the copy theory of traces, S-structure (36a) is thus converted into LF (36b) by deleting the non-operator material from the left periphery (an operation which automatically triggers the consequence that the lexical restriction is "exported" from the trace in (36b), if the trace is understood as an identical copy of the antecedent):

(36) a. Quanti soldi non sai come guadagnare <quanti soldi>
b. Quanti ____ non sai come guadagnare <quanti> soldi

Therefore, at LF the *wh*-dependency in the non-D-linked interpretation is not a DP dependency, but a bare QP dependency, so that mechanism (35) is not available, locality must be met in the strict form of (6iii), and (36b) is correctly ruled out. Following again Frampton (1991) and Chomsky (1995b), we can account for the obligatoriness of reconstruction here by assuming that the principle of Full Interpretation is strong enough to enforce it: the lexical restriction is not licensed by a left-peripheral mechanism in (36), so it must delete in the syntax of LF.

Now, what about D-linked *wh*-phrases, e.g. in (33a)? Following the logic of the argument, the lexical restriction in D-linked *wh*-elements must be allowed to stay in the left periphery at LF, in order to permit a non-local

DP dependency to be established through (35). Why is this legitimate? I continue to assume that D-linked means "pre-established in discourse," hence topic like; of course, topic interpretation licenses elements in the left periphery (e.g. through the formal device discussed in Rizzi 1997), so we can think that the lexical restriction can remain in the left periphery as it is licensed *qua* topic at LF.

In conclusion, the selective sensitivity to *wh*-islands can be reduced to the formal distinction between DP and non-DP dependencies at LF. Among the *wh*-dependencies, only D-linked phrases allow DP dependencies at LF, which can exploit the non-local connecting device (35), and survive across a *wh*-island. Adjunct, predicative, and bare *wh*- (extracted from DP) dependencies are not DP dependencies, so they must obey RM; non-D-linked *wh*-dependencies like (36) are DP dependencies at S-structure, but not at LF, the level where RM applies, so that they are expected to obey strict locality under this approach.

5 A′-Chains: The Interveners

It was observed in the early 1990s that the class of possible interveners triggering minimality effects is not coextensive with the class of target positions, but significantly wider. For instance, asymmetries of the kind illustrated by (29) are also determined by an intervening negation:

(37) a. Combien de problèmes ne sais-tu pas résoudre ____?
"How many of problems can't you solve?"
b. *Combien ne sais-tu pas résoudre [____ de problèmes]?
"How many can't you solve of problems?"

This is a particular case of the selective islands induced by negation, which non-arguments are generally sensitive to (Ross 1983 and, for recent critical discussion, Szabolcsi and Zwarts 1997, Kuno and Takami 1997, and the references cited there).

Certain kinds of quantificational adverb expressing the frequency of an action, or the intensity of a state, determine similar asymmetries in French (Obenauer 1983, 1994):

(38) a. Combien de livres a-t-il beaucoup consultés _____?
"How many of books has he a lot consulted?"
b. * Combien a-t-il beaucoup consulté ____ de livres?
"How many has he a lot consulted of books?"
c. Combien de films a-t-elle peu aimés _____
"How many films did she little like?"
d. * Combien a-t-elle peu aimé [_____ de films]?
"How many did she little like of films?"

Given the width of the blocking effects, it seemed natural to define the structural typology relevant for RM in a very broad way. As *wh*, negation, and quantificational adverbs like *beaucoup*, *peu*, *souvent*, etc. plausibly have in common the fact of occupying an A'-specifier position, the formulation of the principle in Rizzi (1990) referred to the sole distinction between A-and A'-specifiers to express the typology of elements triggering minimality effects at the XP level.

On the other hand, the plausibility of such a purely geometric approach was immediately threatened by the observation that non-quantificational adverbs do not induce a similar Minimality effect (Obenauer 1983, 1994, Laenzlinger 1996): compare (36) with the following:

(39) a. Combien de livres a-t-il attentivement consultés ____?
"How many of books did he carefully consult?"
b. Combien a-t-il attentivement consulté [____ de livres]?
"How many did he carefully consult of books?"

Now, it appears unlikely that the position of a non-quantificational adverb like *attentivement* differs enough in tree geometry from the position of *beaucoup*, *peu*, etc. to allow us to maintain a purely geometric approach. This is even more so in view of recent advances on the study of adverbial positions qua specifiers of particular functional heads (Cinque 1999, Laenzlinger 1996) and on the opportunity of eliminating the distinction between specifier and adjoined position (Kayne 1994). If these approaches are on the right track, then the theory of phrase structure has no resources to differentiate the position of these adverbs uniquely in terms of configurations.

Clearly, a more selective characterization of the Minimality inducing factor is needed. An extremely selective characterization is in fact provided in the reinterpretation of RM effects in Chomsky (1995b). According to Chomsky, movement is triggered by feature attraction: a head endowed with a certain feature attracts a phrase bearing the same specification to its immediate structural domain (say, in traditional X-bar terminology, to occupy its specifier position). This attract operation is phrased in such a way that only the closest "attractee" can move:

(40) **Minimal Link Condition**:
K attracts a only if there is no b, b closer to K than a, such that K attracts b. (Chomsky 1995b: 311)

(40) differs from (4) in two major respects. First, it is a principle that operates on derivations, not a well-formedness condition on representations, so it requires one to take the "movement metaphor" literally, whereas (4) does not. Moreover, it makes the Minimality effect sensitive to identity of features; i.e., in the derivation of (41) the higher C endowed with the *wh*-feature (element K in (40)) fails to attract the *wh*-phrase *how* from the embedded clause due to the intervention of a closer attractee, the *wh*-phrase in the embedded Spec of C:

(41) C you wonder [which problem C [to solve how]]

Here I will not address the important distinction between derivational and representational approaches to locality (but see n. 6), and will focus on the different selectivity of the two approaches. It is clear that (40) suffers from the opposite problem with respect to (4): it is too selective to account for cases of Minimality such as (37b) and (38b-d), in which the intervener bears a feature different (formally and interpretively) from the one of the attractor. If we want to maintain that a genuine generalization underlies (29b) and these other examples we cannot adopt this approach to RM effects.

What seems to be needed is an intermediate position between the geometric approach and the one based on identity of features. Features determining chain formation seem to cluster into natural classes, such that Minimality effects are determined within classes, but not across them.

5.3 思考和练习

1. 本章提到了划分词类的三个标准：形态标准、分布标准、意义标准。请问这些标准适用于划分汉语普通话的词吗？汉语词类该如何划分？

2. 请用 X-标杆理论，举例说明汉语中常见的动词短语（VP）结构、名词短语（NP）结构、形容词短语（AP）结构、介词短语（PP）结构等分别是怎样的。

3. 下列句子（短语）都有歧义。请使用 X-标杆理论说明这句话的歧义来源。

  张三骑累了马。

  鲁迅的照片。

  咬死了猎人的狗。

4. 请用汉语实例说明什么是句法的结构依存性？

5. 什么是句法的层级性？什么是句法的递归性？举例说明。

6. 关于汉语实词和虚词的划分有不同的观点，其中一个争议之处在于副词应当归属为实词还是虚词。请结合英语中区分词汇范畴和功能范畴的标准，谈谈你对这一问题的看法。

7. 什么是原则与参数理论？如何将原则与参数理论应用于汉语方言语

法的比较研究?

5.4 延伸阅读

Adger, D. 2003. *Core Syntax*. Oxford: Oxford University Press.

Baker, M. C. 2003. *Lexical Categories*. Cambridge: Cambridge University Press.

Baltin, M. & C. Collins (eds.). 2001. *The Handbook of Contemporary Syntactic Theory*. Oxford: Blackwell.

Carnie, A. 2013. *Syntax: A Generative Introduction* (Third edition). Oxford: Blackwell.

Chomsky, N. 1965. *Aspects of the Theory of Syntax*. Cambridge, Mass.: The MIT Press.

Chomsky, N. 1970. Remarks on nominalization. In R. Jacobs & P. Rosenbaum (eds.), *Readings in English Transformational Grammar*, 184–221. Ginn.

Chomsky, N. 1981. *Lectures on Government and Binding*. Dordrecht: Foris.

Chomsky, N. 1995. *The Minimalist Program*. Cambridge, Mass.: The MIT Press.

Grimshaw, J. 1990. *Argument Structure*. Cambridge, Mass.: The MIT Press.

Huang, C.-T. J. 1982. *Logical Relations in Chinese and Theory of Grammar*. Ph.D. dissertation, MIT. Jackendoff, R. 1977. *X-bar Syntax: A Theory of Phrase Structure*. Cambridge, Mass.: The MIT Press.

Kayne, R. 1994. *The Antisymmetry of Syntax*. Cambridge, Mass.: The MIT Press.

Manzini, M. R. 1992. *Locality: A Theory and Some of Its Empirical Consequences*. Cambridge, Mass.: The MIT Press.

O'Grady, W., Archibald, J., Aronoff, M. & J. Rees-Miller. 2017. *Con-

temporary Linguistics: *An Introduction* (*the 7th edition*). Boston: Bedford/St. Martin's.

Radford, A. 1997. *Syntax*: *A Minimalist Introduction*. Cambridge: Cambridge University Press.

Rizzi, L. 1990. *Relativized Minimality*. Cambridge, Mass.: The MIT Press.

第六章 语义学

6.1 导引

- 语义概说
- 词之间的意义关系
- 句子之间的意义关系
- 真值条件语义学
- 组合性原则
- 题元角色
- 小结

6.1.1 语义概说

语言是一个符号系统,是形式(form)和意义(meaning)的结合体。语言使用要想达成交际功能,语言必须具有某种内容(content)。语言的这种内容就是意义。语义学就是研究自然语言意义的一门学科。实际上,在语言学独立成为一门学科之前,人类就开始思考意义的本质。几千年以来,关乎意义本质的问题一直是哲学的中心议题,远至古希腊的柏拉图和亚里士多德,近至20世纪的罗素(Bertrand Russell),都对这个问题有过深邃的思考。在这一章,我们将简要介绍语义学中用于分析词与句子意义的一些基本概念。

6.1.2 词之间的意义关系

词和短语的意义不是孤立的,它们通常会和其它词以及短语组成各种各样的意义关系。最常见的意义关系有：同义关系（synonymy）、反义关系（antonymy）、多义关系（polysemy）以及同音同形异义关系（homophony）。

同义关系　指的是语言表达式在某些或所有语境中具有相同或相近的意义。"奢侈、奢华""有钱、富有""漂亮、美丽"，每一对都是同义词。汉语中表示人类去世的词，如"死、辞世、逝世、去世、离世、亡故、一命呜呼、升天、驾崩、离开、去西天"等，都是同义词。"榛子"在英语中既可以是 filbert，也可以是 hazelnut；"青年"可以是 youth，也可以是 adolescent；"汽车"可以是 car，也可以是 automobile；"回忆"可以是 remember，也可以是 recall；"买"可以是 purchase，也可以是 buy；"大"可以说成 big，也可以说成 large。

从语言使用的有效性来说，意义完全相同的词（如"礼拜天"和"星期天"、"的士"和"出租车"）不能说不存在，但一定是极为稀有的。英语中 large 和 big 都可以表示大，但是只有后者可以修饰程度，如：a big mistake/*a large mistake。youth 和 adolescent 虽然都表示年龄不大，但只有 adolescent 含有"不成熟"之义，youth 没有这一层涵义。同义词之间，有可能在感情色彩、语体、程度、适用对象等方面存在差异。

反义关系　指的是语言表达式在某一意义上存在相反性（opposite）的现象。常见的反义词有："光明—黑暗、真—假、男—女、高—矮、生—死、聚—散、离—合、胜利—失败、前进—后退、美—丑"等。下列英语中的例子也都构成反义关系：

（1）dark-light、boy-girl、hot-cold、up-down、in-out、come-go、alive-dead

这些例子都在至少一个方面存在对立："boy"与"girl"在性别上存在对立，"come"和"go"在方向上存在对立，"tall"和"short"在高度上存在对立，等等。

多义关系　指的是语言表达式具有两个或多个意义，并且这些意义之间存在内在联系。多义词一般具有一个本义，其它义都是在本义的基础上衍生出来的。如"深"，本义是指物体在垂直空间上以平面为起点往下的长度，可以进一步引申为水平空间的距离（"庭院深深深几许"），进而引申为感情的强度（"小张对外公的感情很深"）。英语中的"bright"本义是指光线明亮，可以引申为聪明(intelligent)的意思;"glare"本义是光线强烈,可以引申为愤怒地注视(to stare angrily)之义;"deposit"本义是地球上的矿物,引申义为银行的存款。很多时候,引申义往往比本义使用得更为频繁,逐渐成了主要意义,如用"deposit"表示银行存款,而非矿物。

同音同形异义关系 指的是两个或多个表达式的读音或/和拼写完全一样,但是意义不同,并且这些意义之间不存在内在联系。最常见的同音同形异义词如"bank",既可以表示金融机构(银行),也可以表示河岸。同音同形异义词通常会导致词汇歧义(lexical ambiguity),如下面的例子:

(2) Q: Why is the river always rich?
A: Because it has two banks.

河流有两岸(bank),但同时 bank 也表示银行,拥有两个银行,自然很富有。(2)的幽默效果巧妙利用了 bank 的同音同形异义现象。同理,下面的例(3)也有两个意思:

(3) Liz bought a pen. (pen 可以表示钢笔,也可以表示围栏)

在实际使用中,词汇歧义通常可以通过语境因素得以消解。下面的例子一般不会导致歧义:

(4) He got a loan from the *bank*. (他从银行得到了一笔贷款)(bank=银行)

(5) She sat on the *bank* of the river and watched the boats go by. (她坐在河岸上,看船只穿梭)(bank = 河岸)

6.1.3 句子之间的意义关系

释义(paraphrase) 如果两个句子 a 和 b,a 为真,同时 b 也为真,反之亦然,则称 a 和 b 同义,a 和 b 互为对方的释义。下面的句子互为释义:

(6) a. The police chased the burglar.（警察追小偷。）

　　b. The burglar was chased by the police.（小偷被警察追。）

(7) a. Paul bought a car from Sue.（Paul 从 Sue 处买了一辆车。）

　　b. Sue sold a car to Paul.（Sue 卖了一辆车给 Paul。）

(8) a. The game will begin at 3:30 p.m.

　　b. At 3:30 p.m., the game will begin.

如果警察追小偷为真，则小偷被警察追也必然为真，反之亦然。互为释义的两个句子具有同样的真值条件。用"="表示释义，a=b 当且仅当 a 和 b 的真值条件完全相同。

衍推（entailment）　当一个句子 a 为真，另外一个句子 b 也为真，但反之不然的时候，a 衍推 b，记为：a ⇒ b。衍推关系是一种逻辑关系。衍推关系必须满足如下属性：

(9) a 衍推 b(a ⇒ b) 当且仅当

　　(i) 句子 a 为真，句子 b 必定为真；

　　(ii) 句子 b 为假，句子 a 一定为假；

　　(iii) 句子 a 为假，句子 b 的真值不能确定(可以为真也可以为假)。

以(10)的例子来说明(假设说话人和听话人知道南京是江苏的一部分)：

(10) a. 小张去过南京。

　　 b. 小张去过江苏。

(10a)和(10b)之间的语义关系满足(9)的定义：如果小张去过南京，则小张一定去过江苏(因为南京⊂江苏)；反之，如果小张没去过江苏，则小张一定没去过南京；如果小张没去过南京，小张可能去过江苏，也可能没去过江苏。下面的例子中，a 句都衍推 b 句：

(11) a. Liz dances swiftly.
   b. Liz dances.

(12) a. Prince is a dog.
   b. Prince is an animal.

衍推关系与同义关系：衍推关系是非对称的，a 衍推 b 不代表 b 衍推 a。如果 a 和 b 相互衍推（a⇔b），则 a 和 b 具有同样的真值条件：a＝b。

矛盾(contradiction)　如果句子 a 为真，句子 b 必然为假，反之亦然，则 a 和 b 互为矛盾关系。下面例(13)中的 a 和 b 互为矛盾关系：

(13) a. John is dead.
   b. John is alive.

如果 John 还活着，则他没有死；如果他死了，则他没有活着。"男—女""真—假""对—错""单身—已婚"等都是矛盾关系。

预设(presupposition)　如果句子 b 为真以 a 的存在为前提，则 a 是 b 的预设。预设关系满足下面的定义：

(14) b 预设 a 当且仅当
   (i) 句子 b 为真，句子 a 必定为真；
   (ii) 句子 a 为假，句子 b 一定为假；
   (iii) 句子 b 为假，句子 a 仍然为真。

考虑下面的句子：

(15) a. John has a bike.
   b. John's bike is broken.
   c. John's bike is not broken.

很明显，句子(a)为真是(b)成立的前提：John 的自行车坏了，则 John 必然拥有一辆自行车。如果 John 没有自行车，则"John 的自行车坏了"这个句子没有真值[这种情况叫做预设失败(presuppositional failure)]。预设是否定维持,即不管John的自行车坏了还是没坏,John有一辆自行车都是前提条件。(15a)是(15b)和(15c)的预设。

下面的句子中,(16b)是(16a)的预设:

(16) a. The king of France is bald.
　　 b. France has a king.

6.1.4　真值条件语义学

我们的语言知识允许我们确定一个句子是真还是假,一个句子的真值是否蕴含另一个句子的真值,一个句子是否具有多个意义等等。刻画这一部分语言知识可以通过构拟相应的语义规则实现。这些语义规则既要考虑到句子的组成部分的意义,也要考虑句子的各个组成部分的组配方式(句法规则)。这样的一种思路叫做真值条件语义学(Truth-Conditional Semantics)。因为这一种思路是通过计算句子的组成部分的语义来确定整个句子的真值的,所以也叫组合语义学(Compositional Semantics)。

真值条件语义学认为句子的外延(意义)即句子的真值条件。如果句子的意义与现实情况相吻合,则该句子为真,否则为假。我们知道一个句子的真值,并不意味着我们一定要知道这个句子是为真还是为假,我们只需要知道这个句子为真还是为假的条件就足够了。换言之,我们只需要知道如何确定句子的真值就足够了。如下面的句子:

(17) a. Liz dances beautifully.
　　 b. Liz bought a cake yesterday.

如果说话人知道有个人叫Liz,她是个舞蹈演员,舞跳得很好,则(17a)为真,否则为假。同理,(17b)描述说话时间的前一天Liz买了一个蛋糕的事实,属实则为真,不属实则为假。其它的信息,譬如Liz是学生还是老师、Liz住在哪里、Liz当天穿什么衣服等,都不是相关的信息。特别的,真值条件语义学用下面的表达式来刻画句子的真值条件:

(18) 真值条件语义学的表达方式
"P"为真（或："P"=1），当且仅当，P。

这一表达式是逻辑学家 Alfred Tarski 提出来的，因而又叫"T-表达式"。注意第一个 P 加了引号，说明这是目标语言（object language），是被讨论的对象；第二个 P 没加引号，是元语言（metalanguage），是用来讨论的语言。不区分元语言和目标语言容易导致很多逻辑学和语言哲学上的混乱。

下面都是使用"T-表达式"来表达真值条件意义的例子：

(19) a. "雪是白的"为真当且仅当雪是白的。
b. "Snow is white" is true if and only if snow is white.
c. "Schnee ist weiß" is true if and only if snow is white.

真值条件语义学（又叫形式语义学）是当今的主流语义学理论。这一语义学理论的主要目标就是用数理逻辑的手段刻画形形色色的句子的真值条件。

6.1.5 组合性原则

真值条件语义学的基石是组合性原则（Principle of Compositionality）。根据组合性原则，一个复杂表达式的意义由它的组成部分的意义以及组成部分的组合方式共同决定。组合性原则是著名逻辑学家弗雷格（Gottlob Frege）在 19 世纪末提出的，因而又叫"弗雷格方案"（Frege's Program）。特别的，组合性原则可以表述如下：

(20) 组合性原则
一个复杂表达式的意义是它的组成部分的意义以及组成部分的组合方式的函数。

注意如果要确定一个复杂表达式的语义，两个因素都要考虑进去：(1) 组成部分的意义；(2) 组成部分的组合方式。组成部分一模一样，但是组合方式不同，意义也会不同。考虑下面的例子：

(21) a. The cat is under the mat.
　　 b. The mat is under the cat.

(21a)和(21b)两个句子的组成部分完全相同,都包含"the cat、be under、the mat"。但这两个句子的真值条件完全不同。(21a)描述的是猫在垫子下这一情形,而(21b)描述的是垫子在猫的下面这一情形。组成部分完全相同,但是组合方式(句法构造)不同,也会导致语义不同。

当代形式语义学理论是围绕组合性原则展开的。语言学家通过分析不同语言单位(名词、动词、形容词、各种虚词等)的意义以及它们的结合方式,计算句子的真值条件。这一原则一百年来影响不衰,推动着语义研究不断向前发展。

6.1.6　题元角色

对句子做出语义解释,还要考虑句子的各个组成部分(NP、VP、PP等)在句子所描述的事件/情景中所扮演的角色。以(22)为例:

(22) 快递公司把文件从北京寄到南京。

要充分理解这个句子,必须明白以下内容:快递公司是寄快递动作的承担者,快递的东西是文件,快递的起点是北京,快递的终点是南京。语言学家用"题元角色"(thematic roles)来描述句子的组成部分在句子所描述的事件中所扮演的角色。

到底有多少题元角色? 各家观点不一。一般而言,以下的题元角色是各家理论所公认的。根据题元角色所涉及的层次,可以分为动作层(action tier)、事件层(event tier)、心理层(psycho tier)三个层面,每个层面又可分为若干子类。

动作层:为多数理论所公认的主要有施事(agent)和受事(patient)。

(23) 小张买了一套新房子。(施事＝小张)
(24) 老师批评了小张。(受事＝小张)

事件层：涉及事件在空间中的行动或定位，也可以是隐喻意义上的行动；分为客体(theme)、来源(source)、路径(path)、目标(goal)、处所(location)等。其中目标又可以细分为：空间域的目标、与事（领属域的目标）、受益者（领属域之意向目标）三类。

(25) a. 小张从南京来到了北京。（施事＝小张；来源＝南京；目标＝北京）
b. 小张把书给了小李。［施事＝小张；客体＝书；目标（与事）＝小李］
c. 小张沿着大路跑到了学校。（施事＝小张；路径＝大路；目标＝学校）
d. 小张在厨房洗碗。（施事＝小张；处所＝厨房）

心理层：分为感事(experiencer)和激事(stimulus)。

(26) a. 小张对这篇论文很不满意。（感事＝小张；激事＝这篇论文）
b. 这篇论文让小张很生气。（激事＝这篇论文；感事＝小张）

题元角色规定了许多具体的词汇语义特征。题元角色不是单独成立的，而是与相应的动词信息密切相关。题元角色可以解释动词的特点和方式，对于认识事件的本质有直接的帮助，所以题元角色通常被视为句法—语义接口研究中的重要课题。

6.1.7 小结

一个句子的外延（意义）是句子的真值(truth value)，即句子为真为假的条件。基于真值条件的语义学理论叫做真值条件语义学（也叫形式语义学）。真值条件语义学的基石是组合性原则。根据组合性原则，一个复杂表达式的语义是它的组成部分的意义以及各部分组合方式的函数。正是因为组合性原则的存在，我们可以从句子的各个部分的语义计算出整个句子的意义，进而确定句子为真或为假的条件。真值条件语义学一般借鉴数理逻辑的工具来分析自然语言意义。真值条件语义学发展至今已经有一百多年的历史,是当前语义研究中的主流思潮。

6.2 选读

- Russell（1905）"On denoting"选读
- Heim & Kratzer（1998）*Semantics in Generative Grammar* 选读
- Partee（2004）*Compositionality in Formal Semantics* 选读

Russell（1905）"On denoting"选读①

◆ 作者简介

伯特兰·阿瑟·威廉·罗素②(Bertrand Arthur William Russell,1872—1970),英国哲学家、数学家、逻辑学家、历史学家、文学家、政治活动家,诺贝尔文学奖获得者。罗素出生在曼摩兹郡一个贵族家庭,1893 年在剑桥大学三一学院获学士学位,后曾两度在该校任教。1908 年他当选为皇家学会会员。罗素被认为是现代分析哲学的创始人之一,他在数学逻辑方面也有具有巨大的贡献,和怀特海合著的《数学原理》被公认为是现代数理逻辑的基础,他所提出的"罗素悖论"也推动了 20 世纪逻辑学的发展。

◆ 正文节选

By a 'denoting phrase' I mean a phrase such as any one of the following: a man, some man, any man, every man, all men, the present King of

---

① Russell, B. (1905). "On denoting." *Mind* 14, 479–493. Reprinted in R. C. Marsh, ed. (1956). *Logic and Knowledge*. London: George Allen & Unwin. 41–56.

② 图片来源:https://en.wikipedia.org/wiki/Bertrand_Russell#/media/File:Bertrand_Russell_transparent_bg.png。

England, the present King of France, the center of mass in the solar system at the first instant of the twentieth century, the revolution of the earth round the sun, the revolution of the sun round the earth. Thus a phrase is denoting solely in virtue of its *form*. We may distinguish three cases: (1) A phrase may be denoting, and yet not denote anything; e.g., 'the present King of France'. (2) A phrase may denote one definite object, e.g., 'the present King of England' denotes a certain man. (3) A phrase may denote ambiguously; e.g., 'a man' denotes not many men, but an ambiguous man. The interpretation of such phrases is a matter of considerable difficulty; indeed, it is very hard to frame any theory not susceptible of formal refutation. All the difficulties with which I am acquainted are met, so far as I can discover, by the theory which I am about to explain.

The subject of denoting is of very great importance, not only in logic and mathematics, but also in theory of knowledge. For example, we know that the center of mass of the solar system at a definite instant is some definite point, and we can affirm a number of propositions about it; but we have no immediate *acquaintance* with this point, which is only known to us by description. The distinction between *acquaintance* and *knowledge about* is the distinction between the things we have presentations of, and the things we only reach by denoting phrases. It often happens that we know that a certain phrase denotes unambiguously, although we have no acquaintance with what it denotes; this occurs in the above case of the center of mass. In perception we have acquaintance with the objects of perception, and in thought we have acquaintance with objects of a more abstract logical character; but we do not necessarily have acquaintance with the objects denoted by phrases composed of words with whose meanings we are acquainted. To take a very important instance: there seems no reason to believe that we are ever acquainted with other people's minds, seeing that these are not directly perceived; hence what we know about them is obtained through denoting. All thinking has to start from acquaintance, but it succeeds in thinking *about* many things with which we have no acquaintance.

The course of my argument will be as follows. I shall begin by stating the theory I intend to advocate;① I shall then discuss the theories of Frege and Meinong, showing why neither of them satisfies me; then I shall give the grounds in favor of my theory; and finally I shall briefly indicate the philosophical consequences of my theory.

My theory, briefly, is as follows. I take the notion of the *variable* as fundamental; I use '$C(x)$' to mean a proposition② in which x is a constituent, where x, the variable, is essentially and wholly undetermined. Then we can consider the two notions '$C(x)$ is always true' and '$C(x)$ is sometimes true.'③ Then *everything* and *nothing* and *something* (which are the most primitive of denoting phrases) are to be interpreted as follows:

C (everything) means '$C(x)$ is always true';

C (nothing) means '"$C(x)$ is false" is always **true**';

C (something) means 'It is false that "$C(x)$ is false" is always true'.④

Here the notion '$C(x)$ is always true' is taken as ultimate and indefinable, and the others are defined by means of it. *Everything*, *nothing*, and *something* are not assumed to have any meaning in isolation, but a meaning is assigned to *every* proposition in which they occur. This is the principle of the theory of denoting I wish to advocate: that denoting phrases never have any meaning in themselves, but that every proposition in whose verbal ex-

---

① I have discussed this subject in *Principles of Mathematics*, Chap. V, and § 476. The theory there advocated is very nearly the same as Frege's, and is quite different from the theory to be advocated in what follows.
② More exactly, a propositional function.
③ The second of these can be defined by means of the first, if we take it to mean, 'It is not true that "$C(x)$ is false" is always true'.
④ I shall sometimes use, instead of this complicated phrase, the phrase '$C(x)$ is not always false', or '$C(x)$ is sometimes true', supposed *defined* to mean the same as the complicated phrase.

pression they occur has a meaning. The difficulties concerning denoting are, I believe, all the result of a wrong analysis of propositions whose verbal expressions contain denoting phrases. The proper analysis, if I am not mistaken, may be further set forth as follows.

Suppose now we wish to interpret the proposition, 'I met a man'. If this is true, I met some definite man; but that is not what I affirm. What I affirm is, according to the theory I advocate:

'"I met x, and x is human" is not always false'.

Generally, defining the class of men as the class of objects having the predicate human, we say that:

'C (a man)' means '"$C(x)$ and x is human" is not always false'.

This leaves 'a man', by itself, wholly destitute of meaning, but gives a meaning to every proposition in whose verbal expression 'a man' occurs.

Consider next the proposition 'all men are mortal'. This proposition[①] is really hypothetical and states that *if* anything is a man, it is mortal. That is, it states that if x is a man, x is mortal, whatever x may be. Hence, substituting 'x is human' for 'x is a man', we find:

'All men are mortal' means ' "If x is human, x is mortal" is always true'

This is what is expressed in symbolic logic by saying that 'all men are mortal' means '"x is human" implies "x is mortal" for all values of x'. More generally, we say:

---

① As has been ably argued in Mr. Bradley's *Logic*, Book Ⅰ, Chap. Ⅱ.

'C (all men)' means ' "If x is human, then $C(x)$ is true" is always true'.

Similarly

'C (no men)' means ' "If x is human, then $C(x)$ is false" is always true'.

'C (some men)' will mean the same as 'C (a man)',① and

'C (a man)' means 'It is false that "$C(x)$ and x is human" is always false'.

'C (every man)' will mean the same as 'C (all men)'.

It remains to interpret phrases containing *the*. These are by far the most interesting and difficult of denoting phrases. Take as an example 'the father of Charles Ⅱ was executed'. This asserts that there was an x who was the father of Charles Ⅱ and was executed. Now, *the*, when it is strictly used, involves uniqueness; we do, it is true, speak of '*the son* of So-and-so' even when So-and-so has several sons, but it would be more correct to say '*a* son of So-and-so'. Thus for our purposes we take *the* as involving uniqueness. Thus when we say 'x was *the* father of Charles Ⅱ' we not only assert that x had a certain relation to Charles Ⅱ, but also that nothing else had this relation. The relation in question, without the assumption of uniquenessd, and without any denoting phrases, is expressed by 'x begat Charles Ⅱ'. To get an equivalent of 'x was the father of Charles Ⅱ', we must add, 'If y is other than x, y did not beget Charles Ⅱ', or what is equivalent, 'If y begat Charles Ⅱ, y is identical with x'. Hence, 'x is the father of Charles Ⅱ' becomes: 'x begat Charles Ⅱ; and "if y begat Charles Ⅱ, y is identical with x" is always true of y'.

---

① Psychologically 'C (a man)' has a suggestion of *only* one, and 'C (some men)' has a suggestion of *more than one*; but we may neglect these suggestions in a preliminary sketch.

Thus 'the father of Charles Ⅱ was executed' becomes:

'It is not always false of x that x begat Charles Ⅱ and that x was executed and that "if y begat Charles Ⅱ, y is identical with x" is always true of y'.

This may seem a somewhat incredible interpretation; but I am not at present giving reasons, I am merely *stating* the theory.

To interpret 'C (the father of Charles Ⅱ)', where C stands for any statement about him, we have only to substitute $C(x)$ for 'x was executed' in the above. Observe that, according to the above interpretation C may be, 'C (the father of Charles Ⅱ)' implies:

'It is not always false of x that "if y begat Charles Ⅱ, y is identical with x" is always true of y',

which is what is expressed in common language by 'Charles Ⅱ had one father and no more'. Consequently if this condition fails, *every* proposition of the form 'C (the father of Charles Ⅱ)' is false. Thus e.g. every proposition of the form 'C (the present King of France)' is false. This is a great advantage in the present theory. I shall show later that it is not contrary to the law of contradiction, as might be at first supposed.

The above gives a reduction of all propositions in which denoting phrases occur to forms in which no such phrases occur. Why it is imperative to effect such a reduction, the subsequent discussion will endeavor to show. The evidence for the above theory is derived from the difficulties which seem unavoidable if we regard denoting phrases as standing for genuine constituents of the propositions in whose verbal expressions they occur. Of the possible theories which admit such constituents the simplest is that of Meinong.[①] This theory regards any grammatically correct denoting

---

① See *Untersuchungen zur Gegenstandstheorie und Psychologie* (Leipzig, 1904) the first three articles (by Meinong, Ameseder, and Mally respectively).

phrase as standing for an *object*. Thus 'the present King of France', 'the round square', etc., are supposed to be genuine objects. It is admitted that such objects do not *subsist*, but nevertheless they are supposed to be objects. This is in itself a difficult view; but the chief objection is that such objects, admittedly, are apt to infringe the law of contradiction. It is contended, for example, that the existent present King of France exists, and also does not exist; that the round square is round, and also not round, etc. But this is intolerable; and if any theory can be found to avoid this result, it is surely to be preferred. The above breach of the law of contradiction is avoided by Frege's theory. He distinguishes, in a denoting phrase, two elements, which we may call the *meaning* and the *denotation*.① Thus 'the center of mass of the solar system at the beginning of the twentieth century' is highly complex in *meaning*, but its *denotation* is a certain point, which is simple. The solar system, the twentieth century, etc., are constituents of the *meaning*; but the *denotation* has no constituents at all.② One advantage of this distinction is that it shows why it is often worthwhile to assert identity. If we say 'Scott is the author of *Waverley*', we assert an identity of denotation with a difference of meaning. I shall, however, not repeat the grounds in favor of this theory, as I have urged its claims elsewhere (Joe. cit.), and am now concerned to dispute those claims.

One of the first difficulties that confronts us, when we adopt the view that denoting phrases *express* a meaning and *denote* a denotation,③ concerns

---

① See his "Ueber Sinn und Bedeutung," *Zeitschrift fur Phil. und Phil. Kritik*, 100.
② Frege distinguishes the two elements of meaning and denotation everywhere, and not only in complex denoting phrases. Thus it is the *meanings* of the constituents of a denoting complex that enter into its *meaning*, not their *denotation*. In the proposition 'Mont Blanc is over 1,000 metres high', it is, according to him the *meaning* of 'Mont Blanc', not the actual mountain, that is a constituent of the *meaning* of the proposition.
③ In this theory, we shall say that the denoting phrase *expresses* a meaning; and we shall say both of the phrase and of the meaning that they *denote* a denotation. In the other theory, which I advocate, there is no *meaning*, and only sometimes a *denotation*.

the cases in which the denotation appears to be absent. If we say 'the King of England is bald', that is, it would seem, not a statement about the complex *meaning* 'the King of England', but about the actual man denoted by the meaning. But now consider 'the King of France is bald'. By parity of form, this also ought to be about the denotation of the phrase 'the King of France'. But this phrase, though it has a *meaning* provided 'the King of England' has a meaning, has certainly no denotation, at least in any obvious sense. Hence one would suppose that 'the King of France is bald' ought to be nonsense; but it is not nonsense, since it is plainly false. Or again consider such a proposition as the following: 'If u is a class which has only one member, then that one member is a member of u', or, as we may state it, 'If u is a unit class, the u is a u'. This proposition ought to be *always* true, since the conclusion is true whenever the hypothesis is true. But 'the u' is a denoting phrase, and it is the denotation, not the meaning, that is said to be a u. Now if u is *not* a unit class, "the u" seems to denote nothing; hence our proposition would seem to become nonsense as soon as u is not a unit class.

Now it is plain that such propositions do *not* become nonsense merely because their hypotheses are false. The king in *The Tempest* might say, 'If Ferdinand is not drowned, Ferdinand is my only son'. Now 'my only son' is a denoting phrase, which, on the face of it, has a denotation when, and only when, I have exactly one son. But the above statement would nevertheless have remained true if Ferdinand had been in fact drowned. Thus we must either provide a denotation in cases in which it is at first sight absent, or we must abandon the view that the denotation is what is concerned in propositions which contain denoting phrases. The latter is the course that I advocate. The former course may be taken, as by Meinong, by admitting objects which do not subsist, and denying that they obey the law of contradiction; this, however, is to be avoided if possible. Another way of taking the same course (so far as our present alternative is concerned) is adopted by Frege, who provides by definition some purely conventional denotations for the cases in which otherwise there would be none. Thus 'the King of France', is to denote the null-class; 'the only son of Mr. So-and-so' (who has a fine family of ten), is to denote the class of all his sons; and so on. But this procedure, though it may not lead to actual logical error, is plainly artificial, and does not give an exact analysis of the matter. Thus if we allow that denoting phrases, in general, have the two sides of meaning and denotation, the cases where there seems to be no denotation cause difficulties both on the assumption that there really is a denotation and on the assumption that there really is none.

A logical theory may be tested by its capacity for dealing with puzzles, and it is a wholesome plan, in thinking about logic, to stock the mind with as many puzzles as possible, since these serve much the same purpose as is served by experiments in physical science. I shall therefore state three puzzles which a theory as to denoting ought to be able to solve; and I shall show later that my theory solves them.

(1) If a is identical with b, whatever is true of the one is true of the other, and either may be substituted for the other in any proposition without altering the truth or falsehood of that proposition. Now George IV wished to know whether Scott was the author of *Waverley*; and in fact *Scott* was the author of *Waverley*. Hence we may substitute *Scott* for *the author of 'Waverley'*, and thereby prove that George IV wished to know whether Scott was Scott. Yet an interest in the law of identity can hardly be attributed to the first gentleman of Europe.

(2) By the law of excluded middle, either 'A is B' or 'A is not B' must be true. Hence either 'the present King of France is bald' or 'the present King of France is not bald' must be true. Yet if we enumerated the things that are bald, and then the things that are not bald, we should not find the present King of France in either list. Hegelians, who love a synthesis, will probably conclude that he wears a wig.

(3) Consider the proposition 'A differs from B'. If this is true, there is a difference between A and B, which fact may be expressed in the form 'the

difference between A and B subsists'. But if it is false that A differs from B, then there is no difference between A and B, which fact may be expressed in the form 'the difference between A and B does not subsist'. But how can a non-entity be the subject of a proposition? 'I think, therefore I am' is no more evident than 'I am the subject of a proposition, therefore I am', provided 'I am' is taken to assert subsistence or being,① not existence. Hence, it would appear, it must always be self-contradictory to deny the being of anything; but we have seen, in connection with Meinong, that to admit being also sometimes leads to contradictions. Thus, if A and B do not differ, to suppose either that there is, or that there is not, such an object as 'the difference between A and B' seems equally impossible.

The relation of the meaning to the denotation involves certain rather curious difficulties, which seem in themselves sufficient to prove that the theory which leads to such difficulties must be wrong.

When we wish to speak about the *meaning* of a denoting phrase, as opposed to its *denotation*, the natural mode of doing so is by inverted commas. Thus we say:

The center of mass of the solar system is a point, not a denoting complex;

'The center of mass of the solar system' is a denoting complex, not a point

Or again,

The first line of Gray's Elegy states a proposition.

"The first line of Gray's Elegy" does not state a proposition. Thus taking any denoting phrase, say C, we wish to consider the relation between C and 'C', where the difference of the two is the kind exemplified in the above two instances.

---

① I use these as synonyms.

Heim & Kratzer (1998) *Semantics in Generative Grammar* 选读①

◆ 作者简介

艾琳·罗斯威塔·海姆(Irene Roswitha Heim),当代著名的语义学家,1982年在马萨诸塞大学阿默斯特分校获得博士学位,有关无定名词短语的博士论文产生了巨大反响。她曾先后在德克萨斯大学奥斯汀分校、加州大学洛杉矶分校和麻省理工学院执教。

安吉丽卡·克拉泽(Angelika Kratzer),出生于德国,1979年在康斯坦茨大学获得博士学位,现为马萨诸塞大学阿默斯特分校语言学系教授。她在情态、条件句、情境语义学、论元结构以及诸多句法—语义接口课题上做出了突出贡献。

海姆和克拉泽合著的《生成语法的语义学》是形式语义学最具有影响力的课本之一。

◆ 正文节选

Chapter 1　Truth-conditional Semantics and the Fregean Program

1.1　Truth-conditional semantics

To know the meaning of a sentence is to know its truth-conditions. If I say to you

(1) There is a bag of potatoes in my pantry

you may not know whether what I said is true. What you do know, however, is what the world would have to be like for it to be true. There has to be a bag of potatoes in my pantry. The truth of (1) can come about in

---

① Heim, I. and Kratzer, A. 1998. *Semantics in Generative Grammar*. Cambridge, MA: The MIT Press.

ever so many ways. The bag may be paper or plastic, big or small. It may be sitting on the floor or hiding behind a basket of onions on the shelf. The potatoes may come from Idaho or northern Maine. There may even be more than a single bag. Change the situation as you please. As long as there is a bag of potatoes in my pantry, sentence (1) is true.

A theory of meaning, then, pairs sentences with their truth-conditions. The results are statements of the following form:

Truth-conditions

The sentence "There is a bag of potatoes in my pantry" is true if and only if there is a bag of potatoes in my pantry.

The apparent banality of such statements has puzzled generations of students since they first appeared in Alfred Tarski's 1935 paper "The Concept of Truth in Formalized Languages". Pairing English sentences with their truth-conditions seems to be an easy task that can be accomplished with the help of a single schema:

Schema for truth-conditions

The sentence "_____" is true if and only if _____

A theory that produces such schemata would indeed be trivial if there wasn't another property of natural language that it has to capture: namely, that we understand sentences we have never heard before. We are able to compute the meaning of sentences from the meanings of their parts. Every meaningful part of a sentence contributes to its truth-conditions in a systematic way. As Donald Davidson put it:

> The theory reveals nothing new about the conditions under which an individual sentence is true; it does not make those conditions any clearer than the sentence itself does. The work of the theory is in relating the known truth conditions of each sentence to those aspects ("words") of the sentence that recur in other sentences, and can be assigned identical roles in other sentences. Empirical power in such a theory depends on success in recovering the

structure of a very complicated ability—the ability to speak and understand a language.

In the chapters that follow, we will develop a theory of meaning composition. We will look at sentences and break them down into their parts. And we will think about the contribution of each part to the truth-conditions of the whole.

1.2 Frege on compositionality

The semantic insights we rely on in this book are essentially those of Gottlob Frege, whose work in the late nineteenth century marked the beginning of both symbolic logic and the formal semantics of natural language. The first worked-out versions of a Fregean semantics for fragments of English w ere by Lewis, Montague, and Cresswell.

It is astonishing what language accomplishes. With a few syllables it expresses a countless number of thoughts, and even for a thought grasped for the first time by a human it provides a clothing in which it can be recognized by another to whom it is entirely new. This would not be possible if we could not distinguish parts in the thought that correspond to parts of the sentence, so that the construction of the sentence can be taken to mirror the construction of the thought.... If we thus view thoughts as composed of simple parts and take these, in turn, to correspond t o simple sentence-parts, we can understand how a few sentence-parts can go to make up a great multitude of sentences to which, in turn, there correspond a great multitude of thoughts. The question now arises how the construction of the thought proceeds, and by what means the parts are put together so that the whole is something more than the isolated parts. In my essay "Negation", I considered the case of a thought that appears to be composed of one part which is in need of completion or, as one might say, unsaturated, and whose linguistic correlate is the negative particle, and another part which is a thought. We cannot negate without negating something, and this something is a thought. Because this thought saturates the unsaturated part or, as one might say, completes what is in need of completion, the whole hangs together. And it is a natural conjecture that logical combination of parts into a whole is always a matter of saturating something unsaturated.

Frege, like Aristotle and his successors before him, was interested in the semantic composition of sentences. In the above passage, he conjectured that semantic composition may always consist in the saturation of an unsaturated meaning component. But what are saturated and unsaturated meanings, and what is saturation? Here is what Frege had to say in another one of his papers.

Statements in general, just like equations or inequalities or expressions in Analysis, can be imagined to be split up into two parts; one complete in itself, and the other in need of supplementation, or "unsaturated". Thus, e. g., we split up the sentence "Caesar conquered Gaul" into "Caesar" and "conquered Gaul". The second part is "unsaturated"—it contains an empty place; only when this place is filled up with a proper name, or with an expression that replaces a proper name, does a complete sense appear. Here too I give the name "function" to what this "unsaturated" part stands for. In this case the argument is Caesar.

Frege construed unsaturated meanings as functions. Unsaturated meanings, then, take arguments, and saturation consists in the application of a function to its arguments. Technically, functions are sets of a certain kind. We will therefore conclude this chapter with a very informal introduction to set theory. The same material can be found in the textbook by Partee et al. and countless other sources. If you are already familiar with it, you can skip this section and go straight to the next chapter.

Chapter 2 Executing the Fregean Program

In the pages to follow, we will execute the Fregean program for a fragment of English. Although we will stay very close to Frege's proposals at the beginning, we are not interested in an exegesis of Frege, but in the systematic development of a semantic theory for natural language. Once we get beyond the most basic cases, there will be many small and some not-so-small departures from the semantic analyses that Frege actually defended. But his treatment of semantic composition as functional application (*Frege's Conjecture*), will remain a leading idea throughout.

Modern syntactic theory has taught us show to think about sentences and their parts. Sentences are represented as phrase structure trees. The parts of a sentence are subtrees of phrase structure trees. In this chapter, we begin to explore ways of interpreting phrase structure trees of the kind familiar in linguistics. We will proceed slowly. Our first fragment of English will be limited to simple intransitive and transitive sentences (with only proper names as subjects and objects), and extremely naive assumptions will be made about their structures. Our main concern will be with the process of meaning composition. We will see how a precise characterization of this process depends on, and in turn constrains, what we say about the interpretation of individual words.

This chapter, too, has sections which are not devoted to semantics proper, but to the mathematical tools on which this discipline relies. Depending on the reader's prior mathematical experience, these may be supplemented by exercises from other sources or 'skimmed for a quick review.

2.1 First example of a Fregean interpretation

We begin by limiting our attention to sentences that consist of a proper name plus an intransitive verb. Let us assume that the syntax of English associates these with phrase structures like that in (1).

(1)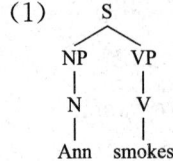

We want to formulate a set of semantic rules which will provide denotations for all trees and subtrees in this kind of structure. How shall we go about this? What sorts of entities shall we employ as denotations? Let us be guided by Frege.

Frege took the denotations of sentences to be truth-values, and we will follow him in this respect. But wait. Can this be right? The previous chapter began with the statement "To know the meaning of a sentence is to know its truth-conditions". We emphasized that the meaning of a sentence is not its actual truth-value, and concluded that a theory of meaning for natural language should pair sentences with their truth-*conditions* and explain how this can be done in a compositional way. Why, then, are we proposing truth-*values* as the denotations for sentences? Bear with us. Once we spell out the complete proposal, you'll see that we will end up with truth-conditions after all.

The Fregean denotations that we are in the midst of introducing are also called "*extensions*", a term of art which is often safer to use because it has no potentially interfering non-technical usage. The extension of a sentence, then, is its actual truth-value. What are truth-values? Let us identify them with the numbers 1 (True) and 0 (False). Since the extensions of sentences are not functions, they are saturated in Frege's sense. The extensions of proper names like "Ann" and "Jan" don't seem to be functions either. "Ann" denotes Ann, and "Jan" denotes Jan.

We are now ready to think about suitable extensions for intransitive verbs like "smokes". Look at the above tree. We saw that the extension for the lexical item "Ann" is the individual Ann. The node dominating "Ann" is a non-branching N-node. This means that it should inherit the denotation of its daughter node 1. The N-node is again dominated by a non-branching node. This NP-node, then, will inherit its denotation from the N-node. So the denotation of the NP-node in the above tree is the individual Ann. The NP-node is dominated by a branching S-node. The denotation of the S-node, then, is calculated from the denotation of the NP-node and the denotation of the VP-node. We know that the denotation of the NP-node is Ann, hence saturated. Recall now that Frege conjectured that all semantic composition amounts to functional application. If that is so, we must conclude that the denotation of the VP-node must be unsaturated, hence a function. What kind of function? Well, we know what kinds of things its arguments and its values are. Its arguments are individuals like Ann, and its values are truth-values. The extension of an intransitive verb like "smokes", then, should be a function from individuals to truth-values.

Let's put this all together in an explicit formformulation. Our semantics for the fragment of English under consideration consists of three components. First, we define our inventory of denotations. Second, we provide a lexicon which specifies the denotation of each item that may occupy a terminal node. Third, we give a semantic rule for each possible type of non-terminal node. When we want to talk about the denotation of a lexical item or tree, we enclose it in double brackets. For any expression α, then, $[\![α]\!]$ is the denotation of α. We can think of $[\![\ ]\!]$ as a function (the *interpretation function*) that assigns appropriate denotations to linguistic expressions. In this and most of the following chapters, the denotations of expressions are extensions. The resulting semantic system is an *extensional semantics*. Towards the end of this book, we will encounter phenomena that cannot be handled within an extensional semantics. We will then revise our system of denotations and introduce intensions.

A. Inventory of denotations

Let D be the set of all individuals that exist in the real world. Possible denotations are:

Elements of D, the set of actual individuals.
Elements of {0, 1}, the set of truth-values.
Functions from D to {0, 1}.

B. Lexicon

[[**Ann**]] = Ann

[[**Jan**]] = Jan

etc. for other proper names.

[[**works**]] = f : D → {0, 1}
  For all x ∈D, f(x) = 1 iff x works.

[[**smokes**]] = f : D → {0, 1}
  For all x ∈D, f(x)=1 iff x smokes.

etc. for other intransitive verbs.

C. Rules for non-terminal nodes

In what follows, Greek letters are used as variables for trees and sub-trees.

(S1) If α has the form $\begin{array}{c}S\\ \wedge\\ \beta\ \gamma\end{array}$, then [[α]]=[[γ]]([[β]]).

(S2) If α has the form $\begin{array}{c}NP\\ |\\ \beta\end{array}$, then [[α]]=[[β]].

(S3) If α has the form $\begin{array}{c}VP\\ |\\ \beta\end{array}$, then [[α]]=[[β]].

(S4) If α has the form $\begin{array}{c}N\\ |\\ \beta\end{array}$, then [[α]]=[[β]].

(S5) If α has the form $\begin{array}{c}V\\ |\\ \beta\end{array}$, then [[α]]=[[β]].

2.1.1 Applying the semantics to an example

Does this set of semantic rules predict the correct truth-conditions for "Ann smokes"? That is, is "Ann smokes" predicted to be true if and only if Ann smokes? "Of course", you will say, "that's obvious". It's pretty obvious indeed, but we are still going to take the trouble to give an explicit proof of it. As matters get more complex in the chapters to come, it will be less and less obvious whether a given set of proposed rules predict the judgments it is supposed to predict. But you can always find out for sure if you draw your trees and work through them node by node, applying one rule at a time. It is best to get used to this while the calculations are still simple. If you have some experience with computations of this kind, you may skip this subsection.

We begin with a precise statement of the claim we want to prove:

Claim:

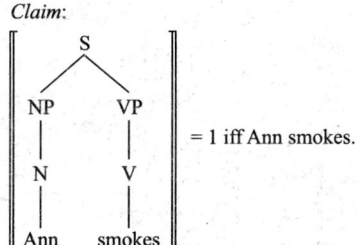

We want to deduce this claim from our lexical entries and semantic rules (S1)-(S5). Each of these rules refers to trees of a certain form. The tree

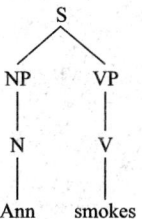

is of the form specified by rule (S1), repeated here, so let's see what (S1) says about it.

(S1) If α has the form $\underset{\beta\ \gamma}{\overset{S}{\wedge}}$, then $[[\alpha]]=[[\gamma]]([[\beta]])$.

When we apply a general rule to a concrete tree, we must first match up the variables in the rule with the particular constituents that correspond to them in the application. In this instance, α is

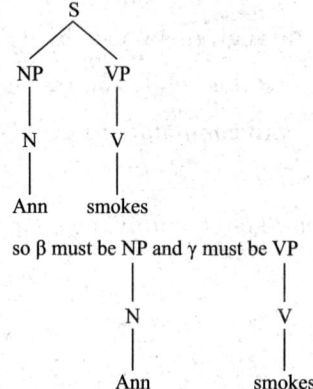

so β must be NP and γ must be VP

The rule says that $[[\alpha]] = [[\gamma]]([[\beta]])$, so this means in the present application that

(2) $\begin{bmatrix} S \\ NP\ VP \\ |\ \ \ | \\ N\ \ \ V \\ |\ \ \ | \\ Ann\ smokes \end{bmatrix} = \begin{bmatrix} VP \\ | \\ V \\ | \\ smokes \end{bmatrix} \left(\begin{bmatrix} NP \\ | \\ N \\ | \\ Ann \end{bmatrix} \right)$

Now we apply rule (S3) to the tree

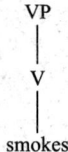

(This time, we skip the detailed justification of why and how this rule fits this tree.) What we obtain from this is

(3) $\begin{bmatrix} VP \\ | \\ V \\ | \\ smokes \end{bmatrix} = \begin{bmatrix} V \\ | \\ smokes \end{bmatrix}$

From (2) and (3), by substituting equals for equals, we infer (4).

(4) $\left[\!\!\left[\begin{array}{c} S \\ \diagup\diagdown \\ NP \quad VP \\ | \quad\quad | \\ N \quad\quad V \\ | \quad\quad | \\ Ann \;\; smokes \end{array} \right]\!\!\right] = \left[\!\!\left[\begin{array}{c} V \\ | \\ smokes \end{array} \right]\!\!\right] \left(\left[\!\!\left[\begin{array}{c} NP \\ | \\ N \\ | \\ Ann \end{array} \right]\!\!\right]\right)$

Now we apply rule (S5) to the appropriate subtree and use the resulting equation for another substitution in (4):

(5) $\left[\!\!\left[\begin{array}{c} S \\ \diagup\diagdown \\ NP \quad VP \\ | \quad\quad | \\ N \quad\quad V \\ | \quad\quad | \\ Ann \;\; smokes \end{array} \right]\!\!\right] = \left[\!\!\left[\, smokes \,\right]\!\!\right] \left(\left[\!\!\left[\begin{array}{c} NP \\ | \\ N \\ | \\ Ann \end{array} \right]\!\!\right]\right)$

Now we use rule (S2) and then (s4), and after substituting the results there of in (5), we have (6).

(6) $\left[\!\!\left[\begin{array}{c} S \\ \diagup\diagdown \\ NP \quad VP \\ | \quad\quad | \\ N \quad\quad V \\ | \quad\quad | \\ Ann \;\; smokes \end{array} \right]\!\!\right] = \left[\!\!\left[\, smokes \,\right]\!\!\right] \left(\left[\!\!\left[\, Ann \,\right]\!\!\right]\right)$

At this point, we look up the lexical entries for **Ann** and **smokes**. If we just use these to substitute equals for equals in (6), we get (7).

(7) $\left[\!\!\left[\begin{array}{c} S \\ \diagup\diagdown \\ NP \quad VP \\ | \quad\quad | \\ N \quad\quad V_i \\ | \quad\quad | \\ Ann \;\; smokes \end{array} \right]\!\!\right] = \left[\begin{array}{c} f : D \to \{0, 1\} \\ \text{For all } x \in D, f(x) = 1 \text{ iff } x \text{ smokes} \end{array} \right] (Ann)$

Let's take a close look at the right-hand side of this equation. It has the gross form "function (argument)", so it denotes the value that a certain function yields for a certain argument. The argument is Ann, and the function is the one which maps those who smoke to 1 and all others to 0. If we apply this function to Ann, we will get 1 if Ann smokes and 0 if she doesn't. To summarize what we have just determined:

(8) $\begin{bmatrix} f: D \to \{0, 1\} \\ \text{For all } x \in D, f(x) = 1 \text{ iff } x \text{ smokes} \end{bmatrix}$(Ann) = 1 iff Ann somkes.

And now we have reached the goal of our proof: (7) and (8) together imply exactly the claim which we stated at the beginning. QED.

This was not the only way in which we could have constructed the proof of this claim. What matters is (a) that we use each applicable rule or lexical entry to obtain an equation regarding the denotation of a certain subtree; (b) that we keep using some of these equations to substitute equals for equals in others, thereby getting closer and closer to the target equation in our claim; and (c) that we employ the definitions of functions that we find in the lexicon to calculate their values for specified arguments. There is no unique specified order in which we must perform these steps. We can apply rules to the smallest subtrees first, or start at the top of the tree, or anywhere in the middle. We can collect a long list of separate equations before we begin to draw conclusions from any two of them, or else we can keep alternating applications of semantic rules with substitutions in equations derived previously. The sowldness of the proof is not affected by these choices (although, of course, some strategies may be easier than others to follow through without getting confused).

We have used the word "proof" a number of times in this section. What exactly do we mean by this term? The notion of "proof" has been made precise in various ways in the history of logic. The most rigorous notion equates a proof with a syntactic derivation in an axiomatic or natural deduction system. Above, we relied on a less regimented notion of "proof" that is common in mathematics. Mathematical proofs are rarely algorithmic derivations. They are usually written in plain English (or some other natural language), supplemented by technical vocabulary that has been introduced through definitions. Conclusions are licensed by inference patterns that are known to be valid but are not spelled out formally. The proofs in this book are all "semi-formal" in this way. The standards of rigor followed in mathematics should be good enough for what we want to accomplish here.

Partee (2004) *Compositionality in Formal Semantics* 选读①

◆ **作者简介**

芭芭拉·帕蒂②(Barbara Partee, 1940—),著名语义学家,被视为美国当代形式语义学的奠基人。她曾在斯沃斯莫尔学院主修数学,辅修俄语和哲学,随后进入麻省理工学院师从乔姆斯基学习,1965 年取得博士学位。她曾先后在加州大学洛杉矶分校和马萨诸塞大学阿默斯特分校执教,并培养了不少语义学学者,如 Gennaro Chierchia 和 Irene Heim。她在生成语言学、形式逻辑和分析哲学方面做出了突出的学术贡献。

◆ **正文节选**

Chapter 7 Compositionality

7.1 The Principle and its Theory-relativity

7.1.1 Introduction

The compositionality principle, in its most general form, can be expressed as follows:

> The meaning of an expression is a function of the meanings of its parts and of the way they are syntactically combined.

The principle is usually attributed to Frege, and is often called "Frege's

---

① Partee, Barbara H. Hoboken: Wiley-Blackwell, 2004.
② 图片来源: https://en.wikipedia.org/wiki/Barbara_Partee#/media/File: Barbara_partee.jpg。

principle" (but cf. Janssen 1983 for some problems with this attribution). In its most general form, the principle is nearly uncontroversial; some version of it would appear to be an essential part of any account of how meanings are assigned to novel sentences.

But the principle can be made precise only in conjunction with an explicit theory of meaning and of syntax, together with a fuller specification of what is required by the relation "is a function of". If the syntax is sufficiently unconstrained and meanings are sufficiently rich, there seems no doubt that natural languages can be described compositionally. Challenges to the principle generally involve either explicit or implicit arguments to the effect that it conflicts with other well-motivated constraints on syntax and/or on the mapping from syntax to meaning. Ultimately the question of how strong a form of the principle can reasonably be maintained is a matter of overall theory comparison, so we cannot expect it to be settled very soon or easily.

I have several goals in this chapter. One is to emphasize how many versions of the principle there can be, since I think some arguments about it are clouded by assumptions that it is more clearcut than it is (or that compositionality equals Montague's theory of grammar). The second is to examine a number of challenges to various forms of the principle from both broad and narrow perspectives, trying to sort out what real arguments there may be for doubting the principle, particularly Montague's strong version of it. And finally I want to explore some questions about context-dependency, ambiguity, and "invisible variables" that I don't know how to resolve but which have potentially important consequences for how strong a version of the compositionality principle we can reasonably expect to maintain.

7.1.2 Versions of the principle

Given the extreme theory-dependence of the compositionality principle and the diversity of existing (pieces of) theories, it would be hopeless to try to enumerate all its possible versions. In what follows, I will be focusing mainly on the following kinds of differences (not exhaustive): (1) in the nature of "meanings": model-theoretic objects or linguistic representations of some sort? Intensions? Functions from contexts (what are those? do they include assignments to free variables?) to intensions? (2) in assumptions about the syntax: must it be "independently motivated?" or is compositionality itself one of the constraints? Is the relevant part-whole relation "configurational" or "derivational" ("rule-by-rule")? (Cf. Bach 1976.) What kinds of abstractness and invisibilia are allowed? (3) in the construal of "is a function of": how locally must compositionality hold? What kinds of functions are allowed, and are there constraints on what kinds of functions interpret what kinds of syntactic combinations? (Cf. Partee 1979a, 1979b; Landman and Moerdijk 1983; Sag and Klein 1982.) Is compositionality necessarily purely "bottom-up"? Must the functions be single-valued, and if so, how are ambiguity and context-dependence allowed for? Does functionality preclude non-dispensable intermediate levels of representation?

This is just a sample of the kinds of questions to which different answers yield different versions of the principle. In the following section we will review some of Montague's answers, and then turn to considering alternatives and challenges.

7.1.3 Montague's "universal grammar"

An explicit version of the compositionality principle which has fueled a lot of subsequent research is that embodied in Montague (1970) ("UG"; expositions can be found in Halvorsen and Ladusaw 1979, Link 1979, and Dowty, Wall, and Peters 1981, ch. 8.) A brief review will summarize what I will subsequently refer to as "Montague's strong version of the compositionality principal", or MCP.

(1) Meanings can be anything you like, as long as they form an algebra homomorphic to the syntactic algebra. ("Intermediate levels" must therefore be in principle dispensable.) For the more restricted notion of "Fregean interpretations" (part of the "theory of reference" for Montague), meanings are functions from possible worlds *and context of use* to possible denotations based on the familiar typed domains with primitive types *e* and

t. (2) The syntax is given as an algebraic characterization of a disambiguated language plus an "ambiguating relation", with no constraints on the substance of the syntactic operations. The compositionality principle is a fundamental constraint on grammar construction; Montague was not interested in syntax "except as a preliminary to semantics", and believed that syntactic evidence alone was unlikely to determine a unique syntax. (UG, the (in)famous footnote 2.) The relevant part-whole relation is given by the syntactic derivation in the syntax of the disambiguated language ("rule-by-rule interpretation"). "Parts" must be "immediate parts" (derivationally), but they need not be "visible parts" of the resulting expression—the syntactic operations can delete or replace things, and the ambiguating relation can effect further deletions after the derivation of an expression in the disambiguated language is complete. (3) "is a function of" is interpreted as the requirement of a homomorphism from the syntactic algebra to the semantic algebra. There are no further constraints on the nature of this function. Interpretation is purely "bottom-up". Ambiguity arises only via the ambiguating relation; there is no ambiguity within the disambiguated language. Context-dependence is treated entirely as indexicality and built into the notion of meanings as functions from possible worlds *and context of use*; there is no provision for dependence on context effects between parts of a single sentence.

Since the issue of compositionality *vis-à-vis* context-dependence is a major concern in this chapter, I will quote what Montague said about it in UG:

> Thus *meanings* are functions of two arguments—a possible world and a context of use. The second argument is introduced in order to permit a treatment, in the manner of [Montague (1968)], of such indexical locutions as demonstratives, first- and second-person singular pronouns, and free variables (which are treated in Section 6 below as a kind of demonstrative). *Senses* on the other

hand... are functions of only one argument, regarded as a possible world. The intuitive distinction is this: meanings are those entities that serve as interpretations of expressions (and hence, if the interpretation of a compound is always to be a function of the interpretations of its components, cannot be identified with functions of possible worlds alone), while senses are those intensional entities that are sometimes *denoted* by expressions. No such distinction was necessary in [Frege (1892)], because there consideration of indexical locutions was deliberately avoided. (UG, p. 228)

It is clear from this passage that Montague took compositionality as a guiding principle in determining what sorts of things meanings should be and not as an independently falsifiable claim. Janssen (1983) gives a number of detailed illustrations of how *prima facie* challenges to the compositionality principle can be met by suitably enriching the entities that are to serve as meanings, following the methodological principle articulated by Montague in the passage just quoted.

7.1.4 Theoretical alternatives

In some approaches to semantics, meanings are identified with expressions of some sort—"semantic representations" (Katz and Fodor 1963; Katz 1972; Jackendoff 1972) or "logical forms". The compositionality principle can still be formulated for such systems, but it then becomes a much more syntactic notion, basically a constraint on the translation rules which map syntactic representations on to semantic ones. It is difficult to compare such systems straightforwardly with model-theoretic semantics, although one can probably say that Jackendoff's theory was less locally compositional (given that some parts of semantic interpretation were to be determined at deep structure, others at surface structure) than that of Fodor and Katz (an early model of "rule-by-rule" interpretation). It seems to me that one of the biggest open issues in semantics is the status of a possible linguistic level of semantic representation of some sort; Montague's theory allows such a level but requires that it be in principle dispensable, but one serious alternative is to posit an intermediate level of representation such that its own semantics is compositional (which might justify calling it "logical form") while the rules mapping syntactic representations on to it are not compositional or only weakly so—or vice versa.

Even within the tradition of Montague grammar not all analyses have adhered to MCP. Cooper (1975) proposed the mechanism now known as "Cooper storage" as a means of generating multiple interpretations, differing with respect to quantifier scope, corresponding to a single syntactic structure; Bach and Partee (1980), extending Cooper's mechanism still further, suggested that a limited weakening of the compositionality constraint was a reasonable tradeoff for the strong syntactic constraints of a phrase structure grammar obeying the well-formedness constraint (Partee 1979a). Landman and Moerdijk (1983) have shown how results corresponding to those of Bach and Partee can be achieved in a system which preserves MCP but reinstates quantifying-in rules in the syntax; one of the major points at issue is the need for a level of translation or "logical form", particularly with respect to the indexing of pronouns—if quantifier scope and pronoun indexing are not represented in the syntax, then it appears that an additional level is needed where they are represented. It appears then that MCP is closely bound up with the possibility (and desirability) of giving a direct model-theoretic interpretation for natural languages. This is a crucial issue, but one for which I have no resolution to offer. It will recur at various points below, and is likely to be a major issue for some time to come.

7.2 Broad Challenges to Montague's Version of Compositionality

In addition to the fact that not all current theoretical approaches to syntax and semantics are as strictly compositional as Montague's, there have been a number of explicit challenges to MCP. In this section I will discuss some which involve challenges to Montague's whole framework.

Chomsky's skepticism towards the compositionality principle, expressed in Chomsky (1975) and elsewhere, seems to stem from two convictions: the "autonomy of syntax" thesis and the idea that the organization of grammar is best viewed as involving a number of relatively independent subsystems, each with its own principles and constraints, which interact to jointly constrain the final output—a view of grammar very different from Montague's, which when extended to phonology as in Bach and Wheeler (1981) presents a grammar as a simultaneous recursive definition of well-formed, phonologically and semantically interpreted, expressions of the language—starting from the smallest units and building up larger ones with phonological, syntactic, and semantic rules working hand in hand to construct and interpret complex expressions compositionally from their parts. Filters, for example, play a large role in Chomsky's theories but have virtually no place in Montague's: given the requirement of a homomorphism from the syntax to the semantics, if an expression is generated by the syntax, it must be interpretable by the semantics. The "autonomy of syntax" thesis is a complex issue which I have discussed elsewhere (Partee 1975b); at the level of description, Montague's theory does include an autonomous syntax. But if the thesis is taken to assert that the syntax of a language should be learnable in isolation from the semantics, then while Montague's theory takes no direct stand on the question, MCP makes such a thesis quite implausible. In a compositionally organized grammar any information about either syntax or semantics would provide some evidence about the other, and an optimal learning mechanism would presumably exploit all availableevidence. These tenets of Chomsky's are, like the compositionality principle itself, too global to be straightforwardly evaluated; and the resulting theories differ in too many ways for grammars constructed within them to be directly comparable. As Landman and Moerdijk (1983) point out, Chomsky's particular arguments against compositionality (as in Chomsky 1975) consist of non-compositional analyses of certain phenomena, and while such cases can provide valuable challenges (which may reasonably sway opinions if unmet), they neither settle the issue nor provide an alternative account of what the limits are on the relation of semantics to syntax.

Bresnan's Lexical-functional Grammar (Bresnan 1978; Kaplan and Bresnan 1982) provides challenges to compositionality which are in a sense more interesting because the theories are more nearly comparable. From the perspective of Montague grammar, her arguments for the level of functional structure can be seen as arguments against direct model-theoretic interpretation of syntactic structure and for the value of an intermediate level of representation. Halvorsen (1983) has provided rules for mapping Bresnan's functional structures onto formulas of intensional logic, making the system model-theoretically interpretable; but since the functional structures are apparently not homomorphically related to either the syntactic algebra or the model-theoretic interpretation, the resulting system violates MCP.

Of particular interest is Bresnan's treatment of idioms and dummy *there*, and their interaction with passives, Raising structures, and the like. On her treatment, an NP which is part of an idiom, such as *tabs* in *keep tabs on*, has no meaning of its own; only the complete idiom has a meaning. Within the Montague framework the fact that such "meaningless" elements appear as NPs presents a problem, since they then should have NP-type meanings, at least if they are independently generated in their surface positions. It is possible to maintain compositionality for such cases by providing special meanings for the "meaningless" pieces (see Sag 1982; Sag and Klein 1982). But one should also consider the possibility that a less compositional but more natural treatment (analogous to Bresnan's) might be achieved in a Montague grammar with a non-dispensable level of translation containing "dummy constants" with no fixed interpretations of their own but subject to meaning postulates specifying the meanings of the relevant larger units that contain them.

Another sort of challenge to MCP concerns "bottom-up" vs. "top-down" interpretations; this is discussed in Hintikka (1980) (as "inside-out" vs. "outside-in") and arises also in connection with recent work of Kamp (1981) and Heim (1982) as well as some of the proposals of Barwise and Perry. Kamp and Heim both provide explicit treatments of syntax as well as semantics, so I will focus on where their theories depart from Montague's. Simplifying considerably and selecting a single feature for comparison, both of their theories (let me call them jointly in this respect the K-H theory) introduce an intermediate level of representation ("discourse representations" (Kamp) or "file cards" (Heim)) such that occurrences of certain kinds of noun phrases in the syntactic structure affect global properties of the intermediate representations. Indefinite noun phrases, for instance, are interpreted "in the long run" as existentially quantified, but what the scope of the existential quantifier is is not determined locally, "bottom-up" but by properties of the larger configuration in which the corresponding variable ("discourse referent") appears at the intermediate level; the scope may end up over a whole discourse, and in the case of the treatment of "donkey-sentences", the operation of the rules for determining the truth-conditions for intermediate representations do not yield a standard "scope" interpretation at all (although they are well-defined). In the K-H theory, *every* and *if* are more alike than *every* and *a*; not only does this depart from Montague's category-to-type correspondences, but the if in effect introduces an "unselective" or variably polyadic universal quantifier which binds everything which occurs within a certain configuration at the intermediate level; what this configuration will be is not a simple function of the syntactic structure, but depends as well on what sorts of noun phrases occur within the *if*-clause (*a*-type or *every*-type). The fact that these treatments do not conform to MCP does not prove, of course, that no MCP-compatible treatment is possible; but the novel solution to the *donkey*-sentence problem provided in the new frameworks does not appear to be expressible in a pure Montague grammar and it poses a serious challenge to the thesis of direct compositional model-theoretic interpretability, since it seems (to me at least) to be superior to any of the many analyses of *donkey*-sentences proposed within Montague's (or any other) framework.

6.3 思考和练习

1. 什么是语义的组合性原则?

2. 什么是真值条件语义学?这一语义学和你理解的意义的研究有什么区别?

3. 什么是衍推?什么是预设?它们之间的区别是什么?

4. 如何用真值条件语义学来表述含有形容词谓语句的语义?下列句子的语义该如何用真值条件语义学表述?

  张三很高。

  张三很聪明。

  张三很小气。

5. 语义学的发展和语言哲学有着密不可分的联系。请仔细阅读 Russell (1905)关于指称的论文,感受语言哲学的相关思考是如何影响语义理论的发展的。

6.4 延伸阅读

Chierchia, G. & S. McConnell-Ginet. 1990. *Meaning and Grammar: An Introduction to Semantics*. Cambridge, Mass.: The MIT Press.

Chomsky, N. 1970. Deep structure, surface structure, and semantic interpretation. In R. Jakobson and S. Kawamoto (eds.), *Studies in General and Oriental Linguistics*. Tokyo: TEC Corporation.

Frege, G. 1891/1980. Function and concept. In P. T. Geach and Max Black (eds.), *Translations from the Philosophical Writings of Gottlob Frege*, 22-41. Trans. P. T. Geach, 3rd edition. Oxford: Blackwell.

Hale, K. & Keyser, S. J. 2002. *Prolegomenon to a Theory of Argument Structure*. Cambridge, Mass.: The MIT Press.

Heim, I. & A. Kratzer. 1998. *Semantics in Generative Grammar*. Cambridge, Mass.: The MIT Press.

Jackendoff, R. 1983. *Semantics and Cognition*. Cambridge, Mass.: The MIT Press.

Kearns, K. 2002. *Semantics (2nd edition)*. New York: Palgrave Macmillan.

Lappin, S. (ed.).1996. *The Handbook of Contemporary Semantic Theory*. Oxford: Blackwell.

Parsons, T. P. 1990. *Events in the Semantics of English*. Cambridge, Mass.: The MIT Press.

Portner, P. & Partee, B. H. 2002. *Formal Semantics: The essential readings*. Oxford: Blackwell.

Saeed, J. I. 1997. *Semantics*. Oxford: Blackwell.

第七章 语用学

7.1 导引

- 语用概说
- 语用的规律性
- 预设与衍推
- 会话涵义
- 言语行为
- 小结

7.1.1 语用概说

语用学(Pragmatics)研究语言在使用中的意义。何谓"语言使用"现象呢？我们在第一章中提到了语言和语言研究的区别。作为语言研究分支的"语言使用"研究，和文体学修辞学等研究不同，语用学研究的侧重点不是教人们怎么得体地使用语言，而是探索人们使用语言时的潜意识的知识，也就说，探索人类语言使用背后的规则。就像句法和语义的研究目的是为了揭示人类潜意识的语言知识(语言能力)一样，研究语言使用的主要目标也是为了揭示人类潜意识的语言能力。

作为语言研究分支之一的语言使用研究，主要是为了研究语言在使用中的意义。在日常语言使用中，句子的字面意义很多时候并不是说话人想要向听话人传递的真正信息。比如中国人经常见面打招呼"你吃了吗"，其实说话人并不关心对方吃了与否，英国人见面喜欢聊天气"The weather is nice, isn't it?",也不是一定要就天气的好坏展开讨论。这两种用法在语言使用的共通之处在于:说话人希望通过这样的打招呼的方式,向听话人表示"寒暄"(phatic),让听话人意识到说话人在乎他的存在。可以这么说,语用就是研究语言的"言外之意"、"言外有意"的。过去半个多世纪以来的语言研究表明,就像语音、结构和语义总是遵循一定的规律一样,我们对语言语用意义的理解也总是遵循一定的规律的。对这些规律进行系统性考察的语言学分支叫"语用学"。

语言学对语用学的定义是:语用学研究语用义,或者说,语用学研究语言在使用中的意义。语用学是当代语言研究的重要分支之一。语义学和语用学有共通之处。从广义的角度来说,语用和语义都关注语言的意义。但是,作为语言学分支的"语用学"和"语义学",它们对意义关注的侧重点有所不同。语义学关注的是语言形式和该形式在客观世界所对应的事物之间的关系,而语用学关注的则是语言形式和语言使用者之间的关系。

要了解一个句子的意义,首先我们需要了解这个句子的组成成分的意义和它们的组成方式(包括语序及其它层级结构)。组成成分的意义即语言形式在客观世界中的所指。比如在"天鹅是白的"这个句子中,"天鹅"的意义即"天鹅"在客观世界所指称的对象(也就是客观世界中的天鹅),"白的"表示客观世界中所有白色的事物。联系词"是"可以看作一种类属关系。我们知道"天鹅是白的"是什么意思,是因为我们知道这个句子什么时候为真,什么时候为假:"天鹅是白的"为真当且仅当"天鹅"是"白色的事物"的一个子集。这一语义的表述通常用如下的形式进行:

(1) 语义的表述形式:S 为真当且仅当 q
例:"天鹅是白的"为真当且仅当天鹅是白的。

上述表达式中的 S 表示句子,q 表示命题。为方便说明,我们会对"命题"的定义做简单的处理,认为命题是句子所表达的意义。命题是抽象的意义,是脱离了语言使用环境的意义。在日常语言使用中,人们知道句子的命题意义,但并不足以完全明白句子的意义。思考下面的对话:

(2) A:周末我们一起去看电影吧?
B:动物园新引进了一批非洲来的斑马。

当 A 听到了 B 的回答之后，他会做如下的推理：B 的回答是有意义的，B 通过说"动物园新引进了一批非洲来的斑马"来传递某个信息；B 所传递的信息受(4)这个对话所发生的时间、地点和情景的影响，同时还受 A 和 B 之间关系的影响；B 要向 A 传递的信息肯定不是"动物园新引进了一批非洲来的斑马"这个句子的命题意义，而是"言外有意"；这"言外有意"才是 B 说出这个句子所要表达的真正意图。通过这样的推理之后，A 可以听出 B 的"言外有意"：B 通过一个不相关的回答来拒绝 A 的邀请，但同时也向 A 发出一个新的提议："一起去动物园看斑马吧"。这个意义，正是语用所关注的内容。这个例子表明，要充分理解"言外之意"，需要考虑更多的因素。

影响语用义的理解的因素是多方面的。首先，实际语言使用中总是有说话人和听话人。对意义的理解因而也包括听话人怎么理解说话人意义的过程。从这一点说，语用义也是说话人的意义。

其次，语用义总是依赖于语言使用的特定的语境(context)。语言使用总是发生在特定的语境之中(说话人和听话人所处的空间、时间以及他们对相关话题的背景知识的理解)，对语用义的理解因而也总是依赖特定的语境进行。即使是同样的语言表示式，在不同的语境中，也会有不同的意义。比如：

(3) A：他进来了。
　　B：我去给他打个招呼。

"语境"在语言学中有不同的定义。表达式所出现的上下文通常也叫做语境。也就是说，语境分为语言语境(上下文)和非语言语境。(3)的例子中有两个人称代词"他"。语法知识告诉我们，"他"的语义是第三人称单数。我们虽然具有这样的语法知识，但是离开了具体的语境，我们仍然不知道这个例子中"他"的所指。很多时间状语也有类似的用法。如在商场里看到下面的广告："明天全场清货"。如果今天是 2018 年 10 月 10 日，那么明天指的是 2018 年 10 月 11 日；如果今天是 2017 年 9 月 3 日，那么明天就是 2017 年 9 月 4 日。"明天"的语义完全依赖于语境。只有当"今天"被说话人指定之后，"明天"的意义才能确定。

类似的还有空间指示词。空间指示词如"这里""那里""上""下""左""右"等的确定的语义所指都受到语境的限制：一方面，它们总是依赖于一定的语境来获得确定的意义;另一方面,在不同的语境中,同样的表达式也会有不同的意义。

然后,人们对语用义的理解的过程通常也是对人们对通过语言传递的信息的理解的过程。在日常语言使用中,说话人总是通过语言表达式来传递一定的信息。这一信息往往超过了语言表达式本身的意义。听话人需要对说话人的意图加以揣测和推理。这个意义,就是人们所称的"言外之意"。

综上,语言的使用总是受到各种因素的影响。语用义也受到一系列因素的影响。影响人们理解语用义的因素除了语言表达式本身的字面意义外,还包括(但不限于):

a. 说话人和听话人的身份、他们之间的亲疏关系、话语发生的地点和时间;

b. 说话人的意愿:说话人希望通过一定的话语所要传递给听话人的信息;

c. 说话人和听话人所具有的某一话题的背景知识;

d. 话语所发生的社会性场合,如结婚场合、法庭场合、开幕式场合等等。

7.1.2 语用的规律性

"言外之意"受到语言使用环境的影响。语言使用的具体环境也是千差万别,因人因地因时间而异。但是,为什么在绝大多数情况下,人与人之间通过语言的交流和沟通仍然可以顺利地进行呢?俗语说"物以类聚,人以群分",就是说,具有同样背景的人具有相似的世界观、价值观和知识结构,这些共同的背景部分决定了谁和谁在一起,确保了沟通的进行,也保证了说话人向听话人传递的信息能够被正确地理解和执行。我们可以进一步说,语言使用的规则具有一定的普遍性。这种普遍性独立于语言系统,和人类的社会准则、交际行为密切关联。事实上,人类对语言使用的规则性的认识,有着漫长的历史发展过程。这一探索最早可以追溯到古代希腊和罗马时期("语用学"的英文名称"pragmatics"一词就来源于拉丁语中的"pragmaticus"和古希腊语中的"pragmaticos",意为"实用")。经过许多代学者的努力,人们已经认识到,相当一部分的语用现象——人们怎么理解"言外之意"——是受到一定规律的制约的。语用义的规律性有一些深刻的原因。

首先,在社会生活中,人们会倾向于用符合规定的方式来使用语言。作为语言使用者的个人总是生活在一定的社会群体之中。作为这个社会群体的一员,他/她总是会遵循社会群体的一些约定的规则。这种规则的来源可能是文化,也可能是社会习俗。只要找出一定社会群体所遵循的规则,自然也就能找到人们使用语言的规则。

其次,在一个特定的语言社区中,大多数人会有对世界的一些共同的认识,共享一些非语言的信息。语言使用者所具有的这些共享的知识和信仰也是语用义规律性的来源之一。比如下面的例子:

(4) I found an old bicycle lying on the ground. The chain was rusted and the tires were flat.

看到这句话,人们不会因为第二个分句中突然出现的车链(the chain)和车胎(the tires)感到惊讶,因为在人们共享的世界知识中,自行车必定有车链和车胎,也就是说,人们会作一个假设:如果 X 是一部自行车,那么 X 必定有车链和轮胎。这个信息是(4)这个例子的前提性条件,是不需要说出来的。比较(4)和(5):

(5) I found an old bicycle. <u>A bicycle has a chain</u>. The chain was rusted. <u>A bicycle has two tires</u>. The tires are flat.

例(5)显得比较奇怪。这个例子中的下划线部分是冗余的信息,因为这些信息是说话人和听话人在开展对话之前都具有的背景知识,不需要明确说出来。听话人听到这个句子,要么认为说话人故弄玄虚,要么认为自己被当作了白痴(不知道"自行车有链条和轮胎"这么浅显的知识)。

所以,人们在使用语言的时候,"说"语言和通过语言"交流"总是会遵循一定的规则。很容易就能举出一个现代汉语的例子:

(6) a. 小明有一个鼻子。他的鼻子上有一个红色的斑点。
    b. 小明的鼻子上有一个红色的斑点。

说汉语的人会觉得(6a)很奇怪,原因就在于其中出现的冗余的信息。

"人有一个鼻子"是大家都有的知识。通常这样的知识是不需要明确说出来的。说出来会导致语言形式和"信息传递"之间的冲突,因而违反了语用规则。

语用义的规律性的第三个来源是人们共同的生活经验。在经典的命题逻辑中,p and q 为真的充分必要条件是:p 为真,同时 q 为真。"and"满足交换律:p and q 和 q and p 的逻辑意义是完全等同的。但是,在很多实际情况下,语言使用的情况并不遵循这一逻辑规律:

(7) a. p and q 为真当且仅当 p 为真并且 q 为真
    b. p and q = q and p
(8) a. 小狗跑向小明,并且舔了他。
    b. #小狗舔了小明,并且跑向他。

根据逻辑规律,(8a)和(8b)这两个句子不应该有差别。但是,实际上则是例(8a)是合格的汉语句子,(8b)则比较奇怪。(8b)让人们感到奇怪的原因是因为它违反了语用规则。因为根据人们的生活经验,事件有先后之分,同样的,语言形式的排列也反应了人们对事件发生先后顺序的认识。我们可以构拟出一条语用规则来解释(8a)和(8b)之间的对立。这条规则可以表述如下:

◆ 语言形式的先后顺序与事件发生顺序的对应规则:
1 语言形式出现的顺序反映了事件发生的顺序。

根据上述规则,"小狗舔了小明"这个事件应该发生在"小狗跑向小明"之后。所以,(8a)是遵守这个规则的,而(8b)则违反了这个规则。

虽然影响语用义的因素众多,但是,这并不会妨碍我们寻找语用现象背后的规律。和语音、结构和语义受规则制约一样,语用现象(至少很大一部分的语用现象)是受规则制约的。哲学家保罗·格莱斯(Paul Grice)的经典之作《逻辑与会话》("Logic and Conversation")就可以看出学者们是如何努力地用形式化、规则的手段来处理语用义的。

7.1.3　预设与衍推

言外之意分为不同的类型。首先需要区分的是预设和衍推。前面的例子(6a),说汉语的人会觉得不自然,是因为其中的信息"小明有一个鼻子"是冗余的。为什么我们会觉得这个信息是冗余的呢?"小明的鼻子上有一个红色的斑点"这个句子为真的必要前提是"小明有一个鼻子"。说话人在说(6b)的时候,已经假定会话的参与方(说话人和听话人)知道这个信息。也就是说,这是双方共享的已知信息。说话人在说某一个话语之前,假定说话人和听话人都共享的信息就叫做预设。这是比较宽泛的定义。另外一个对"预设"的狭义的定义是某一句子所表达的命题为真的必要前提。这两个定义的共同之处在于"预设"是一种背景知识,是听话人和说话人在进行某一语言交际之前共有的、已知的背景知识。

和衍推不同的是,预设通常通过一些特定的表达式或者句法结构来标记。这样的表达式就叫"预设触发语"(presupposition trigger)。现代汉语中比较常见的预设触发语包括"的"字结构、事实陈述性动词,以及一些特殊的动词性结构。它们引发的预设分别叫做"存在预设"、"事实预设"和"词汇预设"。用逻辑符号"⊨"表示预设,p,q,r 等表示命题,这些预设义表示如下:

(9)"的"字结构和限定表达式的"存在预设":
 a. <u>张三的钱包</u>不见了(p)。张三有钱包(q)。
  (预设关系:p⊨q)
 b. <u>张三的耳朵</u>被冻红了(p)。张三有耳朵(q)。
  (预设关系:p⊨q)
 c. <u>那辆汽车的轮胎</u>被人扎破了(p)。那里有一辆汽车(q)。
  (预设关系:p⊨q)

(10)"事实陈述性动词"和事实预设:
 a. 我没<u>注意</u>到张三的耳朵冻红了(p)。张三的耳朵冻红了(q)。
  (预设关系:p⊨q)
 b. 张三没有把小明偷偷回家的事情<u>报告</u>给老师(p)。小明偷偷回家了(q)。
  (预设关系:p⊨q)

c. 张三很后悔没有早点回家(p)。张三没有早点回家(q)。

(预设关系：p⊨q)

(11) 词汇预设

a. 张三终于戒烟了(p)。张三以前抽烟(q)。

(预设关系：p⊨q)

b. 同学们开始抗议学校的不合理的政策了(p)。同学们以前不抗议(q)。

(预设关系：p⊨q)

c. 你又迟到了(p)。你以前迟到过 (q)。

(预设关系：p⊨q)

在上面的例子中,标记为 q 的句子都是标记为 p 的句子的预设。比如"张三的耳朵"必定预设"张三有耳朵",副词"又"预设某事件之前发生过等等。下面是一则关于词汇预设的经典故事:一位法官审理一桩夫妻纠纷案。妻子起诉丈夫经常家暴,所以忍无可忍,要求离婚。丈夫百般抵赖。最后法官问他:

(12) 法官：When did you stop beating your wife?

丈夫：I haven't beaten her since she left home.

从丈夫的回答中,法官断定丈夫有罪,从而判决这对夫妻离婚。在这里,法官就使用了预设。法官的问题包括了"you beat your wife"的预设,丈夫没有对这个预设提出反驳,可见丈夫也是认可这个事实。这个事实成立的话,妻子的指控就有证据了。

特别需要指出的是,预设和衍推是不同的语义概念,两者不可混淆。下列(13a)和(13b)这两个句子之间的语义关系是衍推关系:

(13) a. 我今天早上看见了一只麻雀。

b. 我今天早上看见了一只鸟。

(13a)和(13b)之间的语义联系在于:如果(13a)为真,(13b)一定为真。衍

推是一种逻辑关系。命题 p 衍推 q,则说明 p 和 q 之间存在三种语义联系:

- 如果 p 为真,q 一定为真
  即:如果我早上看见了一只麻雀,我一定看见了一只鸟。
- 如果 p 不为真,q 的真值不能确定
  即:如果我早上没看见一只麻雀,我可能看见了一只鸟(别的种类),也可能没看见。
- 如果 q 为假,p 一定为假
  如果我没有看见一只鸟,我肯定没有看见一只麻雀。

衍推和预设的区别可以用否定来检验。因为预设是命题具有真值判定的必要前提,所以,即使否定了相关命题,预设同样存在。但是,否定了相关命题,衍推义不一定还能继续保存。预设的这个现象叫做"否定保存现象":

(14) a. 我的自行车坏了。
（预设:我有一辆自行车。）
b. 我的自行车没坏。
（预设:我有一辆自行车。）
(15) a. 小王去过北京。
（衍推:小王去过中国。）
b. 小王没去过北京。(不一定)
（衍推:小王没去过中国。）

在(14)的例子中,不管我的自行车坏没坏,都存在"我有一辆自行车"的预设。但是(15)则不同,如果小王没有去过北京,那么命题"小王没去过中国"无法确定真值。

预设义和衍推义并非命题意义的全部。还有一些意义,并非预设,也不是衍推。这些意义是在特定的语境中产生的。语境产生的这种特定的意义是语用研究的重要内容。

7.1.4　会话涵义

平时我们说沟通不顺、信息没有得到有效传递的时候，通常用"鸡同鸭讲"来描述。鸡为什么不能和鸭交流呢？仅仅是因为鸡和鸭属于不同的种类吗？不是的。主要是鸡和鸭作为不同的种类，未必会遵守会话的规范。人们在使用语言的时候，都自觉地遵守一定的规范和原则，这是语言交际能够顺利进行的保障。顾名思义，会话原则是会话过程中说话人和听话人都遵守的原则。再仔细体会前文提到的例子：

（16）A：周末我们一起去看电影吧？
　　　B：动物园新引进了一批非洲来的斑马。

在(16)的例子中，B通过一个和A的问题不相关的回答来向A发出一个新的提议（"我们去动物园吧"）。B所传递的这个信息并非预设，也不是蕴含。这个意义和A与B的话语的本身的意义也没有关系。这种意义是一种字面意义之外的隐含意义。为了和前面的意义相区别，我们把这种意义叫做涵义（implicature）。因为这种涵义是在会话中产生的，所以也叫做会话涵义（conversational implicature）。会话涵义是基于某一特定语境而产生的意义。

会话涵义进入语言研究的视野得益于1960年代兴起的牛津日常语言哲学学派（Oxford Ordinary Language Philosophy）。这个学派的学者们对日常语言的使用中的意义来进行大量的研究，提出日常语言的使用语义也可以借由逻辑的方式来刻画。1967年，哲学家格莱斯在哈佛大学发表了一系列的William James讲座，尝试用逻辑手段来分析会话结构，理解说话人的言外之意。格莱斯假定说话人和听话人在会话中为了保证语言交际的有效性，都遵守"合作原则"（Cooperative Principle, CP）。合作原则是会话得以进行的默认原则。

格莱斯对"合作原则"做了这样的定义：会话参与方对话语的贡献应该符合话语交际的目的和方向的要求。格莱斯把"合作原则"细分为四项准则，分别是"量的准则"（Maxim of Quantity）、"质的准则"（Maxim of Quality）、"方式准则"（Maxim of Manner）和"关联准则"（Maxim of Relevance）。

(17)"合作原则"四准则

　　a. 质的准则:使你的贡献为真。
　　　(i) 不要提供你认为是假的的信息;
　　　(ii) 不要提供你缺乏足够证据的信息。
　　b. 量的准则:
　　　(i) 你的话语的信息量要符合交际的需要;
　　　(ii) 你的话语的信息量不要超过当前交际的需要。
　　c. 方式准则:清晰、具体。
　　　(i) 避免模糊
　　　(ii) 避免歧义
　　　(iii) 要简洁
　　　(iv) 要有序
　　d. 关联准则:让你的贡献与话语话题相关。

格莱斯的合作原则和会话准则为帮助我们理解语言在使用中的意义提供了一扇全新的窗口。通过这个机制,原来很多难以解释的语言使用现象都得到了更清楚的分析。实际上,格莱斯的合作原则和会话准则的影响力早已超越了哲学和语言学,对其他相关学科(如文学、心理学、社会学等)产生了深远的影响。

一般情况下,人们总是会遵守会话原则。但是也有一些特定的情形,参与会话的一方故意违反某一会话准则。这时就会产生会话涵义。会话涵义的产生可以分为下面的几种情形:

(一)违反"量的准则"的情形

有一些会话涵义是违反"量的准则"产生的。比如下面的例子:

　　(18) War is war.

(18)是同义反复(A is A)。同义反复的命题不提供新的信息(违反了"量的准则")。但是,人们觉得是有意义的。战争发生的时候,肯定会自然发生一些可怕的事情,而人们通常无法阻止这类事情的发生。这一会话涵义就是违反"量的准则"产生的。

格莱斯本人还提到了一个经典的例子。一个学生申请一份学术方面的工作，去找某教授写推荐信。教授经过思考后，写了下面这样的一封推荐信：

(19) Dear Sir,
Mr. X's command of English is excellent and his attendance at the tutorials has been regular.
Yours, etc.

这封信违反了"量的准则"：推荐人没有就 X 的学术能力和表现提供评价。聘任方看到了这封信后，会做如下的推理：
"这位教授是遵守合作原则的；
如果他遵守合作原则，他一定会提供有关 X 的学术能力和表现的评价；
作为 X 的老师，他是知道 X 的学术能力和表现的；
但是他在信里没有提供这方面的信息，这并不是这位老师的无知或者不配合；
他可能是不愿意提供关于 X 的学术能力和表现的评语；
他不提供评语的原因可能是这些评语会对 X 不利；
对 X 不利的信息可能显示 X 的学术能力和表象并不能胜任这份工作。
所以：X 无法胜任这份工作。"
聘任方在阅读这封信，做了上述的推理后，做出了婉拒 X 求职申请的决定。这个决定，是基于他们对推荐信的会话涵义的推理做出的。

（二）违反"质的准则"的情形

还有一些会话涵义是因为违反"质的准则"产生的。很多日常生活中的语言的用法，比如夸张，隐喻，拟人，反讽等，在表面都违背了"质的准则"。这些表达式一般都有特定的会话涵义。比如下面的例子：

(20) 这个女人是铁石心肠。

这个世界上的人都不可能是"铁石心肠"的。所以从语义上来讲，(20)在我们所生活的世界中是不可能发生的，是假的。这违反了"质的准则"（不要提供说话人认为是假的的信息）。如果语言的合作者都遵守"合作原则"，那么,"质的准则"的违反肯定有别的原因。这个"别的原因"就是这个句子的会话涵义。(20)表示的是这个女人像铁石一样冷漠无情。

（三）违反"方式准则"的情形

"方式准则"要求说话人的表达要简洁、有序、避免歧义。一些生活中的语言使用现象显然是有意不遵守这个准则而导致会话涵义的产生。在听完《我是歌手》现场张靓颖的演唱后,有人问听众张靓颖表现怎么样。听众想了想,回答道：

(21)哦,我觉得张靓颖唱歌的时候忘记了跳舞,跳舞的时候忘记了唱歌。

如果听众认为张靓颖的舞台表现很好,是歌舞合一型的选手,他会直接说"张靓颖能歌善舞"。他之所以没这么直接回答,而是选用了违反"方式准则"的(21),表明他在向听话人传递一些别的信息。这一语境下的会话涵义就是：张靓颖不能歌舞合一,舞台表现还有待加强。

（四）违反"关联准则"的情形

格莱斯认为"关联准则"很重要,但同时对这个准则的定义却不那么明确。格莱斯认为"关联准则"遵守与否主要看相关的话语是否会引起会话焦点的改变。一个典型的例子如(22)所示：

(22) A:老师回来了吗？
　　　B:电脑是开的。

A 在听到 B 的回答之后,会做如下的推理：
"应该会遵守合作原则,所以他说的话应该和我说的话相关；
因为我问的是问题,所以 B 肯定提供了一个答案；
B 说的话不是直接对我的问题的直接回应；
因为 B 是合作的,所以有可能是他没法提供更明确的信息来回应我的问题,但是显然 B 愿意提供他所知道的信息来帮助我。
所以：老师可能回来过。"

根据上述的推理,"老师回来过"就是(22B)的会话涵义。但是,因为"关联准则"的不确定性,(22B)的回答也可能是对话题的转移。比如 B 认为 A 应该关心别的事情(比如保护电脑数据)而不是寻找老师的下落等等。这种可能性表明对会话涵义的准确解读是依赖于语境的。

会话涵义的产生可以总结如下:

(23) 会话涵义
　　说话人通过说 p 产生会话涵义 q 如果:
　　说话人遵守会话准则,或者至少他/她的态度是合作的;
　　说话人清楚说 p 会带来某种涵义;
　　说话人相信听话人有能力理解这种涵义;
　　听话人通过结合语境因素与背景知识理解会话涵义 q。

会话涵义和预设、衍推不同。预设是说话人和听话人共有的背景知识,是不能取消的。衍推则是句子之间在意义上的逻辑联系。与之相对,会话涵义具有可计算性、可取消性、可加强性和不可分割性的特征。

会话涵义并非话语本身的语义,而是言外之意。它是说话人要向听话人传递的信息。这种意义的理解离不开具体的语境。没有了一定的语境,就得不到特定的会话涵义;不同的语境,也会导致不同的会话涵义。所以这种会话涵义也叫做"特定语境涵义"。格莱斯把会话涵义分为两类:特定语境涵义和规约性涵义。一般我们所指的会话涵义都是特定语境涵义。这类意义的一个主要特征是可计算性。也就是说,会话涵义必须能够被听话人觉察并且理解,或者用格莱斯的话说:"会话涵义必须可以被计算出来"(Grice 1989: 31),也就是说,会话参与方通过对语境、共同背景等知识的把握可以得知某一话语的会话涵义。比如下面例子,很容易得出它的涵义是"张三只有三个儿子"。

(24) 张三有三个儿子。
　　涵义:张三只有三个儿子。

会话涵义是依赖于语境的,是说话人想要向听话人传递的信息,因而这种信息可以被取消,或者反过来,可以被强化。比如(24)的涵义可以取消,如25(a)。(25b)则可以看作是这一涵义的强化:

(25) a. 张三有三个儿子,实际上,他有四个儿子。
　　　b. 张三有三个儿子,其他人一般只有一个儿子。

下面的(26)是另一个会话涵义被取消的例子:

(26) 玛丽昨天晚上去见了一个男人——她丈夫刚从国外回来。

(26)的前半部分"玛丽昨天晚上去见了一个男人"有会话涵义——"这个男人不是她最亲密的人"。因为如果是玛丽最亲密的人,根据"质的准则",说话人肯定会说"玛丽昨天晚上去见了她丈夫"。之所以没有选择这个表达式,是因为说话人对这个事实不确定,因而产生了"玛丽见的人不是她丈夫"的会话涵义。这个涵义可以被取消。会话涵义可以被取消,或者被加强,这是由会话涵义的语境依赖性决定的。

会话涵义的另一个特征是它的不可分割性。这主要体现在两个同义的表达式(具有相同的真值条件)会导致不同的会话涵义:

(27) a.《红楼梦》的作者是曹雪芹。
　　　b.《红楼梦》的作者是曹寅的孙子。

假设我们的历史知识——曹雪芹确实是曹寅的孙子,而且曹寅只有一个孙子——是正确的,那么(27a)和(27b)的语义是相同的:它们具有相同的真值条件。但是,这两个句子有不同的会话涵义。(27b)的可能的会话涵义是表示说话人对历史的精通(可能会让人觉得是在故弄玄虚),而(27a)却没有这样的会话涵义。

自从格莱斯提出会话合作原则和会话四准则后,语言哲学家和语言学家一直想要尽量简化格莱斯的会话准则。这样的思潮叫做"新格莱斯主义"。我们在这一小节简单介绍部分代表性思想。

美国耶鲁大学语言学家 Laurence Horn 曾经努力用"量原则"(他称之为

"Q-Principle")和"关系原则"(R-principle)来推导会话涵义。"量原则"要求说话人要提供尽可能多的信息,而"关系原则"则要求说话人的表达尽量简单。Horn 认为通过这两个原则,我们可以对会话涵义的推导获得新的解释(Horn 1985)。剑桥大学语言学家 Steven Levison 则认为,对会话涵义的推导,不但包括对说话人的要求,也包括听话人是如何理解说话人的。根据这个区分,他提出来两条新的原则:"量原则"(Q－原则)和"理解原则"(I－原则)。"Q－原则"认为,听话人相信说话人提供的信息是尽可能多的;"I－原则"认为,说话人会采取尽可能简单的语言表达,听话人需要结合已知的信息和世界知识为理解说话人的话语提供背景。这两条原则的操作如下所示:

(28) a. 张三停下了车子。
   通过"I－原则"推理的涵义:张三用脚踩刹车停下了车子。
   推理过程:因为"用脚踩刹车停车"是我们停车的背景知识。听话人认为说话人具有这样的背景知识,这背景知识无需说出来。
   b. 张三使得车子停了下来。
   通过"Q－原则"推理的涵义:张三用非惯例的手段使得车子停了下来,比如用手刹停车。
   推理过程:听话人认为说话人要提供尽可能多的信息。如果说话人想要表达张三用惯常的手段停车,比如用脚刹,他会选择另一个表达式"张三停车"。听话人没有选择这个表达式,说明他没有采用惯常的刹车手段。结论就是:他用手刹,而不是脚刹停的车。

"新格莱斯主义"并非是在会话涵义理论基础上发展出来的唯一的理论。当前语言研究中对会话涵义理论的另一重要进展是量级蕴含理论。有些涵义只能在某些特定的语境中得到,某些涵义却似乎可以独立于语境而存在。格莱斯本人对这也有清楚的认识,所以他区分了"会话涵义"和"规约性涵义"。多年的研究表明,"规约性涵义"和语法、语义有着千丝万缕的联系。越来越多的研究表明,许多语义规律源于语用规律的约定俗成化。而这些约定俗成化了的规律,又成为语言使用和交际的基础。语用和语义的界限往往不那么清楚。越来越多的规约性涵义的推导可以借由语义推导的方式来进行。量级蕴含理论就是这样的一种理论。

量级蕴含的理论基础是"信息量原则"。"信息量原则"对信息量的定义基于前述的"衍推"的概念：

(29) 信息量：P 比 Q 更具信息量当且仅当 P 蕴含于 Q。

"信息量原则"能直接与数理逻辑中的相关操作(比如集合的"上集和子集"关系)建立联系，这是它最大的优点。一般来说，子集比上集具体，也更有信息量。假设 X={x:x 是麻雀}是"麻雀"的集合，Y={y:y 是鸟}是"鸟"的集合，很容易证明，X 是 Y 的子集，也就是说，X 比 Y 更具有信息量。同理，{北京}是{中国}的子集，"北京"因而比"中国"更有信息量。下面两个命题之间具有非对称的蕴含关系(请参考前文提到的"衍推"关系)：

(30) P：小明去了北京。
     Q：小明去了中国。

P 比 Q 更具有信息量。根据定义，P 是 Q 的子集，即如果"小明去了北京"为真，则"小明去了中国"自然为真。

在自然语言中，不但存在"麻雀"和"鸟"这样存在上下义关系的表达式，也存在语义之间有量级差异的表达式。比如：

(31) ⟨一、二、三、四、五⟩
     ⟨few, some, many, most, all⟩
     ⟨sometimes, often, always⟩
     ⟨有时候，经常，总是，一直⟩
     ⟨好，优秀，出色，卓越⟩
     ⟨不坏，好，优秀⟩
     ⟨不笨，正常，聪明，天才⟩

这些表达式有一个特点：右边的表达式总是具有更多的信息量。依据前

面提出的信息量原则的定义,"二"比"一"更有信息量:

(32)"张三有两个苹果"衍推"张三有一个苹果"

理解:"张三有两个苹果"为真,则"张三有一个苹果"一定为真。
同理,"三"比"二"更有信息量,"四"比"三"更有信息量,依此类推。和会话涵义不同,这种意义之间的(非对称)衍推关系是不依赖于语境的。表达式自身的词汇语义足以帮助我们建立这些语义联系。有了这些语义联系,就能够建立量级涵义。其定义如(33)所示:

(33)量级涵义:就具有不对称信息量的一组表达式而言,对信息量弱的表达式的选择意味着对信息量强的表达式表达的意义的否定。

在实际的语言使用中,大量的对意义的理解依赖于对量级涵义的推导。比如张三是 A 和 B 的同事。谈起张三的工作表现,他的两位同事有下面的对话:

(34) A:张三经常去办公室吗?
B:张三有时候去。
(量级涵义:张三不经常去办公室。)

理解(34B)的意义,听话人在心中先建立了一个量级序列:〈有时候,经常,总是,一直〉。在这个序列中,右边的词项在意义上总是衍推左边的词项,比如"张三总是去办公室"衍推"张三有时候去办公室",当前者为真,后者必然为真。因为"经常"比"有时候"具有更多的信息量。根据"量级涵义",说话人选择了"有时候",意味着他对"张三经常去办公室"缺乏足够的证据。所以,他认为张三没有经常去办公室。

衍推关系是我们理解意义最重要的手段之一。语言中很多现象都可以经由衍推关系建立起意义上的联系。从某种角度上说,对语用现象的分析,离开了衍推关系、量级涵义等概念是不可能进行的。

7.1.5 言语行为

人们使用语言进行交际,传递信息。但是很多时候,传递信息并不是语言交际的唯一目的。考试的时候,监考人员说"不许舞弊",监考人员在传递信息的同时,还表达了某种"命令"。中国人见面就问,"你吃了吗",除了字面意义之外,还表达了"寒暄"。除此之外,人们还通过语言带来一定的行动效力。也就是说,某个语句一旦说出,就会带来外部世界的某种改变。胡锦涛主席宣布"我命名这艘航空母舰'辽宁号'",这句话说出之后,中国的第一艘航空母舰就被正式命名为"辽宁号"。2014 年 8 月 16 日晚上 8 点整,习近平主席在南京青奥会现场宣布:"我宣布第二届奥林匹克青年运动会正式开幕。"他的话也是有行为效力的:习主席说完这句话之后,青奥会就正式开幕了。在办公室,老板对员工咆哮"你被解雇了",也产生了行为效力:员工被解雇了。在法庭的场合,庭审完毕后,法官对被告宣布:"你被证明有罪,根据××法××条,判决你监禁 6 个月。"法官的话会产生判决的效力,被告的身份也会由嫌疑人变成了有罪的人。很多类似的现象表明,人们使用语言,语言像行为一样,会带来外部世界的某种改动(从一个状态到另外一个状态),会产生效力。

日常生活中的言语行为几乎无处不在。在餐桌上,Sally 对 Polly 说"Could you please give me a hand?"Polly 不会真的把自己的手给 Sally,因为他理解 Sally 说这句话的目的是向他发出一个"请求"的行为。哈佛大学心理学系著名教授品克(Steven Pinker)曾经提到一个著名的例子。人类发明的机器人因为不明白言语行为,当听到"Could you please give me a hand?"这句话的时候,真的会把自己的胳膊卸下来递给对方。吃饭的时候,丈夫对妻子说"能把酱油递给我吗",也不是咨询妻子是否有能力把酱汁递过来,而是发出"请求"的行为。妈妈对想要去摸开关的孩子说"别碰",是对孩子发出"命令"的行为。日常生活中对语言的使用充斥着像这样用语言发出行为的例子。

牛津日常语言哲学学派的另一个哲学家奥斯丁(John Austin)在 20 世纪 60 年代对人们如何使用语言发出行为和产生效力进行了系统的研究。相关研究在他去世后发表[Austin 本人于 1960 年去世,他的专著《如何以言行事》(*how to do things with words*) 在 1967 年发表]。这些研究奠定了言语行为理论(Speech Act Theory)的基础。言语行为理论进一步表明了语用义的规律性。人们通过话语发出的行为叫"言语行为"。和会话涵义一样,言语行为也会受到语境的影响。同样的话语,在不同的语境中,会产生不同的行为:

(35) 茶真凉!

如果是在寒冷的冬天说这句话,(35)发出的行为极可能是"抱怨",但是如果是炎热的夏天,(35)可能是"表扬"。"抱怨"和"表扬"都是言语行为。

根据奥斯丁的分类,每一个话语都包含三种言语行为:言内行为(locutionary act),言外行为(illocutionary act)和言后行为(perlocutionary act)。值得注意的是,这不是说言语行为分为三种类型,而是话语同时具有这三种不同的行为。人们组织句子,进而说出一个有意义的语言表达式的过程就是言内行为。言内行为由句子本身组成成分的意义和结构决定。正常情况下,人们不会无缘无故说话。人们说的话语一般都包含一定的目的,包含说话人向听话人传递的信息,或者说话人的意愿。人们通过话语产生的目的性叫做言外行为。上文提到的例子,如开幕式开幕、法庭宣判、请求、抱怨、命令、表扬等,都是言外行为。人们组织语言,说出某一个表达式(言内行为),并且抱着一定的目的,或者向听话人传递某一个信息(言外行为),自然还希望这个表达式能产生一定的效果。听话人对这个效果的实现就是言后行为。比如在妈妈命令孩子别碰电源插座的情景中,孩子的手离开插座的结果就是"别碰"的言后行为。下面的实例来说明。

(36) 场景:教室
教师:现在开始上课。

在(36)例中,言内行为是教师说出的"现在开始上课"这句话。教师知道这是一个有意义的表达式。教师说这句话是有目的的,这个目的就是言外行为。这个目的可以是命令(同学们必须安静,拿出教材,专心听讲等等)。教师通过说这句话希望达到某种效果,而这种效果的实现就是言后行为。(36)的言后行为就是课堂正式开始。

很多言语行为都包含一个表述词。表述词的出现可以看作对言语行为的明确说明。现代汉语中的"就此""正式""从此""兹""特此"等都属于表述词。下面的例子包含明确的表述词：

(37) 兹证明……
特此说明……
××正式开始……
中国人民从此站起来了。
这艘船就此命名为"辽宁号"。

同样的表达式在不同的语境中会有不同的言语行为。同时，表达式的言语行为要被听话人正确理解（言内行为）和执行（言后行为）也只能发生在说话人和听话人所期待的或者适当的环境中。这就是言语行为的适应性条件。比如下面的句子(38)要产生有效的言内和言外行为，必须发生在法庭，而且必须出自法官之口，而且只能是法官对被告说才是适当的：

(38) 本法庭判处你 6 年有期徒刑。

如果不满足上述的适应性条件，(38)就会失去这个意义。从语用上说，就是不适当或者被人们当作一个笑话。很多幽默效果也因此产生。小王向小丽求婚说："我从此以后成为你的囚犯，甘愿终生服刑"就有很强的幽默效果。这种幽默效果的产生是因为没有满足言语行为的适应性条件，导致了会话涵义的产生。

言语行为的适应性条件可以分为以下几种类型：

通用性条件　听话人和说话人对语言的理解正常；听话人和说话人具有正常的心智；话语发生在正常的场合（比如会话参与方没有参与戏剧角色扮演）等。

内容性条件　具体言语行为产生必须满足的条件。比如"承诺"和"警告"的言语行为都要求相关事件是在未来发生的事件（已经发生的事件不能算承诺），而"承诺"则更进一步要求这个事件必须由说话人在未来的某一个时间亲自来完成。

先决性条件　具体言语行为成立的客观条件。比如"承诺"有两个先决性条件:首先,这个事件不会自己发生;其次,这个事件会对听话人带来有利效果。"警告"的言语行为有三个先决性条件:首先,对听话人来说,他可能知道,也可能不知道,相关的事件会发生;其次,对说话人来说,他相信事件会发生;最后,事件发生以后不会带来有利效果。

真诚性条件 说话人必须有诚意。对"承诺"来说,说话人必须有足够的诚意在未来的某个时间完成相关的事件;对"警告"来说,说话人必须真诚地相信某个事件在未来某个时间发生不会带来有利效果。

实质性条件 言语行为能产生实质性的作用,比如会带来状态的改变。如"承诺",说话人发出"承诺"的言语行为,表示他会具有相关的义务。承诺一旦发出,说话人也会发生状态的改变:从没有义务到具有义务的改变。"警告"的实质性条件则是:一旦发出这个言语行为,说话人会发生状态的改变,从没有知会听话人相关事件不会带来有利效果的状态到已知会的状态。实质性条件是对话语内容、语境、说话人意愿和相关言语行为在适当情况下发生的具体规定的总和。

奥斯丁提出的言外行为包括"陈述、命令、请求、道歉、感慨、祝贺、禁止、疑问、邀请"等等。奥斯丁本人承认,这一名单可以扩大到"至少几百个"。言语行为太多无疑会影响分析的严谨性和系统性。为了解决这一问题,语言哲学家索尔(John Searle)对言语行为重新进行了分类,极大地简化了言语行为的类型。索尔提出言语行为可以分为五类:陈述行为(declaration)、表达行为(representative)、感知行为(expressive)、指示行为(directive)和许诺行为(commissive)。为了和奥斯丁的言语行为理论区别开来,一些学者把索尔的理论叫做"新言语行为理论"。这五类言语行为的定义如下:

(一) **陈述行为** 通过话语对世界的某种状态做出改变的言语行为。在婚礼场合,牧师宣布"I now pronounce you husband and wife",会导致一对恋人从没有结婚的状态改变到结婚的状态;在球场,裁判对球员说"你下去",会导致球员从场上状态到场下状态的改变;在法庭,法官对被告说"本庭认为被告有罪",会导致被告从嫌疑人到罪犯的状态改变。这类言语行为一般需要特定的场合和社会习俗,发生在特定的说话人和听话人之间。

(二) **表达行为** 说话人通过话语对相关事实的真伪做出判定的言语行为。对事实做描述、断言、总结的话语所产生的言语行为大都属于这一类:

(39) a. 地球是平的。
    b. 莫言没有写过《红楼梦》。
    c. 今天很暖和。

（三）感知行为　表达说话人情感状态的言语行为。表达心理状态的话语（如高兴、喜欢、憎恨、悔恨、悲伤、痛苦等）所产生的言语行为属于这一类：

(40) a. 我很难过。
    b. 祝贺！
    c. 啊，太好了，加油！

（四）指示行为　说话人要求其他人做某事的言语行为。表达"命令、请求、建议"等的话语所产生的言语行为属于这一类：

(41) a. 给我一杯咖啡。
    b. 别碰！
    c. 能帮我带点水果回来吗？

（五）许诺行为　说话人自身对未来发生行为的承诺。"承诺,发誓,威胁"等属于这一类：

(42) a. 我会再回来的！
    b. 下次我一定要努力！
    c. 我们不要再去了,好吧？

　　除了上述的言语行为的分类之外,我们还应该注意到：话语形式和言语行为之间存在一定的对应性。一般来说,陈述句表示陈述类言语行为,祈使句表示指示类言语行为,感叹句表示感知类言语行为。下面的表格说明了这种对应性：

表 7.1　话语形式和言语行为之间的对应性

言语行为类型	话语形式(S:说话人;X:情景)
陈述言语行为	S 导致 X
表达言语行为	S 相信 X
感知言语行为	S 感觉 X
指示言语行为	S 想要 X
许诺言语行为	S 愿意 X

如果话语形式和言语行为之间的关系是直接对应关系,这类言语行为叫直接言语行为;如果话语形式和言语行为之间的关系不是直接的对应关系,这类行为叫做间接言语行为。比如说,陈述句本来是表示陈述的,陈述句表示"陈述"是直接言语行为,但是用陈述句来表示"请求"就是间接言语行为。妈妈让孩子出门,孩子说"外面太冷了"。这是一个陈述句,但是孩子通过这个陈述句表示请求"不要出门好不好"。日常生活中的很多言语行为都是间接言语行为。炒菜的时候,爸爸对妈妈说"帮我把盐递过来好吗",也是间接言语行为。疑问句一般用来表示疑问,但是在这个例子里,爸爸其实是向妈妈发出了"请求"的言语行为。用疑问句表示请求,就是间接言语行为。

有时候,可以用不同的话语形式表示同样的言语行为。比如说话人想让听话人不要站在电视机面前,他可以选择下面两种话语形式:

(43) a. 祈使句:走开!
　　　b. 感叹句:比起电视,你的身影太高大了。

现在回到本章开始的问题——"问路的学问"。人们在问路时选择哪种语言形式可以通过言语行为理论得到进一步的阐述。人们选用直接言语行为还是间接言语行为,很大程度上受说话人和听话人之间"距离/亲疏关系"的影响。亲疏关系包括"亲密""熟悉"和"陌生"。说话人和听话人之间的关系越亲密,越可能使用直接的言语行为(比如用祈使句或者命令句表示"请求");说话人和听话人之间的关系越疏远,越可能使用间接的言语行为(比如用疑问句表示"请求")。孩子对妈妈发出"想喝水"的请求,极有可能使用(44a);而在医院的病房,病人对不熟悉的护士发出"想喝水"的请求,极有可能

使用(44b):

(44) a. 妈妈,我要喝水。
　　 b. 护士小姐,介意给我倒一杯水吗?

间接的言语行为通常伴随着更复杂的语言形式,比如"支持性表达式结构"、更多的理由、对自我的降低等。在陌生的城市向陌生人问路,一般要说"请问/打扰/不好意思,请问一下"等,都是为了产生间接言语行为,使得说话人的表达更有礼貌:

(45) 请问/打扰一下/不好意思,可以打扰一下吗,请问×地怎么走?

言语行为理论是重要的语用现象之一,现在仍然是语言学家关注的重点。有兴趣的同学可以阅读相关参考文献以掌握更多的新发展。

7.1.6　小结

了解和掌握语言的规律,不但包括对语言结构的规律的掌握,还包括对语言使用的规律的掌握。语用就是研究语言使用的规律的。人们使用语言,通过语言传递信息、表达意义,都遵守一定的规律。人们通过语言传递信息和说话人、听话人有关,和语言使用的时间、地点、目的等因素有关。总之,和语境有关。语用研究的是语言在语境中产生的意义,换言之,研究语言在字面意义之外的"言外之意"。本章重点介绍了三个关于语用的重要理论假设和研究领域:(一) 在句子和命题意义的层面,本章介绍了预设和衍推的概念。预设是命题为真的必要前提,而衍推是两个命题之间的逻辑联系。人们对意义的理解和推理,很多情况下都基于这一组概念进行的;(二) 在会话的层面,本章介绍了会话原则和会话涵义。人们对会话原则的遵守导致了会话涵义的产生。会话原则包括量的准则、质的准则、方式准则和关联准则四个部分。一些情况下,语言使用者会故意违反会话原则而产生一定的言外之意。这种言外之意就是会话涵义。会话涵义是语用中一个极为重要的研究领域;(三) 人们除了通过语言来传递信息,还通过语言来改变世界。人们通过语言对世界状态的改变就是言语行为。言语行为可以分为言内行为,言外行为和言后行为。言后行为的实现需要满足一定的适应性条件。言语行为还可以分为直接言语行为和间接言语行为。

7.2 选读

莱文森(1986)《语用学》选读

◆ **作者简介**

史蒂芬·莱文森①(Stephen C. Levinson,1947—),英国社会科学家,以对文化、语言、认知的关系研究闻名。他曾在剑桥国王学院获得考古学、社会人类学学士学位,在加州大学伯克利分校获得语言人类学的博士学位,他曾在剑桥大学、斯坦福大学、澳大利亚国立大学任教,现为马克斯—普朗特心理语言学研究所(荷兰)主任。他曾致力于研究互动社会语言学,并在1983年出版了第一本系统性的语用学教材,  他扩展了格莱斯的会话含义,创建了礼貌理论。他研究兴趣广泛,在认知科学的诸多领域都有所涉猎。

◆ **正文节选**

第一章 预 设②

1. 历史背景

对语用学里这个论题的关注起源于哲学上的争议,特别是关于所指和指别词语的争议。近代第一个探讨这类问题的哲学家是 G. Frege。他提出的许

---

① 图片来源:https://www.mpg.de/372359/。
② S. C. Levinson 著,沈家煊译,《语用学论题之一:预设》,《国外语言学》,1986 年第 1 期。

多问题后来成为预设讨论的中心。例如,他说:"在任何命题中总是有一个明显的预设——使用的简单或复合专名是有所指的。因此如果断言'凯普勒死得很惨',存在一个预设即名称'凯普勒'有所指。"他还说:"名称'凯普勒'有所指既是'凯普勒死得很惨'的预设也是它的相反(否定)命题的预设。"(Frege,1892)

随后,B. Russell 在 1905 年的论著中认为 Frege 的观点是根本错误的。他在致力于解决指别理论中同样一些问题时得出很不相同的结论。其中一个问题是如何解释像(1)那种没有专指的句子会有意义:

(1) 法国国王很聪明

Frege 提出的解答是把意义和所指加以区分:这类句子即使没有所指因而没有真假值仍然保持句子的意义。但是 Russell 争论说 Frege 的观点导致异常现象,他相反提出了著名的"描写理论",这一理论后来支配这方面研究达四十五年之久。他认为像"某某人"这些定指描写根本不像想象的那样只有简单的逻辑对应形式。它们在自然语言中虽然像(1)里以主语出现,但在逻辑形式中根本不是逻辑主语,而是对应于一系列命题的联接。因此(1)的逻辑式不是(2)而是复杂的(3):

(2) 聪明(法国国王)
(3) $\exists x$ (法国国王(x) & $\sim\exists y$ $(y\neq x)$ & 法国国王(u)) & 聪明(x))
(存在一个法国国王,并且没有其他人是法国国王,并且他是聪明的)

按照这种解释,(1)有意义是因为(1)根本是假的;通过 Russell 对"法国国王"这个短语的扩充,(1)是一个同时断言存在一个个体的命题。Russell 在自己的分析中发现一个特别的好处是容许我们今天称为"辖域歧义"的现象。例如否定句(4)有两种解释:

(4) 法国国王不聪明

一种理解是设定存在一个法国国王,断言他不聪明,另一种理解(不很通常)是对存在一个法国国王并且他是聪明的真实性都加以否定。句子(5)只能作第二种理解:

(5) 法国国王不聪明——因为根本没有这样一个人。

Russell 的逻辑式(3)可以用(至少)两个插入否定词的空档来解释这种歧义。

在 P. F. Strawson 1950 年提出一种很不一样的处理方式之前,Russell 的分析基本上没有受到挑战。Strawson 争论说,有许多疑难问题的产生是由于没有区分句子和句子的使用。句子没有真假,只有句子作出的陈述才有真假。因此(1)的陈述很可能在公元 1670 年是真的,在公元 1770 年是假的,而在 1970 年则谈不上什么真假:因为 1970 年不存在一个法国国王,不会产生真假问题。Strawson 因而声称在(1)和(6)之间有一种特殊关系:

(6) 现在有一个法国国王

即(6)是判断(1)真假的前提。他称这种关系为"预设",并且认为这是一种特殊的语用推理,不同于逻辑含义或蕴含,而是从指别词语的使用规约得出的一种推理。Strawson 跟 Russell 的分歧引起一个后果,由于放弃定指描写的复杂逻辑形式,他也失去了解释像(5)那种否定句的手段,因为(5)的预设本身被否定了。

因此,跟 Russell 的有定描写相对立,Strawson 和 Frege 持十分相似的观点。当然各种预设理论有一种显著的吸引力:它们看来更加符合我们的语言直觉。例如,当我们说出(1)时有一个处于前景的命题,即某一个人是聪明的;而那个人的存在是某种背景假设,根据这个背景,命题才有意义。显然 Russell 没有说明这种直觉。

当 Strawson 的预设概念开始受到语言学家的注意时,它似乎开拓了一种新的有意义的可能性。在这之前,语言学家一直特别利用一种至关紧要的语义关系即蕴含(entailment)①。语义蕴含可以定义如下：

(7) A 在语义上蕴含 B (写作 A||-B)，当而且仅当每一个使 A 真的情形都使 B 真。

预设的概念开拓的有意义的可能性在于，我们或许可以在各种现存的众所周知的语义关系之外再增加一种新的不同性质的语义关系。关于语义预设的最简单的观点建立在以下定义的基础上：

(8) 句子 A 在语义上预设另一个句子 B，当而且仅当
　　a. 凡是 A 是真的情形，B 是真的(A||-B)
　　b. 凡是 A 是假的情形，B 也是真的(～A||-B)

由于这样的预设理论的全部意义在于处理预设消失的现象，并且解释当句子的预设消失时句子无真假可言这一直觉，这就必须放弃某些传统的逻辑假设。最简单的办法是放弃只有真假二值的假设，代之以真、假、无真假三值（最后一值适用于预设是假的句子）。

这些学术上的进展适合于称为"生成语义学"的语言理论(在 1968—75 年间很盛行)，因为持这种理论的学者关心如何扩展和修改语义学的逻辑模式，使它们能包容自然语言中尽可能多的区别性特征，因此把语用现象纳入有条理的语义学的范围成了他们的目的。但是人们不久就发现有某些类似于预设的现象，它们的表现方式跟语义预设的概念所要求的很不一样。例如，Keenan (1971)曾指出法语句子里使用代词 tu(你)似乎预设"听话人是一个动物，孩子，社会地位低于说话人或与说话人个人关系亲密"。关于说话人和听话人之间关系的"预设"根本不影响真值条件，Keenan 据此认为这样的例子组成一类独立的性质不同的语用推理，把它叫做"语用预设"。因此人们曾一度建议自然语言有两类性质不同的预设：语义预设和语用预设。它们各自独立存在。但是从 1973 年起变得越来越明显，语义预设的概念问题太多，语言

---

① "entailment"学界存在不同翻译，如"衍推"、"蕴含"等，教材正文多使用"衍推"。——编者注

理论(特别是语义学)最好放弃这个概念。放弃的理由是以在适当的探索后发现的某些现象的性质和特性为依据的。

2. 对一切现象的初步考察

Frege 和 Strawson 认为预设在否定句或否定陈述中仍然保持,这为我们鉴别预设提供了一个初步的操作性测试。我们可以拿过一个句子来,把它否定,然后看看哪些推理继续保持,即为肯定句和否定句所共有。例如:

(9) John managed to stop in time (约翰设法及时停了下来)

从(9)可以推断出:

(10) 约翰停了下来
(11) 约翰试图停下来

现取(9)的否定得出(12):

(12) John didn't manage to stop in time (约翰没有能及时停住)

从(12)我们不能得出推理(10),实际上(12)的主要意思是否定(10)。但是推理(11)仍然保持,为(9)和(12)所共有。因此根据否定测试,(11)是(9)和(12)共同的预设。注意只要(9)是真的,(10)必真,但当(12)是真的时,(10)不必真。根据蕴含的定义,(9)蕴含(10),而(12)不蕴含(10)。显然,否定(9)得出(12)后,(9)的蕴含不再是(12)的蕴含。总之,否定使句子的蕴含改变而使预设保持不变。在否定情形里的表现显示了预设和蕴含的根本区别。

(9)的预设的来源是什么? 当然来自 manage 一词。如果(9)里用 tried 代替,虽然推理(11)继续保持,但从否定句(13)可以看出(11)现在成了蕴含:

(13) John didn't try to stop in time (约翰没有试图及时停住)

由此看来预设跟某些特定的词相联系,我们将把这些产生预设的词语称作预设触发语。Karttunen 已经收集了 31 种这样的触发语,下面是一些选例：(肯定和否定用/隔开以便核查推理；预设触发语用斜体；≫表示"预设")

① 定指描写 (definite description)
John saw/didn't see *the man with two heads* (约翰看见/没有看见有两个头的人)
≫ 存在一个有两个头的人

② 叙实动词 (factive verbs)
Martha *regrets*/doesn't *regret* drinking John's home brew (玛莎后悔/不后悔喝了约翰自家酿造的啤酒)
≫ 玛莎喝了约翰自家酿造的啤酒

③ 含义动词 (implicative verbs)
John *forgot*/didn't *forget* to lock the door (约翰忘了/没有忘记锁门)
≫ 约翰本来应该锁门或打算锁门

④ 状态变化动词 (change of state verbs)
John *stopped*/didn't *stop* beating his wife (约翰不再/没有停止打老婆)
≫ 约翰过去一直打老婆

⑤ 表示重复的词 (iteratives)
The flying saucer came/didn't come *again* (飞碟又来了/没有再来)
≫ 飞碟过去来过

⑥ 判断动词 (verbs of judging)
Agatha *accused*/didn't *accuse* Ian of plagiarism (阿加莎指责/没有指责伊恩剽窃)
≫ 阿加莎认为剽窃不道德

⑦ 时间从句

While Chomsky was revolutionizing linguistics, the rest of social science was/wasn't asleep（当乔姆斯基正实行语言学的革命时，其他社会科学处于/没有处于沉睡中）

≫乔姆斯基正实行言学的革命

⑧ 分裂句（cleft sentences）

It was/wasn't Henry that kissed Rosie（跟萝茜接吻的是/不是亨利）

≫有人跟萝茜接吻

⑨ 带重音成分的隐性分裂句

John did/didn't compete in the OLYMPICS（约翰确实参加/没有参加奥运会的比赛）

≫约翰参加了某种比赛

⑩ 比较和对比

Marianna called Adolph a male chauvinist, and then HE insulted HER（玛丽安娜叫阿道夫大男子主义者，然后他也侮辱了她）

≫玛丽安娜叫阿道夫大男子主义，这是对他的侮辱

⑪ 非限制性关系从句

The Proto-Harrapans, who flourished 2800 - 2650 B.C., were/were not great temple builders（原始海拉盆人——生活在公元前2800—2650年间——是/不是高明的庙宇建造者）

≫原始海拉盆人生活在公元前2800—2650年间

⑫ 违反实际的条件句（counterfactual conditionals）

If Hannibal had only twelve more elephants, the Romance languages would/would not this day exist（要是海尼鲍尔多有12头大象的话，罗曼诸语言今天还会/不会存在）

≫海尼鲍尔没有多有12头大象

⑬ 疑问句（是非问句、选择问句、特殊问句）
Who is the professor of linguistics at MIT?（谁是麻省理工学院的语言学教授?）
≫某人是麻省理工学院的语言学教授

以上一系列例子也许包括了通常认为是预设的核心现象。但是必须记住,这种现象的取舍取决于我们对预设的定义。比如,假如仅仅把否定保持作为定义准则,像下面一些现象也属于预设,虽然用语用学理论的其他方面来解释它们更加合适:

(14) Do/don't close the door（关门/别关门）
　　≫？门开着(可用祈使句的适用条件来解释)
(15) The planet Pluto is/isn't larger than Ceres（冥王星比/不比谷神星大）
　　≫说话人相信自己表达的命题(可用 Grice 会话合作原则中的"质"准则来解释)

也可以放弃否定保持作为鉴别预设的测试,(像 Karttunen(1973)所建议的)改用在 if... then 复句中的表现来测试,这样我们可能会得出 only, even, just 等词也是预设触发语的结论。理由是虽然这些词产生的推理不能在否定句里保持,但确实在不保持蕴涵的条件句语境里得以保持,例如:

(16) If *only* Harry failed the exam, it must have been easy
　　（如果只有哈里考试不及格,考试一定很容易）
　　≫？哈里考试不及格
　　（比较否定句 If only Harry didn't fail the exam, it must have been easy
　　≫？哈里考试没有不及格）

因此对预设现象的范围的划定取决于对预设的定义。但是对任何预设理论的合理要求是至少能处理上述大部分的例子。

3. 一些有疑问的特性

要鉴别出一系列连贯的相同性质的推理,否定保持实际上不是一个充分的定义。如果我们考察上述核心现象,我们很快发现实际上预设确实还表现出其他一些显著的特性:

(i) 预设在(a)某些言谈语境(b)某些句子内部语境中是可以消除的;

(ii) 预设显然跟表层结构的某些方面有关

第一个特性将证明任何关于预设的语义理论是站不住的,而第二个特性能把预设跟语用推理的另一种主要形式会话含义区别开来。

3.1 可取消性(defeasibility)

预设的独特的特性之一是在一定的语境里会消失,无论是在直接的上下文、不太直接的言谈语境,还是作出相反假设的语境里。

如果交谈双方都知道某些事实不成立,即使在其他情况下所说的句子可能预设这些事实,还是不会得出相应的预设。例如,交谈双方都知道约翰的博士课程考试不及格,我们可以说(17),尽管 regret 通常预设它的补语:

(17) At least John won't have to regret that he did a PhD(至少约翰不必为获得博士学位而后悔)

注意,在某他语境里,例如约翰刚巧在获得博士学位后最终找到了工作,通常的预设是成立的。再考虑另一个例子。由 before-从句表达的命题一般是预设。因此如果我说(18)就表示我知道(19):

(18) Sue cried before she finished her thesis(苏在完成她的论文前哭了)

(19) 苏完成了她的论文

但比较(20):

(20) Sue died before she finished her thesis(苏在完成她的论

文前死了）

(20)当然不会预设(19)，相反表达苏永远没有完成她的论文。因此在(20)里预设(19)消失。其原因看来是：(20)断言苏的死亡事件发生在（预期的）完成她论文的事件之前；由于我们普遍认为人死后不能再干什么，因此她不可能已完成她的论文。这种根据句子的蕴含和对凡人的背景假设得出的推理与预设(19)相冲突；因此在这个语境或一系列信仰背景里该预设被消除。还有一类在某些言谈语境中产生的取消现象。例如：

(21) You say that someone in this room will betray you. Well maybe so. But it won't be Luke who will betray you, it won't be Paul, it won't be Matthew, and it certainly won't be John. Therefore no one in this room is actually going to betray you（你说这间屋子里有人将背叛你。好吧，也许是这样。但是将背叛你的不会是卢克，不会是保罗，不会是马修，肯定也不会是约翰。因此这间屋子里没有人真的要背叛你）

这里每一个分裂句(It won't be Luke 等)本来应该预设存在某个将背叛听话人的人。但是(21)这段话的整个意图如结论所说的显然是说服对方没有人将会背叛他。因此预设又一次被消除。

3.2 投射问题(the problem of projection)

最初 Langendoen & Savin (1971)曾假设复句的各预设的集合是各分句预设的简单相加，就是说，如果 S_0 是由分句 S_1，S_2，…S_n 组成的复句，那么，"S_0 的预设＝S_1 的预设＋S_2 的预设…＋S_n 的预设"。但是这种对复句预设的简单处理远不是正确的。要制定一种理论，对各分句的预设有哪些在组合成的复句中实际上得以继承作出正确的预测，事实表明这是极其困难的。这个组合问题就是所谓预设的"投射问题"。投射问题有两个方面。一个方面是预设在语境中保持而蕴含消失。另一个方面是在我们也许能期望预设保持的语境里预设消失而蕴含保持。

首先，预设保持而蕴含消失的最明显的一类语境显然是否定句。但是还有其他语境。其一是模态语境，即嵌入像 possible（可能），there's a chance that（有可能）等模态词的语境。例如：

(22) It's possible that the chief constable arrested three men（有可能警长逮捕了三个人）
(23) 存在一个警长
(24) 警长逮捕了两个人

(22)继续预设(23)，但显然不再蕴含(24)，因为不能仅仅根据事态的可能性作出事态的任何部分都是真的这样的逻辑推理。另一组很不相同的语境是由连词 and（和），or（或），if...then（如果……那么）和其他对等词构成的复句。例如：

(25) If the two thieves were caught again last night, P. C. Katch will get an honourable mention（如果两个贼昨晚再次被捕获，凯奇将得到表扬）
(26) 有一个贼昨晚再次被捕获
(27) 两个贼过去曾被捕获过

(26)不再是(25)的蕴含，而预设(27)保持不变。Karttunen (1973)列出很长的一张词语清单，他称之为渗漏词（holes），因为它们允许各预设向上渗透到整个复句，但使蕴含受阻。这个清单包括叙实动词，模态词，否定词等等。这样就可以不再把预设定义为仅仅在否定下保持的推理，还包括在一系列其他不保持蕴含的语境里都保持的推理。

现在来看投射问题的另一个方面。预设在复句中消失的最直接的情形发生在句子的预设在并列句中被公开否认。例如：

(28) John doesn't regret doing a useless PhD in linguistics because in fact he never did do one!（约翰不后悔得了一个无用的语言学博士学位，因为事实上他从来没有得过）

除了公开否认预设外，还有一种可能性，Horn (1972)称之为中止（suspension）。使用后续的 if-从句可以很自然地中止说话人理应表达的预设。例如：

(29) John didn't cheat again, if indeed he ever did（约翰没有再一次诈骗，如果他曾确实诈骗过的话）

另一类有更多争议的语境是某些表达命题态度的动词如 want（想要），believe（相信），imagine（想象），dream（梦想），和所有表示说话的动词如 say（说），tell（告诉），mumble（咕哝），retort（反驳）等。例如(30)似乎没有预期的预设(31)：

(30) Loony old Harry believes he's the Kine of France（傻瓜老哈里认为自己是法国国王）

(31) 现在有一个法国国王

鉴于这种表现，Karttunen (1973)把这类动词取名为堵塞词(plugs)，因为跟渗漏词不同，它们阻塞低层句子的预设向上提升为整个句子的预设。但是还远不清楚情况是否普遍如此，例：

(32) The mechanic didn't tell me that my car would never run properly again（机修工没有跟我说我的汽车将再也不会正常运行）

(33) 我的汽车过去一般运行正常

尽管有堵塞词，(32)继续预设(33)。因此我们只能认为堵塞词的存在是很有疑问的。

现在谈到投射问题最麻烦的方面，即预设在连词 and，or，if...then 构成的复句和包含 but（但是），alternatively（或者），suppose that（假定）等等的语句中的表现。前面早已提到这些词语是允许预设保持的渗漏词，但实际上不是如此，例如：

(34) If John does linguistics, he will regret doing it（如果约翰

搞语言学,他会后悔的)

(35) 约翰将搞语言学

(34)里的结果从句本身就预设(35),但整个条件句不预设(35)。这显然是由于在第一个从句里提到这个预设而又同时把它作为一个假设。Karttunen(1973)给这些连词取名为过滤词(filters):它们允许某些预设通过,同时又阻塞其他的预设。

4. 几种解释

我们将首先表明没有一种关于预设的语义理论有成立的可能,然后着手评价已经提出的三种主要的语用理论。

4.1 语义预设

目前语言学家可以利用两种主要的语义理论,一种是真值条件理论,另一种是假设所有语义关系都可以按照句子分解而成的原子概念或语义特征来定义。为了把预设纳入真值条件理论,必须像上述(8)把预设的性质确定为一种特殊的蕴含。我们指出过这样的理论必须对语义理论的整个逻辑结构作根本的修正。如果这样做可以解释预设的各项特性,这种修正也许是合理的。但是不难看出任何这样的理论原则上都不会成功。使这种预设理论注定失败的因素是预设表现的两个基本特性:可取消性和投射问题的特殊性质。可取消性的要点在于预设在某些言谈语境里不总是保持的,而语义预设必须是一种不变的关系:如果 p 在语义上预设 q,则 p 总是在语义上预设 q。

试图把预设纳入以原子概念或语义特征为基础的语义理论又怎么样呢?这种语义理论的特性远不像逻辑模式有明确的定义,这在某种程度上使它能适应处理新假设的语义关系。因此 Katz & Langendoen (1976)认为语义预设是一个完全可行的概念,并且当它纳入特征分析的语义学时实际上是唯一可行的概念。但事实已经表明他们的建议根本不能处理投射问题。这类理论的目的在于把我们关于语言的语义的知识跟关于世界的知识强行分离开来,划定较小的一组原子概念仅仅满足语义学的描写需要。这种观点的语义学关心的是不受语境约束的、稳定的词义和句义,而把某些语境里特有的推理留给语用学处理。因此很明显,预设属于语用学而不是语义学,因为预设不是意义中稳定的不受语境约束的部分。

4.2 预设的语用理论

已经提出各种关于语用预设的理论。最早的是纲领性的,只是用语用概念提出预设可能有的各种定义。这些定义尽管术语不同,都特别使用两个基本概念:合适性(appropriateness 或 felicity)和共有知识。定义方式如下:

(36) 如果一句话 A 只有当命题 B 是交谈双方的共同知识时才是合适的,则 A 在语用上预设 B

Sadock 曾指出,共同知识的条件过于严格:在对方预先不知道预设(38)的情形下完全可以说(37):

(37) I'm sorry I'm late, I'm afraid my car broke down(对不起,我迟到了,怕是我的汽车坏了)

(38) 说话人有一辆汽车

Gazdar(1979a)指出预设只要跟语境假设的命题一致就够了。这类问题表明像(36)的定义至少需要修正。但从长远来看,我们感兴趣的不是定义而是某种模式,它能准确地预测预设的表现并解释特别是可取消性和投射这些有疑问的特性。实际上只有两种复杂的正规模式接近于解释观察到的事实。这两种理论都假设预设是词语的规约意义(conventional meaning)的一部分,但并不把预设看作语义推理。

第一种这样的规约理论是 Karttunen 和 Peters(1975, 1979)提出的。该理论用蒙太鸠语法的框架来表达。按照这种语法理论,语义表达式的建立是一步一步地跟自然语言表层形式的建立并行的。因此每个词、句子或句法变换都有一个相关联的语义表达式或外延表达式(extention expression)。这种理论的基本思想就是按蒙太鸠语法的框架在句子成分构成句子的过程中再增加一组意义表达式,其生成方式跟外延表达式相同。这种意义表达式只跟所谓预设触发词的词语相联系。跟外延表达式不同,这些预设表达式一般不起规定真值条件的作用,它们的功能纯粹是表示出成分的预设。Karttunen 和 Peters 把这种解释预设的意义表达式称为含义表达式(implicature expression)。按照他们的理论,预设实际上是不可消除的。因为除了含义表达式外,每个成分还有一个关联的承继表达式(heritage expression)它唯一的作用是支配含义表达式表达预设的投射过程。按这种方式,Karttunen(1973)对内嵌结构的分类即堵塞词、过滤词和渗漏词都可以纳入蒙太鸠语法。例如,当一个内嵌补语是堵塞词时,它有一个阻止预设提升到整个句子的承继表达式。例如(39)没有预设(40),因为claim(声称)一词有一个阻止预设(40)的承继表达式:

(39) Nato claims that the nuclear deterrent is vital(北约组织声称核威慑力量至关重要)

(40) 存在一种核威慑力量

按照这种理论,预设实际上不是被消除,只是在生成过程中被阻止,不能在整个句子里出现而已。

另一种处理投射问题的复杂方式能够处理语境造成的可取消性问题。这种理论是由Gazdar(1979 a,b)提出的。他的理论也假设预设属于语义的非真值条件方面。但跟前一种理论相反,在Gazdar的理论里预设实际上是可消除的。首先,一个句子的全部潜在预设(potential presuppositions)整套地生成。在这个阶段,复句的预设由各部分的预设组成。然后一个取消机制开始起作用,在一整套潜在预设中挑选出将予保留的在特定语境中说出该句子的实际预设(actual presuppositions)。取消机制以这样的方式起作用:语境由交谈双方都知道的一系列命题组成,至少双方对这些命题都接受,没有争议。在交谈时双方通过增加表达的命题来扩大语境。关键在于这种扩大应以一种特定的次序进行:先增加句子的蕴含,然后增加会话含义,最后才增加预设。这个次序很重要,因为语境增加新的命题有一个重要的制约:在每一个步骤,只有跟语境已有的全部命题一致的命题才可以增加。例如(41)由于结果从句里的定指描写而具有潜在预设(42),但(42)由于条件主从句具有的含义(43)而被消除:

(41) If there is a King of France, the King of France doesn't any longer live in Versailles(如果现在有一个法国国王,那么这个法国国王不再住在凡尔塞)

(42) 说话人知道存在一个法国国王

(43) 不存在一个法国国王,这跟说话人的全部知识相一致

因为(43)在潜在预设(42)之前已加入语境,因此阻止跟(43)矛盾的(42)再加入语境。

第三章　会话含义①

1. 会话含义的特征

Grice 认为会话含义的基本特征大致可以预言。他分析出五个特征。第一个特征也许最重要:会话含义是可以取消的。如果在原有前提上附加某些前提就能使一个推理消除,那末该推理就是"可取消的"。例如(1)具有"量"含义(2)和蕴含(3):

(1) John has three cows（约翰有三条奶牛）

(2) 约翰只有三条奶牛

(3) 约翰有两条奶牛

(1) 在增加一个相应的 if-从句后会话含义就被消除:

(4) John has three cows, if not more（约翰有三条奶牛,如果没有更多的话）

(4) 不再具有含义(2)。注意蕴含是不可取消的:

(5) ? John has three cows, if not two（约翰有三条奶牛,如果没有两条的话）

---

① S. C. Levinson 著,沈家煊译,《语用学论题之二:会话含义》,《国外语言学》,1986 年第 2 期。

这方面会话含义看来跟逻辑推理很不一样,因此不能参照表示蕴含的语义关系的模式。

第二个重要特征是"不可分离性"。会话含义附属于说话的语义内容,不属于语言形式,因此仅仅用同义词替换并不能使会话含义脱离说的话。但至少有一些语用推理似乎附属于说话的形式而不是意义,例如"预设"。

(6) John's a genius(约翰是位天才)
(7) 约翰是个白痴

(6)具有类似讽刺性质的含义(7),在会话双方都知道(6)确实是假的语境里,如果换说其他句子如 John's a mental prodigy(约翰是位智力奇才),John's an exceptionally clever human being(约翰是个特别聪明的人),John's an enormous intellect(约翰是位大有才智的人),John's a big brain(约翰是位智囊)等,这些不同的说法表达的命题能产生相同的讽刺含义。因此会话含义一般是不可分离的,只有"方式"准则产生的含义是例外,因为表达方式专门跟说话的形式相关联。

第三个特征是会话含义可以推导出来。对于每一个假定的会话含义,都可以构建一个如(8)的推导过程,表明如何一方面根据说话的字面意义,另一方面根据合作原则和各项准则,听话人推导出相应的含义:

(8) 说话人 S 说的话 p 具有会话含义 q,当而且仅当:
(i) S 说了 p;
(ii) 没有理由认为 S 不遵守各项会话准则,至少 S 得遵守合作原则;
(iii) S 说 p 而又要遵守会话准则和合作原则,因此 S 必定想要表达 q;
(iv) S 必定知道:双方都知道如果认为 S 是合作的,必须假设 q;S 没有采取任何行动来阻止我(听话人)作 q 的理解;
(v) 因此 S 想要我作 q 的理解,即说 p 时的含义是 q。

第四个特征:会话含义是非规约性的,即不属于语句的规约意义(conventional meaning）。既然必须在知道句子的字面意义之后才能在语境中推导出它的含义，这种含义就不可能属于字面意义。此外，我们发现一句话的含义虽然是假的，这句话仍然可以是真的，反过来也一样。例如根据"量"准则(9)具有含义(10)：

(9) Herb hit Sally（赫伯打了萨莉）

(10) 赫伯打了萨莉但没有打死她（如果赫伯打死了萨莉,说话人只说(9),这表明他取不合作态度故意隐瞒消息）

但是在(9)是真的而(10)是假的情形里，说话人仍然可以说(9),意在蒙蔽对方。

最后一个重要特征是：具有单一意义的词语在不同的场合可以产生不同的会话含义，而且在任何场合,这组含义实际上无法确定，例如：

(11) John's a machine（约翰是一架机器）

(11)会话含义可以是：约翰是冷漠的，或能干的，或不停地工作，或不停地喘气，或不会动脑筋，或这些含义都有。因此会话含义至少在有些情形里有某种不确定性，与各种语义理论通常假设的确定不变的意义不相同。

2. 会话含义的测试

理解会话含义的特征，然后用可靠的方式把会话含义跟其他种类的语义和语用推理区别开来，这是很重要的。然而，Grice提出的会话含义的特征每一个都有问题。例如，假定我们根据(14)能够取消(13)这一点认定(12)具有含义(13)。

(12) Joe taunted Ralph and Ralph hit him（乔嘲笑拉尔夫，拉尔夫打了他）

(13) 乔先嘲笑拉尔夫，然后拉尔夫打了他

(14) Joe taunted Ralph and Ralph hit him, but not necessarily in that order（乔嘲笑拉尔夫，拉尔夫打了他，但谁先谁后不一定是这样）

有怀疑的人可以提出：(12)里的 and 有歧义，一个意思相当于逻辑词 &，另一个意思相当于"and then"（然后），(14)的例子只不过是表明"and then"不是要表达的意思，从而消除 and 的歧义。

同样，用不可分离性作为一个特征给会话含义下定义也成问题。Sadock 曾指出，要测试不可分离性，必须有一组同义的语句，它们有共同的会话含义。但是假定所谓的含义实际上属于每个语句的语义内容，那么它的不可分离性并不是由于它是会话含义而具备的。更糟的是，甚至是最明显的会话含义的例子也有问题。例如，通常认为(15)具有含义(16)，而(15)的意义大致跟(17)等同（即两者的真值条件相同）：

(15) Some Of the boys went to the soccer match（有一些男孩去看足球赛）

(16) 男孩们没有都去看足球赛

(17) Some and perhaps all of the boys went to the soccer match（有一些也许是全部男孩都去看足球赛）

既然(15)和(17)的意义（真值条件）等同，应该有共同的会话含义。但实际不是这样，只有(15)有含义(16)。

如果把各项特征放在一起作为必要条件，总体上满足这些条件就足以判定一个推理是会话含义，那么上述这类问题实际上有许多就不存在了。例如对于(12)我们还发现推理(13)是可以根据"方式"准则推导出来的；用 but 取代 and 或干脆不用连词，推理(13)仍然不能和(12)分离；根据这些事实我们有理由放弃 and 有歧义的说法。其他一些问题，例如跟(15)和(17)有关的问题得服从某些相反的论点。像 Gazdar 曾提出某些特定的会话含义能取消其他一些含义。(17)由于有短语 perhaps all（也许全部）而具有另一个含义(18)：

(18) 也许不是全部

含义(18)能取消由量词 some（一些）产生的含义(16)。（详见 Gazdar 1979a）。

此外，随着研究的进展，我们也许能发现会话含义还有别的特征。例如,Sadock 指出,会话含义似乎是唯一的一类可以自由强化的语用或语义推理,即可以跟一个说明这种含义的陈述并联而不会有异常的冗余感。试比较:

(19) Some of the boys went to the soccer match but not all
(有一些男孩去看足球赛,但不是全部)

(20) ? Some of the boys went to the soccer match but not none (有一些男孩去看足球赛,但不是一个都没去)

一般性会话含义(见以下第4节)还有一个重要特性,我们预期它们对所有的语言有普遍性。这种普遍性来自这样的理论:如果各项会话准则是从合理的合作原则推导出来的,我们理应预期这些准则的应用具有普遍性。

3. 会话含义和逻辑形式

会话语义是从(a)说的话(b)至少遵守合作原则的假设这两个方面推导出来的。但是会话含义究竟跟"说的话"的哪些方面有关?确切地说,推导会话含义必须参照语言的哪个或哪些层次?有相当详尽的论据可以证明,除了根据"方式"准则得出的含义外,其他会话含义都必须从语义表达层次,包括某种逻辑形式中推导出来。它们不能从未加解释的表层结构推导出来,也不能仅仅从所说句子的真值条件推导出来。首先,有许多语句的表层结构不同,但却有共同的会话含义。其次,形式为"A 不都是 B"的语句具有一般性会话含义"有一些 A 是 B"。但是众所周知,(21)有歧义(即辖域(scope)歧义),两种意思的逻辑形式分别为(22)和(23):

(21) All of the arrows didn't hit the target
(22) $\sim(\forall x (A(x) \rightarrow Hit (x, the\ target)))$ 不是所有的箭都射中了靶子
(23) $\forall x (A(x) \rightarrow \sim(Hit (x, the\ target)))$ 所有的箭都没有射中靶子

(22)的意思就是"A 不都是 B"的意思,因此具有含义"有一些 A 是 B",即(24):

(24) 有一些箭射中了靶子

既然(21)的两种意思中只有一种即(22)具有含义(24),可见会话含义必定不是从未加解释的表层结构(21)推导出来的,而是从表达某种意思的语义表达式推导出来的。

我们还可以证明,会话含义往往不能仅仅从真值条件推导出来。试考虑形式为(25)和(26)的语句:

(25) p
(26) p,并且如果 p 则 p

显然,这两个语句有共同的真值条件:当 p 为真时,(26)也是真的,反过来也一样。但是比较具体例子(27)和(28):

(27) It's done(完结了)
(28) It's done and if it's done, it's done(完结了,要是完结了也就完结了)

只有(28)具有大致是(29)的独特含义:

(29) 已经发生的事情再后悔也没有用了

因此至少有一些会话含义不是仅仅从真值条件推导出来的,虽然真值条件也有关系。由"方式"准则的两个次准则即"避免晦涩"和"避免歧义"推导出来的会话含义是例外,因为它们必须参照语句的表层形式。

4. 含义的种类

我们强调区别两种会话含义,一种是从简单地假设说话人遵守会话准则推导出来的(称为标准会话含义),另一种是以较复杂的方式根据说话人藐视或利用会话准则推导出来的。这种区分的依据是一般认为有些特殊的语句采用修辞手段。Grice 从另一个方面区分两种会话含义:一般性会话含义是不需要特殊语境或背景就能推导出来的,而特殊性会话含义需要依靠特殊的语境。例如，一般说来(30)总是具有含义(31)：

(30) I walked into a house（我走进一所房子）
(31) 那所房子不是我的

与此不同，(32)只有在(34)那样特殊的语境里出现才具有含义(33)：

(32) The dog is looking very happy（那条狗看上去很得意）
(33) 也许那条狗把烤牛肉吃了
(34) A：What on earth has happened to the roast beef?（烤牛肉到底怎么了?）
　　　B：The dog is looking happy.

含义(33)因此属于特殊性会话含义。大部分藐视或利用会话准则得出的含义是特殊性会话含义，例如讽刺需要特定的背景假设来排除字面解释。但是或许可以说，像(35)的隐喻或(36)的同义反复表达的会话含义不大受语境的制约：

(35) England is a sinking ship（英国是一条正在沉没的船）
(36) War is war（战争就是战争）

总之，从上述两个方面对会话含义作出的区分是互相交叉的。但重要的是，那些既遵守会话准则又属于一般性的会话含义对语言理论有特殊的重要性，因为正是这些含义很难跟语句的语义内容区分开来，它们通常在所有的语境里跟有关的语句相联系。Grice 在会话含义即根据会话准则推导出来的含义之外还想到一种完全不同的非真值条件的推理，即规约含义。规约含义不是从会话准则那种高层次的语用原则推导出来的，而是简单地根据规约附属于特定的词项或语句。Grice 提供了两个例子：but（但是）这个词跟 and（和）有相同的真值条件，但 but 还有附加的规约含义，即表明两个连接成分之间存在某种对立。还有一个例子是 therefore（因此），这个词对所在语句的真值条件也不起作用。可以预料，在我们已经列出的会话含义的五个特征上，规约含义跟会话含义都是对立的。有大量的指示词语似乎都以规约含义作为中心意义成分。对于 however（可是），besides（此外），although（虽然），Oh（哦）这类话语指示词和 sir（先生），madam（夫人），your honour（阁下），hey（嗨）这类社会性指称词来说尤其是这样。例如法语里代词 tu（你）/vous（您）的区别表达的并不是真值条件的区别，而只是表达说话人和听话人之间社会关系的区别。

Grice 认为另外还存在一些非规约性的推理，它们是根据语言使用中其他不同的准则或原则推导出来的。例如下文将提到一条"信息充量原则"，它产生的含义有时跟"量"准则产生的含义相矛盾。还有一些礼貌原则产生一系列十分复杂的推理。实际上，很可能有一条总的原则：对于语言使用中双方假设的每一种制约而言，总是相应地存在一组潜在的推理，这些推理是由于说话人遵守或貌视这些制约而产生的。如果真是这样，就还会有许多种类的含义有待发现。含义种类的多样性提醒我们，近来语用学的进展得出一个结论，就是对意义的性质应持"混合的"观点。按照 Grice 的观点，一句话的全部意义或信息交流内容可以作有如下图的分解。从图中我们可以看出一句话的真值条件内容(图中的"字面意义")可能只是全部意义中很小的一部分。

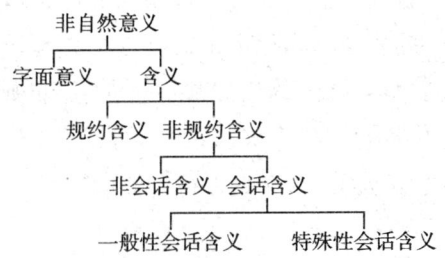

5. 一般性"量"含义

会话含义这个概念最有吸引力的一点在于它有可能大大简化语义学。为了说明 Grice 的理论在这方面有多么深远的意义，我们需要更严格地说明会话准则是如何起作用的。因此，我们集中讨论某些一般性"量"含义，因为对这些含义我们目前似乎了解得最充分。按照 Gazdar（1979a）的方式，我们考虑两个特殊而重要的次类："层阶量含义"和"主从句量含义"。

一个语言层阶(scale)由一组可以交替的语言成分组成，这些成分可以按照提供信息的强弱或语义强度以线性顺序排列。这个层阶具有按次序排列的词语集合的一般形式：

(37) $\langle e_1, e_2, e_3, \cdots e_n \rangle$

如果在句子框架 A 中填入 e_1 或 e_2 等，我们得到合格的句子 $A(e_1)$，$A(e_2)$等，其中$A(e_1)$蕴含$A(e_2)$，$A(e_2)$蕴含$A(e_3)$，依次类推，但逆向蕴含不成立。例如英语的量词 all(所有的)和 some(有些)，它们组成一个含义的层阶$\langle$all, some$\rangle$，因为凡是像(38)的句子都蕴含(39)，但(39)不蕴含(38)：

(38) All the boys went to the party (所有男孩都参加了聚会)
(39) Some of the boys went to the party (有些男孩参加了聚会)

确定这样一个层阶后，根据一条普遍的规则就能得出一组量含义。这条规则是：如果说话人断言层阶中较低或较弱的一项(即层阶中靠右的一项)是成立的，那么他的含义是较高或较强的一项(即层阶中靠左的一项)不成立。例如，假如说话人断言(39)，他的含义就是并非所有的男孩都参加了聚会。这条规则实际上体现这样的观点：层阶中较弱项的语义与可以成立的较强项的真值并不互相排斥，而较强项实际上不成立这个推理只是一种含义。例如 some 跟 all 并不互相排斥，some 的语义并不包含"并非所有"，"并非所有"是属于跟 some 有固定联系的层阶含义。读者如把上述规则应用于以下诸层阶，可以检查由上述规则得出的含义是否符合他们的直觉：

(40) $\langle$all(所有的), most(大多数), many(许多), some(有些), few(少数)$\rangle$
$\langle$and(和), or(或)$\rangle$
$\langle$hot(热), warm(暖和)$\rangle$
$\langle$always(总是), often(经常), sometimes(有时)$\rangle$
$\langle$necessarily p(必定是 p), possibly p(可能是 p)$\rangle$
$\langle$must(必须), should(应该), may(可以)$\rangle$

现在来谈主从句含义。它表示这样一种直觉：如果说话人宁肯使用某个复合语句而不使用另一个可供使用的语义上较强的复合语句,后者使他必须断言某个内含的命题而前者不必如此,那么可以认为他的含义是他不能够作出语义较强的断言。例如:

(41) I believe John is away（我相信约翰走了）
(42) I know John is away（我知道约翰走了）

如果说(41)而不说(42),说话人的含义是:有可能约翰实际上没有走。也就是说,说较弱的"a believes p"而不说较强的"a knows p",说话人的含义是{$Pp, P\sim p$}（P 表示"可能"）。其他类似的结构还有:

(43) (a) 较强形式　　(b) 较弱形式　　(c)(b) 的含义
　　　p and q　　　　p or q　　　　{$Pp, P\sim p, Pq, P\sim q$}
　　　a revealed p　　a said p　　　{$Pp, P\sim p$}
　　　necessarily p　　possibly p　　　{$Pp, P\sim p$}

现在我们可以来说明这类一般性量含义的发现如何有助于简化语义学。语义学有一个普遍问题:有大量的词语似乎要么认为它们只有一种变化无常的意义(即意义随语境而变化),要么认为有许许多多不同的但是密切相关的意义。这两种观点都不太合意。会话含义提供了一种更可取的解决办法:词语一般有一个中心意义,中心意义可以有规律地增加各种受语境支配因而可以消除的会话含义。例如,在许多自然语言中,选言判断句似乎有歧义,一种意思是只有一个选言肢是真的(不相容的析取,记作 V),另一种意思是一个或者两个选言肢都是真的(相容的析取,记作 v),按照这种解释,如果加上 or both 就能使(44)消除歧义:

(44) Ronald is a movie star or a politician, or both（罗纳德是个电影明星或政治家,或者两者都是）

但是 Gazdar 提出歧义的说法是不对的。会话含义的解释可以替代技义说。有一个层阶〈and, or〉,and 的意思相当于逻辑词 &（合取）,or 的意思相当于逻辑词 v(析取)。说"*p* or *q*"的含义是层阶中较强的一项不成立,即～(p & q)。这样,英语或一般自然语言里的 or 的意义可以理解为只有一个意思,即相容的析取,而不相容的析取属于一般性会话含义。

但是有一些其他种类的量含义或语用推理有时跟层阶含义和主从句含义相抵触。例如:

(45) He turned on the switch and the motor started(他合上电闸,马达起动了)

通常我们按提供的信息尽可能多的方式来理解,即两个并联句可能具有以下联系:

(46) (i) p 然后 q　　　　(ii) p 是 q 的原因

(i)的推理可以用"方式"准则来解释,但是这并不能解释(ii)表示因果关系的推理。出现的问题是,按照"量"的准则不可以从(45)得出(46ii)的推理。因为我要是想提供信息较丰富的(46ii)就会这么说了,而没有这么说是由于我的含义是据我所知(46ii)不成立。这当然是不对的。看来另外存在一条原则或准则,可以称为"信息充量原则",跟"量"的准则相反,它在有些情形下允许我们按提供尽量多的信息来理解说的话。

6. 会话含义和语言结构

会话含义理论是关于语言使用的理论,但是它跟语言结构的研究很有关系。很容易发现,对语素和词项的语言学描写有时必须参照会话含义的概念。例如英语里的话语助词 well,oh,ah,so,anyway,actually,still,after all 等,它们向听话人表明冠以这类词的话以什么方式符合合作原则。R. Lakoff 曾指出 well 至少有一个意思可以确定为:表示说话人知道自己不能完全满足"量"准则的要求。(47)中不充分的回答里出现的 well 是很典型的:

(47) A: Where are my glasses?(我的眼镜在哪儿)
　　　B: Well, they're not here(嗯,不在这儿)

同样，anyway 一词至少有些用法似乎是暗示冠以这个词的话跟上文较前面的话的联系要比跟上文紧挨着的话更直接。例如：

(48) A：Oh I thought it was good（哦，我以为那样不错）
　　 B：Anyway, can we get back to the point?（不管怎样，还是回到正题上来，行吗?）

会话含义跟词汇还有一种联系更有理论意义。会话含义对自然语言中可能有的词项施加有系统的制约：如果一个概念是一种语言中某个现成词语的一般性含义，那末这个概念不能直接用词项来表示。例如英语里的 none, never, nor, impossible 等词把否定成分包容在一个词项里。实际上否定成分能不能包容在词项里是有规律的：

(49)　否定短语　　　　　　包含否定的词
　　　not possible　　　　impossible　　（不可能）
　　　not necessary　　　*innecessary　（不必）
　　　not some　　　　　none　　　　　（一个没有）
　　　not all　　　　　　*nall　　　　　（不是所有）
　　　not sometimes　　　never　　　　（从来不）
　　　not always　　　　*nalways　　　（不总是）
　　　not or　　　　　　nor　　　　　　（也不）
　　　not and　　　　　*nand　　　　　（不是还有）

〈necessary, possible〉〈all, some〉〈always, sometimes〉〈and, or〉都是(40)里提到的层阶，因此断言层阶中右边的词项，它的含义是较强的词项不适用，即"not necessary"，"not all"，"not always"，"not and"。按照上述制约，这些含义不能直接用词项表示。

句法受到的语用制约是否有的属于会话含义的制约？这是个有意思的问题。有好几种制约很可能属于这种情形。例如 G. Lakoff 曾提请注意(50)那样的"混合句"其中有些句子片断掺合在另一个句子中：

(50) John invited *you'll never guess how many people to you can't imagine what kind of* a party(约翰邀请了你决猜想不到有多少的人参加你无法想象是怎样的一个聚会)

(51) John invited *a lot of people to a weird* party(约翰邀请了许多人参加一个离奇的聚会)

Lakoff 指出(50)跟(51)密切相关。但是并不是任何句子片断都可以出现在(51)的斜体部分。其中起作用的制约大致是:假定句子(50)具有会话含义(51),那么就可以用间接问句 *you'll never guess how many people* 替代名词短语 *a lot of people*,后者是前者的含义。(*weird* 的替代与此类同——译者)

还有其他的例子也属于句法结构受会话含义制约的情形。例如我们熟悉的非对称并联结构,其中两个并联成分必须按照所陈述的事件发生的先后顺序依次排列,为的是遵守"方式"准则。此外,非限制性关系从句在会话中受"相关性"的制约;内嵌从句跟当时会话的主题的关联程度不得超过主句。

会话含义跟语言结构的互相作用最后还表现在被忽略的语言演变方面。大家知道隐喻和其他比喻是词义随着时间推移发生重大转变的部分原因。例如委婉语开始是一种礼貌的隐喻,但不久就获得了它们原先的含义。夸张,如英语里 frightfully, awfully, terribly 的用法也能诱发新的意义。中古英语里 starve 的意思是"死亡",现在大多数英语方言里已变成"挨饿"的意思。虽然这种变化有文献记载,但我们并不确切知道是如何起变化的:由会话含义转变为规约意义是一下子实现的还是逐渐完成的? 不管怎样,会话含义显然在语言演变中起重要作用。

第五章 言语行为[①]

1. 哲学背景

本世纪三十年代,逻辑实证主义的学说盛行,这个学说的中心信条是:除

---

① S. C. Levinson 著,沈家煊译,《语用学论题之三:言语行为》,《国外语言学》,1986 年第 4 期。

非一个句子至少在原则上可以证实（即验证它的真假），严格地说它是没有意义的。针对这种思潮，L. Wittgenstein 在他的晚期著作《哲学探讨》中发起积极的攻击，提出了"意义就是使用"的口号，并且坚持认为只有联系各项活动或语言博弈（language-games）才能解释所说的话。在同一时期，J. L. Austin 提出了言语行为的理论。Austin 坚持认为"在全体言语环境里的全体言语行为是我们作为最后一着试图阐明的唯一实际现象"。这跟 Wittgenstein 强调语言使用和语言博弈非常相似。在《论言有所为》中，Austin 着手推翻认为真值条件是语言理解的中心的观点。他的方法是：首先，他指出某些一般的陈述句的使用显然不是为了作出真或假的陈叙。例如：

(1) I bet you six pence it will rain tomorrow（我跟你打赌六个便士，明天会下雨）
I sentence you to ten years of hard labour（我宣判你服十年苦役）
I give you my word（我向你保证）

这些句子的特点在于它们不只是有所述，而是有所为。Austin 把这类句子称作"有所为之言"（performatives，以下译作"行为句"），跟"有所述之言"（constatives，以下译作"叙述句"）相对立。接着 Austin 提出虽然行为句不能有真假，但它们有可能不合适。他提出行为句要确有所为必须满足的条件的种类，并称之为"合适条件"（felicity conditions）。例如，假定一个英国公民对妻子说" I hereby divorce you "（我就此跟你离婚），他并不能就此达到离婚的目的，因为没有这样一种传统的做法。然而在穆斯林文化里，说三遍这样的话确能构成离婚。

《论言有所为》开头部分提出的行为句理论到末尾变成关于各种语句的一般理论。前后在定义或概念上有两个重要变化：第一，最初的观点是，行为句是专门一类有特殊句法和语用特征的句子，后来的观点是，它们是有普遍性的一类句子，包括显性行为句（即原先所说的行为句）和隐性行为句，后者包括许多其他种类的语句。第二，最初区分了行为句和叙述句，后来发展成"示言外之力"的一般理论，各种行为句和叙述句只不过是其中的特殊次类。Austin 指出，以上(1)里所列范例的特征似乎是：它们是简单现在时态的第一人称直陈式主动句。但是具有这种特征的句子还有好多其他用法，例如 I now beat the egg fluffy（我现在把鸡蛋打匀）这句话可以边示范边说，报告一项正在进行的动作。我们或许可以求助词汇来下定义：看来只有某些动词可以用在行为句里，而只有用在行为句里的动词可以跟副词 hereby（就此）同时出现，因此可以根据能不能带 hereby 这一点划分出一类行为动词（performative verbs）：

(2) a. I hereby declare you Mayor of Casterbridge（我特此宣布你为卡斯特桥市市长）
   b. ? I hereby now beat the eggs till fluffy.

其中 Declare 是行为动词，而 beat 不是。但是这么办还是不行。例如像 I find you guilty of doing it（我判决你有犯罪行为）那样的行为句不也同样可以用 You did it（你有那种行为）或 Guilty!（有罪！）来表达吗？Austin 实际要表达的意思是：显性行为句其实只是用较特殊的方式使表达明确无误，或具体表明说话时实施哪种行为。如果不用显性句，还可以用较粗略的不太明确和具体的方式，例如语式的变换（用 Shut it "把它关上"替换 I order you to shut it "我命令你把它关上"），或使用语助词（用 Therefore, X "因此, X"替换 I conclude that X "我推断出 X"也可以借助语调把 It's going to charge（它就要朝前冲了）区别为提出警告、疑问或抗议，或者还可以干脆让语境来消除歧义。既然行为句的范围已经扩大到包含隐性行为句，那么无所为的语句就只剩下陈叙句或叙述句了。但是陈叙句是不是也有所为呢？像 I state that I am alone responsible（我声明只有我一个人应负责任）这样的陈叙句不也是行为句的通常形式吗？所以现在认为所有语句除了有所述之外还都通过"示言外之力"而有所为。

Austin 区分三种同时实施的行为：(i) 言之发，(ii) 示言外之力，(iii) 收言后之果。示言外之力是通过跟言之发相联系的规约直接获得的，因而是确定的；而收言后之果是跟言之发的特定环境相联系的，因而不是通过规约获得的，它包括各种有意无意产生的效果，常常是不确定的。例如 You can't do that（你不能做那件事）可能表示抗议的言外之力，而言后之果可能是阻止听话人行动，或使他醒悟，或只是惹他生气。第二种行为即示言外之力显然是

Austin 关注的中心,而"言语行为"这个术语已用来专门指这种行为。

继 Austin 做出的贡献之后出现的大量哲学论著中,有两个方面的进展特别值得一提。一个是 J. R. Searle 将 Austin 的学说加以系统化,很有影响。Searle 的论著使言语行为理论也许对语言学产生了它最大的影响。另一方面的进展体现了试图把 Grice 的非自然意义跟言语行为紧密联系起来的思路。

Searle 借助 J. Rawls(1955)作出的两类规则的区分:控制性规则(regulative rules)和构成性规则(constitutive rules)。前者控制已经存在的活动,如交通规则;后者是创造或构成活动本身的规则,如游戏规则,它具有"实行 X 算作 Y"的概念形式,例如足球赛把球踢进或用头顶进球门算得分。显性行为句和其他示言外之力的手段按规约表示相应的言语行为,基本上就是用的构成性规则:如果我警告你不要碰那条狗,这个警告就构成一项保证,即碰那条狗肯定对你不利。Searle 因此提出,各种言语行为实际上是由一些合适条件共同构成的,并且可以用合适条件作为标准来比较各种不同的言语行为。Searle 根据合适条件如何对四个方面作出规定而把它们相应地分成四类:(i)命题内容,(ii)先决条件,(iii)真诚条件,(iv)基本条件。下面的表列出了提出要求和提出警告在四个方面的比较:

合适条件	提出要求	提出警告
命题内容	听话人 H 将来的行动 A	将来的事件 E
先决条件	1. 说话人 S 相信 H 能做 A 2. 如不提出要求,H 是否会做 A,不清楚	1. S 认为 E 将发生,并对 H 不利 2. S 认为 H 不清楚 E 将发生
真诚条件	S 想要 H 做 A	S 相信 E 对 H 不利
基本条件	算作一种企图,即使 H 做 A	算作一项保证,即 E 对 H 不利

根据各类合适条件,Searle 进而提出,通过以下五种语句可以实施五种基本的言语行为:

(i) 表述句(representative)：说话人保证所表述的命题是真的（范例：作出断言，作出结论）

(ii) 指令句(directive)：说话人企图让听话人做某件事(范例：提出要求，提出疑问)

(iii) 受约句(comissive)：说话人保证将来采取某些行动(范例：提出保证，作出威胁，提供帮助)

(iv) 表情句(expressive)：表达一种心理状态(范例：表示感谢，表示歉意，表示欢迎，表示祝贺)

(v) 宣布句(declaration)：立即引起规约事态的变化，一般要依赖语言以外的各种规约(范例：开除教籍，宣战，命名，解雇)

但是这种分类缺乏原则依据。没有理由认为这种分类是最后确定的和穷尽的，实际上已经有许多其他分类方式在跟它抗衡。Strawson(1964)曾提出，人类信息交流的"基本部分"并不是通过规约的和受文化制约的言语行为来进行的，而是通过 Grice 提出的各种具体的"信息交流意图"进行的。这种观点认为，每种言语行为的合适条件可以从合理性和合作意图的一般角度来解释，例如可用 Grice 提出的会话准则来解释。

2. 两种对立的理论

通过 Austin 的著作并主要通过 Searle 加以系统化后，出现了系统的言语行为理论，我们称之为"不可约论"。它的中心原则是：言语行为是广义的意义的一个方面，不能简约为真假问题，就是说，言语行为构成意义中不能用真值条件语义学来说明的那一部分。言语行为应该用合适条件来描述，它们确定地属于行为(action)的领域，适合于它们的分析方法也应来自行为理论，而不是来自按照真值条件理解的狭义的语义理论。

跟不可约论直接对立的理论是"可约论"。可约论认为没有必要专门建立言语行为理论，因为 Austin 所探究的现象可以纳入一般的句法和真值条件语义学。Austin 的基本论点是 I bet you six pence 这样的语句不能判断真假，但是为什么不能认为出说这句话的本身就使它成为真的呢？在这方面行为句跟其他只要说出来就能证明是真的句子相类似，例如 I am here(我在这儿)，I can speak this loud(我说话声音能有这么大)，I can speak some English(我能讲点英语)。可约论者提出"行为句假设"来处理隐性行为句。按照这个假设,每个句子在它的深层或底层结构有一个最高层次的小句,相当于显性行为句的句首行为小句。这种分析能够作出一系列不然无法作出的句法上的概括。从句法上提出的论据主要有两类,第一类是复指(anaphoric)过程。例如下面(3)里出现反身代词 himself(他自己)取决于高层句里的先行名词短语 the President(总统),但是(4)里的 myself(我自己)似乎没有对应的先行成分:

(6) The President said that solar energy was invented by God and himself. (总统说太阳能是上帝和他自己发明的)
(7) Solar energy was invented by God and myself. (太阳能是上帝和我自己发明的)

如果按照行为句假设,(4)是由(5)通过有规律的"行为小句删略"派生而成,这种疑难就消失了。

(5) I say to you that solar energy was invented by God and myself. (我跟你说,太阳能是上帝和我自己发明的)

另一类句法上的论据是根据这样的事实:在没有显性行为小句出现的句子里,有些副词似乎修饰隐性行为小句:

(6) Frankly, I prefer the white meat. (老实说,我倒喜欢那胸脯肉)
(7) What's the time, because I've got to go out at eight? (几点了,因为我八点钟得出去?)

自然的理解是,(6)里的副词 frankly(老实说)修饰隐性句首行为小句 I tell you(我告诉你),(7)里的 because-从句是修饰隐性的句首行为小句 I ask you(我问你)的状语。

但是,几乎可以肯定,可约论是站不住脚的,因为它在语义学和句法两方面都遇到不可克服的困难。

I. 语义学上的困难

按照可约论的假设,(8)只要在合适的条件下说出来就是真的,并且(9)具有大致相当(8)的底层形式:

(8) I state to you that the world is flat. (我对你陈述地球是扁平的)

(9) The world is falt. (地球是扁平的)

按照假设(8)和(9)应有相同的直值条件,因此(9)也只要说出来就是真的。显然这等于用归谬论证原假设的谬误,因为不管我们对(8)的直觉是什么,(9)肯定是假的。

像 frankly 这类似乎修饰行为动词的副词,也有语义学上的重大困难。首先,这种副词在显性行为句、隐性行为句和报导性行为句中的意义到底是否一样还根本不清楚:

(10) I tell you frankly you're a swine. (我老实告诉你,你是个下流坯)

(11) Frankly, you're a swine. (老实说,你是个下流坯)

(12) John told Bill frankly that he was a swine. (约翰坦率地告诉比尔,他是个下流坯)

按照行为句假设,三个句子里的 frankly 应该以同样的方式修饰动词 tell (告诉)。但是 frankly 在(11)里似乎是在发出预告:即将提出批评;(12)里它修饰告诉的方式;而在(10)这个显性行为句里它也许可以有这两种作用。其次,有些副词只能修饰显性行为句,最突出的是 hereby:

(13) I hereby order you to polish your boots. (我现在命令你擦亮你的靴子)

? Hereby polish your boots

再其次,有人认为像(14)中的状语从句是支持行为句假设的证据,但是很明显 because-从句实际上并不是修饰隐性的 I state(我陈述)或 I claim(我

声称),而是修饰 I know(我知道):

(14) John's at Sue's house, because his car's outside.(约翰在苏的家里,因为他的汽车停在外面)

(15) I know John's at Sue's house, because his car's outside.

Ⅱ. 句法上的困难

有许多例子表明显性行为句不能归诸于说话人,例如:

(16) The company hereby undertakes to replace any can of Doggo-Meat that falls to please, with no question asked.(本公司特此保证狗餐罐头如不讨喜欢,不予询问一律更换)

(17) It is herewith disclosed that the value of the estate left by Marcus T. Bloomingdale was 4,785,758 dollars.(马库斯·布卢明代尔的遗产共计 4785758 美元,特此公布)

不论怎样处理这类例句,肯定会使行为句假设大为复杂。因为行为小句须有可以严格定义的特征才可能在句法上作出明确的规定,不然,适用于行为小句的十分特殊的句法规则(如删略整个行为小句)就无法加以适当的限制。还有许多句子似乎涉及不止一种言语行为,例如(18)有一个非限制性关系从句,这个从句显然是作出断言,但它却嵌在一个问句中。

(18) Does John, who could never learn elementary calculus, really intend to do a PhD in mathematics?(约翰连基本运算都学不会,难道他真的想要攻读数学博士学位吗?)

如果每个句子只能有一个行为小句,那么就得把两个性质不同的派生过程"合并"才能得出(18)。再例如(19)的底层结构类似(20):

(19) Why don't you become an astronaut?(你为什么不当个

宇航员?)

(20) I asked you why you don't become an astronaut, and if you can think of no good reason why not, I suggest that you do.（我问你为什么不当个宇航员,如果你想不出不当的理由,我建议你还是当好）

但是(20)在句法上跟(19)没有联系,因此用句法结构来反映言语行为有明显的局限。

3. 间接言语行为

不可约论和可约论都面临的一个重大问题是所谓"间接言语行为"的现象。要理解这个概念,先得接受"字面用意"(literal force)的概念,即言外之力（用意）是句子形式所固有的。但是句子还有推断出来的间接用意,而大多数用意都是间接的。例如,英语很少用命令句来提出要求,而是喜欢使用间接提出要求的句子。这种间接用法的句子有很多变化。下面的句子都是间接地要求听话人把门关上,这样的句子可以无限地开列下去:

(21) I want you to close the door.（我要你把门关上）
I'd be much obliged if you'd close the door.（如你愿把门关上,我很感激）
Can you close the door?（你能把门关上）
You ought to close the door.（你应该把门关上）
May I ask you to close the door?（我能不能请你把门关上?）
Did you forget the door?（你有没有忘了关门?）
How about a bit less breeze?（让风小一点怎么样?）

从表面上看,句子的用意似乎不受表层形式（即句型）的限制。但是,间接言语行为往往在句法上有反映,这种反映不仅跟表层句型（因而跟字面用意）相关,而且跟间接用意或有效用意相关。首先,please(请)这个词在动词前的分布很受限制,它出现在直接提出要求的(22)里,不能出现在不是提出要求的(23)里:

(22) Please shut the door/you please shut the door（(你)请把门关上）

(23) The sun please rises in the West（太阳请从西边升起）

但是 please 还能在某些间接提出要求的句子里出现在动词前：

(25) Can you please close the door?
Would you please close the door?
I want you to please close the door

因此，要想简洁地描写英语里这个语素的分布，看来需要参照一个专门的功能类，即一类有效的要求（直接或间接提出的）。同样，像 obviously（显然）的副词或像 I believe（我相信）之类的插入语似乎限于有断言用意的语句，不管这些语句是什么句型：

(26) The square root of a quarter is, obviously, a half.（显然，1/4的平方根是1/2）
Is, obviously, the square root of a quarter a half?（显然，1/4 的平方根是不是1/2?）
May I tell you that, obviously, the square root of a quarter is a half?（我能不能告诉你，显然1/4 的平方根是1/2?）

跟间接言语行为相关的另一类分布方式是缩略或删略，例：

(27) a. Why don't you read in bed?（你为什么不在床上看书？）
b. Why not read in bed?（为什么不在床上看书?）

(a) 既可真的用来要求对方说明原因，又可用来提出建议,而删略 do 的

(b)似乎只能作提出建议的理解。同样,(28)里的(a)缩略为(b)后也只能作提出建议的理解:

(28) a. You ought to pay your bills on time.(你应该按时付账)
b. Oughta pay your bills on time.(该按时付你的账)

还有多种这样明显的情形,表明句法和间接言语行为之间的相互作用。Ross(1975)因此认为,句子的句法派生过程必须参照语用制约。他还提议:正像生成语义学认为应该有"语义句法"(semantax)一样,以上事实也是建立一般的"语用句法"(pragmantax)的理由。

字面用意的假设因此面临两个方面的问题:一方面它似乎对按照句子形式分配用意作出的预测是错误的,另一方面,它需要对句子如何和为什么具有表示间接用意的句法标记或分布标记作出解释。为了挽救这一假设,已经提出的理论有两种:成语论和推理论。

成语论认为,像上面(21)里那一类形式实际上都是成语,在语义上相当于"I hereby request you to close the door"(气我现在要求你把门关上),这就像 kick the bucket(翘辫子)是表示 die(死亡)的成语。成语不能作成分分析,而是作为整体记录在词汇里。Sadock(1974)特别认真地坚持成语论,但是它有着不可解决的一些问题。首先,对语句的回答可以针对字面用意同时又针对所谓成语用意:

(29) A: Can you please lift that suitcase down for me?(你能不能请把那只手提箱替我拿下来?)
B: Sure I can; here you are. (当然行,给你)

其次,如果把这些形式都看作成语,词汇部分就会包含无限多的成语。再其次,像 Can you VP? 之类的句子有多重意思,听话人怎么知道是哪种意思呢? 实际上成语论还需要有说服力的语用理论作补充才能解释在不同的语境里作不同的理解。最后,按照定义,成语不可作成分分析,它们跟词汇的音义结合的任意性一样属于言语社团的个异特征。但是大多数表达间接言语行为的基本结构在各种语言里互相类似,这显然证明间接言语行为基本上不是成语。

推理论的基本观点是:间接言语行为具有跟句子表层形式相联系的字面用意,例如 Can you VP? 具有疑问句的字面用意;此外,根据语境条件加以推理还可以得出提出要求的间接用意。最先提出推理论的是 Gordon & Lakoff (1971,1975)。他们提出的推理规则是:如果说话人在不可能有提问意图的语境里说出 Can you VP?,那么说这句话就相当于说 I request you to VP。他们还进一步作出概括:如果语境不允许一个陈叙句或疑问句得出字面用意,那么对一种言语行为的合适条件作出陈叙或提出疑问就算实施该种言语行为。举例来说,(30)是对从说话人出发的合适条件加以陈叙,(31)是对从听话人出发的合适条件提出疑问:

(30) I want more ice-cream.(我还要一点冰淇淋)
(31) Can you pass me the ice-cream please?(你能不能请把冰淇淋递给我?)

Searle(1975)提出另一种推理论,他用 Grice 的会话含义的一般理论提出推理的原则。因为 Grice 的理论是关于语用推理的一般理论,因此 Searle 的路子跟 Gordon & Lakoff 的不同,他提议把间接言语行为纳入更广阔的范围,这个范围还包括隐喻、讽刺等等说话人的意图和句子意义有重大变异的其他现象。

4. 语境改变理论

其实,还有第三种解决间接言语行为问题的办法,它比成语论和推理论更彻底,即根本否认句子有字面意义的基本假设,因此也就不存在间接言语行为和这方面的问题;言语行为完全是语用性质的,跟句子形式或句子意义没有直接的简单的联系。有一种理论可以算作这样的语用理论。其观点是把言对语行为当作语境的运算(operations,集合论概念),即从语境到语境的函数。这里的语境必须理解为一系列命题的集合,这些命题描写言谈参与者的信仰、知识、保证等。基本的直觉很简单:一个句子说出来时不仅表达了它的意义,而且还改变了一系列背景假设组成的集合。一句话引起的这种语境改变就是它的言语行为(用意)。例如,如果我断言 p,我就在语境中增加了我对 p 的保证。按照这种观点,大多数言语行为在语境中增加某些命题,例如做出判断、做出许诺、发出命令等就是如此。还有一些言语行为在语境中取消某些命题,例如表示许可、撤回声明、宣布废除、拒绝承认等就是如此。具体地说,表示许可就是从 p 事态被禁止的语境改变为不再被禁止的语境。这种分析还可以做更细致的改进,一些细节可参看 Hamblin(1971),Ballmer(1978),Stainaker(1978)和 Gazdar(1981)的论著。语境改变论的主要吸引力之一在于它能用集合论的概念做出严格的表达。

5. 超越言语行为理论的研究

有充分的理由可以认为言语行为理论可能逐渐被解决语句功能问题的更加复杂的多方面的语用研究所取代。任何言语行为理论基本上关注的是语句如何映现为各种言语行为。问题在于要么认为这种映现是通过法规(例如通过字面用意的假设)完成的琐细任务,要么试图按语境对句子的功能做出准确的预测。如果采用后一种办法,很明显,语境因素本身就十分丰富复杂,留给言语行为理论去解决的将所剩无几。

由于跟自然语言使用的经验研究有关的一些学科的发展,言语行为理论的基础从外部受到削弱。除了会话分析外,有两门传统的学科关注的是跟言语行为理论有关的实际语言使用的详细情形。一门是言语民族学(ethnography of speaking),对语言使用做跨文化的研究(参看 Bauman & Sherzer(1974)编辑的代表性论集)。这部论集的中心概念是"言语事件"(speech event),即在文化上得到承认的社会活动(如课堂教学,教堂礼拜),其中语言起一种特殊的作用。既然这类文化事件制约语言的使用,也就有相应的推理规则部分地根据谈话发生的社会环境给语句分配适当的功能。例如,在课堂上,下面的对话可以有一种跟所说的内容大相庭径的自然解释:

(32) Teacher:What are you laughing at?(教师:你们笑什么?)
　　　Child:Nothing.(学童:没笑什么)

大致说来，这是教师发出停止嬉笑的命令和学童接受这项命令。这种理解依据的假设是嬉笑在课堂上是一种受到限制的活动。在食品杂货店里，手指着莴苣，(33)可以理解为要求供应这种蔬菜并保证购买：

(33) That's a nice one.（那种蔬菜不错）

下面这句话由学生对房东太太说出是征求同意，而由房东太太对学生说出则是要求采取行动。

(34) Can we move the fridge?（我们能不能移动这个冰箱？）

这类例子说明 Wittgenstein 的"语言博弈"的概念是有效的。他不认为语言只有一套有限的功能或可实施的言语行为。相反，在无限多变的语言博弈中人类可以创造多少角色也就会有多少言语行为。语言博弈概念必然被解释为推理图式或参照系(frame)的概念，这个概念目前在人工智能和认知心理学中广为流行。参照系是指为理解一句话提供推理基础而唤起的知识群体。也许可以认为在理解(32—34)这类句子和分配用意和功能时参照了教学、购物等等言语事件的参照系。

第二门主要的经验性传统学科是语言习得的研究。近来这方面的研究有重大进展，重点不再是儿童早期话语的语法系统，而是转向语句的功能和语句同语境的交互作用。从某种意义上说，言语行为的习得先于言语的习得。由此产生的一个重要观点是言语行为概念的习得是语言本身习得的先决条件。但是最近的研究并不真正支持言语行为是一个重要概念。相反，这些研究强调了信息交流的意图、语句的功能和起交互作用的语境在语言习得过程中的基本作用。实际上 Grice 关于信息交流意图的观点比以规约为根据的解释更适合于描述语言习得过程。此外，最近的研究强调共同产生话语的母亲和儿童之间的交互作用。成人对儿童说的话的解释所起的作用得到确认：正是通过成人按这种解释作出的反应，儿童才"学会如何表达意义"。

最后，言语行为理论的前途很可能取决于字面用意的假设是不是站得住脚。如果能够继续维持形式和用意之间的严格对应关系,因而使预测的用意符合实际,那么言语行为理论很可能继续在语言使用的一般理论中起作用;如果不能找到这样一种字面用意假设的理论,那就没有什么理由专门分出一个言语行为的层次以区别于语句的功能、目的或意图的其他方面。

7.3 思考和练习

1. 怎么理解语用研究的目的在于"解释"？你还学过其他以"解释"为目的的学科吗？

2. 考虑下面两个对话。请从话语的使用环境,说话人和听话人之间关系的亲密程度,说话人和听话人的身份、地位、各自的需求和意愿等因素来分析这两个对话所反应出来的语用现象。

    a. 商场售货员:您好,需要帮忙吗？
       顾客:我想看看这个。
    b. 银行职员:你好,要办什么业务？
       顾客:您好,请问这款理财产品……

3. 你是如何理解语用现象的规律性的？试观察身边语言使用的情况,举例说明符合现代汉语句法和语义,但是违反语用的语言现象。

4. 现代汉语中的指示现象分为"人称指示现象""空间指示现象"和"时间指示现象",所涉及的相关表达式分别叫做"人称指示词""空间指示词"和"时间指示词",这类词的共同特征体现在对它们的意义的确定通常都要依赖于某一特定的语境。试举例说说现代汉语中各有哪些指示词。

5. 请指出下列句子所包含的预设义:
    太阳每天升起。
    我后悔离开太早了。
    他假装很高兴。
    他成功逃脱了。
    小明的姥姥什么时候去世的？
    如果不是塞车的话,小明肯定不会迟到的。

6. (思考)现代汉语有一些特殊的词语,如"才""就""也""只"等。它们的语义分析是汉语语法研究的热门领域之一。请尝试用本课所学到的相关概念分析下列句子的语义现象：

张三才喝了三瓶酒。

张三四点就来了。

张三也买了这本书。

张三只买了王五写的书。

7. 请用合作原则的相关理论（提示：合作原则四准则：质的准则、量的准则、方式准则、关联准则），分析下列对话的会话含义。

a. A：王教授家住在哪里？
B：中国南方某个省的一个城市里。

b. A：我昨天买的牛排去哪里了？
B：你的小狗看上去很满足的样子。

c. 某教授给某谋求语言学研究的学生的推荐信：

×××主任：

您好！我的推荐对象曾旁听过我的一门课。他的英语很好，到课率很高。

此致！

YY 教授

d. 姨妈：晨晨的历史考试通过了吗？
妈妈：可怜的孩子！老师问的都是他出生以前发生的事情！

e. A：某某老太太简直就是一只疯狗！
B：天气真好，不是吗？

f. 郑州火车站一代售处，央视记者采访一位排队的小伙子：
央视：你幸福吗？
受访者：接受你采访，队被人插了。

g. 电影《大话西游》中的对白：
菩提：爱一个人需要理由吗？
至尊宝：不需要吗？
菩提：需要吗？
至尊宝：不需要吗？
菩提：需要吗？

至尊宝:不需要吗?

菩提:哎,我是跟你研究研究,干嘛那么认真呢?需要吗?

8. 用言语行为理论的言内行为、言外行为和言后行为分析下列语言使用现象。

场景一:水果摊

小王:老板,给我来三斤苹果。

场景二:小丽和同学在通电话

小丽:晚上我不能和你去看电影了。

场景三:学生敲门

学生:我能进来吗?

场景四:法庭,庭审结束

法官:我现在宣布,被告人无罪释放。

场景五:开学典礼

校长:我宣布开学典礼现在开始。

场景六:××大学××大楼奠基仪式

主持人:让我们热烈欢迎本大楼的捐赠者,××大学荣誉校董Y先生讲话。

9. 阅读下面的证明信回答问题:

致所有相关机构和人士:

兹证明张三是我校中文系汉语言文字学专业2013级学生!

此致

敬礼

××大学中文系

2014年5月8日

回答问题:

(1) 上述信件中有"表述词"吗?

(2) 如果有,相关表述行为的适应性条件是什么?

10. 用"量级涵义"的理论分析下面对话:

A:尚雯婕唱歌怎么样?

B:还好,有时候不跑调。

11. 会话涵义的重要特征在于它们是可以被取消的。结合下面的例子，思考"量级涵义"能否被取消？

张三偶尔去办公室——其实他经常去的。

这种药要在冷藏环境下保存，冰冻环境更好。

专业登山队员爬乔戈里峰都很吃力，业余的那就更不用说了。

12. 辨析下列语言使用中的言语行为（提示：抱怨、命令、请求、邀请、疑问等）。

秦始皇统一了中国。

恋爱中的男女：女对男说：你真讨厌！

食堂的菜真难吃！

嗨，你好！

老师好！

把门关上！

幼儿园阿姨：小朋友们，饭前要洗手！

朋友之间：你身上钱够吗？

语用学很有意思，超级喜欢语用学！

GRE考满分可以申请到美国一流的语言学系吗？

13. 当你听到句子"我看到一个黑影溜进了老王的家里"的时候，会做两个推理：首先，这件事情发生在晚上；其次，进去的人不是老王（或者老王的熟人）。这两个推理一个是预设，一个是涵义。请指出哪个是预设，哪个是涵义？请列出你的分析依据。

14. 在地铁中，经常可以看到下面的提示：禁止吸烟，违者罚款100。请用本课学到的相关知识，分析这一标记的语用意义。（提示：可以从言语行为理论的角度思考）

7.4 延伸阅读

Austin, J. L. 1962. *How to Do Things with words*. Cambridge, Mass.: The MIT Press.

Grice, P. 1989. *Studies in the Way of Words*. Cambridge, Mass.: The MIT Press.

Horn, L. 1985. Metalinguistic negation and pragmatic ambiguity. *Language* 61: 121-174.

Levinson, S. 1983. *Pragmatics*. Cambridge: Cambridge University Press.

Levinson, S. 2000. *Presumptive meanings: The Theory of Generalized Conversational Implicature*. Cambridge, Mass.: The MIT Press.

Searle, J. 1979. *Expression and Meaning: Studies in the Theory of Speech Acts*. Cambridge: Cambridge University Press.

Yule, G. 1996. *Pragmatics*. Oxford: Oxford University Press.

第八章 语言习得

8.1 导引

- 引言
- 语言发展的几个理论
- 基于使用的语言观
- 第一语言发展
- 第二语言习得
- 语言习得的研究方法
- 小结

8.1.1 引言

关于人类语言习得的理论,其最大的争议点聚焦在语言能力是先天赋予还是后天习得。关于这方面的讨论并不是从现代语言学才开始的,而是可以回溯到17世纪欧洲关于知识本体的讨论。先天论的代表人物是笛卡尔,他认为人是生而具有某种天赋的,知识并不是来自于感觉经验,而是来自于思考的主体本身。而洛克的观点却恰恰相反,他认为人心的初始应是空如白纸的,所谓的人性是人的社会本性,是受后天环境的影响塑造出来的。

以下我们将介绍20世纪几个主要的语言习得与发展理论。总体而言,无论是哪种观点,它们都承认人的语言习得既有先天的成分又有后天的因素。正常的人类大脑先天具有发展语言能力的生理基础,这点是不可否认的,这也是人与动物的重要差异,是人能习得语言而高级灵长类动物却未能发展出语言能力的重要原因。但是这些理论的关键区别在于，后天环境在多大程度上影响或决定了人类语言习得的过程和结果。

8.1.2 语言发展的几个理论

8.1.2.1 行为论

美国心理学家斯金纳（B. F. Skinner）在20世纪50年代提出用行为论（Behaviorism）解释人类语言的习得，称人的言语行为（verbal behavior）与动物的行为类似，是一种习惯的形成，是个体对于来自环境中的刺激的反应。斯金纳认为，儿童的语言习得始于对成年人语言的模仿，来自成年人的反应会强化正确的语言行为、抑制错误的语言行为。譬如，当儿童正确地发出"奶"这样的字眼，父母就会给予正面反馈（比如给小孩奶喝），因此会让儿童开始强化从声音到行为"'奶'→喂奶"的关联，并且通过多次的反馈不断强化这种关联；反之，如果儿童没能给出正确的发音，父母会纠正其发音或不满足他的要求（斯金纳称之为一种"惩罚"），通过不断的负面反馈最终阻断错误的言语行为的产生。对斯金纳而言，儿童言语行为的形成是周围人惩罚、激励、刺激与行为结果对其强化（reinforcement）的过程；人类的语言习得与小鼠通过"奖励惩罚"机制学会按杠取食的本质无异。

斯金纳的语言习得行为论受到诸多诟病。按照斯金纳的假设，如果儿童的言语全部来自模仿，那如何解释语言创造能力？另一个明显的漏洞是，现实中父母对儿童言语行为的反应与斯纳金描述的奖惩制度并不一致：家长不会总是纠正孩子的错误发音，并且恰恰相反，家长甚至可能会对孩子错误的言语行为给予正面的行为反应（比如面对发音错误的索食要求）。乔姆斯基就曾发表一篇文章，逐一痛斥了斯纳金言语行为理论的各个漏洞。本章节选了这篇檄文的部分内容。

8.1.2.2 天赋论

按照斯金纳的理论，如果人类语言习得是一个"尝试—错误"（trial and error）的过程，那么习得任何一种复杂的人类语言大概都需要耗费很长的时间。但事实上，儿童学语言的速度非常快，基本上3岁就能掌握语言主要的结构。儿童不仅不需要太多反馈，甚至对于语言输入的质量和数量要求都不高；儿童有时只需听过一次某个单词，就可以开始准确无误地使用；而且考虑到日常的语言输入其实都是支离破碎甚至错误百出的，儿童最终能掌握一门语言并且正确地使用,其实是非常惊人的。基于儿童语言习得的"刺激贫乏"的观察,乔姆斯基提出,人的语言行为不可能只是应对外界刺激的行为,而必须内在已具有结构化的语言知识才可能如此快速、顺利、准确地掌握语言。

在此基础上,乔姆斯基提出了关于语言习得的理论假设,这就是语言官能(language faculty)。他认为,就像人脑具有控制运动、控制感官的系统一样,人脑具有一个"语言习得机制"(Language Acquisition Device, LAD),是专门负责语言的学习和处理的特殊模块。这个模块内置了语言知识体系,包含了各种语言的原则和参数——即"普遍语法"(Universal Grammar)。先天论认为,普遍语法是人类先天共有的。一个人学习语言的过程并不是习得新的规则,而是通过语言经验,在外界因素的触发、诱导作用下,激发内在的语言知识并适当地调整条件和规则,使普遍语法最终达到稳定状态的过程。正因为有普遍语法的存在,所以儿童能够快速准确地习得语言。一些语言习得研究者发现,不同语言背景的儿童会呈现出具有共性的语言发展轨迹,这是普遍语法存在的另一个有力证明。

8.1.2.3 建构主义

建构主义(Constructivism)对行为论的语言习得"被动说",以及生成学派的"先天论"都做出了否定。建构主义对语言习得的基本观点是,儿童的语言习得是一个个体主动参与建构的过程,是在与环境的相互作用中实现的;它是个体主动参与的结果,而不是被动的反应,因此它也是后天形成的,而不是先天具有的。

建构主义的主要理论来自皮亚杰(Jean Piaget)的认知建构理论以及维果茨基(Lev Vygotsky)的社会建构理论。皮亚杰认为认知发展是一个有序的过程,儿童通过与世界的经验形成图式(schema),建构知识,并在与世界的不断交互中发展自己的认知。其中,语言的发展必须基于认知能力的发展。语言是个体认知发展到一定阶段的产物,而语法的规则和表达式只是个体在认知过程中对语言的抽象和知识提取,是更普遍的基本认知过程的一些副现象。社会建构理论更强调社会在语言习得中扮演的重要作用。建构主义认为,对于儿童的认知发展起关键作用的"世界经验",其实是与其他社会成员的社会交互(social interaction),特别是与比如父母、教师这些更具有知识的社会成员的对话。反过来,语言对于认知发展和知识的构建起到关键的作用,因为社会交互大部分都是通过语言实现的。

建构主义最有影响力的一个理论,是对认知发展具有阶段性特征的阐发。人类的认知发展是一个循序渐进的过程,每一个阶段的发展都必须在上一个发展阶段的基础上进行。教育学中的一个重要理论——近侧发展区间(zone of proximal development)便是脱胎于此。近侧发展区间指向的是一个能力范围,即学习者能独立完成的任务,以及需要协助才能完成的任务之间的一个能力区间。这个区间是最有效的学习范围,因为在这个区间内,学生可以在协助下逐渐学会独立完成之前无法完成的任务,因此实现了能力的发展。近侧发展区间的理论对一语习得和二语习得理论都有很大的启发。

8.1.2.4 联结主义

联结主义(Connectionism)是一种以大脑结构为样本的认知模型。大脑由大量的神经细胞构成,每一个都可以看成一个简单的信息处理器;这些细胞互相之间存在联结,为神经细胞之间传递信号,人的大脑大概有 10^{11} 个神经元,它们之间形成了大概 10^{14} 个联结,这些联结的总和形成一个网络。这是大脑的基本结构。联结主义便是以这样的一个模板为理念提出的一种神经网络模型。在这个模型中,神经网络由具有互相联结的节点(node)构成,其中的每一个节点既可以从外界收集信息,也可以向另外的节点发送信号。每个节点有两种状态:激活和非激活状态,当节点接受信号时便处于激活的状态。

人的思维活动相当于是在神经网络中散播信号,激活不同的节点;而知识是不同的节点激活状态的组合。某些节点储存的信息有可能是一个概念、一个影像、一个声音、一个味道,一个具体或抽象的知识通常是多个节点同时激活。比如关于"狗"的这个概念,在这种模型中可能是许多不同节点的激活,一个节点可能是"狗"这个字发音,另一个是"狗"这个字形,其它的节点可能分别是狗的不同特征,比如狗的皮毛、狗用四肢跑步、狗的吠声,甚至可能有些节点是具体某条狗的影像和记忆——当然,每一个节点并不一定是专属于某个概念的,它们也有可能在别的思维活动中被激活。

在联结主义的理论中,知识习得(包括语言习得)的过程就是调整不同节点间联结权重(weight)的过程——这就意味着,节点间联结的权重不仅是不一致的,而且联结的权重是可以不断地被改变的。造成权重改变的是外界信号的输入。不同内容、不同类型的信息,以不同的频次输入,不断调整联结的权重(见图8.1)。这种基于数据的学习方法也称为数据学习(statistical learning)。

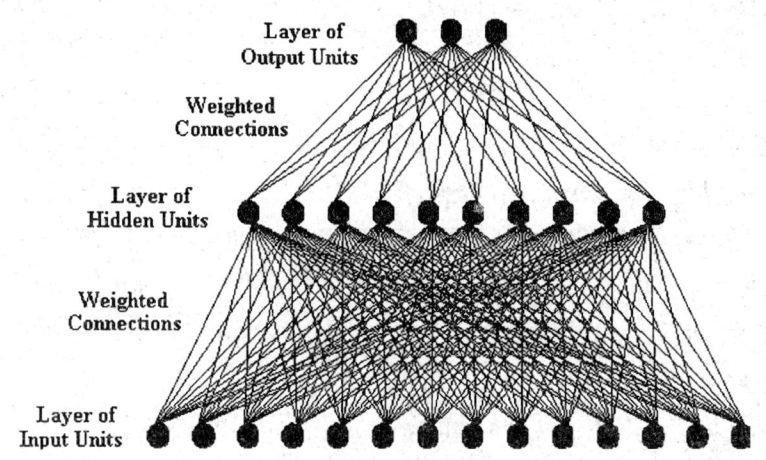

图 8.1　一个简化的联结主义模型的图示①
最下层为输入层，最上层为输入层，中间可能有多个隐藏的节点。
节点之间的联结权重会被不断调整、改变。

联结主义模型的一个最突出的特点是它可以用计算机进行模拟。MacWhinney 就曾以联结主义的模型搭建了一个学习程序，用来模拟人学习语言规则的过程，其选取的知识点是规则相当复杂的德语冠词使用（德语中有 6 个冠词，其使用由名词的性、数、格决定）。实验者在输入层设置了 35 个特征节点，在中间的隐藏层又有更多的节点组合，模拟联结主义的网络。这个程序在反复学习了 102 个德语名词的冠词搭配后，形成了一个代表使用规则的权重联结网络，最终，这个程序能准确判断名词的冠词使用（已知名词准确率达 98%，新名词准确率也高达 92%）②。诸如此类的实验还有很多，它们验证了联结主义模型作为人类认知模型的一种现实可能性。

8.1.3　基于使用的语言观

基于使用的语言观（Usage-based Theory）是上世纪 90 年代由托马塞洛（Michael Tomasello）、拜比（Joan Bybee）等一批语言学家基于大量语言事实

---

①　图片来源：http://www.ucs.louisiana.edu/~isb9112/dept/phil341/myths/IMG00001.GIF。
②　MacWhinney B. 1989. Competition and lexical categorization. In *Linguistic Categorization*, ed. R Corrigan, F Eckman, M Noonan, pp. 195 – 242. New York：Benjamins.

提出的一种语言观。从许多的语言习得的实证研究中,他们发现儿童习得语言的过程并不符合先天论"普遍语法"的假设。举两个最简单的例子:按照普遍语法的理论,语法范畴应该先天就已存在于儿童的语法知识中,只需稍微经过语言激活便可使用;但研究发现儿童在语言习得的初期并没有形成明晰的语法范畴的概念。又比如,按照普遍语法的假设,儿童如果开始使用某个句式,可默认这部分语法知识已被激活,儿童应该能自如灵活地使用;但实际上,幼儿开始使用某个句式时只会固定地使用某些词汇,而不会把自己掌握的所有词汇都轮番套用到这个句式中。也就是说,儿童并不具有成年人的语法知识。

该理论的基本观点是:人类的语言是在使用中形成的;语言习得、语言(信息)处理、语言变化都是在使用中发生的。人的语言知识来自于语言在现实中的使用,既有具体的部分,也有抽象的部分。成年人的语法知识是从无数多的使用场景中归纳出来的抽象模式(abstract pattern),它们来自于具体的语言使用,也在具体的语言使用中体现。与基于使用的语言观一致的语法理论是构式语法(Construction Grammar)。

基于使用的语言观反对先天论的普遍语法理论,但对其它的语言习得理论大多有批判地接受:

(1) 沿袭了建构主义"社会性"的基本观点。基于使用的语言观认为,语言知识的传授与习得是借由沟通行为发生的。当成人与儿童发生行为上的互动时,儿童会把此时发生的语言与行为关联起来,比如"吃吧"这个口令和(对方把东西递过来放到"我"嘴里)这个动作,或者"我看看"这句话和(对方拿起某个东西在面前端详)这个动作。当然,语言形式和语言功能关联的前提是儿童具有能读懂对方行为意图的能力。这种"读懂(对方)意图"(intention-reading)的能力是人类所独有的,也是语言能力发展的关键能力之一。

(2) 认同建构主义关于语言能力本质的观点,即语言能力无异于学习其它知识的认知能力。人的语法知识(即词汇组合或句子需遵循的规律)的形成需要动用的认知能力,比如范畴化(categorization)、组块化(chunking)、翔实记忆(rich memory)、类比(analogy)和跨模态关联(cross-modal association)等,都属于一般领域(domain-general)的学习机制,并不是先天论所说的特定领域的"语言习得机制"。这些认知能力的联合作用使人具有发现模式(pattern-finding)的能力,人们对当下和以往类似的语言使用情境做出比较、分类,提取出语言使用的规律。语言使用规律的总和构成了语法。

(3) 语言系统的形成类似于行为主义和联结主义的关联"强化"。前面提到,语法知识的形成其实是语言使用规律逐步稳定的过程,这个过程需要有足够多的数据——语言材料输入——对规律进行反复检验和调整。抽象和具体的构式的形成都需要非常高的频率。一个抽象构式的形成需要多个不同的具体语言例证的出现;一个具体构式的形成则需要某个具体的词汇、短语或句子的反复出现。如果用类似大脑结构的联结主义模型来表示,就是节点之间的联结通过一次次的激活不断增强。基于使用的语言学习是基于频率的学习(frequency-based learning)和数据学习。

综上,基于使用的语言观认为语言学习过程是后天的,但是学习语言的认知能力是先天的。

8.1.4 第一语言发展

8.1.4.1 关键时期

在发展生理学和发展心理学中,有一个关于生物发展"关键时期"(Critical Period)的理论,大概可以理解为生物行为和功能的发展有一定的有效期限。生物在关键时期内如果适用(或不适用)某些功能,就会产生永久及不可逆的效果。比如鸡鸭等鸟类的"印刻现象"(imprinting)就受到关键时期的制约。在孵化后几个小时内,鸡鸭会对看见的第一个物体进行"印刻",认定这是母亲并从此尾随,一旦"印刻"便无法改变。另一个例子是动物视觉神经系统的激活。曾有研究者对初生的小猫进行了实验,缝合了它的一只眼睛;三个月后拆线时发现小猫没缝合的眼睛视力正常,但缝合的眼睛永久失去了视力。

有人提出人类的语言同样受到关键时期的制约,语言习得的关键时期大概在12岁左右。以此往上,一个人的年龄越大,学习语言的能力越差;单从二语习得的例子来看,我们发现从小就学外语的人比成人后才学的讲起来更地道。至于一语习得是否同样存在关键时期,出于道德的考量,我们不可能用实验的方法去验证。但从以前一些"野孩子"的案例来看,从小就被剥夺了语言环境的儿童长大后语言能力会严重受损,Genie 就是一个这样的女孩。上世纪70年代,Genie 在美国加州的一个小城被发现,时年13岁的她从一岁多开始就被有精神病的父亲长期关在地下室,未跟任何人有过语言接触。在逃出生天后 Genie 开始接受语言教育,但最终却未能发展出正常人的语言能力。Genie 被认为是语言能力存在关键时期的一个力证。但是在二语习得中,我们经常也能看到一些过了所谓的关键时期但仍能成功掌握一门外语的外语学习者。

8.1.4.2 发展轨迹

正常儿童第一语言的发展通常是有规律的,按照一定的顺序,遵循一定的时间。在这里我们仅从语言特征角度来看儿童的语言发展。

儿童的语音和词汇发展是先于语法发展的。基本上,元音会早于辅音出现,而辅音根据其发音的难易程度,可能有些要到 7—8 岁才能学会。儿童大概在 1 岁时会说出第一个真正的词,在 2—3 岁期间,词汇量会飞速地发展。语法的发展基本从 2 岁开始。不管什么语言背景的儿童,基本上在 5 岁能掌握母语的语法。

美国心理学家布朗(Roger Brown)发明了一种以平均语句长度(mean length of utterance, MLU)来测量儿童语言发展的方法;语句长度在某个层面上也反映了句子的复杂度。基本上,以英语为母语的儿童 2 岁后开始出现有某种语法的句子。2 岁时的 MLU 是 2—6 个词,出现单词句;3 岁是 3—8 个词,出现"电报句",4 岁是 5—20 个词,使用简单句和一些复杂句,到 5 岁时能使用各种复杂句型。

研究汉语儿童语言发展的学者则认为,布朗的 MLU 不适合用于分析汉语的语言发展,而应着重儿童合成句子的能力,也就是从句子的结构表现对语言发展进行分类。由此,有学者把汉语儿童语言发展分为四个阶段:(1)前结构阶段(0—2 岁);(2)简单结构阶段(2—4 岁);(3)合成结构阶段(4—6 岁);(4)嵌置结构阶段(6—8 岁)[①]。

8.1.5 第二语言习得

无论什么语言背景,人的母语习得的轨迹和结果大体是一致的。相比之下,学习第二门语言的轨迹和成果千差万别,是由哪些因素造成的?外语学习已经成了现代中国教育的一个重要部分,那么坊间流传的"学语言需要天赋""学外语从娃娃抓起"之类的说法,是否有科学根据?作为一个研究课题,

---

[①] 周兢,1997,《汉语儿童语言发展阶段新说》,南京师范大学学报:社会科学版 58—64。

二语习得通过实证方法探究可能导致二语习得最终成果差别的各种因素,其研究成果能直接作用于二语学习,指导我们如何改善二语学习的条件,从而提高二语习得的效率,取得最终成果。

8.1.5.1 影响二语习得的内在因素

二语学习者本身的生理因素和心理(认知)因素有可能会影响二语习得。由于篇幅的限制,我们在这里快速地了解几个已知的内在因素,包括二语学习者的年龄、天赋、动机和学习类型。

在我们的周围似乎不难观察到这样的现象:越晚开始学习外语母语口音越重,语法也越难掌握。上面提到"关键时期"影响母语的习得(一般认为12岁或9岁之前是儿童学习母语的黄金时间),那么它是否也影响二语的习得?许多研究确认开始学习二语的年龄确实对二语的发音纯正度有影响(越晚开始学口音越不纯正),但对于句法准确度的影响目前并没有定论;开始学习二语的年龄对于学习者最终能达到的水平有影响(儿童最终能比成年人达到更高的水平),可成年人在初学阶段却能比儿童学得更快。目前唯一可以确定的是,年龄对二语习得的最终成果不起决定性的作用,但随着年龄增长,大脑发生的变化以及学习环境的变化却对学习过程有不可小觑的影响。关于"关键时期",我们既能看到支持的例证,也能听到反对的声音,现把主要观点和证据总结如下:

表 8.1 二语习得是否存在"关键时期"的正反面的证据

正面	反面
·越早开始学二语最终能达到的水平越高; ·随着年龄的增长,大脑会渐渐失去其可塑性而影响总体的学习能力; ·儿童甄别语音的能力一般在5—7岁之间定型;因此对之后出现的语音失去了先前敏锐的甄别能力。	·比较"关键时期"前后开始学习二语儿童的语言能力,并未发现在某个时间点出现能力的急剧下降; ·有些个案研究表明,即使不接受常规的二语教育,成人的二语学习者也可以达到母语者水平的发音和语法; ·年龄的差别会导致语言学习的环境和语言输入的质和量,因此间接影响二语习得; ·相比儿童,成年人可能会从主观上抗拒学习(或学好)第二门语言。

生活中,我们也经常听到关于"语言天赋"的论断:有"语言天赋"的人学起外语来不仅快,而且发音地道。上世纪50年代由美国心理学家John Carroll 制定的《现代语言学能测试》(The Modern Language Aptitude Test,

MLAT)就是一套测试所谓外语学习天赋的题。它的确能较为准确地预测受试者学外语的速度,并在世界范围内(尤其是许多政府机关部门)广泛使用。但是"语言天赋"的本质到底是什么? MLAT测试的其中一项能力,后来也被研究者普遍验证的与二语习得有关的能力是短期记忆(short-term memory)或者工作记忆的容量(working memory capacity);能记住的最长句子长度是体现这一能力的指标。此外,发现语言规律的能力、控制提取语言知识和控制语言产出的能力、组成词块的能力等,都属于影响二语习得的"天赋"能力。这几个方面的能力都和母语语言能力有关,因此有研究者发现,儿童在婴幼儿时期展现的语言能力也能较为准确地预测以后二语习得的能力。

学习动机对于二语习得的影响或许毋需多言。强烈的学习动机可以让二语学习者投入更多的时间、精力、资源进行学习。一个人或者出于工作学习娱乐的需求,或者由于搬到了一个新的语言环境,都可能产生强烈的二语学习动机。虽然我们把动机认为是一个学习者自身的心理状态,但必须认识到,动机并非完全由学习者自己掌控,它也受到很多外界因素的影响。试想如果二语的学习环境恶劣,学习遭到来自周围亲人朋友的反对,甚至学习者对二语的社区没有认同感,都极有可能会打击学习二语的动力。二语学习动机的缺失或许可以由改善外部环境来扭转。

二语学习的类型和方法是多种多样的,而个体对于这些方法的接受度也是因人而异的。有些人喜欢从局部到整体;有些人喜欢从具体到抽象;有些人对知识喜欢细吞慢咽,有些人则喜欢囫囵吞枣;有些人反应快,有些人反应慢;有些人喜欢视觉上的刺激,有些人则喜欢听觉上的输入。如果二语学习的方式可以按自己习惯、擅长的方式展开,二语学习就能够事半功倍。

8.1.5.2 影响二语习得的外在因素

影响二语习得的外因,这里特指外部语言环境,比如它提供了什么样的二语输入和二语输出的机会。既然是外部因素,就说明这些是教师可以人为进行改变的因素。外部因素的研究通常以"行动研究"(action research)的方式开展。

语言输入(input)是语言习得最重要的前提。然而,并不是所有的语言输入都是有效的。Stephen Krashen 提出,只有可理解的输入(comprehensible input),才能被学习者理解并产生内化;并且,有效的语言输入应该是稍高于学生目前水平的。因此,二语教学的有效输入必须是建立在对学生目前水平的了解之上，假设学生的水平为"i"，提供的语言输入应该位于"i+1"的水平。

有效的语言输入的理想结果是使学生发现新的语言规律并对其进行内化，但如此也仅代表学生能够理解；从语言知识变成语言技能还需要经过不断的练习，才能成为自然的语言习惯。如果缺乏充分的语言输出，就不能保证语言输出的准确性。Merrill Swain 在加拿大的英法双语学校观察到，虽然英语母语的学生们在学校有充分及合适的法语输入，但他们仍会在输出语言时发生基本的语法错误。Swain 由此提出了可理解输出（comprehensible output）的假说。她认为，只有创造一些使用场景迫使学生使用特定的语法结构（如果使用错误可能会导致交际失败）并多加练习，才能使学生真正习得并能应用语法结构知识。

可理解输出的假说也呼应了 Michael Long 的互动假说（Interaction Hypothesis）。语言的本质形式既然是互动，就应该通过互动来习得，儿童对母语的习得也是通过与父母的互动完成的。Long 认为，母语者在与二语学习者沟通的过程中，会按照二语学习的水平对自己的语言进行调节，对二语学习者而言这是"可理解的输入"，是恰到好处的学习材料；而当学习者需要对母语者进行回应时，就是检验语言输入有效性的机会。Long 把在互动过程中对自己语言不断调整以完成沟通目的的行为称为"语义协商"（negotiate for meaning）。互动假说在很大程度上推动了美国语言课堂的转型，使课堂从传统的"以教为主，教师中心"转变为"以练为主，学生中心"。

此外，二语学习者的注意力对于语言的习得也非常关键。Richard Schmidt 提出的"注意假说"（Noticing Hypothesis）认为，无论是语音、词汇、语法还是语用的习得，都需要学习者意识到他们遇到了一个新的语言材料。即使最初只是单纯地"注意到"而未加理解分析，也会对后期的进一步学习有所帮助。引起二语学习者对某个语言现象的注意有很多种方式。除了直接讲解，还可以通过提问、文本（语音）强化等方式；甚至教师的纠正也是引起注意的一种有效的方法。

8.1.5.3 二语习得的发展历程

二语习得的研究者认定语言存在某种正确形式，并以此为参照对二语学习者的语言输出进行分析；与正确形式发生偏离的语言输出称为偏误（error）。理想状态下二语最终的发展状态是目标语，也就是说二语习得的过程是从有偏误的二语向无偏误的目标语发展的过程。中介语（interlanguage），也就是未达到目标语之前的二语,是二语习得的一个重要课题。中介语研究通常基于偏误研究。

研究者发现偏误发生主要有两个原因。一个是母语的迁移(transfer)。语言之间存在对应的成分,但往往不对等。比如,英文的"or"在中文就有"或者"以及"还是"两个截然不同的用法,一旦学中文的英语母语者把英语的"or"和中文的任意一个用法对等起来,就会发生迁移的偏误。另一个造成偏误的原因是由语言发展的必然规律造成的。例如,有研究者发现,无论英语学习者的语言背景是什么,他们习得英文常用词素的顺序是:(1)进行时-ing,复数-s,述词 be;(2)助动词 be,冠词 a/the;(3)动词的不规则过去式;(4)动词的规则过去式,第三人称-s,所有格 's。当然,有一种解释是,这个所谓发展的规律和顺序,其实与这些词素的出现频率有关——出现的频率越高,输入越多,越早掌握。

8.1.6 语言习得的研究方法

语言习得研究的基本思路是,某个变量会不会引起习得结果的变化,因此二语习得的研究可以用类似科学实验的方法进行,即:在严格控制某一个或多个变量的同时,观察语言水平是否随之发生变化。

首先,研究者需选取可靠的测量方法,确定受试者在实验前后语言水平的变化;同时,还需设置参照组,对比不同条件下语言水平变化的区别。有些实验会对受试者进行长期的追踪,称为"追踪研究"(longitudinal study),适用于观察习得的长期效果。在二语习得中,实验往往是在课堂中进行,称为"行动研究",通常在一个学期内完成。

除此以外,还有许多语言习得的语料库可供使用。在一语发展方面,"儿童语言交流系统"(Child Language Data Exchange System,CHILDES)就是一个囊括了世界上 25 种语言的儿童语料库。在二语习得方面,也有许多公开的口语及书面语料库可供研究使用。

8.1.7 小结

由于本章的内容较多但篇幅有限,大部分内容只是做了最基本的介绍而无法一一讲述。以上提到的每一个研究方向都有更多的内容等待读者发现和探索,感兴趣的读者可以参见"延伸阅读"中的书目。

8.2 选读

● 乔姆斯基(1959)《评斯金纳著〈言语行为〉》选读
● Ibbotson & Tomasello (2018) "Evidence Rebuts Chomsky's Theory of Language Learning"选读
● Schmidt (1983) "Interaction, Acculturation, and the Acquisition of Communicative Competence: A Case Study of An Adult"选读

乔姆斯基(1959)《评斯金纳著〈言语行为〉》选读[①]

◆ **正文节选**

本文的第 1—10 部分是乔姆斯基对斯纳金"言语行为"的理论框架和主要概念的批判,特别是对其所举例证的批判。第 11 部分是对自己的语言观的阐发。

[正文 1—4 部分介绍了斯金纳行为论的一些主要概念,如"反应""刺激""强化""内驱力"等概念,并引用了一些斯纳金给出的言语行为作为"反应"和"刺激"产物,以及言语行为需要通过"强化"保持的例子进行批判。——编者注]

5. 斯金纳这书有许多地方以不同方式说了这样的话:语言学习的一个必要条件,是语言社团对强化所需的东西作出了细心的安排。这话所根据的不是实际观察,而是从对较低等的生物机体做试验后得出的类比,所以看看他这个根本主张在实验心理学本身有无学术地位,是重要的。关于强化,最常见的说法(即斯金纳所明显反对的说法)是说其时内驱力(drive)降低了。这

[①] 译文分三部分发表于 1982 年第 2—4 期《国外语言学》(现《当代语言学》)。本章节选部分主要来自后两部分译文。N. Chomsky 著、王宗炎译,评斯金纳著《言语行为》(上),《国外语言学》,1982 年第 2 期;N. Chomsky 著、王宗炎译,评斯金纳著《言语行为》(中),《国外语言学》,1982 年第 3 期;N. Chomsky 著、王宗炎译,评斯金纳著《言语行为》(下),《国外语言学》,1982 年第 4 期。

种说法的实质,是认为有那么一种内驱力,不管事实上学习的是什么,它都存在。如果假定,有内驱力是因为学习确是在进行着,那么说学习必须经过强化的说法就是无意义的,而在斯金纳学说的框架里,正是如此,到底学习时是否内驱力不一定降低,——这就是潜学习(latent learning),——这个问题已有不少文献讨论过。最"经典性"的实验是布罗杰特(Blodgett)的实验,它证明无需给什么奖赏就自动探究迷箱内情的白鼠(与没有探究过的白鼠比较),在有食物奖赏时迷路次数大为减少。这说明在饥饿内驱力未衰退时,白鼠已经弄清了迷箱的结构了。主张强化必须内驱力减少的理论家则说,除饥饿内驱力外还有探究内驱力,它在白鼠未有食物奖赏就进行学习时已经衰退;他们认为,在给予食物奖赏之前,白鼠走错路的次数已经略为减少了。按相似的设计,人们做过各式各样的实验,结果很不一致。但是事实上有这种现象存在,已经没有多少研究者仍然怀疑了。希尔加德(Hilgard)对学习理论作了总评述,他说,在适当情况下,潜学习信而有征,这一点已不容置疑了。

近来有更多的研究工作证明:刺激如果新鲜多样,就能引起白鼠的好奇心,推动它(用视觉)去探究迷箱的内情,事实上就是去学习(因为如给它两种刺激,一种新的,一种旧的,白鼠就注意那新的);虽然除走路外没有什么好处,白鼠也会挑选那单一选择性迷箱,从而走进那复杂的迷箱;虽然用视觉探索(从窗口外望三十秒钟)是唯一的奖赏,猴子也会学习分辨实物,并且始终维持在高效率水平上;也许更突出的例子是,即使探究和操纵是唯一的诱因(incentives),如把带有相当复杂的操纵问题和分辨问题的东西放进笼子,猿猴也要把它处理妥当。在这些案例中,解决问题显然是唯一的奖赏。强化论者如要说明这些实验结果,就必须承认有好奇内驱力、探究内驱力、操纵内驱力存在,就必须思索内驱力是否也可以学习得来,而关于学习得来的内驱力,我们除看到学习行为确实发生之外,还别无佐证呢。

为了反对学习必须内驱力减少的论点,已有人提出许多其他证据。有人做过把一种感觉作为另一种感觉的条件(sensory-sensory conditioning)的实验,拿所得结果作为学习无须内驱力减少的明证。奥尔德斯(Olds)报告说,直接对脑子施加刺激,就有强化作用,因此他断言奖赏不必满足什么生理需要,也不必取消内驱力刺激。在这里,动物学家早已看到的铭记(imprinting)现象是特别引起人们的兴趣的。特别值得注意的是鸟类。鸟类那些最复杂的行为模式,有些是以关键性的幼稚时期所接触过的实物和动物为其榜样的。动物有先天的爱在某些方面学习的倾向，碰到某些模式和实物就做出适当的反应，而且常常远在原先的学习活动早已完成之后。关于这一点，铭记是最强有力的证据。所以我们说，铭记是无须奖赏的学习，虽则动物行为的最后模式会因强化而得到改进。鸣禽学唱那些典型的鸟歌，有的也是由于铭记。杜伯（Thorpe）说，他的研究证明，"在鸣禽很小很小，还不会唱整支歌以前，已经懂得鸟类通常所唱的歌里边的那些特征了。"关于铭记现象，近来已在实验室里用人工控制的方法来进行研究，并取得了积极成果。

在日常经验中，下面这种平凡现象无疑是屡见不鲜的。有些人，有些地点，我们并不怎么特别加以注意，可是认得出来。我们可能查书找资料，把其中一些东西记得清清楚楚，可是这样干只不过为了反驳强化论，或者闲极无聊，或者只是为了好奇。搞科学研究的人都有过这样的经验：抱着极大的长时间的兴奋心情去写一篇谁也不要看的论文，或解决一个谁也不觉得重要的问题，完成之后毫无奖赏，甚至还可能使别人以为自己为无关紧要的事浪费了时间。白鼠和猴子同样也不为奖赏就学习起来，这个事实值得注意，在精心设计的实验中证明这一点，是很重要的。事实上，研究上述种种行为，是有独立的积极意义的；它固然也会使人怀疑学习时是否内驱力必然减退，但是那只是次要的作用。要是这样放大视野来研究动物行为，在研究像言语行为这样复杂的活动方面，我们很可能获得十分有用的知识，而这种知识，强化论至今还不能提供。不管怎样，从现有证据看来，很少人会仍然坚持强化是学习的必要条件，如果所谓强化指的是不用看后来行为有什么变化就可以识别的东西。

同样，小孩们学到许多言语行为和其他行为，也是由于无意中观察和模仿成人和别的小孩所致，这似乎是无疑的。决不能说，小孩学语言，必须成人"无微不至地给他小心布置一番"，即通过谨慎的差别强化（differential reinforcement）来给小孩准备若干言语项目（虽则在知识分子家庭中，成人往往有留神教小孩学语言的习惯）。人所共见，移民的幼儿能神速地在街上从别的小孩那里学会第二语言，把话说得流畅无误。第二语言的微妙之处，这些幼儿会极其熟悉，而他们的父母虽然想学，不断学，还是学不到。小孩的大部分词汇和对句法结构的敏感性，可能是从电视、读书、听成人说话等等学来的。甚至一个年纪很小，连说半句全新的话所需的语言材料也没学会的孩子，在学说一个词时也可能一学就学好，根本用不着父母来教导。大家也分明看到,过了一些时候,这小孩就会构成全新的话语,也听得懂全新的话语,而这些话语按本国语习惯都是可以接受的。一个成人读报,每次都会碰到无数的全新句子,这些句子在声音方面与过去听过的完全不同,可是他认得出这些是句子,懂得它的意思;如果句子稍稍写错印错,他也辨认得出是错了。在这些实例中,还谈什么"刺激的泛化"(stimulus generalization),那不过是用新名称来保存旧神话罢了。人们能这样做,必有能不依赖环境所给的"反馈"(feedback)的重要心理过程。斯金纳和别的一些人说,要通过差别强化才能逐步好好地形成言语行为,我找不出任何佐证。如果强化论者真的要假定学语言必须倚靠如此小心周密的安排,这样的话最好视为显示强化论如何谬误的反证。斯金纳还说,使言语行为强度稳定的唯一因素是由语言社团提供强化所需的条件,这话也难于找到根据(实则也没有什么意义内容)。言语行为的"强度"来源何在,目前还完全不明。强化在这里有其重大作用,可是此外起作用的还有许许多多促进性因素。就人类而言,对这些促进性因素我们所知还太少了。

就语言习得来说,强化、无意中的观察、天然的好奇心(再加上爱模仿的强烈倾向),都是重要因素。小孩会概括,会假设,会以各种非常特殊并且显然极其复杂的方式来"处理信息",这也是个重要因素。这些方式我们现在还描写不出,或者根本不懂;它也许大部分是先天得来的,或者是通过学习或神经系统逐步成熟而发展起来的。以上因素在语言学习中怎么起作用和互相感应,现在还完全不懂。在这种情况下,需要的显然是研究,而不是从类比得来的武断和完全任意做出的主张。因为,这种类比推论的来源,不过是我们偶然注意到的实验文献中的一小部分而已。

天生的生理结构,个人的成熟程度和所进行的学习,各在什么程度上成为熟练而复杂的作业的起因,大家都知道难以确定。只要想想这一点,就晓得斯金纳那些话多么没有意义。这里只要举出一个例子:一个在巢里安睡的小斑鸫,在第一阶段,有什么东西碰一下它的巢,它就把嘴张开;再往下一个阶段,如有某种体积、形状和位置的东西向它这个巢移动,它也会作出同样的反应。在这第二阶段,它的反应是向那起刺激作用的实物的一部分发出的,即它的妈妈的头。这些刺激如何合为一个复杂的整体,我们可以精密地描写出来。凭着这一点,人们就能提出个想当然的学习理论,说小斑鸫这一系列行为模式是通过差别强化过程发展出来的。训练白鼠,无疑也能产生同类的结果。可是，我们似乎有证据证明，这些随着相当复杂的"符号刺激"（sign stimuli）而作出的反应，是先天决定的，无需学习就成熟起来的。这个可能性分明存在，我们不可低估。小孩模仿新词，也可与此相比，现在让我们看着吧。最初，我们可能发现，小孩只是模仿得大致不差。再过一些时候，我们发现小孩虽然把话复述得不准确（这就是说，不是依样仿制，这本身就是一个有趣的事实），可是造成本族语语音结构的那些发音特征，小孩已把它弄成非常复杂的型式，一一说出来了。这里人们同样可以想当然地说，凭着给强化所需的条件做出周密的安排，可以获得这一结果。可是，小孩能从复杂的听觉输入中选出那合乎语音系统的特征，这种能力也许主要不是靠强化发展起来，而是靠先天决定的成熟过程得来的。如果这样看不错的话，那么要说明行为如何发展，行为的原因是什么，却又不考虑生物机体本身的结构，就不能说明行为的实际过程是怎样的了。

　　人们常常说，小孩在什么语言社团里生活，就说那个社团的语言，所以决定语言习得的特征的头等重要因素一定是经验，而不是以某些方式处理信息的天生能力。可是这种说法是很肤浅的。如果我们只是从事推测，我们不妨设想，人们的脑子现在已经演化到这样一个程度，只要若干被观察到的汉语句子输入，它就（用分明是惊人地复杂而且突然的"归纳法"）创造出汉语语法"规则"来；只要有若干被观察到的英语句子输入，它就（也许用完全相同的归纳法）创造出英语语法规则来；只要观察到某一名称运用于某些例子，它就自动地预测，这个用法可以引申来用于与这个例子有复杂关系的其他例子。要是我们这样清楚地认识问题的话，那么这种推测就不是毫无理由或者异想天开，也不是不能进行科学研究的。现在自然还不知道有什么神经结构能按特殊方式来完成作业（虽则观察那后来做出的行为会使我们有此假设）；可是，谈到学习问题，甚至最简单的学习是由什么生理结构进行的，也还没人能查明呢。

　　把这一节的简短讨论总结起来，似乎可以说，在语言习得过程中，环境所给的"反馈"和"生物机体的独立作用"二者，到底哪个更重要，目前既没有实验例证，也没有已知的理由来让我们做出判断。

　　6. 我们现在转过来讨论斯金纳专为描写言语行为而建立的那个体系。这体系既然以"刺激"、"反应"、"强化"等等观念为基础，根据上头那几节所说，我们不妨断定，它必是含糊的，任意立论的。但是，由于本文第 1 节已经说过的原因，我想现在还必须仔细看看，只用这些观念来分析言语行为是多么不着边际，用这个体系来描写言语行为的各种事实是多么劳而无功。

让我们先研究一下"言语行为"这个术语本身吧。关于这，斯金纳所给的定义是，"由于他人的媒介而获得加强的行为"（2 页）。显而易见，这个定义太宽了。按这条定义，白鼠在迷箱里按杠，小孩刷自己的牙齿，拳击家在对手面前倒退，机工修理汽车，将无一不是言语行为。而且在这个意义上，通常所谓言语行为到底有多少还能算是"言语行为"，也大成问题。也许，像我在上头所说，只有其中一小部分可以算是"言语"，如果我们赋予"强化"这个词以实在意义的话。斯金纳后来又把定义弄得精密一点，加上了这么个规定：起强化作用的人（听话者）的有媒介作用的反应（mediating response）必须"有条件性，即正好强化那说话者的行为"（225 页，着重号是原来有的）。这个规定仍然会把上述各例包括进来，要是我们假定做实验的心理学家，刷牙小孩的父亲，与拳击家对打的人，出钱请人修汽车的人之所以能作出"起强化作用的"行为，都是由于受过适当训练的话（这样假定还可能不无道理）。另一方面，定义一改，原来能包括进去的一些言语行为，却有一大部分要被排除出去了。比方说，在过马路时，我听见有人大喊"当心汽车"，就立即跳开。很难说我这一跳（按斯金纳的说法，这是有媒介作用和强化作用的反应），是基于某些条件（即我受过训练要这样跳），跳一下是为了正好强化那说话者的行为。同样的例子极多。斯金纳说，这样把定义修改一下，"我们就把我们的题目缩小，限于传统上所说的言语范围了"（225 页），这话看来是大错特错。

［正文 7—10 部分主要批判了斯纳金对言语行为的所谓功能进行的分类，包括："触发反应"、"回声反应"、"自相反应"等。——编者注］

11. 斯金纳的描写体系中所提出的主要概念，上文已经都讨论过了。我讨论这些概念，为的是指出在斯金纳的每一个实例中，要是把他所用的术语按本义来理解，言语行为的任何侧面都没有描写出来；要是按转义来理解，这样的描写却又并不比各种传统说法强。他那些从实验心理学借用的术语，一引申起来就再也没有客观性，而是跟常用词语同样地含糊了。斯金纳只用不多几个术语来代替旧词语，这就使得许多旧词语原有的重要区别看不清了。我想，我们这样分析斯金纳的学说，能证明第 1 节所表示的观点无误，这就是说,要是把发言者和学话者本人的独立作用一笔抹杀(斯金纳认为这样做很重要,见 311—2 页),必然把斯金纳的描写体系中的一切重大意义也抹杀掉,结果只是疏略而粗陋地描写一番,以致连对最浅的问题也提不出任何答案。斯金纳所致力思考的问题,是一些过早提出,毫无解决希望的问题。还不懂言语行为的特征是什么,就要研究言语行为的原因,这是白费力气;还不大了解学到的语言是什么,就猜想语言如何学到,这也是无的放矢。

不论是语言学家、心理学家还是哲学家,谁要真的想研究言语行为,一定会很快看出,想要提出一个能规定研究范围,而所谈既非细枝末节,又非今天的认识和技术所负担得起的任务,是如何困难。斯金纳提出功能分析作为自己要解决的问题,这是心余力绌。拉施里(K.S. Lashley)在一篇有趣而又有见识的论文中①含蓄地规定了语言学家和心理学家都可以卓有成效地研究的一类问题。要弄清斯金纳所谈的那些问题,先要弄清拉施里所提的那些。拉施里看出(谁要是认真考虑有关资料都会看出),构成并说出话语(utterance)不是只把那由外界刺激和言内联想(intraverbal association)所控制的一序列反应串起来,话语的句法组织也不能由它的有形结构本身以简单方式作为直接代表。他做过许多观察,从而断定句法结构是"加于不断出现的具体行动的统一模式","考虑句子结构和其他运动序列(motor sequences)会显示……在那明白说出的序列后面还有许多整合过程(integrative process),这些过程是什么,只能从它的活动的最后结果来推断"。他还指出,想要断定在实际构成话语时有什么"选择机制",是十分困难的。

当代的语言学虽然还不能精密描写这些整合过程、外加模式和选择机制,但是至少也能把——说明这些东西的特征作为自己的任务。我们有理由设想,L 语言的语法是一种机制,它把 L 语言中的一切句子——列举,好像演绎原理把一组定理——列举那样。(在这个意义上,"语法"也包括语音。)而且,语言原理可以认为是若干种语法的形式方面的性质的研究,语法在做出了精密的表述以后,就能根据它生成某一句子的过程来提出统一的方法来定下结构描写法,从而帮助人们看清句子是怎么用的,怎么理解的。简言之,从

---

① Lashley 论文题目是《行为顺序问题》(The Problem of Serial Order in Behavior),收入杰列斯主编的《行为神经机制赫讯座谈会文集》(Jeffries, ed.), *Hixon Symposium on Celebral Mechanisms in Behavior*, New York, 1951。

正确表述出来的语法，应该能推导出外加于那构成话语的具体活动的整合过程和统一模式。具有适当形式的语法里边的规则，应该分为两类，一类是任选的，另一类是必需的。在生成句子时，只是应用那些必需规则。至于语法的任选规则，可以看做是说出某一话语时的选择机制。如何详细说明这些整合过程和选择机制不是无关紧要的问题，也不是无法研究的问题。正如拉施里所说，这种研究的结果，对心理学和神经学说来，本身就饶有兴趣。（反过来说，对这种研究说来，心理学和神经学本身也饶有兴趣。）即使研究成功了，也还不能回答与意义研究和行为原因研究有关的各个重大问题，可是它与这些问题决不会毫无关系的，而且，现在一切语言研究都要倚赖"意义泛化"(semantic generalization)这样的概念，这些概念可能是隐藏着一些复杂事物和一个特殊的推理结构，与句法学所能研究和显示的结构差不多，因此句法研究得到的结果所具有的普遍性，也许能把意义理论那些简单化研究法纠正过来。

说话者、听话者、学话者的行为，自然是语言研究的真实资料。编成一部语法，列举若干句子，使得每一个句子都能由有意义的结构描写来决定，这件事情本身还没有说明什么能成为真实的言语行为。它只不过把懂得一种语言的人能辨别什么是句子，什么不是句子，能（部分地）听懂全新的句子，以及能看出某些含糊不清之处等等的本领抽象地勾勒出来。这些本领是非常值得注意的。我们经常读到听到许许多多全新的词语序列，可是能认得出那是句子，也能了解这些句子的意思。很容易证明，我们承认并且理解为句子的那些新的言语事件，它跟我们已经熟悉的言语事件能联系起来，但是那并不是靠形式上（语义上或统计上）相似或语法框架相同。在这种情况下谈论什么"泛化"是无意义的，空洞的。我们能辨识出一个全新的语言项目是一个句子，似乎不是由于这个项目与那些已经熟悉的项目有什么简单的符合一致关系，而是由于每个人都以某种方法、某种形式把语法内在化(internalized)，从而生成句子。我们能部分地理解一个全新的句子，也是因为我们多多少少能够决定从这部语法推导出这个句子的过程。

如果我们能构造出有上述性质的若干种语法，那又怎么样呢？如果能做到这一点，我们就能试着去描写和研究说话者、听话者、学话者所做出的事情。我们必须假定，说话者和听话者已经具有语法所抽象描述的那些能力。说话者的工作是选择一组互相协调的任选规则。要是我们从语法研究知道说话者有多少选择,这些选择如要彼此协调又要有什么条件,我们就能有意义地进而研究使说话者做出选择的因素。听话者(或读者)也必须按碰到的话语来决定对方在造成话语时挑选出了哪些任选规则。必须承认,一个人怎么能这样做,这是远远超过我们现有的认识的。学会一种语言的小孩,在某种意义上是根据他所观察到的句子和不成为句子的东西(即看自己的语言社团要改哪些说法,不改哪些说法),给自己编成了一部语法。研究了一个说话者确有能力区分句子和非句子,区分意义含糊之处,等等,我们就不得不断定,这部语法是极复杂、极抽象的,也不得不断定小孩已能进行至少从形式看来是非常可观的理论建设工作。而且,这项工作的完成,时间短得惊人,多半又不管本人的智力高低如何,而且个个小孩都是这样做的。我们的学习理论,必须能说明这些事实才行。

我们说,小孩能构造出极复杂的机制来生成一组句子(其中有些是他听人说过的),成人也能立即决定(如果能够,他是怎么决定的?)某一项目是否由这生成句子的机制生成的(抽象的演绎原理的许多性质,这机制都有),——以上这种看法,人们是不易接受的。可是对于说话者、听话者学话者的所作所为,这似乎是正确的描写。如果这话对,那么我们就能预言,想直接说明说话者、听话者、学话者的真实行为而不首先了解语法如何建立,这是不会成功的。正如拉施里所指出,这部语法应该认为是说话者和听话者的行为的一个组成部分,它可以从后来做出的有形结果推想出来。一切正常的小孩都很快就能学会极复杂的大致相同的语法,这个事实让我们想到,人类大概是天生如此的,即他有天生的处理材料或"构成假说"的能力,其性质和复杂程度现在大家还不懂。研究语言结构,最后可能使我们对这个问题获得了不起的认识。现在这个问题还不能郑重地提出,可是信息处理(假说构成)系统要有个什么内装结构(built-in structure)才能在有限的时间内根据有限的资料就弄出一部语法,这个问题也许原则上是可以研究的。不管怎么样,排除说话者本身的作用只会造成一个"心灵主义"描写体系,这个体系只会把传统上的重大区别弄混。不肯研究小孩在语言学习中的个人作用,也只会把语言习得理解得很肤浅,把大量未经分析的个人作用都归入所谓"刺激泛化"。但是学习过程中一切有趣的东西其实都在这里了。如果语言研究只限于这样做,言语行为的各重要方面似乎必然是弄不清楚的。

Ibbotson & Tomasello(2018)"Evidence Rebuts Chomsky's Theory of Language Learning"选读[1]

◆ **作者简介**

迈克尔·托马塞洛[2](Michael Tomasello),美国发展与比较心理学家,德国马克普朗克进化人类学研究院联合院长,德国莱比锡大学心理学系、美国杜克大学、英国曼切斯特大学荣誉教授。托马塞洛被公认为当代最权威的发展与比较心理学家,是世界范围内少数被多学科领域认可的学术权威之一。他关于社会认知起源的先锋性研究,开启了发展心理学与灵长类认知研究的独特视角,代表作有《人类思维的自然史》(*A Natural History of Human Thinking*, 2014)。在语言发展方面,他提出了"基于使用的"语言观并进行了大量的一语习得研究,大部分研究成果可参见他的著作《构建一门语言》(*Constructing a Language*, 2003)。

Paul Ibbotson,英国公开大学发展心理学系讲师,主要研究影响儿童语言习得的心理和认知因素。

◆ **正文节选**

The idea that we have brains hardwired with a mental template for learning grammar—famously espoused by Noam Chomsky of the Massachusetts Institute of Technology—has dominated linguistics for almost half a century. Recently, though, cognitive scientists and linguists have abandoned Chomsky's "universal grammar" theory in droves because of new research examining many different languages—and the way young children learn to

---

[1] Tomasello, M. and Ibbotson, P. "Evidence Rebuts Chomsky's Theory of Language Learning." *Scientific American*, Special Edition Volume 27 Issue 3s, July 2018. First appeared online Sep 7, 2016: https://www.scientificamerican.com/article/evidence-rebuts-chomsky-s-theory-of-language-learning/.

[2] Michael-Tomasello 出处 https://www.psychologicalscience.org/observer/michael-tomasello-honored-for-influential-cooperation-research.

understand and speak the tongues of their communities. That work fails to support Chomsky's assertions.

The research suggests a radically different view, in which learning of a child's first language does not rely on an innate grammar module. Instead the new research shows that young children use various types of thinking that may not be specific to language at all—such as the ability to classify the world into categories (people or objects, for instance) and to understand the relations among things. These capabilities, coupled with a unique human ability to grasp what others intend to communicate, allow language to happen. The new findings indicate that if researchers truly want to understand how children, and others, learn languages, they need to look outside of Chomsky's theory for guidance.

This conclusion is important because the study of language plays a central role in diverse disciplines—from poetry to artificial intelligence to linguistics itself; misguided methods lead to questionable results. Further, language is used by humans in ways no animal can match; if you understand what language is, you comprehend a little bit more about human nature.

Chomsky's first version of his theory, put forward in the mid-20th century, meshed with two emerging trends in Western intellectual life. First, he posited that the languages people use to communicate in everyday life behaved like mathematically based languages of the newly emerging field of computer science. His research looked for the underlying computational structure of language and proposed a set of procedures that would create "well-formed" sentences. The revolutionary idea was that a computerlike program could produce sentences real people thought were grammatical. That program could also purportedly explain as well the way people generated their sentences. This way of talking about language resonated with many scholars eager to embrace a computational approach to ... well ... everything.

As Chomsky was developing his computational theories, he was simultaneously proposing that they were rooted in human biology. In the second half of the 20th century, it was becoming ever clearer that our unique evolutionary history was responsible for many aspects of our unique human psychology, and so the theory resonated on that level as well. His universal grammar was put forward as an innate component of the human mind—and it promised to reveal the deep biological underpinnings of the world's 6,000-plus human languages. The most powerful, not to mention the most beautiful, theories in science reveal hidden unity underneath surface diversity, and so this theory held immediate appeal.

But evidence has overtaken Chomsky's theory, which has been inching toward a slow death for years. It is dying so slowly because, as physicist Max Planck once noted, older scholars tend to hang on to the old ways: "Science progresses one funeral at a time."

In the Beginning

The earliest incarnations of universal grammar in the 1960s took the underlying structure of "standard average European" languages as their starting point—the ones spoken by most of the linguists working on them. Thus, the universal grammar program operated on chunks of language, such as noun phrases ("The nice dogs") and verb phrases ("like cats").

Fairly soon, however, linguistic comparisons among multiple languages began rolling in that did not fit with this neat schema. Some native Australian languages, such as Warlpiri, had grammatical elements scattered all over the sentence—noun and verb phrases that were not "neatly packaged" so that they could be plugged into Chomsky's universal grammar—and some sentences had no verb phrase at all.

These so-called outliers were difficult to reconcile with the universal grammar that was built on examples from European languages. Other exceptions to Chomsky's theory came from the study of "ergative" languages, such as Basque or Urdu, in which the way a sentence subject is used is very different from that in many European languages, again challenging the idea of a universal grammar.

"Noam-enclature" and the New Linguistics

Noam Chomsky took the linguistics community by storm more than 50 years ago. The idea was simple. Underlying language is a set of rules innate to every child that generates grammatical sentences from the earliest age. Chomsky set out to define those rules and how they work. Without this universal grammar, he thought, it would be impossible for a child to learn any language. In the ensuing years, Chomsky's theory has gradually been challenged by new theories asserting that language is acquired as children discern patterns in the language they hear around them.

Chomsky's Universal Grammar

Chomsky's universal grammar equipped the child with rules that worked on phrases ("the nice dogs") and rules for transforming those phrases ("Cats are liked by the nice dogs"). The theory has evolved in recent years but still retains the essential idea that children are born with the ability to make words conform to a grammatical template.

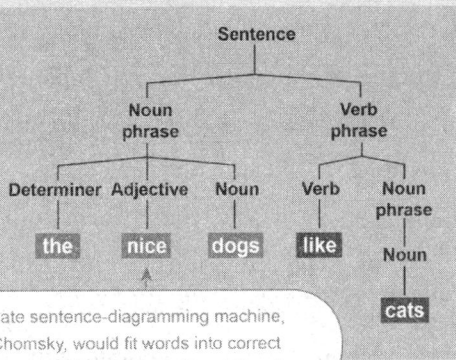

The brain's innate sentence-diagramming machine, according to Chomsky, would fit words into correct grammatical slots—"nice" (adjective), "dogs" (noun).

Usage-based Learning

New approaches to linguistics and psychology suggest that children's natural ability to intuit what others think, combined with powerful learning mechanisms in the developing brain, diminishes the need for a universal grammar. Through listening, the child learns patterns of usage that can be applied to different sentences. The word "food" might replace the word "ball" after the phrase "The dog wants." Studies show that this theory of building up knowledge of word meaning and grammar approximates the way that two- and three-year-olds actually learn language.

插图作者：Lucy ReadingIkkanda

These findings, along with theoretical linguistic work, led Chomsky and his followers to a wholesale revision of the notion of universal grammar during the 1980s. The new version of the theory, called principles and parameters, replaced a single universal grammar for all the world's languages with a set of "universal" principles governing the structure of language. These principles manifested themselves differently in each language. An analogy might be that we are all born with a basic set of tastes (sweet, sour, bitter, salty and umami) that interact with culture, history and geography to produce the present-day variations in world cuisine. The principles and parameters were a linguistic analogy to tastes. They interacted with culture (whether a child was learning Japanese or English) to produce today's variation in languages as well as defined the set of human languages that were possible.

Languages such as Spanish form fully grammatical sentences without the need for separate subjects—for example, *Tengo zapatos* ("I have shoes"), in which the person who has the shoes, "I", is indicated not by a separate word but by the "o" ending at the end of the verb. Chomsky contended that as soon as children encountered a few sentences of this type, their brains would set a switch to "on", indicating that the sentence subject should be dropped. Then they would know that they could drop the subject in all their sentences.

The "subject-drop" parameter supposedly also determined other structural features of the language. This notion of universal principles fits many European languages reasonably well. But data from non-European languages turned out not to fit the revised version of Chomsky's theory. Indeed, the research that had at tempted to identify parameters, such as the subject-drop, ultimately led to the abandonment of the second incarnation of universal grammar because of its failure to stand up to scrutiny.

More recently, in a famous paper published in *Science* in 2002, Chomsky and his coauthors described a universal grammar that included only one feature, called computational recursion (although many advocates of universal grammar still prefer to assume there are many universal principles and parameters). This new shift permitted a limited number of words and rules to be combined to make an unlimited number of sentences.

The endless possibilities exist because of the way recursion embeds a phrase *within* another phrase of the same type. For example, English can embed phrases to the right ("John hopes Mary knows Peter is lying") or embed centrally ("The dog that the cat that the boy saw chased barked"). In theory, it is possible to go on embedding these phases infinitely. In practice, understanding starts to break down when the phrases are stacked on top of one another as in these examples. Chomsky thought this breakdown was not directly related to language per se. Rather it was a limitation of human memory. More important, Chomsky proposed that this recursive ability is what sets language apart from other types of thinking such as categorization and perceiving the relations among things. He also proposed recently this ability arose from a single genetic mutation that occurred between 100,000 and 50,000 years ago.

As before, when linguists actually went looking at the variation in languages across the world, they found counterexamples to the claim that this type of recursion was an essential property of language. Some languages—the Amazonian Pirahã, for instance—seem to get by without Chomskyan recursion.

As with all linguistic theories, Chomsky's universal grammar tries to perform a balancing act. The theory has to be simple enough to be worth having. That is, it must predict some things that are not in the theory itself (otherwise it is just a list of facts). But neither can the theory be so simple that it cannot explain things it should. Take Chomsky's idea that sentences in all the world's languages have a "subject". The problem is the concept of a subject is more like a "family resemblance" of features than a neat category. About 30 different grammatical features define the characteristics of a subject. Any one language will have only a subset of these features—and the subsets often do not overlap with those of other languages.

Chomsky tried to define the components of the essential tool kit of language—the kinds of mental machinery that allow human language to happen. Where counterexamples have been found, some Chomsky defenders have responded that just be cause a language lacks a certain tool—recursion, for example—does not mean that it is not in the tool kit. In the same way, just because a culture lacks salt to season food does not mean salty is not in its basic taste repertoire. Unfortunately, this line of reasoning makes Chomsky's proposals difficult to test in practice, and in places they verge on the unfalsifiable.

Death Knells

A key flaw in Chomsky's theories is that when applied to language learning, they stipulate that young children come equipped with the capacity to form sentences using abstract grammatical rules. (The precise ones depend on which version of the theory is in voked.) Yet much research now shows that language acquisition does not take place this way. Rather young children begin by learning simple grammatical patterns; then, gradually, they intuit the rules behind them bit by bit.

Thus, young children initially speak with only concrete and simple grammatical constructions based on specific patterns of words: "Where's the X?"; "I wanna X"; "More X"; "It's an X"; "I'm X-ing it"; "Put X here"; "Mommy's X-ing it"; "Let's X it"; "Throw X"; "X gone"; "Mommy X"; "I Xed it"; "Sit on the X"; "Open X"; "X here"; "There's an X"; "X broken." Later, children combine these early patterns into more complex ones, such as "Where's the X that Mommy Xed?"

Many proponents of universal grammar accept this characterization of children's early grammatical development. But then they assume that when more complex constructions emerge, this new stage reflects the maturing of a cognitive capacity that uses universal grammar and its abstract grammatical categories and principles.

For example, most universal grammar approaches postulate that a child forms a question by following a set of rules based on grammatical categories such as "What (object) did (auxiliary) you (subject) lose (verb)?" Answer: "I (subject) lost (verb) something (object)." If this postulate is correct, then at a given developmental period children should make similar errors across all wh-question sentences alike. But children's errors do not fit this prediction. Many of them early in development make errors such as "Why he can't come?" but at the same time as they make this error—failing to put the "can't" before the "he"—they correctly form other questions with other "wh-words" and auxiliary verbs, such as the sentence "What does he want?"

Experimental studies confirm that children produce correct question sentences most often with particular wh-words and auxiliary verbs (often those with which they have most experience, such as "What does ..."), while continuing to make errors with question sentences containing other (often less frequent) combinations of wh-words and auxiliary verbs: "Why he can't come?"

The main response of universal grammarians to such findings is that children have the competence with grammar but that other factors can impede their performance and thus both hide the true nature of their grammar and get in the way of studying the "pure" grammar posited by Chomsky's linguistics. Among the factors that mask the underlying grammar, they say, include immature memory, attention and social capacities.

Yet the Chomskyan interpretation of the children's behavior is not the only possibility. Memory, attention and social abilities may not mask the true status of grammar; rather they may well be integral to building a language in the first place. For example, a recent study co-authored by one of us (Ibbotson) showed that children's ability to produce a correct irregular past tense verb—such as "Every day I fly, yesterday I flew" (not "flyed")—was associated with their ability to inhibit a tempting response that was unrelated to grammar. (For example, to say the word "moon" while looking at a picture of the sun.) Rather than memory, mental analogies, attention and reasoning about social situations getting in the way of children expressing the pure grammar of Chomskyan linguistics, those mental faculties may explain why language develops as it does.

As with the retreat from the cross-linguistic data and the tool-kit argument, the idea of performance masking competence is also pretty much unfalsifiable. Retreats to this type of claim are common in declining scientific paradigms that lack a strong empirical base—consider, for instance, Freudian psychology and Marxist interpretations of history.

Even beyond these empirical challenges to universal grammar, psycholinguists who work with children have difficulty conceiving theoretically of a process in which children start with the same algebraic grammatical rules for all languages and then proceed to figure out how a particular language—whether English or Swahili—connects with that rule scheme. Linguists call this conundrum the linking problem, and a rare systematic attempt to solve it in the context of universal grammar was made by Harvard University psychologist Steven Pinker for sentence subjects. Pinker's account, however, turned out not to agree with data from child de velopment studies or to be applicable to grammatical categories other than subjects. And so the linking problem—which should be the central problem in applying universal grammar to language learning—has never been solved or even seriously confronted.

An Alternative View

All of this leads ineluctably to the view that the notion of universal grammar is plain wrong. Of course, scientists never give up on their favorite theory, even in the face of contradictory evidence, until a reasonable alternative appears. Such an alternative, called usage-based linguistics, has now arrived. The theory, which takes a number of forms, proposes that grammatical structure is not in nate. Instead grammar is the product of history (the processes that shape how languages are passed from one generation to the next) and human psychology (the set of social and cognitive capacities that allow generations to learn a language in the first place). More important, this theory proposes that language recruits brain systems that may not have evolved specifically for that purpose and so is a different idea to Chomsky's single-gene mutation for recursion.

In the new usage-based approach (which includes ideas from functional linguistics, cognitive linguistics and construction grammar), children are not born with a universal, dedicated tool for learning grammar. Instead they inherit the mental equivalent of a Swiss Army knife: a set of general-purpose tools—such as categorization, the reading of communicative intentions, and analogy making, with which children build grammatical categories and rules from the language they hear around them.

For instance, English-speaking children understand "The cat ate the rabbit," and by analogy they also understand "The goat tickled the fairy". They generalize from hearing one example to another. After enough examples of this kind, they might even be able to guess who did what to whom in the sentence "The *gazzer* mibbed the toma," even though some of the words are literally nonsensical. The grammar must be something they discern beyond the words themselves, given that the sentences share little in common at the word level.

The meaning in language emerges through an interaction between the potential meaning of the words themselves (such as the things that the word "ate" can mean) and the meaning of the grammatical construction into which they are plugged. For example, even though "sneeze" is in the dictionary as an intransitive verb that only goes with a single actor (the one who sneezes), if one forces it into a ditransitive construction—one able to take both a direct and indirect object—the result might be "She sneezed him the napkin," in which "sneeze" is construed as an action of transfer (that is to say, she made the napkin go to him). The sentence shows that grammatical structure can make as strong a contribution to the meaning of the utterance as do the words. Contrast this idea with that of Chomsky, who argued there are levels of grammar that are free of meaning entirely.

The concept of the Swiss Army knife also explains language learning without any need to invoke two phenomena required by the universal grammar theory. One is a series of algebraic rules for combining symbols—a so-called core grammar hardwired in the brain. The second is a lexicon—a list of exceptions that cover all of the other idioms and idiosyncrasies of natural languages that must be learned. The problem with this dual-route approach is that some grammatical constructions are partially rule-based and also partially not—for example, "Him a presidential candidate?!" in which the subject "him" retains the form of a direct object but with the elements of the sentence not in the proper order. A native English speaker can generate an infinite variety of sentences using the same approach: "Her go to ballet?!" or "That guy a doctor?!" So the question becomes, are these utterances part of the core grammar or the list of exceptions? If they are not part of a core grammar, then they must be learned individually as separate items. But if children can learn these part-rule, part-exception utterances, then why can they not learn the rest of language the same way? In other words, why do they need universal grammar at all?

In fact, the idea of universal grammar contradicts evidence showing that children learn language through social interaction and gain practice using sentence constructions that have been created by linguistic communities over time. In some cases, we have good data on exactly how such learning happens. For example, relative clauses are quite common in the world's languages and often derive from a meshing of separate sentences. Thus, we might say, "My brother.... He lives over in Arkansas.... He likes to play piano." Because of various cognitive-processing mechanisms—with names such as schematization, habituation, decontextualization and automatization— these phrases evolve over long periods into a more complex construction: "My brother, who lives over in Arkansas, likes to play the piano." Or they might turn sentences such as "I pulled the door, and it shut" gradually into "I pulled the door shut."

What is more, we seem to have a species-specific ability to de code others' communicative intentions—what a speaker intends to say. For example, I could say, "She gave/bequeathed/sent/loaned/sold the library some books" but not "She donated the library some books." Recent research has shown that there are several mechanisms that lead children to constrain these types of inappropriate analogies. For example, children do not make analogies that make no sense. So they would never be tempted to say "She ate the library some books." In addition, if children hear quite often "She donated some books to the library," then this usage preempts the temptation to say "She donated the library some books."

Such constraining mechanisms vastly cut down the possible analogies a child could make to those that align the communicative intentions of the person he or she is trying to understand. We all use this kind of intention reading when we understand "Can you open the door for me?" as a request for help rather than an inquiry into door-opening abilities.

Chomsky allowed for this kind of "pragmatics"—how we use language in context—in his general theory of how language worked. Given how ambiguous language is, he had to. But he appeared to treat the role of pragmatics as peripheral to the main job of grammar. In a way, the contributions from usage-based approaches have shifted the debate in the other direction to how much pragmatics can do for language before speakers need to turn to the rules of syntax.

Usage-based theories arefar from offering a complete account of how language works. Meaningful generalizations that children make from hearing spoken sentences and phrases are not the whole story of how children construct sentences either—there are generalizations that make sense but are not grammatical (for example, "He disappeared the rabbit"). Out of all the possible meaningful yet ungrammatical generalizations children could make, they appear to make very few. The reason seems to be they are sensitive to the fact that the language community to which they belong conforms to a norm and communicates an idea in just "this way." They strike a delicate balance, though, as the language of children is both creative ("I goed to the shops") and conformative to grammatical norms ("I went to the shops"). There is much work to be done by usage-based theorists to explain how these forces interact in childhood in a way that exactly explains the path of language development.

A Look Ahead

At the time the Chomskyan paradigm was proposed, it was a radical break from the more informal approaches prevalent at the time, and it drew attention to all the cognitive complexities in volved in becoming competent at speaking and understanding language. But at the same time that theories such as Chomsky's allowed us to see new things, they also blinded us to other aspects of language. In linguistics and allied fields, many researchers are be coming ever more dissatisfied with a totally formal language approach such as universal grammar—not to mention the empirical inadequacies of the theory. Moreover, many modern researchers are also unhappy with armchair theoretical analyses, when there are large corpora of linguistic data—many now available online—that can be analyzed to test a theory.

The paradigm shift is certainly not complete, but to many it seems that a breath of fresh air has entered the field of linguistics. There are exciting new discoveries to be made by investigating the details of the world's different languages, how they are similar to and different from one another, how they change historically, and how young children acquire competence in one or more of them.

Universal grammar appears to have reached a final impasse. In its place, research on usage-based linguistics can provide a path forward for empirical studies of learning, use and historical development of the world's 6,000 languages.

Schmidt(1983)"Interaction, Acculturation, and the Acquisition of Communicative Competence: A Case Study of An Adult"选读[①]

◆ 作者简介

Richard Schmidt(1941—2017),美国夏威夷大学语言系终身荣誉教授,主要研究领域是成人二语习得及影响习得的认知和情感因素,提出的重要理论有"注意假说"。

该选文是二语习得研究中的一篇经典文献。本文以一例个案研究讨论了 acculturation model 的局限性,其调查的对象 Wes 也因作者翔实、全面的报告和其独特的语言习得情况被二语习得研究反复引用和讨论,俨然是一名二语习得研究界的"名人"。

◆ 正文节选

文章的前半部分详细描述了被调查者 Wes 各方面的语言能力,最后的一小部分是从这例个案出发对 acculturation model 的思考。在此分别做了部分的节选。——编者注

[…]

The present case study attempts to provide relevant evidence for the acculturation model by looking at the development of English ability of an adult with generally low social and psychological distance from target language speakers, acquiring English without formal instruction over a 3-year period characterized by steadily increasing interaction and communicative need. In addition, this study attempts to provide a broader and more global (though still partial) analysis of what is acquired than is usually the case, analyzing the learner's accomplishments in terms of a four-part framework

---

① Schmidt, R. 1983. "Interaction, acculturation, and the acquisition of communicative competence: A case study of an adult." In N. Wolfson and E. Judd (eds.) *Sociolinguistics and Language Acquisition*, 137 – 174. Rowley, MA: Newbury House Publishers, Inc.

of the components of communicative competence suggested by Michael Canale(forthcoming); grammatical competence, sociolinguistic competence, discourse competence, and strategic competence.

SUBJECT

The subject of this study is a 33-year-old native speaker of Japanese named Wes, who first visited the United States (Hawaii) as a tourist in late 1977 and shortly afterward decided to emigrate from Tokyo to Honolulu. His initial motivations were varied, ranging from the attractions of the climate and the relaxed way of life in Hawaii to personal ties with Japanese friends who had made the same move earlier and a general attraction to the people of Hawaii. Opportunities for professional development, initially not a factor in the decision to move to the United States, soon after became an additional major consideration. Wes is an artist, very successful in Japan, with a growing international reputation, and Honolulu is a significant international art market which proved to be an ideal location for further growth and recognition. During the period of observation, Wes spent increasing amounts of time in Hawaii—3 months in 1978, 6 months in 1979, 8 months in 1980—and finally achieved permanent resident status in early 1981.

Wes has had no significant formal instruction in English, as he left school in Japan to be apprenticed to a well-known artist at age 15, just about the time when English teaching in Japan begins in earnest. He claims to remember nothing from the limited instruction he did receive except the useless sentence, "I have five pencils in my hand," and reports that he was a poor English student. He was not a complete beginner in English when he arrived in the United States for the first time, however, as he had already developed relationships with numerous American and European art collectors in Japan, beginning about 1974. It is not clear how much of this interaction took place in English and how much in Japanese, but it is clear that when Wes first arrived in the United States his ability to communicate in English was minimal. He did not need to speak much English at first, however, as Japanese is widely spoken in Hawaii and Japanese friends could translate for him when necessary and handle any problems which arose.

The past three years have been characterized by steadily increasing demands on Wes's ability to communicate in English, and he now lives in an Englishspeaking world. An extremely friendly and outgoing person, he has a wide circle of friends and acquaintances who are monolingual English speakers, including an American roommate. Contacts with other Japanese speakers have shrunk rather than grown, and with some Japanese he will speak English if there is a monolingual English speaker present, something which he would not do and greatly disapproved of several years ago. His professional life has also required steadily increasing interaction with English speakers in a variety of situations, for while the creation of art may be a solitary act, the promotion of an artist's career is not and in fact depends nearly as much on personal and communicative qualities as on innate talent, imagination, and developed teclmique. While I have no data to defend the claim, I would estimate very roughly that something between 75 and 90 percent of all of Wes's meaningful interactions at the present time are in English.

In terms of the acculturation model for SLA, the following factors are relevant:

[作者在此讨论了 age, aptitude, length of education, social distance factors, psychological distance factors。该部分内容可大致参见表一中作者的总结。——编者注]

Table 1 Social and Psychological Distance Factors, Evaluation of Subject Characteristics, and Predicted Effects on SLA by the Acculturation Model

Social and psychological factors	Wes	Predicted influence on SLA
Age	33	Neutral if other factors positive
Formal study of L2	Insignificant	Not relevant
Language aptitude	Possibly low	Not relevant
Communicative need	High, increasing	Facilitative

续 表

Social and psychological factors	Wes	Predicted influence on SLA
Interaction, type and amount	Varied, increasing	Facilitative
Social dominance pattern	Equal	Facilitative
Social interaction pattern	Adaptive	Facilitative
Enclosure, cohesiveness	Low	Facilitative
Similarity of cultures	Different	Negative
Attitudes toward L2 group	Positive	Facilitative
Intended length of residence	Indefinite/permanent	Facilitative
Culture shock	Low	Facilitative
Language shock	Low	Facilitative
Empathy, social outreach	High	Facilitative
Inhibition, fear of appearing foolish	Low	Facilitative
Motivation type	Integrative	Facilitative
Motivation, drive for communication	Very high	Facilitative
Motivation for formal language study	Very low	Possibly negative
Preferred learning style	Natural acquisition	Facilitative

Data and Analysis

[...]

The following more detailed analysis is based primarily on 18 one-hour tape recordings concerning business and daily activities which Wes recorded in Japan and mailed to the United States on each of six trips which he made to Tokyo during the 3-year period of transition from being a Tokyo resident vacationing in Hawaii to establishing full-time permanent residence in Honolulu. The length of these visits back to Japan varied from 1 to 3 months at a time, and the amount of taped material varies from 1 to 5 hours per visit. One of the major advantages of these tapes is that they were not recorded for the purposes of linguistic analysis and consist of authentic, meaningful, and often important material, both professional and personal. A major disadvantage for the present analysis is that they are monologues. In addition, it might be suggested that Wes has a Tokyo English grammar, which emerges on each tape recorded in Japan and does not reflect changes in his developing Honolulu grammar. This does not seem to be the case, however, as Wes's grammar appears remarkably stable whether one compares early and late tapes or tapes recorded in Japan with recent, more limited recordings (3 hours total) made in Honolulu in which Wes is engaged in informal conversations with native speakers, including friends and, in one case, brand-new acquaintances. An additional source of data used in the analysis has been extensive but irregular field notes gathered by me over the entire period of observation, June 1978 to June 1981.

Grammatical Competence

In the four-component model of communicative competence proposed by Canale, grammatical competence is concerned with mastery of vocabulary and rules of word formation, sentential grammar, linguistic semantics, pronunciation, and spelling, i.e., the elements and rules of the language code itself. Because Wes does not read or write English, spelling is not an issue, and specifying his semantic system is a formidable task which I will not attempt here.

Impressionistically, Wes's pronunciation of English is good, though clearly not native. In addition to substitutions in the segmental phonology, most final consonant clusters are reduced, far more often by consonant deletion than by vowel insertion (epenthesis). Wes articulates clearly and enjoys practicing difficult words: *banana split*, *patty melt*, *Ann Margret*, and *Cheryl Ladd* are among his favorite lexical items for such practice. Intonation is noticeably better than that of the average Japanese graduate student whom I have encountered, and no doubt contributes highly to the overall impression of fluency which native speakers often report.

Proficiency in grammar is another story, as indicated in Table 2, which shows the general lack of progress in acquiring nine commonly studied grammatical morphemes.

Table 2 Accuracy Order for Nine Grammatical Morphemes in Obligatory Contexts

	July 1978	*November 1980*
1. Copula BE	Acquired, present only	No change
2. Progressive ING	Acquired(?)	No change
3. Auxiliary BE	Acquired(?)	No change
4. Past irregular	25%	55%
5. Plural	5%	43%/33%
6. 3rd singular	0%	21%
7. Article	0%	19%/6%
8. Possessive	0%	8%
9. Past regular	0%	0%

Source: First and last monologue tapes.

[...]

Sociolinguistic Competence

In Canale's framework, sociolinguistic competence has to do with the extent to which utterances are produced and understood appropriately in different sociolinguistic contexts, depending on contextual factors such as status of participants, purposes of the interaction, and norms or conventions of interaction. Appropriateness has two dimensions, meaning and form. Appropriateness of meaning concerns what one does in particular situations, what communicative functions or acts may be expressed. For example, in English one does not normally ask strangers their age, marital status, or salary on first meeting (excluding job interviews and other special interactions), though these may be acceptable first questions, social openers, in other cultures. Appropriateness of form concerns the extent to which a given communicative meaning is represented in an appropriate grammatical form and style.

A partial picture of Wes's command of English communicative functions and forms and his development in this respect over the 3-year observational period can be gained from looking in some detail at a sample of his directives, a major category of speech act (Searle 1976, Schmidt and Richards 1980). A directive is any utterance whose principal point is that it counts as an attempt on the part of the speaker to get the hearer to do something. The category thus includes orders, requests, pleas, hints, and suggestions, though these subtypes of directives may differ in the intensity of expression or other dimensions of the act.

The following are some of Wes's early directives, taken from my 1978 field notes:

1. shall we go?

2. ah, I have a Big Mac, n I have a french fries, small, and Coke, that's all.

3. can I have a banana spi..lit, please?

4. NS: you wanna go eat?

Wes: uh, what you ever like'?

NS: you mean "whatever you like"?

Wes: yes, please.

Examples 1, 2, and 3 indicate Wes's reliance from the beginning on speech-act formulas for directives. In these examples, the formulas are both topically appropriate ("shall we go?" is thoroughly idiomatic as a suggestion) and situationally appropriate ("I'll have X" and "Can I have X?" are normal restaurant patterns). The phonological distortions (*I have* for "I'll have"; occasionally *shall (w)e go?*) indicate that in some cases these formulas may not be analyzed into literal meanings and parts, but other examples such as 4, in which Wes is groping for a formula which is not yet mastered, indicate that there is some analysis into constituent parts even with idiomatic expressions.

[...]

In summary, Wes's early directives reflected a heavy reliance on a limited number of speech formulas, many of which were not available for productive use outside of the wholly fixed expressions in which they first occurred, an incorrect identification of *-ing* form with request function, a reliance on lexical clues such as *please* and *maybe*, and transfer of Japanese norms regarding both which speech acts are acceptable in particular situations (complaint example) and the linguistic strategies which are commonly used to convey such acts (hinting example).

Since I have indicated that Wes is highly motivated to engage in interaction and communication and in general has developed considerable control of the formulaic language that acts as social grease in interaction, we might expect that he would show more development over time in the area of sociolinguistic competence compared with his very limited development of grammatical competence. This is, in general, the case. By the end of the observation period, gross errors in the performance of directives had largely been eliminated: progressive forms were no longer used for directive function with any frequency, while the use of imperatives increased (*please next month send orders more quick*); "shall we?" and "let's" were used productively as patterns for a great many different requests; and in general Wes's directives showed a great deal more elaboration (*shall we maybe go out coffee now, or you want later?*; *Ok, if you have time please send two handbag, but if you're too busy, forget it*).

Appropriateness of meaning is one area in which Wes has shown clear evidence of acculturation. Although there are certainly still cases in which his messages are more appropriate by Japanese than by American norms for particular contexts (e.g., he tends to open many phone calls with an immediate *thank you* for some recent service rendered, while Americans tend to delay such thanks to later in the conversation), he is no longer reticent, for example, about expressing complaints to waiters (*excuse me, this milk is no good, sour I think*). He often comments on differences between the United States and Japan with respect to such norms of speaking. For example, in response to an item on a test of verbal routines designed by Scarcella

(1979), he noted the following difference:

> Item: Greg told his friend, Sllvia, that he would see her in the cafeteria at 12:00. Greg arrives late. He feels bad. When Greg sees Sllvia, he says, "Hi! .... "
> Wes: "Hi! I'm sorry. Somebody call." No, this is Japan need two story. Here I'm only just say "Hi, sorry, you waiting long time?"

[...]

While Wes's learning accomplishments appear on the whole better in the area of sociolinguistic than grammatical competence, this should not be overestimated. For example, he is able to a limited extent to provide alternate forms for a speech act appropriate to different addressees:

> Item: Robert is a waiter. He is taking an order. When he finishes taking the order, he checks to be sure that his customer doesn't want to order more. Robert asks his customer, "................. "
> Wes: "Would you like something more?" But home you know I'm only just say "do you want." Don't need so polite.

However, this ability is limited, and Wes does not have extensive control of different registers for talking about the same things differently in different settings or with different hearers: bodily functions, sex, and other taboo topics are discussable rather crudely or not at all. The forms of speech-act realizations, though much improved, are still far from perfect also, with the mesh between productive utilization of patterns and idiomaticity still to be realized. In fact, Wes's most productive extension of a speech-act pattern, the clearest case of creative construction arising from a decomposed formula that I can find in all the data, leads to some clearly inappropriate utterances:

    1. can I getting some more coffee? (at home, intended as request)
    2. can I have a light? ("turn on the light," not "give me a match")
    3. if you back to room, can I bring cigarette? ("please bring me")
    4. uh, can I? ("would you?")

(field notes, 1980)

[...]

Discourse Competence

Both grammatical and sociolinguistic competence, as discussed so far, deal with the learner's language at the level of the single sentence or utterance. In Canale's framework of the components of communicative competence, discourse competence concerns mastery of the ways in which grammatical forms and meanings combine to achieve unified spoken or written texts. As Wes does not write English, I will be concerned in this section only with spoken discourse. Since spoken discourse other than monologue is a cooperative effort by all parties to a conversation, I will also be dealing with *conversational* competence and what we might consider *interactional* competence.

Discourse competence seems to me to be Wes's greatest strength in his use of English, compensating to an extent for his weaknesses in other aspects of language form and use.[...]

Discourse competence is also the area in which the greatest improvement has been evidenced over time in Wes's use of English. The texture of the early tapes is choppy. [...]

Descriptions and narratives in the later tapes are, by contrast, much easier to comprehend. Increased redundancy and the use of structuring elements such as *well*, *anyway*, *so*, and *then* clearly play some part in this [...]

Wes is a good listener as well as a good talker. He is interested in people and what they have to say. He signals his comprehension of ongoing conversation frequently, using feedback signals such as *uh huh*, *I see*, *really?*, *really!*, *yeah*, *I know what you mean*, *my goodness*, as well as repetitions of fragments of his interlocutors' utterances. While many Japanese learners of English, even those with a high level of grammatical competence, retain the use of Japanese conversational fillers, accompanied in varying degrees by Japanese body language, Wes does not. His paralinguistic behavior is dramatically different depending on whether he is speaking English or Japanese.

Strategic Competence

[...]

Disucssion

Wes: I know I'm speaking funny English/because I'm never learning/I'm only just listen/then talk/but people understand/well/some people confuse/before OK/but now is little bit difficult/because many people I'm meeting only just one time/you know demonstrations everybody's first time/sometime so difficult/you know what I mean? /well/I really need English more/I really want speak more polite English/before I'm always I hate school/ but I need studying I maybe school/ I don't have time/but maybe better/ whaddya think? /I need it, right?

(monologue tape, November 1980)

Whether one considers Wes to be a good language learner or a poor language learner depends very much on one's definition of language and of the content of SLA. If language is seen as a means of initiating, maintaining, and regulating relationships and carrying on the business of living, then perhaps Wes is a good learner. If one views language as a system of elements and rules, with syntax playing a major role, then Wes is clearly a very poor learner. Friends and acquaintances who are not in the language or language teaching business generally evaluate Wes's English favorably, pointing out, for exan1ple, that "I understand him a lot better than X, who's been here over twenty years." Several sociolinguists with whom I have discussed his case have given similar evaluations, sometimes proclaiming him a superior language learner who just doesn't care about grammatical do-dads, most of which are eliminated in normal speech anyway. Grammar teachers, on the other hand, generally consider him a disaster, possibly beyond rescue. Wes's own evaluation of his English ability is mixed, recognizing both strengths and weaknesses. He is quite clearly proud of what he has accomplished and knows that he can communicate much better in English than many nonnative speakers with much greater linguistic knowledge. On one occasion Wes introduced me to some Japanese friends honeymooning in Hawaii, for whom he was acting as guide and interpreter, friends who by all appearances knew no English. Yet in subsequent encounters, with Wes not present, it turned out that the husband at least knew English quite well, had a large vocabulary, and spoke very grammatically, but was simply too shy to attempt much conversation and had some difficulty comprehending what native speakers said to him. On several different occasions I have heard Wes give impromptu English lessons to other Japanese, explaining what to say in a particular circumstance, supplying forms which were almost always wrong but which had worked for him. At the same time, Wes knows that he speaks *funny* English, that there are many things he wants to say that he can communicate only with great difficulty, that people do sometimes have a difficult time understanding him, and that his command of English is not adequate to his needs.

Wes is a different type of learner from many others with the same language background, for example, the Japanese graduate student at an American university who has studied English for many years and can write well, perhaps even at the scholarly level, but who is barely comprehensible in conversation. However, the major point of this paper is that Wes is also unlike Alberto, who lived in an Hispanic/Portuguese ghetto, Zoila, who never wanted to come to the United States, and the Vietnamese mother suffering from intense culture shock. It seems to me quite clear that Wes's failure to learn much of the grammatical component of his second language cannot be attributed to social distance factors, to lack of need for or interest in meaningful communication and interaction, to personality factors such as self-consciousness, or to poor attitudes toward target language speakers. Low social distance, positive attitudes toward the second language community, and high integrative motivation to use the second language for communication have led to a considerable increase in overall *communicative* competence but have had little effect on improved *grammatical* competence. I conclude, therefore, that the hypothesis that "the degree of acculturation toward the 'model' language group seems to be the primary consideration in attempting to account for the varied levels of *linguistic* achievement reached by second language learners" (Stauble 1978, p. 46, emphasis mine) is false.

There are, of course, a number of ways in which one might attempt to explain away or modify this conclusion. It is possible that the period of observation reported here might not be the relevant time span in which to observe the effect of social and psychological variables on SLA. The acculturation model might be relevant to explaining Wes's acquisition of a limited form of English in Tokyo, but perhaps once such a system has developed and has been perceived as adequate for a period of time it fossilizes, so that changes will not be effected simply by changes in social and psychological distance factors. Such a rationalization would explain not only Wes's case but also the case of Angela, an Italian immigrant reported on by Bruzzese (1977). Angela came to the United States when she was 37 and initially lived in an Italian neighborhood in New York. Twenty-three years later, she moved to California and integrated into an English-speaking community, but this did not result in defossilization of her very limited linguistic system. If this kind of explanation is accepted, however, it restricts the importance of the acculturation model to a very limited time span.

[...]

The factors which appear to best explain Wes's failure to acquire much grammar are therefore partly psychological, but these have less to do with social or psychological distance from target language speakers than with cognitive style, personality characteristics, and attitudes which are specifically relevant to learning the grammatical code. While the acculturation model predicts that such factors will interact with acculturation but will not dominate it (Schumann 1978b, p. 48), this appears to have happened in Wes's case.

8.3 思考和练习

1. 乔姆斯基批判斯金纳的文中(第 11 部分第 4 段)有这样一句话:"我们经常读到、听到许许多多全新的词语序列,可是能认得出那是句子,也能了解这些句子的意思。很容易证明,我们承认并且理解为句子的那些新的言语事件,它们跟我们已经熟悉的言语事件能联系起来,但是那并不是靠形式上(语义上或统计上)相似或语法框架相同。"结合你对儿童和成年人的语言习得的观察以及第二篇选文,你对这句话有什么看法?

2. 以下是一位以英语为母语的儿童 Andrew 早期语言发展阶段出现的一些词语组合(见下页)①。你认为 Andrew 在这个阶段具有什么样的语法知识?他是否已经具有创造语言的能力?请给出你的证据。(表下方的标注是 Andrew 想表达的真正含义)

---

① 资料来源:Braine, M. D. and Bowerman, M., 1976. Children's first word combinations. *Monographs of the Society for Research in Child Development*, p.7。

more car[a]	no bed	other bib	boot off	see baby
more cereal	no down[c]	other bread	light off	see pretty
more cookie	no fix	other milk	pants off	see train
more fish	no home	other pants	shirt off	
more high[b]	no mama[d]	other part	shoe off	hi Calico
more hot	no more	other piece	water off	hi mama
more juice	no pee	other pocket	off bib	hi papa
more read	no plug	other shirt		
more sing	no water	other shoe	airplane all gone	airplane by[h]
more toast	no wet[e]	other side	Calico all gone[f]	siren by
more walk			Calico all done[f]	mail come
outside more	down there		all done milk	mama come
	clock on there		all done now	what's that
all broke	up on there		all gone juice	what's this
all buttoned	hot in there		all gone outside[g]	mail man
all clean	milk in there		all gone pacifier	mail car
all done	light up there		salt all shut	our car
all dressed	fall down there			our door
all dry	kitty down there		byebye back	papa away
all fix	more down there		byebye Calico	look at this
all gone	sit down there		byebye car	pants change
all messy	cover down there		byebye papa	dry pants
all shut	other cover down there		Calico byebye	
all through	up on there some more		papa byebye	
all wet				

a "Drive around some more."
b "There's more up there."
c "Don't put me down."
d "I don't want to go to mama."
e "I'm not wet!"
f Said after the death of Calico the cat.
g Said when the door is shut: "The outside is all gone."
h "A plane is flying past."

3. 根据你对本章论及的不同的语言习得观的理解，它们对于二语教学可能有什么样的启示？

4. 一个学英语的汉语母语者可能会出现哪些正迁移（positive transfer）和负迁移（negative transfer）？学汉语的英语母语者呢？

8.4 延伸阅读

Hoff, E. 2009. *Language Development (Fourth Edition)*. Boston: Wadsworth/Cengage Learning.

Ingram, D. 1989. *First Language Acquisition: Method, Descrption and Explanation*. Cambridge: Cambridge University Press.

Locke, J. 1983. *Phonological Acquisition and Change*. New York: Academic Press.

O'Grady, W. 1997. *Syntactic Development*. Chicago: University of Chicago Press.

Ortega, L. 2009. *Understanding Second Language Acquisition*, London: Hodder Education.

Tomasello, M. 2003. *Constructing a Language: a Usage-based Theory of Language Acquisition*, Cambridge, Mass.: Harvard University Press.

第九章 语言与社会

9.1 导引

- 引言
- 变异社会语言学
- 话语分析
- 广义社会语言学

9.1.1 引言

美国语言学家乔姆斯基提出了生成语法,关注的是理想状态下的语言能力,而非语言表现。但是我们发现,在社会生活中,生成语法研究范式下的所谓的理想状态几乎不存在;真正的交际中的语言和生成语法所描摹的语法规则也相差颇多,并且这些"不合乎语法规则"的语言并不妨碍语言实现交际功能。举一个比较极端的例子,即使是牙牙学语的儿童或外语水平不高的游客,都可以用他们支离破碎的语言达到交际的目的。交际能力(communicative competence)的概念,由海默斯(Dell Hymes)在60年代提出,与乔姆斯基的"语言能力"相对立。"交际能力"强调的是,单纯用语法规则来界定语言的使用、讨论语言是否"合乎语法规则"过于片面;语言使用的"正确"与否也包含一个人在什么样的场合、对什么样的人、有什么样的交际目的时,应该说什么样的话。如果说语言存在语法规则,那么语言同时也有交际规则,这些交际规则受到语言交际发生时直接相关甚至看似不相关的各种社会因素影响,例如语言交际发生的时间地点、沟通的媒介、会话者的身份、会话者的意图等等。语言的社会属性不可否认。海默斯"交际能力"的提出深刻地影响了此后语言学研究的导向。在生成语法对理想状态下的语言研究之后,对社会的考量被重新纳入了语言学研究的体系。一部分语言学家们开始意识到:脱离了对社会的考量,我们无法准确地、全面地去把握语言现象。

广义的社会语言学研究即从这个角度出发,语言的使用乃是在社会语境下进行的。这个理论前提(premise)决定了社会语言学的研究方法和研究对象具有社会属性。从研究方法上看,社会语言学必须取材于语言在社会中的真实使用,而不能由语言学家进行臆想生造;研究的关注点也不能局限于语言的形式和表象,而应该考虑语言交际发生时的各种现实因素,比如交际参与者的情况,交际的情境等等。广义的社会语言学研究并没有系统的研究方法和具体的研究目标,它泛指的是各种具有以上理论导向的研究。以近几年社会语言学类学术期刊和会议的一些研究为例,我们可以看出社会语言学所涉及的研究话题甚广,比如:

- "后多语时代"对传统汉字书写体系带来的挑战
- 全球化时代英语作为国际通用语所发挥的重要作用
- 媒体中食物话语体呈现出的精英身份的构建
- 英国城市青少年"th"的塞音化
- 死亡话语与社会变迁的关系
- 中国高校外语教育政策

可见,广义的社会语言学研究包括城市语言调查、语言教育规划、领域语言与领域服务、语言政策与语言规划、国别语言研究、语言态度与语言认知、方言与民族语言等领域。而狭义的社会语言学研究特指兴起于美国 60 年代的变异社会语言学(Variationist Sociolinguistics)。它是社会语言学中最早形成的一个有独立体系的研究分支,也是最旗帜鲜明的一个研究分支。

9.1.2 变异社会语言学

上世纪 60 年代,美国语言学家拉波夫(William Labov)观察到人们的语音似乎和社会经济地位相关,于是他在纽约市进行了一系列的语言调查。其中最有名的调查是他在纽约市的几个百货商场进行的元音后"r"卷舌音发音情况的调查。拉波夫假装顾客向百货商场的店员问问题，诱导他们说出"the fourth floor"这个词，并偷偷记录下发音人的发音情况（第一次回答和重复答案时"r"有没有发卷舌音），以及他们的性别、年龄、职务、种族等特征。这三个商场有明显的定位差别，于是拉波夫分别用他们代表社会等级中的上等、中等和下等。调查结果显示，面向上等阶层的百货公司里使用或部分使用"r"卷舌音的售货员占该公司售货员总数的 62%，而面向中等阶层和下等阶层的百货公司的这一比例分别为 51% 和 20%。也就是说，社会经济地位越高的阶层，他的发音中的"r"卷舌音出现的比例就越高。同时他也发现，越是正式的场合（或者说越是需要注意语音准确性的场合），"r"卷舌音出现的比例也越高。本章的第一篇选文报告的就是这个研究。

9.1.2.1　研究方法

拉波夫等学者由此提出，语言是"有序的异质体"（orderly heterogeneity）。早期社会语言学研究的目的是建立语言形式与社会因素的关系，因此采取了类似社会学的定量分析方法（quantitative analysis），通过抽样（sample）收集大量的数据，最后用统计分析建立不同语言形式和不同社会因素之间的相关性（correlation）。VARBRUL、GoldVarb 或者基于 R 的 Rbrul 都是可以直接对数据进行变项规则分析的程序。

变异社会语言学的语料收集，一方面需要取自不同的语言使用者。另一方面，拉波夫发现语体也会影响语言表现（见图 9.1），因此他采用不同的方法搜集不同语体的语料，从像百货商场调查中的日常会话，到稍微正式的访谈，再到让受访者念语段或者词表。在进行访谈时，调查者要想办法让受访者能放松自在地讲话，这样才能取得比较自然的语料。拉波夫常用的一个办法是问受访者他们"死里逃生"的经历（Death Story），当受访者绘声绘色地讲起自己的一段难忘的经历的时候，通常就会忘记访谈的紧张气氛。

相较而言，后期的变异社会语言学研究采用更激进的方法去获得真实的语料。比如，民俗学研究所采用的参与观察法（participant-observer technique）让调查者可以深入到被调查对象的实际生活中，参与其言语活动，观察、搜集所需的资料。这种方法不仅可以获得大量真实的语料，而且能体验、感受到该群体的语言习惯、交际方式、文化特点等。也有一些研究采取的办法是在征得被调查对象同意的情况下，设置录音录像设备，在取得所有材料后再进行分析。

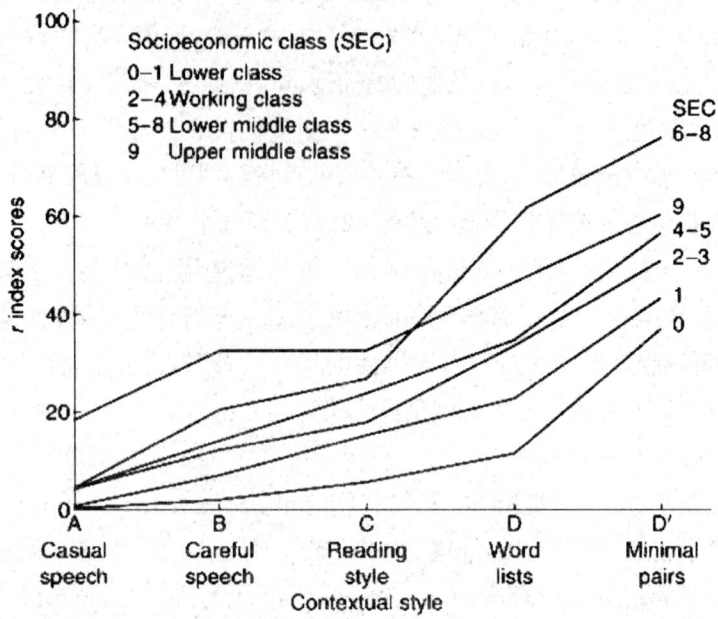

图 9.1　"r"卷舌音在纽约市不同人群的发音情况（横轴代表不同正式程度的语体）①

9.1.2.2　基本概念

在拉波夫的纽约百货商场调查中，他调查的是元音后的"r"是否发卷舌音。这里的"r"就是变异社会语言学中的语言变项（linguistic variable），也就是会随着社会情境改变表达情况的语言单元；而"r"发音与否就是语言变式（variant），一个人可能在不同的社会情境会表达出不同的语言变式。"r"在美国的社会语言学研究中是一个比较有效的语言变项，此外还有比如 dog 和 caught 的元音"o"，thin 和 three 的"th"。在英国较常出现的语言变项有：现在分词-ing 韵尾是发-in 还是-ing，词尾的 t/d 如 bet 是否发音。在汉语中，中国北方较为明显的语言变项则是儿化音的使用。本章选取的另一篇选文考察的就是儿化音的社会意义。此外，声调的高低、词汇和句型的使用，都可以是语言变项。

变异社会语言学的研究发现，语言变式的出现与分布除了和使用语言的

---

① Wardhaugh, R. & Fuller, Janet M. 2015. *An Introduction to Sociolinguistics* (*Seventh Edition*). Chichester, West Sussex, UK；Malden, MA, USA：Wiley Blackwell. p.174.

场合有关系以外,也与受调查者的社会属性有关系。因此,拉波夫的调查也包括与语言使用相关的社会变项(social variable),如社会阶层、年龄、性别、种族等,并且他主要将职业、学历、住宅的价格作为划分社会阶层的标准。

关于两者为何会具备这种相关性,拉波夫的理论是,一个社会的中上阶层定义着语言的"标准"形式。他们所使用的语言变式具有"显威望"(overt prestige),使得中上以下阶层的人们模仿学习,最终导致社会的语言整体向"显威望"语言形式的方向发展。这种变化常常是从中下阶层,特别是从他们中的女性开始的。但在正式的场合,无论男性或女性总是力图向文雅高贵的标准形式看齐。简而言之,中上阶层所使用的语言变式被当作具有标记社会属性的标记物(marker)使用。

9.1.2.3 三个浪潮

反观变异社会语言学的发展脉络,后世学者认为变异社会语言学的发展经历了三个浪潮。第一个浪潮以拉波夫在纽约市的研究为代表,其研究结果指向社会变项与语言变项的关系。其它著名的研究包括 Shuy 和 Wolfram 60 年代在美国底特律的调查(其中的一个语言变项是双重否定),以及特鲁吉尔(Peter Trudgill)在英国诺里奇城(Norwich)的调查。特鲁吉尔的研究发现,工人阶级的年轻男性语言并不是向中上阶层的语言形式靠拢,反而是增加了社会较底层的非标准语言形式的使用。特鲁吉尔认为非标准的语言形式具有"隐威望"(covert prestige),它的使用表明工人对自己所处团体的认同。

社会阶层是第一个浪潮研究中的核心概念,但是对如何定义社会阶层却存在明显的分歧。一种观点认为,人在社会中是多面的;一个人在社会生活的不同方面,可能会故意表现出与其所属社会阶层不相符的特征。在这种情况下,用社会阶层来和语言形式做相关性研究是否可靠?另一种质疑则是,即使我们假设拉波夫的研究中,社会阶层的确可以通过经济水平和社会地位两个因素来界定,在其它类型的社会和社区里,这种界定的方法是否仍然适用?是否可以直接复制?

变异社会语言学的第二个浪潮是以米尔罗伊夫妇——Leslie Milroy 和 James Milroy——为代表的"社会网络"(social networks)模型。英国社会语言学家 Leslie Milroy 在 1975 年至 1977 年间花了近两年的时间对贝尔法斯特市(Belfast)三个工人居住区的居民的语言状况进行了观察调查。她首先深入到一些家庭的生活中,成为他们的朋友,然后通过这些家庭的关系网络,接触这个社区更多的人。通过这次调查，Milroy 发现人们使用语言变项的情况和社区的紧密程度有关。一个人与社区的关系越紧密，使用当地的语言特征就越多；一个内部关系越紧密的社区，人们总体表现的当地语言特征就越多。Milroy 认为，社区是由社会关系网络所维系的；一个内部关系紧密的社交网络是维护当地方言的重要社会机制，它能有效地抵御由中上阶层主导、被广泛社会认可的语言规则。因此，社会关系网络是一个研究语言传播的模型，它能用于解释语言维持和变化的现象。

第三个浪潮则反映于近期的研究中，更注重语言变异在说话者身份构建中发挥的作用。如果说前两个浪潮将研究重点放在语言如何反映社会属性上，第三个浪潮的研究则试图表明语言如何构建身份认同。美国华人学者 Zhang Qing 就曾研究过中国都市白领"雅皮士"如何使用港台腔进行身份构建，北京的"京油子"又如何有意地使用儿化音等"京腔京调"来呈现自己的"京油子"人格面具 (persona)（见本章选文）。在第三个浪潮的研究中，学者们反对用社会阶层对个体的社会属性进行简单化地一维归类，反而认为一个人的社会属性可能是多面的；并且个体的社会属性亦非静态的、一成不变的，而是可以进行主观改造的。除了对生活方式、消费方式的选择，语言也是一个进行身份构建的有力工具。在方法上，第三个浪潮的研究不仅搜集语言变量，也搜集其它能够帮助其实现社会或风格目的的语言材料，同时更注重说话者的行为。

上述变异社会语言学三个浪潮的发展，每一个新的浪潮都是在前一次浪潮的基础上产生的。新的浪潮并未宣告前一次浪潮的终止，三者之间是互为补充、相互促进的关系。

9.1.3　话语分析

话语分析 (discourse analysis) 是社会语言学的另一种主要的研究思路。它与变异社会语言学最大的区别在于，语料不再是个别单词的发音，或者某个语法结构的呈现，而是一个语篇语段，或者是多个语篇语段的呈现。话语分析研究的是作为交际行为的语言，因此也需要考虑交际双方的关系，了解该言语社区内部的一些交际规则以及交际发生时的更广的社会语境。就分析手段而言，话语分析更倾向于采用定性分析 (qualitative analysis) 的方法。

9.1.3.1 会话分析

会话分析(conversation analysis, CA, 以下简称 CA)是一个具有鲜明特点以及系统性的研究方法,通常被认为是话语分析方法的一种。会话分析 20 世纪 60 年代诞生于美国,其主要的架构者包括萨克斯(Harvey Sacks)、施格洛夫(Emanuel Schegloff)和杰佛逊(Gail Jefferson)。关于会话分析,施格洛夫有一句名言:"言谈应对是人类社会性初始之地"(Talk-in-interaction is the primordial site of human sociality)。社会得以运行、文化得以传播、身份得以构建、社会结构得以产生,全都有赖于会话来实现。CA 认为会话比文本更能体现人类语言交际的真相,而且只有在自然情况下发生的会话才具有真实性;由于观察者悖论(the observer's paradox)的存在,通过采访、观察和实验手段获得的会话都被 CA 研究者认为是不真实、不自然的。因此 CA 的研究材料必须是日常生活中自然发生的真实会话,研究者一般对会话进行录音或者录像,然后对会话进行转写(transcribe)。CA 的分析都是在转写的基础上进行的。转写的内容不仅包括会话参与者的语言内容,也包括停顿、重叠、插话、言语打断、音量的高低、音节的拖长等伴语言资源(paralinguistic features),甚至包括眼神、手势、肢体等交际行为动作。CA 认为,人类的言谈应对通常都是发生在具体的语境下,是交际者在具体的语境下进行交流的产物;因此,交际发生的时间和地点,交际者的性别、身份等都是影响交际者构建自己的话轮和理解对方话轮的重要因素,这些也是必须记录下来的内容。

CA 的一个基本理论假设是,言谈应对像任何一种社会行为一样,是有组织有结构的,具有一定的序列组织(sequence organization)。任何一个话语都与前后的话语具有序列方面的相关性;每一个话语都要受到前面话语的影响和制约。举例来说,如果前面的话语是个问题的话,那么接下来的话语应该是对前面问题的回答,而当下一个话语并没有对前面的问题做出回答,这就是值得探讨的问题了。又比如,正常情况下,会话的参与者会轮流参与会话,每个人有自己的话轮(turn),并且几乎不会出现重叠的现象;但一旦出现了话轮转换(turn-taking)的问题,那就是值得研究的现象。

较诸其它的社会语言学研究,CA 具有高度的实用价值。通过研究特定交际情境下的会话,CA 可以发现交际出现问题的症结所在,并提出如何改善交际的做法。到目前为止,CA 在医患对话、课堂教学、语言治疗、客服热线等领域均有成功运用。

9.1.3.2 批判话语分析

批判话语分析(critical discourse analysis, CDA, 以下简称 CDA)是话语分析的另一个重要的流派。CDA 并没有系统的研究方法；准确的说，它是一种看待话语的社会作用的视角，其理论基础可以追溯到福柯(Foucault)的话语权力观。CDA 最有影响力的研究来自费尔克劳(Norman Fairclough)、Teun A. van Dijk 和 Ruth Wodak，他们主要的论点包括：社会群体相互之间的关系是通过话语构建的，话语可以固化，也可以改变这种关系；话语的使用可以反映群体之间的关系；控制话语的群体可以通过话语影响受众的意识形态和行为，这种操纵话语的行为的实质是一种霸权(hegemony)。例如，美国种族歧视的形成、欧洲国粹主义的兴起、不同社会对女性的歧视等等，都可以从这种视角加以解释。

CDA 的研究对象是一切的话语，包括文本和言谈(text and talk)。CDA 研究的出发点是语言，但是落脚点是社会关系和权力结构，因此在研究时会从四个不同的层面的去考量话语的语境(context)，包括(1) 某个说法或者观点的上下文，(2) 该文本或言谈与其它相关文本的关联性，(3) 话语发出的具体社会语境，比如是谁发出的，在什么场合发出的，(4) 话语所处的历史语境和社会政治语境等宏观的语境。

CDA 的研究方法更灵活地吸取了语言学研究的各家之长。除了细致的文本分析以外，也有定量和定性的分析方法。比如，从语用学的角度分析竞选中的政治口号的使用；利用语料库语言学(Corpus Linguistics)的基本方法(比如共现、频率等)，佐证欧洲难民危机中媒体如何通过把难民比作"洪水"引导舆论。

9.1.4 广义社会语言学

广义的社会语言学研究的对象，是语言在社会生活各个方面的使用情况。研究者通过对语言情况进行描述、思考，适当地提出建议。可以说，社会语言学是具有社会服务使命的语言学分支。

9.1.4.1 语言政策与语言规划

当前，全球化和现代化进程深刻地改变了语言使用的面貌。一方面，人口迁移以前所未有的规模发生，出现了新的语言接触；另一方面，沟通的需求使区域内产生强势语言，挤压了其它语言的生存空间。语言规划和语言政策的研究就是针对这些现象进行分析,提出应对的政策。以下是《Routledge全球社会语言学手册》中10个国家和地区社会语言学研究的关键词,从中可以看出,语言规划和语言政策是广泛关注的研究话题。

表9.1　10个国家和地区社会语言学研究关键词①

洲别	国别或地区	研究关键词
北美	美国	美国非裔英语、多语制、语言变异
	加拿大	移民语言、城市语言研究、英法语言接触、语言变异
亚洲	新加坡、马来西亚、印尼、菲律宾	认同、语言选择与语言转用、语言使用、语言多样性、华语、新英语
	伊朗	借词、语言选择、转用式双言制
大洋洲	澳大利亚	认同、语言濒危、移民语言、语言转用
	新西兰	变异社会语言学
非洲	南非	语码转换、语言转用、语言濒危、语言变异、认同、多语制与语言接触
	中东和北非	语码转换、双言制、语言转用、语言使用、变异社会语言学
欧洲	不列颠群岛	双语、语码选择、比较社会语言学、语言接触、语言变异
	俄联邦诸国	语言态度、语言接触、语言濒危、语言复兴、语言转用、语言意识形态、官方语言、少数民族语言

其中,移民国家(比如美加澳新)面临的问题是如何妥善处理官方语言和移民的本族语言的关系,在推进多元文化的同时,是否应该推进多语政策以及如何推进多语政策。在多民族国家(比如南非和前苏联诸国),官方语言渗透到了生活的方方面面,少数民族语言的使用范围缩小,有些甚至已经到了濒临消亡的边缘;在实行双言制的中东和北非国家,双言制能否长期维持、应该如何维持,也是个值得关注的问题。总体来讲,如何兼顾语言的流通性和多样性,是目前各个国家普遍需要处理的问题。

---

① 来源:郭熙、祝晓宏,2016,《语言生活研究十年》,《语言战略研究》1(3):24—33。

我国的语言使用情况面临的情况更为复杂，因此更需要语言规划与语言政策研究的指导。对内，中国是一个多民族国家，并且按照民族志（Ethnologue）的分法，境内现存的语言有 299 种，其中有 32 种濒临灭亡。在推广普通话和汉字作为流通文字的时候，一个急迫的议题就是：我们应该如何做好汉语方言和少数民族语言的保护工作？如果我们已面临一些语言的逐渐消亡，我们能否及时地进行记录及保护，甚至开始语言复兴的工程？对外，中国作为一个积极参与全球化进程的国家，也需要制定好国内的外语教育政策以及海外的汉语教育项目，培养足够多的外语人才，才能保证"一带一路"等国际合作倡议能顺利开展。所有这些语言规划及语言政策的制定，都必须基于对语言使用事实的调查研究，因此就需要研究者们用具有科学性的语言学方法进行描述，才可能提出具有参考性的建议。

9.1.4.2 语言生活

"语言生活"是中国特色的社会语言学的一个关键词，它体现了我国从国家层面对社会语言的高度关注，这种关注即使在世界范围内也是少有的。"语言生活"指的是运用、学习和研究语言文字、语言知识和语言技术的各种活动。教育部语言文字信息管理司从 2006 年开始每年出版《中国语言生活报告》，有计划地报道各领域（如教育、行政、媒体、医疗卫生、商贸等）以及各民族地区的语言生活状况，呈现语言生活热点、反映语言生活的问题。同时，我国也成立了多个语言资源监测与研究中心，对平面媒体、有声媒体、网络媒体及教材语言进行统计分析，每年公布高频网络新词、媒体新词等；另也设有机构通过网络来获取数据，分析研判网络舆情，及早预警和发现语言矛盾。

语言既是实现社会交际的工具，也是一面反映社会的棱镜。研究社会中的语言是我们了解所处社会的另一种手段。

9.2 选读

- Labov (1972) "The Social Stratification of (r) in New York City Department Stores" 选读
- 鲍明炜 (1980)《六十年来南京方音向普通话靠拢情况的考察》选读

● Zhang (2008)"Rhotacization and the 'Beijing Smooth Operator': The social meaning of a linguistic variable"选读

Labov(1972)"The Social Stratification of (r) in New York City Department Stores"选读①

◆ **作者简介**

拉波夫②(William Labov, 1927—),美国语言学家,宾夕法尼亚大学终身荣誉教授,变异社会语言学派的创始人,主要研究社会语言学、语言变化和方言。拉波夫是第一个把社会学的变量和定量分析方法引入应用到语言学研究的人。他的主要著作有《语言变化原理》(*Principles of Language Change*),分"内部因素"和"社会因素"两辑(1994,2001),以及合著《北美英语地图集:语音、音系及语音变化》(*Atlas of North American English: Phonetics, Phonology, and Sound Change*)。

◆ **正文全文**

Anyone who begins to study language in its social context immediately encounters the classic methodological problem: the means used to gather the data interfere with the data to be gathered. The primary means of obtaining a large body of reliable data on the speech of one person is the individual tape-recorded interview. Interview speech is formal speech—not by any absolute measure, but by comparison with the vernacular of everyday life. On the whole, the interview is public speech—monitored and controlled in response to the presence of an outside observer. But even within that defini-

---

① Labov, W. 1972. "The social stratification of (r) in New York City department stores." In *Sociolinguistic Patterns*, pp. 43 - 54. Philadelphia, PA: University of Pennsylvania Press.

② 图片来源:https://www.altalang.com/beyond-words/2016/03/11/7-questions-linguist-william-labov-false-idols-language/。

tion, the investigator may wonder if the responses in a tape-recorded interview are not a special product of the interaction between the interviewer and the subject. One way of controlling for this is to study the subject in his own natural social context—interacting with his family or peer group (Labov, Cohen, Robins, and Lewis 1968). Another way is to observe the public use of language in everyday life apart from any interview situation to see how people use language in context when there is no explicit observation. This chapter is an account of the systematic use of rapid and anonymous observations in a study of the sociolinguistic structure of the speech community.①

This chapter deals primarily with the sociolinguistic study of New York City. The main base for that study (Labov 1966) was a secondary random sample of the Lower East Side. But before the systematic study was carried out, there was an extensive series of preliminary investigations. These included 70 individual interviews and a great many anonymous observations in public places. These preliminary studies led to the definition of the major phonological variables which were to be studied, including (r): the presence or absence of consonantal [r] in postvocalic position in *car*, *card*, *four*, *fourth*, etc. This particular variable appeared to be extraordinarily sensitive to any measure of social or stylistic stratification. On the basis of the exploratory interviews, it seemed possible to carry out an empirical test of two general notions: first, that the linguistic variable (r) is a social differentiator in all levels of New York City speech, and second, that rapid and anonymous speech events could be used as the basis for a systematic study of language. The study of (r) in New York City department stores which I will report here was conducted in November 1962 as a test of these ideas.

We can hardly consider the social distribution of language in New York City without encountering the pattern of social stratification which pervades

---

① I am indebted to Frank Anshen and Marvin Maverick Harris for reference to illuminating replications of this study (Allen 1968, Harris 1968).

the life of the city. This concept is analyzed in some detail in the major study of the Lower East Side; here we may briefly consider the definition given by Bernard Barber: social stratification is the product of social differentiation and social evaluation (1957:1 - 3). The use of this term does not imply any specific type of class or caste, but simply that the normal workings of society have produced systematic differences between certain institutions or people, and that these differentiated forms have been ranked in status or prestige by general agreement.

We begin with the general hypothesis suggested by exploratory interviews: *if any two subgroups of New York City speakers are ranked in a scale of social stratification, then they will be ranked in the same order by their differential use of (r).*

It would be easy to test this hypothesis by comparing occupational groups, which are among the most important indexes of social stratification. We could, for example, take a group of lawyers, a group of file clerks, and a group of janitors. But this would hardly go beyond the indications of the exploratory interviews, and such an extreme example of differentiation would not provide a very exacting test of the hypothesis. It should be possible to show that the hypothesis is so general, and the differential use of (r) pervades New York City so thoroughly, that fine social differences will be reflected in the index as well as gross ones.

It therefore seemed best to construct a very severe test by finding a subtle case of stratification within a single occupational group: in this case, the sales people of large department stores in Manhattan. If we select three large department stores, from the top, middle, and bottom of the price and fashion scale, we can expect that the customers will be socially stratified. Would we expect the sales people to show a comparable stratification? Such a position would depend upon two correlations: between the status ranking of the stores and the ranking of parallel jobs in the three stores; and between the jobs and the behavior of the persons who hold those jobs. These are not unreasonable assumptions. C. Wright Mills points out that salesgirls in large department stores tend to borrow prestige from their customers, or at least make an effort in that direction.① It appears that a person's own occupation is more closely correlated with his linguistic behavior—for those working actively—than any other single social characteristic. The evidence presented here indicates that the stores are objectively differentiated in a fixed order, and that jobs in these stores are evaluated by employees in that order. Since the product of social differentiation and evaluation, no matter how minor, is social stratification of the employees in the three stores, the hypothesis will predict the following result: salespeople in the highest ranked store will have the highest values of (r); those in the middle-ranked store will have intermediate values of (r); and those in the lowest-ranked store will show the lowest values. If this result holds true, the hypothesis will have received confirmation in proportion to the severity of the test.

The three stores which were selected are Saks Fifth Avenue, Macy's, and S. Klein. The differential ranking of these stores may be illustrated in many ways. Their locations are one important point:

Highest-ranking: Saks Fifth Avenue
    at 50th St and 5th Ave., near the center of the high fashion shopping district, along with other high-prestige stores such as Bonwit Teller, Henri Bendel, Lord and Taylor

---

① C. Wright Mills, *White Collar* (New York: Oxford University Press, 1956), p. 173. See also p. 243: 'The tendency of white-collar people to borrow status from higher elements is so strong that it has carried over to all social contacts and features of the workplace. Salespeople in department stores...frequently attempt, although often unsuccessfully, to borrow prestige from their contact with customers, and to cash it in among work colleagues as well as friends off the job. In the big city the girl who works on 34th Street cannot successfully claim as much prestige as the one who works on Fifth Avenue or 57th Street.'

Middle-ranking: Macy's

Herald Square, 34th St and Sixth Ave., near the garment district, along with Gimbels and Saks-34th St, other middle-range stores in price and prestige.

Lowest-ranking: S. Klein

Union Square, 14th St and Broadway, not far from the Lower East Side.

The advertising and price policies of the stores are very clearly stratified. Perhaps no other element of class behavior is so sharply differentiated in New York City as that of the newspaper which people read; many surveys have shown that the *Daily News* is the paper read first and foremost by working-class people, while the *New York Times* draws its readership from the middle-class.[①] These two newspapers were examined for the advertising copy in October 24 – 27, 1962: Saks and Macy's advertised in the *New York Times*, where Kleins was represented only by a very small item; in the *News*, however, Saks does not appear at all, while both Macy's and Kleins are heavy advertisers.

No. of pages of advertising October 24 – 27, 1962

	NY Times	Daily News
Saks	2	0
Macy's	2	15
S. Klein	1/4	10

We may also consider the prices of the goods advertised during those four days. Since Saks usually does not list prices, we can only compare

---

① This statement is fully confirmed by answers to a question on newspaper readership in the Mobilization for Youth Survey of the Lower East Side. The readership of the *Daily News and Daily Mirror* (now defunct) on the one hand, and the *New York Times* and *Herald Tribune* (now defunct) on the other hand is almost complementary in distribution by social class.

prices for all three stores on one item: women's coats. Saks: $90, Macy's: $79.95, Kleins: $23. On four items, we can compare Kleins and Macy's:

	Macy's	S. Klein
dresses	$14.95	$5.00
girls' coats	$16.99	$12.00
stockings	$0.89	$0.45
men's suits	$49.95 – $64.95	$26.00 – $66.00

　　The emphasis on prices is also different. Saks either does not mention prices, or buries the figure in small type at the foot of the page. Macy's features the prices in large type, but often adds the slogan, 'You get more than low prices.' Kleins, on the other hand, is often content to let the prices speak for themselves. The form of the prices is also different: Saks gives prices in round figures, such as $120; Macy's always shows a few cents off the dollar: $49.95; Kleins usually prices its goods in round numbers, and adds the retail price which is always much higher, and shown in Macy's style: '$23.00, marked down from $49.95.'

　　The physical plant of the stores also serves to differentiate them. Saks is the most spacious, especially on the upper floors, with the least amount of goods displayed. Many of the floors are carpeted, and on some of them, a receptionist is stationed to greet the customers. Kleins, at the other extreme, is a maze of annexes, sloping concrete floors, low ceilings; it has the maximum amount of goods displayed at the least possible expense.

　　The principal stratifying effect upon the employees is the prestige of the store, and the working conditions. Wages do not stratify the employees in the same order. On the contrary, there is every indication that high-prestige stores such as Saks paylower wages than Macy's.

　　Saks is a non-union store, and the general wage structure is not a matter of public record. However, conversations with a number of men and women who have worked in New York department stores, including Saks and Macy's, show general agreement on the direction of the wage differential.① Some of the incidents reflect a willingness of sales people to accept much lower wages from the store with greater prestige. The executives of the prestige stores pay a great deal of attention to employee relations, and take many unusual measures to ensure that the sales people feel that they share in the general prestige of the store.② One of the Lower East Side informants who worked at Saks was chiefly impressed with the fact that she could buy Saks clothes at a 25 percent discount. A similar concession from a lower prestige store would have been of little interest to her.

From the point of view of Macy's employees, a job in Kleins is well below the horizon. Working conditions and wages are generally considered to be worse, and the prestige of Kleins is very low indeed. As we will see, the ethnic composition of the store employees reflects these differences quite accurately.

A socioeconomic index which ranked New Yorkers on occupation would show the employees of the three stores at the same level; an income scale would probably find Macy's employees somewhat higher than the others;

---

① Macy's sales employees are represented by a strong labor union, while Saks is not unionized. One former Macy's employee considered it a matter of common knowledge that Saks wages were lower than Macy's, and that the prestige of the store helped to maintain its nonunion position. Bonuses and other increments are said to enter into the picture. It appears that it is more difficult for a young girl to get a job at Saks than at Macy's. Thus Saks has more leeway in hiring policies, and the tendency of the store officials to select girls who speak in a certain way will play a part in the stratification of language, as well as the adjustment made by the employees to their situation. Both influences converge to produce stratification.

② A former Macy's employee told me of an incident that occurred shortly before Christmas several years ago. As she was shopping in Lord and Taylor's, she saw the president of the company making the rounds of every aisle and shaking hands with every employee. When she told her fellow employees at Macy's about this scene, the most common remark was, 'How else do you get someone to work for that kind of money?' One can say that not only do the employees of higher-status stores borrow prestige from their employer—it is also deliberately loaned to them.

education is the only objective scale which might differentiate the groups in the same order as the prestige of the stores, though there is no evidence on this point. However, the working conditions of sales jobs in the three stores stratify them in the order: Saks, Macy's, Kleins; the prestige of the stores leads to a social evaluation of these jobs in the same order. Thus the two aspects of social stratification—differentiation and evaluation—are to be seen in the relations of the three stores and their employees.

The normal approach to a survey of department-store employees requires that one enumerate the sales people of each store, draw random samples in each store, make appointments to speak with each employee at home, interview the respondents, then segregate the native New Yorkers, analyze and resample the non-respondents, and so on. This is an expensive and time-consuming procedure, but for most purposes there is no short cut which will give accurate and reliable results. In this case, a simpler method which relies upon the extreme generality of the linguistic behavior of the subjects was used to gather a very limited type of data. This method is dependent upon the systematic sampling of casual and anonymous speech events. Applied in a poorly defined environment, such a method is open to many biases and it would be difficult to say what population had been studied. In this case, our population is well-defined as the sales people (or more generally, any employee whose speech might be heard by a customer) in three specific stores at a specific time. The result will be a view of the role that speech would play in the overall social imprint of the employees upon the customer. It is surprising that this simple and economical approach achieves results with a high degree of consistency and regularity, and allows us to test the original hypothesis in a number of subtle ways.

THE METHOD

The application of the study of casual and anonymous speech events to the department store situation was relatively simple. The interviewer approached the informant in the role of a customer asking for directions to a particular department. The department was one which was located on the fourth floor. When the interviewer asked, 'Excuse me, where are the women's shoes?' the answer would normally be, 'Fourth floor.'

The interviewer then leaned forward and said, 'Excuse me?' He would usually then obtain another utterance, '*Fourth floor*,' spoken in careful style under emphatic stress.①

The interviewer would then move along the aisle of the store to a point immediately beyond the informant's view, and make a written note of the data. The following independent variables were included:

the store
floor within the store②
sex
age (estimated in units of five years)
occupation (floorwalker, sales, cashier, stock boy)
race
foreign or regional accent, if any

The dependent variable is the use of (r) in four occurrences:

casual: fou<u>r</u>th floo<u>r</u>
emphatic: *fou<u>r</u>th floo<u>r</u>*

Thus we have preconsonantal and final position, in both casual and emphatic styles of speech. In addition, all other uses of (r) by the informant were noted, from remarks overheard or contained in the interview. For each plainly constricted value of the variable, (r-1) was entered; for uncon-

---

① The interviewer in all cases was myself. I was dressed in middleclass style, with, white shirt and tie, and used my normal pronunciation as a college-educated native of New Jersey (r-pronouncing).
② Notes were also made on the department in which the employee was located, but the numbers for individual departments are not large enough to allow comparison.

structed schwa, lengthened vowel, or no representation, (r - 0) was entered. Doubtful cases or partial constriction were symbolized d and were not used in the final tabulation.

Also noted were instances of affricates or stops used in the word fourth for the final consonant, and any other examples of nonstandard (th) variants used by the speaker.

This method of interviewing was applied in each aisle on the floor as many times as possible before the spacing of the informants became so close that it was noticed that the same question had been asked before. Each floor of the store was investigated in the same way. On the fourth floor, the form of the question was necessarily different:

'Excuse me, what floor is this?'

Following this method, 68 interviews were obtained in Saks, 125 in Macy's, and 71 in Kleins. Total interviewing time for the 264 subjects was approximately 6.5 hours.

At this point, we might consider the nature of these 264 interviews in more general terms. They were speech events which had entirely different social significance for the two participants. As far as the informant was concerned, the exchange was a normal salesman-customer interaction, almost below the level of conscious attention, in which relations of the speakers were so casual an anonymous that they may hardly have been said to have met. This tenuous relationship was the minimum intrusion upon the behavior of the subject; language and the use of language never appeared at all.

From the point of view of the interviewer, the exchange was a systematic elicitation of the exact forms required, in the desired context, the desired order, and with the desired contrast of style.

OVERALL STRATIFICATION OF (r)

The results of the study showed clear and consistent stratification of (r) in the three stores. In Figure 13.1, the use of (r) by employees of Saks, Macy's and Kleins is compared by means of a bar graph. Since the data for most informants consist of only four items, we will not use a continuous numerical index for (r), but rather divide all informants into three categories.

all (r-1): those whose records show only (r-1) and no (r-0)
some (r-1): those whose records show at least one (r-1) and one (r-0)
no (r-1): those whose records showed only (r-0)

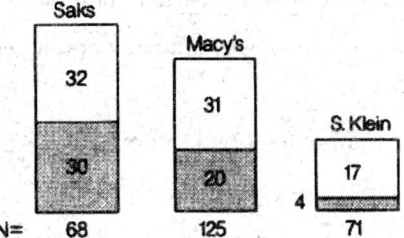

Figure 13.1　Overall stratification of (r) by store. Shaded area= % all (r-1); unshanded area= % some (r-1); % no (r-1) not shown. N = total number of cases

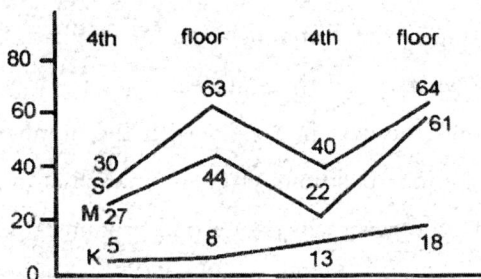

Figure 13.2　Percentage of all (r-1) by store for four positions
(S= Saks, M = Macy's, K = Kleins)

From Figure 13.1 we see that a total of 62 percent of Saks employees, 51 percent of Macy's, and 20 percent of Kleins used all or some (r-1). The stratification is even sharper for the percentages of all (r-1). As the hypothesis predicted, the groups are ranked by their differential use of (r-1) in the same order as their stratification by extralinguistic factors.

Next, we may wish to examine the distribution of (r) in each of the four standard positions. Figure 13.2 shows this type of display, where once again, the stores are differentiated in the same order, and for each position. There is a considerable difference between Macy's and Kleins at each position, but the difference between Macy's and Saks varies. In emphatic pronunciation of the final (r), Macy's employees come very close to the mark set by Saks. It would seem that r-pronunciation is the norm at which a majority of Macy employees aim, yet not the one they use most often. In Saks, we see a shift between casual and emphatic pronunciation, but it is much less marked. In other words, Saks employees have more *security* in a linguistic sense.

The fact that the figures for (r-1) at Kleins are low should not obscure the fact that Kleins employees also participate in the same pattern of stylistic variation of (r) as the other stores. The percentage of r-pronunciation rises at Kleins from 5 to 18 percent as the context becomes more emphatic: a much greater rise in percentage than in the other stores, and a more regular increase as well. It will be important to bear in mind that this attitude—that (r-1) is the most appropriate pronunciation for emphatic speech—is shared by at least some speakers in all three stores.

Table 13.1 shows the data in detail, with the number of instances obtained for each of the four positions of (r), for each store. It may be noted that the number of occurrences in the second pronunciation of *four* is considerably reduced, primarily as a result of some speakers' tendency to answer a second time, 'Fourth.'

Table 13.1 Detailed distribution of (r) by store and word position

(r)	Saks		Macy's		S.Klein	
	Casual 4th floor	Emphatic 4th floor	Casual 4th floor	Emphatic 4th floor	Casual 4th floor	Emphatic 4th floor
(r-1)	17 31	16 21	33 48	13 31	3 5	6 7
(r-0)	39 18	24 12	81 62	48 20	63 59	40 33

(r)	Saks		Macy's		S.Klein	
	Casual 4th floor	Emphatic 4th floor	Casual 4th floor	Emphatic 4th floor	Casual 4th floor	Emphatic 4th floor
d	4　5	4　4	0　3	1　0	1　1	3　3
No data*	8/68　14/68	24/68　31/68	11/125　12/125	63/125　74/125	4/71　6/71	22/71　28/71
Total no.						

* The 'no data' category for Macy's shows relatively high values under the emphatic category. This discrepancy is due to the fact that the procedure for requesting repetition was not standardized in the investigation of the ground floor at Macy's, and values for emphatic response were not regularly obtained. The effects of this loss are checked in Table 13.2, where only complete responses are compared.

Since the numbers in the fourth position are somewhat smaller than the second, it might be suspected that those who use [r] in Saks and Macy's tend to give fuller responses, thus giving rise to a spurious impression of increase in (r) values in those positions. We can check this point by comparing only those who gave a complete response. Their responses can be symbolized by a four-digit number, representing the pronunciation in each of the four positionsrespectively (see Table 13.2).

Thus we see that the pattern of differential ranking in the use of (r) is preserved in this subgroup of complete responses, and omission of the final 'floor' by some respondents was not a factor in this pattern.

Table 13.2   Distribution of (r) for complete responses

(r)					% of total responses in		
					Saks	Macy's	S.Klein
All(r-1)	1	1	1	1	24	22	6
Some(r-1)	0	1	1	1	46	37	12
	0	0	1	1			
	0	1	0	1 etc.			
No(r-1)	0	0	0	0	30/100	41/100	82/100
N=					33	48	34

鲍明炜(1980)《六十年来南京方音向普通话靠拢情况的考察》选读[①]

◆ **作者简介**

鲍明炜(1919—2007),著名语言学家,南京大学文学院教授,1946年于国立中央大学(现南京大学)文学院毕业后后留校任教,曾任江苏省语言学会会长、南京大学语言与语言工程研究中心主任。

鲍明炜主要致力于汉语方言学、音韵学、现代汉语普通话等领域的研究,著有《唐代诗文韵部研究》《初唐诗文的韵系》《南京方言中几个问题的调查》《六朝金陵吴语辩》《江淮方言的特点》《江苏省·方言志》(主编)等论著。

《六十年来南京方音向普通话靠拢情况的考察》一文报告了20世纪80年代在中国南京进行的方言语音调查,是继20年代高本汉、赵元任,50年代作者本人之后对南京方言进行的第四次系统语音调查。虽然这篇文章并未采用变异社会语言学的社会学研究方法,但通过代际之间的语音变化,再把现今的调查和早前的结果进行对比,从"显像时间"(apparent time)和"真实时间"(real time)两个维度展示了南京方音的变化。另外值得注意的是,作者在这篇文章中并未只针对某一语音变量进行考察,而是按照汉语音韵系统的实际情况以及南京方言的特色对某几个韵进行考察。这两方面的做法都非常值得借鉴。

◆ **正文节选**

一 引 言

南京话属汉语北方方言系统中江淮次方言。南京是江淮地区政治、经济、文化的中心。由于人们的频繁交往,南京话对江淮各地方言有很大的影响,各地方言对南京话的变化也起了不小的作用。因此,南京话在江淮次方言中居于中心地位。

大半个世纪以来,南京人口常有剧烈的变动,二十年代只有三十多万人,三十年代已接近百万,抗日战争时期曾大量减少,建国初期又增至一百五十万左右,现在拥有二百五十万人。人口的变动,自然带来语言的交流和发展。

[①] 鲍明炜,《六十年来南京方音向普通话靠拢情况的考察》,《中国语文》,1980年第4期。

南京人口增加的来源主要是苏北和皖北。南京居民中，世代居住南京的只占很少一部分，老南京话处在被包围的状态之中，深受外地话（主要是苏北话和皖北话）的影响，时刻起着变化。建国以来，由于大力推广普通话，南京话向普通话靠拢的速度是很快的。

六十年来，对南京话有过几次调查研究，比较有价值的有三次。第一次是瑞典高本汉《方言字汇》《中国音韵学研究》第4卷第8章），共记音二千一百二十五个单字，出版于1926年，调查当在二十年代以前。第二次是赵元任《南京音系》（《科学》杂志13卷8期，1929年），根据的材料是1907年至1927年间作者的调查记录。第三次是1957年的方言普查（以下称普查），调查报告的主要部分收进《江苏省和上海市方言概况》一书中。另外还有一次，是我在1957年和同学们一起进行的专题调查，从《南京音系》提出的南京话的派别和特点出发，在市区分三十八个点进行了比较全面的调查，以观察自《南京音系》以来三四十年间南京音系的发展变化，调查报告见《南京方音中几个问题的调查》（《方言与普通话集刊》第8本，1961年）。这次调查是继上次之后又作一次类似的调查，以观察这二十多年来南京话新的发展变化。从高本汉和赵元任在本世纪初对南京所作的调查以来，至今约六十年。六十年来，随着社会的发展，南京话发生了急剧的变化。不需要很久，老南京话将归于消失。在老南京话的消亡过程中，分阶段作几次调查研究，比较详细地了解语言的各种要素的发生、发展和消亡的过程是有意义的。

以往几次调查的规模和深度各不相同。高本汉的《方言字汇》记录了三千多字的读音，用严式音标记音，在《中国音韵学研究》译本中又经译者的校正，但没归纳出声韵系统，看不出声韵配合的关系。赵元任的调查是很精细的，用严式音标，并归纳出声韵系统和声韵配合的关系。高、赵两次调查时间距离很近，调查结果也接近，这两次调查可作为一次看待。普查是比较全面的，除了语音，还有词汇。至于1957年的专题调查，其特点是调查点多，能了解南京音的概貌。

这次调查仍限于语音。记音用国际音标。南京话有五个声调：阴平˩31、阳平˩13、上声˩22、去声˥44、入声˥5。调类分配，除入声外，和普通话相同。记音一般不标调，要知调值，按调类补入即可。本该附列南京话声韵调系统，也省去了，读者可参看《南京音系》与《江苏省和上海市方言概况》。

二 调查方法

（一）调查内容：仍用1957年专题调查的十类例字，以便前后比较，此外又加了一些读音有些特殊的字。

（二）调查对象：这次调查是1957年专题调查的继续，目的在于了解南京话的现状，以便与前两次调查结果相比较，观察南京话向普通话靠拢的情况。这次调查的对象以出生在南京的青少年为主，因为他们说的话才足以代表今天南京话的面貌。青少年中有的世代居住南京，有的父母（或其一）是外地人（这种情况比前者多得多），这种不同情况，在调查时都问明，分别对待。还能说老南京话的老年人也附带调查了一些，看他们的话和以往是否有什么变化，在多大程度上还能保持老南京话的特点，他们之间有什么共同点和差异。这些差异是不是在不知不觉中又向普通话靠拢了。在调查时特别强调平时怎么说就怎么读字音，不要有意多说老南京话或普通话。另外还特意调查了几家世代居住南京的父子、父女和祖孙三代的语言情况，以观察在同一家庭中两代人或三代人所说的南京话的异同和发展。从小生长在父母身边的子女，一般跟父母（当然也跟社会）学说话并且学得很好（若父母来自外地说外地话，自是例外），但是说老南京话的父母对其子女的语言能有多大影响呢？这是一个具有一般语言学意义的问题。人们从小学习其本民族的语言，如果家庭语言环境和社会语言环境不同，家庭给他的影响大，还是社会给他的影响大？这是一个值得注意、值得深入调查的问题。

这次还调查了几个其父母说不同于南京话的北方方言的青少年，看他们接受父母口语的影响有多大，从而了解外地方言（包括普通话）怎样影响老南京话。两个语言或方言一旦发生接触，在什么情况下二者互相影响，互相渗透，在什么情况下一个战胜另一个，其相互消长的过程怎么样。这也是具有一般语言学意义的问题。

（三）调查点的分布：这次调查以城区为主，比较着重南部中华门内外和水西门内外。北部的调查点也不少，但是地区广大，实际上比南部少。郊区更少，最远的是浦镇。不能再远了，再远就和江宁、江浦、六合各郊县相混了，例如"跃"字，浦镇有人读 z_o 去声，这是六合音。

三 专题考察

（一）n、l 的分混：《南京音系》说："l 母略带鼻音，碰到 i、y 音时几乎变成 n 音。"普查报告说："n、l 不分，n 和 l 可以任意互换。总的来说，用 l 的时候比较多。"这次调查和上次基本相同,仍分三种情况,有的全是 l,有的全是 n,有的混用,l 占优势。南京话的 n、l 是一个音位,可以任意互换,甚至一个人可以一会儿读 n,一会儿读 l,自己并不感到不同,在与 i、y 拼时,既像 n,又像 l,实际上是一种很软的略带鼻音的舌尖音。这个音外地人很难模仿,但南京儿童(不管其家庭语言环境如何)则学得很好。据说这个声母的发音可以作为辨别真假南京人的标准,非常有效。这次调查发现有一个中学生因受家庭语言环境的影响,能正确辨别"拿"和"拉"、"耐"和"赖"、"脑"和"老"、"南"和"兰"、"农"和"龙"、"尼"和"离"、"女"和"吕"的声母,但是"牛"和"流"、"娘"和"良"、"怒"和"路"、"内"和"类"的声母仍不能辨别,"内"和"类"都读为 n 母,其余全是 l 母。另有一个十七岁的中学生能辨别"拿"和"拉"、"脑"和"老"、"南"和"兰"、"尼"和"离"、"牛"和"流"、"娘"和"良"的声母,但"耐"和"赖"、"农"和"龙"、"怒"和"路"、"内"和"类"、"女"和"吕"的声母仍不能辨别,"女和吕"都读 n 母,其余全读 l 母。这种情况在中年以上的人中没有发现,在青少年中为数也很少。既然是在青少年中才开始有这种现象,应是一种新的发展趋势。相信调查更多的人,可以证实这一点。再过几年这种趋势将更明显。六十年来,南京话这个音位没有很显著的变化。

(二) 尖团音的分混:早期的调查报告一致认为南京话分尖团音。老南京话确实分尖团,如"齐 tsʻi、旗 tɕʻi","尖 tsē、肩 tɕiē","浅 tsʻē、遣 tɕʻiē"。普查报告说分三派:第一派全分尖团,第二派多数不分,第三派完全不分;青少年多数不分尖团,这是主流。上次专题调查的结果是:城内南部老年人几乎全部能分,中年以下几乎全部不分。这次调查结果,已经全部不分尖团音了,这和上次调查的结果是相符合的。二十多年以前的老年人,现在多已去世;现在的老年人,二十多年以前正是中年人,符合"中年以下几乎全部不分"的情况。六十年来,南京话的尖音读法消失了,全部读为团音:齐=旗 tɕʻi、尖=肩 tɕiē、浅=遣 tɕʻiē。

(三) a、ai 两韵的开齐问题:老南京话有些人把 a、ai 两韵在 tʂ、tʂʻ、ʂ 声母后的开口字和在 tɕ、tɕʻ、ɕ 声母后的齐齿字的读音混同了,一律读成 tʂ、tʂʻ、ʂ 的开口,如"渣、家"tʂɒ,"叉、卡"tʂʻɒ,"沙、虾"ʂɒ,"斋、街"tʂɛ,"筛、蟹"ʂɛ。上次调查结果,个别老年人还保持这种读法,中年人已渐不能保持,青年人则已无此种读法,与普通话相同。普查报告以青年人为准,不存在这个问题。这次调查仍有两三位老年人保持这种读法,但他们的读法并不相同,如"家、揸、虾"三字有的读为 tʂɒ、tʂʻɒ、ʂɒ（"揸"字韵母是 ɒ，前进了一步），有的读为 tʂa、tʂʻa、ʂa，有的读为 tɕia、tɕʻia、ɕia（"家"字读音已向普通话靠拢），内部很不一致。还有的人一字两读，如"架" tʂa、tɕia，"下" ʂa、ɕia，逐步向普通话靠拢。看来"家"这类字音的演变过程是 tʂɒ→tʂa→tɕia。我们注意到这类字音的保持者，他们的子女并没有继承这种读法（读音），他们说："我们学不来。"这种读音将随着老年人的死亡而归于消失。六十年来，南京话的这个特点已濒于消失，大约再过二十年将不复存在。

（四）撮口韵的有无：南京话无撮口韵，是突出的特点。人们一提起南京话，总是和"吃鱼"说成"吃姨"联系起来。其实有无撮口韵是南京话的内部分歧，并非全无撮口韵。高本汉和赵元任的调查和普查报告，都记录南京话有撮口韵。上次调查结果是：有人撮口韵很完全，有人全无撮口韵，有人撮口韵不完全，总的说有撮口韵的人少，无撮口韵的人多。这次调查仍是上述三种情况，不同的是：无撮口韵和撮口韵不完全的各只有三人，其中有两人是二十一岁，其余都是中年以上的人。在调查的四十一人当中，有撮口韵的占绝大多数。二十年间形势完全反转过来，有撮口韵的人在数量上大大超过无撮口韵的人，向普通话靠近了一大步。照此发展下去，再过二十年，南京话向有撮口韵转变将基本完成。

（五）ɒ 韵的读法：六十年前，南京话的 ɒ 韵很完全，普通话的 a 韵字，南京话都是 ɒ 韵。普查报告和上次专题调查都说：老年人还读 ɒ，中年人不稳定，有的读 ɒ，有的读 a，青年人全读 a。这时 ɒ 韵是整齐的，要读 ɒ，全读 ɒ，同一个人很少兼读 ɒ 和 a。这次调查，ɒ 韵基本上没有了，只有一位老年人还保留在"家 tʂɒ、插 tʂʻɒ、虾 ʂɒ"等字中，其他"巴、马、法、他"等字没有人读成 ɒ 韵。这说明 ɒ 韵已不像以前那样整齐，只残存在几个特殊的字中。二十年前在老年人中 ɒ 韵还占优势，现在随着老年人的死亡，基本上已为 a 韵所取代，中年以下则已无 ɒ 的痕迹了。

（六）e 韵的读法：南京话的 e 韵也是著名的方言特点。普通话读齐齿韵 ie、ian 的字，南京话读开口韵 e，如"爹 te、且 tsʻe、些 se、边 pē、天 tʻē、连 lē"。上次调查结果是：老年人中年人大体保持 e 韵读法，青年人已大见混乱，出入于 e、ie 之间，但居住老南京话区的青年人，e 韵的读法还比较稳固。总之，e 比 ɒ 稳固得多。这次调查的四十一人当中，有四位老年人还保持 e 韵，有七人不完全，其中有四人只个别字还读 e 韵，如"爹 te、别 pe、灭 me"等字，其他绝大多数人已无 e 韵读法,都读同普通话的 ie、ian 了。二十年间 e 韵的变化不小,现在青少年已不再学说这个音,六十年来的发展,e 韵已是强弩之末。

(七) e、ai 两韵的分混:普通话 tʂ、tʂʻ、ʂ 后 ɤ、ai 两韵的字,如"遮、车、奢"和"斋、差(出差)、筛",南京话的读音有分有合。赵元任的记音分两类,高本汉的记音有分有合,普查报告合为一类,"遮"类并入"斋"类。上次专题调查认为大体是分的,可记作 e、ɛ,但两类之间界限不清,各人分法不同,也有人完全不分,并且 e 的读法不稳定,开始向普通话靠拢。这次调查表明大部分是分的,特别是青少年清清楚楚分为 ə、ɛ 两类。只有少数老年人混为一类,还有一些老南京话区的青年人也混为一类,但不甚彻底,一般是"车、扯"读为 tʂʻə 不混,"奢、舍"读为 ʂə,易混。

这个问题实际上是"遮"类字读音的问题,目前读 ə 或 ɛ 不稳定,现在只有小部分人保持这种状态,提请他们略加注意是可以克服的。但是应当指出南京话这个韵音还有一定的稳固性。

(八) 鼻音韵尾的读法:南京话的鼻音韵尾有三种: -ã、-n、-ŋ,和普通话比较,an 和 aŋ 不分,班 = 帮 pã,ən 和 əŋ 不分,分 = 风 fən 或 fəŋ;in 和 iŋ 不分,金 = 经 tɕin 或 tɕiŋ。关于南京话这几个鼻音韵尾,以前的报告都有分析,可以参看,这里不细说。

以前的调查都表明南京话不分前后鼻音韵尾,我们上次的专题调查三十八人当中能够区分的只有一人。这次不同了,四十一人当中有一半能区分 an 和 aŋ 的,这是一个非常可喜的变化,把一类字音区分为两类是不容易的。能区分的多是青少年,不能区分的多是老年人。至于 ən 和 əŋ、in 和 iŋ 现在还不能区分,但已经有少数青少年开始能分辨了,这是一个很好的开始。可以肯定十年二十年以后将有很大的发展。

(九) 其他一些字音:这次调查增加几组南京话读音有些特殊的字,这些字的改读情况可以反映南京话向普通话靠拢的动态,例如"师、士、事"等字,南京话本来读 sɿ,现在已有不少青少年读 ʂʅ。"歌、可、何"等字南京话本来读 ko、kʻo、xo,现在已有不少人读 kə、kʻə、xə,又如"去"字,南京话原读 kʻi,这是南京方言特点之一,现在已基本上都读 tɕʻy,四十一人当中,三人读 tɕʻi,三人读 tɕʻy、kʻi 两读,其余全读 tɕʻy。有一位老年人读 tɕʻy、tɕʻi 两音,他说:"说白了读 kʻi"说明他在口语中还常说成 kʻi,但是已经注意要改说 tɕʻy 了。但是这类字的读音目前改变还不够大,习惯势力还很强,例如"徐"字,南京话读

tɕ‘y 或 tsʻy 或 tɕ‘i，现在小学生读课文时念 ɕy，但一开书本还是说 tɕ‘y（不说 tsʻy, tɕ‘i）。其他"祥、鼠、纯、唇"诸字的读音还在相当剧烈地演变中。对于这几类字来说，在南京话向普通话靠拢的过程中，目前还处在很不稳定的阶段。

四 老南京话与新南京话

经过几十年的发展演变，沿着向普通话靠拢的道路，在老南京话的基础上形成了新南京话，并且已经取得了支配地位，这就是今天在中年以下，特别是青少年中间说的南京话。新南京话保留了旧南京话声韵调的主要部分，按照向普通话靠拢的要求，抛弃了方言性特强的一部分，如尖音并于团音，从 i 韵分出 y 韵，以 ɑ 韵取代 ɒ 韵，以及其他一些特殊的字音。其他区别于普通话的一些特点，如 n、l 不分，an 和 aŋ、ən 和 əŋ、in 和 iŋ 不分，以及仍保留入声调。新南京话还不是普通话，是由老南京话到普通话的一种过渡形式，它将有一定的稳定性。

五 南京话的发展趋势

从《南京音系》的调查至 1957 年方言普查，这三四十年间可分为两个阶段。建国以前是前期，在这个时期中，南京话是自然地向前发展，外路话影响着老南京话，但是老南京话还能自成系统，固守住城南一隅。这一时期发展是缓慢的。建国以后是后期，这一时期原来主要说老南京话的家庭妇女和老年人大多参加工作以及其他社会活动，由于广泛的交际活动，老南京话的最后阵地保不住了。南京开始明确地向普通话靠拢，前进的速度比前一阶段快得多。

1957 年以后，由于普通话的推广，老南京话的特点越来越小。现在，有些在南京出生的青少年甚至已能够分辨 n 和 l、i 和 y、an 和 aŋ 了，只有为数很少的老年人还能说程度不同的老南京话。

残存的老南京话内部不统一，水西门一带的话和夫子庙一带的话就不一样，一个字往往有几种读法。例如：

ₛ寻　ts‘in、ts‘yen、tɕyen、tɕ‘in、sin、suen、ɕyen

ₛ靴　ɕie、ɕy（＝虚）、ɕiē、ɕyē（＝宜）、suei、sie、ɕye

屑ₒ　sue、sye、se、ɕi、ɕie、ɕye、ɕyo

ₒ纯　ʂuen、ʂen、suen、ts‘en、tsʻuen、tʂʻuen

ₒ唇　ʂuen、ʂen、suen、tsʻen、tsʻuen、tɕʻuen、tʂʻuen

ₒ家　tʂɒ、tʂɑ、tɕin、tɕiɑ

₍全 ts'yē、tɕie、tɕye、tɕ'yē

₍元 iē、ye、yē

去° k'i、tɕ'i、tɕ'y

₍给 ki、tɕi、kei

每字最后一个音是现在南京话最普通的读法,除调值以外,和普通话基本相同。一字多音是现阶段南京话的一个特色,这种情况是其他方言少见的。这是南京话在各地方言的包围下交互融合的结果。这种现象很值得进一步调查研究,以观察语音演变的规律。

每一个汉语方言都向普通话集中。由于近几十年来南京人口变动大,南京话受普通话和外地话的影响十分明显,老南京话处于比较急速的变动之中。六十年来,南京话的演变过程是:首先向苏北皖北话靠拢,建国以后向普通话靠拢。由于几方面的交互影响,以致发生读音混乱的现象。这次调查的单音字表中很大一部分是每人一个样,二十多个字,各人读音竟如此不同,在汉语方言中也是罕见的。我们调查了几个长辈还说老南京话的家庭,其子女继承老南京话特点的一个也没有。老南京话已是后继无人。

六 调查记录

[略]

Zhang(2008)"Rhotacization and the 'Beijing Smooth Operator': The social meaning of a linguistic variable"选读[①]

◆ 作者简介

Zhang Qing,美国德州大学奥斯汀校区人类学助理教授,斯坦福大学博士毕业。他的主要研究领域是国际化和社会变迁中语言的构建作用,发表过多篇调查北京都市白领的社会语言学现象的文章。

汉语语言学在过去普遍把儿化音当作一个词素形态层面的语言现象进行研究,而作者却认为儿化音是具有社会标记功能的语言变项。这篇文章无

---

① Zhang, Q. 2008. "Rhotacization and the 'Beijing Smooth Operator': The social meaning of a linguistic variable 1." *Journal of Sociolinguistics*, 12(2), pp.201-222.

论是在方法上还是在视角上都具有社会语言学第三个浪潮研究的典型特征，包括强调定性分析、注重受访者内省等等，并且创新地加入了文学作品作为分析材料的一部分。文章结构分明、行文清晰、论证严谨，值得仔细研读。

◆ 正文节选

1. INTRODUCTION

In recent years, an outpouring of studies have examined linguistic variation as a resource for the construction of identities and styles (e.g. Bucholtz 1996; Coupland 2001a; Eckert 2000; Eckert and Rickford 2001; Schilling-Estes 1998). This focus is part of a broader move in sociolinguistics, particularly variationist sociolinguistics, to adopt practice-based approaches to the study of linguistic variation (e.g. Eckert and McConnell-Ginet 1992). Compared with earlier variationist studies, this strand of research pays more attention to speaker agency and the ways in which social meanings are constructed through deployment of linguistic and other semiotic resources. These studies demonstrate that speakers often draw on pre-existing linguistic resources that are already imbued with social meanings through their association with a social group or character type. When these linguistic features are used to construct a different style or persona, their existent meanings are transformed. Hence, the employment of a pre-existing linguistic element in a new context, or what Bauman and Briggs (1990) call 'recontextualization', is a transformational process wherein new meaning emerges. Although much focus has been on investigating the emergent meanings of linguistic features, more work is needed from sociolinguists to explore the imbued meanings that the recontextualized element brings with it. A better understanding of imbued meanings helps to address a crucial question in the study of style and social meaning: how do linguistic resources become available for appropriation by new groups?

Thus, the main concern of this article is to explore the meanings and sociocultural associations imbued in a salient linguistic feature that make it amenable to stylistic work. Specifically, this article examines rhotacization in Beijing Mandarin, a locally salient sociolinguistic variable. The questions to be addressed are: (1) how does rhotacization take on social saliency and consequently semiotic potential to do stylistic work? and (2) what are the social meanings and associations that this feature carries with it? This empirical investigation draws on insights from the recent work of Agha (2003) on the historical development of the cultural value of Received Pronunciation and those of Johnstone and her associates on the social history of 'Pittsburghese' (Johnstone, Andrus and Danielson 2006; Johnstone, Bhasin and Wittkofski 2002). The goal of this study is to contribute to the ongoing efforts in developing 'a coherent theory of the social meaning of variables' (Eckert 2004: 41).

2. THE SIGNIFICANCE OF IMBUED SOCIAL MEANING

The present study builds on insights from recent sociolinguistic research on the use of linguistic resources in the construction of identities, styles, and personae (Bell 1999, 2001; Bucholtz 1996, 2001; Cameron 2000; Chun 2007; Coupland 2001a, 2001b; Eckert 2000; Mendoza-Denton 2007; Podesva 2007; Schilling-Estes 1998, 2004; Q. Zhang 2005; studies in the *Journal of Sociolinguistics* 1999 special issue on styling). Treating styles and personae as dynamic and motivated semiotic processes, these studies elucidate how social meanings emerge in situated discursive practices, or 'the situated face of meaning' in Eckert and McConnell-Ginet's (1992: 474) terms. In addition, many of the studies cited above attest to a tendency among speakers to draw on a limited set of such resources that are already imbued with social meanings. However, not much attention has been devoted to investigating what the meanings are.

Employing linguistic resources with imbued meanings is a key strategy in Bell's (1984, 2001) conceptualization of initiative style in his audience design framework. As illustrated in his studies of New Zealand television commercials (Bell 1992, 1999), the language varieties and features used in the advertisements are saturated with meanings through their associations with salient social groups and cultural stereotypes. Such meanings and sociocultural associations constitute the indexical potential for these resources to carry out new stylistic work in the advertisements. Similarly, salient dialect features and repertoires of Welsh English with conventionalized meanings are deployed in the stylized performance by two Welsh radio presenters examined in Coupland (2001a). The reworking of existing resources for new purposes in these cases points to what Bakhtin (1981) refers to as the dialogic orientation of language, which both Bell and Coupland draw on in their work on styles (e.g. Bell 2001; Coupland 2001a). According to Bakhtin's (1981: 293) notion of 'dialogism,' language 'lives a socially charged life' and carries tastes of its past uses and users. The Bakhtinian dialogic view of language has profound implications for investigating social meaning beyond the immediate context. As Ochs (1992: 383) notes, '[p]art of the meaning of any utterance (spoken and written) is its social history, its social presence, and its social future.' Bauman and Briggs (1990) operationalize Bakhtin's rather abstract notion of dialogism in terms of decontextualization and recontextualization, two aspects of a transformational process wherein readymade discourse is extracted from one context and fitted into another (Bauman 1996: 301). As Bauman and Briggs (1990: 75) point out, '[b]ecause the process is transformational, we must now determine what the recontextualized text brings with it from its earlier context(s) and what emergent form, function, and meaning it is given as it is recentered.' Sociolinguistic studies on style tend to focus on the transformed, emergent aspect of social meaning. As linguistic features and styles bear traces of their past uses and users real and imagined (Irvine 1996: 151), the sociocultural associations that they bring from their 'socially charged life' (Bakhtin 1981: 293) constitute potential for, aswell as constraints on, their uses in the present and future contexts. Hence, it is important for analysts to explore the meanings imbued in a linguistic feature that make it available for stylistic work.

Particularly relevant to the case presented in this article is work by Agha (2003) and Johnstone, Andrus and Danielson (2006). Agha (2003) traces the 'enregisterment' processes whereby the Received Pronunciation has taken on a specific scheme of cultural values linked to correctness and a prestigious social status. Whereas Agha (2003) examines the historical emergence of a supralocal variety, Johnstone, Andrus and Danielson (2006) explore that of a named local variety, 'Pittsburghese'. Using multiple methods, including historical research, ethnography, discourses analysis, and sociolinguistic interviews, Johnstone, Andrus and Danielson (2006) reveal the historical and ideological processes through which a set of linguistic features have come to take on meanings of localness and to be enregistered as 'Pittsburghese'.

The empirical case investigated in this article is rhotacization, a sociolinguistic variable in Beijing Mandarin. Although the scope of this study is smaller than that of Agha (2003) and Johnstone, Andrus and Danielson (2006), by focusing on one dialect feature, the present investigation explicates how rhotacization takes on semiotic saliency and builds it meaning potential. Before presenting the data and analysis, I provide a brief description of the feature under study.

3. A BRIEF DESCRIPTION OF RHOTACIZATION

[...]

4. DATA AND METHODOLOGICAL CONSIDERATIONS

The analysis to be presented is based largely on data drawn from selected sources in standard written Chinese. They are complemented with a small amount of spoken data—metalinguistic commentaries—from audio recorded sociolinguistic interviews conducted during my fieldwork in 1997—1998 for the study of the linguistic practice of business professionals in Beijing (Q. Zhang 2001). The metalinguistic commentaries from the interviews are included in this study because they provide folk perceptions of the saliency of rhotacization and its sociocultural associations. These commentaries constitute supplementary evidence of the link between the linguistic feature of Beijing speech and social attributes of Beijingers. This association is valorized in other metapragmatic practices, as demonstrated by the written data drawn from two sources: (1) novels and literary works categorized as *jing wei wenxue* 'Beijing-flavor literature,' particularly *jing wei xiaoshuo* 'Beijing-flavor novel'; *and* (2) literary criticisms of Beijing-flavor literature. A list of the literary works and literary criticisms on which the analysis of this study is based is provided in the Appendix.

[...]

5. RHOTACIZATION: SEMIOTIC SALIENCY AND IMBUED MEANINGS

In what follows, I first examine uses of rhotacization in literary works and writings of literary scholars to show how it has come to take on the semiotic saliency of an emblem representing an 'authentic' Beijing style (section 5.1). Second, I examine data from Beijing-flavor literature and explicit metapragmatic discourse from sociolinguistic interviews and writings of literary critics to explicate the meanings and sociocultural associations imbued in Beijing Mandarin and, specifically, rhotacization (section 5.2).

5.1 *Jing qiangr jing diaor*: Rhotacization as an emblem of Beijing vernacular style

Er-hua 'rhotocization', or *er yin* 'r-sound', the Chinese technical terms for rhotacization, are hardly linguistic terms among lay Beijingers. They were used by many participants during my fieldwork interviews to characterize Beijing Mandarin. To them, rhotacization was an object that they had a name for, referred to, and described. In the written data, rhotacization is frequently used in the expressions *jing qiangr*, 'Beijing tune,' *jing diaor*, 'Beijing tone,' both of which are folk linguistic terms for the Beijing accent. For example, rhotacization is used with *jing qiang* in '*Fuhai de jing qiangr*' 'Fuhai's Beijing speech[r]' (J. Zhao 1996: 83) to describe the speech style of the protagonist in Lao She's novel *Zheng Hong Qi Xia*, 'Beneath the Red Banner'. In contrast to *Beijing hua* 'Beijing speech,' a neutral term for the local variety, *jing qiangr* and *jing diaor* are names for an 'authentic' Beijing speech style, distinctive from other local styles. The use of rhotacization adds a perceptual effect to the terms, projecting a 'sound image' of the local style of speech.

Rhotacization is also often used with the term *jing wei*, 'Beijing flavor.' Although *jing qiang* and *jing diao* refer specifically to Beijing speech style, *jing wei* or *jing weir* are more general terms used for anything with a distinctive Beijing style, including the local culture, speech, and cuisine, as illustrated in the following example from Lin Haiyin's essay '*Wo-de jing weir zhi lü*', 'My Beijing-flavored[r] trip' (note the use of rhotacization in the title) (1994: 36).

2. zai Beijing guo-le liu tian 'jing wei**r**' de rizi, ... guo zu-le shuo 'jing wei**r**' de hua, ting 'jing wei**r**' de xi, chi 'jing wei**r**' xi-ao-chi de yin.

[I] spent six 'Beijing-flavored[**r**]' days in Beijing,... enjoyed to my heart's content talking in 'Beijing-flavored[**r**]' speech, watching 'Beijing-flavored[**r**]' plays, and eating 'Beijing-flavored [**r**]' local specialties.

In the above excerpt from the end of the essay in which Lin summarizes what she did on her trip to Beijing, rhotacization is applied to all four occurrences of 'Beijing-flavor.' Such a high frequency of its use brings into prominence and enhances the localness of the writer's touring experiences in Beijing: from talking in the Beijing speech, to listening to the traditional Peking Opera, and to eating the local specialties, all constitutive of the distinctiveness of the local culture.

In addition to its use as a general term for Beijing-specific cultural forms, *jing wei* is used to designate a particular literary style, *jing wei xiaoshuo* 'Beijing-flavor novels,' or *jingwei wenxue* 'Beijing-flavor literature,' whose stylistic characteristics were described in section 4.

[...]

The frequent co-occurrence of rhotacization with key cultural terms, as in example 3, and its repeated use to represent and evoke authentic Beijing-ness, as in example 4, constitute part of the process by which this particular dialect feature comes to take on semiotic saliency as the quintessential emblem of the uniqueness of Beijing vernacular style. Such saliency renders this dialect feature a rich resource for stylistic work, particularly for expressing meanings of localness.

5.2 *Imbued meanings*

In this section, I examine the sociocultural associations imbued in rhotacization through examining metalinguistic comments from sociolinguistic interviews, Beijing-flavor literaryworks and explicit metapragmatic commentaries of literary scholars.

The 'smoothness' of Beijing speech and rhotacization.

[...]

Rhotacization and the 'Beijing Smooth Operator'. The above descriptions (5, 6, and 7) of Beijing speech and rhotacization in terms of 'smoothness' attest toAgha's observation that 'the native speaker's metalinguistic grasp of semioticp henomena is an inherently leaky thing' (1998: 162). In other words, the same metalinguistic description can be applied to different kinds of linguistic objects, for example, words, sentences, and registers (Agha 1998: 162). As demonstrated in the preceding examples (5, 6 and 7), the metalinguistic characterization of 'smoothness' is applied to, or leaks across, different kinds of linguistic objects, namely, the Beijing vernacular style and one of its prominent components, rhotacization. Moreover, such leakage is also exhibited across aspects of speech and speakers such that the 'smoothness' of Beijing speech and rhotacization is identified with a smooth Beijing persona. Such cross-level leakage, prevalent in native speakers' talk about Beijing Mandarin, is illustrated by the comment made by a participant in one of my sociolinguistic interviews, reproduced in 8 below.

8. (Liu, a 38-year-old male chief representative of a foreign bank)

1 qishi, shuo Beijing ren you,
In fact, **Beijingers** are said to be **smooth**,
2 suovei jing you-zi ma,
the so-called **Beijing Smooth Operator**,
3 zhuyao shi yinwei Beijing hua you haoduo er-hua yin.
mainly because **Beijing speech has a lot of rhotacization.**
4 Beijing ren benlai jiu neng shuo,
Beijingers are naturally gifted with gab,
5 zai jiashang er yin zhong,
and with **heavy r-sounding**,
6 na jiu xiande youhua.
then [**Beijingers**] appear to be smooth.
7 ni ting shei shuo guo Guangdong ren you-qiangr hua-diaor a?
Have you heard anybody saying **the Cantonese** have '**oily accent [r], slippery tone[r]**?'
8 na shi yinwei tamen shetou bu hui dawanr
That's because **their tongues can't curl[r].**

Typifying Beijingers as having a smooth personality (line 1), Liu refers to the well-known local character type, *jing you-zi*, 'Beijing Smooth Operator' (line 2). The smooth character is further motivated in relation with rhotacization in line 3. In other words, rhotacization is interpreted as the cause for the smooth character. In lines 4 - 6, another causal relationship is established, where Beijinger's gift of gab and 'heavy r-sounding' speech are construed as effected by their smooth character. In lines 7 and 8, the contrast between the smooth-tongued Beijinger and the Cantonese is considered to be brought about by the fact that the latter's 'tongues can't curl.' The Mandarin idiomatic expression *you-qiangr hua-diaor* 'oily accent, slippery tone' in line 7 means smooth-tongued.

Example 8 thus represents a typical case of 'iconization' (Irvine 2001; Irvine and Gal 2000), a semiotic process whereby 'linguistic differences appear to be iconic representations of the social contrasts they index—as if a linguistic feature somehow depicted or displayed a social group's inherent nature or essence' (Irvine 2001: 33). In 8, the 'smooth' quality of rhotacization and Beijing speech is identified via ideological construal with a corresponding naturalized attribute of Beijingers. In line with what Bell (2001: 142) and Coupland (2001b: 198) have observed, this example demonstrates that linguistic features and styles derive their meanings from their associations with social personae and identities. Therefore, exploring the full import of the salient local character type is necessary for a better understanding of the social meanings of rhotacization. To do this, I turn to works of Beijing-flavor literature in which *jing you-zi* 'Beijing Smooth Operator' is a stock character type. As explained in Q. Zhang (2005: 441):

> Jing in *jing you-zi*, is Beijing. While *you* is the Mandarin word for 'oil,' it is also part of *youhua*, which means literally 'oily' or 'slippery'. When used to describe a personality, *you* connotes smooth and worldly-wise. With the nominalization suffix *-zi*, *you-zi* refers to someone who is versed in the ways of the world.

This local character type is reified by the fact that *jing you-zi* is included in the *Modern Chinese Dictionary*, defined as 'a longtime resident of Beijing who is worldly and slick' (*Xiandai Hanyu Cidian* 1998: 663). Beijing-flavor literature offersmany vivid examples of various kinds of Beijing Smooth Operator characters in different historical periods. The following summary of the five categories of literary representatives of this stock character is based on L. Zhang's analysis (1994: 111 – 125).

[...]

The association between rhotacization and the smooth persona and its characterological attributes becomes even more explicit in the metadiscursive evaluations, or explicit comments about speech, produced by participants in the sociolinguistic interviews as illustrated in example 8 earlier (e.g. 'Beijing speech has a lot of rhotacization...[Beijingers] appear to be smooth'). Similar metadiscursive comments are produced by literary critics, as shown in 11 and 12, both of which are cases of iconization.

[...]

Although explicit metapragmatic comments by the lay native speakers in the sociolinguistic interviews and literary scholars in the genre of literary criticism anchor rhotacization (and Beijing speech) to qualities of 'smoothness' and the Beijing Smooth Operator character type, those produced by the latter group, such as the ones in 11 and 12, are in effect 'expert' evaluations. As Johnstone, Andrus and Danielson (2006) observe in their study of the enregisterment of 'Pittsburghese', published 'expert' testimonies of language scholars and teachers in newspaper articles have an influential effect on 'enregistering and legitimizing' a set of speech forms as a named dialect, 'linked explicitly, via its name, with place' (2006: 97). The 'expert' evaluations of the literary critics cited above revalorize the social meaning of rhotacization and are likely to have a wider reach at a translocal level.

6. CONCLUSION

[...]

9.3 思考和练习

1. 在你生活的地区,能观察到类似于纽约的(r)这样的具有社会标记功能的语言变项吗?

2. 如果要对上题的语言变项进行调查,这个研究应该如何设计?结合本章阅读的三篇文章进行思考。

3. 你的家乡方言是否也存在向普通话靠拢的现象?这种变化是整个音韵系统的变化,还是个别词汇的变化?试讨论导致这种现象的原因。

4.《倒鸭子》是 2011 年在网上爆红的一段大连话报案保险理赔的客服录音。请从社会语言学的角度,试用会话分析(CA)的基本原则分析这段对话。

5. 如果现在有一个 2018 年《人民日报》所有文章及标题的语料库,这份资料可用于做哪些社会语言学研究?

6. 中国教育部语言文字应用管理司(简称语用司)是我国负责制定语言文字方针、政策和规划的政府职能部门。请根据官方网站公开的资讯和信息,概括中国目前语言文字工作的主要目标和几个要点。

9.4 延伸阅读

Baker, P., Gabrielatos, C., Khosravinik, M., Krzyzanowski, M., McEnery, T. & R. Wodak. 2008. A useful methodological synergy? Combining critical discourse analysis and corpus linguistics to examine discourses of refugees and asylum seekers in the UK press. *Discourse & Society* 19(3): 273–306.

Chambers, J. K. & P. Trudgill. 1980. *Dialectology*. New York: Cambridge University Press.

Drew, P., Chatwin, J. & S. Collins. 2001. Conversation analysis: a method for research into interactions between patients and health-care professionals. *Health Expectations* 4(1): 58–70.

Fairclough, N. 2013. *Critical Discourse Analysis: The Critical Study of Language*. London: Routledge.

Hymes, D. H. 1974. *Foundations in Sociolinguistics: an Ethnographic Approach*. Philadelphia: University of Pennsylvania.

Milroy, L. & Llamas, C. 2013. Social networks. In J. Chambers and N. Schilling (eds.) *The Handbook of Language Variation and Change*, 409 – 427. Oxford: Wiley-Blackwell.

Wardhaugh, R. & J. M. Fuller. 2015. *An Introduction to Sociolinguistics (Seventh Edition)*. London: Wiley-Blackwell.

第十章 语言类型学

10.1 导引

- 类型学的研究目的
- 类型学的起源
- 类型学的分类
- 汉语类型学研究
- 类型学的解释
- 类型学的发展

10.1.1 类型学的研究目的

语言类型学通过比较语言各个方面的特征,发现语言之间的共性与差异,以此揭示语言的本质和规律。相比其它语言学的研究分支,语言类型学最突出的特征是采用了跨语言的视角。

10.1.2 类型学的起源

语言类型学的概念最早由19世纪的德国语言学家施勒格尔兄弟(Friedrich von Schlegel & August von Schlegel)和洪堡(Wilhelm von Humboldt)提出,当时关注的是以形态为标准对语言进行分类。这个研究分支的发展并未止步于此。现代类型学研究真正的鼻祖是格林伯格(Joseph Greenberg),他发表于1963年的《某些主要跟语序有关的语法共性》("Some Universals of Grammar with Particular Reference to the Order of Meaningful

Elements")可谓现代类型学研究的开山之作。

在这篇文章中,格林伯格调查了30种语言,发现一个语言的默认语序往往与其它成分的相对顺序呈现相关的关系。譬如,如果看一种语言中一般陈述句里主谓宾(S、V、O)的顺序,"VSO语言通常使用的是前置介词,而SOV语言则通常是后置介词";如果看一种语言的词缀的类型,"如果一种语言只有后缀,那么它使用的是后置介词;如果一种语言只有前缀,那么它使用的是前置介词"等等。格林伯格根据这30种语言的情况总结出了45条与语序有关的语言共性。

格林伯格的这篇文章奠定了现代类型学研究的三个主要研究目的:对语言进行分类、发现语言共性,以及对语言共性做出解释。格林伯格的研究方法也为后世沿用,其基本操作为:在保证均衡性的前提下选取一定语言作为"语种库"(language sample),确定要研究的语言参项后对相关语言特征进行四分表分析,由此建立语言共性及寻找等级序列(hierarchy)。以下表10.1是一个三种类型语言的六分表,其展示的语言共性是"疑问词位于句首的语言是前置介词语言;疑问词位于句末的语言是后置介词语言"。

表10.1 格林伯格(1963)疑问词位置和语序的六分表

疑问词的位置	VSO	SVO	SOV
句首	5	0	0
句末	0	2	5

类型学研究的几个关键概念,比如绝对共性(absolute universals)和蕴涵共性(implicational universals),也是由格林伯格提出的。绝对共性,指的是所有语言中都普遍存在的语言特征,比如"所有语言中都有名词和动词",或者说"所有语言中都有元音和辅音",这都是语言的绝对共性。但是,绝对共性这个概念本身存在逻辑问题,因为我们无法证明我们已经知晓了所有人类语言,因此有些人认为用倾向共性(tendencies)或者数据共性(statistical universals)来表述更加准确。数据共性也可用来表述在大部分语言里观察到的语言事实,比如"主语通常位于宾语之前";这样的表述只是描述了一个大体的情况,而不代表绝对的事实。

蕴涵共性,揭示的则是不同语言特征之间可能存在相互关系的情况,通常用"如果X则Y"或者"如果X并Y则Z"这样的表述式。例如,如果一门语言有塞擦音,则必定有塞音也有擦音。在本章第二部分我们会看到更多有关语言蕴含共性的例子。感兴趣的读者也可查阅由康斯坦茨大学维护的线上"语言共性档案库"(The Universals Archive)[①],上面搜集罗列了2029条语言共性,涉及语音、形态、句法、语用、语段等多个层面。

10.1.3 类型学的分类

类型学的第一个研究任务是对语言进行"分类"。语言分类的标准既可以是形式上的,也可以是功能上的语言特征。语音系统、词素形态(morphology)、语义、句法结构、语用特征等都可以作为语言分类的标准。《语言结构世界地图集》(World Atlas of Language Structure)就集合了2679种语言,比较了包括音系、形态、词类、语序、句法句型、词汇以及手语等方面的192个特征(features)。

下面我们将简要介绍一些常见的分类特征以及跨语言共性。

10.1.3.1 语音系统类型

语言可以按照所具有的元音个数来分类。世界上最普遍的元音系统是五元音系统(/a, e, i, o, u/),也就是仅通过舌位的前后高低便可以对元音进行区分。日语、西班牙语和斯瓦西里语都是这样的元音系统。世界上大部分语言的元音系统有3—9个元音——元音数量比这再多或再少的语言都较为罕见。基于跨语言的观察,类型学家发现元音系统存在一些跨语言的共性。比如,/a, i, u/是元音当中最常见的三个,只有三个元音的系统就是这三个音位。又比如,一般舌位靠后的元音都是圆唇音(譬如/o, u/),而舌位靠前的元音则是不圆唇音(譬如/e, i/);开口元音/a/一般也是不圆唇音。

语言可以按照所具有的辅音进行分类。由于人类语言的辅音库存本身数量较大,类型学家一般不从数量上进行分类,而是从辅音的类型上进行观察。世界上的语言普遍都存在塞音(stop),最常见的几个为/p, t, k/;而擦音当中,/s/是最常见的;绝大部分语言中也至少会有一个鼻音,最常见的是/n/。跨语言的辅音系统内部也能观察到一些蕴含共性,比如:如果一门语言存在浊阻塞音,则必定存在清阻塞音;如果一门语言存在擦音,则必定存在塞

---

① "语言共性档案库"由 Frans Plank 主持建立,由康斯坦茨大学维护。网址:http://typo.uni-konstanz.de/archive/intro/。

音,诸如此类。

语言也可以按照有无声调以及声调类型进行分类。我们在第二章已经介绍过声调语言的定义并给出了一些例子。尽管我们熟悉的大部分印欧语言都不是声调语言,但声调语言也并没有想象的那么罕见。除了中国境内的诸多汉语方言以外,东南亚、非洲、美洲都存在大量声调语言;其中既有像汉语一样有声调曲折的复杂声调系统,也有只分高(中)低音的较为简单的音调系统。图10.1是《语言结构世界地图集》中声调语言的分布图。声调系统内部也有一些语言共性特征。比如,在具有复杂声调系统的语言里,如果存在有声调曲折的声调,则必定有平调。

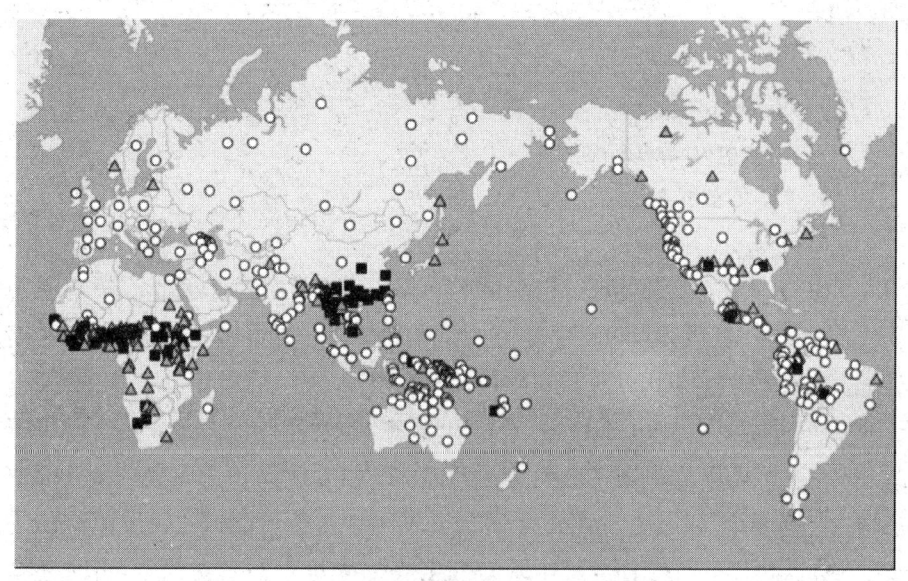

图 10.1　声调语言在全球的分布①

此外,音节重音也有几个类型。有些语言具有固定重音,如斯瓦西里语的重音固定在倒数第二个音节上,而捷克语、芬兰语的重音固定在第一个音节上;而有些语言,如俄语,则没有固定的重音位置。

10.1.3.2　形态学类型

语言还可以根据其形态特征进行分类(详见前文4.1.6的相关介绍)。按照词语构成的特点,语言大体可以分为四种类型:孤立语(isolating

---

① 图片来源:https://wals.info/feature/13A。

language)、屈折语(inflectional language)、黏着语(agglutinative language)和复综语(polysynthetic language)。

孤立语又称分析型语言(analytical language)，汉语和越南语都是典型的孤立语。孤立语的每一个词通常只有一个词素，并且所有词素都是自由词素，可以单独出现，不需要依附其它词素共同出现。

在另外三类语言中，一个完整的词通常由词根和其它黏着语素合成；这三类语言都属于综合型语言(synthetic language)。在黏着语中，词语由词根和多个词素组成，通常一个词素代表一个意思，比如人称、时态。土耳其语、斯瓦西里语都属于较为典型的黏着语。以下是斯瓦西里语的一个词，表示"我在看书"：

  ni-na-soma
  1SG-present-read
  "我在看书"

屈折语的典型例子包括俄语和西班牙语。屈折语的动词变格经常使用一个词素结合表示人称和时态。例如，西班牙语中'Hablo español'意味着"我说西班牙语"，其中动词 hablar 的动词词尾-o 表示的是第一人称现在时；而如果把词尾变成-an 'Hablan español'则意味着"他们说西班牙语"，动词词尾-an 在这里表示的是第三人称复数现在时；如果把动词词尾换成-é 'Hablé español'则表示"我过去说西班牙语"，-é 表第一人称单数过去时。复综语的词语通常由多个词素组成，其中既有屈折类语素也有黏着类语素，有时还会有多个词根。爱斯基摩语族中的很多语言都属于复综语。比如，在西格林兰岛语中，一句话的意思可能用一个词表达出来：

  tusaa-nngit-su-usaar-tuaannar-sinnaa-nngi-vip-putit
  'hear'-NEG-intrans.participle-'pretend'-'all the time'-'can'-NEG-'really'-2SG indicative
  "你不能总假装听不到"

实际上，大部分的语言都不如以上提到的这些语言这么典型。例如，总体来看，英语是个相对孤立的语言，因为每个词都有自己独立的意思；但英语单词中也有高度黏着的例子，例如 antidisestablishmentarianism（"反对解散国教主义者"）这个词就是由 anti-dis-establish-ment-arian-ism 六个词素构成；而英语的人称代词系统则是屈折型的，试比较 he/him 和 she/her，每个单词里包含了格、性、数三重信息。因此在实际操作中，在试图定义一种语言在形态学上属于哪种类型时，要对该语言内不同属性的词进行具体考察、细分。

在形态学方面几个较为显著的蕴涵共性有：

· 如果一种语言存在屈折词素（inflectional morpheme，比如英语中动词标第三人称单数的后缀 -s），则其必有派生词素（derivational morpheme，比如英语的表示否定的前缀 un-）。

· 如果一种语言既存在屈折词素也有派生词素，则派生词素较屈折词素离词根更近。例如，memberships（"会员制"的复数形式）一词中，名词词缀 -ship 是派生词素，就比表复数的屈折词素 -s 更接近词根 member。

10.1.3.3 句法学类型

格林伯格 1963 年发表的文章奠定了现代类型学研究的基本范式，也建立了一种从语序切入语言类型的视角，使句法类型成为类型学研究经久不衰的热点。在这篇文章中，格林伯格主要从"主、谓、宾"（S, V, O）三种句法成分的相对语序切入，归纳出 30 种语言中可能出现的 6 种语序（SVO, SOV, VSO, VOS, OSV 和 OVS，前三种最为常见，后三种极为罕见），及其与其它句子成分的相对顺序的关系（如修饰成分和被修饰成分、名词与介词、动词与助词）。本章节选了这篇文章，具体恕不赘述。

除语序以外，类型学也关注语言在句子层面的其他特征，比如：

· 句型与构式：疑问句的类型；双及物构式、被动构式、使动构式的形态；相互构式与反身构式的异同；关系从句与其它相关句式的异同；

· 句子成分：否定的表现形式；名词之间的连接词、动词之间的连接词；

· 论元的形态句法配列（alignment）：主宾格（nominative-accusative）、作通格（ergative-absolutive）等。

10.1.3.4 语用学类型

上世纪 70 年代,以包括中文在内的东亚语言为样本,美国功能学派语言学家李讷(Charles N. Li)和 Sandra Thompson 提出了"话题突出语言"(topic-prominent language)的概念。他们发现,有些语言不仅以主语架构句子,更常以话题统领句子和串联语篇。例如,中文的复合句中通常使用的是同一话题,比如这句话:"琴叶榕高可达 12 米,茎干直立,极少分枝,叶片密集生长,叶片厚革质、深绿色、具光泽,叶脉凹陷、节间较短。"日语和韩语更是存在对话题成分的语法标记(日语的 wa 和韩语的 neun/eun)。类似的语言还有越南语、马来语、匈牙利语和索马里语。"话题突出语言"这一概念并不是对句子主语的否定,而是类型学研究在语篇组织层面显现的一个跨语言事实。

除此以外,语用学类型学研究的成果目前仍较为有限。语用学研究的对象多是功能上的,缺乏具体的形态作为依据,在定义上很难达到统一,要进行大型的跨语言研究仍有很多工作要做。目前已经进行和正在进行的一些尝试包括:话语标记(discourse marker)、会话结构(conversation structure)与语篇结构以及不同言语行为在语法层面的表现。

10.1.4 汉语类型学研究

中国以其特有的语言资源为类型学研究提供了别样的视角。中国境内有数量繁多的汉语方言和少数民族语言,它们为类型学研究提供了新的语言特征,丰富了类型特征库。汉语中的动词补语(如结果补语、趋向补语)、作为前附加标记的介词(如"在、到、从")、上文提到的"话题突出"、语气词等等,这些特征虽不都为汉语独有,但汉语是研究这些类型学特征的重要材料。

中国是使用书面文字历史最长的国家之一,保留了三千多年的书面语言记录。通过三千多年的历时语料,可以看出语言类型与驱动语言变化的各种因素相互作用的结果。上世纪 70 年代,汉语言学界展开了一场对汉语的基本语序的辩论。依照格林伯格总结的共性来看,现代汉语虽然具有 SVO 的基本语序,但其它许多成分的相对语序呈现的却是 SOV 语言的特征。有学者以古汉语的语料为依据,提出上古汉语其实是 SOV 语言,与其同源的藏缅语语序一致,只是后来语言整体演变成了 SVO 的语序,但仍保留了部分 SOV 语言的语序特征。关于这场论辩可以参见本章延伸阅读推荐的书目。

从另一个方面看,类型学的研究也为汉语内部的研究——特别是汉语方言的分类,提供了新的方法和依据。早期的汉语方言分类(如王力、李方桂)采用方言音韵作为分类标准,罗杰瑞(Jerry Norman)率先提出一套综合考虑音韵、词汇、构词法和语法的分类标准,并据此把中国的七个主要方言分为南、北、中三个大区域。朱德熙、余蔼芹(Anne O. Yue-Hashimoto)、曹茜蕾(Hilary Chappell)也对比研究了汉语方言中大量不同的句法类型,进行汉语方言语法对比描写。

10.1.5 类型学的解释

一些类型学家从生成理论出发,用"原则与参项"解释语言出现共性和差异的原因。生成理论认为,语言发展的实质是对普遍语法的参项进行设置,一门语言之所以会出现 A 现象,而另一门语言会出现 B 现象,仅仅是因为在同一个参项上的设置不同。不同层级的参项都会受到上层的参项设置的影响,在实际语言中便体现为绝对共性和趋向共性。

功能学派的学者则认为语言存在的共性和差异与人的认知能力有关。语言呈现出共性,比如最为普遍的主语在前宾语在后的语序,有利于人们处理语言信息。格林伯格总结出来的关于语序的蕴含共性,体现的是不同语言现象之间的和谐一致性(harmony),这种和谐有助于语言使用者对语言的习得和处理。这种一致性有时是由一定历史原因造成的,比如,某种构式是从另一个构式演化而来的(介词构式往往是从所有格构式发展而来的)。此外,语言共同具有的经济性(economy)和象似性(iconicity),也决定了语言表现形式的相似。

语言是存在于特定时间、空间中的实体。地理上的临近使得语言互相接触,不仅可能导致词汇的借用,也有可能使相邻的语言演化出相似的语言特征。语言地理类型学家桥本万太郎就认为,汉语方言的南北音韵分化、句法结构演变、基本词汇改变,与周边语族的接触有关。语言特征的地理聚集是不争的事实,前文提及的由全球 55 位语言学家参与编撰的《语言结构世界地图集》集合了 2600 多种语言的包括语音、构词、词汇、语法方面近 200 个语言特征(feature),以地图的形式标注出来,呈现出语言特征的地理分布。而有些语言即使地理上相隔甚远,仍有可能因为历史上发源于同一个语言,而拥有共同的语言特征——亚洲印度境内的印地语有可能与欧洲西端意大利的西西里语在类型学上有许多共同的特征,因为两者都发展自原始印欧语。

10.1.6 类型学的发展

近来,类型学研究的发展主要体现在三个方面。一是语种库的扩大。语言类型学的关键是跨语言的研究,必须基于多个语言样本,而不能只考察一种单一的语言。每一个语言样本的出现,都可能揭示新的语言特征,或者为已有的语言特征提供统计学上的支撑。在格林伯格(1963)的研究之后,Hawkins(1983)选取了超过 300 种语言重新验证了格林伯格提出的与语序相关的语言共性;Dryer(1992,1999)更是分别选取了超过 600 和 900 种语言进行调查。当然,语种库的扩大也意味着统计方法的革新,对语种库中不同语言参项标注的规范化的要求也随之提高。第二个发展是对于语类的定义方法的反思。句法层面的类型学研究,在过去基本是从结构和语义层面对语类进行定义,因此会导致每个语言实际取得的类别范围扩大或缩小。比如,格林伯格文章中的"形容词"类,在某些语言中实际包含了表性质特征的动词和关系从句。因此,有学者提出应从功能出发对语类进行考察,一是可以比较同个语类不同功能类别在句法层面的区别,二是可以比较功能相似的不同语类在语言内部和跨语言的相似与区别。类型学第三个方面的发展是利用语义地图(semantic map)来表现语言内部和语言之间相关成分的变异和发展。

最后,语言类型学研究的发展与语言描摹密不可分。一门新的语言的发现、对一门语言的描摹,都有可能发现新的语言特征,或者为已知的语言共性提供新的证据。未来语言类型学的发展,还需要系统的语言描摹的进一步开展。

10.2 选读

- 格林伯格(1963)《某些主要跟语序有关的语法普遍现象》选读
- Charles Li & Sandra Thompson(1976)《主语与主题:一种新的语言类型学》选读
- Hilary Chappell (2001) "Language Contact and Areal Diffusion in Sinitic Languages"选读

格林伯格(1963)《某些主要跟语序有关的语法普遍现象》选读[①]

◆ **作者简介**

约瑟夫·哈罗德·格林伯格[②](Joseph Harold Greenberg, 1915—2001),美国语言学家和人类学家,1940年美国西北大学人类学博士毕业,后历任哥伦比亚大学和斯坦福大学人类学系主任。他最主要的贡献是提出了"语言共性",开创了语言类型学研究。同时,他对非洲语言也有很深的研究,著有《非洲的语言》,书中对非洲语言的分类法已为许多研究者所接受。

◆ **正文节选**

1. 引 言

首先读者要知道本文所提出的结论是尝试性的,由于没有对全球语言作更全面的抽样调查,还不能充分保证这里所断言的大多数普遍现象没有例外,诚如题目所示,我们关注的主要是语素和词序问题,当然绝非仅限于此。作出这样的选择是因为以往的经验已显示了语法的这个专门方面即语序方面的很多规律。本文提出一系列普遍现象,它们大部分是蕴含性的,即它们采取这样的形式:某语言中有现象 x,就必然有现象 y,若不作进一步说明,逆命题即有 y 必有 x 就不能成立。当这两种现象分别具有"有""无"两种可能时,四分表上的典型分布是:四组中有一组是零。就科学方法论而言,这结果无可厚非,理由有二:科学方法手册中描述的最起码的法则恰是这种形式。其次,那些看来是非蕴含性的语言普遍现象,由于它们被语言的定义性特征所蕴含,因此事实上不言而喻,还是蕴含性的[③]。

---

① 格林伯格著,陆丙甫、陆致极译,《某些主要跟语序有关的语法普遍现象》,《国外语言学》,1984年第2期。
② 图片来源:https://www.unm.edu/~wcroft/JHG.html。
③ 指经验上的蕴含,而并不是逻辑上的蕴涵。任何语言都可以观察到这类特征。并且,那些仅存在于语言中的非定义性的普遍现象,它们一定具有蕴含性的附加逻辑性质。同时也被定义性特征所蕴含。

有必要指出的第二种普遍现象,即蕴含在语言定义性特征之中的普遍现象,尽管本文通常不作正式阐述,事实上已包含在各种语言在语法方面是可以比较的这一观念之中,这个观念正是本文所作具体阐述的基础。例如,以下这个叙述就含有一系列通常认为是普遍现象的假设:如果一种语言以主语—宾语为陈述句的基本词序,那么从属的所有格总是跟在核心名词后面。这里已经假定:所有的语言都有主谓结构,有词类之分和所有格结构等等。我很清楚,在确定不同结构的语言中的这些现象时,人们基本上使用的是语义标准。很可能会有形式上的相似点,可以用来归并不同语言中的这类现象。寻求这种相似点尽管很重要,但十分艰难。若全力干这项任务,恐怕无法在这类调查的基础上得到具体的假设,而这些假设具有经验的意义,是非语言学家的主要兴趣所在。况且,给"名词"下的适用于各种语言的定义是否恰当,完全可以依据它所要表达的语义现象的效果来加以验证。例如,假使"名词"的一个形式定义把一种语言中的含有诸如"男孩"、"鼻子"、"房子"那些词项的类同另一种语言中含有"吃"、"喝"、"给"等词项的类等同起来,这样的定义会立刻被排斥,这样做所根据的是语义。事实上,语言中处理此类问题时并无多少疑虑。完全有理由相信,这类判断是十分有效的。譬如说,如果有人对本文所作的某一所有格结构语序类型的安排提出质疑的话,那么,这种安排之所以可以接受或需排斥的依据还是十分明白的。

　　本文的许多描写利用了以下 30 种语言的抽样:欧洲的巴斯克语、塞尔维亚语、威尔士语、挪威语、现代希腊语、意大利语、芬兰语;非洲的约鲁巴语、努比亚语、斯瓦希里语、弗拉尼语、马萨伊语、宋盖语、柏柏尔语;亚洲的土耳其语、希伯来语、布鲁沙斯基语、印地语、坎纳达语、日语、泰语、缅甸语、马来语;美洲印第安人的毛利语、洛里查语(大洋洲);玛雅语、萨波特语、凯楚亚语、奇布查语、瓜拉尼语等。

　　选择这些抽样主要是出于方便。总的来说,它包含了我过去接触过的或我有适当的语法书可以查对的语言。尽管我力图使发生学和地域性方面的包括面大些,但我的选择有所偏好是显而易见的。这个抽样用于两个主要的目的,首先,任何对这 30 种语言适用的陈述很可能会具有普遍性,或者至少接近这样的普遍性。其次,它可以提供某些语法特征之间联系的相对频率。在有些问题上,我大大超出了这 30 种抽样的范围。

　　本文的主要部分是根据语言的经验事实提出种种普遍现象,尽量少作理论性评述。最后一节是探索性的,试图找出一般的原则,至少前几节中的某些概括可以由它们推演出来。理论部分比起阐述普遍现象本身的部分来说,臆测的成分和不确定性要多得多。在某种意义上,我们宁可使获得的普遍现象尽可能少些,而不是尽可能多一些,也就是说,我们希望能够从数量尽可能少的一般原理中推导出普遍现象。然而,建立起相对来说数目较多的经验概括,总是必须跨出的第一步。从一个似乎有效的概括性原理中推导出一种特殊的普遍现象,结果却发现这个概括在经验上并不能成立,这就够麻烦的了。

2. 基本语序类型①

语言学家一般都知道,某些语言总倾向于把修饰或限定成份放在被修饰或被限定的成分之前,而另一些语言又恰恰相反。作为前一种类型的例子,土耳其语把形容词置于被修饰的名词之前,把动词的宾语置于动词之前,从属的所有格置于中心名词之前,副词置于它所修饰的形容词之前,等等。此外,这类语言还倾向于使用意义上相当于英语前置词的后置词。泰语是相反类型的一种语言,它的形容词在名词之后,宾语在动词之后,所有格在中心名词之后,并使用前置词。大多数语言,譬如英语,在这方面并不这么显著。英语像泰语一样,使用前置词,名词宾语在动词之后。另一方面,英语又像土耳其语,形容词在名词之前,而且,所有格结构具有两种语序:John's house 和 the house of John(约翰的房子)。

更细致地考虑这类语序现象以及别的语序现象,不难发现某些因素之间是密切相关的,而另一些因素则相对独立。鉴于以下阐述中会明了的某些原

---

① 某些关于基本语序类型的思想在十九世纪的语言学著作中就可以看到。例如,在 R. Lepsius 的《努比亚语语法》(Berlin, 1880)一书的序言中就已有为人熟知的关于所有格的位置跟前置词/后置词的关系以及某些语言喜欢用"修饰语—被修饰语"这样的语序,而另外一些语自则用相反语序的看法。

这方面作出过的系统的论述见于 W. Schmidt 的《全世界的语系及其区域》(Heidelberg 1926) 以及其他一些著作。Schmidt 的基本结论可简述如下:前置词伴随名词—所有格语序,后置词则伴随相反的语序。名词—所有格语序倾向于出现在 V-O 语言中,而所有格—名词语序则在 O-V 语言中。Schmidt 没有谈及主语—动词的语序,因此没有区分本文论及的 I 型和 II 型。此外,名词—所有格伴随名词—形容词,而所有格—名词则伴随形容词—名词。这种对应关系,尤其是后者,跟其他对应关系相比是不十分明显的。Schmidt 在世界性抽样调查的基础上给出了具体的数字,这跟本文运用的三十种语言抽样所得出的结果十分吻合。这里还要说明 Schmidt 在这方面的主要兴趣是要以此来解释文化史,他在文化史方面的结论就近于异想天开了。

因,最好设立一套涉及某些语序基本因素的类型,可称之为基本语序类型。这可使用三组标准:第一是使用前置词还是后置词,分别标作 Pr 和 Po。第二是带有名词性主语和宾语的陈述句中主语、动词和宾语的相对顺序。绝大多数语言有几种语序变体,但总有一种是占优势的语序。从逻辑上来看,有六种可能出现的语序:SVO,SOV,VSO,VOS,OSV 和 OVS。然而,在这六种之中,只有三种通常作为优势语序而出现。其它三种则根本不发生或极为少见,它们是 VOS,OSV 和 OVS。其共同点是宾语处于主语之前。由此我们得出第一个普遍现象:

普遍现象 1:带和名词性主语和宾语的陈述句中,优势语序几乎总是主语处于宾语之前。①

这样,通常的三种类型是 VSO,SVO 和 SOV,分别标记为类型Ⅰ,Ⅱ,Ⅲ,以示动词的相对位置。

分类的第三种基础是那些表示性质的形容词与名词的相对位置,正如下文要看到的,指示词冠词、数词和指量词(如 some、all)的位置往往跟性质形容词不同。这方面有时也有变化,但绝大多数语言总有一个优势语序。形容词位于名词之前的优势语序标作 A,名词位于形容词之前的标作 N。这样,就有了涉及 2×3×2,即逻辑上十二种可能性的一套类型。在这十二种搭配中,30 种语言的抽样分布如下②:

表 1

	Ⅰ	Ⅱ	Ⅲ
Po — A	0	1	6
Po — N	0	2	5
Pr — A	0	4	0
Pr — N	6	6	0

如表所示,"极端"的类 Po-A 和 Pr-N 分别处于第一和第四行,而Ⅰ型和Ⅲ型显然又是其中的两个极,Ⅰ型跟 Pr-N 密切相关,Ⅲ型跟 Po-A 密切相关。Ⅱ型则更密切地跟 Pr-N 而不是跟 Po-A 相关。形容词的位置比起 Pr/Po 的

---

① 俄勒冈的佩努蒂亚诸语言中的西乌斯罗语和科斯语,以及一种萨利什语言——克尔达伦语,是例外。
② 每种语言的分配方式可以由附录Ⅰ的材料来决定。

对立来说,跟Ⅰ,Ⅱ,Ⅲ型的关系要疏远得多,这也是很明显的。我相信,此表正确地反映了世界范围内的这几种类别的相对频度,Ⅱ型频度最高,Ⅲ型也常见,Ⅰ型则少得多。这意味着在世界上的极大多数语言中名词性主语通常位于动词之前。

考虑一下所有格的位置,或许也可用它来分类,没有用它作标准是因为它跟Pr/Po有密切的对应关系,这是语言学家都知道的。两者实际上是重复的,况且总的来说Pr/Po跟其他的现象的对应程度也较高。在上述30种语言的抽样中,14种用后置词,其中所有格语序皆为所有格处于中心名词之前,无一例外。在用前置词的14(译者注:原文如此。当为16)种语言中,13(译者注:当为15)种是所有格处于中心名词之后,只有挪威语例外,所有格在中心语之前。可见30例中29例符合这条规则。从全球范围来看,例外的情况更要小于1/30。于是我们得出第二个普遍现象:

普遍现象2:使用前置词的语言中,所有格几乎总是后置于中心名词,而使用后置词的语言,所有格几乎总是前置于中心名词。

再回过头来看表1,我们发现明显的证据,说明在诸变项之间有些确定的关系,那就是12种可能搭配中有5种,几乎近一半,在样品中几乎没有例证。这些类或者稀少,或者根本不存在[①]。对Ⅰ型来说,样品中所有的6种语言都为Pr/N,在全球范围内这很少例外。但Ⅰ/Pr/A有少数确凿的例子,可以说,是相当常见的Ⅲ/Po/N的反像。另一方面,就我所知,没有Ⅰ/Po/A或Ⅰ/Po/N的例子,因此我们可以列出下面第三条普遍现象:

普遍现象3:优势语序为VSO的语言,总是使用前置词。

Ⅲ型语言如上所述是Ⅰ型的相反极。正如Ⅰ型中没有用后置词的语言,我们期待Ⅲ型中没有用前置词的语言,这基本上是对的,但我也知道有一些例外[②]。既然像上面所讲的那样,所有格位置跟Pr/Po有严格的对应关系,那么Ⅲ型语言通常应当具有GN(按:G代表领属成分,N代表名词——校者)语序。这也有些例外,不过当所有格语序反常时,形容词语序也会反常。而在Pr/Po方面却并非如此。于是我们得到第四个普遍现象:

普遍现象4:以SOV为正常语序的语言,使用后置词的远在半数以上。

---

① 详见附录Ⅱ——原文注释。
② 伊拉库语(一种南库施特语)、坎蒂语(一种泰语)标准波斯语和阿姆哈拉语。

[略]

3. 句法

[略]

4. 词法

[略]

5. 结论：某些一般原则

在此并不想对前几节所叙述的所有的普遍现象做出解释。不过要提出某些一般原则，它们是一些不同的普遍现象的基础，这些普遍现象可从中推导出来。首先要考虑那些跟基本语序类型关系最为密切的、跟所有格的结构紧密相连的普遍现象。这里要引进两个基本概念：一是某种特定语序压倒其交替语序的优势；二是不同的语序规则之间的和谐的和不和谐的关系。后者显然跟泛化（generalization）这一心理学概念有关。

我们可以用普遍现象 25 为例来说明这样做的理由。根据普遍现象 25，如果代词性宾语后置于动词，那么名词性宾语也同样后置。换言之，在四分表上各组搭配的结果有一栏是空白。因为无论代词性宾语前置或后置，名词性宾语都可以在动词之后，而只有代词前置时名词性宾语才可以在动词之前，我们可以说 VO 比 OV 多，因为 OV 仅在特定条件下出现，即在代词性宾语也前置的条件下出现，而 VO 是不受这类限制的。进一步说，"名词性宾语—动词"的语序跟"代词性宾语—动词"是和谐的，但跟"动词—代词性宾语"不和谐，因为不跟它同时出现。同样，"动词—名词性宾语"的语序跟"动词—代词性宾语"和谐，跟"代词性宾语—动词"不和谐。我们可以使用这些概念来重新表述这个规则：优势的语序总可以出现，而其相反的处于劣势的语序则只有在其和谐结构也出现时才会出现。

注意这里所谓优势并不由出现率高低来决定，而是根据四分表上有一组为零这个因素来决定的。要找一个虽为劣势结构但出现率比优势结构高的例子并不困难。优势地位跟和谐的关系完全可以从这张带有一个零的表上机械地推导出来。构成零的那一组每一个结构都为劣势结构，并且两个结构之间相互也不和谐。

像前面所提到的，和谐和不和谐的关系就是泛化的例子。在相类似的结构中，对应的成分也倾向于使用同样的语序。本例中对应的基础是一目了然的，代词和名词都作动词的宾语，另一对相应的成分都是动词。关于和谐和不和谐关系,根据结构间的转换以及其他关系还可以有相当的伸缩余地,并不仅仅取决于四分表上为零的那一组。

在此基础上,接下来我们来看看普遍现象 3 ,这种普遍现象显然否定了在Ⅰ型语言里使用后置词的可能。既然在Ⅰ型、Ⅱ型、Ⅲ型中都是 S 出现在 O 之前,这跟目前的论题无关。它可以引出以下结论:前置词比起后置词来说是占压倒优势的,SV 语序比起 VS 语序来说也占压倒优势。而且,前置词跟 VS 和谐,跟 SV 不和谐,而后置词跟 SV 和谐,跟 VS 不和谐。

Ⅱ型和Ⅲ型的区别在于Ⅱ型中宾语后置于动词,这特征跟Ⅰ型是相同的。另一方面,Ⅲ型是宾语前置于动词。根据普遍现象 4,绝大多数 SOV 使用后置词,可以得到这样的结论:OV 跟后置词相和谐,而 VO 跟前置词相和谐。证明这结论的类似结构留到下面论及密切相关的所有格结构时再讨论。现在要注意的是,Ⅰ型、Ⅱ型和Ⅱ型跟 Pr/Po 的关系或许可以重新概括如下:Ⅰ型具有 VS 和 SO, VS 和 SO 都跟前置词相和谐,而且前置词是占优势的。事实上,一切Ⅰ型语言都用前置词。Ⅱ型具有跟后置词相和谐的 SV 以及跟前置词相和谐的 VO,而且前置词占优势。事实上,相当多的Ⅱ型语言用前置词。Ⅲ型具有 SV 和 OV,都跟后置词相和谐。然而,前置词是占优势的。事实上,绝大多数Ⅲ型语言用后置词,但也有少数例外。

前置词语言绝大多数是"中心名词—所有格"语序,后置词语言绝大多数是"所有格—中心名词"语序。但两种类型都有一些例外,由此可以得到这样的结论:前置词是跟 NG 相和谐,后置词跟 GN 相和谐。

所有格语序跟 Pr/Po 的密切联系是泛化的一个明显表现。表示所有的关系跟其他的关系概念,如空间关系等相类似。英语里所有格标记"of"是一个前置词,跟 under、above 等等的语序特点一样。并且,这类空间和时间关系常用名词或类似名词的词来表达,如英语的 in back of(……的背后)。许多语言里 behind = the back+所有格,于是: X's back = in back of X 同 X's house (X 的房子)相平行; back of X = in back of X 跟 house of X 相平行。

这些所有格一方面跟与其类似的前置词或后置词短语相联系,另一方面跟"主语—动词"和"宾语—动词"结构相联系,这种联系都是通过所谓的主语所有格和宾语所有格而发生的。注意英语中 Brutus' klling of Caesar started civil war(布鲁图斯的刺杀恺撒引起了一场内战)跟 The fact that Brutus killed Carsar started a civil war 有相同的真值。成分的次序也类似。换言之，在这类转换式里，名词主语或宾语跟所有格对应，而动词同中心名词相对应。事实上，有的语言中动词的主语或宾语用所有格式来表示。例如，在柏柏尔语里，argarz（人）是名词的一般形式。而 urgaz 直接后置于另一词时，既可作从属的所有格，又可作动词的主语。所以 iffer urgaz（人走出去）恰恰跟 axam urgaz（人的房子）相平行。要知道柏柏尔语是Ⅰ型语言，所有格是在名词后的。它更多地使用前置词而不是后置词。

还可以对基本语序类型的各个变化因素之间的关系作进一步探讨，如所有格语序和形容词语序之间的关系。所有格和修饰性形容词都是限制名词的意义的，有更多的事实可证实这一点。有些语言如波斯语，形容词和所有格附加语都用同样的形式手段来标记。至于代词所有格，一些语言使用派生形容词，另一些则用代词的所有格形式，甚至有这样的例子，在第一、第二人称中用形容词，第三人称则用所有格（如挪威语）。

我们可以用所有以下因素间的直接或间接的相互和谐来概述上面的结果：前置词、NG、VS、VO、NA。这里有个总的倾向是把被修饰语放在修饰语之前，这方面处于最"极端"的语言是用 NG、NA 的Ⅰ型语言，有相当一部分语言属于此类。相反的类型是建立在后置词、GN、SV、OV，AN 之间的和谐关系上的。这也是相当广泛的类型，抽样中土耳其语和其他一些语言可以为例。另一方面，NA 语序的总的优势导致了巴斯克语类型（即Ⅲ/Po/NA，并有 GN 语序）的语言，它们跟土耳其语类型语言几乎同样常见。当然也要指出，语言作为高度复杂的结构，还有以上五个因素之外的其他因素在各种场合发生作用。如前面已经提到的指别词同名词的位置就是其中之一。

要解释优势地位比解释和谐关系更困难。例如，解释为什么形容词倾向于放在名词后面。人们可能会想到，同样的因素导致名词—形容词优势语序和主语—动词优势语序。用霍凯特的话来说，话题置于述谓之前是一种总的倾向。有些证据可以证实：名词—形容词确实以这种方式跟主语—动词相平行。在许多语言里，所有形容性的观念都当作不及物动词来处理。于是性质形容词就成了动词的一种关系形式或分词形式。上面谈到过，关系从句比形容词后置于名词的倾向更为强烈。有些语言里，像新几内亚的阿拉帕斯语里，The good man came（好人来了）照字面将译为 The man is-good that-one he came. 形容词—名词（译者注：应为名词—形容词语序）语序于是有点处于两可的地位，因为它类似于其他有修饰语的结构，因此跟 VS 发生间接的和谐,同时,话题—述谓语序的影响又使它跟 SV 相类似。

这一切远非是完备的理论,但无论如何它可以帮助我们去分析那些所有格结构违背通常规则而同 Pr/Po 的选择不相和谐的情况。可以设想在这种情况下所有格结构事实上是受了形容词—名词结构的影响,而形容词—名词结构,如前所述,某种程度上取决于修饰语与被修饰语之间一般和谐关系框架之外的因素。例如,如果我们发现 GN 语序违反一般规则跟前置词一起使用,原因可能是受到了跟 GN 相和谐的 AN 语序的相反影响。换句话说,所有格结构只有当 Pr/Po 跟 AN 语序不相和谐时才跟 Pr/Po 不和谐。这里可以包括某些一种语言同时有两种所有格语序的例子,它们指出了某种可能的类型演变,因为十之八九其中一种所有格语序会比另一种更古老。还可以进一步推测:如果有例外,这些例外的语言很可能是属于 II 型的,因为它同时使用 SV 和 VO 两种不相和谐的语序,这就为两种不同的所有格语序都提供了存在的基础。

注意,就 III 型的后置词语言(它们占绝大多数)来说,普遍现象 5 为上述假设提供了一个例证。因为普遍现象 5 的内容是一种 III 型语言如果有 NG,也就同时有 NA。这样的语言假定是使用后置词的,那么 NG 就跟后置词不和谐,但跟 NA 和谐。如果我们把具有两种所有格语序的语言都包括进来,那么至少可以有六种情况,都是同 NA 而不是同 AN 协调的。索马里语和马巴语都同时有两种所有格语序,而卡努里语、盖尔语、特达语和苏默语都有 SOV、后置词、NG 和 NA。

然而,这个假设还会产生某些进一步的预测。对 III 型的前置词语言来说,这个假设是:如有不同的所有格语序,或有跟前置词不相和谐的 GN,形容词—名词语序将是 AN,我仅知道两个例子,提格里尼亚语有两种所有格语序,阿姆哈拉语是 GN。它们都符合我们的假设,具有 AN。II 型语言中凡使用前置词而又有 GN 的,也应具有 AN,这方面例子有:丹麦语、挪威语、瑞典语(可能只有一种情况),而英语则有两种所有格语序。但它们都具有 AN,所以都符合这个假设。在 II 型的后置词语言中,我们有苏丹的莫鲁—马迪诸语言,以及与其有远亲关系的芒贝图语。它们都有两种所有格语序,也不出所料有 NA。现在我们遇到的仅有的例外就我所知是智利的阿劳堪尼亚语,它有两种所有格语序;高加索的达格斯坦诸语言,其中某些语言像罗吐里亚语那样使用 NG,其他则像塔巴萨兰语那样有两种所有格语序。显然,所有属于Ⅲ型的达格斯坦族语言只有 GN 跟后置词和 AN 相和谐。如果确实如此,这是我们的假设具有充分合理性的一个重要证据。最后既然所有的Ⅰ型语言都是使用前置词的,那么唯一要考虑的是具有 GN 的前置词语言。我仅知道一个例子,就是沃尔夫描写过的纳胡阿特尔语中的米尔帕—阿尔塔方言,像预期的那样,它有 AN。

除了上述已经讨论过的关系之外,普遍现象 20 和 29 显示了另一种类型的关系。也许可以称作"亲近等级"(proximity hiecrarchies)。我们发现有这样一种规则,即某些成分一定比另一些外国成分更亲近中心成分。这中心成分可以是词根语素或词干,或是向心结构中的中心词。这种亲近等级可能跟屈折范畴例子中的蕴含性等级有关。正因为数范畴跟词根的关系总比格范畴来得密切,因此不少语言有数的范畴而没有格的范畴,有格而没有数的语言则极为少见。从亲近等级角度来看,既然数更为密切,它就更容易跟词根融合起来而成为屈折形态。可以认为这种等级是同跟中心成分的逻辑和心理上的亲疏程度有关,但是这些问题本文就不拟再加以探讨了。

同样,这些现象跟中和现象也有关系越是关系密切的范畴,或者说是被蕴含的范畴,表现得越是精密,而不甚密切的范畴或有蕴含的范畴,则倾向于在表现形式上取中和的方式。普遍现象 36 和 37 就是如此。数是被蕴含的范畴。性的范畴在有标记数(非单数)的情况下常被中和,而数在某种特定的性(例如德拉维达诸语言中的中性)被中和的情况则极为少见。至于数和格相比,如上所述,数更亲近,在格出现的情况下数一般都出现,而相反的情况则极少。同样,某些格的区别在无标记数的情况下被中和亦属常见,而相反的情况也许根本就找不到。

从普遍现象 34 中可以发现另一条原则,我们还没有见过以下的系统:有一个表示三数的特定语法范畴,而另一个包括双数以及所有大于三的数。换言之,这方面是不允许分离性或非连续性的。

普遍现象 14 和 15 也许反映了同一条原则。语序是平行于实际经验或知识顺序的。在条件关系中,虽然其真值关系是非时间性的,但逻辑学家总是用像自然语言中那样的"蕴含者—被蕴含者"的顺序把它符号化。如果将前提转换法用于证明,我们会得到遵循推理顺序的实用例子。谁也不会想用颠倒的方式来写出一个证明过程。

普遍现象 7、8 和 40,虽然表面很不同,但看来都同样表现出在单位的末尾而不是起首加以标记的总的趋势。例如,在严格的Ⅲ型次类中,动词标记了句子的结束。当屈折仅出现在名词短语的最后一个成分上时,它就标记了短语的结尾。这或许牵涉到这样的事实:我们总知道某人何时开始讲话;但可悲的经验表明,没有一定的标记,我们无法知道他何时将结束。

有严格的Ⅲ型次类,却没有严格的Ⅰ型次类,这可能还牵涉到另一个因素。一般来说,开首的位置是强调的位置。而当使用其他强调方式(如重音)时,开首的位置就空出来了,于是要予以强调的那个成分就可以首先出现。普遍现象12就是一例。看来似乎所有的语言中表达时间、地点的成分都可以出现在句首的位置上。

在下面这类例子中[如德语的 Gestern ist mein Vater nach Berlin gefahren(我父亲昨天到柏林去了)]常见的谓语的非连续现象,又表明了另一条原则。总的来说,在直接成分层级上越高的结构体,它的直接成分的语序越自由。可以发现实际上所有的语言中各自作为整体的主语和谓语之间的语序,都有某种程度上的自由,只有少数语言的所有格结构的语序可以变动,而且如有变动,也几乎总是伴随有其他的区别,不仅仅是语序不同。在语素结构中,次序最为固定。总的说来,非连续成分比起连续成分来要少得多。

诚如本文第一节所指出的那样,本节所阐述的那些原理仅仅是尝试性的。我希望其中至少有一些原理对进一步的探索是有益的。

Charles Li & Sandra Thompson(1976)
《主语与主题:一种新的语言类型学》选读[①]

◆ 作者简介

李讷(Charles N. Li, 1940—),美国加州大学圣塔芭芭拉校区语言学系终身荣誉教授,早年研究兴趣为汉语语言学。

Sandra A. Thompson(1941—),美国加州大学圣塔芭芭拉校区语言学系终身荣誉教授,曾任国际语用学学会会长。

两人合著有 *Mandarin Chinese:A Functional Reference Grammar*

[①] Li C., Thompson, S.著,李谷城摘译,《主语与主题:一种新的语言类型学》,《国外语言学》,1984年第2期。

(1981),是一本经典的从功能语法的角度探讨汉语的语法书。

◆ **正文节选**

Ⅰ. 引 言

本文试图为建立以主语—谓语(subject-predicate)和主题—述题(topic-comment)这两种语法关系为依据的类型学打下基础。主语这个概念长期来一直被当作语言句子结构中的基本语法关系。然而,我们从某些语言所收集到的证据表明,这些语言中的基本结构表现为主题—述题关系,而不是主语—谓语关系。这种证据不仅表明在各种语法描写中主题这个概念可能同主语概念一样,都是基本的,而且表明各种语言,按其注重的是主题概念还是主语概念,构成句子的方式可能各不相同。根据我们的研究,语言有四种基本类型:1. 注重主语(subject-prominent)的语言;2. 注重主题(topic-prominent)的语言;3. 主语和主题都注重的语言;4. 主语和主题都不注重的语言。在注重主语(下面简作 Sp)的语言中,句子结构便于主要用**主语—谓语**这种语法关系进行描写;在注重主题(下面简作 Tp)的语言中,基本句子结构便于主要用**主题—述题**这种语法关系进行描写。在第 3 类语言中,有两种同等重要而明显不同的句子结构:主语—谓语结构和主题—述题结构;在第 4 类语言中,所有句式中的主语和主题合二为一,难分彼此。我们不妨以两个英语句式为例,分别说明主语—谓语结构和主题—述题结构:

(1) John hit Mary. (约翰打玛丽。)
　　主语　谓语

(2) As for education, John prefers Bertrand Russell's ideas. (至于教育,约翰更喜欢罗素的思想。)
　　主题　　　　　述题

在 Sp 语言中,基本句子结构同句(1)相似;而在 Tp 语言中,基本句子结构则同句(2)相似。但这并不是说在 Tp 语言中不能识别主语,也不是说 Sp 语言就没有主题。事实上,我们所调查的所有语言都有主题—述题结构;虽然并非所有的语言都有主语—谓语结构,但在多数 Tp 语言中似乎总有识别主语的方法。我们的类型学只不过主张:有些语言以主题概念为基础可以描写得更深刻,而另一些语言则以主语概念为基础可以描写得更深刻。

根据我们下面提出的一些标准和我们所调查的一小部分语言,可以列出如下的分类表:

<u>注重主语的语言</u>　　　　　　<u>注重主题的语言</u>
印欧语　　　　　　　　　　　汉语
尼日尔—刚果语　　　　　　　拉祜语(倮倮语—缅甸语)
芬兰—乌戈尔语　　　　　　　傈僳语(倮倮语—缅甸语)等
闪米特语
达依巴尔语(澳大利亚土著语言)
印度尼西亚语　马达加斯加语等

<u>主语和主题都注重的语言</u>　　<u>主语和主题都不注重的语言</u>
日语　　　　　　　　　　　　他加禄语
朝鲜语等　　　　　　　　　　伊洛干诺语等

本文的目的在于确定以注重主语和注重主题这两个概念为基础的类型学的价值和有效性。做法如下:首先根据主语和主题之间许多不是共同具有的特性概述两者之间的区别;接着探讨 Tp 语言的一些特征。然后,证明 Tp 语言中主题—述题结构确实是基本句式;最后说明这种类型学对于研究普遍语法的意义。

Ⅱ. 主语与主题

(a) 有定和无定。主题的主要特征之一是所指的事物必须是有定的,主语则不必是有定的。例如(3)和(4)的主语就是无定的。

(3) A couple of people have arrived. (到了几个人。)

(4) A piece of pie is on the table. (桌上有块馅饼。)

(b) 选择关系。主题的一个重要特性是,它同句中的任何动词无需有选择关系;就是说,主题不必是谓语成分的论元(argument)。主题的这一特性在 Tp 语言中尤为明显,因为那些语言中的主题—述题结构代表其基本句式。考察(5)和(6),句中划底线的成分为主题:

(5) 那场火幸亏消防队来得快。
(6) 那些树木树身大。

这两个句子中的主题同动词没有什么选择关系。同样,日语中带は标记的主题同句子的动词也不必有选择关系,例如:

(7) 学校 は ぼくが 忙しかった。(在学校里我很忙。)
　　学校——主题标记　我——主语标记　忙——过去时

但是,主语总是同句中的某个谓语有选择关系。诚然,某些句子的表层主语可能同表层的主要动词没有选择关系。例如,传统的转换分析①承认下列句子中表层主语 John 同主要谓语 be easy 和 appear 没有选择关系:

(8) John is easy to please. (约翰容易讨好。)
(9) John appears to be angry. (看来约翰很生气。)

然而,这个事实并不违背我们的论断,即句子的主语总是同句中某个谓语有选择关系。在表层结构中,主语也许不紧挨着同其有选择关系的谓语,而且甚至可能跟与其没有选择关系的动词构成新的语法关系。但事实仍然是:一句句子的主语与该句子中某个动词之间必定存在选择关系,而在主题与动词之间就不必存在这种关系。

(c) 动词决定"主语"而不决定"主题"。例如,英语中如果动词同施事和其它名词短语一起出现,施事就成为主语,除非使用诸如被动式那样的"特殊"结构(这种主语化的方法是菲尔墨 1968 年提出的)。如果动词是不及物的,那末根据是状态动词还是动作动词,分别由受事(patient)或施动者充当主语。如果是使役动词,则由使役者充当主语。

但是,主题就不是由动词决定的;主题的选择不取决于动词。话语(discourse)对主题的选择可能起作用,但在话语的制约范围内,说话者仍有相当大的自由来选择充当主题的名词短语,而不用考虑动词的性质。

(d) 功能。在任何句子中,主题的功能始终如一。主题是"注意的中心",

---

① 指乔姆斯基 1965 年《句法理论要略》的分析模式。

它预告话语的话题。这就是为什么主题必须是有定的原因。主题的功能在于确立容纳谓语表述的框架,这就使得主题不可能是不确定的。

考察主语的功能,可以看到两个事实。其一,某些名词短语显然可以定为主语,但在句中不起任何语义作用;这就是说,在许多 Sp 语言中,句子中可能出现"虚位"或"假位"主语。其二,要是主语名词短语不是虚位,主语的功能在句子(而不是话语)的范围内就可以确定。主语的特点可以归纳为:表明动词所表示的动作、经历和状态等等的方向或着眼点。主语与主题之间在功能上的这种区别解释了一个事实,即主语总是动词的一个论元而主题则不一定是论元。

(e) 与动词的一致关系。大家知道,许多语言中的动词同句子的主语表现出强制性的一致关系。然而,主题与谓语之间的一致关系则极为罕见,就我们所知,还没有一种语言普遍存在或非得有这种一致关系。其理由相当清楚:跟主语和动词间的相互联系相比,主题和述题间的联系要松散得多。

(f) 句首位置。我们考察的所有语言在转换而成的表层结构中,主题总是居句首位置,而主语并不限定于句首位置。这可以从话语的结构方式中找到原因。由于言语要把信息按顺序连续传递,这就不难理解代表话语话题的主题应该最先说出。主语概念更多地着眼于句子范围,因此在话语的传递顺序中不必优先传递。

(g) 语法过程。主语在诸如反身代词化、被动化、相同名词短语删除、动词系列化和命令句化等过程中起着重要作用。主题不介入这些过程,部分原因正如前面所述,主题在句法上不依附于句子的其余部分。

Ⅲ. 注重主题的语言的特征

(a) 表层的形式标志。在 Tp 语言中,主题有表层标志,主语则不一定有表层标志。例如,汉语的主题总是在句首;在傈僳语和拉祜语中,主题带有形态标志。在这几种语言中没有一种语言的主语有表层标志,尽管如前面所述,主语在某些语法过程中的作用是可以确定的。

(b) 被动结构。在 Sp 语言中,被动结构很普遍。但在 Tp 语言中,被动化或者根本看不到(如拉祜语、傈僳语),或者看来是一种边缘结构,在讲话中几乎不用(如汉语),或者包含特殊的意义(如日语中的表示"逆境"的被动式)。[①] 在

---

① 汉语和日语中的被动句原来只表示遭受某种不愉快的事情,但由于受英语的影响,这种意义上的限制正在消失。

Tp 语言中,被动式相对来说不太重要,其原因可以这样解释:在 Sp 语言中,主语是个非常基本的概念,如果不是由某个动词指派为主语的名词充当了主语,而是另一个名词变成了主语,那个动词必须带有标志以表示这个主语的选择是"非正常"的。在 Tp 语言中,在句子结构中起更重要作用的是主题,而不是主语。任何名词短语都可以成为句子的主题,而不用给动词带上任何标志。

(c) "假位"主语。Sp 语言可以有"假位"或"虚位"主语,比如英语的 it 和 there,德语的 es,法语的 il 和 ce;而 Tp 语言则没有。这是因为在 Sp 语言中主语不管起不起语义作用,总得有一个。英语的例子有:

  (10) *It* is hot in here.(这里面很热。)
  (11) *There* is a cat in the garden.(有一只猫在花园里。)

在 Tp 语言中,主语概念不起显著作用,就不需要"假位"主语。遇到不要求有主语的情况,Tp 语言的句子完全可以没有主语。(如(10)—(11)中相应的汉语译句。)

(d) "双重主语"。Tp 语言以普遍存在所谓"双重主语"结构而著称。例如:

  (12) 魚は　鯛が　　美味しい　　(鱼数鲷好吃。)
    鱼(主题)　鲷(主语)　好吃
  (13) 那棵树　叶子大。
    (主题)(主语)

(e) 支配互参关系。在 Tp 语言中,对互参成分的删除起支配作用的一般是主题,而不是主语。汉语的例子有:

  (14) 那棵树叶子大,所以我不喜欢_____。

第二个分句中删除的宾语只可理解为主题"那棵树"的互参成分,而不是指主语"叶子"。句(15)说明:主语"消防队"不能支配第二分句中成分的删

除,并且主题"那场火"同该分句不相容,因而语义不连贯:

(15) 那场火消防队来得早,(﹡)所以＿＿＿＿很累。

(f) 动词居句末的语言。Tp 语言往往是动词居句末的语言。日语、朝鲜语、傈僳语和拉祜语无可争辩已经是地道的动词居句末的语言,汉语则还处于变成这种语言的过程中。

(g) 对主题成分的限制。在某些 Sp 语言中,就什么可以作为主题成分而论,主题述题句式受到很大的限制。例如,印度尼西亚语只允许表层主语成分和表层主语成分的所有格作为主题。如果宾语性名词短语作主题,句子就不合语法。

而在 Tp 语言中,对于什么可以作为主题成分则没有限制。

(h) 主题—述题句子的基本性。Tp 语言与非 Tp 语言之间的最突出区别也许在于:在 Tp 语言中主题—述题句在很大程度上可以看作全部基本句式的一部分,而在 Sp 语言中则不是这样。我们将在下一节证明 Tp 语言中主题—述题句子的基本性。

Ⅳ. Tp 语言中主题—述题句子的基本性

我们要在这一节中证明,在 Tp 语言中的主题—述题结构式不可看作是从任何别的句式派生出来的。

先要说明,我们并不是反对据以确立这种派生关系而制定的任何一种公式;我们所反对的是认为这种做法在原则上合乎需要,即在这些语言中把主题—述题句看作是派生的、边缘的、有标志的句式,或者看作是不寻常的句式。就是说,我们并不是说不可能想出某种生成装置来"处理"我们要提供的实例。我们的看法是:把主题—述题句看作基本的而不是派生的句式,就最自然地解释了 Tp 语言所示的现象。

(a) 傈僳语。在傈僳语中可以找到证实这种看法的最明显的语言现象。在傈僳语中,甚至连施事和受事这些语法关系也无法确定,因而无法确定主语这个概念。如果主题—述题句可以说成是从某种主语—谓语句式派生出来的,那么,很清楚,在傈僳语中这种主语—谓语句式根本不存在。

从语法关系来看,傈僳语的句子词序是动词居句末;如果动词前有一个以上的名词短语,那么句子通常产生歧义,不清楚哪个名词短语代表施事或动作者,哪个名词短语代表受事。包含及物动词的简单陈述句结构只表明哪个名词短语是主题,并不表明哪个名词短语是施事。句(16)和(17)是傈僳语中典型的简单陈述句。

(16) làthyu　nya　ánà　khù-a
　　　人　主题标记　狗　咬—陈述句标记
　　"人(主题) {他们咬狗。/狗咬他们。}"

(17) ánà　nyu　làthyu　khù-a
　　　狗　主题标记　人　咬—陈述句标记
　　"狗(主题) {它们咬人。/人咬它们。}"

就施事而论,句(16)和(17)同样含糊不清。两句都可以解释为<u>人咬狗</u>或<u>狗咬人</u>。两句的区别仅在于主题。

(b)汉语。最早提出汉语是 Tp 语言的不是我们。除了其他人外,赵元任(1968:67—104)颇为详细地讨论了主题—述题概念。有必要指出,虽然赵通篇使用主语和谓语这两个名称,但我们可以把这些名称理解为主题和述题。这正是他的本意,这从下面的话中可以看出:

"汉语句子中主语和谓语的语法意义是主题和述题,而不是动作者和动作。"

当然,我们感兴趣的是主题与主语之间的区别及其对于建立语言类型学的含意。

与傈僳语不同,汉语中的确存在可以称作为主语—谓语句的结构。例如:

(18) 我弟弟喜欢吃苹果。(My brother likes to eat apples.)

这个例子的词序同英语译文的词序一致。从这类例句也许可以得出结论:汉语同英语一样,属于主语居于句首的 Sp 语言。此外,虽然如前所述,我们把汉语说成是 Tp 语言,但主语概念显然在某些句子结构中起作用。例如,连动结构就须描写成具有同一个主语的谓语系列:

(19) 张三买了票进去。

我们能够举例证明,要解释这种结构必须借助于主语概念。下面的例子中,两个谓语共用的那个名词是其中一个谓语的施事和另一个谓语的经历者。这就是说,单单用施事来说明同两个谓语的关系是无法描写连动句的。

(20) 我花了钱享受。

再者,(21)—(22)说明主语可以支配反身代词化。

(21) 约翰喜欢他自己。
(22) *约翰,我喜欢他自己。

句(22)表明,当句子包含的主题可以同可称作主语的成分区别开来时,那个主题就不支配反身代词化。因而,汉语语法得用主语来描写反身代词化过程。但是即使对于汉语,反对把主题—述题句看作从主语—谓语句式派生出来的证据仍然非常有力。比如许多正常的主题—述题句中的主题同述题中的动词没有选择关系,这类句子就不能溯源到主语—谓语句式。下面是几个这类的例句:

(23) 那座房子幸亏去年没下雪。
(24) 这件事情你不能光麻烦一个人。

这类句子俯拾即是,这是反对主题化过程的十分明显的证据。

此外,在汉语句子的表层结构中主语没有系统的标志。这就是说,人们可能想要视作主语的名词短语,是无法识别的。作为一个适例,让我们简略地考察一种结构,我们认为这种结构清楚地说明了 Sp 语言与 Tp 语言之间的区别。我们不妨把这种结构叫做"假被动式"(pseudo-passive)。下面是两个例子:

(25) 这件新闻广播了。

(26) 那本书已经出版了。

(c) "双重主语"结构。"双重主语"句子是最典型的主题—述题句,广泛见于汉语、日语、朝鲜语、傈僳语和拉祜语。如果我们能够证明这种句子不是派生的,那末这就非常有力地证实了我们的看法。这些反对从任何别的句式派生出"双重主语"句的论据,恰恰对于我们所考察的所有 Tp 语言都适用。

据我们所知,唯一曾被认为是"双重主语"句来源的句子是这样的一种主谓句式,其中名词短语 1 与名词短语 2 之间表现出领属关系。比如,对于汉语,我们可以说(27)应从(28)派生出来:

(27) 象鼻子长。
(28) 象的鼻子长。

然而,许多"双重主语"句的两个句首名词短语之间并没有领属关系或整体与部分的关系,例如:

(29) 他们谁都不来。

因此,只是对于"双重主语"句的一个次类来说,存在领属关系。那末,把这类句子看作从以领属性短语作主语的主谓句派生出来,并不说明问题。

(d) 分布。有人向我们指出,主题—述题句也许比别的句式在分布上有更多的限制,尤其是不能那么自由地出现在限制性关系从句和非断定补语[①]中。然而,事实上情况并非如此。下面我们举汉语的例子,说明那些须分析成主题—述题结构的分句,可以作为限制性关系从句和作为非断定补语而嵌入。(30)和(32)分别是这两种情况的例子:

---

① 非断定补语(non-asserted complemenet)的定义见 J. Hooper 和 Thompson 合写的: On the applicability of root transformation,刊 *Language Inquiry* 1973 年第 4 期,第 465—497 页。

(30) 我不喜欢那种一斤三十块钱的豆子。

划底线的关系从句出自下面的句子：

(31) 那种豆子一斤三十块钱。

句(31)显然不能分析成为主谓结构。

(32) 我反对他们谁都不来。
同样，划底线的补语只可能是主题—述题分句。

V．类型学及其若干历时意义

我们主张在主题概念起重要作用的语言和主语概念起重要作用的语言之间划分类型，并已经提出证据。当然，同所有类型划分一样，我们讲的显然一种连续体(continuum)。例如傈僳语就比汉语更为注重主题。菲律宾语似乎既非十分注重主语，又非十分注重主题，而日语和朝鲜语则可以说既注重主语，又注重主题。马达加斯加语注重主语的程度不如英语。这些事实可用图解表示如下：

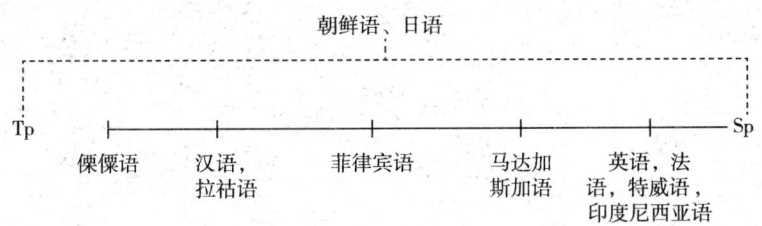

根据共时及历史的语言现象，似乎可以明显看出，主语和主题并非是互不相干的概念。主语实质上是语法化了的主题；主题在纳入动词的格框架（这时我们称之为主语）的过程中，变得有些不纯，某些主题特性削弱了，但其主题性依然可辨。这就是在有些语言中主题的许多特性为主语所共有的原因。例如，有些 Sp 语言不允许无定主语。

我们在这里要提出的看法是，主题这个普遍概念可以以不同方式表现于各语言之中。在有些语言中，比如傈僳语和汉语，主题的特性体现在主题成分中，而且主题—述题句属于这些语言的基本句子结构。在另一些语言中，比如马达加斯加语,主语体现某些主题特性,主语成分跟动词有密切的语法关系,并在描写许多语法过程中起主要作用。

根据我们所示的跨语言证据,我们提出下面的历时图解。

(A) 代表:注重主题的语言。主题概念属于基本句子结构;主题和主语分明。

(B) 代表:主题和主语都不注重的语言。主题较密切地纳入动词的格框架。

(C) 代表:注重主语的语言。主题完全纳入动词格框架成为主语;主语和主题常不分明,主语具有某些非主题特性;带明显主题的句子属于高度"有标记"的句式。

(D) 代表:主语和主题都注重的语言。主题句的"有标记"性减弱,更接近基本句式。

回过头来讲前面提出的问题,为什么 Tp 语言绝大多数都是动词居句末?我们提出如下猜测:一种语言从(C)阶段,经过(D)阶段,进而演变到(A)阶段的过程中,起主要作用的句式是"双重主语"句式。哪种语言使用这种句式越多,它就越接近(A)阶段,因为这种句式是典型的主题—述题结构。要注意,"双重主语"结构总是这样的形式:

```
名词短语1 | 名词短语2   动词
  主题         述题
```

这种形式恰恰是动词居句末的语言的典型句子结构。当名词短语1与名词短语2之间的关系所受的限制越来越少时,这种句式随之渐趋普遍。

最后,我们希望本文已经指向一个新的剧场,去观看一出老戏的上演:共时类型学不过表现为历史循环圈的一个横切面,在这个横切面上,不同的语言处于各种不同的阶段。我们在探索语言普遍现象的过程中领悟到,语言类型实际上是对于达到同样交际目标的各种手段的一种描写。

Hilary Chappell(2001)"Language Contact and Areal Diffusion in Sinitic Languages"选读①

◆ 作者简介

曹茜蕾②(Hilary Chappell),法国社科院东亚语言研究所首席教授,主要从事汉语方言语法和语言类型学研究,对普通话、闽南话、湘语、瓦乡话等有深入研究。1984年她在澳大利亚国立大学获博士学位,1980至1981年攻读博士学位期间她在北京大学留学一年,师从朱德熙和陆俭明两位教授。

曹茜蕾教授同其他研究者一直致力于开拓汉语类型学和汉语方言语法对比描写,旨在探索汉语方言的多样性。她的研究一直努力超越现有诸多对汉语个体方言的描述,而且更进一步,以主要句法结构分析为基础,采用一种宏观的鸟瞰视角来分析汉语方言的共性和个性特点。在过去10年中她收集并整理了口语语料库及诱导性材料作为句法分析的基础,这也是其研究的创新之处。

选文中,作者探讨了中国方言中几个"有特色"的语法现象。作者认为不能简单地把这种"特色"等同于"类型学特征",而应结合语法化和地域类型综合地进行考量。

◆ 正文节选

4. Shared grammaticalization pathways in Sinitic, areal diffusion, and language universals

In this section, I examine five sets of data in Sinitic: the source of the diminutive suffix, the feature of negative existential verbs 'there is not/there are not', the development of complementizers from verbs of saying, adversative passives, and some constructions which express inalienable pos-

---

① Chappell, H. 2001. "Language contact and areal diffusion in Sinitic languages." *Areal Diffusion and Genetic Inheritance: Problems in Comparative Linguistics*, pp. 328 - 357.

② 图片来源:http://xwb.hnedu.gov.cn/c/2017 - 04 - 19/868432.shtml。

session. Some of these phenomena unify Sinitic as a family while others bear witness to the grouping of languages in the South-East and East Asian zone as a *Sprachbund* or linguistic area. In this section, the attempt is made to distinguish which features represent a pathway of grammaticalization that is cross-linguistically unremarkable, which are the result of areal diffusion, and which could be seen as special typological features of Sinitic languages.

4.1 EARLY SOUTHERN MIN DIALECT GRAMMAR AND EVIDENCE FOR GRAMMATICALIZATION: THE DIMINUTIVE

Early seventeenth-century texts on Southern Min dialects provide an invaluable source for the diachronic study of the grammar of their modern counterparts in that they are largely written in the special dialect characters for vernacular Hokkien. Below, I compare the diminutive of modern Southern Min dialects such as Taiwanese and Amoy (Xiamen) with those found in the *Arte de la lengua Chiō-Chiu* (1620), a grammar on the same type of dialect written in Spanish.[①]

In Sinitic languages, the diminutive has its source in various morphemes for 'son' which may have 'child' as a secondary meaning. A morpheme for 'child' is the common source crosslinguistically for diminutives (see Heine, Claudi, and Hilnnemeyer 1991: 79 – 88, 1993: 38). For example, Mandarin uses the suffix ə˞ < *ér* 兒 'son' while Cantonese employs tone sandhi, changing the citation tone to high rising tone, the cheshirization of an earlier segmental morpheme meaning 'son'. Cheshirization refers to the attrition of segmental phonemes, which leave a mere trace of their former phonetic sub-

---

① This work was most likely a collaborative effort of Spanish Dominican missionaries and Chinese interpreters living in a Chinese Sangley community near Manila in the late sixteenth and early seventeenth centuries. On phonological grounds, van der Loon identifies the dialect used in these manuscripts as the vernacular of Hai-cheng as spoken around the turn of the seventeenth century (1967:132). He shows conclusively that it differed in certain phonological features from the dialect of Zhangzhou city, to which prefecture this harbour town belonged. It appears that the Sangleys or Chinese traders had migrated from this port in southern Fujian province during the late sixteenth century, with many eventually settling in and around Manila.

stance, such as the tone.① In Taiwanese Southern Min, the diminutive is formed with the suffix -á. It can be related to the lexeme for 'son', 子 kĭaⁿ used in the *Arte* (1620: 2b, 11a, 12b) and to kiáⁿ 'son' in contemporary Taiwanese and Amoy, for which the character 囝 is used as well.② Note that the stem of the word used for 'child' in the *Arte*—简仔 kĭn nĭa (1620:15) or 囡仔 gín-á ~ gín-ná in contemporary Taiwanese—cannot be the source for this diminutive on phonological grounds (see Lien 1998).

In the early seventeenth-century grammar of Southern Min, the following description is given for the diminutive (1620:10):

(4) *Arte de la lengua Chiō Chiu* (1620)

'The diminutive is formed with the final particle *ia* or *nia* or *guia*:

kéiguìa 圭仔 "little chicken" [*pollito*]

bôguiìa 帽仔 "little hat" [*sonbrerillo*]

tóguìa 刀仔 "little knife" [*guedillito*]'

In contemporary Taiwanese, the three corresponding words are *ke-á* 'chicken, little chicken'; *bō-á* 'hat' and *to-á* 'knife, small knife' respectively, indicating partial bleaching of the diminutive feature.③

I suggest that in this early grammar of Southern Min, the *Arte*, an incipient stage of development for the diminutive can be viewed, where its form can still be clearly related to the morpheme for 'son', unlike contemporary Southern Min where the form has atrophied to -*á* and can be used not

---

① See Matisoff (1991) for more on 'cheshirization', to whom we owe the coining of this evocative term.

② This morpheme kiáⁿ 子 'child, son' is in fact used to exemplify the tone category which is accompanied by nasalization, according to the missionaries' classification. Note that in the Spanish Romanization *k*- is used interchangeably with *gu*- and *qu*- for the unaspirated voiceless velar plosive initial /k/, as seen in the diminutive forms given in (4). Furthermore, nasalization has not been marked for these diminutive forms, suggesting that it had already been lost at this stage, in contrast to its lexical use as 'child'.

③ Note that only one of the variants listed by the *Arte* is illustrated by the examples in (4). This is discussed further in Chappell (2000).

only as a diminutive but also as a marker for the noun category:

(5) Taiwanese Southern Min:
一 张 桌仔　　合 两　张 椅仔
chit tè toh-á　　*kap nn̄g tè　í-á*
one CL table-NOM and two CL chair-NOM
'a table and two chairs' (not: 'a small table and two small chairs')

It is interesting to find that the lexeme *kiá*ⁿ can nonethesless still be used as a kind of suffix to mark the young of animal species, postposed after the reduced diminutive form used as a noun marker:

(6) 牛仔囝　　　狗仔囝
*gû-á-kiá*ⁿ　　*káu-á-kiá*ⁿ
ox-NOM-offspring　dog-NOM-offspring
'calf'　　　　　'puppy'

Further support for the proposed grammaticalization pathway of 'son' > DIMINUTIVE comes from Yang (1991: 166) who points out that the diminutive suffix in the Chaozhou dialect of Southern Min retains the full form of *kiá*ⁿ.

(7) Chaozhou: *tia*ⁿ *kiá*ⁿ contrasting with Xiamen, Zhangzhou, Taiwanese: *tia*ⁿ-*á*
'a small cooking pot'

Yang also quotes the Tang poet Gu Kuang 顾况 who annotates the character 囝, pronounced with an alveopalatal initial /tɕiǎn/ in modern Mandarin, as having the meaning 'son' in colloquial Min in §13 of his poem *Shànggǔ zhī shé*.

(8) 囝　音　蹇，閩　俗　呼　子　為　囝．
　　Jiǎn yīn jiǎn, mǐn sú hū zǐ wéi jiǎn
　　(word) sound jian Min custom call son as jian
　　'The sound of this character is *jiǎn*, the Min usually call "*son*" *jiǎn*'

The more general case of semantic change from 'child' to diminutive morpheme is well attested in other languages of the world, for example, in Jurafsky (1996) and Heine *et al.* (1993: 38) while the use of diminutives with probable source morphemes in sex-specific 'son' is characteristic of Sinitic (for more data, see Huang 1996). The *Arte* provides the hard evidence for this semantic change into a diminutive suffix, affecting the morpheme 'son' in Southern Min (see also Chappell 2000). Given the widespread occurrence of the first type of conceptual shift cross-linguistically, I conclude that while this more semantically specific case may be a shared development in Sinitic languages, it only partially characterizes it typologically.

[...]

4.3 COMPLEMENTIZERS

In Taiwanese Southern Min, a complementizer similar in function to English *that* has grammaticalized out of the verb 'to say' *kóng* 講. Matisoff (1991: 398 – 400) describes this path of grammaticalization as an example of the general category of verbs developing into verb particles in South-East Asian languages, represented by Thai, Khmer, and Lahu. Like these three languages, the Southern Min verb 'say' is also used at the end of a non-final clause and before the intonation break to introduce the complement clause. It is not fully grammaticalized since it may be omitted. Moreover, it forms a kind of verb complex with the preceding matrix verb which must belong to one of the following verb classes: speech act, cognition, or perception, and it directly introduces the embedded clause, as in (11):

(11) Taiwanese Southern Min:

遐 个　　敌对　　　的 武将　　　共　　笑　　讲
Hia ê ⟨MC:díduì⟩ ê búchiòng kā　　chhiò kóng,
that CL opposing　L general PRETR laugh SAY_that

这　是　号作　　⟨J:猴面冠者⟩
che sì　hō-tsò　⟨J:Sarumen Kanja⟩.
this be name.as monkey.face youngster

'Those generals who opposed him mocked him (General Toyotomi) as the one who should be called "monkey-face boy".' (Japanese tales 629–30) (Note: MC = Mandarin Chinese insert; J = Japanese insert)

In this first stage of grammaticalization, when 'say' verbs are used as quotative markers, the lexical meaning is not completely bleached. Examples such as *chhio kóng* could still be rendered as 'laughed (at him) saying' while in the second stage where *kóng* is used with cognitive verbs such as *siū^n* 'think', its literal meaning is less plausible: 'think saying'. The putative path of development is outlined in Chappell (forthcoming e) in addition to other grammaticalized or partially grammaticalized uses of *kóng* as a metalinguistic marker of explanation; an evidential marker of hearsay; a component of a compound conditional marker; a topic introducer and as a clause-final marker of assertions and warnings. It has not yet developed a purposive function, which may indicate that certain of its several grammaticalization pathways are relatively 'young' (Bernd Heine, p.c.).

There has been only very little study of this phenomenon in typological work on Sinitic languages to date. In Chappell (forthcoming e), I show that this development has proceeded as far as the quotative stage in some Yue and Wu dialects and less far in standard Mandarin. For the Yue dialect of Cantonese, ample evidence can be found of the use of *wa^6* 'to speak' in conversational and narrative texts where it functions as such a quotative marker with speech-act verbs. Note, however, that wa^6 does not form a verb complex with the preceding speech-act verb: this is clear in that it can be separated from the verb by a noun denoting the direct object:

(12) Cantonese:
赞 哩 个 男仔 话……
$jaan^3$ lei^5 goh^3 $laam^4jai^2$ wa^6...
praise this CL young.man say...
'(she) praised this young man saying ...'

Although a verb complex with 'say' as V_2 is not a possible strategy for introducing complement clauses in standard Beijing Mandarin, or *pǔtōnghuà* (as opposed to such a use for quotations), it is in the regional variety known as Taiwanese Mandarin. It is striking that Taiwanese Mandarin does not choose the cognate verb for *kóng*, which is *jiǎng* in Mandarin, to create the new syntactic calque but instead makes use of its functional equivalent, the high frequency verb *shuō* 說, in the configuration SUBJECT — $VERB_1$ — *shuō* + CLAUSE:

(13) Taiwanese Mandarin:
那 我 希望 说 这 个 愿望
nà *wǒ* *xīwàng* *shuō* *zhè* *ge* *yuànwàng*
CONJ 1sg hope SAYcomp this CL wish
很 快 就 到 了
hěn *kuài* *jiù* *dào* *le*
very quickly then arrive PFV
'So I hope that this wish will be realized very soon.'

(14) Beijing Mandarin:
*我 希望 说
*wǒ *xīwàng* *shuō*
1SG hope say

However, this does not provide supporting evidence just for the north-south divide for Sinitic languages: it appears that Sinitic is encircled by language families and language isolates (such as Japanese and Korean) that all possess complementizers which have developed from verbs of saying. This feature has been described in the relevant literature for individual languages belonging to Tibeto-Burman, Tai-Kadai, Hmong-Mien, Indic, Dravidian, and Altaic (see Matisoff 1991, Saxena 1988).

Since this semantic change is also cross-linguistically well attested (it occurs widely in various language families of Africa—see Frajzyngier 1996 for Chadic, Amberber 1995 for Amharic, Heine *et al.* 1991: 216 - 17, 246 - 7, Heine *et al.* 1993: 190 - 8 for a larger sample of languages), it seems that the grammaticalization of *kóng* into a complementizer in Taiwanese Southern Min is most likely a language internal development. It has simply drawn on its own resources (Dixon 1997) to recreate a syntactic device which was in fact available in Classical and Middle Chinese, as attested in the written register.

Indeed, earlier periods of written Chinese made use of verbs of saying such as *yuē* 曰 (Classical Chinese) and *dào* 道 (Medieval Chinese) as quotative markers, although not as fully fledged complementizers (described in Chappell forthcoming e). This means that not only does Sinitic have its own inherited language internal devices upon which to analogize but it also has access to patterns and processes which can be imitated from surrounding unrelated language families.

It seems that this has taken place in recent times for sister languages within Sinitic, the case in point being the calquing of the Taiwanese Southern Min complementizer into Taiwanese Mandarin. This is an unusual development in terms of the direction of metatypy from a less prestigious to a more prestigious language, and note that there are many other examples of Taiwanese Southern Min constructions which have been borrowed into the Taiwanese variety of Mandarin (see Kubler 1985). This probably reflects linguistic creativity in transferring favoured syntactic forms and devices into Mandarin where gaps exist, rather than a negative description in terms of interference from the first language.

Further research on dialect materials would be in order to show irrefutable evidence for the view that the development of a complementizer in Taiwanese Southern Min is a purely independent innovation, triggered however by a combination of factors: a conducive environment in terms of areal typological features and the existence of appropriate language-internal characteristics.

Unlike the case for negative existential verbs, the existence of a complementizer in Southern Min and some Wu and Yue dialects tallies well with Matisoff's inclusion of Southern Sinitic in the South-East Asian linguistic area. The theoretical problem remains, however, of distinguishing between areal diffusion and a putative language universal for the development of complementizers from verbs of saying, given the right typological preconditions.

4.4 ADVERSATIVE PASSIVES

Matisoff (1991) points out that verbs of giving typically develop into causatives and benefactives in South-East Asian languages. In Southern Sinitic languages, verbs of giving are also used to form the passive construction. For example, most Hakka dialects use the high frequency verb pun^{44} 'to give' as both the passive and the benefactive marker, while Cantonese does the same with $bei^2 <$ 'give'.

A further characteristic feature of passives which unites Sinitic is that the colloquial forms are both adversative and agentful. This appears to be an unusual development for 'give' (compare this with data in Heine *et al.* 1993: 97 – 103). Such a description applies to standard Mandarin as well where only the *bèi* passive has an agentless form although it has lost its adversative feature in some contexts. Note that the *bèi* passive belongs to more formal discourse, in contrast to the agentive colloquial passives formed by *jiào* 'make' and *ràng* 'let' (see Chappell 1986).

Norman (1982: 245) observes that these two Northern Chinese passives formed with the causative verbs *jiào* 'make' and *ràng* 'let' are unique amongst Sinitic languages, as opposed to the use of verbs of giving. He argues that this is not an independent development in Mandarin but rather is due to Manchu superstrate influence on Chinese. In Manchu and other Altaic languages the same structure can be used for both passive and causative meanings. In support of this view, an earlier study by Hashimoto (1987: 46) contrasts standard Mandarin with Mandarin dialects on the periphery of the Northern Chinese zone which continue to use verbs of giving as passive markers. This suggests that 'give' verbs as passive markers are an older feature.

The adversative feature appears to be an areal feature as not only do South-East Asian languages such as Thai and Vietnamese show this restriction, but also Japanese (see Shibatani 1994). Hence there are different allegiances for each of these features: some evince the north-south divide in Sinitic (verbs of giving versus causative verbs used as passive exponents), some are relevant to the South-East and East Asian area (the adversative feature), while this particular development for 'give' is possibly specific to Southern Sinitic within the Asianzone, and is quite rare cross-linguistically (Bernd Heine, p.c.).

10.3 思考和练习

1. 请根据以下的例子,分析以下几种语言在词素形态上属于哪种语言类型(孤立语、屈折语、黏着语和复综语)。

甲: ev-   ler- im-   de
    house- pl-   my-   in
    'in my houses'

乙: ea   taya na   ŋone na   yalewa
    PAST   hit   the   child the girl
    'the girl hit the child'

丙: chʰatra-ra   monojog   diye   likʰ chʰi-l-o
    student-PL   attention with   write-PROG-PST-3

'students are writing attentively.'

ʧ:wa'-   k-   akya'tawitsher-   ú:n:
PAST- 1SG- dress-   make
'I made a dress.'

2. 浏览《语言结构的世界地图集》在线版的语音特征库（https://wals.info/feature），观察中国方言在语音方面具有哪些共性和差异，列举几个你的发现。

3. 根据你对中国方言的理解，有哪些词素形态和语法方面的特征可以作为对中国方言分区的参考标准？

4. 语言类型学研究的发展与语言描摹密不可分。结合本章的几篇文章，讨论：类型学研究的发展对语言描摹工作有什么启示？一个具有类型学意义的语言描摹应具备哪些要素？

10.4 延伸阅读

Comrie, B. 1989. *Language Universals and Linguistic Typology: Syntax and Morphology* (Second Edition). Chicago: University of Chicago Press.

Croft, W. 1990. *Typology and Universals*. New York: Cambridge University Press.

Greenberg, J. (ed.).1966. *Universals of Language* (Second Edition). Cambridge, Mass.: The MIT Press.

第十一章 历史语言学

11.1 导引

- 引言
- 历史比较语言学
- 语言谱系
- 语言演变的类型
- 语言演变的过程
- 语言演变的动因

11.1.1 引言

历史语言学主要研究三个方面的问题:(1) 构拟语言的原始形式;(2) 确定语言的亲属关系;(3) 发现语言演变的规律。历史语言学研究始于历史比较法,历史比较法奠定了历史语言学的研究方法以及对语言演变的一些基本认知的基础,因此本章将首先阐释历史比较法,再介绍近期关于语言演变的重要理论和热点问题。

11.1.2 历史比较语言学

历史比较语言学是历史语言学的一个重要组成部分,它奠定了历史语言学发展的根基。历史比较语言学发展于 19 世纪的欧洲,其核心是历史比较法。

要了解历史比较法,首先要谈谈历史比较语言学的一个理论预设。我们知道,意大利语、西班牙语、葡萄牙语和法语等欧洲语言虽为不同的语言,但是在词汇、句法上却高度地相似,原因是这些语言都是由通俗拉丁语演变而来的。罗马帝国的统治曾使拉丁语通行于欧洲,但大约在公元1世纪,口头拉丁语在不同的地域出现了分化;随着时间的推移,这些分化日渐累积,不同区域间语言的差别越来越显著,最终形成了今天欧洲的语言格局。

拉丁语和欧洲语言的发展历程体现的正是历史比较语言学的一个理论预设,即一些语言可能具有同一个祖先,它们发源于同一个早期的原始母语(proto-language);在人口的迁移和其它因素的作用下,这种原始母语在不同的地方会发展出新的特征;久而久之,这些特征累积形成了语言和语言的差别。基于这样的假定,历史比较语言学家认为,具有亲属关系的语言(由同一原始母语演变出来的不同语言)很有可能仍保留着原始母语的一些特征,通过比较和分析这些特征便可以确立这些语言的亲属关系——这是历史比较法的第一步;然后,在第一步的基础上,根据同谱系语言共有的特征,可以对它们共同的祖先——原始母语进行构拟。历史比较语言学采用比较分析的方法实现两个研究目标:建立谱系关系和构拟原始母语。

诸拉丁语言的历史发展似乎过于显而易见,有充分的历史文书见证和记录了这一过程。对于那些没有发展出文字记录的语言,或者发生在史前的语言演化,历史比较的方法能够发挥更加重大的作用。

18世纪,当欧洲国家开始向海外扩张,欧洲人开始接触到远在东方的印度文明和各种用梵语书写的经典,有些人发现,这种在遥远东方的语言竟然和他们熟悉的希腊语和拉丁语有惊人的相似之处。1786年"亚洲学会"上,一名供职于东印度公司的英国人William Jones宣读论文,指出梵语和众多欧洲语言的相似之处,提出它们同出一源的猜想;这在当时被许多人视为无稽之谈。但正是由于欧洲语言与梵语在此时的邂逅,引发了语言学家的思考和讨论,催生出了历史比较语言学及其系统的研究方法,致使"印欧语系"及世界几大语系的提出(见图11.2)。

11.1.2.1　主要著作

历史比较语言学的几篇重要奠基之作,始于对印欧语系语言的分析。历史比较语言学发展的第一阶段以波普、拉斯克和格里姆为代表。他们开创了历史比较法,提出并论证了有关印欧语种共同发源的设想,树立了一些历史比较语言学的基本观念。

德国的葆朴(Franz Bopp)有两部重要的著作:《论梵语动词变位系统,与希腊语、拉丁语、波斯语和日耳曼语相比较》(*Über das Conjugationssystem der Sanskritsprache in Vergleichung mit jenem der griechischen, lateinischen, persischen und germanischen Sprache*, 1816)、《比较语法》(*Vergleichende Grammatik des Sanskrit, Zend, Griechischen, Lateinischen, Litthauischen, Gothischen und Deutschen*, 1833),尤其是其中第一本,被认为标志着历史比较语言学的元年。在这两本著作中,通过比较这些语言中具有同样语法功能的变位——第一本主要集中在动词的变位,而第二本则扩展到不同的语法类别,如:名词的变位(性、数、主格、宾格、所有格等)、形容词的格(比较级、最高级)和数词,葆朴主张把这些词语分成"词根-词缀"两部分看待,并着重分析词缀的演变。通过比较分析法,波普不仅构拟了词缀的原始形式,提出词缀来源的假设;并且分析了这些变位词缀的语音变化的规律。波普讨论的历史语音变化规律很大程度上印证了格里姆提出的"格里姆定律"(Grimm's Law)。

	SANSKRIT.	ZEND.	LATIN.	LITHUANIAN.
m.	*vriké-bhyas,*	*vĕhrkaĕi-byô,*	*lupī-s.*	*wilka-m(u)s.**
f.	*jihwá-bhyas,*	*hizvá-byô,*	*terrī-s,*	*ranko-m(u)s.*
m.	*pati-bhyas,*	*paiti-byô,*	*hosti-bus.*	....†
f.	*príti-bhyas,*	*áfríti-byô,*	*messi-bus,*	*awi-m(u)s.*
m.	*bhavishyantí-bhyas,*	*búshyainti-byô,*	....	....
m.	*súnu-bhyas,*	*pasu-byô,*	*pecu-bus,*‡	*sunu-m(u)s,*
f.	*vág-bhyas,*	*vách-e-byô,*	*voc-i-bus.*	....
m.	*bharad-bhyas,*	*barĕn-byô,*§	*ferent-i-bus,*	....
m.	*átma'-bhyas,*	*asma'-byô,*	*sermon-i-bus,*	....
m.	*bhrátri-bhyas,*	*brátar-ĕ-byô,*	*fratr-i-bus,*	....

图 11.1　四种语言中的与格(dative case)变位①

格里姆(Jacob Grimm)对历史比较语言学最大的贡献是他在《德语语法》

---

① 图片来源:Bopp, F., Eastwick, E. B. 1885. *A Comparative Grammar of the Sanskrit, Zend, Greek, Latin, Lithuanian, Gothic, German, and Slavonic languages*. London, UK: Williams. p. 262。

(*Deutsche Grammatik*)(1822)中提出的"格里姆定律"。受到波普(1816)和拉斯克(1818)①研究中不同语言的启发，以及他对日耳曼语语音演变的观察，格里姆提出印欧语言的语音演变是系统的音变，并且具有一定的规律。比如在辅音方面：

- 送气浊塞音变浊塞音或擦音
- 浊塞音变清塞音
- 清塞音变擦音

波普、拉斯克、格里姆等人的发现由此在欧洲掀起了一股历史比较语言学的风潮，词源研究开始兴起，关于"重建"(reconstruction)的研究也开始出现。波特(August Friedrich Pott)的《印度-日耳曼系语言领域内的词源研究》("Etymologische Forschungen auf dem Gebiete der Indogermanischen Sprachen", 1833)是一个较早期的词源研究。施莱赫尔(August Schleicher)的《印度-日耳曼系语言比较语法纲要》("Compendium der Vergleichenden Grammatik der Indogermanischen Sprachen", 1861/62)也是第一次使用"重建"的方法构拟了古印欧语的研究，其构拟的内容包括元音、辅音、词根、词干结构、名词变格等。

所谓"重建"，就是就所比较的语言材料，用历史统计的方法为每个形式、每个词构拟出一个对每种语言来说都适合的"一般历史性的公分母"，用来代表最原始的形式，并表明各有关的个别语言以后的演变。构拟出来的原始形式(一般前加 * 表示)的准确性是无法验证的，它只是一种基于理论的猜测，很难代表当时的准确发音。

历史比较语言学第二个阶段的发展大概可以从 1870 年开始算起。在这个阶段，比较语言学家开始认识到一切语音的演变都是有规律的，并且没有例外——如果有不能被解释的例外，只是因为还没有找到它的规律，这就是

---

① 拉斯克(Rasmus Rask)，丹麦语言学家，主要研究语言为冰岛语，著有《古代北方语或冰岛语起源研究》。此书成书于 1814 年，最后于 1818 年出版。拉斯克与波普不谋而合，在此书中采用了历史比较法，把冰岛语和峨特语、斯拉夫语、立陶宛语、拉丁语和希腊语等作比较，找出了许多词汇上的对应，并整理出一个比较语法。拉斯克对古音演变的规律有很细密的考察，这点对格里姆有尤其大的启发。

"维尔纳定律"(Verner's Law)。维尔纳定律的提出为新语法学派(The Neogrammarians)提供了有力的理论依据,进一步推动了历史比较语言学的发展。

新语法学派中特别值得一提的是法国语言学家梅耶(Antoine Meillet)。他的《历史语言学中的比较方法》(La Méthode Comparative en Linguistique Historique,1925)一般被认为是历史比较法最好的书。本章节选了其中几节,展示历史比较法基本的操作方法。

在此必须指出,语音形式在历史比较语言学研究中始终占据着核心的地位。首先,两个语言间亲属关系的确认必须由同源词(cognates)是否存在对应的规律的语音形式来验证①;其次,词源的构拟也是基于其后代语言的语音的。历史比较法通常不会在构词形态和基本语序上使用——前者极其不稳定,而后者更容易受到其它语言的影响而彻底改变。虽然早前波普的分析是基于变位词缀,但根据波普的推断,这些词缀演变自代词等基本词汇。

11.1.2.2　汉语古音的构拟

20世纪初,瑞典汉学家高本汉(Bernhard Kalgren)把历史比较语言学的方法引入传统的汉语音研究中。高本汉根据《切韵》的音类、现代汉语方言和域外汉字读音,利用历史比较法构拟了中古音,后来赵元任、李方桂、罗常培等学者又对高本汉的构拟做出了修改和订正。高本汉对于汉语中古音的构拟发表于他的博士论文《中国音韵学研究》("Études sur la Phonologie Chinoise",1915)中。本章的第二篇选文总结了迄今为止包括高本汉在内的中古音构拟的一些重要研究。

11.1.3　语言谱系

历史比较语言学的一个巨大贡献,就是推动了世界语言语系的建立。19世纪的历史比较法从不同的方面论证了横跨欧亚大陆的印欧语系(Indo-European)的存在。汉藏语系(Sino-Tibetan)也早在19世纪就有学者提出。除此以外,世界的几大语系中,使用人数较多的语系包括:分布于西亚/北非的亚非语系(Afro-Asiatic,旧称含闪语系),广布于南太平洋、印度洋、南亚诸岛

---

① 语音形式的系统对应通常仅在语言的基本词汇中确立。一般词汇通常不作考虑,因为很多是从非亲属语言中借来的。

的南岛语(Austronesian),分布于非洲西南部的的尼日尔-刚果语系(Niger-Congo)。位于亚洲大陆上的几个主要语系除了汉藏语系,还包括:主要分布于印度中南部的达罗毗荼语系(Dravidian),亚洲南部的侗台语系(Tai-Kadai)和南亚语系(Austro-asiatic),以及亚洲北部的阿尔泰语系(Altaic)。

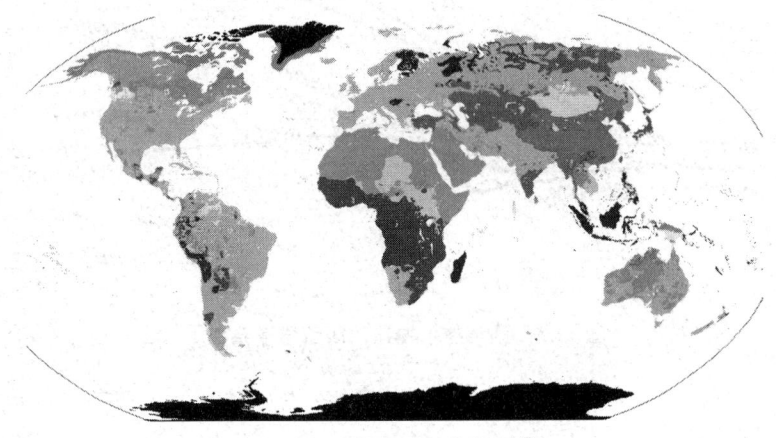

图 11.2　世界语系分布图①

11.1.3.1　谱系树模型

前面提到,两种语言之间的亲属关系可以通过比较法建立。但是一个语系中庞杂的关系应该如何表示呢?施莱赫尔受到达尔文进化论物种演变的启发,以谱系树(Stammbaum)的模型,把不同语言分为语支和语族,以表示同一个语系内不同语言的分化和共同进化(图 11.3)。

谱系树的模型及其反映的语言演变观对历史语言学的影响深刻,以至于有学者提出了与谱系树理论相关的"落叶模型",试图来解释目前还无法厘清关系的汉藏语系的谱系结构(图 11.4)。"落叶模型"的提出者,荷兰语言学家 George van Driem 解释,这种模型并不是反对谱系树模型,而是反映了现阶段语言学家对汉藏语的认识——我们近期才了解了汉藏语大部分语言的全貌;就像看到一棵树满地的落叶一样,还无暇去抬头观察树的枝干。但或许通过观察树干投射在地上的影子,我们能逐渐看到枝干的走势……

---

① https://upload.wikimedia.org/wikipedia/commons/e/ed/Primary_Human_Language_Families_Map.png.

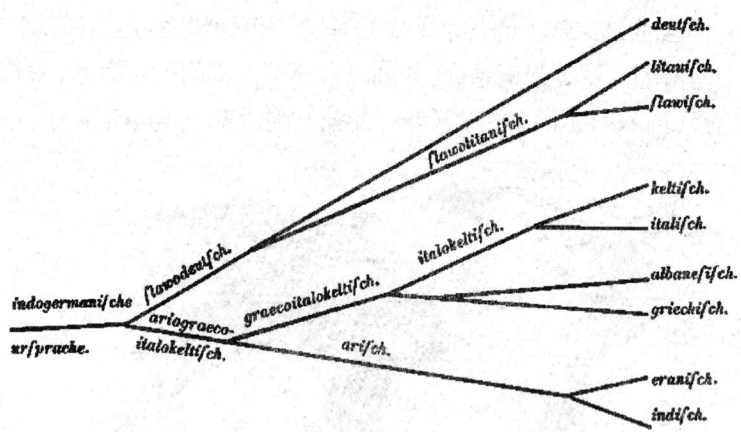

图 11.3 施莱赫尔构建的印欧语谱系树①

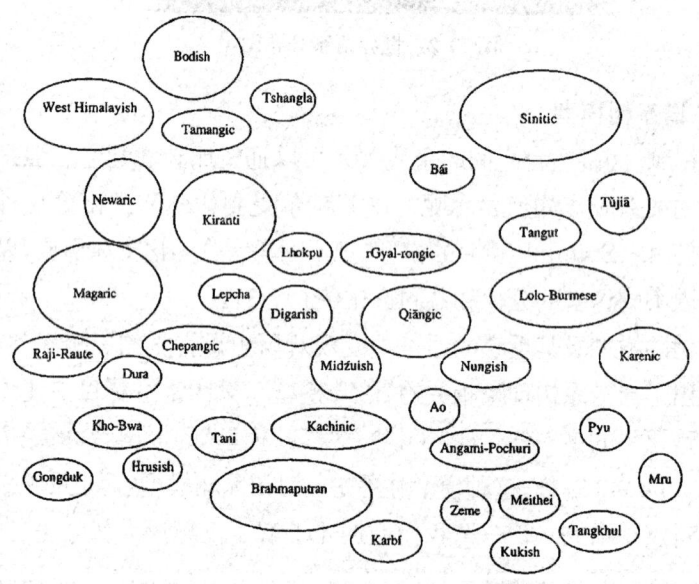

图 11.4 汉藏语系的"落叶模型"②

---

① 图片来源：http://lingulist.de/pyjs/slides/img/schleicher1861.jpg。
② van Driem，G. 2003. Tibeto-Burman v. s Sino-Tibetan. In B. Bauer & G.-J. Pinault (eds.) Language in Time and Space. Berlin: Mouton de Gruyter. p. 111.

11.1.3.2 波浪模型

因为语言演化的实际情况并不是能简单地用谱系树结构来解释的。即使在历史比较法盛行的时期，人们也已经意识到语言之间可能相互影响：互借词汇，甚或影响另一个语言的结构。德国的施密特（Johannes Schmidt）另外提出了"波浪模型"，认为原始印欧语已存在方言，这些不同方言的特点像波浪一样向四周传播扩散，互相影响，形成了印欧语各语族语支中的某些共同点。

11.1.4 语言演变的类型

在这一小节，我们开始跳出历史比较语言学的框架，进入广义的历史语言学研究。现代的、广义的历史语言学研究的内容，除了是对早期语言的一种静态构拟，更多的是一种动态的历时（diachronic）研究，其关注的是语言演化的过程，以及语言演化中呈现的普遍规律和趋势。历史语言学也因此往往需要采用一个跨语言的视角。在这点上，它与类型语言学非常相似，两者也经常有方法上的交叉。

11.1.4.1 语音变化

从新语法学派时期起，语音变化就被认为是规律、系统发生的现象。某个音素的合流、分化、增加、脱落、替换不会孤立地出现在一个或几个词里，而是会普及到语言的整个语音系统中。例如在汉语中，从中古汉语到现代普通话，就有"浊声母清化""知、庄、章三组声母合流""精、见二组声母分化""韵尾合流归并""韵头由繁到简"，以及平上去入声调的变化等发生在整个语音系统的语音变化现象。而在印欧语系的构拟中，则能发现演变过程中元音或辅音在不同位置的增加、脱落、替换和音色的改变（延长、缩短、增强、弱化、颚化等等）。这些音变的发生有时与语流音变有关，或者与人发音和听音的生理基础有关，有时与语言的省力原则有关；但更多的时候，语音变化是一种随机发生、无法预测其方向的现象，所以印欧语言才会出现各种各样的分化。

在语音变化中，有一种特殊的现象，称为链变（chain shift），指的是一个语音系统中一系列相互联系的音位全部改变其语音现实的复杂音系变化。链变的基本假设是，一个语音中的所有音位构成了一个平衡的语音系统，只要其中一部分发生了改变，就会影响整个系统发生改变。音位的移动意味着原语音系统出现空槽，因而产生了填补空槽的需求，这时会由另一个音位的移动来填补，这就是所谓的链变现象。格里姆定律所指向的印欧语历史上发生的系统音变本质上就是一种链变。

11.1.4.2 词汇变化

词汇变化在这里有两个方面的含义。一种词汇变化指的是词义的变化，也就是既有词汇在历史的演变中词义发生了改变。词义变化的类型可分为词义扩大、词义缩小、词义转移，以及词义褒化和贬化。比如古汉语（文言文）中的"行"、"走"以前的词义是"走"和"跑"，这种现象属于词义转移。而在对某些特殊人群的指称中，我们经常会看到一个中性含义的词经历词义贬化的现象，比如中文的"小姐"（原是对年轻女性的称呼，后指从事色情服务行业的女子）、"同志"（原是社会主义体制下对他人的敬称，后指同性恋者），英语的 *mistress*（原义为"女主人"，后指"情妇"）、*madam*（原是对成年女性的尊称，后在某些情形下指"老鸨"）。

另一种词汇变化则指新词汇的发明及旧词汇的淘汰。伴随着社会的兴替，新事物的涌现和旧观念的式微造就了这个意义上的词汇变化。计算机时代的到来产生了许多新事物，也创造了许多新词来描述这些现象：电脑/计算机、芯片、内存、键盘、博客、云计算、弹幕等等，不一而足。还有一类新词，比如网络流行语言"也是醉了"、"十动然拒"则是一种更类似于俚语、诙谐幽默的社会方言。

11.1.4.3 形态句法变化

还有一类语言变化是语法规则的变化。在具有屈折形态的语言中，可能体现为词素形态的变化；在孤立语中，可能体现为新句型（词语的组合序列）的出现；或者是在任何语言中的语序的变化。我们把这一类统称为形态句法变化。形态句法变化往往伴随着词义的变化以及语音的变化。中古汉语六朝之后发生的语序变化，以及由此诱发的动补结构的出现、体标记的产生，可视为形态句法变化的范畴。

语法化（grammaticalization）是形态句法变化中的一个常见的现象，指的是实词演变成语言中具有语法功能成分的一种语言变化。汉语的很多虚词就是从实词语法化而来的，比如体标记"在"、"过"、"着"、"了"都是从动词变化而来的。在汉语这样的孤立语中，语法化之后的成分仍然可视为一个词；但在屈折语言中，实词经历语法化后可能会失去词的地位，而变成附着于词根的词缀，甚至消失。语法化的成分通常读音会变弱；在具有词素形态的语言中，其长度会缩短。比如，英语中的 have 表完成时的时候，可以缩写为 've，在发音上也从一个音节缩为一个辅音[v]。这种语义从实到虚，形态从有到无的变化——也就是语言变化的"单向性"（unidirectionality），曾被认为是语法化的普遍真理，但随着越来越多反例的出现，这种观念已经受到了撼动。当然，语法化的单向性是一个较为普遍的现象，因此语义的虚实和形态特征在某些情形下能帮助我们判断比较语言发展的阶段。

如果仅用虚实之分来描述语法化成分的词义变化未免过于简单。实际上，语法化成分的语义变化就如同我们的语言系统一样，具有一定的随意性。同样语义的实词，在不同语言中可能会演变成不同功能的语法成分；或者说，不同语言中具有类似功能的语法成分，是从不同的实词演变而来的。

但语法化成分的语义变化同时也具有一定的规律性。我们大概会以为，汉字的"把"字句非常特殊（特别是"把"从"握"、"持"的动词义演变为处置构式的一部分），但实际上，在尼日尔-刚果语系中的语言 Twi 和 Nupe 中，都存在具有"拿"义的动词演变成使动结构一部分的例子。上文提到的英文用表"拥有"的动词 have 表示事情的发生和完成，这种用法在中国的某些方言里也能看到，比如受到闽南话影响的台湾普通话"你有没有看到他？"又比如，用个人的客观能力来表示事情发生的可能性，用身体部位来表示方位，用方位词来表示时间等等，都是虽不绝对但是极为普遍的语法化现象①。当这种规律的语义变化同时出现在没有亲属关系、地理上也不毗邻的语言中时，唯一的解释便是人类共有的认知能力和认知倾向造就了这种相似的、有规律的语言变化。

语法化发生的一个重要前提，就是人类喻象思维（metaphorical thinking）的能力。喻象思维，在这里并不限于作为文学创作修辞手法"比喻"，而是更广泛地指向人类跨越概念空间，以一个概念替代另一个概念的一种思维能

---

① 更多的例子可参阅 Heine, B. & Kuteva, Tania, 2002. *World Lexicon of Grammaticalization*, New York, N.Y., USA: Cambridge University Press.

力。时间和空间属于不同的概念空间，主观意愿和客观事实也属于不同的概念空间；但人类运用喻象思维，就可以把两个不同概念空间的概念关联起来——人们为跨空间概念 A 和 B 建立的关联性，使他们可以利用原来专门用于描述 A 的语言来描述 B。而由于人类的生活体验(人周遭的时间、空间，人的生理结构，人的行为，人与人之间的关系)大部分是类似的，人类利用喻象思维建立的关联也是相似的——或者至少是可以被别人理解的。人类的喻象思维是语言创造性的重要来源。

近几年在语法化理论的基础上，有学者结合构式语法理论提出了语言变化的"构式化"(constructionalization)理论。这种理论认为，词义变化以及形态句法的变化都是在"构式"(construction)的框架内进行的。一个构式的组成成分组成了一个整体，决定了构式整体的语义(语用)以及其中各个成分的语法关系和含义。

11.1.5　语言演变的过程

如果从语言的系统性角度来考虑，语言变化的开端总是始于某处的，比如某个具体的搭配、句子或场景。由于语言的规律和系统性特征，一些语言使用者可能会对几个偶然发生的语言变化做出分析，发现它们变化的规则，逐渐推导应用到其它的符合规则的场景中，最终扩及到整个语言系统。类推(analogy)是语言演变发生的一个重要机制。无论是语音变化、词义变化还是形态句法变化，类推都决定了语言变化在整个语言系统的扩散。

如果从语言的社会性这个角度来考虑，语言的变化也是始于某些使用者，然后逐渐扩散到社会的绝大部分使用者。一个新的语言现象之所以能被理解，是因为说话者之间有语用推理(pragmatic inference)的能力。即使是从没接触过的一个新的语言现象，母语者仍能在语境中猜测出它的意思。我们在儿童时期学习语言，甚至在网络时代学习新的流行语言，依靠的都是语用推理的能力。

因此，语言演变的过程是一个既有突变，又有渐变的过程。突变指的是说话者的语言创新以及听者理解的瞬间；渐变指的是这种变化从孤立、个别的现象到系统、普遍的存在的过程。总的来说，语言演变从开始走向完成，是一个使用频率增加、使用场景增加和使用人数增多的过程。

11.1.6 语言演变的动因

语言演变的动因大致可分为内因和外因。内因是指引起语言演变的语言系统内部因素。以上提到的印欧语系语音系统的链变、汉语语序变化而产生的语法变化，包括语言使用者的类推能力、语用推理能力，我们都可以视为内部因素。

在讨论语言演变的外部因素时，通常会考虑到语言使用的社会生态，比如语言接触、语言特征作为社会标记，以及来自官方的语言规划的影响。地理上毗邻语言的相互接触势必会造成一定程度的语言交融，例如，中国各异的方言在一定程度上是历史上汉族人南下迁徙与当地语言（楚国、百越国）交融的结果。但是，接触的两个语言哪一方对另一方的影响更大，则可能与经济实力和文化势力有关。中国在建国之后推广普通话，许多方言都开始向普通话靠拢，这与普通话带来的各种就业、教育、医疗等社会资源不无关系。另一方面，我们也可以把这类语言变化视为一种社会标记，也就是说，不同群体使用"普通化"的方言或本土味的方言，有可能是在试图呈现一种对本地文化的身份认同。来自官方的语言规划对语言变化的作用则更加不可忽视。建国以来，我国对文字书写、发音、甚至语法使用都做出了规范，遏制了一些可能正在进行中的随机语言变化，但这并不意味着语言变化一定按照官方的意志和方向进行。来自上层和底层的语言变化，最终由一代又一代的语言使用者决定其是去是留。

11.2 选读

- 梅耶(1925)《历史语言学中的比较方法》选读
- Jerry Norman (1988) "The Methodology of Middle Chinese Reconstruction"选读
- 梅祖麟(1991)《从汉代的"动、杀"、"动、死"来看动补结构的发展》选读
- Cavalli-Sforza et al. (1988) "Reconstruction of Human Evolution"选读

梅耶(1925)《历史语言学中的比较方法》选读①

◆ 作者简介

安东尼·梅耶②(Antoine Meillet, 1866—1936), 法国历史语言学家。梅耶师从索绪尔, 1891 年任巴黎高级研究学院教授, 1906 年任法兰西学院印欧语比较语法教授。他的研究领域涉及希腊语、拉丁语、日耳曼语、凯尔特语、波罗地语、吐火罗语等诸多领域, 编写过斯拉夫语教材。1924 年他与科恩同编《世界语言》一书, 一生出版专著 24 种、论文 540 篇, 其中《印欧系语言比较研究导论》、《历史语言学中的比较方法》对历史比较语言学产生了重大影响。梅耶构拟出原始印欧语的语音语法系统, 但认为它不可能完全重建。

◆ 正文节选

一、比较方法的定义

进行比较工作有两种不同的方式:一种是从比较中揭示普遍的规律, 一种是从比较中找出历史的情况。这两种类型的比较都是正当的, 又是完全不同的。

世界上各处地方都有一些关于动物的故事:动物与人的相似之点是这样明显, 所以把一些人类固有的行为加到动物身上, 来表明一些不容易直接使人了解的事情, 是很自然的。我们可以比较这些故事, 确定它们的形式、性质和应用范围, 从而建立一个关于动物的故事的一般理论。我们在其中所发现的相同之点, 是由共同的人类心理所造成的;其中的不同之点, 是由文明的类型和程度的差别所造成的。用这样的方法, 我们可以知道人类的共同性质, 但是一点也不能知道人类的历史。

假如我们和一位法国青年学者杜美西尔(Dumézil)先生一同去研究那些关于"长生水"的印度欧罗巴神话, 所得的结果就完全不同了。这种以为有一

---

① 梅耶著, 岑麒祥译,《历史语言学中的比较方法》,《国外语言学论文选译》, 语文出版社 1992 年版。
② 图片来源:法国维基百科 https://fr.wikipedia.org/wiki/Antoine_Meillet。

种水可以使人长生的想法实在太自然了,所以不是什么民族的特点。可是,在每个印欧语民族中,都或多或少的可以遇到这种在一个巨桶里酿造"长生水"的传说,这个传说还加上假未婚妻的故事或神仙和恶魔相斗的说法,可见这里面是包含着许多特殊的事情的。这些特殊的事情之间并没有什么联系,所以它们的结合决不是偶然的。

假如语言所表达的意思和那些用以表示这意思的声音之间有一种或松或紧的自然联系,就是说,假如语言符号可以撇开传统,单用它的音值本身可以使人想到它所表达的概念,那末,语言学家所能采用的就只有这种一般的比较方法,任何语言的历史也就都不会有了。

但是事实上语言的符号是任意规定的:它只有靠传统的力量才能有意义。如果在法语里,大家用 un, une 来表示"一",用 deux 来表示二",……那并不是因为 un, une 和 deux 等词本身和"一"、"二"等意思有什么关系,而只是因为说法语的人教给学法语的人的习惯是这样的。

只是因为语言符号具有这种完全任意的性质,所以才能有现在所要研究的这种历史比较方法。

比方法语、意语、西班牙语的数词是这样的:

	法　语	意　语	西班牙语
一	un, une	uno, una	uno, una
二	deux	due	dos
三	trois	tre	tres
四	quatre	quattro	cuatro
五	cinq	cinque	cinco
六	six	sei	seis
七	sept	sette	siete
八	huit	otto	ocho
九	neuf	nuove	nueve
十	dix	dieci	dies
二十	vingt	venti	veinte
三十	trente	trenta	treinta
四十	quarante	quaranta	cuarenta
一百	cent	cento	ciento

这里面的相符之点决不是出于偶然的；其所以不是偶然的，是因为从一种语言与另一种语言的那些差异中，可以找出一些确定的对应规律来。比方"huit"，"otto"，"ocho""八"等词间的差异初看起来很大，但是这个差异并不是偶然的，因为这样的对应还有很多，如法语的 nuit"夜"，意语的 notte，西班牙语的 noche；或法语的 cuit"煮"，意语的 cotto；以至法语的 lait"乳"，意语的 latte，西班牙语的 leche；法语的 fait"事实"，意语的 fatto，西语的 hecho 等等。这些显而易见的相符之点固然给我们指出了应当遵循的途径，但是可以利用的却只是那些语音对应的规律。

显而易见的相似之点给我们指出了很好的途径的地方，常常有些特殊的细节予以证实。比方 un 和 une 有阴阳性之分，而其他的数词却都没有，这一点是很重要的。

因此，我们可以假定，法、意、西班牙三种语言的数词出于同一个来历。在这种情形之下，经验告诉我们，只有两个可能的来历：一、这三组数词同出一源；二、这三组中有两组的形式是由另外一组借来的。在这个例子里，第二种假设是不可能的，因为在这三种语言中，我们不能用任何一种语言的形式来解释另一种语言的形式。法语的 huit 不能出于意语的 otto 或西班牙语的 ocho，意语的 otto 不能出于法语的 huit 或西班牙语的 ocho，西班牙语的 ocho 也不能出于法语的 huit 或意语的 otto。由此可以证明法、意、西班牙这三种语言的数词有一个共同的出发点，而这出发点不是法语，不是意语，也不是西班牙语。

在以上所举的例子中，相符之点又多又完备，对应的规律又极容易认识，连门外汉也可以马上看得出来，用不着语言学家才看得到它的证明价值。假如我们考察一些在时间上和空间上相隔较远的语言，如梵语、古雅典希腊语、拉丁语和古典亚尔明尼亚语等，相符之点就没有这样显著，对应的规律也就比较难于确定。

	梵语	古雅典希腊语
一	ekah, ékā, ékam	hēs, mia, hen
	拉丁语	亚尔明尼亚语
	ūnus, ūna, ūnum	mi

以上三个形式中，第一个是阳性的，第二个是阴性的，第三个是中性的；亚尔明尼亚语没有这种语法上的性的分别。

	梵语	希腊语	拉丁语	亚尔明尼亚语
二	d(u)vā	dyo	duo	erku

"二"这个数词是有性的分别的,这里只举出阳性的形式;"三"和"四"也是如此。

	梵语	希腊语	拉丁语	亚尔明尼亚语
三	tráyah	trēs	trēs	erekʻ
四	catvārah	téttares	quattuor	čorkʻ
五	páñca	pénte	quinque	hing
六	sát	heks	sex	vec
七	saptá	heptá	septem	ewtʻn
八	ástā①	óktō	octō	utʻn
九	náva	ennéa	nouem	inn
十	dáça	déka	decem	tasn

除了"一"这个数词暂且不论,可以说希腊语、拉丁语以至梵语间的对应大部分是显而易见的,可是亚尔明尼亚语和其他语言间的对应就没有这样明显了。

但是我们把亚尔明尼亚语的各种事实详细考察一下,就可以看到这些相符之点的证明价值。

比方亚尔明尼亚语的 erku"二"和拉丁语的 duo 等是不相似的;不过,一些其他的对应表明 erk-可以与其他语言的 *dw-相当,例如:希腊语有一个词根 dwi-表示"怕"的意思,亚尔明尼亚语也有一个 erki-(erkiw"怕");希腊语有一个很古老的形容词 dwārón,表示"长久",亚尔明尼亚语也有一个 erkar"长"(参看中译本第 26 页。)从这个相符之点可以得出一条一般的对应规律:古代的 *dw-在亚尔明尼亚语变成了 erk-。

作为复合词的第一个成分,希腊语有一个 dwi-,亚尔明尼亚语有一个 erki-。所以有这组特殊的相符之点是不容许我们存任何怀疑的(参看中译本第 91 页)。

亚尔明尼亚语 erkʻ"三"和 čorkʻ"四"等词的形式和希腊语的 trēs, téttares 相差很远;但是它们至少有一部分可以用同类的对应来解释。并且有一种特殊的细节,就是在梵语和希腊语中,"三"和"四"都有正规的格变形式,而自"五"以后的数词却是不变的;在亚尔明尼亚语中,"三"和"四"也有正

---

① 在辅音前的吠陀梵语形式,在元音前变成 ástāv。

规的格变形式，特别是语尾-k'是亚尔明尼亚语多数体格（nominatif）的记号，而这个记号在其他各数词里就找不着了。

由此看来，这些数词形式的相符之点，在梵语、希腊语、拉丁语和亚尔明尼亚语中，初看起来虽没有像在法语、意语和西班牙语中那么明显，其实是同样可靠的。

这些相符之点不能用各语言间互相借用来解释，可以假设它们有一个共同的来源。但是我们还要用一种系统化的方式来解释，这就是比较历史语言学的目的。

二、共同语言

［……］

三、所用的证明

我们要确定一种古代共同语的存在，必须在所比较的语言中尽量找出这种古代语言的那些被保存下来的特性。因此应当研究这种语言的各个成分的作用是怎样的，因为它们并不是以同等的程度保存下来的，也不是以同样的方式保存下来的。任何语言都包含有三个不同的系统，彼此之间有一定的联系，但是大体上这三个系统可以各自独立发生变化。这三个不同的系统就是：形态、语音和词汇。

［……］

可以作为确定"共同语"和后代语间的连续性的证据的，只有那些表现形态的特殊规则。比方大家都知道两个名词的领属关系，可以用一个前置的虚词来表示，如法语的 de，可以用一个后置的成分来表示，如英语的-s。但是这个虚词用 de 的形式还是用-s 的形式，这件事却是有特殊性的；因为这种关系用任何音素来表示都是可以的，只要传统没有决定用别种音素来表示它。所以我们可以说：用放在补语前面的 de 来表示这种关系，是一种法国土语的特性；用放在补语后面的-s 来表示这种关系，却是一种英国土语的特性。

这一类的特殊事实常常是很稳固的。发音尽管起变化，词汇尽管改变，而这些特性却是不变的。比方在现在法国北部的那些土语中，本地的词的形式起了变化来适合法语的形式，词汇有了革新，人们一般地有依照共同法语的习惯来说话的趋势。最后留存的就只有一些形态学上的地方特点；比方阳性与阴性的分别，共同法语说 il dit（他说），elle dit（她说），他们却说 i dit，a dit。这一类的特殊事实，是从小就学到的，不知不觉地成了习惯，其他一切尽管起变化，这些特殊事实却可以不变。

因此，一种形态繁杂的语言，包含着很多的特殊事实，它的亲属关系自然比较容易得到证明；反过来，一种形态简单的语言，只有一些一般的规则，如词的次序，要找出有力的证据就很不容易了。我们差不多用不着去证明一种语言是印欧系的：只要碰到一种大家还不认识的印欧系语言，如最近发现的吐火罗语(tokharien)或喜低特语(hittite)，我们略加考释就可以看出它的印欧语的特性。反过来，远东的那些语言，如汉语和越南语，就差不多没有一点形态上的特点，所以语言学家想从形态的特点上找出一些与汉语或越南语的各种土语有亲属关系的语言，就无所凭借，而想根据汉语、西藏语等后代语言构拟出一种"共同语"，是要遇到一些几乎无法克服的阻力的。

两种语言之间相符的事实愈特殊，这个相符之点的证明力量就愈大。所以例外的形式是最适于用来确定一种"共同语"的形式。

[……]

在语音方面，我们也要把一个古代的系统和新的系统互相对照，这些系统间的差别可以是非常之大的。

但是系统之间的差别并不是乱来的。要认识两种同源的语言之间的有规则的对应，虽然常常是不可能的，然而共同语和从它演变出来的语言之间的对应却有一定的规则。我们可以把它们列成许多确定的公式。这就是所谓"语音规律"。

日耳曼语的 f, p, x(以后变为 h)，以及在某些条件之下的 ƀ, đ, γ 和印欧语的 p, t, k 相对应；日耳曼语的 p, t, k 和印欧语的 b, d, g 相对应；日耳曼语的 b, d, g(在二元音之间则为 ƀ, đ, γ)和印欧语的 bh, dh, gh 相对应。日耳曼语的这套有规则的对应系统，就是所谓"辅音转化"，或格林姆(Grimm)规律(在格林姆之前不久，大部分已经为拉斯克 Rask 所发现，不过到了格林姆①才把它定为规律)。这种原始"共同语"和各个后代语言之间语音对应的规律性，表现出发音的变化并不是孤立的影响某一个词或某一形式，而是影响到整个语音系统的。

根据方法上的原则，可见对应的规则可以在原始语和它的每一种后代语之间拟定，而不能在各种出于同一共同语的后代语之间拟定。我们可以拟定

---

① 现多译为"格里姆"，后文不再一一说明。——编者注

印欧语的首音 p 在希腊语和梵语为 p，在歌特语①为 f，如希腊语的 patěr，梵语的 pit$\frac{1}{a}$ 和歌特语的 fadar（父亲），印欧语的首音 kʷ 后面跟着一个 o 的时候在希腊语为 p，在梵语为 k，在歌特语为 hw，如希腊语的 póteros，梵语的kataráh，歌特语的 hwapar（二者之一）。实际上观察到的这两个对应：

希腊语 p＝梵语 p＝歌特语 f

希腊语 p＝梵语 k＝歌特语 hw

只有在和那个为了解释它们而拟定的印欧语的形式对照之下，才可以理解。

我们比较同族语言时所注意的并不是形式上的相似，而是对应的规律。上文第 5 面已经说过，亚尔明尼亚语的数词"二"是 erku，和古印欧语的 *dwō（或 *duwō）对应。这个对应初看来好像很奇怪。但是亚尔明尼亚语的 erk- 和欧印语的 dw- 相对应，是遵守一个一般的规则的。因为此外我们知道还有两个别的例子。印欧语曾有一个词根 *dwei-（怕），在荷马的希腊语里是广泛的以一些动词形式如 *dedwoa（写作 deidō），dedwoike（写作 deidoike）（我怕）或一些名词形式如 *dweos（写作 deos）（怕）来表现的；亚尔明尼亚语与它对应的就有 erkiwl（怕），erkeay（我曾经怕）。印欧语曾有一个形容词 *dwāro-（长），在希腊语里还显著的保存着，而亚尔明尼亚语也有一个形容词 erkar（长）。所以这个规律有三个明显的相近的例子作为基础。如果我们想到已知的以 *dw-，*duw- 为首音的印欧语的词数目非常少，就可以看出这三个符合的例子同时并存有证明的价值了。

这个对应还可以有解释。舌尖辅音后面跟一个 w 而造成的音组，在亚尔明尼亚语里变成了舌根音：tw 变为 k'-如 k'o（你的），与希腊语的 twe（古雅典语变为 se）之类的形式相对应。这个清音 k 的来源是这样的：在亚尔明尼亚语中和在日耳曼语中一样，从前曾经有过一个由浊塞音变为清塞音的变化，如 d 变为 t，g 变为 k。前面的那个 r，就是这个音组中首音的古代浊辅音性质的一个痕迹②，随后这个 r 又引出一个首音 e，erku。可是如果那个词中间本来有一个 -r-，如 kr-kin（两倍），这个首音 r 就不能产生了（kr-kin 是由古

---

① 现多译为"哥特语"，后文不再一一说明。——编者注

② 详情参看格拉蒙 M. Grammont 在《巴黎语言学会专刊》第 20 种，第 252 页的解释。

代的*kirkin 或*kurkin 变来的）。所以在亚尔明尼亚语的 erk-与*dw-这个非常奇特的对应中，一切都是由亚尔明尼亚语的结构所造成的。任何对应，假如不能得到这样的解释，就是可疑的。

[……]

词汇虽然常常是不稳固的，但是在比较各种语言时，最先引人注意的却是那些词汇上的相符，常常甚至于只是处理词汇。其所以这样做，或者是由于对所考察的那些语言知道得太少，只有从词汇上来找证据；或者是由于所研究的语言语法非常简单，如在远东的各种语言；或者是由于存留下来的形态建立得太晚，是在所拟定的共同时期之后。因此我们要特别细心考察怎样才能证明词汇之间的相符。

上面已经说过，有效的语源上的符合决不是根据一些语言形式间的相似而确定的，而是根据一些对应的规律：我们之所以能够拿亚尔明尼亚语的 erku 来和俄语的 dva 相比较，并不是因为这两个形式相似：在语音方面，它们是毫无共同之点的；而是因为那些对应的规则容许我们这样比较，印欧语的 ō 在斯拉夫语变成了 a，在亚尔明尼亚语变成了 u，印欧语的 duw，在俄语变成了 dv-，在亚尔明尼亚语变成了 erk-。

对应中的不规则的情形，假如不能用某个词的特殊情况来解释，那就或者是由别的语言借来的，或者是由于语源不合。比方古拉丁语的 ca-，在法语变成了 cha-,che-,chè-，例如 campum 变成了 champ（田），carrum 变成了 char（车），caballum 变成了 cheval（马），carum 变成了 cher（亲爱的），等等；至于有个 camp（营地）和 campum 相当，那是因为这个词并不属于法语的旧传统，实际上是由意大利语借来的，并且事实上还知道它是在什么时候、为什么"借来"的。可以与日耳曼语的 b-相对应的是拉丁语的 f，如拉丁语的 flos, flōris 和德语的 Blume（花）；所以德语的 Feuer 和法语的 feu（火）毫无关系：想一想各个罗马族语言中那些与法语的 feu 相对应的词，如意大利语的 fuoco，西班牙语的 fuego，就可以知道 feu 与 Feuer 的相似是不相干的。所以我们进行比较时只能用一些精密的对应公式——并且要小心避开那些借用的成分。

[……]

如果所考察的是一些真正由"共同语"直接变来的词，那么就应当构拟出这种"共同语"的一个各方面都确定的词，而不要满足于比较一些词根上的细小成分。错误的危险性既然很大，所以我们必须用些精密的证据来断定观察到的相符不是偶然的。

　　大家所同意的第一点(如果不是在原则上同意,至少是在事实上同意)就是:一个词源,只有确实符合语音对应规则,或者虽有歧异之点,也能用一些严格确定的特殊情况来解释,这样的一条词源研究才是有效的。

　　不消说,相对应的语音成分数目愈大,相符之点的偶然性的危险就愈小。

　　[……]

　　意义方面的相符也应当与语音方面的相符(根据语音的对应规则)同样正确,同样精密。这并不是说,意义相符的程度应当比语音相符的程度大;而只是说,如果有意义上的分歧,就不应该只用一些含胡的、一般的"可能性"来解释,而必须用一些特殊的情况来解释。法语的 ouaille 是由拉丁语的 ouicula (羊)变来的,ouaille 这个词在现代法语里仅指礼拜堂里的教士的忠实信徒而言,这条语源决不会因此变得可疑。

　　我们知道,一所基督教礼拜堂的忠实信徒是常常被人比作这所礼拜堂的牧师所牧养的羊群的,由于这个原因,这个意义上的比较便得到说明了。此外,ouaille 这个词在法国某些土语里也还有作"羊羔"解的,这一点更可以证明这个词源的正确性。

　　[……]

　　我们要构拟一种原始"共同语"时,必须注意到我们对于某个词所拥有的证据有多少。两种语言之间的相符,如果不是全部的,就会保不定不是偶然的。但是如果相符之点扩充到三种、四种或五种很不相同的语言,偶然的可能性就大大减少了。虽然古波斯语的 rādiy(因为)和斯拉夫语的 radi(因为)在他种语言里找不出来,我们还是毫不迟疑地拿它们来比较,因为这两个词在形式上、意义上和用法的细节上都是完全一致的。除了这一类的例子以外,假如我们只在两种印欧系的语言里找到一组相符的词,而在别的语言里却找不到使它们失掉这个语词的特殊情况,这种相符就是可疑的了。

　　无论那种语言,必定要全体的密切相符之点,确定了所比较的词之所以相似不可能是出于偶然的,才能说词源得到了证明。

　　[……]

　　无论在形态方面语音方面还是词汇方面,我们决不能忽视一条原则,就是:所有的比较,只有合乎严格的规则,才是有效的。语言学家愈是粗心大意,他的比较愈是任意,他的证明也就愈不可靠。

Jerry Norman(1988) "The Methodology of Middle Chinese Reconstruction"选读[1]

◆ 作者简介

罗杰瑞[2](Jerry Lee Norman，1936—2012)，美国汉语言学家，华盛顿大学亚洲语言文学系教授。他早年师从赵元任，后与桥本万太郎、余霭芹等提出普林斯顿假说，主张摆脱《切韵》的框架，先构拟汉语各方言的原始语，在其基础上再构拟原始汉语。在诸多汉语方言中，罗杰瑞对闽语的研究最深。其博士论文题为《闽方言的特征描述》。

本文出自罗杰瑞1988年出版的汉语通论性著作《汉语概说》，这本书也是英语世界汉语语言学教程最通用的教材。

◆ 正文节选

2.4 The methodology of Middle Chinese reconstruction

In his *Compendium of Phonetics in Ancient and Archaic Chinese* (1954) Kalgren gives a succinct description of the methodology used in reconstructing Middle Chinese. Karlgren considered Middle Chinese to be the language reflected in the categories of the *Qièyùn* as they have come down to us in its various redactions. The *Qièyùn* categories in most cases are interpreted in light of the rhyme tables; even though Karlgren admitted that the *Qièyùn zhǐzhǎngtú* was based on a later stage of Chinese, he felt that it was still useful in interpreting the *Qièyùn*, since it was much closer to it in time than the modem dialects. Second in importance to the rhyme tables were the so-called Sinoxenic dialects (a term created by Samuel Martin to refer to the systems of pronouncing Chinese characters in Japan, Korea and

---

[1] Norman, J., 1988. *Chinese*, Cambridge; New York, NY: Cambridge University Press.

[2] 图片来源：https://upload.wikimedia.org/wikipedia/en/4/4a/Jerry_Lee_Norman_%281936％E2％80％932012％29.jpeg。

Vietnam). In all three of these countries Chinese has been studied and used extensively for many centuries, and each country has its own distinctive manner of reading Chinese texts aloud. Karlgren, while recognizing that these foreign dialects were "corrupt" in some respects, considered that they were of paramount importance in reconstructing the language of the *Qièyùn*. Third in importance in Karlgren's view were the native Chinese dialects.

The entire process of reconstructing Middle Chinese was of course vastly complicated, but some simple examples will suffice to illustrate the principles which were employed. A comparative study of the *Guǎngyùn fǎnqiè* formulas reveals that there was a distinct initial consonant in the language represented by eight *fǎnqiè* upper characters pronounced (in Modem Chinese) *tā*, *tuō*, *tǔ*, *tù*, *tōng*, *tiān*, *tái*, *tāng*; this initial corresponds to the rhyme table initial *tòu*, and *tòu* is one of the *shétóu* sounds. Each of the *shétóu* sounds corresponds to a distinctive set of *fǎnqiè* upper characters in the *Guǎngyùn*. The only way phonetic substance can be given to these categories is by comparing them to actual pronunciations in modern Chinese dialects and in the Sinoxenic dialects of Japan, Korean and Vietnam. Table 2.2 gives the readings of several common characters from each of the *shétóu* initials in several Chinese and Sinoxenic dialects. A glance at the table shows that a large majority of the forms are either dental or alveolar stops and nasals. The initial *ní* may be safely reconstructed as a nasal on the basis of the forms given. The initials *duān* and *tòu* are voiceless dental (or alveolar) stops in all the dialects; with the exception of Kanon, which has merged the two series. The remaining dialects have an unaspirated stop for *duān* and an aspirated stop for *tòu*, it is reasonable to suppose that Middle Chinese possessed the same sort of contrast. The only dialect which clearly distinguishes the initial *dìng* from *duān* and *tòu* is Sūzhōu in which *dìng* corresponds to a voiced stop contrasting with the voiceless correspondences for *duān* and *tòu*. Provisionally at least, the initial *dìng* can be considered some kind of

Table 2.2 Dialectal reflexes of the Shétóu initials

	Peking	Sūzhōu	Xiàmèn	Guǎngzhōu	Kanon	Sino-Vietnamese	Sino-Korean
duān 端							
多	tuo¹	təu¹	to¹	to¹	ta	ʔda¹	ta
刀	tau¹	tæ¹	to¹	tou¹	to	ʔdao¹	to
短	tuan³	tø³	tuan³	tyn³	tan	ʔdoan³	tān
tòu 透							
他	tʻa¹	tʻɒ¹	tʻa¹	tʻa¹	ta	tha¹	tʻa
天	tʻien¹	tʻix¹	tʻien¹	tʻin¹	ten	thien¹	chʻŏn
铁	tʻieˀ	tʻiəʔ⁷	tʻiet⁷	tʻit⁷	tetsu	thiet⁷	chʻŏl
dìng 定							
弟	ti⁵	di⁶	ti⁶	tai⁶	tei	ʔde⁶	che
头	tʻou²	dY²	tʻɔ²	tʻau²	tō	ʔdəu²	tu
豆	tou⁵	dY⁶	tɔ⁶	tau⁶	tō	ʔdao⁶	tu
ní 泥							
内	nei⁵	nE⁶	lui⁶	noi⁶	dai	noi⁶	nae
年	nien²	nir²	lian²	nin²	nen	nien²	yŏn
农	nuŋ²	noŋ²	loŋ²	nuŋ²	nō	noŋ²	nong

voiced dental stop in Middle Chinese. Karlgren argued that *dìng* and the other *quánzhuó* initials were voiced aspirates, whereas the present consensus is that at the time of the *Qièyùn* they were voiced unaspirated stops. Once one set of the rhyme table initials has been reconstructed, the meaning of the terms *quánqīng*, *cìqīng*, *quánzhuó* and *cìzhuó* becomes clear, and this information can then be applied to other sets of initials. The above example illustrates in a very simple way how the *Qièyùn* and rhyme table categories, which viewed in isolation were just so many abstract formulas, were given phonetic substance by comparing them with corresponding words in the Modern Chinese dialects and Sinoxenic reading systems. Table 2.3 shows the inventory of Middle Chinese initials as reconstructed by Karlgren and modified by F. K. Li (1971).

Table 2.3 Middle Chinese initials

Bilabials	p	ph	b	m	
Dentals	t	th	d	nl	
Sibilants	ts	tsh	dz		s z
Retroflexes	ṭ	ṭh	ḍ		
Retroflex sibilants	tṣ	tṣh	dẓ		ṣ ẓ
Palatal sibilants	tś	tśh	dź	nź	ś ź
Velars	k	kh	g	ng	x
Glottals	(ʔ)				j φ(zero)

The reconstruction of the finals was carried out in similar fashion: the *děngyùn* categories which were applied to the finals were compared with actual dialect forms, and reconstructed values were postulated. In the case of the finals, however, the rhyme tables do not actually distinguish all the different and distinct rhymes of the *Qièyùn*, so that even after all the rhyme table distinctions are reconstituted, there still remain a considerable number of *Qièyùn* categories which must be dealt with if all the Middle Chinese rhymes are to be distinguished. As indicated above, the most difficult of the rhyme table categories applied to the finals is the notion of *děng* or 'division'. In Table 2.4 the actual pronunciation of a representative sample of words from table 25 of the *Yùnjìng* is shown. (The examples for divisions Ⅰ, Ⅱ and Ⅲ are *píng* tone; a *qù* tone word is used to exemplify the fourth division, since it is a more common word than the corresponding *píng* tone form.) Each of the words is in a different division; they all share the same initial and offglide, so the significance of *děng* must be sought in the remainder of the syllable—in either the medial or the main vowel, or perhaps in both simultaneously.

Table 2.4 The four divisions in the dialects

Division	Ⅰ	Ⅱ	Ⅲ	Ⅳ
dialect	高	交	骄	叫
Peking	kau	tɕiau	tɕiau	tɕiau
Sūzhōu	kæ	kæ	tɕiæ	tɕiæ

续表

Division	I	II	III	IV
Xiàmén	ko	kau	kiau	kiau
Guǎngzhōu	kou	kaau	kiu	kiu
Kanon	kau	kau	keu	keu
Sino-Vietnamese	cao	giao	kiêu	kiêu
Sino-Korean	ko	kyo	kyo	kyo

Using the forms in Table 2.4 as examples, we can now outline the main lines of Karlgren's thinking concerning the reconstruction of the four divisions: (1) The offglide in all the forms is *u*. (2) The main vowels in divisions I and II must be some sort of low vowel like *a*. (3) The four divisions differ not only in the presence or absence of a medial *i*, but also in having several different main vowels in several of the dialects (Xiàmén, Guǎngzhōu, Sino-Vietnamese); hence the divisions differed both by medial and main vowel. (4) Division I is clearly the least palatalized; a low back *â* [ɑ] is postulated as the main vowel. (5) Division II causes palatalization of the preceding velar in some dialects but not in others; this would make sense only if it had some sort of front vowel without an intervening medial *i* (which, as we will see below, is the distinguishing characteristic of divisions II and IV). A low front vowel *a* [a] is reconstructed as the main vowel of this division. (6) Divisions III and IV clearly both had a palatal medial of some sort; and, judging from Kanon and Sino Vietnamese, the nucleus was some kind of mid vowel. (7) The most difficult question to answer is how the third and fourth divisions differed from one another; in the present sample all the dialects have merged them. To resolve this problem, Karlgren had recourse to Sino-Korean where, in a few cases (not illustrated in Table 2.4), fourth division words have a medial *y* where the corresponding third-division words lack this medial: *jiàn* 'to see', a fourth division word, is *kyǒn* [ki̯ən] in Sino-Korean, where *jiàn* 'to construct', a third division word, is *kǒn* [kən]. On the basis of cases like this, Karlgren concluded that the fourth division had a longer and more vocalic medial i, as opposed to a shorter, more consonantal $į$ in the third division. The stronger and more vocalic i survives in Sino-Korean (in some cases at least), whereas the weaker and more consonantal third-division medial $į$ drops out. Finally, since third- and fourth-division finals are different rhymes in the *Qièyùn*, they must be reconstructed with different main vowels in order to preserve their rhyme distinction. Karlgren proposed that the fourth division had a more strongly palatal e [e] as its main vowel, which matched its strongly palatal medial i; by similar reasoning, then, the third division had a somewhat less palatal mainvowel to match its more weakly palatal medial; Karlgren reconstructed this vowel as $ä$ [ɛ]. As a result of this analysis we arrive at the following Middle Chinese forms:

Division	I	II	III	IV
Reconstruction	kâu	kau	kįäu	kieu

A solution to the problem of the nature of the *děng* was of course an immense help in reconstructing the *Qièyùn*, finals, but it did not solve all the problems by any means. Although one could easily classify all the *Qièyùn* rhymes as to division, in some cases the *Qièyùn zhǐzhǎngtú* treated distinct *Qièyùn* rhymes as if they were identical; such rhymes had doubtless merged at an early date, and it was difficult to find evidence for distinguishing them. Generally Karlgren foundhis solution to this problem in marginal distinctions maintained in one or more of the native or foreign dialects which he relied upon. In two cases he was unable to find any evidence for distinguishing two important *Qièyùn* rhymes; in one case he reconstructed two separate rhymes as i; F. K. Li (1971) has proposed that these two rhymes be distinguished as i versus $ï$, on the basis of their separate origins in Old Chinese. Likewise, Karlgren has reconstructed two distinct *Qièyùn* rhymes both as ai; Li distinguishes them as ai and $aï$.

Karlgren's Middle Chinese vowel system is highly complex; it consists of sixteen distinct vowels and four medials, two of which can also function as offglides; his medials are i, $į$, u and w; the difference between i and $į$ is discussed above; u, in contrast to w, is used when the $k\bar{a}i$ and $hé$ variants of a final are put into different *Qièyùn* (or *Guǎngyùn*) rhymes. Since his transcriptional system is a bit strange to most modern linguists (it was based on J. A. Lundell's Swedish dialect alphabet), we will examine all his vowels and medials, describing the phonetic interpretation of each and listing the finals in which each occurs. Bracketed symbols are taken from the International Phonetic Alphabet.

(1) *i*. A high front unrounded vowel, [i]: $(j)i$, $(j)wi$. The first of these two finals actually represents two contrasting rhymes, as we pointed out above. Karlgren writes these finals with the *j* after labials, velars and gutturals; otherwise he generally omits the *j*.

(2) *e*. An upper mid, front unrounded vowel, [e]: *iei*, *iwei*, *ieu*, *iem*, *iep*, *ien*, *iwen*, *iet*, *iwet*, *ieng*, *iweng*, *iek*, *iwek*.

(3) *ĕ*. A shorter variety of vowel (2): *iĕu*, *iĕn*, *iwĕn*, *iĕt*, *iĕu*, *iwĕt*.

(4) *e̯*. Karlgren writes this [e] when it functions as a glide and the preceding or following *i* is to be taken as the main vowel of the final: $(j)e̯i$, $(j)we̯i$, $(j)ie̯$, $(j)wie̯$.

(5) *ä*. A lower mid, front unrounded vowel, [ɛ]: *i̯äi*, *i̯wäi*, *i̯äu*, *i̯äm*, *i̯äp*, *i̯än*, *i̯wän*, *i̯ät*, *i̯wät*, *i̯äng*, *i̯wäng*, *i̯äk*.

(6) *ɛ*. A front unrounded vowel somewhat lower than vowel (5), [æ]: *i̯ɛn*, *i̯ɛt*, *ɛng*, *wɛng*, *ɛk*, *wɛk*.

(7) *a*. A low front unrounded vowel, [a]: *a*, *wa*, *i̯a*, *ai*, *aï*, *wai*, *waï*, *au*, *am*, *ap*, *an*, *wan*, *at*, *wat*, *i̯ang*, *i̯wang*, *i̯ak*, *i̯wak*.

(8) *ă*. A shorter variety of vowel (7): *ăi*, *wăi*, *ăm*, *ăp*, *ăn*, *wăn*, *ăt*, *wăt*.

(9) *ə*. A mid, central unrounded vowell, [ə]: *iəm*, *iəp*, *ən*, *uən*, *uət*, *i̯ən*, *i̯uən*, *i̯ət*, *i̯uət*, *əng*, *wəng*, *i̯əng*.

(10) *ə̯*. A short (non-syllabic) variety of vowel (9): *ə̯u*, *i̯ə̯u*—in these finals *u* is to be taken as the main vowel.

(11) *ɒ*. A lower mid to low unrounded central vowel, [ɐ]: *i̯ɒi*, *i̯wɒi*, *i̯ɒm*, *i̯wɒm*, *i̯ɒp*, *i̯wɒp*, *i̯ɒn*, *i̯wɒn*, *i̯ɒt*, *i̯wɒt*, *ɒng*, *wɒng*, *i̯ɒng*, *i̯wɒng*,

ɒk, wɒk, i̯ɒk.

(12) *u*. A high back rounded vowel, [u]: i̯u, ung, i̯ung, uk, i̯uk.

(13) *o*. An upper mid, back rounded vowel, [o]: uo, i̯wo, uong, i̯wong, uok, i̯wok.

(14) *å*. A lower mid, back rounded vowel, [ɔ]: ång, åk.

(15) *â*. A low back, unrounded vowel, [ɑ]: â, uâ, i̯â, i̯wâ, âi, uâi, âu, âm, âp, ân, uân, ât, uât, âng, wâng, âk, wâk.

(16) *ă*. A shorter variety of vowel (15): ăi, uăi, ăm, ăp.

The four medials may be described as follows:

(1) *i̯*. A short, consonantal palatal onglide, [j]. F. K. Li uses the IPA symbol given here for this medial, a practice which we shall also follow hereafter.

(2) *i*. A palatal glide, longer and more vocalic than medial (1). It also occurs as an offglide.

(3) *w*. A short back rounded medial, [w].

(4) *u*. A back rounded medial, longer and more vocalic than medial (3).

Karlgren's reconstruction of the Middle Chinese finals has been criticized by a number of scholars. Y. R. Chao (1941) examined his system with a view to determining its contrastive elements; in the process he proposed several revisions in he system, some of which were subsequently accepted by Karlgren. Samuel Martin (1953) made a thoroughgoing phonemic analysis of Karlgren's reconstruction, reducing the number of vocalic contrasts to six. Martin treated Karlgren's reconstruction, along with Chao's revisions of it, as a valid phonetic reconstruction of Middle Chinese; his resulting phonemicization, while interesting from the point of view of phonological analysis, did little to advance our knowledge of Middle Chinese itself. Lǐ Róng (1952) and Dǒng Tónghé (1954) subjected Karlgren's reconstruction to a more searching examination, producing in the process fairly drastic revisions of it. Tōdō Akiyasu (1957), taking into account the work of the above-mentioned scholars as well as that of several Japanese predecessors, proposed an even more drastically revised version of Middle Chinese. In 1962 Edwin Pulleyblank, as a preliminary step toward re-examining the probblem of Old Chinese, proposed his own revised reconstruction of Middle Chinese (Pulleyblank 1962a; 1962b). Although all the aforementioned revisions differ from Karlgren's original reconstruction in many important ways, both in interpretation and in substance, from a methodological point of view these revisions depart little (if at all) from Karlgren's views. The differences come about because of a refinement of technique: a closer examination of the sources reveals more distinctions than Karlgren posited; more and better information relevant to reconstructing some of the more difficult contrasts has come to light; the Chinese transcriptions of Buddhist names and terms and Chinese words transcribed in alphabetic scripts (Tibetan, Brahmi, Uygur) have also thrown some light on problems of reconstruction. Such material can be employed, however, without questioning Karlgren's basic methodology. All the reconstructions and revisions of Middle Chinese published up until the present can and should be viewed as products of a single methodological tradition going back to the original work of Bernhard Karlgren and his predecessors.

Pulleyblank (1970) and Miller (1975) have both raised serious questions concerning this traditional methodology. Pulleyblank for the first time rejects the direct relevance of the rhyme table categories to the reconstruction of the *Qièyùn* language; this is because the earliest rhyme tables are based on another dialect, two centuries later in time and based on different geographic standards. In Pulleyblank's view this later form of Chinese should be first reconstructed independently, and only then be used along with other data to reconstruct the categories of the *Qièyùn* language. Miller's objections to the methodology outlined here are much more radical; he describes it as a "highly eclectic, pick-and-choose system" that brings together elements of the traditional historical comparative method with purely intuitive and, at times, arbitrary processes. He finds traditional Chinese linguistic terminology rife with terms chosen for their exemplary function, and even tainted in many cases by philosophical or mystical speculation. As a result, Miller sees little value in most of the reconstructions produced before 1975. While I do not subscribe to this criticism in all its details, I think that Miller's criticism can be accounted useful if it leads to a sober re-examination of the whole question of historical reconstruction in Chinese. It indeed seems that Karlgren's sapproach to this topic has pretty much run its course; pursued further, it can only lead to an unending process of juggling and rejuggling of the same old elements, without any really new insights into the historical process. If Chinese historical linguistics is to be rescued from scholasticism, a thoroughgoing reevaluation of basic assumptions about methodology is essential. Although it is well beyond the scope of a book of this type to carry out such a re-evaluation, I will offer a few preliminary thoughts on the subject. The *Qièyùn* itself must be viewed as the primary source for Middle Chinese, the stable core to which other bodies of information are referred; despite disclaimers to the contrary, Karlgren's reconstruction of "Ancient" Chinese is in its essence a reconstruction of the rhyme table categories. The *Qièyùn* is the basic datum, and the rhyme tables are interpretations of this datum based on later and geographically disparate dialects. We are under no compulsion to accept such interpretations; they are no more than one other type of evidence, to be judged along with other equally valuable types such as modern dialect forms, ancient transcriptions and Sinoxenic readings. The value attributed them because of their early date is offset by the fact that their meaning is anything but clear, and consequently any interpretation of them is of necessity speculative. The native Chinese dialects should take precedence over the Sinoxenic materials: the latter are loanwords taken into a foreign medium, and subject to the internal historical processes of that medium. The Sinoxenic material needs to be studied much more thoroughly before being used to interpret the earlier stages of Chinese. The Chinese dialects are the organic, autochthonous descendants of Middle Chinese, and clearly should be the primary data on which any reconstruction of earlier stages of the language is based. More account needs to be taken of the rich stock of Chinese loanwords in neighboring languages such as Vietnamese, the various Tai languages, Miao-Yao and perhaps others as well. Ancient transcriptional evidence, Buddhist as well as other types, needs to be studied more systematically. Finally there should be a more conscious and rigorous approach to methodology; we should know precisely what we are doing at every stage of the reconstructive process.

Another aspect of Chinese historical linguistics that demands more attention is the distinction between the literary and popular components of the various historical and modern stages of the language. Popular forms are those elements of a language that go back in an unbroken line to the proto-language; literary elements are words or expressions which at some point ceased to be living words in the spoken language. Such literary elements survive in the texts, and are frequently reintroduced into the spoken language. Note that this distinction is not the same as that of colloquial versus literary which one often encounters in works on Chinese dialects; this distinction refers to contemporary usage, while the popular/literary distinction refers to be historical status of the elements in question. A word which is literary in the historical linguistic sense may be colloquial in that it is employed as an everyday word in the spoken language, just as in English many Latin words (clearly of literary origin in the historical sense) are perfectly good everyday colloquial words. A great majority of the words in the *Qièyùn* do not actually reflect the spoken language of the time it was written, but are reading pronunciations of words encountered in texts. In some cases, of course, these reading pronunciations actually coincided with popular spoken forms, but unfortunately the *Qièyùn* makes no distinction between the two types of elements. Chinese historical phonology hitherto has been the study of the development of the various stages of the literary language as codified in traditional dictionaries. Certainly another approach is possible: the reconstruction of the ancestor of the spoken (popular) forms of Chinese, working backward from the present spoken dialects. One important benefit of this approach would be to establish a core of words which has evolved organically from the ancestral form of Chinese down to the present day; in doing this, we would escape from much of the artificiality which plagues the traditional approach. In the process of studying the evolution of spoken Chinese one could integrate much valuable data on the spoken language preserved in historical texts, an area still largely unexplored. An added advantage of this approach would be to give us a better appreciation and better control of the purely literary monuments of Chinese linguistic history.

梅祖麟(1991)《从汉代的"动、杀"、"动、死"来看动补结构的发展》选读①

◆ 作者简介

梅祖麟②(Tsu-Lin Mei，1933—)，美国康奈尔大学中国文学和哲学教授，1962 年获耶鲁大学哲学博士学位，主要研究领域为汉语语法史和汉藏语言比较。其有影响力的主要文章包括《中古汉语的声调与上声的起源》(1970)，以及与罗杰瑞合写的《古代江南的南亚民族：一些词汇证据》(1976)。其主要论著收录于《梅祖麟语言学论文集》(2000)。

◆ 正文节选

引 论

两汉时期产生了"压杀"、"格杀"、"烧杀"等复合动词，同时也产生了"压死"、"格死"、"烧死"等复合动词。"V 杀"是两个他动词组成的并列结构，"V 死"是他动词带着自动词。我们发现从先秦两汉一直到五世纪初年，"V 杀"经常出现于表示受事者的止词前面，"V 死"只能出现于表示受事者的起词

---

① 梅祖麟，《从汉代的"动、杀"、"动、死"来看动补结构的发展——兼论中古时期起词的施受关系的中立化》，《语言学论丛》(第十六辑)，商务印书馆 1991 年版。

② 图片来源：http://www.literature.org.cn/Scholar.aspx? id=794。

后面：

> 岸崩，尽压杀卧者。（《史记·外戚世家》）
> 百余人炭崩尽压死。（《论衡·吉验》）

这个结论主要是根据《史记》、《汉书》、《论衡》，另外我们也参考了一些其他先秦两汉的文献，如《左传》、《庄子》、《韩非子》、《说苑》等。

动补结构的发展，曾经引起不少争论。以王力（1958）、祝敏彻（1981）为代表的早出派认为这种形式前汉已经出现，以太田辰夫（1958）、志村良治（1974）为代表的晚出派认为这种形式大多数产生于唐代。本文继续讨论这个问题，全文分六节：第一节说明两汉时代"V 杀"、"V 死"的出现场合互补。第二节说明五世纪时"V 死"才用作动补结构。第三节讨论动补结构的定义。第四节检验前汉所谓动补结构的例证。第五节讨论动补结构的形成方式和年代。第六节是余论。由于"V 死"在五世纪变成动补结构以后，前面的起词可以是施事者，也可以是受事者，于是以前施受关系的对立在这时中立化。这节举例说明施受关系的中立化是中古语法演变的一般趋势。

一　汉代的"V 杀"和"V 死"

[……]

二　动补结构的"V 死"产生年代

[……]

三　动补结构的定义

3.1　现在回过来讨论动补结构的定义和产生时代。王力先生（1958：403）说：

> 使成式……是一种仂语的结构方式。从形式上说，是外动词带形容词（"修好"、"弄坏"），或者是外动词带着内动词（"打死"、"救活"）；从意义上说，是把行为及其结果在一个动词性仂语中表示出来。这种行为能使受事者得到某种结果，所以叫做使成式。

王先生的"使成式"我们叫做"动补结构"。上面的定义有个地方没说清楚。现代汉语的动补结构可以用在主动句，也可以用在非主动句。

（甲）警察打死了土匪。　　（乙）土匪打死了，大家都很高兴。
老王修好了汽车。　　　　汽车修好了，现在就可以动身了。

按照现代的语感，再看上面的定义，就会觉得(甲)、(乙)两型差不多，动补结构在两种句型中都能出现。但历史的事实并非如此。第一节的例子说明，"V死"在两汉时代只在(乙)型中出现，一直到五世纪，或者更晚，才在(甲)型中出现。换句话说，动补结构的产生，不但是构词层次上的问题，也是句法层次上的问题。

为了弥补这个缺点，我们把动补结构的定义稍微修改一下：

1. 动补结构是由两个成分组成的复合动词。前一个成分是他动词，后一个成分是自动词或形容词。
2. 动补结构出现于主动句：施事者＋动补结构＋受事者。
3. 动补结构的意义是在上列句型中，施事者用他动词所表示的动作使受事者得到自动词或形容词所表示的结果。
4. 唐代以后第二条的限制可以取消。

按照这个定义，"V死"在五世纪以前是复合动词，但不是动补结构；五世纪以后，才变成动补结构。

至于为什么说唐以前动补结构只出现于主动句中，这将在下文加以论证。

3.2 有了这个新定义，还不能断定动补结构的产生时代。问题在于：定义既说动补结构的下字是自动词或形容词，我们怎样去判断下字是否符合这个定义？以前有人举过这样的例子：

（甲）射伤郤克，流血至履。(《史记·齐太公世家》)
从杜南，入蚀中，去辄烧绝栈道。(同上，《高祖本纪》)

"射伤郤克"是"射而伤郤克"，"伤"在后一句算是使动式。从使动式转来的"伤"算是自动词还是他动词？在讨论这个问题以前，先说一下我们一般的看法。

按照现代汉语的观点,动补结构是可以嵌进"得"、"不"的复合动词,例如"打得死"、"打不死"、"修得好"、"修不好"。这种复合动词至少有两个来源。一个是(甲)型句,在两汉时期"射伤"、"烧绝"是并列结构,由两个他动词组成。后来,大概是南北朝,由于多种因素,复合词里的"绝"、"伤"才转成自动词。

另一个来源是(乙)型句里的复合动词:

(乙)百余人炭崩尽压死。(《论衡·吉验》)
(乙')恐帝长大后见怨。(《汉书·云敞传》)
叟,缩也,人及物老皆缩小于旧也。(《释名·释亲属》)

"压死"、"缩小"、"长大"的下字确实是自动词或形容词,但(乙)型的复合词不带宾语。这里又要分作两种情形:"长大"一直不能带宾语,现在也不能说"长大这个孩子"。另一种是"压死"、"缩小",前汉根本不能带宾语,后汉带宾语的例子罕见,如"减轻田租"(《汉书·王莽传》),但"减轻"是否是动补结构也成问题(见下节)。到了五世纪,(乙)型的复合词才带宾语。(甲)、(乙)两型合流以后,就形成后代的动补结构。

四 检验前汉所谓动补结构的例证

4.1 以前的学者曾经举出"推堕"、"激怒"、"射伤"、"伐灭"、"攻出"、"攻下"、"烧绝"、"禁止"、"击败"、"罢退"等复合词,认为是动补结构出现于前汉的证据。下面的例句除了最后的一句以外,都是《史记》里的。

汉王急,推堕孝惠、鲁元车下。(《项羽本纪》)
乃激怒张仪。(《苏秦列传》)
射伤郤克,流血至履。(《齐太公世家》)
二十四年,楚考王伐灭鲁。(《鲁周公世家》)
遂攻出献公,献公奔齐。(《卫康叔世家》)
燕王臧荼反,攻下代地。(《高祖本纪》)
诸侯更相诛伐,周天子弗能禁止。(《始皇本纪》)
从杜南,入蚀中,去辄烧绝栈道。(《高祖本纪》)

与秦击败楚于重丘。(《田敬仲完世家》)

据法以弹咸等,皆罢退之。(《汉书·翟方进传》)

以上除了"弗能禁止"句以外,都是(甲)型句;"弗"字可能是"不……之"。下面要提出三个理由来说明这些复合词在前汉都不是动补结构。

第一个理由是根据"伤"、"灭"、"败"、"绝"等下字的用法。李佐丰(1983:117—144)在这方面做了很有意思的研究。他用时代比较接近的六部作品:《左传》、《论语》、《孟子》、《庄子》、《荀子》、《礼记》,选出若干他所谓的自动词,然后根据这些书的《引得》,观察这些自动词的用法,得出统计数字。我们上面抄录所谓动补结构的例句,就是选择下字在李文中有统计数字的。

李文表中原分四类,为了节省篇幅,删去"带介词补语"一项,这四项加起来的总和等于"用作谓语"下的数字。此外我们还用第一、第二两栏的数字求出每个字自动、他动两种用法的比例,放在第三栏。

例	不带宾语和补语	带使动宾语	他动:自动	带关系宾语	用作谓语
灭	19	115	6.0:1	0	135
败	32	111	3.5:1	0	147
伤	15	52	3.5:1	0	73
绝	4	11	2.8:1	0	16
止	77	83	1.1:1	2	175
出	84	30	1:2.8	41	215
下	29	7	1:3.5	29	66
退	66	10	1:6.6	7	84
怒	83	13	1:6.4	8	105
堕	9	1	1:9	0	11
死	172	4	1:43	37	263

上表有两点值得注意。(1)"灭"、"败"、"伤"、"绝"、"止"五个字都是他动(或使动)用法比自动用法多,这是先秦的情况。前汉离先秦不近,这些字仍是他动性比较强,因此"V 灭"、"V 败"、"V 伤"、"V 绝"、"V 止"在前汉都是并列结构。尤其是"灭"字,"他动:自动"的比例是 6:1。《尚书·盘庚》"若火之燎于原,不可向迩,其犹可扑灭",这句话不时有人引来作为动补结构产生于先秦的证据。其实,"可"字表示受动,"扑灭"是并列结构,这句实在没有做证据的资格。还有 1.2 节引过的《汉书·苏武传》"朝鲜杀汉使者,即时诛灭",这句的"诛灭"也是并列结构复合动。

(2)"死"字的"他动:自动"比例最低,平均要用43次自动式的"死"字才用一次使动式。原因很简单:第一,使动式的功能是制造他动式,"死"字已有他动式"杀"字跟它搭配,不必多此一举。第二,"死+宾语"包含三种意义(李佐丰1983:126—127):

(一)其北陵,文王之所辟风雨也,必死是间。《左·僖三十二年》[死在这里]

(二)然子死晋国,子孙必得志于宋。《左·定六年》[为晋国而死]

(三)"死吾父而专于国,有死而已"。《左·襄二十一年》[弄死了我父亲]

(一)、(二)"死"字后面带的都是关系宾语,例(一)表示处所,例(二)表示原因、目的。例(二)这种句子,是"死"字的特殊用法,先秦文献中常见。上面引过的"尔射死艺"(《左·成十六年》)就是一例。其他如《论语·宪问》"桓公杀公子纠,召忽死之,管仲不死"、《孟子·梁惠王》"君行仁政,其民亲其上,死其长"等也是这种用法。因为"为某某而死"的"死某某"占据了使动式"死某某"的形式位置,而"杀"字又占据了"死"字使动用法的语意位置,所以"死"字的使动用法极少见,九部书只出现4次,例(三)就是其中一例。因此我们可以说,"死"字是道道地地、98%的自动词。

4.2 第二个理由是"推堕"、"激怒"、"攻下"等所谓动补结构在前汉只出现于(甲)型句,不出现于(乙)型句:

(甲)施事者+复合动词+受事者
(乙)起词+复合动词

比方说,"恐帝长大后见怨"出现于《汉书·云敞传》。我们按照类似的形式,用"推堕"、"射伤"造两个句子。*"孝惠推堕车下后,大呼求救"、*"邵克射伤后,流血至履"。这种句子是合乎文言文法的,但根据我们的观察,《史记》里却不出现。这种句子并不是完全没有,前人引过:

父战死于前,子虏伤于后。(《汉书·贾捐之传》)

凡山林之高，非削成而崛起也。(《潜夫论·慎微》)
山谷之卑，非截断而颠陷也。(同上)

这些都是后汉的例。《潜夫论·浮侈》"或纺綵丝而縻，断截以绕臂"，"截断"、"断截"词序相反，两个都是并列结构。其他两例出现场合是平行结构。平行结构对于语法的限制总是放宽些。因此，我们目前认为在两汉时代，"推堕"、"射伤"类的复合词只出现于(甲)型，"V死"、"缩小"类复合词只出现于(乙)型，两者出现场合互补。

为什么"推堕"、"攻下"、"击败"、"射伤"等复合词在两汉时代后面一定要带着宾语？这是因为"堕"、"败"、"伤"等下字在复合词中仍是使动(或他动)用法，后面需要有宾语撑着。

4.3 第三个理由是动补结构"V死"的晚出。这里问题不在动补结构"V死"的出现和其他所谓动补结构有先后之别，而在时间差距何以如此之大。第2节给"施＋V死＋受"断代是用比较宽的标准，它最早也不会早过五世纪初年。如果"推堕"、"击败"等在司马迁(公元前145—前86?)《史记》里出现的复合动词是动补结构，那么动补结构"V死"至少要晚出五百年，尤其是"V死"在先秦两汉文献中俯拾即是，更令人觉得费解。

解决的方法是承认"射伤"、"推堕"等复合词的构成程序和"V死"不同。"射伤"等是先把下字使动化变成他动词，然后附加在"射"、"击"、"推"等上字的后面。"V死"是直接把自动词"死"字附加在"V"的后面。这两种复合构成程序不同，所以词性不同，出现场合也不同。同样的，后汉的带着宾语的"减轻"、"填满"大概也是并列结构。

五 动补结构的形成方式和产生时代

5.1 第2节已经说明五世纪初有"是邻家老黄狗，乃打死之"这样的句子。这是动补结构的来源之一。现在讨论另外的一个来源，也就是"击败"、"射伤"等怎样从"他动＋他动"的并列结构转成"他动＋自动"的动补结构。引起这种转换的因素很多，根据它们的产生年代可以估计第二种动补结构的产生年代。

第一个因素是清浊别义的衰落。"败"、"折"、"断"、"坏"都有两读，清音声母是他动词，浊音声母是自动词或既事式(周祖谟1966:116—118)，例如：

*k-: *g-	见(古甸切):	现(胡甸切)
	解(古买切):	解(胡买切)
	降(古巷切):	降(户江切)
	繫(古谐切):	繫(胡计切)
	坏(音怪):	坏(户怪切)
	挟(古洽切):	挟(侯夹切)
*p-: *b-	败(补败切):	败(薄迈切)
	覆(芳福切):	复(扶富切)
*t-: *d-	折(之舌切):	折(市列切)
	属(章玉切):	属(时玉切)
	著(陟略切):	著(直略切)
	断(都管切):	断(徒管切)

这种用清浊之别来区别词性的构词法我们叫做"清浊别义"。从秦代开始，就有用"败"、"折"、"断"等字作下字的复合动词：

击败 　与秦赤败楚于重丘。(《史记·田敬仲完世家》)
击断 　乃下石乞、壶属攻子路，击断子路之缨。(同上,《仲尼弟子列传》)
啮断 　或斗，啮断人若耳若指若唇，论各可(何)殴(也)。(《睡虎地秦墓竹简》,186)
斗折 　斗折脊项骨，可(何)论？比折支(肢)。(同上，183)
椎坏 　饶燕土果悍，即引斧椎椎坏之。(《汉书·匈奴传》)

据上所论，"击败"的"败"在前汉是他动词，读作"补败切"，帮母。清浊别义衰落后，"败"字只有浊音一读，并母。"击败"的"败"读作并母，对"败"字清浊有别的人来说，"击败(并母)"是他动词带着自动词。这样，并列结构的"击败(帮母)"就转成动补结构的"击败(并母)"。

"败"字从两读变为一读，六世纪的文献里还有记载。陆德明《经典释文》(583—589)《序录》里说：及夫自败蒲迈反败他补败反之殊，自坏呼怪反坏撒音怪之异，此等或近代始分，或古已为别，相仍积习，有自来矣。"颜之推(513—?)《颜氏家训·音辞篇》说:"江南学士读左传口相传述,自为凡例。军自败为败,打破人军曰败_{补败反}……此其穿凿耳。"

  清浊别义可以远溯到汉藏共同语。当清浊别义在口语中活跃时,不必用文字点明,人们自然而然地会按照字的不同用法说出清浊两音,倒是在清浊别义衰落时,才需要在经典的诠释中注明。最早关于清浊别义的记载大概是晋代吕忱的《字林》。《尔雅·释诂》"坏,毁也",《释文》云"《字林》坏自败也,下怪反";《礼记·问丧》"如坏墙然",《释文》云引《字林》云:"坏音怪"。我们知道,《经典释文》是四声别义、清浊别义的总汇。这样看来,清浊别义作为能产的构词法,在东汉已开始衰落,到六世纪渐趋灭亡。

  上面的论证假设"败"字在古代确实曾有清浊两读。《经典释文》里清浊两读的"读破",有些可能是人为的读书音。"败"、"坏"、"断"、"别"等《释文》两读而口语一读的字,口语保存的都是浊音声母的自动词,所以我们相信古代确实曾有两读。退一步着想,清浊别义的衰落是事实,衰落以前一定会有更多的动词可以清浊两读,只要其中有一批从两读变为一读,而仅有一读的是浊音声母的自动性,上面的论证就不受影响。

  [……]

  第二个因素是使动式的衰落。后世的文言,受了先秦典籍的影响,一直在用使动式,所以使动式在口语中衰落的年代不容易直接判断。志村良治(1974)做过一项类似的研究。他的设想是:两汉有"射伤、斫破、击断、椎坏"等复合动词,如果"伤"、"破"、"断"、"坏"等只能用作自动词,这些字就不能用作复合他动词的上字。结果他在东汉到南北朝的佛经里找出若干"断"、"坏"、"破"、"伤"用作上字的例,例如"断截、断除、断绝、断决"、"坏败(也有'败坏')、坏烂(也有'烂坏')、坏破"、"破除、破裂、破碎"、"伤败、伤损",可惜他没有注出这些复合词是否后面带着宾语。

  [……]

  第三个因素是"隔开式"动补结构的产生,如上面引过的"排[扑]船坏耳"(《幽明录》)[……]

  第四个因素是"动+形"式复合词的产生,例如:

    恐帝长大后见怨。(《汉书·云敞传》)

[……]

5.2 现在再讨论三个一般性的问题。

第一,上面谈到的"射伤"、"击败"等复合词从并列结构变成动补结构,这种现象叫做"重新分析"。这就是说,同样的语素,同样的词序,在先后两个不同的阶段,被理解为两种不同的结构。这种现象跟研究现代语法的学者所谈的"结构歧义"相似,例如"在黑板上写字"(朱德熙 1980:169—192);只是我们所谈的是共时性的现象,这里所谈的是历时性的现象。

历史语法学一直有个理论上的问题:当一个新兴的结构出现时,老一辈人的语法里没有这种结构,他们怎么听得懂?"重新分析"论提出了一种解释:字面上没起变化,字面所表示的结构却受了演变的影响在"潜移默化"。这样,老幼两辈虽然用新旧两种不同的结构,说的却是同样的话,照样可以互相了解。

第二,从先秦到唐代,汉语有个"自动词化"的趋势。最极端的例子是吴语"杀"字在复合词中被"死"同化而变成自动词,作为"死"讲。另外"坏、败、断"本来有清浊两读,一是自动,一是他动,而后来只保存了浊音的自动词,这也是"自动词化"的结果。最常见的是一个动词在先秦两汉时自动、他动两用,而且如第 4.1 节的字表所示,"灭"、"败"、"伤"等字他动用例占压倒优势;到了唐代以后只有自动一用,或者自动用法的频率超过他动用法。现代汉语不能说*"破了他的杯子"、*"断了他的铅笔",总得说成"碰破"、"摔破"、"压断"、"掰断",如果没有具体的他动词可用,就说"弄破"、"弄断"。单音节的他动式既然被双音节的动补结构替代,结果是只剩下自动式,或者减低他动式的使用频率。因为我们现代的语感形成于唐代"自动词化"以后,就不免会产生一种错觉,以为"击断"、"击败"等复合动词的下字在前汉也是自动词。

第三,原始汉语有套由各种词缀或声母清浊交替组成的构词法。目前可以证明的有 *-s 后缀(梅祖麟 1980)、*s-前缀(李方桂 1980:24—27)、*-r-中缀(蒲立本 1973:118)以及清浊别义。这些音变构词法逐渐衰落,唐代完全灭亡。这是上古、中古时代很重要的演变,甚至于可以说汉语改变了类型,从藏文那样富有音变构词法的综合类型的语言变成分析类型的语言。

在音变构词法衰落的过程,有若干新兴的形式来替代失去的语法功能。大部分担任补偿作用的新兴形式和古老形式只是功能相称,但没有源流关系。清浊别义似乎结局不同。清浊别义的主要构词功能是分辨他动、自动;

清音声母是他动词,浊音声母是自动词。上面看到清浊别义的衰落是动补结构的产生因素之一,两者之间有源流关系。更有意思的是"折(禅母)"、"断(定母)"、"败(並母)"这种自动词有既事式的含意,给动补结构吸收进去以后,又因为动补结构的结果补语有完成貌的语法意义,在十世纪促成完成貌"了"字的产生(梅祖麟 1981)。套句《文心雕龙》的话,也许可以说"清浊别义告退,而动补结构方滋"。

Cavalli-Sforza et al. (1988) "Reconstruction of Human Evolution"选读[1]

◆ 作者简介

路易吉·路卡·卡瓦利-斯福扎[2](Luigi Luca Cavalli-Sforza, 1922—2018),20 世纪最著名的遗传学家之一,先后任教于意大利帕尔马大学、帕维亚大学及斯坦福大学,为斯坦福大学名誉教授。卡瓦利-斯福扎开创性地提出利用群体基因研究历史上的人口迁移和文化传播,其研究成果对人类学、语言学、考古学、生物进化等不同学科都有启发。在语言学方面,他与王士元(1986)将人口遗传学中的"脚踏石模型"应用到语言演变研究中,使用计量分析方法研究了密克罗尼西亚一系列岛链上的词汇,研究结果反映出词汇在空间上的替代速率与时间上的替代速率具有明显的正相关性。他们的研究为探索语言的横向传递与纵向传递的关系开辟了新的视角。

本文综合对比了来自遗传学、语言学和考古学的成果,追溯了人口的迁移史。

---

[1] Cavalli-Sforza, L.L., Piazza, A., Menozzi, P. and Mountain, J. 1988. "Reconstruction of human evolution: bringing together genetic, archaeological, and linguistic data." *Proceedings of the National Academy of Sciences*, 85(16), pp. 6002-6006.

[2] 图片来源:http://www.affaritaliani.it/static/upl2018_restyle/luig/0000/luigi-luca-cavalli-sforza5.jpg.

◆ 正文节选

The reconstruction of human phylogeny from contemporary genetic information was first attempted (1-4) by the use of gene frequencies of 20 alleles from five major blood-group systems known from 15 populations. The genetic information from all genes was cumulated by calculating a "genetic distance" between pairs of populations. Two independent methods developed for the purpose were used to reconstruct the phylogeny, with very similar results. One of them was based on independence of evolution in the branches resulting after every fission, and the other on maximum parsimony; neither, however, can define an origin (a "root") for the tree. When only information internal to the data set is used, it is necessary to assume constant evolutionary rates for setting a root. When this hypothesis was superimposed on constructed trees, the root separated African plus European populations on one side and the rest of the world on the other. The later addition of more genes (5), including *HLA* (6), caused little change in the shape of the phylogenetic tree.

Many protein and enzyme polymorphisms were detected in the 1960s and 1970s by electrophoretic methods but were initially tested on few samples. By using only three populations (Africans, Europeans, and East Asians), Nei (7) was able to consider many more genes. He concluded that blood groups and enzyme polymorphisms gave different results with respect to the location of the root, with blood groups still showing greater similarity between Africans and Europeans than between Europeans and East Asians, thus confirming earlier results on the position of the root. With enzymes and proteins, however, Europeans were closer to East Asians than to Africans. These markers carried more statistical weight than blood groups, so that the complete data located the root between Africa and Europe plus Asia. The conclusion remained unchanged on extension to other populations (8), but the analysis did not include the rich set of *HLA* data.

Since that time, there have appeared results generated by DNA restriction analysis of mitochondrial DNA (9, 10), β-globin (11), the Y chromosome (12), and 44 nuclear gene markers (13,14). With some contradiction, they tend to confirm the African/non-African split, but they are affected by biological or statistical weaknesses that will be discussed in a separate paper in which we will also present new DNA-marker data. The classical marker data used here confirm this conclusion but are much more abundant, thus allowing us to study human evolution in greater detail and to test agreement with other sources of evolutionary information, both archaeological and linguistic.

Evolutionary Analysis of Classical Genetic Markers

Materials and Methods. The literature data were collected in the course of preparation of an atlas of human variation. Selection of the present material was guided by the desire to study a representative sample of the world aboriginal populations, balancing the need to have as many genes as possible with the need to minimize the number of gaps in the gene × population matrix. Two genetic distances corresponding to different evolutionary models were used for comparing populations in pairs: (i) the most investigated one, a family (15) that also includes distances used in earlier papers (refs.1 - 4; see also ref.16); and (ii) Nei's standard genetic distance (16), always with correction for sample size. The two distances were highly correlated (r = 0.86) and the relation between them was of almost perfect proportionality except at short distances. We found it safe to use gene × population matrices that had gaps, provided these were not too frequent, by calculating distances between pairs of populations only for genes known in both of the populations being compared. Tests of this statement included comparison of results of principal components and tree analysis based on both an incomplete matrix and a complete subset of the same matrix, as well as extensive experiments of simulation of the effect of random gaps on principal component maps, which are highly related to the highest splits in the tree (17). Gaps in the matrix used for the tree of Fig. 1 were 23.7%.

A recently introduced statistical technique, the bootstrap (18), a resampling method for obtaining standard errors that are difficult to estimate di-

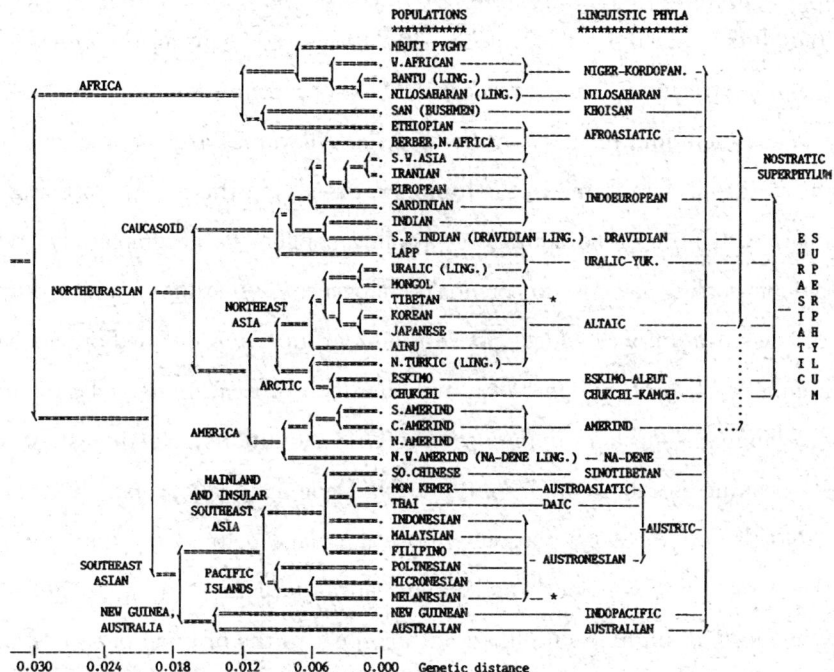

FIG. 1. Comparison of genetic tree and linguistic phyla. See text for details. (Ling.) indicates populations pooled on the basis of linguistic classification. The tree was constructed by average linkage analysis of Nei's genetic distances. Distances were calculated based on 120 allele frequencies from the following systems: $A1A2BO$, MNS, RH, P, LU, K, FY, JK, DI, HP, TF, CC, LE, LP, $PEPA$, $PEPB$, $PEPC$, AG, $HLAA$ (12 alleles), $HLAB$ (17 alleles), PI, CP, ACP, PGD, $PGM1$, MDH, ADA, PTC, EI, $SODA$, GPT, PGK, $C3$, SE, ESD, GLO, KM, BF, LAD, $E2$, GM, and PG.

rectly, proved very useful. According to this method, genes actually used are randomly sampled with replacement, generating a new matrix of genes × populations with the same number of genes as the original, but in which some genes are missing and others are repeated. The procedure is repeated a sufficient number of times ("bootstraps"), each time producing a new matrix. From each matrix a given statistic is calculated; its standard error is the standard deviation of the values taken by the statistic in the bootstrap samples. Felsenstein (19) suggested using the bootstrap to test the reproducibility of the sequence of splits in the tree.

Tree of 42 World Populations. The tree shown in Fig. 1 was generated by average linkage analysis (20) of 42 populations representing the world aborigines: 7 African, 5 American (natives), 5 Oceanian, 6 European, and the rest Asian including insular Southeast Asia. All values are average gene frequencies for all data found in the literature satisfying the criteria of being aboriginal, with little or no admixture, pooling populations geographically. When geographic pooling gave rise to potential heterogeneity, an ethnolinguistic criterion of classification was added. Six of the 42 groups were formed on the basis of linguistic affinity: Nilosaharan and Bantu in Africa; Samoyed and other Uralic language speakers living near the Ural mountains; Northwest Americans speaking northern and southern Na-Dene languages; North Turkic, i.e., Northeast Asian populations whose language belongs to this subgroup of the Altaic phylum; Southeast Indian, speaking Dravidian languages. The tree in Fig. 1 is slightly simplified with respect to the original one of 42 populations in that all Europeans that clustered compactly together (Basque, Dane, English, Greck, and Italian) were pooled to form one population. All analyses, however, were done on the full tree.

The first split in the tree separates Africans from non-Africans and is reproducible, given that in 84 out of 100 bootstrap trees the first split separated from all other populations a cluster containing at least the four "core" African populations (Pygmies, West Africans, Bantu, and Nilo-saharan). In most of the 84 trees the African cluster also contains the other two sub-Saharan African populations (San and Ethiopians). When these two are not with the core Africans they tend to join the Caucasoid group.

The next bifurcation separates two major "superclusters", the first of which, Northeurasian, splits into (i) Caucasoids and then (ii) Northeast Asians plus Amerindians. The Northeast Asian cluster separates further into a small cluster of Arctic populations, including Eskimos, and a cluster including both East Asians and North Asians. Caucasoids form a fairly tight group consisting of 12 populations, 5 of which were pooled as "Europeans" in Fig. 1. Lapps leave the cluster in 32% of the bootstraps, joining Asian Arctic populations. Berbers and Dravidians leave the Caucasoid cluster 20% of the time and tend to join respectively the African and one of the two major East Asian clusters. The Northeast Asian cluster is also reasonably compact, 81% of trees having at least 4 of the 6 populations shown in the tree in Fig.1; most often lost are Tibetans (25%), Uralic speakers (13%), and Ainu (12%). The Arctic Northeast Asian cluster (Chuckchi, Eskimo, and North Turkic) is not very tight but is still well recognizable on bootstrapping. Amerinds are the tightest cluster, as in 79% of bootstraps all 4 populations are together, with Northwest Amerindians (speaking Na-Dene languages) being most easily lost (21%).

The Southeast Asian supercluster splits into (i) Southeast Asians proper (mainland and insular), a fairly tight cluster of the six populations seen in the tree of Fig. 1; on bootstrapping, Filipinos are lost 29% of the time, Malaysians 23%, and Indonesians 7%; (ii) the Pacific islanders, a cluster of three populations, not tight but clearly recognizable; and (iii) New Guineans and Australians, which remain together more than 50% of the time.

The earlier splits are all statistical significant by tests that will be described elsewhere. Of special interest is the second bifurcation shown in Fig. 1, separating Northeurasians from Southeast Asians. This split occurs most often among the bootstraps, but two alternative partions are fairly frequent: one separates Caucasoids from all Asian, Oceanian, and Amerindian populations, and the second separates New Guinean and Australian populations from all other non-African populations. We shall see later that the second bifurcation given in the tree receives support from an independent source as well.

Constant Evolutionary Rates. [...]

Correlations with Archaeology

There has been in the last few years considerable interest in the dating of the earliest anatomically modern humans, *Homo sapiens sapiens*. There seems to have developed some consensus about the validity of dates of early modern humans from the Border Caves and the Klasies River Mouth, both in South Africa, now dated at more than 100 kyr (100,000 years ago), with a date of 125 kyr for Laetoli in Tanzania (23) and 130 kyr for Omo I (24). In the rest of the world, findings are very poorly dated; however, a recent analysis of modern human remains from the Qafzeh cave in Israel suggests the date of 92 ± 5 kyr (25). This is about twice as old as the very approximate previous results. If the current archaeological data are accepted at face value, the origin of modem humans was in Africa and the expansion to the rest of the world started there. Naturally, considering the paucity of samples and the uncertainties in their dating, one cannot exclude the possibility that new archaeological discoveries may alter this picture.

The timing of the steps in the expansion can be very useful for calibrating the process of genetic differentiation and testing the constancy of evolutionary rates in our tree. Dates used for this aim in Table 1 are as follows:

(*i*) A time$\geqslant$92 kyr for the split between African and non-African has been matched with the genetic differentiation due to the first split of the tree.

(*ii*) The first entry to Australia took place at least 40 kyr (26), and the first settlement of New Guinea took place from Australia. We have matched this time with the node connecting Australia plus New Guinea with Southeast Asia (the third split in the tree).

(*iii*) The disappearance of Neanderthals and the first appearance of modern humans in southwestern Europe occurred 30 – 35 kyr, and somewhat earlier in Eastern Europe (27), for which data are less satisfactory. A time of 35 kyr was matched with the separation of Caucasoids from Northeast Asia.

Table 1 Comparison of genetic distances and archaeological time data

Clusters defining fission	Genetic distance (G)*	Time (T), Kyr	G/T
African/non-African	29.7±6.8	92	0.32±0.07
Australian/S.E. Asian	18.4±3.4	≥40	0.46±0.09
Caucasoid/(N.E.Asian+Amerind)	16.6±3.5	35	0.47±0.10
N.E.Asian/Amerind	12.1±1.8	15—35	0.81±0.12 —0.35±0.05
N.Amerind/S.and C.Amerind	4.2±1.0	15—35	0.28±0.07 —0.12±0.03

* Nei's distances×1000, with standard errors.

(iv) Two possible dates for the entry to America are 35 kyr and 15 kyr (28, 29). There seems to be more consensus for the second, later date, and in any case this is likely to have had greater demographic weight, given the relative number of sites. There is also uncertainty as to the best match in the genetic tree. Use of the fission between Northeast Asia and the Americas generates a genetic distance that is too large, if the tree has no direct descendants of the Northeast Asians who went to America. The fission between North Amerinds and Central plus South Amerinds generates a distance that is probably too small but that is at least uncomplicated by admixture with later arrivals to North America.

Table 1 shows the clusters defining the fissions listed above, the average genetic distances (G) between the clusters defining each fission, and the archaeological separation dates (T). If the evolutionary rates are constant, the G/T ratios should be constant. Leaving aside the Americas, for which there is uncertainty, we see that there is satisfactory agreement between the three values that are more dependable, as shown by standard errors. The older fission used for America seems to accord with the older date, and the younger one with the younger date. At least one can say that the American data are not inconsistent with the conclusions from the other three dates, from which the average G/T of 0.40±0.05 was calculated. This is valid for long time intervals, for which there is the advantage that many distances are averaged and the distorting effects of admixture and drift may even partially compensate for each other. For shorter intervals this G/T value should be used with caution.

Correlation with Linguistic Classification

There are approximately 5000 languages spoken today, and in a recent taxonomic effort they have been classified in 17 families or phyla (30). The phyla of the languages spoken by the populations studied in the genetic tree are listed in Fig. 1. Of the 17 phyla proposed by Ruhlen (30), only one, Caucasian, is missing for lack of adequate genetic data, but the limited genetic information available suggests that Caucasians are very similar to neighbors and would not generate anomalies if inserted into the tree. Inspection of Fig. 1 shows that every linguistic phylum corresponds to only one of six major genetic clusters defined by the tree. Exceptions are Mbuti Pygmies, who have lost their original language; Basques, who have kept their original language, which is an isolate (30); and Melanesians (starred in Fig. 1), who speak in part also Indopacific languages. More important exceptions are the folliong. (i) Ethiopians are classified genetically in the African cluster although they speak Afroasiatic languages, also spoken in North Africa and the Near East by people who are genetically Caucasoid. The evidence for genetic admixture of Ethiopians can explain the anomaly. (ii) Lapps associate linguistically with speakers of Uralic languages but genetically with Caucasoids and again have important genetic admixture. (iii) Tibetans (starred in Fig. 1) are associated genetically with the Northeast Asian cluster but linguistically with the Sinotibetan phylum, which is spoken in all of China. According to Chinese historians, the Tibetans originated from pastoral nomads of the steppes north of China; this origin explains their genetic association with the Northeast Asian cluster.

The correspondence between linguistic phyla and genetic clusters shows that they have similar origins, but phyla, being contained in the clusters, must have developed later. This suggests a time frame for their origin. Also of great interestare the "superfamilies" of languages recently proposed by some linguists. Greenberg (31) has classified all the many preexisting phyla of American native languages into three, which are incorporated in the Ruhlen classification shown in Fig. 1: a superphylum including all languages of Central and South America and many of North America, a phylum (Na-Dene) of languages spoken in the Northwest, and the Eskimo-Aleut phylum. It is interesting that the Austric superfamily postulated by Ruhlen (30) includes almost all of the Southeast Asian cluster, leaving out only the southern Chinese, who speak Sinotibetan languages.

Two other superfamilies have been suggested and are indicated at the extreme right of Fig.1: Nostratic and Eurasiatic. The first follows a proposal by Soviet linguists (summarized in ref. 30) and includes six phyla that all belong to the North Eurasian major cluster; the sixth phylum, South Caucasian, is not given in Fig. 1 for reasons already discussed. The other superfamily, Eurasiatic, proposed by Greenberg and summarized by Ruhlen (30), overlaps but does not coincide with Nostratic; it includes other phyla also belonging to the North Eurasian cluster. A link of Nostratic with Amerind (dotted vertical line in Fig. 1) was recently suggested by Shevoroshkin (32). It is most striking that the union of Eurasiatic and Nostratic, with the Amerind extension, includes all, and only, the languages spoken in our major Northeurasian cluster, with the exception of Na-Dene, the origin of which is less clear. Greenberg (33) noted that the apparent contradictions between his Eurasiatic superfamily and the Russians' Nostratic superfamily can be resolved by considering time levels of separation.

Languages evolve more rapidly than genes. They can also undergo rapid replacement, even if the new language is imposed by an invading minority, provided this minority has adequate political and military organization, as in the "elite dominance" model (34). When this happens it may be difficult to find genetic traces of the invasion. Elites have developed only recently, however, rarely being older than 5000 years, and therefore episodes of rapid language replacement are relatively recent and often accounted for historically. In the more remote past, replacement was more rare, justifying the stability of the relation between linguistic phyla and genetic clusters.

The Process of Expansion of Modern Humans

Reconstruction of human evolution can be truly satisfactory only if information from all relevant sources of acceptable reliability gives a coherent answer. The present data and analysis offer an attempt at a detailed joint approach. The tree of Fig.1 may be wrong in details; it would be surprising if a tree of this size based on current information were completely correct. Any change in the archaeological, genetic, or linguistic conclusions will require adjustment. Current agreement remains nevertheless very encouraging.

The model we use (1-4) clearly assumes expansion of modern humans from a nuclear area and replacement of other local preexisting populations, a model that has found resistance in some anthropological circles. The major evidence cited against the replacement model comes from the continuity of some traits in fossil crania from East Asia. This evidence has prompted Wolpoff *et al*. (35) to suggest an alternative model, which they call "the theory of multiregional evolution", based on an almost continuous population network (36) and standard clinal theory. But the multiregional model cannot provide an explanation of the most important phenomenon, the rapid expansion of modern humans to the whole Earth. Its inability to do so derives from its assumption that genetic populations are at equilibrium, whereas a rapid expansion is a disruption of a former equilibrium. Another hypothesis on which the model rests, the maintenance of potential interfertility among all living humans for very long periods, may be correct, but if interfertility can help to explain the local performance of aome traits, it does not help to understand the expansion of a new type.

First, one must explain the expansion. There are several examples of expansions, some easier to study because they took place in historic time (37). Archaeologists in the early 20th century postulated migrations in a facile way, often on the basis of inadequate evidence. Today they have reacted with a strongly antimigrationist stance, but they certainly do not deny all expansions; the important point is to find in every case whether there were conditions conducive to expansion and its maintenance (34). The Neolithic expansions were due to the introduction of new technologies of food production, allowing a substantial increase in the carrying capacity of the land. The introduction of farming in West Asia was the stimulus and the support for the Neolithic expansion to Europe and most probably in other directions (38). The introduction of farming in the Sahel, in addition to the introduction of iron technology, stimulated and supported the Bantu expansion to central and southern Africa (39). Pastoral nomadism, coupled with new social structures and with new social structures and with new techniques of transportation and warfare, mostly using the horse, supported the expansions in which the steppe nomads have been major actors until very recently and for several millennia (40). A rapid expansion can be viewed as a punctuationist (41) episode in evolution, and such events are likely to occur repeatedly in general and not only in human evolution.

Which stimuli determined, and which technologies helped, expansions of modern humans to the whole Earth? It seems very likely that an important role was played by a biological advantage that may have developed slowly over millions of years and undergone a final step only with the appearance of modern humans: a fully developed language. Isaac (42) has indicated archaeological evidence in favor of this hypothesis. From a speculative point of view, it seems reasonable that more efficient communication can improve foraging and hunting techniques, favor stronger social ties, and facilitate the spread of information useful for migratory movements. It also makes it easier to understand the rapid disappearance of Neanderthals, if they were biologically provided with speech of more modest quality than modern humans. In our society, until 100 – 150 years ago, deaf-mute people had very little chance of reproducing because of strong adverse social selection (43). Even if interfertility was potentially complete and there was little or no impingement, Neanderthals must have been at a substantial disadvantage at both the between- and the within-population level.

11.3　思考和练习

1. 学界对于《切韵》所反映的是什么语音至今仍存在较大的争论,而中古汉语的构拟基本是参照《切韵》进行,这会造成什么问题?结合 Norman 的文章进行讨论。

2. 有些方言存在文白异读现象。利用方言音进行古音构拟的话,应该怎么处理文白两个读音?

3. 根据以下历史语料,试分析"V 个 VP"结构及"个"语法化的过程和相关机制①。

(1) 譬如群兽然,<u>一个</u>负矢,将百群皆奔。(《国语·吴语》)
(2) 有<u>个</u>人家儿子,问着无有道不得底。(《景德传灯录》)
(3) 人不辨<u>个</u>大小轻重无鉴识。(陆九渊《象山先生集》)
(4) 你看我<u>寻个自尽</u>、<u>觅个自刎</u>(《元曲选·曲江池》)
(5) 消消停停的,就<u>有个青红皂白</u>了。(《红楼梦》三十四回)
(6) 黛玉说着,便<u>撕了个粉碎</u>,递与丫头们说:"快烧了罢。"
(《红楼梦》二十二回)

4. 根据本章最后一篇选文的思路,结合亚洲特别是东亚地区的群体基因及人口迁移方面的资料,探讨中国方言的形成与发展史。

11.4　延伸阅读

Chambers, J. K. & Trudgill, P. 1980. *Dialectology*. New York: Cambridge University Press.

Hopper, P. J. & T. Closs, 2003. *Grammaticalization*（Second Edition）.

---

① 资料来源:张谊生,2013,《从量词到助词——量词"个"语法化过程的个案分析》,《当代语言学》(第五期), 193—205。

New York: Cambridge University Press.

Labov, W. 1992. *Principles of Linguistics Change*. Oxford: Blackwell.

Lehmann, W. P. 1992. *Historical Linguistics*. London: Routledge.

Sun, C. 1996. *Word-order Change and Grammaticalization in the History of Chinese*. Stanford, Calif.: Stanford University Press.

Traugott, E. C. & Trousdale, G. 2013. *Constructionalization and Constructional Changes*. Oxford: Oxford University Press.

第十二章　语言与大脑

12.1　导　引

- 引言
- 大脑皮层的语言区
- 大脑语言区的几个理论
- 大脑语言区对语言理论的启示
- 脑功能成像技术
- 语言与电脑

12.1.1　引言

神经语言学(neurolinguistics)或许是与研究"语言与大脑"关系最为密切的一个学科。作为一个新兴的交叉学科，神经语言学横跨脑科学、语言学、心理学与认知科学，以人类大脑为研究材料，探索与语言信息处理、储存有关的大脑结构和神经机制。本章仅介绍神经语言学最基本的概念，以及一些常用的研究方法及工具。

12.1.2　大脑皮层的语言区

大概在150年前，科学家就发现了大脑的两个与语言功能密切相关的区域：布洛卡区(Broca's area)和威尼克区(Wernicke's area)。这两个区域的发现都源于对失语症的研究。

布洛卡区位于左侧大脑半球额叶，通常被认为是主要负责语言表达的中枢。该区域若受损会出现"表达性失语症":患者只能讲出短句,或一些支离破碎、没有章法的句子,而无法完整地表达长句;在理解长句,特别是复杂句的时候,也会有一定的困难。比如,病人可能能理解"Mary gave John balloons"这样的句法关系简单的句子,但同样的意思,如果表述成"The balloons were given to John by Mary"这种既包含被动又包含状语、具有多个成分相对复杂的句子,就可能会造成患者的理解困难。布洛卡区受损的患者通常读写能力也会受损,即使能够保留阅读的能力,写字的能力也会严重受损。

威尼克区位于左侧大脑半球颞叶,通常被认为是负责语言理解的中枢。该区域受损会出现"接受性失语症",在语言理解方面通常有很大的困难:有时一个简单的句子甚或一个词也有可能听不懂。在表达方面,这种患者与上一种失语症患者不同,能够讲出语流顺畅、语法无误的句子,并且词汇量丰富;但因为所用的词语与谈话的内容毫无关系,甚至有时候是一些生造出来的词,这些流利的话听起来更像是没有任何含义的胡言乱语,而讲话者本身对此却毫无知觉——他们受损的理解能力也影响到了对自己语言输出的判断能力。

布洛卡区和威尼克区之间由弓状神经束(arcuate fasciculus)相互联系,担负着在两个区域间传输信号的功能。例如,我们在认读单词的时候,一旦威尼克区开始处理信息,信号便经由弓状神经束向布洛卡区传送信号,由布洛卡区去负责语言输出。若这种神经联系受损则会出现传导性失语症,患者不能正常对话,出现用词不当或答非所问等错误。

与语言处理相关的还有一个重要的中枢是角回(angular gyrus),位于威尼克区上方、顶枕叶交界处。角回是大脑后部一个重要的联合区,是大脑视觉中枢与威尼克区之间的中介,与处理语言的视觉信息有很大的关系。当要说出一个书面文字的词时,认读的视觉信息传到大脑皮层视区产生该词的视觉形象,接着神经冲动再传到角回,使视觉形象转换为该词的听觉形式,然后再传给威尼克区转化为理解的语言信息。当我们听到一个词的时候,威尼克区接受的听觉信息也将送到角回,再做处理。若角回损伤就会出现失读症,患者不能正确阅读书面文字,因为文字的视觉与听觉分离,使威尼克区得不到书面词语的听觉形式,而不能转化为理解性的语言信息。

12.1.3 大脑语言区的几个理论

布洛卡区和威尼克区是分别以他们的发现者布洛卡和威尼克命名的。19世纪,当布洛卡和威尼克发现这两个区域的时候,对于大脑的分析探测技术手段还极其有限,他们是在失语症患者死后,通过对其大脑进行尸检才做出了推断。随着现代科技的发展,当时由于实验手段的局限性而提出的一些假说也被新研究一一做出补充、修订和完善。

12.1.3.1 单侧化

大脑在结构上具有不对称性,左右两个半球在功能上也存在一定的分工。布洛卡在发现位于大脑左半球的布洛卡区时就提出,人是由大脑左半球处理语言。这就是所谓的语言中枢的"单侧化"(lateralization)。这种观点认为大脑语言功能主要集中在左半球,左半脑是语言加工的"优势半球"。

"优势半球"的观点持续了一个世纪,直到20世纪中期才开始转变。当时,医学界开始施行裂脑手术(split brain),认为切断连接大脑两半球的胼胝体是治疗癫痫病的一种措施。在切断胼胝体以后,大脑左右半球失去沟通的机制,因而通过分别对左右脑进行实验刺激,研究者便可探明大脑两半球的分工技能。20世纪中期,一系列的裂脑实验和对脑损伤病人的临床医学观察一致表明:两侧大脑半球之间是分工合作的关系,二者各有所长,相互补充,共同完成大脑的整体功能;大脑两半球各有优势,称为"双势理论"。

近期的研究更是表明,右半球在对语言生成和理解也起着重要作用。右半球不仅仅在篇章理解等方面有重要作用,在非直义语言、语义、语篇加工等方面也占有重要地位。大脑右半球受损者在语用方面有许多缺陷,包括对隐喻、幽默、习语和讥讽语的过度字面诠释等。在口语加工过程中,右半球同样起着重要作用,如情感语韵等方面。目前研究证明,情感语韵加工的优势半球为右半球。

从语言习得的证据来看,有人认为,语言区单侧化就是"关键时期"的生理基础。人在6—7岁就已经形成语言单侧化,在此之前主要靠左半球学习语言,但在此之后学习第二语言主要靠右脑,因而此后学习的语言无法达到母语的水平。近期的研究也表明,如果儿童在早年就学习第二语言,第二语言的激活区域会和第一语言习得激活的区域出现部分重合。但同时,研究也发现,婴儿两侧大脑有同等的语言潜力,在2—3岁以后才逐渐形成差异。有研究曾报道过,儿童如果在 3 岁前损伤一侧大脑,另一侧也可以发展语言功能,甚至在 8—10 岁以前左脑损伤仍可由右脑补偿而逐渐恢复语言功能。语言功能的左脑单侧化不是绝对固定不变的。

12.1.3.2 威尼克-格施温德模型

威尼克-格施温德模型是语言信息处理的神经模型的"经典模型"(见图 12.1),这个模型的重要组成部分包括布洛克区和威尼克区以及串联这两个区域的弓状神经束形成的回路。从威尼克提出这个模型的基本理念,到上世纪 70 年代格施温德的修订,这个模型已有至少 150 年的历史;然而时至今日,在神经科学、心理学、语言学的大学教材中,这个模型依旧被奉为经典;在顶尖的脑科学研究中仍然将该模型引为研究的基本理论的根据。最前沿的研究成果已在各个方面呈现出应摒弃该模型的力证,包括以下几方面:

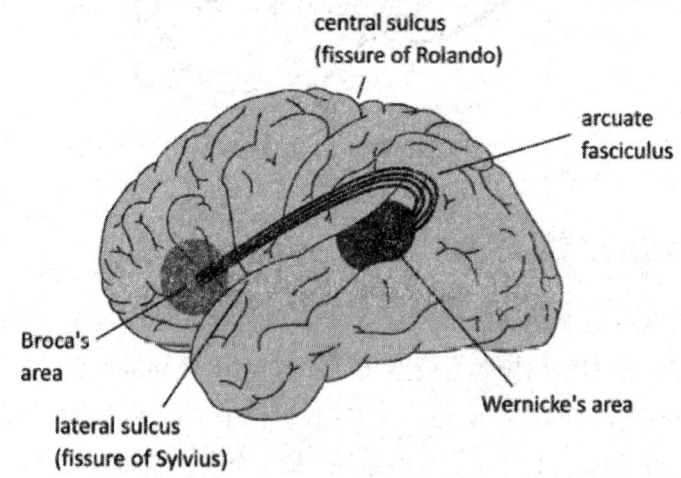

图 12.1 "威尼克-格施温德模型"[①]

第一,大脑的语言信息处理区域不仅限于布洛卡区和威尼克区,而可能分布在大脑的更广泛的区域内;第二,自始至终,科学界对布洛卡区和威尼克区的具体位置和功能就没有达成一致的定义和意见;第三,这个过于简化的模型不能体现已经公认的神经网络的联结性,特别是语言与大脑其它区域的连接;第四,这个模型简单的构造已远远脱离了目前我们对大脑解剖结构的

---

① 图片来源:https://www.ncbi.nlm.nih.gov/pmc/articles/PMC3709422/bin/fpsyg-04-00416-g0001.jpg。

认知。近几年的研究表明,布洛卡区的内部有更为细致的分区,可能存在语言区和非语言区,并且信息处理的回路不止有一条;第五,这个模型仅关注了大脑皮层的区域,完全忽视了皮层下的结构和联结。

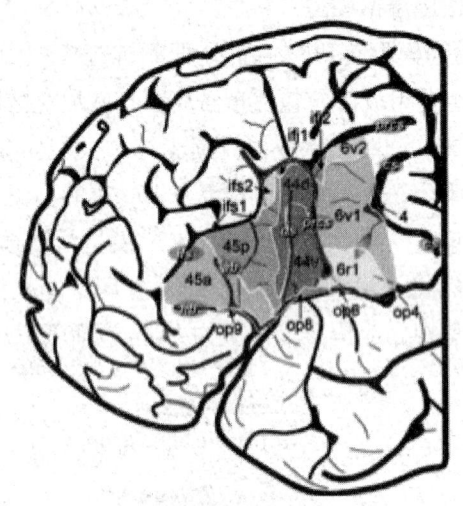

图 12.2　布洛卡区的分区①

12.1.4　大脑语言区对语言理论的启示

　　脑科学对于大脑语言区日益深入和准确的了解对语言学理论意味着什么?停留在"威尼克-格施温德模型"阶段的布洛卡区和威尼克区的讨论无疑是对普遍语法理论的有力支撑。一方面,它似乎证明了语言的"模块性"观点,也就是,人的语言是一个自主的系统,是一个在功能和神经结构上都有别于其它高层皮质的机能。有许多案例也表明,认知机能受损的人可能仍有完好的语言功能,而语言功能受损的人也可能有完好的认知机能,由此证明人使用语言的能力是独立于普通的认知机能的。这类证据恰恰反驳了认知语言派的观点。另一方面,有一些学者提出,布洛卡区控制的是语言的语法,而威尼克区是储存词汇的中心,这种脑神经结构印证了普遍语法的"语法-词汇"分立的观点,反驳了类似于构式语法所提出的"语法-词汇是一个连续体"这样

---

① 图片来源:https://www.ncbi.nlm.nih.gov/pmc/articles/PMC3495005/bin/nihms-414436-f0002.jpg。

的观点。最近的一个研究似乎也证明了语言存在生成语法的"层级结构"(见本章选文)。大部分的脑科学研究似乎都更支持普遍语法(生成语法)的语言理论。

但是,以上所提到的关于布洛卡区分区的新发现似乎也部分支持了认知语言学家的观点,即人的语言的能力和一般领域的认知领域相关。另外,神经语言学也进行了有关构式语法的研究,证明了大脑所储存的语言信息不只有词汇和语法,也包括从具体语言使用中形成的抽象语言构式[①]。目前,我们对大脑如何实现语言功能还知之甚少。希望随着科学技术的发展,有一天我们能够掌握充分的证据,探明人类语言知识的构成形式。

12.1.5　脑功能成像技术

现代的大脑成像技术使研究者采用无创手段,在时间和空间两个维度上对于大脑执行语言功能时的激活状态有更精确的反映和体现。目前主流的大脑功能性成像技术按工作原理区分可分为血流动力学成像和电磁成像。另外,Wada 测试也是一种用于临床快速确定大脑语言优势侧的方法,但并不属于脑功能成像技术。

12.1.5.1　Wada 测试

Wada 测试又称异戊巴比妥钠实验,即向颈动脉或股动脉注入一定量的异戊巴比妥钠溶剂,达到暂时选择性地麻醉一侧大脑半球功能。在用于语言功能测试的时候,通过对患者进行提问并观察患者的回答,可以由此确定患者的语言优势侧。如果麻醉剂注入的是优势侧,患者通常停止语言 2 分钟,随后出现语言障碍,且不能正常命名和顺序计数。

Wada 测试是一种最早的脑功能测试手段,目前多用于癫痫病人脑科学手术前定位语言优势侧。Wada 测试的结果和临床应用表明人和人的语言功能区定位存在巨大的差异。

12.1.5.2　脑功能血流动力学成像技术

血流动力学成像技术的基本原理是,大脑在进行认知任务时需要增强神

---

① Pulvermüller, F., Cappelle, B., and Shtyrov, Y. 2013. Brain basis of meaning, words, constructions, and grammar. In: G. Trousdale and T. Hoffmann (eds.), Oxford Handbook of Construction Grammar. Oxford: Oxford University Press, 397 – 416.

经活动,被激活大脑区域的糖分和氧供应也随之增加。这种变化可以通过局部脑血流量反映出来。

利用该原理的几种常用的成像技术包括 PET(正电子释放成像)、fMRI(功能磁共振成像)、fNIRS(功能性近红外光光谱仪)。总体来说,这几种技术的优点是不仅能检测到脑皮层的活动,也能检测到皮层下的活动,并且通常可以多种技术搭配使用;但其明显的缺点是在空间和时间上的精确性不足——首先,必须认识到,局部脑血流量的变化只是大脑工作区域的间接反映。同时,血流动力学还存在一个严重的滞后问题,也就是当检测到激活区域时,有可能语言活动已发生几秒甚至几十秒。另外,这几项技术在便携性、时间和空间分辨率上又分别有各自的一些优势和劣势。比如,PET 技术在使用时需要向受试者大脑注射放射性液体,因此不适合频繁对同一受试者进行测试;fNIRS 尽管具有造价低、便携性好、无噪音等优点,空间分辨率目前仍不太理想;fMRI 的空间分辨率很高,但是时间分辨率较差,并且在测试时受试者必须处于一个固定的位置。

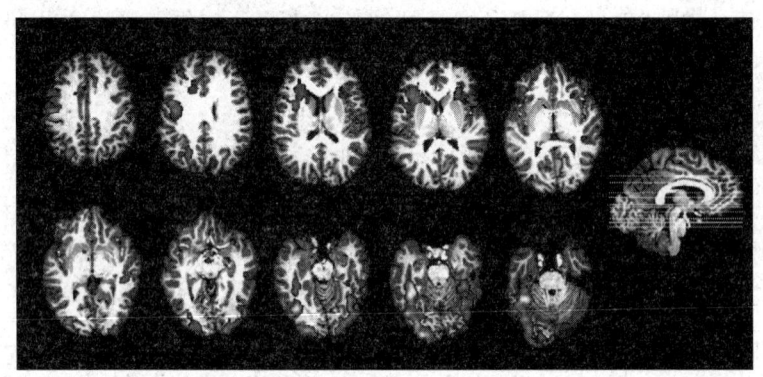

图 12.3　听单词时不同大脑区域激活情况(fMRI 图像)[①]

12.1.5.3　脑功能电磁成像技术

电磁成像技术的基本原理是,大脑在进行认知任务时会引起大脑中的电化学变化。通过在头皮安放电磁成像技术,便可以把这种变化记录下来。

利用该原理的几种常用的成像技术包括 EEG(脑电图)、MEG(脑磁图)和 ERPs(事件相关电位)三种。总体来说,电磁技术的优点是它能直接地测

---

① 图片来源:https://med.nyu.edu/thesenlab/wp-content/uploads/2014/04/fmri1-1024x477.jpg。

量某一认知活动发生时大脑的电磁变化,也就是时间分辨率高;但缺点是它仅能检测到大脑皮层的活动而不能检测到皮层下的活动,空间分辨率较低。由于这种时间上的精确性,电磁成像技术的结果通常以带有峰值的波形图显示。

12.1.6　语言与电脑

尽管我们对大脑处理、储存语言机制的了解仍然非常有限,但随着计算机技术的飞速发展,我们有可能在破译人脑的语言功能之前,提前实现用基于算法的"电脑"使计算机实现人类的语言功能。虽然本章的主题是"语言与人脑",但是在人工智能成为时代热词的当下,"语言与电脑"是一个我们绕不开的话题,而且电脑与人脑和自然语言的关系其实极为密切。

我们对人类认知模型的构建一方面推进着计算机认知模型的发展,例如,本书第八章介绍的"联结主义"神经网络模型已被广泛并成功地使用于各种计算机学习,包括语言学习;反过来,这种模型在计算机上的验证也推进着我们对人脑认知功能的了解。本章的最后一篇选文便介绍了几种目前计算机实现基于自然语言的交流的策略,读者可自行比较这些方法和人类真实的语言能力的差别之处。目前看来,计算机自然语言处理的能力对算法的依赖性很大,但随着算力越来越强大的机器的出现,计算机语言能力已经出现了几次巨大的飞跃。计算机自然语言能力接下来会有怎样的发展,我们拭目以待。

12.2　选读

- 祖里夫(1990)《语言与大脑》选读
- Ding et al. (2016) "Cortical Tracking of Hierarchical Linguistic Structures in Connected Speech"选读
- 迈因策耳(2018)《人工智能与机器学习》选读

祖里夫(1990)《语言与大脑》选读[①]

◆ 作者简介

埃德加·祖里夫(Edgar Zurif),曾任职于美国布兰戴斯大学心理学系、波士顿大学医学院失语症研究中心,其主要研究领域为神经语言学,特别是失语症。

◆ 正文节选

本文讨论语言能力组织和神经系统组织之间的关系,可说是"语言的神经理论"。

这种理论可从不同角度去探究。其一是寻找一个以大脑功能为基础的语言处理动态模型,以了解语言的运算怎样转变为神经活动,这就必须研究语言处理和大脑活动的时空型式的相互关系。要在目前勾勒出这个模型的动态特征还为时过早,故只在文后稍作介绍。

本文主要从另一方面,从失语症分析的角度去建立语言与大脑关系的理论。失语症指由于病灶性脑损伤而引起的各种语言紊乱。值得注意的是,这些病灶性损伤并没有引起语言能力的全面衰退,它们对语言能力的破坏是有选择性的。我们要研究的是,能否用某种语言理论去解释这种选择性。正常的语言能力由许多部分天衣无缝地组合在一起,它们在脑损伤后能否显露出来?失语症病人的语言能力的展示是否有助于科学地了解语言?有些观察者相信,语言障碍的选择性和脑受损的区域有关,我们不妨先看看脑的哪些部分对语言处理是至关重要的。

1. 失语症

1.1 语言活动与大脑定位

测定语言行为变化与大脑各个区域损伤的关系是神经学中一个老问题,已有100多年的历史。研究这个问题的神经学家大都有些哲学癖好,而且喜欢思考心理问题。失语症有两点事实颇惹人深思:一是引起语言紊乱的损伤往往也引起其他认知活动的障碍,这就促使各种关于语言和思维的关系的假设的产生;二是语言障碍本身有选择性;不同位置的损伤会从不同方面损害

[①] Edgar Zurif 著,桂诗春译述,《语言与大脑》,《国外语言学》1992 年第 3 期。

语言能力,这使人去推测正常语言能力究竟由大脑哪些部分组成。

在 1870 年代所建立的大脑与语言关系的模型就是考虑了后一点而提出来的,这个模型集中对待与大脑两个损伤区有联系的两种选择性语言障碍:一种是以 19 世纪神经学家 Paul Broca 的名字命名的 Broca 失语症,他发现脑的左前叶区(处于管辖唇、舌、腭、声带、膈的主要肌动区前面的部分大脑皮质)受损,病人的理解能力虽仍较完好,但说话有困难。他们的言语是"语法失能的"(agrammatic):往往略去封闭性词类(如限定词、助动词、功能词),而依赖开放性词类(多数为名词,也有一点名词化的动词)来表达自己(Goodglass & Kaplan 1972; Locours, Lhermitte, & Bryans 1983)。

另一种是以 19 世纪德国神经学家 Carl Wernicke 的名字命名的 Wernicke 失语症,这种失语症来自左半球后面的区域,与听力有关的皮质区相邻。犯这种失语症的人说话无甚困难,也不会略去封闭性词类或功能词,但由于选择实义词和句子处理有困难,说话不正常。他们主要的困难是理解言语(Goodglass Kaplan 1972; Locours, Lhermitte, & Bryans 1983)。

应怎样使用和解释这些发现呢?Wernicke 等人的解释是直截了当的:语言的大脑表征就是一些可以在左半球观察到的、相互联系的区域,这些区域按其和听(理解)或说(产生)的能力的不同联系而区分开来(Lichtheim 1885; Wernicke 1874/1977),而不是按其和各种语言信息(句法、语义、语音)的不同联系而区分开来。这种论点的核心是:既然 Broca 区支配肌动功能,而 Wernicke 区支配听觉功能,那么依赖于肌动功能的语言产生和依赖于听觉功能的语言理解就应该区分开来。这种观点还进一步认为,词的使用依赖于词的视觉表象或肌动表象。Wernicke 区是存储听觉表象的(即口语的单词记忆),而 Broca 区是存储肌动表象的(即关于把单词编码成发音形式的记忆),因此,单词的听觉形式对正确引导单词产生是不可少的,Wernicke 区受损,不但会使理解产生缺陷,而且还会带来输出不正常的综合病征。

这种理论有两个明显的问题:一是它不涉及语言知识和使用,更说不上对它们作出预测,但是语言知识能够对很多抽象信息(如句法、语义、语音信息)作出区别;二是它甚至也解释不了语言破坏本身的某些重要问题,例如为什么功能词会被略去?为什么会出现名词化动词的倾向?人们从一开始就注意到这种理论的缺陷,因此以后研究失语症的历史都试图对 Wernicke 理论作出反应。

1.2 从语言活动到符号能力

一种反映来自19世纪神经学家John Hughlings Jackson，他坚持认为，语言的主要单位是命题，而不是词，失语症反映了构成命题的能力受到损害(Jackson 1884; 见选集 1958)。脑损伤释放了高级皮质控制机制的低级区域的活动,因而释放了一些原始的行为。

这种看法导致另一种观点：失语症不是语言受到破坏，而是一种更为一般的概念性局限在语言中的反映。因此失语症被解释为"抽象态度的损失"(Goldstin, 1948), "失符号症"(Finkcelnburg, 见 Bay, 1964), "概念思维紊乱"(Bay, 1964)。

这种一般的概念性局限可解释为什么很多行为都受到破坏，但是因为缺乏证据,失语症和其他"符号性的"破坏的关系仍然不甚了了。失语症可单独发生；其他的破坏也可单独发生；如果由于左脑受损，两者亦可同时发生。失语病症候表现为 Goldstein (1948) 所说的"呼名"缺陷——即不能说出物体、事件的名称。但是相反的,也有一些失语病症候与这种相互关系无甚关系,例如语法变形。即使是有些行为从直觉上看是有联系的,如给出名称和用手势指出物体,两者都表示把符号和指称对象联系起来,我们仍然可以认为它们在神经上是有区别的：一个是支持指称关系的系统，一个是表示语法知识的语言系统。

从另一个角度看,这种粗略的概括也是站得住的。我们可以不必从哪一种失语症源于哪一种病灶性损害,而是从导致认知功能削弱(即所谓痴呆)的扩散脑损害所引起的效应来看。一般来说,符号性手势、有目的性动作、给出名称的紊乱都被看成是痴呆的早期症候,而语法能力受破坏则不是(Curtiss & Kempler 1982; Schwartz, Marin & Saffran 1979)。事实上,即使是认知能力受到严重损坏,语法能力仍能保持下来(Curtiss & Kempler 1982)。

因此大脑左半球并非仅存储一些无区别的符号能力,而且似乎也保存了一些作为独特的神经实体的语法能力。

1.3 从语言活动到抽象信息类型

把认知固定在大脑左半球的企图仅是对 Wernicke 理论作出的一种反应,另外一派人对 Wernicke 的以词为基础、以活动为中心的分析感到不满,仍坚持把失语症看成独特的语言现象。所不同的是,他们把分析单位从词转移到句子,而且对 Broca 失语症的语法失能现象和 Wernicke 失语症的句子层次错误现象都同样重视。

这种转移相当早就出现了,见于 Pick 和 Salomon 的著作(De Bleser 1987 曾作评论)。但在近年来,对句子层次分析又出现了明显的修正。从表述的角度看,现在正在使用转换语法框架里的一些原则来对待失语症的分析;从处理的角度看,分析转向那些为了交际目的而表达语言信息的实际运作。

这些新方法源于 1970 年代一系列对 Broca 失语症中理解的研究,这些研究试图决定什么是尚未受损害的理解能力的基础(如 Caramazza & Zurif 1976; Heilman & Scholes 1976; von Stockert & Bader 1976; Zurif, Caramazza & Myerson 1972)。它们一般使用句子/图画匹配的实验方法,先向失语症病人显示一个句子,让他们根据对句子的理解指出正确的图画(放在几幅供选择的图画中)。这些研究通过系统地观察语义和语法提示,以观察病人对语义提示的反常的依赖,以及他们无法执行正常句法分析的困难。Broca 失语症病人可以理解像 The apple that the boy is eating is red.（男孩正在吃的苹果是红色的）,他们的理解建立在语义制约上面:男孩可以吃苹果,苹果不能吃男孩。如果没有这些制约,他们就会有麻烦。他们理解不了像这样的句子 The girl whom the boy is pushing is tall.（那个男孩正在推的女孩很高）,因为两个实体都可以做同样动作,他们弄不清楚谁对谁干什么(Caramazza & Zurif 1976)。

另外一些试验指出,Broca 失语症病人碰到句子理解必须依赖对冠词 the 的处理的场合,也会相对地出现困难(Goodenough, Zurif & Weintraub 1977; Heilman & Scholes 1976)。例如 Heilman & Scholes 发现病人难以区别 He showed her baby the pictures.（他把照片给她的宝宝看）和 He showed her the baby picture.（他把宝宝的照片给她看）这两个句子的意义。

总的来说,这些分析指出,关于 Broca 失语症病人的理解能力相对无损的说法多少是一种假象。他们似乎不能使用句子形式的特征来帮助他们理解。当时的一种更为彻底的说法是,Broca 病人在听和说方面都犯了同样的语法无能症。左前脑损伤的病人虽然可以保存执行语义推理的能力,但却产生了严重的句法局限。一种较为乐观的说法是,Wernicke 和他的同事当时已正确找出语言区的位置,后来的研究无非是重新定义这些区域的功能:Broca 区似乎是管句法的,而 Wernicke 区则可能支持语义推理。

1.4 复杂化

事物要复杂得多。首先,从表述方面来看,我们可以只用语法用语来解释句法局限的概念,而无需从处理受到破坏的角度去说明产生局限的原因。

按照原来的说法,犯语法无能症的 Broca 失语症病人似乎没有完全依赖语义和语用提示。他们的句法并非完全丧失,只是部分受损:即使没有语境和语义提示来帮助他们绕过句法分析,他们仍能解释某些句子。例如在像 The girl whom the boy is pushing is tall 那样的宾语—关系结构里,病人找不出施事者。但是如果把男孩和女孩的关系调整为主语—关系结构,The boy who is pushing the girl is tall,病人却表现出一种接近正常的理解能力,知道谁对谁干什么(Grodzinsky 1984;Wulfeck 1984)。

类似的情况还有两例:语法无能症的病人理解被动语态句子无甚把握(The girl was pushed by the boy.[女孩被男孩推]),但对理解相应的主动语态句子却无大问题(The boy pushed the girl.[男孩推女孩])。他们虽然难以理解宾语分裂句(It is the girl whom the boy is pushing.[男孩正在推的是那个女孩]),但理解主语分裂句(It is the boy who is pushing the girl.[是男孩在推女孩])却毫无问题。

1.5 Broca 失语症的语法无能症的虚迹理论分析

[……]

1.6 表征理论与脑定位

[……]

1.7 处理分析

[……]

1.8 失语症中对开放性和封闭性词类的处理

[……]

1.9 失语症的启动型式

只用封闭性词类来描述 Broca-Wernicke 处理的区别易使人误解。Broca 病人不能正常使用这种词类,可能是因为他们根本就不能正常提取任何有限制的词汇,而不能提取封闭性词类,仅是最敏感的一种反映。

词汇启动研究在这方面提供了数据。启动(priming)指的是决定一个目标词所需的时间会因为词的前面为有意义联系的词项而加快。这种型式表明相关的词被激话,或被联系上了。

这种启动试验因为目标不同，而有不同的变种，这里只谈两种有关的。Milberg & Blumstein 研究孤立词的启动效应，以分析脑损伤病灶对提取语义信息的影响（Milberg & Blumstein 1981；Blumstein, Milberg & Shrier 1982；Milberg, Blumstein & Dworetsky 1987）。此外 Swinney 等人（1985）Swinney, Zurif, & Nicol (1989) 又采用交叉方式启动（cross-modal priming）技术来研究脑损伤对句子理解中词汇提取的影响（Zurif, Swinney & Garrett, 正在出版）。

交叉方式启动技术是研究自动处理机制的一种重要工具。这种技术在句子中包括一些有两个或更多的意义的词——潜在的歧义词。在句子语境只与一个意义有关的情况下，单词的两个意义都被启动。例如，在句子 The man saw several spiders, roaches, and other bugs in the corner of the room.［那个男人在房间角落里看见几个蜘蛛，蟑螂，臭虫］里，bugs 的两个意义都被启动——一个是与语境有关的"虫子"，另一个是与语境无关的"窃听器"。在第一种情况下，我们标出字符串 ANT 的词汇决定时间，在第二种情况下，我们标出字符串 SPY 的词汇决定时间；然后再拿这两种反应时间和别的与 bugs 的两个意义都无关字符串的反应时间相比较。

当正常的受试身上，反复出现两种现象。首先，当受试听到放出来的句子中的 bugs，而又马上在屏幕上看到启动字符串时，它的两个意义——ANT 和 SPY，都得到启动。其次，如果决定词汇的试探词延缓出现——即字符串在听到 bugs 的一秒半钟后才显示，只有和语境有关的那个意义（ANT）才有启动效应（Swinney 1983）。所以，在正常句子理解中，词汇提取是一个自动化过程，不会被语境信息所穿透；词汇提取牵涉到一个词项的所有意义的检索；只有在词汇提取后，语境信息才会对词汇处理发生影响。

让我们再看看失语症病人的情况，可简单归纳如下：对 Wernicke 病人来说，他们在孤立单词和交叉方式两种启动情况下，表现与正常人一样。在孤立单词试验里，他们对前面为语义相关的启动词的目标词的反应时间要快于前面为语义无关的启动词（Milberg & Blumstein 1981）；在交叉方式的句子试验里，当试探词紧接着歧义词，它的两个意义都得到启动（Swinney 等 1985；Swinney, Zurif & Nicol 1989）。

Broca 病人的情况则截然不同。在孤立单词试验里，他们得不到启动（Milberg & Blumstein 1981）；在交叉方式向子试验里，不管什么语境，得到启动是那些歧义词的最常见的意义,(Swinney 1985; Swinney, Zurif & Nicol 1989)。我们可概括地说,虽然 Broca 病人知道一个词的意义(这一点在进行启动研究前都已弄清楚的),但他们不能正常地提取。

这个处理失败的具体过程是怎样的,还有待于进一步弄清楚,但它是在句子处理时出现的。研究者的任务是怎样把这种异常的词汇提取型式和病人照例能理解含有歧义启动词的句子的事实调和起来。Broca 病人要理解句子,就必须理解句子中的词,包括歧义词,但是他们只有对那些歧义词的最常见的意义才能启动。

一种可能的解释建筑在对正常处理的理解上面:(1)一个歧义词的几个意义的集合是采用序列检索的形式进行的;(2)检索的次序是受意义出现的频率所控制的;(3)如果集合中的意义数量很少,检索的速度很快,就难以用目前的技术来测量。根据这种观点,语法失能症病人的词汇检索机制是以低于正常的速度运作的,在在线试验所容许的时间内,他们只能处理最常见的意义。因此在 Broca 病人身上,一个歧义词的所有意义的启动应该明显地晚一点。

语法失能症病人在处理封闭性词类时所出现的缺陷,也可以看成是处理器缓慢的问题。这也许是因为句子结构主要是依赖封闭性词类的分布,这类词受较严格的时间限制,最易受影响。不管怎样解释,Broca 病人提取词项(包括开放性和封闭性)的困难不能看成是表征存储的失败,而应看成是处理的失败:也就是说,在处理过程中,不能在需要的时间提取这些因素。至于处理的失败怎样会引起全面的表征后果,还是个悬而未决的问题。

最后一点是,作为一种类别,语法失能症病人的快速处理机制都受到破坏,这很可能是他们的这些机制都依赖于基本的肌动系统,因为肌动系统是处理机制的根源。如果这是事实的话,我们就要部分回到 Wernicke 的公式:大脑的语言处理是那些在脑中具有明确位置的感觉·肌动运作的延长。这种解释不能理解为新瓶装旧酒:虽然处理器可能源于具有明确皮质位置的感觉·肌动活动,但是这些处理器必须首先根据它们所提取的信息来确定。而且由于它们在处理过程中被压缩,这些处理器只能专管这一种或那一种信息。因此我们可从两个方面来评估处理机制:一是它们的可定位的感觉·肌动源;二是它们的运算操作和目标。

2. 大脑—语言关系的动态分析

前面的失语定分析使用的都是静态的神经解剖事实。在下面,我们将集中讨论脑活动的动态特征,即对参与处理信息的数以百万计的神经元所引起的电化活动进行分析。这种分析使我们更接近神经生理学,即我们语言能力所赖以实现的机械码。它也可与心理语言学分析的目标相一致:从信息处理系统的实时运作的角度去描写语言能力。

其实这就是在神经语言理论方面,用电化生理研究方法去取代以失语症为中心的研究方法,但这与目前电化生理分析的水平有关,现在一时还做不到。

2.1 一些假定和问题

神经活动是一个生化过程,我们关于与语言有关的神经传导的知识来自一些电化结果的记录,最使人感兴趣的是"与事件有关的潜能"(event-related potentials,简称ERP)。ERP是由数百万个活动的神经元所产生、通过放在头皮上的电极所测到的短暂的电压波动。它们之所以被称为ERP是因为它们是一些与特定的认知活动(如人们处理语言输入的活动)同时发生的电信号。

使用ERP研究大脑在语言处理中的作用是从这样的假定出发的:神经活动的某一部分所产生的头皮潜能在认知活动中的某些方面起功能作用。因此,我们必须找寻ERP参数和认知过程的相互关系。

研究者根据对某些输入的字符串进行句法分析的需要,设计试验来操纵变量,从而引起波形变化,通过对其变化的研究就能探索这个过程是否独立地反映在大脑里。如果这个过程能够分离出来,我们还可观察它在句子理解中相对于其他过程所需的时间,了解它是否受其他输入信息的影响。

表面看来,这不算是什么复杂的事情,其实不然。首先,如果在一段时间内分析一个事件,ERP容量太小,不能从正在进行的电化活动中分离出来。因此要从背景噪声中区别出ERP来,就必须作多次尝试,然后取其平均。随机的"噪声"是分散的,随机的高峰和低槽互相抵销,而常数的高峰和低槽就变得容易辨认。

即算是采用了这种手段,对ERP的解释仍有不少问题,下面三点是有代表性的(根据Picton & Stuss 1984所列出的清单):第一,在头皮所记录到的电场可以来自很多人为的根源,如眼睛、头皮、肌肉、皮肤、舌头。第二,头皮

ERP 只代表那些在较远距离产生电场的皮质活动,要产生这些电场,神经活动必须是同步的、定向的。但是在神经元身上产生的皮质活动并非同步和定向激活的;它们虽然对所估量的认知过程至为重要,但却与头皮记录无甚关系。第三,在头皮所记录的任何 ERP,可以由几种在时间和空间上互相重叠的电场所产生,因此在头皮处所记录的高峰不一定反映一个独立的皮质过程。

后一点是意料中的,因为语言过程可独立地反映在大脑里的这种说法依赖于 ERP 参数与认知过程之间存在某些对应关系。这种关系不一定是直接的,一组神经元不一定和某一语言过程相呼应。

2.2 某些实验研究

ERP 作为一种测量复杂的相互关系的工具仍不够完善。但有些研究人员对它的潜力持乐观的态度,只要小心地减少人为信号并使用合适的统计技术把次波形和产生波形的根源分离出来,ERP 可以为研究语言处理提供一种重要的生理石芯试验。

他们也许是对的。但是这种石芯试验只是用于对目前语言理论价值不很高的一般的区分。例如,让受试听句子中的目标词,判断它是名词还是动词(Sit by the fire [坐在火炉边]与 Ready, aim, fire [预备,瞄准,开火])的时候,在头皮左前区可测量出一种稳定的 ERP 差异(Brown, Marsh & Smith 1973)。这些差异是由于两个 fire 的意义不同而引起的? 还是因为它们反映了句法处理机制所找出的词汇范畴的差异? 研究人员并不清楚。

也有一些证据表明,有某些电波型式与句子处理的需要特别相关。所以,通过视觉逐词显示的句子如果是由语义不合适的词来结束,就会产生一个约 400 毫秒的波形高峰。但是如果句子是由语义合适的词结尾,就不会出现高峰。而且这个"意外"成份并没有对所有类型的"意外句子"都作出回应。如果"意外"是视觉显示的,例如句子最后的一个词是用不同的字体显示的,波形是一个推迟出现的低槽,而不是一个高峰。而且当同一词是语义不合适,或是用不同字体显示时,它会引起明显不同的 ERP 效应——高峰或低槽(Kutas & Hillyard 1984)。

这方面的工作还很难说是能够支持目前理论语言学的需要,但它起码表明大脑是怎样把语言和非语言处理需要区分开来的。

也有一些令人鼓舞的进展,例如有一项研究从功能结构的区别来直接考察开放性词类和封闭性词类的区别。其发现是:不管是显示在句子(Kutas &

Hillyard 1984)里,还是单独地显示(Neville 1984,Kutas & Hillyard 1984 引用),开放性词类的处理比封闭性词类的处理与更为积极的成份相联系。所以,ERP 的发现和失语症研究的数据是相一致的,大脑在某一神经组织的平面上,把两种词类的处理分别对待。而且 ERP 用一种十分明显的方式来表示这种神经组织。

Ding et al.(2016)"Cortical Tracking of Hierarchical Linguistic Structures in Connected Speech"选读①

◆ **作者简介**

Nai Ding,任职于美国纽约大学心理学系及中国浙江大学。

Lucia Melloni,任职于美国纽约大学 Langone 医学中心神经学系、德国马克普朗克研究所及美国哥伦比亚大学。

Hang Zhang,任职于美国纽约大学心理学系、北京大学及上海纽大。

Xing Tian,任职于美国纽约大学心理学系及上海纽大。

David Poeppel,美国纽约大学及德国马克普朗克研究所。

◆ **正文节选**

Introduction

To understand connected speech, listeners must construct a hierarchy of linguistic structures of different sizes, including syllables, words, phrases, and sentences. It remains puzzling how the brain simultaneously handles the distinct timescales of the different linguistic structures, for example, from a few hundred milliseconds for syllables to a few seconds for sentences. Previous studies have suggested that cortical activity is synchronized to acoustic features of speech, approximately at the syllabic rate, providing an initial timescale for speech processing. But how the brain utilizes such syllabic-level

---

① Ding, N., Melloni, L., Zhang, H., Tian, X., & Poeppel, D. 2015. "Cortical tracking of hierarchical linguistic structures in connected speech." *Nature Neuroscience*, 19(1), 158–164.

phonological representations closely aligned with the physical input to build multiple levels of abstract linguistic structure, and represent these concurrently, is not known. We hypothesized that cortical dynamics emerge at all timescales required for the processing of different linguistic levels, including the timescales corresponding to larger linguistic structures such as phrases and sentences, and that the neural representation of each linguistic level corresponds to timescales matching the timescales of the respective linguistic level.

Although linguistic structure building can clearly benefit from prosodic, or statistical cues, it can also be achieved purely based on the listeners' grammatical knowledge. To experimentally isolate the neural representation of the internally constructed hierarchical linguistic structure, we developed new speech materials in which the linguistic constituent structure was dissociated from prosodic or statistical cues. By manipulating the levels of linguistic abstraction, we found separable neural encoding of each different linguistic level.

Results

Cortical Tracking of Phrasal and Sentential Structures

In the first set of experiments, we sought to determine the neural representation of hierarchical linguistic structure in the absence of prosodic cues. We constructed hierarchical linguistic structures using an isochronous, 4-Hz sequence of syllables that were independently synthesized (**Fig. 1a, b, Supplementary Fig. 1** and **Supplementary Table 1**). As a result of the acoustic independence between syllables (that is, no co-articulation), the linguistic constituent structure could only be extracted using lexical, syntactic, and semantic knowledge, and not prosodic cues. The materials were first developed in Mandarin Chinese, in which syllables are relatively uniform in duration and are also the basic morphological unit (always morphemes and, in most cases, monosyllabic words). Cortical activity was recorded from native listeners of Mandarin Chinese using magnetoencephalography (MEG). Given that different linguistic levels, that is, the monosyllabic morphemes, phrases and sentences, were presented at unique and constant rates, the hypothesized neural tracking of hierarchical linguistic structure was tagged at distinct frequencies.

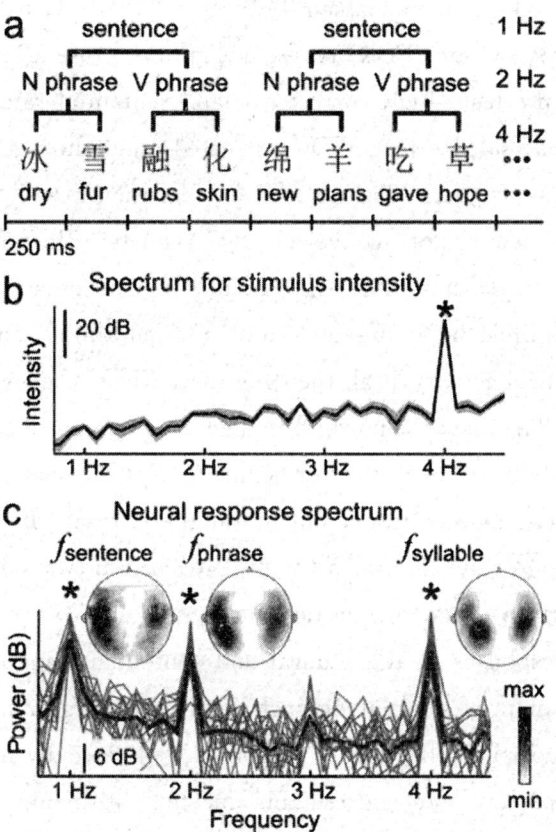

Figure 1 Neural tracking of hierarchical linguistic structures.
(a), Sequences of Chinese or English monosyllabic words are presented isochronously, forming phrases and sentences. (b) Spectrum of stimulus intensity fluctuation revealed syllabic rhythm, but no phrasal or sentential modulation. The shaded area covers 2 s.e.m. across stimuli. (c) MEG-derived cortical response spectrum for Chinese listeners and materials (bold curve: grand average; thin curves: individual listeners, $N = 16$; 0.11 - Hz frequency resolution). Neural tracking of syllabic, phrasal, and sentential rhythms was reflected by spectral peaks at corresponding frequencies. Frequency bins with significantly stronger power than neighbors (0.5 Hz range) are marked (* $P <$ 0.001, paired one-sided t-test, FDR corrected). The topographical maps of response power across sensors are shown for the peak frequencies.

The MEG response was analyzed in the frequency domain, and we extracted response power in every frequency bin using an optimal spatial filter (Online Methods). Consistent with our hypothesis, the response spectrum showed three peaks at the syllabic rate [$P = 1.4 \times 10^{-5}$, paired one-sided t test, false discovery rate (FDR) corrected], phrasal rate ($P = 1.6 \times 10^{-4}$, paired one-sided t test, FDR corrected), and sentential rate ($P = 9.6 \times 10^{-7}$, paired one-sided t test, FDR corrected) and the response is highly consistent across listeners (**Fig. 1c**). Given that the phrasal- and sentential-rate rhythms were not conveyed by acoustic fluctuations at the corresponding frequencies (**Fig. 1b**), cortical responses at the phrasal and sentential rates must be a consequence of internal online structure building processes. Cortical activity at all the three peak frequencies was seen bilaterally (**Fig. 1c**). The response power averaged over sensors in each hemisphere was significantly stronger in the left hemisphere at the sentential rate ($P = 0.014$, paired two-sided t test), but not at the phrasal ($P = 0.20$, paired two-sided t test) or syllabic rates ($P = 0.40$, paired two-sided t test).

Dependence on Syntactic Structures

Are the responses at the phrasal and sentential rates indeed separate neural indices of processing at distinct linguistic levels or are they merely sub-harmonics of the syllabic rate response, generated by intrinsic cortical dynamical properties? We address this question by manipulating different levels of linguistic structure in the input. When the stimulus is a sequence of random syllables that preserves the acoustic properties of Chinese sentences (**Fig. 2** and **Supplementary Fig. 2**), but eliminates the phrasal/sentential structure, only syllabic (acoustic) level tracking occurs ($P = 1.1 \times 10^{-4}$ at 4 Hz, paired one-sided t test, FDR corrected; **Fig. 2a**). Furthermore, this manipulation preserves the position of each syllable in a sentence (Online Methods) and therefore further demonstrates that the phrasal- and sentential-rate responses are not a result of possible acoustic differences between the syllables in a sentence. When two adjacent syllables and morphemes combine into verb phrases, but there is no four-element sentential structure, phrasal-level tracking emerges at half of the syllabic rate ($P = 8.6 \times 10^{-4}$ at 2 Hz and $P = 2.7 \times 10^{-4}$ at 4 Hz, paired one-sided t test, FDR corrected; **Fig. 2b**). Similar responses are observed for noun phrases (**Supplementary Fig. 3**).

To test whether the phrase-level responses segregate from the sentence level, we constructed longer verb phrases that were unevenly divided into a monosyllabic verb followed by a three-syllable noun phrase (**Fig. 2c**). We expect that the neural responses to the long verb phrase to be tagged at 1 Hz, whereas the neural responses to the monosyllabic verb and the three-syllable noun phrase will present as harmonics of 1 Hz. Consistent with our hypothesis, cortical dynamics emerged at one-fourth of the syllabic rate while the response at half of the syllabic rate is no longer detectable ($P = 1.9 \times 10^{-4}$, 1.7×10^{-4}, and 9.3×10^{-4} at 1, 3, and 4 Hz, respectively, paired one-sided t test, FDR corrected).

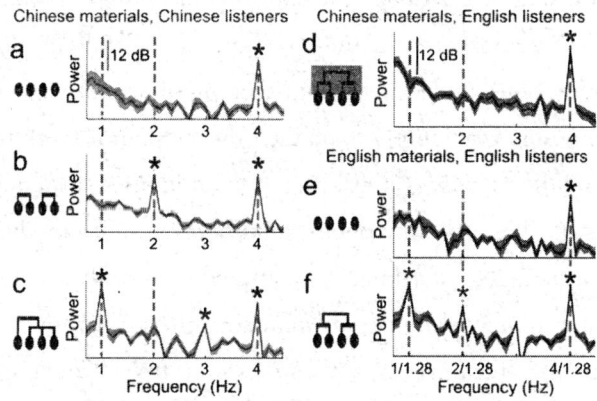

Figure 2 Tracking of different linguistic structures. Each panel shows syntactic structure repeating in the stimulus (left) and the cortical response spectrum (right; shaded area indicates 2SEM over listeners, $N = 8$). (**a**) Chinese listeners, Chinese materials: syllables were syntactically independent and cortical activity encoded only acoustic/syllabic rhythm. (**b, c**) b, c, Additional tracking emerged with larger linguistic structures. Spectral peaks marked by a star (black: $P < 0.001$; gray: $P < 0.005$; paired one-sided t test, FDR corrected). (**d**) English listeners, Chinese materials from **Figure 1**: acoustic tracking only, as there was no parsable structure. (**e, f**) English listeners, English materials: syllabic rate (4/1.28 Hz) and sentential and phrasal rate responses to parsable structure in stimulus.

Dependence on Language Comprehension

When listening to Chinese sentences (**Fig. 1a**), listeners who did not understand Chinese only showed responses to the syllabic (acoustic) rhythm ($P = 3.0 \times 10^{-5}$ at 4 Hz, paired one-sided t test, FDR corrected **Fig. 2d**), further supporting the argument that cortical responses to larger, abstract linguistic structures is a direct consequence of language comprehension.

If aligning cortical dynamics to the time course of linguistic constituent structure is a general mechanism required for comprehension, it must apply across languages. Indeed, when native English speakers were tested with English materials (**Fig. 1a**), their cortical activity also followed the time course of larger linguistic structures, that is, phrases and sentences ($P = 4.1 \times 10^{-5}$, syllabic rate; **Fig. 2e**; $P = 3.9 \times 10^{-3}$, 4.3×10^{-3}, and 6.8×10^{-6} at the sentential, phrasal, and syllabic rates respectively; **Fig. 2f**; paired one-sided t test, FDR corrected).

Neural Tracking of Linguistic Structures Rather than Probability Cues

We found that concurrent neural tracking of multiple levels of linguistic structure was not confounded with the encoding of acoustic cues (**Figs. 1 and and 2**). However, is this simply explained by the neural tracking of the predictability of smaller units? As a larger linguistic structure, such as a sentence, unfolds in time, its component units become more predictable. Thus, cortical networks solely tracking transitional probabilities across smaller units could show temporal dynamics matching the timescale of larger structures. To test this alternative hypothesis, we crafted a constant transitional probability Markovian Sentence Set (MSS) in which the transitional probability of lower level units was dissociated from the higher, level structures (**Fig. 3a, Supplementary Fig. 1e, f**). The constant transitional probability MSS is contrasted with a varying transitional probability MSS, in which the transitional probability is low across sentential boundaries and high in a sentence (**Fig. 3b, c**). If cortical activity only encodes the transitional probability between lower level units (for example, acoustic chunks in the MSS) independent of the underlying syntactic structure, it can show tracking of the sentential structure for the varying probability MSS, but not for the constant probability MSS. In contrast with this prediction, indistinguishable neural responses to sentences were observed for both MSS (**Fig. 3d**), demonstrating that neural tracking of sentences is not confounded by transitional probability. Specifically, for the constant transitional probability MSS, the response was statistically significant at the sentential rate, twice the sentential rate and the syllable rate ($P = 1.8 \times 10^{-4}$, 2.3×10^{-4}, and 2.7×10^{-6}, respectively). For the varying transitional probability MSS, the response was statistically significant at the sentential rate, twice the sentential rate and the syllable rate ($P = 7.1 \times 10^{-4}$, 7.1×10^{-4}, and 4.8×10^{-6}, respectively).

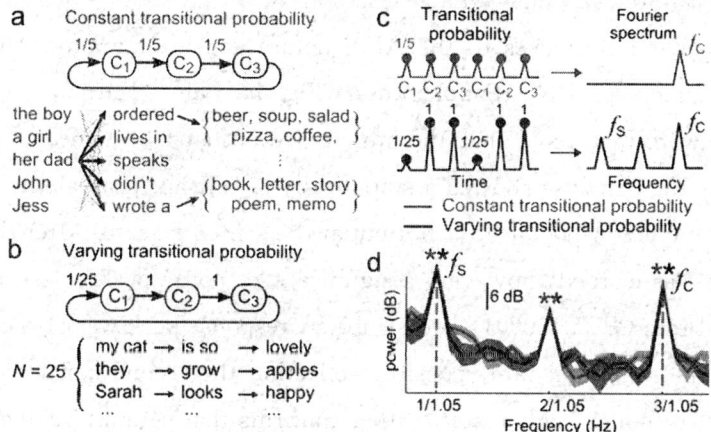

Figure 3 Dissociating sentential structures and transitional probability. (**a**, **b**) Grammar of an artificial Markovian stimulus set with constant (**a**) or variable (**b**) transitional probability. Each sentence consists of three acoustic chunks, each containing 1 - 2 English words. The listeners memorized the grammar before experiments. (**c**) Schematic timecourse and spectrum of the transitional probability. (**d**) Neural response spectrum shaded area covers 2 s.e.m. over listeners, $N = 8$). Significant neural responses to sentences were seen for both languages. Spectral peaks are shown by an asterisk ($P<0.001$, paired one-sided t test, FDR corrected, same color code as the spectrum). Responses were not significantly different between the two languages in any frequency bin (paired two-sided t test, $P>0.09$, uncorrected).

Given that the MSS involved real English sentences, listeners had prior knowledge of the transitional probabilities between acoustic chunks. To control for the effect of such prior knowledge, we created a set of Artificial Markovian Sentences(AMS). In the AMS, the transitional probability between syllables was the same in and across sentences (**Supplementary Fig. 4a**). The AMS was composed of Chinese syllables, but no meaningful Chinese expressions were embedded in the AMS sequences. As the AMS was not based on the grammar of Chinese, the listeners had to learn the AMS grammar in order to segment sentences. By comparing the neural responses to the AMS sequences before and after the grammar was learned, we were able to separate the effect of prior knowledge of transitional probability and the effect of grammar learning. Here, the grammar of the AMS indicates the set of rules that governs the sequencing of the AMS, that is, the rule which syllables can follow which syllables.

The neural responses to the AMS before and after grammar learning were analyzed separately (**Supplementary Fig. 4**). Before learning, when the listeners were instructed that the stimulus was just a sequence of random syllables, the response showed a statistically significant peak at the syllabic rate ($P = 0.0003$, bootstrap), but not at the sentential rate. After the AMS grammar was learned, however, a significant response peak emerged at the sentential rate ($P = 0.0001$, bootstrap). A response peak was also observed at twice the sentential rate, possibly reflecting the second harmonic of the sentential response. This result further confirms that neural tracking of sentences is not confounded by neural tracking of transitional probability.

Neural Tracking of Sentences Varying in Duration and Structure

These results are based on sequences of sentences that have uniform duration and syntactic structure. We next address whether cortical tracking of larger linguistic structures generalizes to sentences that are variable in duration (4 - 8 syllables) and syntactic structures. These sentences were again built on isochronous Chinese syllables, intermixed and sequentially presented without any acoustic gap at the sentence boundaries. Examples translated into English include "Don't be nervous," "The book is hard to read," and "Over the street is a museum."

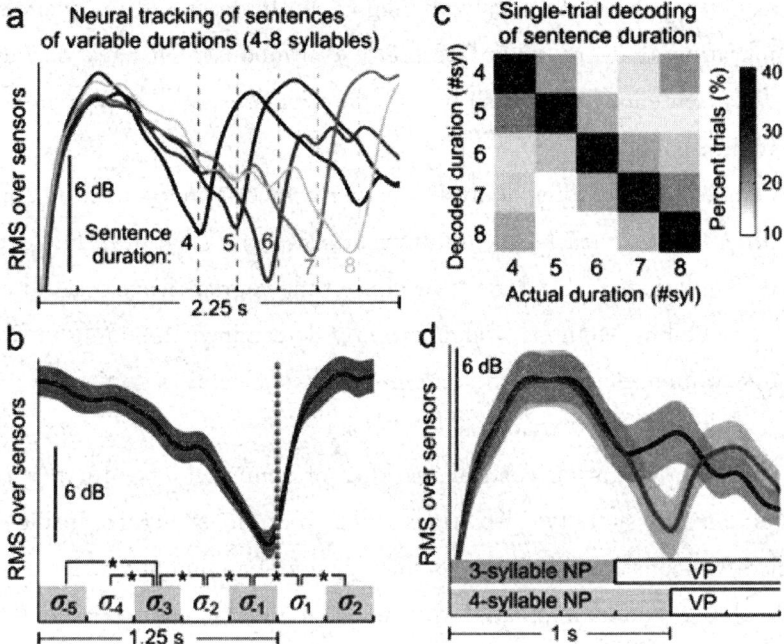

Figure 4 Neural tracking of sentences of varying structures. (a) Neural activity tracked the sentence duration, even when the sentence boundaries (dotted lines) were not separated by acoustic gaps. (b) Averaged response near a sentential boundary (dotted line). The power continuously changed throughout the duration of a sentence. Shaded area covers 2 s.e.m. over listeners ($N = 8$). Significance power differences between time bins (shaded squares) are marked by a steriks ($P = 0.01$, one-sided t test, FDR corrected). (c) Confusion matrix for neural decoding of the sentence duration. (d) Neural activity tracks noun phrase duration (shown in the bottom). Yellow areas show significant differences between curves ($P = 0.005$, bootstrap, FDR corrected).

As these sentences have irregular durations that are not tagged by frequency, the MEG responses were analyzed in the time domain by averaging sentences of the same duration. To focus on sentential level processing, we low-pass filtered the response at 3.5 Hz. The MEG response (root mean square, r.m.s., over all sensors) rapidly increased after a sentence boundary and continuously changed throughout the duration of a sentence (**Fig. 4a**). To illustrate the detailed temporal dynamics, we averaged the r.m.s. response over all sentences containing six or more syllables after aligning them to the sentence offset (**Fig. 4b**). During the last four syllables of a sentence, the r.m.s. response continuously and significantly decreased for every syllable, indicating that the neural response continuously changes during the course of a sentence rather than being a transient response only occurring at the sentence boundary.

A single-trial decoding analysis was performed to independently confirm that cortical activity tracks the duration of sentences (**Fig. 4c**). The decoder applied template matching for the response time course (leave-one-out cross-validation, Online Methods), and correctly determined the duration of 34.9 ± 0.6% sentences (mean ± s.e.m. over subjects, significantly above chance, $P = 1.3 \times 10^{-7}$, one-sided t test).

After demonstrating cortical tracking of sentences, we further tested whether cortical activity also tracks the phrasal structure inside of a sentence. We constructed sentences that consist of a noun phrase followed by a verb phrase and manipulated the duration of the noun phrase (three-syllable or four-syllable). The cortical responses closely follow the duration of the noun phrase: the s.e.m. response gradually decreased within the noun phrase, then showed a transient increase after the onset of the verb phrase (**Fig. 4d**).

Neural Source Localization using Electrocorticography (ECoG)

We found that large-scale neural activity measured by MEG concurrently follows the hierarchical linguistic structure of speech, but which neural networks generate such activity? To address this question, we recorded the ECoG responses to English sentences (**Fig. 2e**) and an acoustic control (**Fig. 2f**). ECoG signals are mesoscopic neurophysiological signals recorded by intracranial electrodes implanted in epilepsy patients for clinical evaluation (see **Supplementary Fig. 5** for the electrode coverage), and they possess better spatial resolution than MEG. We first analyzed the power of the ECoG signal in the high gamma band (70 - 200 Hz), as it highly correlats with multiunit firing[23]. The electrodes exhibiting significant sentential, phrasal and syllabic rate fluctuations in high gamma power are shown separately (**Fig. 5**). The sentential rate response clustered over the posterior and middle superior temporal gyrus (pSTG), bilaterally, with a second cluster over the left inferior frontal gyrus (IFG). Phrasal rate responses were also observed over the pSTG bilaterally. Notably, although the sentential and phrasal rate responses were observed in similar cortical areas, electrodes showing phrasal rate responses only partially overlapped with electrodes showing sentential rate responses in the pSTG (**Fig. 6**). For electrodes showing a significant response at either the sentential rate or the phrasal rate, the strength of the sentential rate response was negatively correlated with the strength of the phrasal rate response ($R = -0.32$, $P = 0.004$, bootstrap). This phenomenon demonstrates spatially dissociable neural tracking of the sentential and phrasal structures.

Furthermore, some electrodes with a significant sentential or phrasal rate response showde no significant syllabic rate response ($P<0.05$, FDR corrected, **Fig. 6**). In other words, there are cortical circuits specifically encoding larger, abstract linguistic structures without responding to syllabic-level acoustic features of speech. In addition, although the syllabic responses were not significantly different ($P>0.05$, FDR corrected) for English sentences and the acoustic control in the MEG results, they were dissociable spatially in the ECoG results (**Fig. 7**). Electrodes showing significant syllabic responses ($P<0.05$, FDR corrected) to sentences, but not the acoustic control, were seen in bilateral pSTG, bilateral anterior STG (aSTG), and left IFG.

We then analyzed neural tracking of the sentential, phrasal, and syllabic rhythms in the low-frequency ECoG waveform (**Fig. 5**), which is a close neural correlate of MEG activity. Fourier analysis was directly applied to the ECoG waveform and the Fourier coefficients at 1, 2, and 4 Hz are extracted. Low-frequency ECoG activity is usually viewed as the dendritic input to a cortical area[24]. The low-frequency responses are more distributed than high-gamma activity, possibly reflecting the fact that the neural representations of different levels of linguistic structures serve as inputs to broad cortical areas. Sentential and phrasal rate responses are strong in STG, IFG,

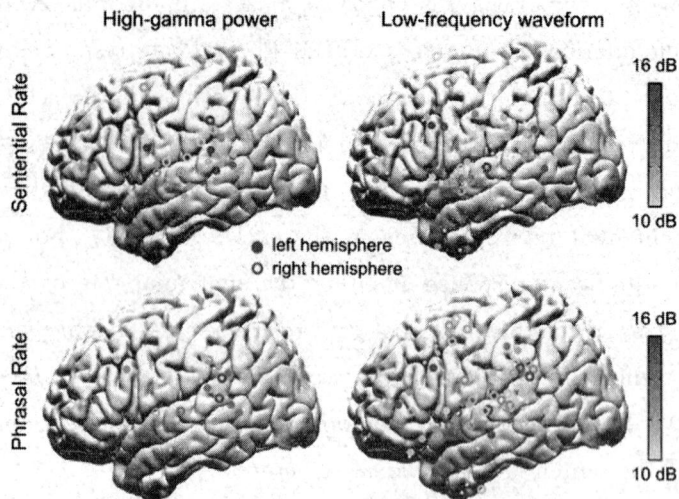

Figure 5 Localizing cortical sources of the sentential and phrasal rate responses using ECoG ($N = 5$). Left, power envelope of high-gamma activity. Right, waveform of low-frequency activity. Electrodes in the right hemisphere were projected to the left hemisphere, and right hemisphere (left hemisphere) electrodes are shown by hollow (filled) circles.

The figure only displays electrodes that showed statistically significant neural responses to sentences in **Figure 2e** and no significant response to the acoustic control shown in **Figure 2f**. Significance was determined by bootstrap (FDR-corrected) and the significance level is 0.05. The response strength, that is, the response at the target frequency relative to the mean response averaged over a 1-Hz wide neighboring region, is color-coded. Electrodes with response strength less than 10 dB are shown by smaller symbols. The sentential and phrasal rate responses were seen in bilateral pSTG, TPJ, and left IFG.

and temporoparietal junction (TPJ). Compared with the acoustic control, the syllabic-rate response to sentences was stronger in broad cortical areas, including the temporal and frontal lobes (**Fig. 7**). Similar to the high-gamma activity, the low-frequency responses to the sentential and phrasal structures were not reflected in the same set of electrodes (**Fig. 6**). For electrodes showing a significant response at either the sentential rate or the phrasal rate, the strength of the sentential rate response was also negatively correlated with the strength of the phrasal rate response ($R = -0.21$, significantly greater than 0, $P = 0.023$, bootstrap).

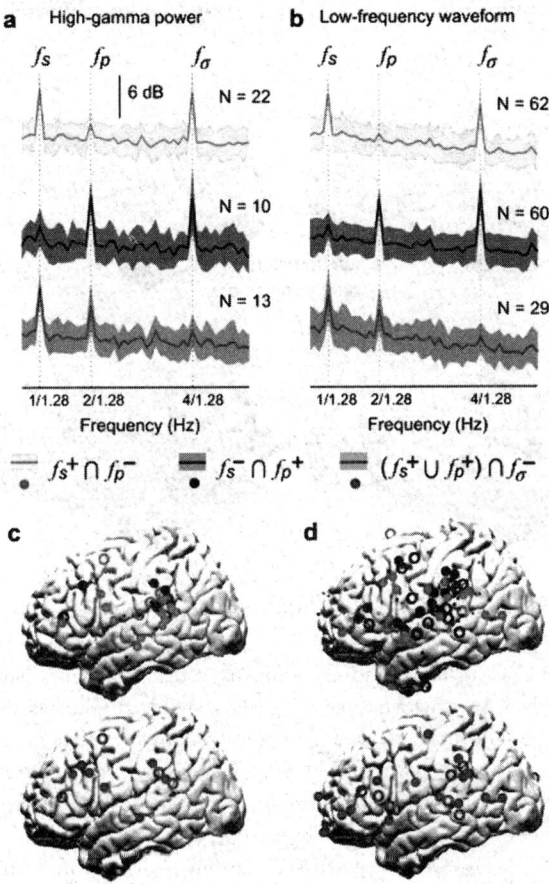

Figure 6 Spatial dissociation between sentential-rate, phrasal-rate, and syllabic-rate responses ($N = 5$). (**a**) The power spectrum of the power envelope of high-gamma activity. (**b**) The power spectrum of low-frequency ECoG waveform. The top panels (green curves) show the response averaged over all electrodes that show a significant sentential-rate response but not a significant phrasal-rate response. Significance was determined by bootstrap (FDR-corrected) and the significance level is 0.05. The shaded area is 1 s.d. over electrodes on each side. The blue curves show the response averaged over all electrodes that showed a significant phrasal-rate response, but not a significant sentential-rate response. The red curves show a significant sentential-rate or a significant phrasal-rate response, but not a significant syllabic response. (**c**, **d**) The topographic distribution of the three groups of electrodes analyzed in (**a**) and (**b**). As in **Figure 5**, electrodes showing a response greater than 10 dB are shown by larger symbols than electrodes showing a response weaker than 10 dB.

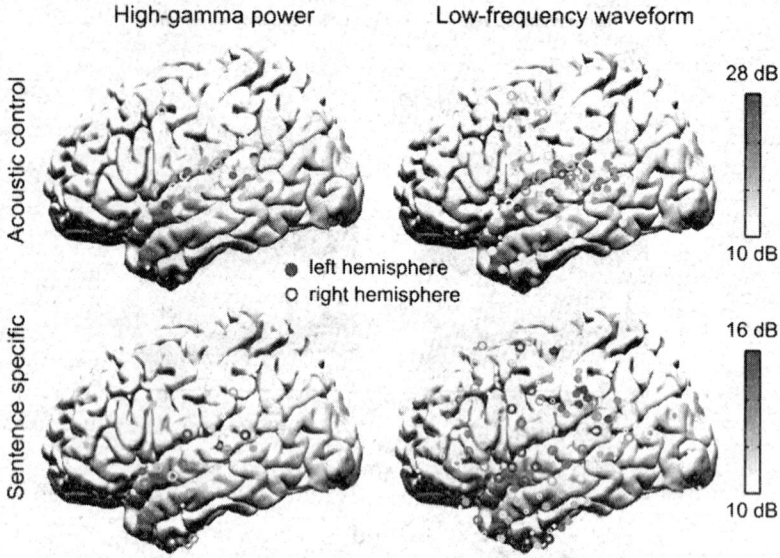

Figure 7 Syllabic-rate ECoG responses to English sentences and the acoustic control ($N = 5$). Top, electrodes showing statistically significant syllabic-rate ECoG responses to the acoustic control, that is, shuffled sequences, which had the same acoustic and syllabic rhythm as the English sentences, but contained no hierarchical linguistic structures (**Figure 2f**). Significance was determined by bootstrap (FDR-corrected) and the significance level is 0.05. The responses were most strongly seen in bilateral STG for both high-gamma and low-frequency activity and in bilateral premotor areas for low-frequency activity. Bottom, syllabic-rate ECoG responses to English sentences. The electrodes displayed are those that showed statistically significant neural responses to sentences and no significant response to the acoustic control. The syllabic rate responses specific to sentences were strong along bilateral STG for high-gamma activity and were widely distributed in the frontal and temporal lobes for low-frequency activity.

迈因策尔(2018)《人工智能与机器学习》选读[①]

◆ **作者简介**

克劳斯·迈因策尔[②]（Klaus Mainzer，1947— ），欧洲科学院院士，德国工程院院士，德国慕尼黑工业大学教育学院哲学与社会教席荣休教授。主要著作有《几何学史》(1980)、《大自然的对称性》(1980)、《复杂性中的思维》(1994)、《大脑、计算机和复杂性》(1997)等。

◆ **正文节选**

一、什么是人工智能？

人工智能(AI)在很多人不知情的情况下统治我们的生活很久了。与我们说话的智能手机、记录我们健康数据的手表、自动安排的工作程序、自动驾驶的汽车和飞机、有自主逻辑的交通和能量系统，以及探测远方星球的机器人，都是连接成网的智能系统世界的例证。它们向我们展示了人们的日常生活是如何受到人工智能功能影响的。

艾伦·麦席森·图灵(1912—1954)在后来以其姓命名的测试中定义一个系统是否具有智能性的判断校准为：如果该系统的回答和反应与人类的无法区别时，则该系统是智能的。这个定义的不足之处是用人类作为测试标准。很多生物体也是智能系统的范例，它们和人类一样，在进化中出现并能够或多或少地、独立有效地解决问题。有时自然是技术发展的模板。但是信息科学和工程技术科学也经常会找到一些与自然界不同甚至更好、更高效的解决问题的方法。所以，图灵所定义的智能并不严谨，智能应是指通过技术或自然系统有效而自动地解决问题的程度或者等级。因此，笔者为一个系统的智能性提出一个暂时的工作概念，如果一个系统能独立而有效地解决问题，则它就是智能的。一个系统的智能度由系统的独立性程度、问题的复杂

[①] 克劳斯·迈因策尔著，贾积有译，2018，《人工智能与机器学习：算法基础和哲学观点》，《上海师范大学学报：哲学社会科学版 47》，13—24。

[②] 图片来源：https://ipk.nyu.edu/people/klaus-mainzer/。

程度以及解决问题过程的效率大小决定:智能度我们能够测量。据此,动物(和人类)的意识和感觉对于智能来说并非必需的。

二、从图灵到符号主义人工智能和自动证明

1956年,受到图灵"机器会思考吗"这一问题的启发,约翰·麦卡锡(John McCarthy)、艾伦·纽厄尔(Alen Newell)、赫伯特·西蒙(Herbet Simon)等多位权威研究人员出席了在达特茅斯举行的有关机器智能的会议。人工智能研究的第一阶段至少在于形式逻辑中探求解决问题的通用方法上取得了成就。为了证明公式的逻辑上的普遍适用性,设计了一种机械的处理方法。这种处理方法可以被计算机程序执行,也将自动定理证明引入了计算机科学。

在实践中论证一个逻辑推论的普遍适用性可能会非常复杂。因此,1965年鲁滨逊(J. A. Robinson)提出了所谓的归结方法,借此能够推导出逻辑驳议过程的证明。人们从对立的猜测(否定),即逻辑推论不具有普遍适用性开始;接着证明这一假设的所有可能的应用实例都将导致自相矛盾的结果。否定之否定和逻辑推论的否定是普遍有效的。鲁滨逊的归结方法使用了逻辑化简法,据此人们可以将所有逻辑公式转换成合取范式。在命题逻辑中一个合取范式由可以否定的和不可否定的命题变量(字符串)组成,这些变量由合取(∧)和析取(∨)符号连接起来。一个常规公式的组成元素被称为子句。

对于谓词逻辑的公式来说,也有一个通用的归结过程,以便再次从一个公式的一般无效假设推导出矛盾。为此,一个谓词逻辑的公式必须被变换为一个常规形式,从它的子句中可以机械地推断出矛盾。但是,因为在谓词逻辑中(不同于命题逻辑)一般不能判断一个公式的普遍适用性,所以,有可能发生归结过程无法结束的情况。计算机程序就这样无限制地运行下去。因此,重要的是找到一些子类,其中的过程不仅有效而且能够结束。机器智能提高并加速决定过程的效率,但机器智能像人类智能一样受制于逻辑决定性的原则界限。

在逻辑学和数学中,公式(也是字符串)是一步步被推导出来的,直到完成一个命题的论证。计算机程序的运行归根结底就像论证。程序根据确定的规则一步步推导出字符串,直到找到一个解决问题答案的形式表达。类似地,我们想象流水线上某个工件的组装过程,相应的计算机程序规定了预设的零件如何一步步地根据规则组装成这个工件。一个顾客想从一个计算机科学研究者那里得到一个能解决这样问题的程序,在一个非常复杂又不清晰

的生产过程中,顾客一定想先得到这个程序能正确运行的证据。可能发生的错误是危险的,也可能带来巨大的额外费用。计算机科学研究者依据一种软件,这种软件可以自动从问题的形式特征中提取出证据。就像被投入到"数据挖掘"中寻找数据或者数据相关性的软件一样,相应的软件也被投入到证据的自动寻找中。

这就产生了一个问题,软件自动提取证据是否可靠。在一个准确地预先确定的框架内,能够对以此为基础的软件进行可靠性论证,顾客就能确定这个计算机程序是否能够正确工作以解决问题。这种"自动证明"不仅对现代软件技术有巨大的影响,还导致了深刻的哲学问题,即数学的思维可以被自动化到什么程度。但是,这种软件的正确性论证却是由一个数学家进行的。如果我们想要使这种证明自动化,一个基本的认识论的问题就产生了:这是否将我们引入一个回归,它的终点是人类(必须是人类)?

三、从一般问题解决器到专家系统

人工智能研究的第一阶段大约在20世纪50年代中期到60年代中期,仍被欣快的期待所刺激着。人们应用计算机来设计通用问题解决方法,但是实践的结果令人非常失望。大约在20世纪70年代中期到80年代中期,以知识为基础的专家系统进入人们视野,这是人工智能的第一次实际应用。有限而明确的人类专家的专业知识,比如工程和医学等领域的专业知识被写进专家系统,应用到日常生活领域。

以知识为基础的专家系统作为一种人工智能程序,储存相关领域的知识并根据这些知识自动进行推理,以便找出正确答案或者提供某些情形下的诊断。专家系统与人类专家的不同之处在于,专家系统的知识被限制在专门的信息基础里,没有结构化的、关于世界的常识性知识。要建造一个专家系统,必须首先将专家的知识用规则表达出来,然后翻译成程序语言,并用问题解决策略进行处理。

四、人工智能与自然语言:魏泽鲍姆的 ELIZA

以上策略同样适用于用计算机实现基于自然语言的交流。约瑟夫·魏泽鲍姆(Joseph Weizenbaum)设计的语言程序 ELIZA 就是一个例子。ELIZA 模拟人类专家中的女精神病医师与病人聊天。该程序涉及一些规则,指挥一个"女精神病医师"用怎样的句子模板对病人的某些特定的句子模板做出反应,基本上是根据各种情况对规则进行识别和分类。最简单的情况是确定两个符号结构的等价性,就像它们在符号编程语言 USP 中被函数 EQUAL 确定一样。如果常量和变量被包含在符号表达式中,则出现一些扩展。比如:

  (xBC)
  (ABy)

这两个项相互匹配,因为变量 x 和原子 A、变量 y 和原子 C 互相对应。通过引入变量可以使一个模板的结构通过模式比较被识别。

为此,可以在 LISP 编程语言中定义一个特殊的运算符 MATCH。一个数据和一个结构对应的最简单的情况是常量的相等性,比如列表 AB 和 AB 的相等性:

  (MATCH '(AB) '(AB)) = T

符号" ' "表示后面的列表不是函数定义,而是应当理解为符号的排列。

为了实现分类,可以使用各种各样的生成符号,就像逻辑学或数论中的变量那样。比如可以用符号"?"来引导出任何对象:

  (MATCH '(? B) '(AB)) = T
  (MATCH '(? B) '((AB)B)) = T

这个结构将每一个包含两个子列 A 和 B 的列表与其中的第二个列表 B 匹配。

生成符号"*"表示任意多个符号构成的字符串(包括空串)。比如:

  (MATCH '(* B) '(B)) = T
  (MATCH (* B) (ABCB)) = T

这样给出的结构表示与所有在尾部包含 B 的列表相匹配。

以上结构就可以说明 ELIZA 系统的本质算法结构,它反映了"精神病医师"的知识库内容。请看病人 P 和 ELIZA(简称 E)之间的对话：

  P：MEN ARE ALL ALIKE.(男人们全都一样。)

  E：IN WHAT WAY?(在哪些方面?)

  P：THEY'RE ALWAYS BUCGING US ABOUT SOMETHING OR OTHER.(他们总找借口躲避我们。)

  E：CAN YOU THINK OF A SPECIFIC EXAMPLE?(你能举个例子吗?)

  P：WELL, MY BOYFRIEND MADE ME COME HERE.(好吧,我的男朋友要我到你这里来。)

  E：YOUR BOYFRIEND MADE YOU COME HERE.(你的男朋友要你到我这里来。)

  P：YES, I AM VERY SAD.(是的,我很伤心。)

  E：YOU ARE VERY SAD.(你很伤心。)

  P：SAD AND DEPRESSED.(伤心而沮丧。)

  E：PLEASE GO ON.(请继续。)

下列规则可以推导出 ELIZA 的回答,因为它们可以识别病人和 ELIZA 使用的某些特定的句子模式：

  '((((* AM * B) →(APPEND '(YOU ARE) B))

  ((* ARE *)→'(IN WHAT WAY))

  ((* ALWAYS *)→'(CAN YOU THINK OF A SPECIFIC EXAMPLE))

  ((* MY * BME * C) → (APPEND '(YOUR)(APPEND B (CONS 'YOU C)))

  ((* L)→'(PLEASE GO ON)))

第二个规则规定:当在句子中存在 ARE 这个关键词,而在其左右的内容为任意时,用"IN WHAT WAY"作为回答。在句子"MEN ARE ALL ALIKE"中,ARE 前的 * 是"MEN", ARE 后的是"ALL ALIKE"。

第四个规则是：当病人的句子中单词 MY 和 ME 通过列表 * B 被分开，并以列表 * C 结束时，ELIZA 的回答首先由 YOU 和 C 部分（CONS 'YOU C）构成，然后使用 B 部分，最后是 YOUR。

一段用户与 ELIZA 之间的对话，与我们所举的编程语言 LISP 中的句法符号列表没什么不同。在语义学上要尽量使用与日常聊天习惯相符的结构。

最后一个规则是典型的随机响应，就像我们在日常聊天中经常遇到的一样：如果专家无法识别一个任意的符号列表（* L），他就说"请继续（PLEASE GO ON）"。

五、从 ELIZA 到 WATSON 系统

自约瑟夫·魏泽鲍姆的 ELIZA 之后，以模式识别为基础的文本比较方法被人们熟知。现在的软件将句子拆分成单独的短语进行分析，迅速计算出对于提出的问题合适的答案模式或者在另一种语言中找出合适的翻译。1993—2000 年间由德国人工智能研究中心（DFKI）研发的 VERBMOBIL 就是一个高效的翻译程序。

人类的语言处理过程包括不同的层次。技术也在这些层次上得到实现。在计算语言学中，这种处理方式被称作管道模型，从声音信息出发到文本形式，相应的字母字符串波概括为单词和句子。形态分析要得到单词的词根。基于乔姆斯基语法体系的语法学分析要得到句子的语法组成单元，比如主语、表语、宾语等。语义分析则关注句子的含义。最后，对话和话语分析则研究文本包含的问题与答案、目的、企图、意图等。高效的技术解决方案并不需要经过这个管道模型的所有阶段。当今强大的计算能力以及机器学习和搜索算法可以用于各个层次的语言分析中。人类的语法分析过程通常与意识相关，而这并非必要的。

IBM 公司研制的 WATSON 系统是一个语义层面上的自动问答系统。它基于并行计算机的强大计算能力和维基（Wikipedia）网站所存储的海量知识，综合应用了语言语法、专家系统、搜索算法、大数据处理等多种技术。与 EILIZA 不同，WATSON 理解某些背景知识和语言的语义，能够理解自然语言的提问，并快速在海量知识库中找到相应的知识和回答。WATSON 一方面是 IBM 公司发明的认知工具平台，另一方面也意味着在经济和企业界的广泛应用可能。按照摩尔定律，WATSON 的功能在可以预计的时期内不再需要超级计算机了。一部智能手机上的一个 App 应用就可以具备这样的功能。

不必通过键盘输入来完成这样的操作,而是通过智能语音程序就可以实现自然语言进行的对话。对话中所包含的人类情感也能够被程序识别,就像魏泽鲍姆早就担心的那样。

2013年斯派克·琼斯(Spike Jonze)摄制的美国科幻片《她》(her)描绘了一个内向而害羞的男人爱上了一个语言程序。他的职业是给那些难以向别人解释他们感受的人写信。为了减轻工作负担,他得到了一个新的操作系统,该系统配备了女性身份和愉快的声音。使用头戴式耳机和摄像头,他与这个自称为萨曼莎(Samantha)的系统交流。萨曼莎很快就学会了社交互动,并表现得越来越人性化。在频繁而长期的对话中,亲密的情感关系得以发展。

智能写作程序(或称"写作机器人")不仅被媒体和新闻业用于处理常规文本,比如商业新闻、体育报道或小报消息,同样可以应用在行政管理或法律领域的常规文本写作中。我们也将体验到在科研领域中使用智能写作程序。在医学、技术和自然科学领域专业刊物上的论文出版量已经变得如此巨大,以至于各个专业研究领域的专家都没有时间详细阅读这些文章。研究结果必须以极快的速度出版才具有竞争力。完全可以想象,将来科学家只需要在某个论文结构中输入数据参数和结果,智能系统就能按照其写作风格写出一篇规范的论文。

写作机器人在金融行业也应用得越来越普遍。可以在几秒钟内生成多个原来靠人类专家才能完成的报告,比如公司简介。可以提示客户、基金经理采用何种策略投资股票市场以及基金如何发展。保险公司使用智能写作程序来衡量销售业绩并提出改进建议。自动创建的文本可以确认客户的投资策略是否能够取得成功。自动编写程序提供的支持还可以为客户提供更多的个人建议。人力投资顾问并没有被取代,但数字产品的发展速度与IT工具的指数增长一样迅速。

六、神经网络和机器

生物体的自组织大脑则与可编程计算机不同。在演化进程中,网络最开始以复杂基因及蛋白质网络中的亚细胞供应、控制和信息系统的身份出现。基于神经化学信号处理功能的神经细胞的信息、控制和供应系统不断进化。蚂蚁种群的发展就像人类大脑和人类社会的网络物理系统一样。

根据我们的工作定义,如果一个系统能够独立而有效地解决某种问题,那么这个系统就是智能的。传统上我们把在进化过程中发展起来的自然系统和在技术上引入的技术("人工")系统区分开来。智能度取决于数学复杂性理论中可以测量的问题的复杂性。

自然进化中产生的有效解决问题的方法并没有通过计算机模型中的符号方法进行表示。亚细胞、细胞和神经元自组装产生适当的复杂网络。神经元由图形网络的节点表示，触连接由图形网络的连线表示。神经化学连接的强度由连接权重来表示。学习在神经元的开关模式建构过程中产生，受到神经网络的学习算法指导。强烈的突触耦合产生了神经元的开关模式，与一个生物体的大脑情感或者肢体动作状态相适应。这个过程也可以通过计算机模型来模拟，这种模拟基于神经网络、自动机与计算机之间的基本的数学等价性。已经得到证明，一个 McCulloch-Pitts 网络可以通过一个能够终止的自动机模拟。可终止的自动机包括一些简单的系统，比如火车站的自动购票机，它能够识别一些简单的指令语言代码。反过来，一个可终止的自动机的功能也可以由一个 McCulloch-Pitts 网络来实现。数学上，这样的网络可以通过实数加权。也可以这样说，一个由 MeCulloch-Pitts 网络类型的神经网络系统构成的生物体，只能解决具有这种复杂性的问题，即能够被一个可终止的自动机解决的问题。在这个意义上说，一个这样的生物体的智能与一个可终止的自动机的智能是同等程度的。

不过哪些神经网络相当于图灵机，也就是相当于根据丘奇(Church)论题可以编程控制的计算机呢？这些机器和神经网络可以识别哪些语言呢？这些语言涉及某些自然语言，它们可以通过乔姆斯基语法体系推导出来，也就是可以递归地建构起来。可以证明，图灵机依据这种语言识别功能能精确地模拟那些突触权重为有理数且有反馈环的神经网络。反过来说，图灵机可以被具有突触权重为有理数的识别递归语言的神经网络精确地模拟出来。

如果我们把图灵机作为程序控制计算机的原型，那么根据这个证明，一个具有有限的突触强度的大脑可以被一个计算机模拟。相反，一个图灵机(即一个计算机)的工作过程可以被一个具有有限的突触强度大小的大脑追踪。换句话说，这种大脑的智能度对应于图灵机的智能度。

这样的神经网络原则上可以在适当的计算机上模拟。事实上实际应用(例如模式识别)的大部分神经网络仍然是在数字计算机(例如诺伊曼机器)上模拟实现的。只有神经形态的计算机才能直接构建神经元网络。

但是，如果神经网络的突触权重不仅允许是有理数(即大小有限的数字，例如 2.3715，其中小数点位数有限），而且还可以使用任意实数（即小数无限多的小数点，例如 2.3715……这也是不可计算的）的话，将导致怎样的结果呢？从技术上讲，这样的网络不仅可以执行数字计算，而且可以进行模拟计算。

在信号理论中，模拟信号被理解为具有连续且不间断的过程的信号。在数学上，模拟信号被定义为无限可微分的连续的平滑函数。显然，这样一个函数的图形没有不可微分的拐角和断点。因此一个模拟信号形式的物理量的时间连续过程可以被描述出来。模拟-数字转换器将时间连续的输入信号离散成单独的离散样本。

事实上，在一个自然的有机体中，许多过程可以被认为是模拟的。因此，视觉信号处理可以通过触发传感器的连续电磁场来描述。听觉的声学也是基于稳定的声波的。触觉上，皮肤传感器也能提供稳定连续而不是数字化的感觉。现在有人会争辩说，在有限的物理世界中的测量值是有限的，因此原则上是可数字化的。然而对于人工智能具有非常重要意义的是模拟性的神经网络的理论结果。在数学上，如果拥有关于实数的数学理论，突触权重为任意实数的模拟神经网络也可以被明确地定义出来。核心问题是模拟神经网络是否可以比具有有理数的神经网络且因此比图灵机或数字计算机做得"更多"。这可能是人工智能辩论中的一个中心论点，也就是说，具有实数的数学比仅具有比特数的计算机科学可以做得"更多"。

自动机和机器的核心特征是对形式语言的认识和理解。如果一个自动机经过有限多的步骤之后进入一个可以接受的状态并终止了，它就将一个读入的单词识别为某种形式的符号序列。自动机可以接受的语言仅包含可被它识别的词汇。可以证明，有限状态自动机正是可以识别规则语言的简单符号序列。上下文无关语言使用的规则推导出的符号与背景符号无关，它们被更强大的具有特殊存储结构的自动机识别。递归可枚举语言非常复杂，只能被图灵机识别。

具有有理数突触权重的神经网络（以及图灵机）也可以识别递归可枚举的语言。这可以是生物体的自然神经元系统，也可以是符合具有有理数突触权重的递归神经网络的规律的人造神经形态计算机。现在可以证明：模拟的神经网络（具有实数的突触权重）原则上可以在指数大小的时间内识别不可计算的语言。通过将自然数和有理数的可计算性概念扩展到实数上，这种证明在数学上是可能的。可以用差分方程代替数字过程，也可以用差分方程来描述连续的实际过程。换句话说，所有类型的动态系统，例如物理学中的流动、化学反应和生物界的组织，原则上都可以用相应的、扩展了的、具有实数的模拟系统来表示。

当然模拟神经网络在多项式时间内不能解决 NP 困难问题。可以证明，旅行商问题（TSP）也是关于实数的 NP 困难问题。另一方面，根据逻辑学家阿尔弗雷德·塔斯基（Alfred Tarski）的证明，任何在实数域上可以定义的数量是有确定性的。相反，在整数域上可定义的集合，是不可确定的。这是哥德尔的算术不完全性定理的一个结论。实数上的可计算性显然在一定程度上比整数域上的数字可计算性"更简单"。

无论如何，推广到实数域的普遍性的（模拟性的）可计算性的优点是，它比较客观地概括了生物体、大脑和神经形态计算机中的模拟过程。在这里可以清晰地观察到与进化、数学和技术方法非常相近的一个等价说法，它依赖于丘奇推论的扩展性：不仅数字化上的有效过程可以被计算机模型表示出来，自然过程中模拟有效过程也可以。这是一个关于复杂动态性系统的统一理论的核心。计算机中带有数字的符号代码只是我们的一种信息处理方式，它代表了原子、分子、细胞和进化的过程。

可以这样来区分可计算性的程度：一个非确定性图灵机在计算过程中，除了使用通常的有效计算的基本操作外，还使用随机决策。为此，我们借用图灵定义的 ψ 预言机扩展了图灵机的概念：对于 ψ 预言机而言，除了一个确定性的图灵机的命令，一个操作 ψ 也是可以的，例如给 $\psi(x)$ 的 x 赋值，尽管我们不知道它是否可以计算。这样，这种计算就依赖于这个预言 ψ。大自然中的一个例子是 DNA 信息有效处理过程中的随机变化。这就是相对可计算性：一个函数相对于 ψ 是可计算的，如果它通过一个 ψ 预言机是可计算的话。

相应地，一个相对化版本的丘奇推论可以这样来定义：所有相对于 ψ 有效的过程可以被一个（通用）ψ 预言机来模拟。一个扩展的对于实数的模拟版本的丘奇推论也可以被定义。已经证明了：一个模拟神经网络在多项式时间内能够识别一个合适的 ψ 预言机在多项式时间内能够识别的语言。根据我们对人工智能的定义，一个具有相应的模拟神经元的神经系统的自然有机体或者一个具有相应技术的神经系统，和 ψ 预言机一样地智能。

人类的知识与意识联系在一起。来自长期记忆的相应数据和规则被放置到短期记忆中，可以被象征性地表示为：我知道我是个知道能够或做了某事的人。原则上不能排除人工智能系统将来会有类似意识的能力。这样的系统会创造出与人类截然不同的它们自身的体验、经历和身份。所以，如果将人工智能研究仅仅局限在具有与人类相似的意识的人工智能系统上，将是进入了一个死胡同。

12.3　思考和练习

1. 请在下图中圈出人类大脑的几个主要语言区域①。

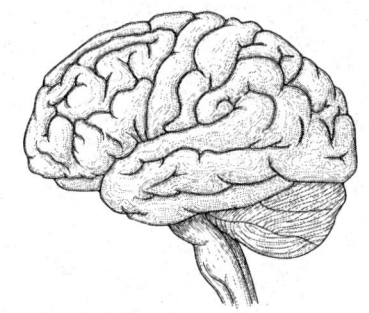

2. 试比较几种不同的大脑成像技术的优点和缺点。
3. 通过失语症研究正常人类大脑的语言功能存在哪些有效性和局限性？
4. 仔细阅读第二篇选文，介绍该文章中包含的几个实验设计和每个实验的主要发现。

12.4　延伸阅读

Deacon, T. W. 1997. *The Symbolic Species：the Co-evolution of Language and the Brain*. New York：W. W. Norton.

Ingram, J. C. L. 2007. *Neurolinguistics：an Introduction to Spoken*

---

① 图片来源：https://www.123rf.com/photo_83670431_stock-vector-anatomical-brain-heart-hand-drawn-sketch-medicine-vector-illustration-poster-anatomical-high-detaile.html.

Language Processing and its Disorders. New York: Cambridge University Press.

Schnelle, H. 2010. *Language in the Brain*. New York: Cambridge University Press.

附录：基本术语中英文对照表

（按音序排列）

中文	英文	页码
阿尔泰语系	Altaic	519
班图语系	Bantu	54
伴语言资源	paralinguistic feature	434
本土语言	indigenous language	1
鼻音	nasal	48,52,53,56
边擦音	lateral fricative	48
变通音	lateral approximate	48
变异社会语言学	Variationist Sociolinguistics	430,432,433
变音符号	diacritic	50
表层表征	surface representation(SR)	93,95
表达行为	representative	329
波形图	sound waveform	55—57
补足语	complement	210,211,214—216
布洛卡区	Broca's area	570—575
擦音	fricative	48,50
参与观察法	participant-observer technique	431
层级性	hierarchy	3,92,156,205,207,308
颤音	trill	48
超音段标记	suprasegmental	53
超音段特征	suprasegmental feature	53
陈述行为	declaration	329

续表

中文	英文	页码
成分	constituent	206
成分测试	constituent test	206
程度副词	degree word(Deg)	202,204
齿龈音	alveolar	48
齿音	dental	48
抽象模式	abstract pattern	384
处所	location	274
唇齿音	labiodental	48
词	word	3,201
词干/词基	stem/base	147—148
词根语素	root	147
词汇范畴	lexical category	200—203,205,217
词汇歧义	lexical ambiguity	268
词库	lexicon	6
词缀	affix	146,473
搭嘴音	click	51
达罗毗荼语系	Dravidian	519
替代法	replacement test	206,207
单侧化	lateralization	572
单向性	unidirectionality	523
单元音	monophthong	51
定量分析法	quantitative analysis	432
定性分析	qualitative analysis	435
动词	verb(V)	237,239,240
动作层	action tier	273
侗台语系	Tai-Kadai	519
独立法	stand-alone test	205
短期记忆	short-term memory	387

续 表

中文	英文	页码
短语	phrase	3,208
短语结构规则	phrase structure rule(PSR)	208
多义关系	polysemy	266,267
儿童语言交流系统	Child Language Data Exchange System (CHILDES)	389
发现模式	pattern-finding	383
发音语音学	Articulatory Phonetics	45,46
反义关系	antonymy	265,267
范畴化	categorization	383
方式准则	Maxim of Manner	316,319
非肺部气流音	non-pulmonic consonant	50
肺部气流音	pulmonic consonant	47
分析型	analytic	157
弗雷格方案	Frege's Program	271
辅音	consonant	47—50,86,90
辅音串	consonant cluster	90
复合元音(滑动元音)	gliding vowel	50
复综型	polysynthetic	157—159
复综语	polysynthetic language	474
副词	adverb(Adv)	200
感事	experiencer	273
感知行为	expressive	328
格里姆定律	Grimm's Law	514
工作记忆的容量	working memory capacity	387
弓状神经束	arcuate fasciculus	568,570
功能范畴	functional category	200,204
共时语言学	Synchronic Linguistics	2
构式	construction	522

续 表

中文	英文	页码
构式化	constructionalization	522
构式语法	Construction Grammar	383
孤立语	isolating language	157,473
关键时期	Critical Period	384
关联原则	Maxim of Relevance	316,319,320
关系原则	Q-principle	322
观察者悖论	the observer's paradox	434
规定语法	Prescriptive Grammar	7
国际音标	International Phonetic Alphabet (IPA)	46,47,49,50,53
涵义	implicature	316
汉藏语系	Sino-Tibetan	516
合作原则	Co-operative Principle(CP)	316
后缀	suffix	146
互补分布	complementary distribution	88
话轮	turn	434
话轮转换	turn-taking	434
话题突出语言	topic-prominent language	476
话语标记	discourse marker	476
话语分析	discourse analysis	433
环缀	circumfix	146,148
会话分析	conversation analysis(CA)	433
会话涵义	conversational implicature	316
会话结构	conversation structure	476
基于频率的学习	frequency-based learning	384
基于使用的语言观	Usage-based Theory	382
激事	stimulus	273
挤喉音	ejective	50

续 表

中文	英文	页码
建构主义	Constructivism	380,381
交际能力	communicative competence	428
角回	angular gyrus	568
教学语法	Teaching Grammar	7
节点	node	381
解释充分	explanatory adequacy	2
介词	preposition(P)	200
近侧发展区间	zone of proximal development	381
经济性	economy	477
句法范畴/词类	syntactic category/parts of speech	200—204
句法树/树形图	tree-diagram	151,155,209
句法学	Syntax	6,200
句子	sentence	3
卷舌音	retroflex	47
绝对共性	absolute universals	471
科依桑语系	Khoisan languages	50
可理解输出	comprehensible output	388
可理解输入	comprehensible input	387
客体	theme	273
龈后音	postalveolar	47
跨模块关联	cross-modal association	383
来源	source	273
类比	analogy	383
类推	analogy	522
历时的	diachronic	519
历史语言学	Diachronic Linguistics	2
连词	conjunction(Conj)	201
联结主义	Connectionism	381,382

续表

中文	英文	页码
链变	chain shift	519
量的准则	Maxim of Quantity	316—318
量原则	R-principle	322
路径	path	273
论元的形态句法配列	alignment	475
矛盾关系	contradiction	269
描写充分	descriptive adequacy	2
描写语法	Descriptive Grammar	6
民族志	Ethnologue	436
名词	noun(N)	200
目标	goal	273
目标语言	object language	271
南岛语	Austronesian	516
南亚语系	Austro-Asiatic	517
内爆音	voiced implosive	50
尼日尔-刚果语系	Niger-Congo	516
黏着型	agglutinating	157,158
黏着语	agglutinative language	473
黏着语素	bound morpheme	145,146,474
牛津日常语言哲学学派	Oxford Ordinary Language Philosophy	316
派生	derivation	148
派生词	derived word	149
派生形态	derivational morphology	144,148—152
批判话语分析	critical discourse analysis(CDA)	434
偏误	error	388
频谱图	spectrogram	54,56
平均语句长度	mean length of utterance(MLU)	385

续　表

中文	英文	页码
普遍语法	Universal Grammar(UG)	3,8,200,214,380,383
谱系树	Stammbaum	517
迁移	transfer	389
前缀	prefix	146
倾向共性	tendencies	471
屈折	inflection	149
屈折形态	inflectional morphology	144,152—155
屈折语	inflectional language	473
屈折语素	inflectional morpheme	152,475
溶合型	fusional	157,158
软腭音	velar	47
萨丕尔·沃尔夫假说	Sapir-Whorf Hypothesis	8,9
塞音	plosive	47
塞音	stop	472
三元音	triphthong	50
闪音	flap/tap	47
社会变项	social variable	432
社会交互	social interaction	380
社会语言学	Sociolinguistics	4
神经语言学	Neurolinguistics	567
生成语法	Generative Grammar	2
声调语言	tonal language	52
声门音	glottal	47
声母	onset	52
声学语音学	Acoustic Phonetics	45,54
时态	tense	203
实词	content word	204
事件层	event tier	273,274

续 表

中文	英文	页码
释义	paraphrase	267
输入	input	387
数据共性	statistical universals	471
数据学习	statistical learning	381
双唇音	bilabial	47
双分叉结构	binary branching	209
双元音	diphthong	50
特殊语法	Special Grammar	8
特征矩阵	feature matrix	90
体态	aspect	203
听觉语音学	Auditory Phonetics	45,57
通音	approximate	47
通用语法	General Grammar	8
同义关系	synonymy	265,266
同音同形异义关系	homophony	266,268
同源词	cognates	516
投射	projection	209
图式	schema	380
威尼克区	Wernicke's area	567
维尔纳定律	Verner's Law	514
位移法	displacement test	205,206
先行语	antecedent	207
显威望	overt prestige	432
现代语言学能测试	The Modern Language Aptitude Test(MLAT)	387
线性排列	linear sequencing	200
限定词	determiner(Det)	201
翔实记忆	rich memory	383

续 表

中文	英文	页码
象似性	iconicity	477
小舌音	uvular	47
心理层	psycho tier	272,273
新语法学派	The Neogrammarians	515
行动研究	action research	387
行为论	Behaviorism	379
形容词	adjective(A)	200
形式	form	265
形态学	Morphology	6,144
虚词	function word	204
许诺行为	commissive	328
序列组织	sequence organization	434
亚非语系	Afro-Asiatic	516
言后行为	perlocutionary act	326
言内行为	locutionary act	326
言外行为	illocutionary act	326
言语(索绪尔)	parole	2
言语行为	verbal behavior	379
言语行为理论	Speech Act Theory	325
派生词素	derivational morpheme	475
衍推(蕴含)	entailment	268,314,320,323,324
咽音	pharyngeal	47
一般领域	domain-general	383
一致性	harmony	477
依附成分	clitic	145
意义	meaning	265
音段	segment	86
音节	syllable	51,90,91

续表

中文	英文	页码
音节化	syllabification	92
音素	phone	46,85
音位	phoneme	51,85—90,92
音位变体	allophone	51,86—90,92
音系表征	phonological representation	92
音系学	Phonology	6,85
隐威望	covert prestige	432
印客现象	imprinting	384
印欧语系	Indo-European	516
硬腭音	palatal	47
有序的异质体	orderly heterogeneity	430
语法范畴	grammatical category	6
语法化	grammaticalization	4,520
语法原则	grammatical principles	5
语境	context	309,320—322,435
语料库语言学	Corpus Linguistics	435
语素	morpheme	3,144
语言(索绪尔)	langue	2
语言变项	linguistic variable	431
语言表现	linguistic performance	3,428
语言共性档案库	The Universals Archive	472
语言官能	language faculty	380
语言官能	faculty of language	8
语言类型学	Linguistic Typology	4,157,470—472
语言能力	linguistic competence	3,428
语言人类学	Linguistic Anthropology	4
语言习得机制	Language Acquisition Device (LAD)	380

续 表

中文	英文	页码
语言相对论	Linguistic Relativism	9
语义地图	semantic map	477
语义学	Semantics	6,200,265
语音表征	underlying representation(UR)	92
语用推理	pragmatic inference	522
语用学	pragmatics	307,310,475,476
语种库	language sample	471
预设	presupposition	269,313,320
预设触发语	presupposition trigger	313
元音	vowel	47,50,51,86,90
元语言	metalanguage	271
原始母语	proto-language	513
原则与参数理论	Principles and Parameters(P&P)	215
韵核	nucleus	91
韵母/韵部	rhyme	52,91
韵尾	coda	51
蕴涵共性	implicational universals	159,471,472
真值	truth value	273
真值语义学	Truth-Conditional Semantics	270—272
甄别性特征	distinctive feature	89
指示行为	directive	328
指示行为	directive	328
指示语	specifier	209,214
质的准则	Maxim of Quality	317,319,320
中介语	interlanguage	389
中心语	head	209,214
中缀	infix	146
主宾格	nominative-accusative	475

续 表

中文	英文	页码
主谓呼应	agreement	208
助动词	auxiliary verb(Aux)	201,207
注意假说	Noticing Hypothesis	388
转写	transcribe	434
追踪研究	longitudinal study	390
浊塞音	voiced obstruent	89
自然类	natural class	200
自由语素	free morphone	146
综合型	synthetic	157
综合型语言	synthetic language	474
组合性原则	Principle of Compositionality	271
组合语义学	Compositional Semantics	270
组块化	chunking	383
最小对立对	minimal pair	54,88
作通格	ergative-absolutive	475
X-标杆理论	X-bar Theory	210,215

全书正文遵循术语首次出现注释英文的原则，除个别术语为行文中新、老概念对比需要，一般不再多次作注。

图书在版编目(CIP)数据

语言学 / 罗琼鹏,彭馨葭编. —南京:南京大学出版社,2019.8(2021.5重印)

汉语言文学本科专业核心课程研究导引教材/徐兴无,徐雁平主编

ISBN 978-7-305-22475-1

Ⅰ.①语… Ⅱ.①罗… ②彭… Ⅲ.①语言学-高等学校-教材 Ⅳ.①H0

中国版本图书馆 CIP 数据核字(2019)第 150943 号

敬告作者

为编写《汉语言文学本科专业核心课程研究导引教材》,选编了一些优秀作品,得到许多作者的大力支持,我们表示衷心感谢!由于地址不详等方面的困难,未能与一些作者或译者取得联系,谨表歉意。敬请有著作权的作者与我们联系,以便按国家有关规定支付稿酬并赠送样书。

出版发行	南京大学出版社
社　　址	南京市汉口路 22 号　邮　编 210093
出 版 人	金鑫荣
书　　名	**语言学**
编　　者	罗琼鹏　彭馨葭
责任编辑	柏　雪　马蓝婕
照　　排	南京紫藤制版印务中心
印　　刷	南京京新印刷有限公司
开　　本	718×1000　1/16　印张 40.5　字数 656 千
版　　次	2019 年 8 月第 1 版　2021 年 5 月第 2 次印刷
ISBN	978-7-305-22475-1
定　　价	140.00 元

网址:http://www.njupco.com
官方微博:http://weibo.com/njupco
微信服务号:njupress
销售咨询热线:(025)83594756

* 版权所有,侵权必究
* 凡购买南大版图书,如有印装质量问题,请与所购
　图书销售部门联系调换